June 24–27, 2013
London, United Kingdom

I0027574

**Association for
Computing Machinery**

Advancing Computing as a Science & Profession

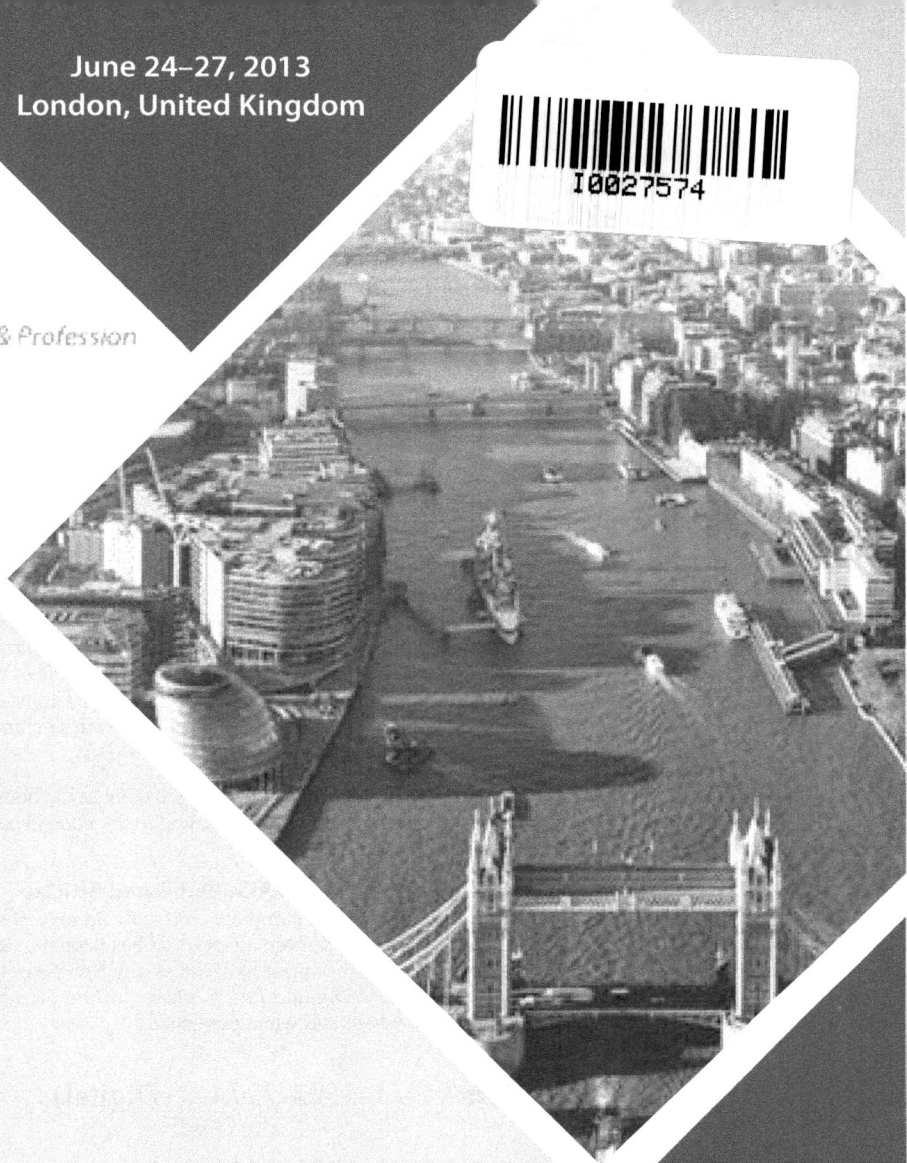

EICS'13

Proceedings of the ACM SIGCHI Symposium on
Engineering Interactive Computing Systems

Sponsored by:
SIGCHI

Supported by:
CITY University London, Springer, & IFIP Working Group

**Association for
Computing Machinery**

Advancing Computing as a Science & Profession

The Association for Computing Machinery
2 Penn Plaza, Suite 701
New York, New York 10121-0701

Notice to Past Authors of ACM-Published Articles
ACM intends to create a complete electronic archive of all articles and/or other material previously published by ACM. If you have written a work that has been previously published by ACM in any journal or conference proceedings prior to 1978, or any SIG Newsletter at any time, and you do NOT want this work to appear in the ACM Digital Library, please inform permissions@acm.org, stating the title of the work, the author(s), and where and when published.

ISBN: 978-1-4503-2214-0 (Digital)

ISBN: 978-1-4503-2443-4 (Print)

Additional copies may be ordered prepaid from:

ACM Order Department
PO Box 30777
New York, NY 10087-0777, USA

Phone: 1-800-342-6626 (USA and Canada)
+1-212-626-0500 (Global)
Fax: +1-212-944-1318
E-mail: acmhelp@acm.org
Hours of Operation: 8:30 am – 4:30 pm ET

Printed in the USA

EICS 2013 Chairs' Introduction

The 5th ACM SIGCHI Symposium on Engineering Interactive Computing Systems (EICS), 2013, was held at City University London. EICS addresses all aspects relating to the *engineering* of usable and effective *interactive computing systems*. The work presented here describes recent innovations in the development of interactive systems. It has a particular focus on tools, techniques and methods for analysis, design and development. EICS brings together researchers and practitioners who engineer interactive systems.

The International Program Committee consisted of 35 experts from the field. It selected 20 full papers from 86 submissions and 13 Late Breaking Results out of 28 submissions. To allow a thorough evaluation and appropriate prioritisation of the broad range of submitted papers, the committee met for the first time this year as a physical meeting. We hope that as a result you will find this year's programme particularly interesting and thought provoking. Besides research papers, the EICS 2013 programme also contained three workshops, a tutorial, a doctoral consortium, demonstrations and posters. Three keynote speakers offered different perspectives on engineering interactive computing systems: Ann Blandford, Patrick Healey and Jeffrey Nichols.

We would like to thank the reviewers, PC members, all chairs and the local organisation for their hard work. We are grateful to our sponsors, ACM SIGCHI and IFIP WG 2.7/13.4, who have continued to support and endorse EICS symposia. Special thanks are due to City University London for providing excellent facilities and to Springer Publishers for providing financial support and, last but not least, the authors who submitted their work.

Peter Forbrig	**Michael Harrison**	**Carmen Santoro**
Prasun Dewan	**Kris Luyten**	**Simone DJ Barbosa**
General co-chairs	Long paper chairs	Late-Breaking Results chairs

Table of Contents

Session 1: Keynote Address

Session 2: Adaptation

Session 3: Design and Implementation Process

Session 4: Analysis

Session 5: Keynote Address

Session 6: Posters and Demonstrations

Session 7: Doctoral Consortium

Session 8: Gesture, Multi-touch, Tangibles, and Speech

Session 9: Callaboration

Session 10: Empirical Techniques

Session 11: Keynote Address

Session 12: Measures and Metrics

Session 13: Design and Implementation Experience

Session 14: Tutorial

Session 15: Workshops

EICS 2013 Symposium Organization

General Chairs: Peter Forbrig *(University of Rostock, Germany)*
Prasun Dewan *(University of North Carolina, Chapel Hill, USA)*

Papers Chairs: Michael Harrison *(Queen Mary University London)*
Kris Luyten *(Hasselt University, Belgium)*

Late Breaking Results Chairs: Simone Barbosa *(PUC Rio, Brazil)*
Carmen Santoro *(CNR-ISTI, Italy)*

Demonstrations Chairs: Nick Graham *(Queen's University, Canada)*
Sara Jones *(City University London)*

Doctoral Consortium Chairs: José C. Campos *(University of Minho, Portugal)*
Jean Vanderdonckt *(Université Catholique de Louvain, Belgium)*

Workshops Chairs: Bob Fields *(Middlesex University, UK)*
Marco Winckler *(University Paul Sabatier, France)*

Tutorial Chairs: Simone Stumpf *(City University London, UK)*
Philippe Palanque *(University of Toulouse 3, France)*

Local Organization Chairs: Stephanie Wilson *(City University London, UK)*
Julia Galliers *(City University London, UK)*

Publicity Chairs: Gaëlle Calvary *(University of Grenoble, France)*
Greg Phillips *(Royal Military College of Canada)*

Sponsorship Chairs: Gerrit Meixner *(Heilbronn University, Germany)*
Thomas Roth-Berghofer *(University of West London, UK)*

Program Committee: Simone Barbosa *(PUC-Rio, Brazil)*
Marco Blumendorf *(yetu AG, Germany)*
Matthew Bolton *(NASA, Human Systems Integration Division, USA)*
Judy Bowen *(University of Waikato, New Zealand)*
Gaëlle Calvary *(University of Grenoble, France)*
José C. Campos *(University of Minho, Portugal)*
Stéphane Chatty *(ENAC, France)*
Keith Cheverst *(Lancaster University, UK)*
Karin Coninx *(Hasselt University, Belgium)*
Paul Curzon *(Queen Mary University London, UK)*
Anke Dittmar *(University of Rostock, Germany)*
Nick Graham *(Queen's University, Canada)*
Christian Kray *(University of Münster, Germany)*
Panos Markopoulos *(Eindhoven University of Technology,*
   The Netherlands)
Mieke Massink *(CNR-ISTI, Pisa, Italy)*
Gerrit Meixner *(Heilbronn University, Germany)*
Jeffrey Nichols *(IBM Research, Almaden, USA)*
Laurence Nigay *(Université Joseph Fourier, Grenoble, France)*
Philippe Palanque *(University of Toulouse 3, France)*
Fabio Paternò *(ISTI-CNR, Italy)*
Greg Phillips *(Royal Military College of Canada, Canada)*
Andreas Pleuss Lero *(The Irish Software Engineering Research Centre,*
   Limerick, Ireland)
Steve Reeves *(University of Waikato, New Zealand)*
Nicolas Roussel *(Inria, Lille, France)*
José Rui *(University of Minho, Portugal)*
Carmen Santoro *(CNR-ISTI, Pisa, Italy)*
Anthony Savadis *(University of Crete, Greece)*
Orit Shaer *(Wellesley College, USA)*
Piyawadee Sukaviriya *(IBM T. Watson Research Center, USA)*
Jan Van den Bergh *(Hasselt University, Belgium)*
Jean Vanderdonckt *(Université Catholique de Louvain, Belgium)*
Marco Winckler *(University of Toulouse 3, France)*
Jürgen Ziegler *(Universität Duisburg-Essen, Germany)*

Additional reviewers:

Theophanis Tsandilas
Brygg Ullmer
Arie van Deursen
Davy Vanacken
Jo Vermeulen
Joël Vogt
Heli Väätäjä
Andrew Webb
Anthony Whitehead
Daniel Wigdor
Doug Wightman
Judy Wilson
Nelson Wong
Min Wu
Stanislaw Zabramski
Nelson Zagalo
Jun Zheng
Caroline Appert
Regina Bernhaupt
George Buchanan
Joelle Coutaz
Alexandre Demeure
Vijay Duddu
Bruno Dumas
Florian Echtler
Mirko Fetter
Vivian Genaro Motti
Mieke Haesen

Steffen Hess
Jochen Huber
Stephane Huot
Antonio Krüger
Yann Laurillau
Alexandre Lemort
Agnes Lisowska Masson
Cosmin Munteanu
Celeste Paul
Vinícius Segura
Shamus Smith
Sandra Smith
Jean-Sébastien Sottet
Simon Tucker
Radu-Daniel Vatavu
Colin Venters
Markel Vigo
Juergen Vogel
Gerhard Weber
Arnaud Blouin
Matthias Kranz
Paolo Masci
Michael Nebeling
Mario Romero
Rami Tabbah
David England
Lucio Davide Spano
David Navarre

EICS 2013 Sponsorship & Support

Sponsors:  SIGCHI

 CITY UNIVERSITY LONDON

Springer

Supporter:

 **IFIP working group 2.7 / 13.4 on User Interface Engineering**

Using the Crowd to Understand and Adapt User Interfaces

Jeffrey Nichols
IBM Research – Almaden
650 Harry Rd, San Jose, CA 95120
jwnichols@us.ibm.com

ABSTRACT

Engineering user interfaces has long implied careful design carried out using formal methods applied by human experts and automated systems. While these methods have advantages, especially for creating interfaces that have the flexibility to adapt to users and situations, they can also be time consuming, expensive, and there are relatively few experts able to apply them effectively. In particular, many engineering methods require the construction of one or more models, each of which can only be created through many hours of work by an expert. In this keynote, I will explore how social and human computation methods can be applied to reduce the barriers to achieving user interface flexibility and ultimately to using engineering methods. In a first example, I will illustrate how groups of users can work together to modify and improve user interfaces through end-user programming examples from the CoScripter and Highlight projects. I will then discuss some initial work on using a crowd of novice workers to create models of existing user interfaces. I hope this keynote will inspire the engineering community to consider alternate approaches that creatively combine formal methods with the power of crowds.

Author Keywords

Human computation; end-user programming; model-based user interfaces; crowd computing; social media; CoScripter; Highlight; qCrowd;

ACM Classification Keywords

H.5.2

BIO

Jeffrey Nichols is a Research Staff Member and Manager of the Social Media & Crowd Research group at IBM Research – Almaden. He leads research efforts on crowdsourcing, social media analysis and social engagement. He joined IBM in 2006 after receiving his Ph.D. from the Human-Computer Interaction Institute in Carnegie Mellon University's School of Computer Science. He has worked in the areas of mobile computing, automated design, and end-user programming. He is the author of more than 25 publications in academic conferences and journals, and co-edited the book *No Code Required: Giving Users Tools to Transform the Web*, published by Morgan Kaufmann in 2010. He is also the Information Director and an Associate Editor for ACM Transactions on Computer-Human Interaction (ToCHI), the premier journal in the field of human-computer interaction. He taught introductory human-computer interaction courses at the University of California, Berkeley in 2009 and 2010.

EICS'13, June 24–27, 2013, London, United Kingdom.
ACM 978-1-4503-2138-9/13/06.

RBUIS: Simplifying Enterprise Application User Interfaces through Engineering Role-Based Adaptive Behavior

Pierre A. Akiki, Arosha K. Bandara, and Yijun Yu
Computing Department, The Open University
Walton Hall, Milton Keynes, United Kingdom
{pierre.akiki, a.k.bandara, y.yu}@open.ac.uk

ABSTRACT

Enterprise applications such as customer relationship management (CRM) and enterprise resource planning (ERP) are very large scale, encompassing millions of lines-of-code and thousands of user interfaces (UI). These applications have to be sold as feature-bloated off-the-shelf products to be used by people with diverse needs in required feature-set and layout preferences based on aspects such as skills, culture, etc. Although several approaches have been proposed for adapting UIs to various contexts-of-use, little work has focused on simplifying enterprise application UIs through engineering adaptive behavior. We define UI *simplification* as a mechanism for increasing usability through *adaptive* behavior by providing users with a minimal feature-set and an optimal layout based on the context-of-use. In this paper we present Role-Based UI Simplification (RBUIS), a tool supported approach based on our CEDAR architecture for simplifying enterprise application UIs through engineering role-based adaptive behavior. RBUIS is integrated in our general-purpose platform for developing adaptive model-driven enterprise UIs. Our approach is validated from the technical and end-user perspectives by applying it to developing a prototype enterprise application and user-testing the outcome.

Author Keywords

Simplification; Adaptive user interfaces; Role-based; Enterprise applications; Model-driven engineering

ACM Classification Keywords

[Software Engineering]: D.2.11 Software Architectures - Domain-specific architectures; D.2.2 Design Tools and Techniques - User interfaces; [Information Interfaces and Presentation]: H.5.2 User Interfaces – User-centered design

General Terms

Design; Human Factors

INTRODUCTION

The functionality of software applications tends to increase with every release increasing the visual complexity. This

phenomenon, referred to as "bloatware" [22], has a negative impact on usability especially for users who do not require the complete feature-set. Also, users have different layout preferences. Both feature-set and layout related choices could be affected by several aspects such as skills [30], culture [27], etc. This paper presents Role-Based UI *Simplification* (RBUIS), a mechanism for increasing usability by providing users with a minimal feature-set and an optimal layout based on the context-of-use (user, platform, and environment). We define a feature as a functionality of the software system and a minimal feature-set as the set with the least features required by a user to perform a job. An optimal layout is the one that maximizes satisfaction of the constraints imposed by a set of aspects. An optimal layout is achieved by adapting the properties of concrete widgets (e.g., type, grouping, size, location, etc.).

Feature-bloated *enterprise applications* are sold as off-the-shelf products to be used by people whose diverse needs in required feature-set and layout preferences are affected by multiple aspects. These applications serve various purposes in an enterprise's functional business areas (e.g., inventory, accounting, etc.). The literature clearly indicates that these systems suffer from usability problems. One example is given by a study carried out in the Nordic countries [20], which showed that almost 40% of the users find enterprise applications difficult to use to a certain extent. UI *simplification* could enhance the usability of these applications by catering to the variable user needs.

One method to achieve UI *simplification* is for enterprise applications to become adaptive/adaptable, respectively referring to the ability of tailoring software applications automatically/manually. Adapting a UI's feature-set could enhance user satisfaction [21] and make complex applications easier to use on mobile devices and by cognitively impaired users [16]. Also, adaptive/adaptable behavior has been used for tailoring the UI layout based on various aspects such as: "Accessibility" [24], "Platform" [7], "Natural Context" [6], etc. However, to meet enterprise application needs we propose the following criteria, for implementing UI simplification, based on the scale and complexity of these applications and the existing literature:

- providing a **scalable**, **extensible**, and **tool supported** mechanism capable of integrating in the development and post-development phases of enterprise applications and accommodating multiple adaptation aspects;

- programming **role-based** adaptive behavior through both **visual** and **code** constructs hence allowing developers as well as I.T. personnel to define and reuse it;
- **preserving designer input** [26] on concrete UIs during adaptation instead of a fully mechanized UI generation;
- **reducing user confusion** [21] by proposing the adapted UI as a simplified alternative to the initial design rather than adapting it while the user is working;

We intend to meet the proposed criteria by using interpreted runtime models that allow more advanced adaptations and could be integrated as part of a generic solution offered as a service. The approach is based on our CEDAR architecture [1]. This paper makes the following contributions:

- An approach called Role-Based User Interface Simplification (RBUIS) composed of the following:
  - A mechanism for minimizing the feature-set at runtime by applying roles on task models
  - A mechanism for optimizing the layout by executing adaptive behavior workflows (visual and code-based constructs) on concrete UI (CUI) models
- *Cedar Studio*, our Integrated Development Environment (IDE) for devising adaptive model-driven enterprise UIs, provides tool support for our approach
- An evaluation of our approach with a set of studies based on two criteria: (1) technical feasibility and scalability, and (2) end-user satisfaction and efficiency

The remainder of this paper is structured as follows. We discuss the related work and briefly explain of our CEDAR architecture. Then, we elaborate on how RBUIS could be applied for minimizing a UI's feature-set and optimizing its layout based on CEDAR. Next, we provide an overview of our IDE *Cedar Studio*, and an example on building adaptive behavior models for use in our approach. Finally, we highlight the results of a study for evaluating RBUIS.

BACKGROUND AND RELATED WORK

This section briefly discusses existing work in terms of the four criteria we established in the introduction. We categorize existing work into feature-set minimization and layout optimization. These categories make up the *simplification* process and address the variable user needs in enterprise UIs. Additionally, we provide a brief overview of the CEDAR architecture based on which RBUIS is based.

Feature-Set Minimization

The *simplification* process should start by providing each user with a *minimal feature-set* to reduce unnecessary "bloat" [22] present in feature-rich enterprise applications.

Providing a multi-layered user interface design is promoted for achieving universal usability [28]. Other researchers propose using two UI versions, one fully-featured and another personalized, in bloated applications [21]. An earlier research work proposes the use of a "training wheels" UI that blocks advanced functionality from novice users [9]. These works present a sound theoretical basis, useful for providing the users of feature-bloated software applications with a minimal feature-set. Yet, the given examples, a basic text editor [28] and the Word 2000 menu [21], are not as complex as enterprise applications. Also, a generic, scalable, extensible, and tool supported mechanism is needed for applying feature-set minimization in practice.

Approaches from product-line (SPL) engineering [26] are used to tailor software applications and some particularly address tailoring UIs. MANTRA [7] adapts UIs to multiple platforms by generating code particular to each platform from an abstract UI model. Although SPLs can be dynamic [3], the SPL-based approaches for UI adaptation focus on design-time (product-based) adaptation whereas runtime (role-based) adaptive behavior is not addressed.

Role-based tailoring of the feature-set is sought after in commercial enterprise applications. Dynamics CRM 2011 [31] and SAP GuiXT [32] offer such a mechanism, yet it is not generic enough to be used with other applications and it requires maintaining multiple UI copies manually. Our approach is generic because it works at the model level.

Layout Optimization

Providing an *optimal layout* based on the context-of-use complements the *simplification* process. For example, SAP's usability (world's leading ERP [17]) is mostly affected by "Navigation" and "Presentation" [29] and its UI does not adapt to the user's skills [30]. Many existing works target the adaptation of the user interface layout, yet each uses a different approach to handle the adaptive functionality.

Fully mechanized UI construction has been criticized in favor of applying the intelligence of human designers for achieving higher usability [26]. It would be better if the designer could manipulate a concrete object rather than its abstraction [12]. Supple is a system for automatically generating UIs adapted to each user's motor abilities [16]. This automation prevents designer input on the concrete UI (CUI), which is the representation as concrete widgets (e.g., button, text box, etc.), making the system difficult to adopt for enterprise applications. Also, this approach has been criticized [24] for exceeding acceptable performance times.

Providing the adapted UI as an alternative version while maintaining access to the original full-scale UI, was shown to have higher user acceptance [21]. Yet, many platforms perform the adaptations while the UI is in use. MASP targets ubiquitous UIs in smart environments by adapting the UI whenever a context change is detected [6]. The MyUI platform also opts for adapting UIs while the user is working in order to prompt for user confirmation [24]. The choice of this adaptation mode is due to the ubiquitous nature of the target systems (e.g., Smart Homes). Since enterprise applications have a less ubiquitous nature with more complex WIMP style UIs, proposing the adapted UI as an alternative helps in avoiding confusion.

Scalability is important when targeting adaptive enterprise UIs. DynaMo-AID supports the development of adaptable context-aware UIs by generating what is referred to as a task tree forest [10]. As another work indicates [5], since each tree corresponds to a context's tasks, the combinatorial explosion makes the approach hard to scale.

The CEDAR Architecture

We created the CEDAR architecture [1] (Figure 1) as an approach for devising adaptive enterprise application UIs based on interpreted runtime models instead of code generation. The dynamic nature of these models gives more flexibility in performing UI adaptations and allows us to implement CEDAR as a **generic service oriented solution** that can be consumed by APIs using different technologies. These characteristics make CEDAR appropriate as a basis for our Role-Based UI Simplification mechanism (RBUIS).

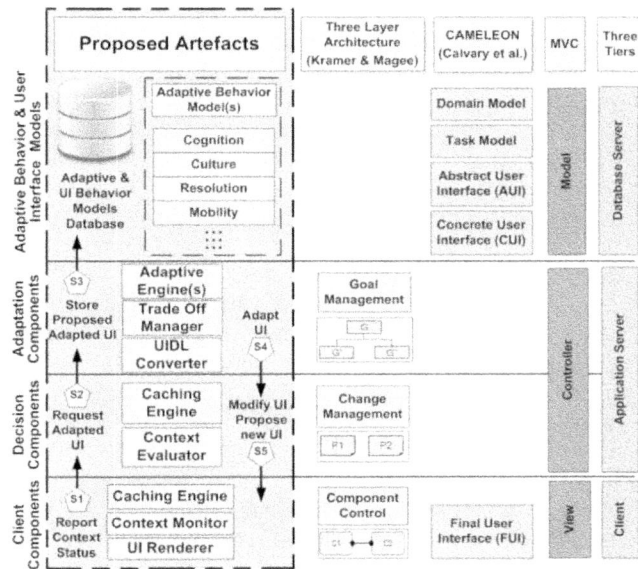

Figure 1. The CEDAR Architecture

We based CEDAR on the: (1) CAMELEON [8] reference framework (*UI Abstraction*), (2) Three Layer Architecture [18] (*Adaptive System Layering*), and (3) Model-View-Controller (MVC) paradigm (*Implementation*).

The coming sections show how RBUIS addresses the four criteria established in the introduction.

ROLE-BASED UI SIMPLIFICATION (RBUIS)

To simplify UIs, we need to provide a minimal feature-set and an optimal layout based on the context-of-use. The feasibility of adapting a single UI designed for the least constrained profile was demonstrated in previous research [15]. Our simplification mechanism will follow the same approach. In the case of the feature-set, the initial UI contains all the features hence it is without constraints. Yet, initial designer layout related choices (e.g., widget type, grouping, etc.) have to be the least constrained (e.g., in terms of screen size). The designer will devise the UI for

the least constrained profile at design-time. Afterwards, a role-based approach is used to simplify the UI at runtime based on the context-of-use. Role-based modeling has been used for adapting the components of software applications [25], yet our approach is oriented towards merging access control with model-driven UIs to achieve UI simplification.

The standard for role-based access control (RBAC) could be utilized by enterprises for protecting their digital resources [13]. In RBAC, "Users" are assigned "Roles", which in turn are assigned permissions on "Resources". In our case the *users* are the enterprise employees logging into the system with their accounts, and the *resources* that we want to apply roles to, are the UI and adaptive behavior models. We merged the role-based approach with UI simplification to create Role-Based User Interface Simplification (RBUIS), in the spirit of RBAC. In RBUIS, *roles* are divided into groups representing the aspects based on which the UI will be simplified (e.g., literacy level, job title, etc.). RBUIS is applied after deploying the software in the enterprise. Managing this process could be a joint work between personnel from the software company in charge of the deployment process and the enterprise's I.T. personnel.

RBUIS comprises the following elements that support feature-set minimization and layout optimization:

Role-Based UI Models support *feature-set minimization* by assigning roles to task models (e.g., ConcurTaskTrees (CTT) [23]) to provide a minimal feature-set based on the context-of-use. This approach allows a practical realization of the concept of multi-layer interface design [28].

Role-Based Adaptive Behavior Models support *layout optimization* through workflows that represent adaptive UI behavior visually and through code. The adaptation is applied on the concrete user interface (CUI) models. Afterwards, adaptive behavior models are tied to roles to specify how the UI will be optimized for each set of users.

User Feedback for Refinement allows the users to reverse feature-set minimizations and layout optimizations, and to choose possible alternative layout optimizations. Keeping users involved increases their UI *control* [21] and *feature-awareness* [14] affected by adaptive/reduction mechanisms.

The following sections describe our approach in detail.

MINIMIZING THE FEATURE-SET

In order to minimize the feature-set we will rely on the concept of multi-layer interface design. This concept allows the users to control different sub-sets of the UI at any moment. For example, novice users could be given access to layer 1 and as they develop expertise could gain access to the upper layers at any time. RBUIS provides a practical approach for controlling the different UI layers. The meta-model for applying RBUIS on task models (CTT) is shown in Figure 2. CTTs were chosen to represent the task models due to their support of temporal constraints, which help in determining if simplifying a task could affect other tasks. Our approach in using temporal operators to check for task dependencies is similar to that of other researchers [4].

Feature-Set Minimization with RBUIS

Applying RBUIS on task models allows the minimization of the feature-set by revoking access to tasks based on roles hence achieving a role-based multi-layer interface design. Since we are initially designing the UI for the least constrained profile, the default policy will grant all roles access to all the tasks. This could be considered as a layer containing all the features. Afterwards, access could be revoked by allocating roles to tasks thereby creating separate layers, which users could gain role-based access to. Since users could be allocated multiple roles from the existing role categories, priorities will be used to provide enough flexibility to specify how roles override each other. Upon assigning the access rights to block tasks based on roles, a property (*concrete operation*) will specify whether to make a task invisible, disable it (keep data visible / protect data), or fade it until first use. The task model is mapped to the Abstract UI (AUI), which is in turn mapped to the CUI to hide, disable, or fade the relevant UI widgets.

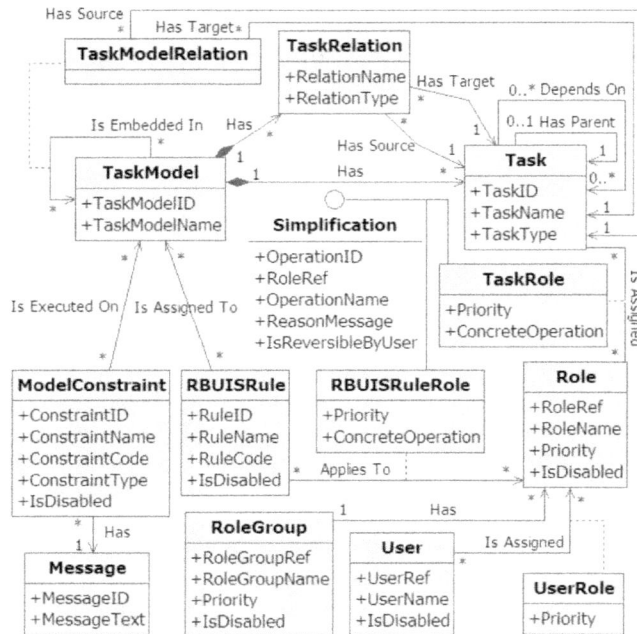

Figure 2. Meta-Model of Applying RBUIS on Task Model

Less Time Consuming Access Rights Allocation

Since enterprise applications encompass a large number of tasks that are used by hundreds of users, we need to make the allocation of access rights on the task models as little time consuming as possible. Traditionally, enterprise application users are allocated roles. This could be considered as a positive starting point. We will resort to the following features to minimize the time taken to allocate roles to tasks in the task models:

- A *default policy* grants access to all roles on all the application's task models hence making it only necessary to override this policy where access should be revoked. Each task will be implicitly allocated a fixed role called

"All-Roles", which represents all the roles in the system and is granted access to execute the task. Access to the task will be revoked to all other explicitly assigned roles.

- Sub-tasks will *inherit* the access rights of the parent tasks while maintaining the ability to override these rights.

- In some cases the same functionality is replicated in many places within the application. Usually developers create visual components (CUI level) that could be reused in different places. By making task models *reusable* within one another, access rights allocated to a task model could roam with it whenever it is used again while maintaining the ability to override the initial rights. This feature is illustrated in Figure 2 with the recursive relationship *"Is Embedded In"* on the *"TaskModel"* class. Each embedded task model is connected to a source and a target task as shown on the *"TaskModelRelation"* class.

- *Rules* could be defined and applied to sets of task models based on each task's properties (ID, name, type, etc.). RBUIS rules are defined through our support tool (*Cedar Studio*) in the form of conditions using SQL syntax. Also, check lists are given to associate task models and roles with each rule. One basic example would be to revoke access to the role *"Cashier"* on all *"Interaction"* tasks with the words *"Enter Discount"* in the task name.

Applying RBUIS to Task Models at Runtime

Based on the CEDAR architecture, the UI models will be loaded on the server and the adaptive engine will apply RBUIS at runtime. To apply the concrete operations on the CUI, the Task Model is mapped to the AUI, which is in turn mapped to the CUI. A certain order should be followed to perform the elimination since each user could be allocated multiple roles simultaneously. The meta-model allows the assignment of priorities on different levels. The designer could specify where the priority is read from (*"RoleGroup"*, *"Role"*, *"TaskRole"*, *"UserRole"*). Task-based assignments have a higher priority than rule-based ones unless specified otherwise. The following example demonstrates the process assuming the priorities were set at the *"TaskRole"* level:

- *UserA*: Novice, Manager
- *TaskX*: **1.** All-Roles (Allow) **2.** Accountant (Deny-Hide) **3.** Novice (Deny-Disable)

An excerpt of our algorithm is shown in Algorithm 1, the full version is included in a separate report [2]. Following this algorithm *"UserA"* is allowed to perform *"TaskX"* since *"Manager"* has the highest priority. In contrast, if *"Novice"* had a higher priority than *"All-Roles"*, then *"UserA"* would have been denied access to *"TaskX"* hence disabling its CUI as indicated by the concrete operation.

The running time of our algorithm is estimated to be polynomial: $O\ (m \times (n \times l \times p \times (2\ j \log j + k) + n))$, where m = Num. of Task Models, n = Num. of Tasks in a Task Model, j = Num. of User Roles, k = Num. of Blocked CUI Elements for a Task, p = Num. of Parent Tasks for a Task, and l = Num. of Task Roles.

Algorithm 1. Feature-Set Minimization (Excerpt)

```
1. Simplify-Task (TaskID, UserRoles[ ], TaskRoles[ ], UIModel)
2.   foreach ur in UserRoles // Determine the Primary Role
3.     tr ← TaskRoles.GetRole(ur.RoleRef)
4.     if tr = null then tr ← TaskRoles.GetRole(All-Roles)
5.     ur.Priority ← tr.Priority;
6.   UserRoles.OrderBy(Priority)
7.   PrimaryRole ← UserRoles.First()
8.   if PrimaryRole.RoleRef ≠ All-Roles // Apply Concrete Operation to CUI
9.     blkdAUI←GetBlckdAUI(TaskID, UIModel.TMToAUIMap)
10.    blkdCUI←GetBlckdCUI(blkdAUI, UIModel.UIToCUIMap, UIModel.CUI)
11.    foreach element in blkdCUI
12.      switch PrimaryRole.ConcreteOperation
13.        case Hide: element.Visible ← false; break;
14.        case Disable: element.ReadOnly ← true; break;
15.        case Protect: element.ReadOnly ← true;
16.               element.MaskChar ← '*'; break;
17.        case Fade: element.Opacity ← '30%'; break;
```

Model Checking using SQL

Since the access rights are being allocated by humans, model checking is needed to ensure that critical constraints are not violated. This allows our tool to issue appropriate warnings and errors. Several techniques exist for defining and evaluating constraints on models. For example, the Object Constraint Language (OCL) could be used to define constraints on UML diagrams. Furthermore, there are numerous tools that could be used for model checking (e.g., Z3, Spec#, Formula, etc.). In our case we need to define constraints on task models represented by CTTs. Since our approach is based on the CEDAR architecture, all the models are being stored in a relational database. This allows the model checking to be performed using SQL, which is more familiar to many developers and I.T. personnel than constraint languages such as OCL. The following example shows a constraint and its SQL-based solution in Listing 1.

Constraint: A sub-task should not be blocked for all the assigned roles because it will not be accessible by any user

Listing 1. Task Model Constraint Example using SQL

```
With SelTasks as (Select TM.TaskModelID, TM.TaskModelName, TK.TaskID,
TK.TaskName From TaskModel as TM Inner Join TaskModelTask as TK On
TM.TaskModelID = TK.TaskModelID Where TaskModelID in (@ModelIDs))

UserAccessOnTasks as (Select TaskModelID, TaskID, COUNT(case
UR.CanExecuteTask when 1 then 1 else null end) as CanExecuteCount
From SelTasks Cross Apply LoadSortedUserRoles(TaskModelID,TaskID)
as UR Where UR.UserRolePriority = 1 Group ByTaskModelID,TaskID)

Select SelTasks.* From SelTasks ST Inner Join UserAccessOnTasks UAT
On ST.TaskID = UAT.TaskID and ST.TaskModelID = UAT.TaskModelID
Where CanExecCount = 0
```

Constraints are defined in *Cedar Studio* and associated with task models through a system variable ("*@ModelIDs*"). Predefined functions such as "*LoadSortedUserRoles*" could be used in model constraints and extended when necessary. In this case the function loads the users and their assigned roles sorted by the priority of execution according to a certain task. The SQL statement would return the tasks that are violating the constraint, to be displayed on the screen.

Feature-Set Minimization Example

Although enterprise applications contain many complex examples, a basic example has been purposefully chosen in order to accommodate screen shots in the paper. Complex real-life examples were considered in our evaluation.

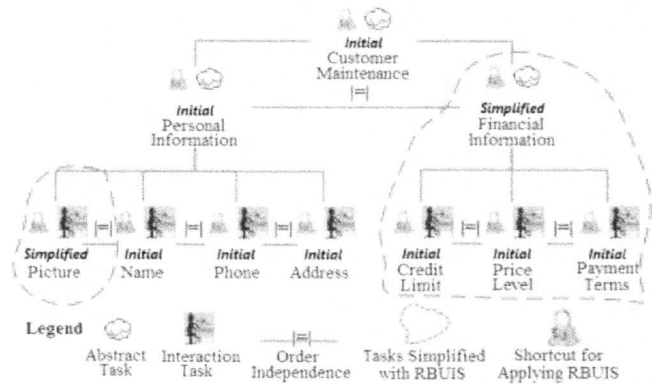

Figure 3. Simplified Customer Maintenance Task Model

The example illustrated in Figure 3 shows part of a task model built in *Cedar Studio* for a "*Customer Maintenance*" UI common in ERP systems. The lock-shaped buttons allow the application of RBUIS on any task. In this case, the tasks called "*Financial Information*" and "*Picture*" encircled in a dashed line are marked as **simplified** indicating that RBUIS has been applied. In the case of "*Financial Info.*" the access rights will get inherited by its sub-tasks. We considered a role called "*Cashier*" requiring a version of the UI showing only the "*Name*", "*Phone*", and "*Address*". This allows users working as cashiers to enter the initial information for a new customer on the counter without having to handle other details that could be added later. The initial version of the Final UI (FUI) is illustrated in Figure 4 (a), and the one simplified for the role "*Cashier*" is illustrated in Figure 4 (b). In this example, the concrete operation in RBUIS was set to "*Hide*" hence the widgets became invisible.

(a) Initial Fully-Featured Version

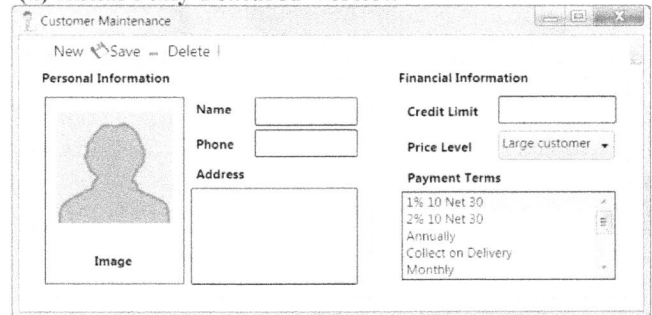

(b) Minimized Feature-Set Version for Role "Cashier"

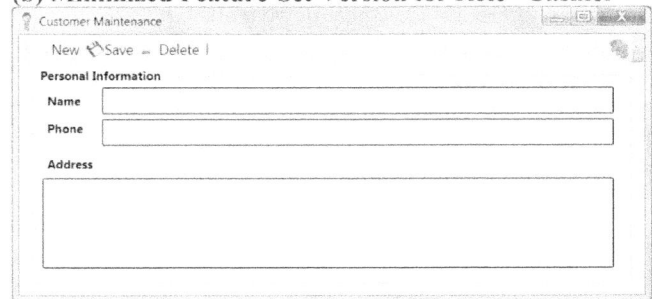

Figure 4. Feature-Set Minimization of Customer UI

OPTIMIZING THE LAYOUT

Providing users with an optimal layout could be based on various aspects (e.g., computer literacy, cognition, screen-size, etc.). In this section we present our generic mechanism for devising adaptive behavior for such criteria. Enterprise applications require an approach that allows developers as well as I.T. personnel to implement adaptive behavior. Our feature-set minimization mechanism allows RBUIS to be applied visually and through code-based rules. Similarly, our layout optimization mechanism allows the definition of adaptive behavior using a mix of visual and code constructs embedded in adaptation workflows. The meta-model for applying this mechanism on the CUI is shown in Figure 5.

Layout Optimization with RBUIS and Workflows

The representation of adaptive behavior has a great impact on the extensibility of any adaptive system. Most adaptive UI state of the art systems tend to employ an arbitrary design that hardcodes adaptation behavior within the software application, severely minimizing its reusability and extensibility. A graphical tool is suggested for hiding the complexity of defining UI adaptation rules [19]. This tool might not be able to handle all possible scenarios due to the limited use of a high level visual representation.

To balance between ease of use and flexibility, our approach combines high level adaptation operations and low level programming constructs by using both visual and code-based representations. Workflows are not strange to enterprise applications due to their use for devising customizable and reusable business rules that could be separated from the software code. With appropriate tool support, workflows could also provide visual programming constructs (e.g., control structures, error handling, etc.). Additionally, it is possible to define code-based adaptation operations that integrate within the visual workflow.

Our approach uses tool supported workflows, which could represent adaptive behavior with: (1) visual programming constructs, (2) compiled code libraries and dynamically interpreted scripts. The workflows are executed at runtime on the CUI models to perform the necessary adaptation.

To implement the workflows in practice we are using the Windows Workflow Foundation (WF), which is part of the .NET framework. WF provides a visual design tool, which we integrated into *Cedar Studio*. This design tool provides the ability to visually design activity workflows using a rich set of constructs, which could be saved in an XML-based format then reloaded and executed when an adaptation is needed. Furthermore, the supported constructs could be extended through external compiled class libraries developed in C# or VB.NET and dynamically integrated with our tool. We have used this capability to develop a construct capable of integrating within a workflow and executing non-compiled script code. We currently support Iron Python but other scripting or transformation languages (e.g., XSLT) could be integrated in the future.

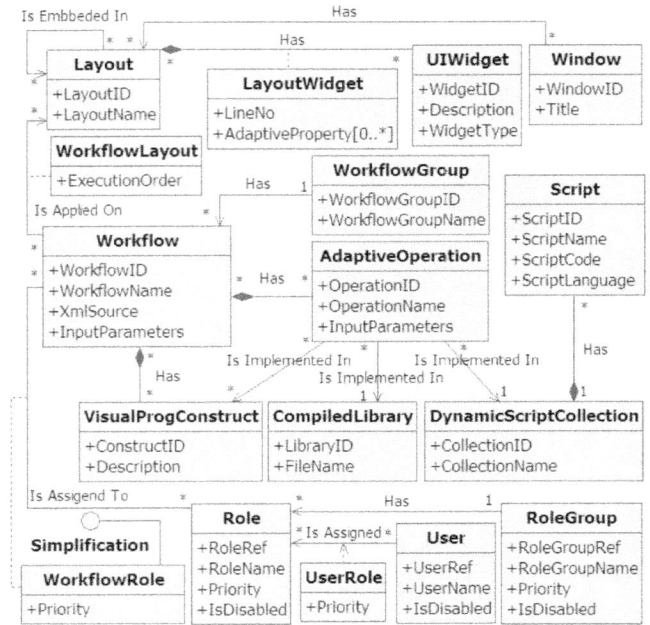

Figure 5. Meta-Model for RBUIS and Workflows on CUI

Applying RBUIS with Workflows at Runtime

Layout optimization is also based on our CEDAR architecture. After the feature-set is minimized, the workflows will be executed on the CUI by the adaptation engine. Afterwards, the FUI will be transferred to the client to be rendered on the screen. The process of selecting the workflows to be applied based on the user's role is illustrated in Algorithm 2 through an excerpt of our algorithm assuming the priority is read from the "*Roles*" class. The running time of our algorithm is established to be polynomial: $O(2\ m \log m + 2\ n \log n)$, where $\mathbf{m}$ = Num. of User Roles and $\mathbf{n}$ = Num. of Workflows to be Executed.

Algorithm 2. Layout Optimization (Excerpt)

```
1. Optimize-Layout (UserRoles[ ], Roles[ ], UIModel, LayoutID)
2.    foreach ur in UserRoles // Determine the Primary Role
3.       tr ← Roles.GetRole(ur.RoleRef)
4.       if tr = null then tr ← Roles.GetRole(All-Roles)
5.       ur.Priority ← tr.Priority;
6.    UserRoles.OrderBy(Priority)
7.    PrimaryRole ← UserRoles.First()
8.    WorkflowsToExecute[ ] ← GetWorkflows(PrimaryRole, LayoutID)
9.    WorkflowsToExecute.OrderBy(ExecutionOrder)
10.   foreach workflow in WorkflowsToExecute // Execute Workflows
11.      workflow.Execute(UIModel) // Execution Time Depends on Content
```

Layout Optimization Example

This example builds on the previous one illustrated in the feature-set minimization section. We consider two roles "*Sales Officer*" and "*Novice*". The "*Sales Officer*" requires the fully-featured UI illustrated in Figure 4 (a). The "*Novice*" requires layout optimizations that make functions accessible through on-screen buttons rather than a context-menu, and trading list boxes for radio buttons to fit more items on the screen. The workflow illustrated in Figure 6, represents the adaptive behavior by using three different techniques: (a) list boxes are substituted with radio button groups using visual programming constructs, (b) function accessibility is set to high by calling an Iron Python script, and (c) the UI is refitted by calling a C# layout algorithm.

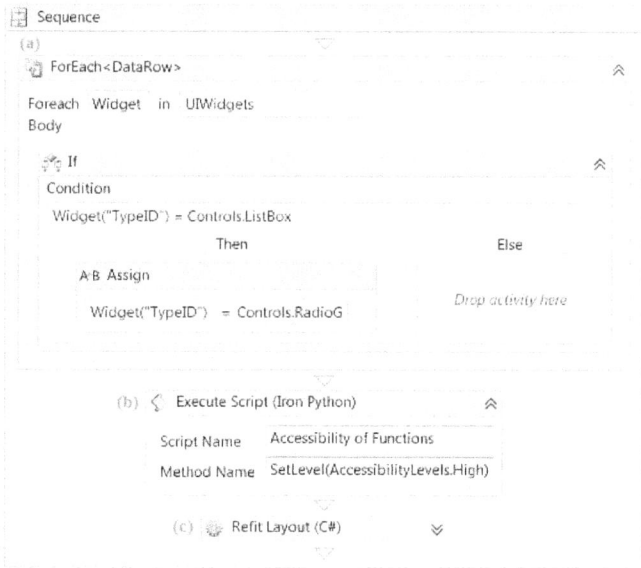

Figure 6. Layout Optimization Adaptive Workflow

The optimized UI in Figure 7 shows the functions for the image (add, remove, etc.) and address text-area (bold, italic, etc.) on the screen. In contrast, the version in Figure 4 (a) provided these functions through a context-menu. Also, the payment terms list box was substituted with a radio button group that displays more items on the screen. Some factors (e.g., access. of functions) are set by "*Adaptive Properties*" on the "*LayoutWidget*" class in the meta-model (Figure 5). In this case, the implementation of the adaptation behavior is part of the widget and it is just triggered from the workflow.

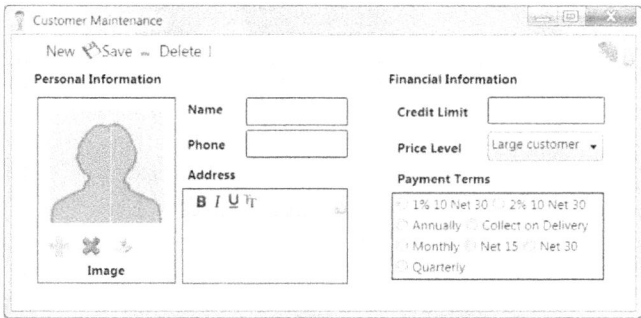

Figure 7. Optimized Layout of Customer FUI

USER FEEDBACK FOR REFINEMENT

Keeping the users involved in the adaptive process provides awareness of adaptive decisions and the ability to override role-based adaptations per user when necessary. In order to achieve this in practice we chose to transmit the final UI to the client with a list of the applied simplification operations. We denote such operations by the UML interface called "*Simplification*" shown in both meta-models. Our approach has two types of operations: *Feature-set minimization* and

layout optimization identified by "*RoleRef*" and "*TaskID*" / "*WorkflowID*" respectively. The meta-model in Figure 2 shows "*ReasonMessage*" and "*IsReversibleByUser*" as attributes of the "*Simplification*" UML interface (same for Figure 5). These attributes indicate the reason behind the simplification and whether it its reversible by the users.

The users can click the chameleon icon in the top right corner of the UI (Figure 4 (b), and Figure 7) to show a list of the applied adaptation operations as illustrated in Figure 8. Afterwards, the users can uncheck any reversible operation (feature-set minimization or layout optimization) and apply the changes for one time only or for future use as well. Furthermore, layout optimizations have another feature that allows the users to choose from possible alternatives. This is achieved by assigning workflows to groups as shown in the meta-model (Figure 5). Workflows in the same group could serve as alternatives. For example, a group could encompass several workflows for adapting the selection widget (e.g., combo box, list box, radio buttons, etc.). After the user applies the changes, a request will be sent to the server to re-simplify the UI and exclude the operations that he or she unchecked. In case the user decides to keep the changes for future use, based on the CEDAR architecture, the changes would get stored and he or she will gain access to an alternative version of the UI. The example operations illustrated in Figure 8 are related to the simplified UI in Figure 4 (b). The operations inform the user that the UI parts pertaining to the *financial information* and *image* are unused by the user's role (*Cashier*) hence were eliminated. In this example, if the user unchecks both operations and applies the changes, the simplified UI in Figure 4 (b) will revert back to the original version in Figure 4 (a). If an operation is set as "irreversible by users" (e.g., due to security reasons) the check box would be disabled and a message would notify the user of the reason. If a feature depends on other disabled features, the user is informed that these features should be enabled as well. The dependency is determined from the CTT temporal operators and is defined on the meta-model (Figure 2) through the recursive relationship "*Depends On*" on the "*Task*" class.

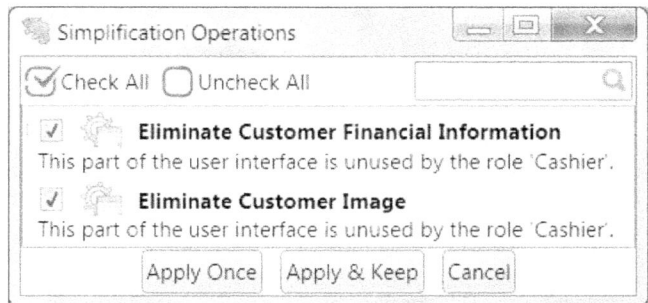

Figure 8. User Feedback - Simplification Operations

Even though in the case of feedback the UI is changing while the user is working, the user's initiation of the action reduces confusion due to the awareness and understating of the adaptation that is going to take place.

DEVELOPING APPLICATIONS WITH CEDAR STUDIO

Cedar Studio is our Integrated Development Environment (IDE) that supports the development of adaptive model-driven UIs for enterprise applications based on the CEDAR architecture. Due to space limits we will briefly describe its features in this paper. Interested readers could get more details from a separate report [2] and observe the tool in operation through online demo videos [33].

We created *Cedar Studio* in the form of an IDE to provide developers and I.T. personnel with an ease of access to all the visual-design and editing tools in one place. Currently, it supports visual design tools for: (1) Task Model, (2) Domain Model, (3) AUI Model, (4) CUI Model, and (5) Workflows. Also, it supports a combination of visual design and code editing tools for (1) Task Role Assignments and RBUIS Rules, (2) Model Constraints, and (3) Dynamic Scripts. One of the supported design tools (task model) is illustrated in Figure 9. Additionally, *Cedar Studio* supports automatic generation and synchronization between the various levels of abstraction (Task Model, AUI, and CUI) with the possibility to make manual changes at any of these levels.

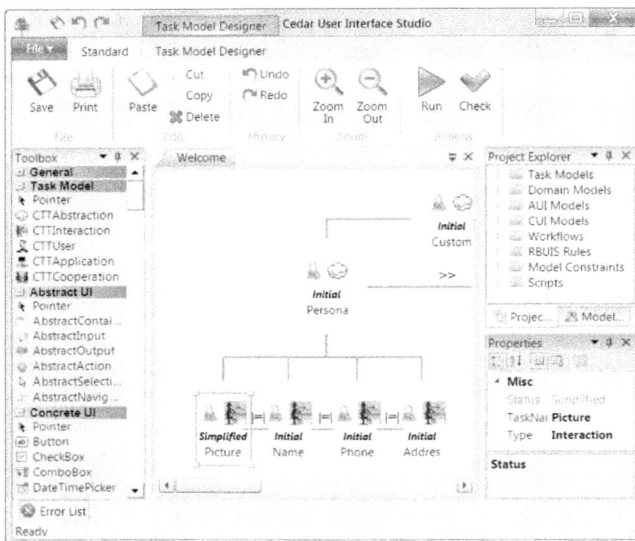

Figure 9. *Cedar Studio* **- Our IDE Support Tool**

Cedar Studio was designed as a tool for supporting our CEDAR architecture through UI and adaptive behavior models that would get stored in a relational database to provide easier runtime management and interpretation. The implementation of CEDAR is provided as a service that is consumed by *Cedar Studio* and technology specific APIs that allow enterprise applications to integrate with our solution. An API would include the client components illustrated in Figure 1. To test our approach we developed an API and a Toolkit in C# for the Windows Presentation Foundation. APIs for other presentation technologies (e.g., HTML, Java Swing, etc.) could be devised by anyone and used in combination with *Cedar Studio* for developing adaptive enterprise applications capable of benefitting from our simplification mechanism and any future extensions.

Adaptive UI behavior (e.g., widget hiding, substitution, etc.) could leave gaps and deformations in the layout, which are not esthetically desirable and could increase the navigation time (Fitts's Law). We required a mechanism to maintain plasticity, denoting the UI's ability to adapt to the context-of-use while preserving its usability [11]. Hence, we devised an algorithm to refit the layout based on its initial manual design by filling the gaps and adjusting the widgets' positions based on their new sizes and initial locations chosen by the designer. This technique creates a balance between fully automated approaches that generate the UI from an abstract model [16] and manual approaches that require developing and maintaining multiple CUI versions [32].

Cedar Studio is meant to be used during the development and post-development phases by developers, deployment teams, and I.T. personnel. The UI models are devised at the development phase and the simplification behavior could be added during the deployment phase according to the needs of each enterprise. This behavior could be based on user models such as the one described in the coming section.

BUILDING ADAPTIVE BEHAVIOR MODELS

One way to build adaptive behavior models for our system is to determine an aspect that influences enterprise application usability, statistically test its effect on UI alternatives, and implement the adaptive behavior for the alternatives using *Cedar Studio*. The outcome would be a general role-based adaptive model that could be refined by our feedback mechanism for particular tasks and users.

One such aspect discussed in the literature is "Computer Literacy" [29]. We setup a list of factors based on which the UI could be adapted and ran an online interactive survey to statistically test the effect of computer literacy on user preferences [2]. Although the list is not comprehensive it allows us to test our system against factors discussed in the literature and relevant to enterprise applications. We grouped the factors under categories that impact enterprise application usability ("*Presentation*" and "*Navigation*"):

Presentation: **Layout Grouping** (*Tab Page, Sub-Window, Group Box*), **Multi-Record Visualization** (*Grid, Carousel, Detailed Form*), **Simple Selection Widget** (*Combo, Slider, Radios*), **Multi-Record Input** (*Scrolling Grid, Non-Scroll. Grid, Form*), **Accessibility of Functions** (*High, Medium, Low*), **Information Density** (*High, Medium, Low*), **Text versus Graphics** (*Text Only, Image Only, Image & Text*)
Navigation: **Multi-Doc. UI** (*New Window, New Page, New Tab*), **Search the UI** (*Go to Widget, Filter, Filter & Re-layout*) **Navigation Structure** (*Menu, Tree, Panel*)

One should note that from a technical perspective adaptive behavior for all the factors is devisable using our platform. Yet, factors could vary based on different aspects. For example, our survey showed that computer literacy impacts "*Multi-Document UI*", "*Navigation Structure*", and "*Layout Grouping*", whereas "*Accessibility of Functions*" and "*Info. Density*" were shown to be impacted by culture [27].

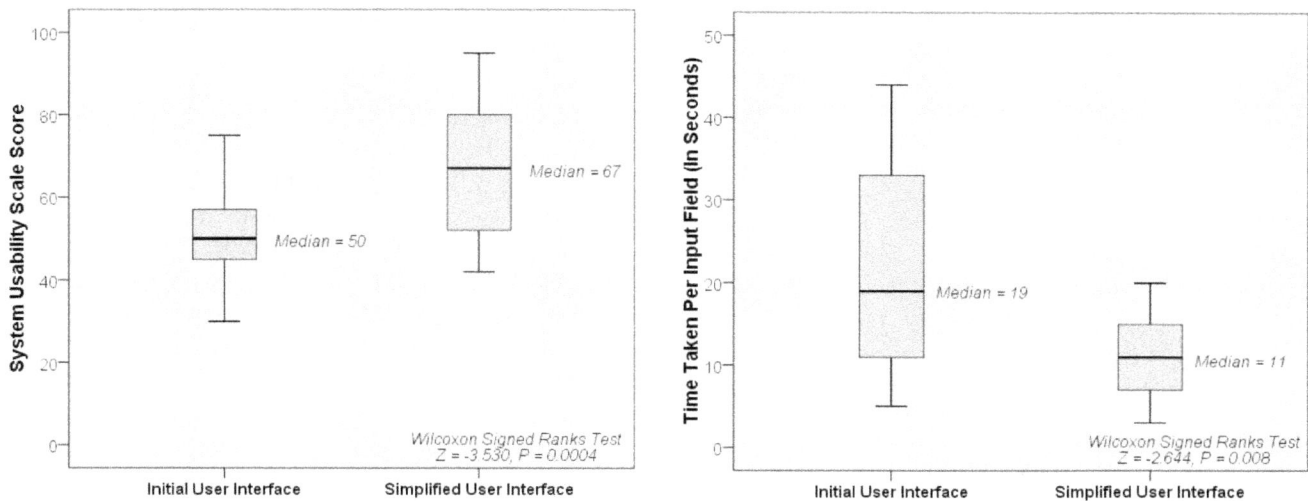

Figure 10. Evaluation Results for Role-Based UI Simplification

EVALUATING ROLE-BASED UI SIMPLIFICATION

Our simplification mechanism was evaluated [2] using an online interactive survey with a UI pair composed of an initial and a simplified UI. We selected the *"Customer Maintenance"* form of the SAP ERP. The initial version contains numerous nested tab pages and dozens of fields. Yet, users with different roles in the enterprise require a simpler version for managing basic customer records.

We developed a copy of SAP's UI alongside a simplified version containing the fields used to create a basic customer record. The fields were selected based on the variability in SAP's user needs [32]. The concrete operation was set to *"Hide"* with some fields being reversible by the user, and the widgets were regrouped accordingly.

Participants were asked to fill a set of fields required for creating a basic customer record using both UI versions. In the case of the simplified UI some of the fields had to be retrieved through the user feedback screen, allowing us to test how participants react to this feature.

In some cases, participants prefer the first UI option they see hence creating certain bias in a study's outcome. To avoid this potential bias we presented half of the participants with the initial UI first and the other half with the simplified one first. After each task, participants were asked to answer the System Usability Scale (SUS) questions, which allow us to detect usability differences between the two UI versions. Also, the time taken to complete each task was recorded.

We hypothesize that simplifying enterprise application UIs based on roles improves user satisfaction and efficiency.

The participants (n=25) never used the selected UI before. A Wilcoxon Signed Ranks Test showed that simplifying the user interface based on roles elicited a statistically significant improvement (Figure 10) in both SUS usability score ($Z = -3.530$, $P = 0.0004$) and task completion time ($Z = -2.644$, $P = 0.008$) hence confirming our hypothesis.

The median SUS score was 50 for the initial UI and 67 for the simplified one. The median time taken to complete the task (seconds per input field) was 19 for the initial UI and 11 for the simplified one. The results were also reflected in the comments of some participants about the simplified version being more efficient whereas the initial UI made it complicated to locate fields. Also, the ease of use of the feedback mechanism was reflected by the fact that 80% of the participants were able to use it by only referring to a few words of instruction on its purpose.

CONCLUSIONS AND FUTURE WORK

We presented our Role-Based UI Simplification (RBUIS) approach, comprising feature-set minimization and layout optimization. RBUIS is based on our CEDAR architecture that is offered as a generic extensible service allowing the addition of adaptive behavior as needed. The scalability of our mechanism was shown by our complexity analysis.

Additionally, we introduced *Cedar Studio* our IDE that provides tool support for developing and maintaining adaptive enterprise UIs. We described how it can be used to represent role-based adaptive behavior visually (role assignment, and constructs in workflows) and through code (RBUIS rules, and compiled code/scripts in workflows).

Finally, we conducted a user study to evaluate RBUIS. The study showed a statistically significant improvement in user satisfaction and efficiency for simplified UIs. The outcome of the study also reflects the importance of a model-based approach that preserves designer input, made on the CUI, during adaptation. Also, by offering the UI as a role-based alternative our approach reduces confusion created by adaptations conducted while the user is working.

In the future we will extend our mechanism to support UI simplification in scenarios that require the use of multiple user interfaces for fulfilling a task. Additionally, more user studies will be conducted using eye-tracking in addition to measuring user satisfaction and efficiency.

ACKNOWLEDGMENTS
We would like to thank Prof. Helen Sharp and Dr. Sheep Dalton for their input on early drafts of this paper, Prof. Marian Petre for her comments on the video figure, and the anonymous reviewers for their valuable suggestions. This work is partially funded by ERC Advanced Grant 291652.

REFERENCES

1. Akiki, P.A., Bandara, A.K., and Yu, Y. Using Interpreted Runtime Models for Devising Adaptive User Interfaces of Enterprise Applications. ICEIS'12, SciTePress (2012), 72-77.

2. Akiki, P.A., Bandara, A.K., and Yu, Y. Cedar: Engineering Role-Based Adaptive User Interfaces for Enterprise Applications (2012). http://computing-reports.open.ac.uk/2012/TR2012-08.pdf

3. Bencomo, N., Sawyer, P., Blair, G.S., and Grace, P. Dynamically Adaptive Systems are Product Lines too: Using Model-Driven Techniques to Capture Dynamic Variability of Adaptive Systems. SPLC'08, Lero (2008), 23-32.

4. Bergh, J., Sahni, D., and Coninx, K. Task Models for Safe Software Evolution and Adaptation. TAMODIA'09, Springer (2010), 72-77.

5. Blouin, A., Morin, B., Beaudoux, O., Nain, G., Albers, P., and Jézéquel, J.-M. Combining Aspect-Oriented Modeling with Property-Based Reasoning to Improve User Interface Adaptation. EICS'11, ACM (2011),85-94.

6. Blumendorf, M., Lehmann, G., and Albayrak, S. Bridging Models and Systems at Runtime to Build Adaptive User Interfaces. EICS'10, ACM (2010), 9-18.

7. Botterweck, G. Multi Front-End Engineering. Model-Driven Development of Advanced User Interfaces, Springer (2011), 27-42.

8. Calvary, G., Coutaz, J., Thevenin, D., Limbourg, Q., Bouillon, L., and Vanderdonckt, J. A Unifying Reference Framework for Multi-Target User Interfaces. Interacting with Computers 15, 3, Elsevier (2003), 289-308.

9. Carroll, J.M. and Carrithers, C. Training Wheels in a User Interface. CACM 27, 8, ACM (1984), 800-806.

10. Clerckx, T., Vandervelpen, C., Luyten, K., and Coninx, K. A Task-Driven User Interface Architecture for Ambient Intelligent Environments. IUI'06, ACM (2006), 309-311.

11. Coutaz, J. User Interface Plasticity: Model Driven Engineering to the Limit! EICS'10, ACM (2010), 1-8.

12. Demeure, A., Meskens, J., Luyten, K., and Coninx, K. Design by Example of Graphical User Interfaces Adapting to Available Screen Size. Computer-Aided Design of User Interfaces VI, Springer (2009), 277-282.

13. Ferraiolo, D.F., Sandhu, R., Gavrila, S., Kuhn, D.R., and Chandramouli, R. Proposed NIST Standard for Role-Based Access Control. TISSEC, ACM (2001), 224-274.

14. Findlater, L. and McGrenere, J. Evaluating Reduced-Functionality Interfaces According to Feature Findability and Awareness. INTERACT'07, ACM (2007), 592-605.

15. Florins, M. and Vanderdonckt, J. Graceful Degradation of User Interfaces as a Design Method for Multiplatform Systems. IUI'04, ACM (2004), 140-147.

16. Gajos, K.Z., Weld, D.S., and Wobbrock, J.O. Automatically Generating Personalized User Interfaces with Supple. Artificial Intelligence, Elsevier (2010), 910-950.

17. Jacobson, S., Shepherd, J., D'Aquila, M., and Carter, K. The ERP Market Sizing Report. AMR Research (2007).

18. Kramer, J. and Magee, J. Self-Managed Systems: an Architectural Challenge. FOSE'07, IEEE (2007), 259-268.

19. López-Jaquero, V., Montero, F., and Real, F. Designing User Interface Adaptation Rules with T:XML. IUI'09, ACM (2009), 383-388.

20. Lykkegaard, B. and Elbak, A. IDC - Document at a Glance - LC52T. International Data Corporation (2011).

21. McGrenere, J., Baecker, R.M., and Booth, K.S. An Evaluation of a Multiple Interface Design Solution for Bloated Software. CHI'02, ACM (2002), 164-170.

22. McGrenere, J. "Bloat": The Objective and Subject Dimensions. CHI'00, ACM (2000), 337-338.

23. Paterno, F. Model-based Design and Evaluation of Interactive Applications. Springer-Verlag (1999).

24. Peissner, M., Häbe, D., Janssen, D., and Sellner, T. MyUI: Generating Accessible User Interfaces from Multimodal Design Patterns. EICS'12, ACM (2012), 81-90.

25. Piechnick, C., Richly, S., Götz, S., Wilke, C., and Aßmann, U. Using Role-Based Composition to Support Unanticipated, Dynamic Adaptation - Smart Application Grids. ADAPTIVE'12, IARIA (2012), 93-102.

26. Pleuss, A., Botterweck, G., and Dhungana, D. Integrating Automated Product Derivation and Individual User Interface Design. VaMoS'10, Universitat Duisburg-Essen (2010), 69-76.

27. Reinecke, K. and Bernstein, A. Improving Performance, Perceived Usability, and Aesthetics with Culturally Adaptive User Interfaces. TOCHI 18, ACM (2011), 1-29.

28. Shneiderman, B. Promoting Universal Usability with Multi-Layer Interface Design. CUU'03, ACM (2003), 1-8.

29. Singh, A. and Wesson, J. Evaluation Criteria for Assessing the Usability of ERP systems. SAICSIT '09, ACM (2009), 87-95.

30. Uflacker, M. and Busse, D. Complexity in Enterprise Applications vs. Simplicity in User Experience. HCI'07, Springer-Verlag (2007), 778-787.

31. Dynamics CRM 2011 - Role-Based UI. http://bit.ly/DynamicsRoleBasedUI.

32. GuiXT - Simplify and Optimize the SAP ERP UI. http://bit.ly/SAPGuiXTSimplifyUI.

33. Cedar Studio - Demo Videos. http://adaptiveui.pierreakiki.com.

Model-driven Development and Evolution of Customized User Interfaces

Andreas Pleuss
Lero
University of Limerick, Ireland
andreas.pleuss@lero.ie

Stefan Wollny
University of Augsburg,
Germany
stefanwollny@googlemail.de

Goetz Botterweck
Lero
University of Limerick, Ireland
goetz.botterweck@lero.ie

ABSTRACT

One of the main benefits of model-driven development of User Interfaces (UIs) is the increase in efficiency and consistency when developing multiple variants of a UI. For instance, multiple UIs for different target users, platforms, devices, or for whole product families can be generated from the same abstract models. However, purely generated UIs are not always sufficient as there is often need for customizing the individual UI variants, e.g., due to usability issues or specific customer requirements.

In this paper we present a model-driven approach for the development of *UI families* with systematic support for customizations. The approach supports customizing all aspects of a UI (UI elements, screens, navigation, etc.) and storing the customizations in specific models. As a result, a UI family can be evolved more efficiently because individual UI variants can be re-generated (after some changes have been applied to the family) without losing any previously made customizations. We demonstrate this by thirty highly customized real-world products from a commercial family of web information systems called *HIS-GX/QIS*.

Author Keywords

User Interface Engineering; Model-driven development; Software Product Lines; Usability Engineering

ACM Classification Keywords

D.2.2 Software Engineering: Design Tools and Techniques—*User interfaces*; D.2.9 Software Engineering: Management—*Software configuration management*; H.5.2 Information Interfaces and Presentation: User Interfaces—*Theory and methods*

INTRODUCTION

While classic user interface engineering approaches address mainly the quality of the User Interface (UI), other engineering goals, e.g., efficiency, robustness, and maintainability

require application of additional software engineering concepts. For instance, concepts from *Model-driven Development* (MDD) [24] have been applied to UIs in various approaches [13, 10]. In MDD, the system to be developed is specified in terms of abstract *models* (e.g., using UML or domain-specific languages), which are transformed stepwise by automated *model transformations* into more concrete models and finally into the implementation code (i.e., code generation).

However, when applying software engineering concepts to UIs, it is important to take the specific characteristics of UIs into account and to ensure that there are concrete benefits of applying these techniques. For instance, MDE supports efficiency and consistency when developing multiple variants of a UIs from the same abstract models. Many existing approaches address the development of UIs for multiple target platforms [4, 9]. Similar scenarios are development of multiple UIs for different users, devices, or contexts of use. Another important scenario is the development of multiple different variants of an application (*product family*) as addressed in software product line engineering [8, 20]. All these scenarios can be addressed with MDD by generating multiple variants of a UI from the same abstract model. To generalize from these concrete scenarios, we introduce in this paper the term *UI family* that refers to multiple different variants of a UI in general and show an MDD approach for UI family development.

Beyond variability in UI families, MDD can also help with *maintenance and evolution* [14], e.g., addressing the need to adapt software over time according to changing market and user requirements. Here, again MDD can help by providing the ability to perform changes on an abstract model level and then to just (re-)generate the new version of the UIs. We demonstrate this here as part of our evaluation.

At the same time, however, the special characteristics of UIs have to be considered. For instance, UIs developed by purely automated approaches are not always optimal in terms of quality [2]. In particular, specific users, customers, or target devices can raise unforeseen requirements on the UI that need to be addressed by manual customizations [18, 19]. Hence, there is a need to support manual customizations within a model-driven UI development process.

In this paper we aim to push the boundaries of model-driven UI development further by tackling these issues: We aim to provide a model-driven development approach for whole families of similar UIs. For this, we introduce a notion of

UI families that generalizes from specific aspects, e.g., multi-platform or multi-user UIs. To support customized high-quality UIs, we introduce a novel concept to integrate manual UI customization into the MDD process. Inspired by stylesheets for HTML UIs, the manual customizations can be stored in separate, modular models. In this way, customizations can be added, combined and reused over multiple products and multiple product versions. In contrast to stylesheets, which cover mainly the visual appearance, our models support customizing *all* aspects of the UI including navigation, layout or the decomposition of the UI into screens.

We evaluate the approach using a commercial web information system for university management *HIS-GX/QIS*[1]. This is a product family where each product (an individual instance of the software for a particular university) is highly customized according to the individual needs of the university – often by third parties or the university itself. We have performed a detailed analysis of the UI customizations in this UI family [19] showing that customizations are spread all over the UI and cover each aspect of the UI. Our evaluation shows for thirty real-world product instances, that all these individually customized UIs can be developed from a single abstract model using our approach. In particular, we demonstrate the benefits of MDD for software evolution: Changes on the UI family, like adding or removing UI elements, need to be performed only on the single abstract model. By regenerating the UIs, the changes can be automatically propagated to all products without loosing any previously specified customizations. We demonstrate this again for all thirty real-world product instances.

The remainder of the paper is structured as follows: The next section introduces the concept of *UI families* that generalizes from multi-target UI development (as in existing model-driven UI development approaches) and product family development (as in software product lines). Next, we introduce our concept for integrating manual customizations into an MDD process for UIs. Subsequently, we show the concrete realization of our approach followed by a comprehensive evaluation using HIS-GX/QIS. Finally, we discuss related work and present conclusions and an outlook.

DEVELOPMENT OF MULTIPLE UIS – UI FAMILIES

Development of different UIs depending on the context of use has become an important issue in UI engineering research, e.g., in the context of ubiquitous computing [15]. For instance, it can be required to vary a UI according to different target devices, user groups, or usage context. The area of *Model-based UI Development* (*MBUID*)provides modeling concepts that can be used to address these challenges. On the other hand, development of families of systems is also an important issue in software engineering as many software products have to be provided in different variations. This is addressed by the area of *Software Product Line Engineering* (*SPLE*). As both concepts require the development of multiple related UIs and can be supported by MDD, we integrate these concepts by introducing *UI families* as a more general term for multiple related UIs.

---

[1]http://www.his.de/english/organisation

The following sections first introduce MBUID, then SPLE, and finally our concept of UI families.

MBUID Concepts

The area of Model-based UI Development [25] addresses model-based (including model-driven) development of UIs[2]. There have been various approaches using models for different purposes but one of the most important goals has become the development of UIs for multiple contexts of use. For instance, UIs for multiple target platforms, devices, users, or situations are developed from the same abstract UI models (often called multi-platform, multi-user, etc. UIs).

Figure 1a shows the common concepts for such approaches based on [25, 6]. The left-hand side shows the different models used to specify a UI in MBUID. The right-hand side shows the context of use that influences the UI development. In the following we first explain the models on the left-hand side.

The most abstract models are the *Domain Model* and the *Task Model*. The *Domain Model* is a conventional model used to describe domain concepts and the corresponding application structure, e.g., in terms of a UML class diagram. A *Task Model* describes the user tasks to be supported by the application and temporal operators between them (e.g., if two tasks are performed sequentially or concurrently). A concrete approach for task models is, e.g., CTT [16].

An *Abstract UI Model* describes the UI in terms of abstract UI elements that are platform- and often even modality-independent abstractions of UI widgets, like *input* element, *output* element, *selection* element, or *action* element (abstraction of a button). Each abstract UI element realizes tasks from the *Task Model* and is associated with properties or operations from the Domain Model. Abstract UI Elements are contained in *presentation units*, which are top-level containers, e.g., Windows/Frames, and other *UI containers* (abstractions of, e.g., panels). The *Abstract UI Model* also describes the navigation between the *Presentation Units* and an (abstract) layout.

A *Concrete User Interface Model* refines and concretizes the *Abstract UI Model* by specifying concrete UI elements, i.e., concrete UI widgets, and their layout. It can still abstract from a specific GUI API (e.g., providing a generalized "List Box" widget).

The final implementation is referred to as the *Final UI*. It can either be a model that represents the final implementation code (potentially interpreted at runtime) or the final code itself.

The context of use for a UI can be defined by *user*, *platform*, and *environment* (models). A UI can be adapted to the context of use either at development time (e.g., developing multiple UIs for different target platforms) or at runtime (i.e., context-adaptive UIs). Here we focus on the former case as runtime adaptation is outside the scope of this paper. The (type of)

---

[2]"Model-based" usually refers to usage of models in a general sense while "model-driven" more specifically refers to usage of models for (semi-)automated code generation.

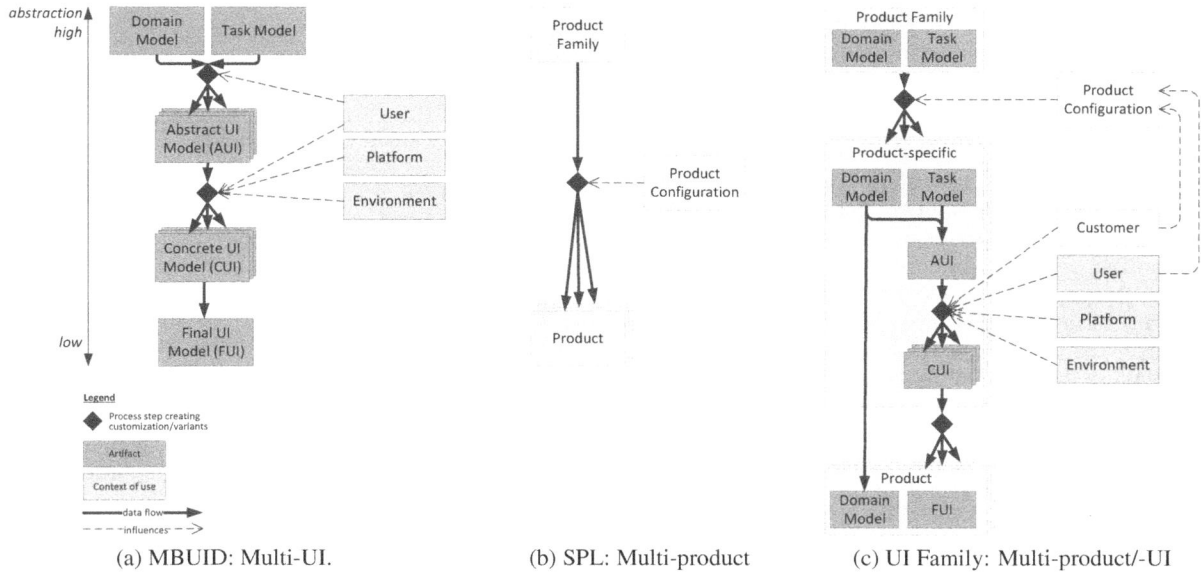

(a) MBUID: Multi-UI. (b) SPL: Multi-product (c) UI Family: Multi-product/-UI

Figure 1. Families of related UIs and influencing factors.

user can influence the AUI as, e.g., some tasks are not intended for all users. It can also influence the CUI development as, e.g., an elderly user might require like larger size of UI elements. The platform and environment influence mainly the CUI, like selected widget types and layout.

Basically, the steps from task and domain model to FUI can be performed manually or in an automated way, depending on the particular MBUID approach. In MDD, these steps are performed automatically by model transformations. The context models are then used as additional input for the model transformations, e.g., by parameterizing and/or selecting between different transformation rules.

SPLE Concepts

The area of *Software Product Line Engineering* (*SPLE*) [8, 20] addresses the development of a whole family of similar software products from a common set of shared software assets. Software Product Lines (SPL) have been applied by many companies in various industry domains [23]. A common example is online shop software: As different online shops have large *commonalities* in their functionality they can potentially all be built from a common set of software assets. However, there are also *variations* between them, like the supported payment methods or the way the articles sold in the shop are organized.

The commonalities and variability in a SPL are usually specified in terms of a variability model. For instance, a variability model for an online shop SPL might specify that each online shop must support at least one payment method (commonality) which can be credit card payment, purchase order, or cash on delivery (variability). A concrete product is then defined by a *product configuration*, i.e., a selection of variants. For instance, there might be an online shop that supports credit card payment only, while another one supports all three payment methods.

Each variant in the product line is associated with an implementation. For instance, each of the payment methods might be associated with a software component that implements the payment method. Using model-driven techniques, it is then possible to automatically generate a product implementation by automated composition of the implementation assets that are associated with selected variants.

Figure 1b summarizes the main concepts: on SPL level, the whole *product family* is specified, i.e., the superset of all implementation assets for all potential variants. A *product configuration* defines which variants have been selected for this product. Different product configurations result in multiple products.

As shown in [18], SPL concepts can also be applied to the UI of an application: On product family level, all UI elements for all potential product variants are specified. A concrete product contains only those UI elements for those variants that have been selected for this product. For instance, UI elements for input of credit card information are only included into the UI if credit card payment has been selected in the product configuration.

UI Families

The MBUID and SPLE concepts introduced in the previous sections can both be used for model-driven development of multiple UIs from the same abstract models. The difference between them is that SPLE focuses on the whole application and mainly *functional* differences (e.g., support of credit card payment or not) while MBUID focuses on the UI and mainly *non-functional* differences (e.g., usability when using a particular device). However, one can easily imagine that both concepts in combination can be required in practice: For instance, an online shop cannot only vary in its functionality (SPLE) but also has to vary according to the context of use (MBUID), e.g., provide support for multiple target platforms.

15

From the viewpoint of a general MDD process there is no need to exclude one of these two possibilities, hence, we combine both concepts. For this we introduce the term *UI family* as a general means to refer to a set of related UIs that vary according to SPLE concepts and/or the context of use.

Figure 1c shows the combined concepts: The family model specifies the UI (and other parts of the application like the domain model) for the whole family. The UI is defined as task model, containing the superset of all tasks supported in the product family. The product derivation influences the functionality of the product (by selecting variants) which results in a selection of tasks to be supported by a concrete product, i.e. a product-specific task model. Hence, in contrast to Figure 1a, adapting the available tasks to different users can be handled by different product configurations as well[3]. Based on the product-specific task model, the common MBUID concepts can be applied like generating multiple UIs for the specific product based on different contexts of use. In summary, this results in multiple products (e.g., different online shops), each with (potentially) multiple UIs (e.g., each shop has multiple UIs for different target devices).

In an SPL scenario, the context of use has to be extended by an additional stakeholder: In addition to the end user there is now also the *customer* who owns a concrete product. Often, this is not the end user itself. For instance, in case of online shops, the customer is the shop owner for which the particular shop has been built for. Often the customer defines not only the product configuration but also influences the UI design. For instance, each UI of an online shop can be strongly influenced by the branding, the business goals, and marketing strategy of the shop owner.

UI CUSTOMIZATION WITHIN MDD
In the previous chapter we have shown a general model-driven process to develop UI families from abstract models. This process can be fully automated, starting from a task model and optional models for the context of use. However, in practice, UIs sometimes require manual customization for two reasons [18]: First, for usability reasons. For instance, automatic distribution of UI elements onto presentation units (e.g., screens) is sometimes difficult and can lead to overfull or too empty presentation units [5]. Second, there can be very specific customer requirements beyond generic rules. For instance, [3] reports that providers of online shops often ask for very specific UI customizations that cannot be foreseen. Hence, we aim to support manual UI customization within our approach.

To support manual UI customization in an efficient way within a model-driven approach we aim to address the following requirements:

- The manual customization is optional only; i.e., there is a default automated UI provided that can be used directly if there is no need for customizations.

UI Aspect	Customization Specification
Tasks and Temporal Operators	Product Derivation
Abstract UI (AUI) Elements	Product Derivation
Relationships to Domain Model	Product Derivation
Presentation Units	AUI Model
Navigation	AUI Model
Layout	AUI Model
Concrete UI (CUI) Elements	AUI to CUI Transformation
Visual Appearance & Adornments	AUI to CUI Transformation OR Stylesheets

Table 1. UI aspects and development step where to specify customizations.

- It must be possible to store customizations so that they can be reused, for instance, when re-generating the application during software evolution.

- Customizations should be stored in a modularized way to support easier reuse. For instance, it should be possible to apply a specific customized layout to multiple UIs without modifying their other properties.

- The specification of customizations should be as efficient as possible. For instance, it should not only be possible to customize single elements but also multiple elements that are, e.g., of the same type.

A successful concept are CSS stylesheets as commonly used for HTML UIs. Stylesheets fulfill the requirements above as they can be added, removed, and combined in a flexible way without modifying the HTML code itself. However, stylesheets mainly influence a UI's *visual* appearance while other aspects of the UI cannot be modified, e.g., the distribution of UI elements onto presentation units. Hence, we propose to fill this gap by supporting additional models that can customize *all* aspects of the UI and can be added, removed, and combined within the MDD process similar to stylesheets.

In [18] we classified the properties of a UI into different *UI aspects*, e.g., navigation, layout, visual appearance, etc. These aspects are derived from MBUID concepts and shown in the left column of Table 1. In [19] we perform a empirical case study about which of these aspects are customized in practice using the commercial product family of web applications *HIS QIS/GX* (which we also use for the evaluation in this paper). It shows that customizations for *all* these UI aspects can be found in practice and, hence, need to be supported by a generic model-driven process.[4]

The right column of Table 1 shows for each aspect at which step in a common MBUID process it can be customized. The task model specifies the basic functionality of the UI (*tasks and temporal operators*). According to the general framework in Figure 1 this information can be modified during product derivation (as modifying functionality is considered as creating a different product). The same holds for the *AUI elements* and their *relationships to the domain model* as they are directly related to tasks. The distribution of UI elements onto *presentation units*, the *navigation* between presentation units, and their *layout* are defined on the AUI level and, hence, also customized on this level. *CUI elements* and their *visual*

---

[3]This can be different for runtime adaptation which is outside the scope of this paper.

[4]We have updated Table 1 accordingly compared to its initial version in [18].

appearance are defined on CUI level. However, customizations on the CUI level often apply to multiple elements. For instance, *all* buttons should have a certain design or *all* selections with less than three choices should be represented by a radio button. Hence, such customizations are best supported by adapting the transformation from the AUI to the CUI. Common model transformation languages like ATL[5] or ETL[6] support defining conditional mapping rules for fine-grained customizations.

In the next section we show a concrete and generic realization of a MDD approach that supports all customizations according to Table 1.

DETAILED APPROACH

This section presents a concrete realization of the concepts discussed so far, i.e., a MDD process for UI families with support for customization. The approach extends and generalizes the process in [17]. Further details on the proposed solution and tool support can be found in [26]. We focus here on manual customizations to adapt the UIs to the context of use; the approach might further be augmented with heuristics [4, 21] to improve the results of the automated transformations but this is not further discussed here. In the following we explain the process as shown in Figure 2.

Product Derivation

The process starts with product derivation (**A** to **B** in Figure 2) as in SPLE: First, the models on the level of the whole *product family* **A** are created. They specify a superset of all potential product variants, i.e., all model elements that can appear in any of the products (except additional customizations). We focus here on the UI part of the products, while all other models (e.g., domain models and other models to specify an application) are summarized as *application logic* and not discussed further. Regarding the UI, the tasks and temporal operators, the AUI elements, and their relationships to the domain model are customized during product derivation (see Table 1). However, as AUI elements are a more concrete representation of tasks, the tasks can be omitted here and product derivation can be performed directly on the AUI elements. However, we still require the temporal operators from the task model for the further steps of the process (e.g., calculating the presentation units for the specific product). Hence, we use a specific AUI model for the product derivation that contains AUI elements, their relationships to the domain model, and temporal operators.

Figure 3 shows a sample AUI model for an example product family of online shop applications. Analogous to task models like CTT [16], the model consists of a tree structure; siblings are connected by temporal operators. The leaf nodes are AUI elements, like *input*, *output*, or *selection*. The non-leaf nodes are UI containers. An exception are selection elements which can be used as non-leaf nodes to represent selections of complex objects. For instance in the example, articleSelection enables to select one or more articles. It is also possible to

[5]http://www.eclipse.org/atl/
[6]http://www.eclipse.org/gmt/epsilon/doc/etl/

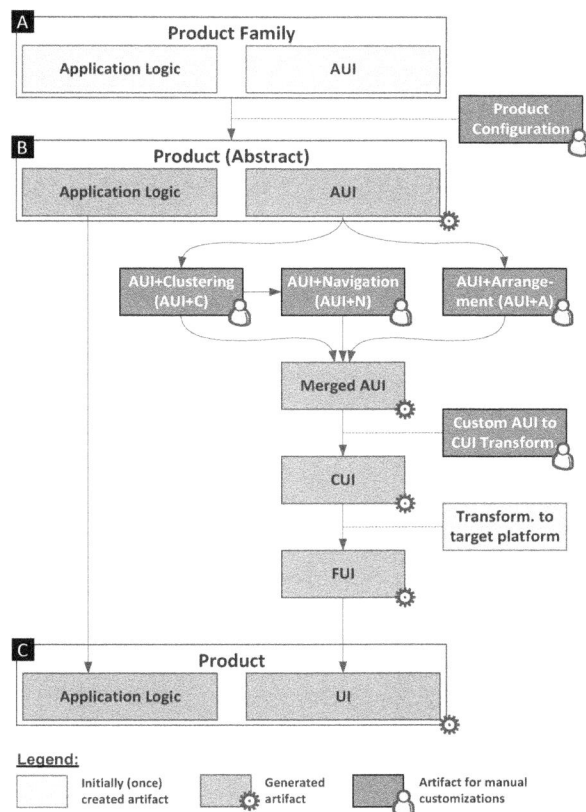

Figure 2. Detailed model-driven development process with customizations.

specify multiplicities for elements whose number is not specified yet as it is either product-specific or calculated at runtime (like the number of articles in articleSelection). In addition, it is possible to reuse a container multiple times within the model. For instance, shippingAddress and billingAddress are both copies of a container *Address* (which is defined elsewhere). The relationships to the domain model are stored with the AUI elements but not shown in the diagram.

Once the product family model is defined, concrete products are derived by defining *product configurations*. A product configuration specifies which elements are present in a concrete product. For instance, if a concrete online shop does not support credit card payment, all corresponding AUI elements (here the UI container creditCard) are deleted from the model (see [18] for details and how to ensure consistency). The result of this process step is a product-specific model **B** that includes a product-specific AUI. An example is shown later in Figure 4, where, e.g., the UI container credit card was removed. The next process steps address customizing the product-specific AUI (according to Table 1).

AUI+Clustering Model

The *AUI+Clustering* model (AUI+C) is used to customize the decomposition of the UI into presentation units. This is specified by clustering AUI elements. A cluster contains AUI elements and can either be an *AUICluster* an *AUIFragment*. An AUICluster represents a presentation unit. An AUIFragment

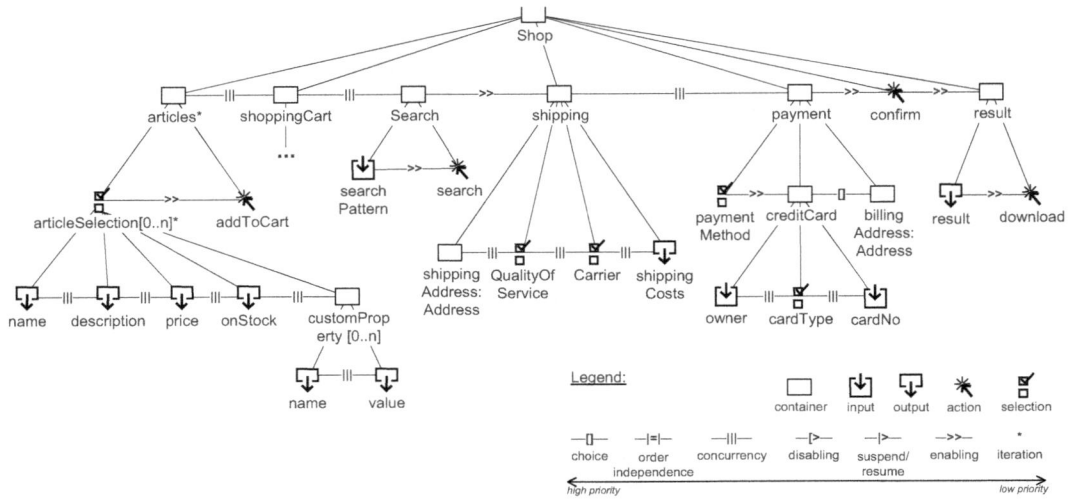

Figure 3. Example AUI for a product family of online shops.

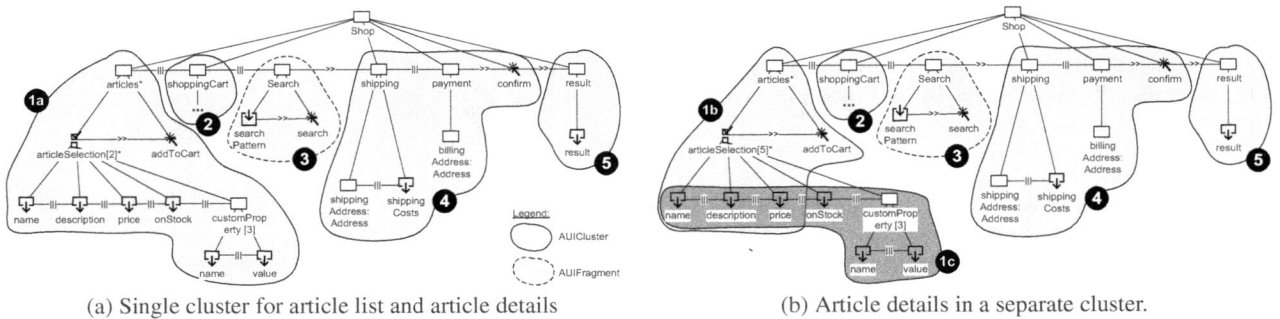

(a) Single cluster for article list and article details   (b) Article details in a separate cluster.

Figure 4. Two alternative AUI+C models for an example product-specific UI.

represents a container which is embedded into multiple other presentation units (which is calculated based on the temporal operators). For instance, a search bar might be embedded into multiple presentation units and, hence, clustered into an AUIFragment.

Figure 4 gives an example for two alternative clusterings of a product-specific AUI: The cluster ❸ is an AUIFragment (here the search bar) and will hence be embedded into other presentation units. All other clusters are AUIClusters which will result in presentation units. The two alternatives differ in the clustering of articles: in Figure 4a, article information is displayed on a single presentation unit ❶a while in Figure 4b one presentation unit is used for the list of articles ❶b while article details are presented in a separate presentation unit ❶c. Customization of the clustering is an essential step when adapting to various platforms, e.g., due to varying display sizes.

AUI+Navigation Model

The *AUI+Navigation* model (*AUI+N*) specifies the navigation between presentation units. It is automatically calculated based on the clusterings (from the AUI+C) and the temporal operators (from the AUI) using an algorithm presented in [12]. The resulting AUI+N model contains the *navigation links* between the presentation units and *fragment inclu-*

sion dependencies, which specify the embedding of AUIFragments into presentation units.

The AUI+N model can be customized by adding or removing links or dependencies (while presentation units and fragments itself are customized in the AUI+C model only).

AUI+Arrangement

The *AUI+Arrangement* model (*AUI+A*) specifies the abstract layout with respect to how AUI elements are arranged within a presentation unit (the size of UI elements is defined later on CUI level). We use the concepts from [11]: The abstract layout is defined by an *order* of elements and an *orientation* constraint. The orientation constraint defines the relative placement to the previous element and is either "*horizontal-to*" or "*vertical-to*".

To keep the customization models (AUI+C, AUI+N, and AUI+A) modular, they do not contain AUI elements directly but only references to the AUI elements in the AUI model. In this way, they can be edited independently from the AUI model and each other. It is also possible to reuse them by applying them to other product-specific AUI models.

Merged AUI and Transformation to CUI

The *Merged AUI* model integrates the information from the AUI+C, AUI+N, and AUI+A models into a single model.

This is not necessary in a technical sense but considered as helpful for the developer to get an overview on the resulting AUI. It is used as starting point for the AUI to CUI transformation.

The *AUI to CUI transformation* maps the presentation units and AUI elements to CUI elements (e.g., a selection element becomes a list box). It also sets the properties of CUI elements like size, default values, or a reference to a style definition in a stylesheet. The transformation is currently specified using the declarative model transformation language *Epsilon Transformation Language (ETL)*[7]. The advantage of using a transformation language instead of a simple mapping model is the support for defining complex generic rules and conditions. For instance, it can be specified that selections should be mapped differently depending on certain conditions. The transformation language also allows to manipulate the mapping of individual elements (by specifying a condition over a name). The transformation is customized by adding rules. Transformation languages like ETL also support mechanisms like inheritance and modularization which eases structuring and reuse of the transformation rules.

Final Code Generation and Tool Support
Finally, the final UI code (*FUI* and resulting final product **C**) is generated. Here, the developer has to select a transformation to the desired target platform. Currently we have implemented a transformation which generates HTML5 code. Feasibility of similar transformations for other platforms has been shown, e.g., in [4].

The whole process has been implemented and tool-supported based on the *Eclipse Modeling Framework (EMF)*[8]. All models are specified as metamodels compliant to *Ecore*, an Eclipse-based implementation of the *MOF* standard[9]. All model transformation are implemented using the model transformation language ETL.

We also implemented a first version of a modeling tool for all models (based on Eclipse). Currently, the tool only provides tree-oriented representations of the models (no graph-oriented representation yet), but eases the creation and management of the models and guides the development process. For instance, it provides a screen showing an overview over all models and supports to run the model transformations. Figure 5 shows a screenshot. The main screen consists of multiple tabs, one for each model. The screenshot shows the tab for the AUI+C model which supports creation and management of AUIClusters and AUIFragments and the assignment of AUI elements to them.

EVALUATION
We have evaluated our approach using the UIs from a commercial web information system *HIS-GX/QIS* by the company *HIS*[10]. It is a system for the management of universities currently used by 145 German universities. We focus on a

[7]http://www.eclipse.org/gmt/epsilon/doc/etl/
[8]http://www.eclipse.org/modeling/emf/
[9]http://www.omg.org/mof/
[10]http://www.his.de/english/organisation

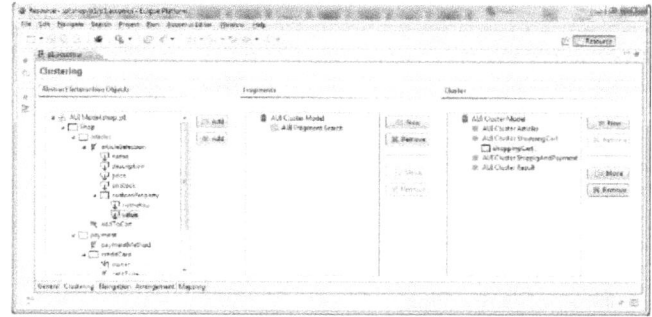

Figure 5. Screenshot from our modeling tool showing an AUI+C model.

specific part of the application, the web-based *online application*, where prospective students can apply for a course of study. The system guides the user through various forms to enter detailed information like personal data, previous education, and decisions about the course of study to apply for. It is a purely HTML-based UI that consists by default of 13 screens with 111 UI elements. By "UI element" we refer to interactive elements like input fields or buttons while static content like text and graphic is not further considered in the study.

HIS-GX/QIS can be considered as a family of products. There is a basic product version that contains all common functionality for applying at a university. However, all product instances which are in use online[11] are customized to a wide variety of usage contexts: On the one hand there are different types of universities, from full universities to small art schools. On the other hand, universities in Germany are subject to the different laws by the 16 federal states in Germany. For this reasons, HIS supports the universities in customizing their products, including the UI. Customizations are performed by HIS itself, by the universities, and sometimes also by third party companies.

The study in [19] analyses the UI customizations in detail based on 30 products (running at 30 different universities). It turns out that all products are highly customized. Moreover, customizations are spread over most parts of the UI (77.5 % of the UI elements) and over *all* UI aspects (those listed in Table 1). This includes both, functional customizations like in product derivation (adding and removing UI elements) but also UI-specific customizations (see [19]). This includes complex customizations like changing types of UI elements (e.g., from list box to radio buttons), changing the order of UI elements, merging and splitting screens, or changing the navigation path.

To evaluate our approach using real-world UIs, we extracted the HTML UIs from the existing HIS-GX/QIS products using an extraction tool from our previous study [19]. Based on the extracted data, we aim to address the following research questions:

[11]See, for instance, https://qisweb.hispro.de/fab/rds?stg=n&state=wimma&imma=einl and https://sbservice.tu-chemnitz.de/qisserver2/rds?state=wimma&stg=f&imma=einl for two examples.

1. *RQ1 – Development of Customized UIs:* Can all of these customized UIs be generated using our approach?

2. *RQ2 – Evolution of Customized UIs:* Can all of these customized UIs be modified by making changes on the abstract product family model without loosing any customizations?

The next section describes the general setup for the study, followed by two sections on these two research questions.

Evaluation Approach

Figure 6 shows the approach for the evaluation. Starting point are the HTML UIs ❶ from the HIS-GX/QIS online application system running at thirty universities. We created a tool based on *Selenium*[12], a framework for browser automation, to extract all relevant information about the UIs. Our tool traverses the HTML forms at a given URL and extracts ❷ the desired data from the HTML and CSS code into data tables. For each screen (presentation unit) we extract its name and its position in the navigation path and its contained UI elements. For each UI element we identified its name and type and all other properties like size, style or default values. Extracting the layout is more difficult as it can be influenced by multiple factors like the stylesheets and the screen size. Hence, we divide the screen into a virtual grid and defined the relative position of each element by a row and a column value. Static content like text and images is not extracted but just represented by a placeholder. Our tool does not interpret JavaScript. This does not limit the results as JavaScript is *not* used in HIS-GX/QIS due to German accessibility laws for universities. A little restriction is that we cannot ensure that there are dynamic branches in the navigation path depending on the input; our tool just follows the sequential standard navigation path that results from the default values which we use as input to the forms. As a result we get a data table for each product containing the extracted UI information ❸.

The next step is to automatically create the models for our MDD process from the extracted UI specifications ❹. All identified UI elements are mapped to a AUI element in the product family model ❺. As all UI elements in HIS-GX/QIS have a unique id that is consistent over all products, we can identify identical UI elements within different products. The resulting product family AUI model is the superset of all different UI elements extracted. Note that the generated AUI model is less structured than a manually created one as all UI elements are just placed as children of the root node and connected by the *concurrency* operator which is the most generic temporal operator, but this is sufficient for our purpose.

In addition, for each product we generate the product-specific customization models ❻ from the extracted data: For each product we store the information which AUI elements are present in the product (product configuration). We generate a product-specific AUI+C model that specifies the presentation units and the AUI elements they contain. We generate an AUI+N model to define the product-specific navigation. The navigation in HIS-GX/QIS is sequential in general, but the order of screens is sometimes customized so this is stored in the

[12]http://seleniumhq.org/

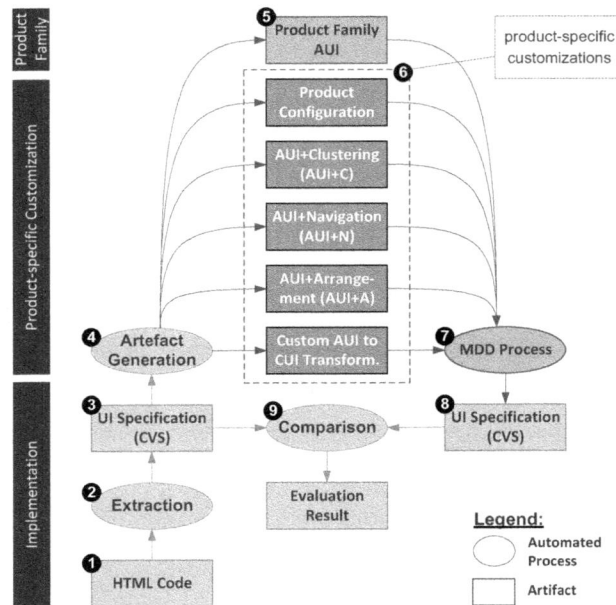

Figure 6. Approach for the evaluation.

AUI+N. We generate an AUI+A model that defines the order and relative position of each UI element based on the virtual grid we used for the layout extraction. Finally, we generate an AUI to CUI transformation for each product which is a simple mapping for each AUI element to a CUI element assigning the product-specific properties to the CUI element (the extracted properties like size, style or default value). Again, the generated transformation has a somewhat trivial structure and is less readable than more generic transformation rules created by a human developer. Nevertheless the result is sufficient for our study. Altogether the artifact generation step results in a single product family AUI model ❺ and a set of product-specific customization models ❻ for each product.

RQ1: Development of Customized UIs

The result of the previous steps are a AUI model for the HIS-GX/QIS product family and a set of customization models for each product. We now aim to show that this information is correct and sufficient to generate the product-specific UIs. Hence, we perform the UI generation ❼ based on the extracted models using our MDD process as shown in Figure 2. We can use our HTML code generator to generate real executable HTML implementations from the models. However, based on the HTML code it is not possible to automatically compare the generated UIs with the initial real-world UIs as the generated code differs syntactically from the manually written code in the real-world applications. Hence, we generate the UIs in the UI specification format that we used for the extraction ❽ as this enables automated comparison. This is sufficient for our evaluation assuming that the extracted UI Specification is an exact representation of the HTML UIs.

The last step is to compare the generated UI specifications with the extracted ones ❾. This is performed using a file comparison tool. It turns out that there are no differences between them. Consequently, we have shown that our approach is sufficient to generate a family of real-world customized UIs based on a single abstract product family model.

RQ2: Evolution of Customized UIs

In a second part of our evaluation we study the support for evolution. We aim to perform changes on the product family model (e.g., adding or removing UI elements) and to re-generate the product-specific UIs. We want to show that the changes are reflected in the re-generated UIs while all product-specific UI customizations remain. We aim to perform three evolution steps in which different modifications should be performed on the whole product family. For this, we specified fictitious evolution scenarios:

Scenario 1: Due to a new law, it is no longer allowed to ask for the date of birth and gender of a student. Hence, the corresponding UI elements are removed. Instead, for administrate reasons a social insurance number should be requested now. So a corresponding text input field should be added on the same screen where users put their name.

Scenario 2: The universities now aim to support multiple alternative email addresses. So new input fields for a second and a third email address should be added on the same screen where the primary email is requested. In addition, the previous input field for email has to be renamed to primary email. Moreover, the universities now want to support social media like Facebook, Twitter, and Skype. So a new UI container should be added containing corresponding input fields.

Scenario 3: The law from scenario 1 is withdrawn and date of birth and gender input fields should be restored on the same screen where they were located before. Moreover, two output fields used to show some extra information should be added to the same screen.

The scenarios should be realized in three evolution steps. For each step, the corresponding changes are performed on the product family AUI (❺ in Figure 6). By default, our MDD process puts new AUI elements (which have not been manually clustered into a presentation unit) into the same presentation unit as their previous sibling in the AUI model. This means, e.g., in scenario 1, that the new AUI element social insurance number must be inserted after the AUI element name in the product family AUI to be automatically put into the same presentation unit.

Once the product family AUI has been modified according to a scenario, the corresponding modified UIs are automatically generated ❼ without any further manual intervention. Like in the first part of the evaluation, we generate the UI in our UI specification format ❽ to enable easy automated comparison of the updated UIs with the original extracted one ❾. In case of evolution, the modified UIs should be identical with the initial ones except the modifications exactly as specified in the scenarios.

As a result all thirty generated product-specific UIs showed the expected structure for all three evolution steps: they were exactly identical to the original ones (including all product-specific customizations) except the modifications specified in the scenarios. Also, all expected modifications were found in all the generated UIs.

As an additional test, we also generated HTML UIs for the modified UIs. This worked as well and the updated UIs contained all changes defined on the product family AUI. Of course, the generated HTML UIs look different as we did not store static content (text/graphics) and the original stylesheets during the extraction. However, this could easily be added (by adding model elements for static content) if desired. This means that our approach enables to modify a whole family of tens (or hundreds) of UIs by just modifying a single product family AUI.

Discussion

The evaluation has shown some clear benefits of MDD for UIs: Modifications need to be performed just once on the abstract product family model and can be automatically propagated to tens or hundreds of customized real-world UI without the need for any manual intervention. But there are of course also some limitations and open issues of our approach.

First, the evaluation is currently restricted to purely HTML-based UIs. This was helpful for the automated extraction of the real-world UIs as reverse engineering of dynamic JavaScript-based UIs is difficult. In general, the specification of dynamic behaviour in our MDD approach is currently restricted to temporal operators and the corresponding navigation between presentation units. In the future we plan to extend our approach towards more dynamic UIs like Java-based UIs and to gain further experience by performing case studies with other UI families.

Another important aspect is the usability and efficiency of the proposed models. This has not been addressed by the evaluation yet. As described in our detailed approach, we have implemented a basic Eclipse-based tool to create, manage, and apply the models and the model transformations. While a tool like this seems to be usable for developers with background in modeling, it seems not sufficient for UI designers who are used to visual design tools. Hence, in the future there is need for visual tool support that hides the models in the background and provides direct visual feedback about the customizations specified (e.g., an immediate preview). Related to this, there is also a need to get more experience with developers in practice to evaluate whether the customization models are efficient to specify and use, and to which extent they can be reused across different products (e.g., which granularity is most appropriate for reuse). The models and the corresponding tool support have then to be refined accordingly.

CONCLUSIONS AND OUTLOOK

In this paper, we have presented an MDD approach for families of customized UIs. We have provided a generic notion of UI families, have presented tool support, and have evaluated our approach by application to a commercial real-world UI family. In particular, we have demonstrated the benefits for evolution of UI families: Modifications need to be performed *just once* on the abstract product family model and can be automatically propagated to numerous individually customized products without loss of customizations.

The presented approach continues and extends our previous work in [17, 18]. To the best of our knowledge, supporting families of customized UIs has not been addressed in related work yet. Also practical evaluation of MDD for UIs is addressed only in a few publications: [7, 1, 2, 21] evaluate the quality of UIs developed using MDD. While they show that it is possible to generate acceptable results there is an agreement that manual customization is often still desirable. An important approach besides our work to support such manual customization is [22]: It presents visual tool support to specify presentation units and their content within a MDD process. However, other UI aspects like the navigation are not considered yet in this approach.

In future work, we aim to address the issues discussed in the previous sections: enhanced visual tool support (e.g., like in [22]), more dynamic UIs beyond HTML including the specification of UI behavior, and management and reuse of customization models.

Acknowledgments

This work was supported, in part, by Science Foundation Ireland grant 10/CE/I1855 to Lero – the Irish Software Engineering Research Centre http://www.lero.ie/.

REFERENCES

1. S. Abrahão, E. Iborra, and J. Vanderdonckt. Usability evaluation of user interfaces generated with a model-driven architecture tool. In *Maturing Usability*, pages 3–32. Springer, 2008.

2. N. Aquino, J. Vanderdonckt, N. Condori-Fernández, O. Dieste, and O. Pastor. Usability evaluation of multi-device/platform user interfaces generated by model-driven engineering. In *ESEM 2010*, pages 30:1–30:10. ACM, 2010.

3. P. Bell. A practical high volume software product line. In *OOPSLA'07*, pages 994–1003. ACM, 2007.

4. G. Botterweck. A model-driven approach to the engineering of multiple user interfaces. In *MoDELS Workshops*, pages 106–115. Springer, 2006.

5. H. Brummermann, M. Keunecke, and K. Schmid. Variability issues in the evolution of information system ecosystems. In *VaMoS'11*, pages 159–164, 2011.

6. G. Calvary, J. Coutaz, D. Thevenin, Q. Limbourg, L. Bouillon, and J. Vanderdonckt. A unifying reference framework for multi-target user interfaces. *Interacting with Computers*, 15(3):289–308, 2003.

7. C. Chesta, F. Paternò, and C. Santoro. Methods and tools for designing and developing usable multi-platform interactive applications. *PsychNology Journal*, 2(1):123 – 139, 2004.

8. P. Clements and L. M. Northrop. *Software Product Lines: Practices and Patterns*. Addison-Wesley, 2002.

9. B. Collignon, J. Vanderdonckt, and G. Calvary. Model-driven engineering of multi-target plastic user interfaces. In *ICAS'08*, pages 7–14. IEEE, 2008.

10. J. V. den Bergh, S. Sauer, K. Breiner, H. Hussmann, G. Meixner, and A. Pleuss, editors. *Proceedings of the 5th International Workshop on Model Driven Development of Advanced User Interfaces (MDDAUI 2010): Bridging between User Experience and UI Engineering*, volume 617. CEUR Proceedings, 2010.

11. S. Feuerstack, M. Blumendorf, V. Schwartze, and S. Albayrak. Model-based layout generation. In *AVI '08*, pages 217–224. ACM, 2008.

12. B. Hauptmann. Supporting derivation and customization of user interfaces in software product lines using the example of web applications. Master's thesis, Technische Universität München, Germany, 2010.

13. H. Hussmann, G. Meixner, and D. Zuehlke, editors. *Model-Driven Development of Advanced User Interfaces*. Springer, 2011.

14. T. Mens and S. Demeyer, editors. *Software Evolution*. Springer, 2008.

15. B. A. Myers, S. E. Hudson, and R. F. Pausch. Past, present, and future of user interface software tools. *ACM Trans. Comput.-Hum. Interact.*, 7(1):3–28, 2000.

16. F. Paternò. *Model-Based Design and Evaluation of Interactive Applications*. Springer, 2000.

17. A. Pleuss, G. Botterweck, and D. Dhungana. Integrating automated product derivation and individual user interface design. In *VAMOS'10*, pages 69–76, 2010.

18. A. Pleuss, B. Hauptmann, D. Dhungana, and G. Botterweck. User interface engineering for software product lines – the dilemma between automation and usability. In *EICS 2012*, pages 25–34, 2012.

19. A. Pleuss, B. Hauptmann, M. Keunecke, and G. Botterweck. A case study on variability in user interfaces. In *SPLC 2012*, pages 6–10. ACM, 2012.

20. K. Pohl, G. Böckle, and F. van der Linden. *Software Product Line Engineering*. Springer, 2005.

21. D. Raneburger, R. Popp, H. Kaindl, J. Falb, and D. Ertl. Automated generation of device-specific WIMP UIs: weaving of structural and behavioral models. In *EICS 2011*, pages 41–46. ACM, 2011.

22. A. Schramm, A. Preußner, M. Heinrich, and L. Vogel. Rapid UI development for enterprise applications: combining manual and model-driven techniques. In *MODELS'10*, pages 271–285. Springer, 2010.

23. Software Engineering Institute. SPL Hall of Fame, 2008. http://splc.net/fame.html.

24. T. Stahl and M. Voelter. *Model-driven software development : technology, engineering, management*. John Wiley, 2006.

25. P. A. Szekely. Retrospective and challenges for model-based interface development. In *DSV-IS*, pages 1–27. Springer, 1996.

26. S. Wollny. Model-driven support for user interface evolution in software product lines. Master's thesis, University of Augsburg, Germany, 2013.

CrowdAdapt: Enabling Crowdsourced Web Page Adaptation for Individual Viewing Conditions and Preferences

Michael Nebeling, Maximilian Speicher and Moira C. Norrie
Institute of Information Systems, ETH Zurich
CH-8092 Zurich, Switzerland
{nebeling,norrie}@inf.ethz.ch, maximilianspeicher@gmx.de

(a) Original design of the CNN web site
(b) Crowdsourced adaptation

Figure 1: Juxtaposing the original CNN web site viewed on a medium-size screen at 1680x1050 pixels and the best-matching, highest-ranked crowdsourced layout that uses more screen real estate and increases the amount of text visible without scrolling.

ABSTRACT

The range and growing diversity of new devices makes it increasingly difficult to design suitable web interfaces for every browsing client. We present *CrowdAdapt*—a context-aware web design tool that supports developers in the creation of adaptive layout solutions for a wide variety of use contexts by crowdsourcing web site adaptations designed for individual viewing conditions and preferences. We focus on one experiment we conducted for an existing news web site using CrowdAdapt (i) to explore the design space in terms of layout alternatives created by the crowd, (ii) to identify adaptation preferences with respect to different viewing situations, and (iii) to assess the perceived quality of crowd-generated layouts in terms of reading comfort and efficiency. The results suggest that crowdsourced adaptation could lead to very flexible web interfaces informed by individual end-user requirements. In particular, scenarios such as the adaptation to large-screen contexts that the majority of web sites fail to address could be supported with relatively little effort.

Author Keywords

Adaptive layout; responsive web design; crowdsourcing.

ACM Classification Keywords

H.5.2 User Interfaces: Screen design

INTRODUCTION

The growing range and increased diversity of new devices that vary widely, not only in terms of screen size and resolution, but also supported input and output modalities, makes it difficult to design web interfaces that adapt well to every browsing client. Many of the existing methods for automatic adaptation provide little control for developers and are typically tailored to very specific scenarios such as desktop-to-mobile adaptation [8] and therefore not easily extended for other use cases. On the other hand, more comprehensive solutions to accommodate a much wider range of use contexts require advanced layout generation techniques [18] that are, however, often not feasible in a web context.

Given the need for more flexible web interfaces, but the high design effort and costs required to create them, our goal is

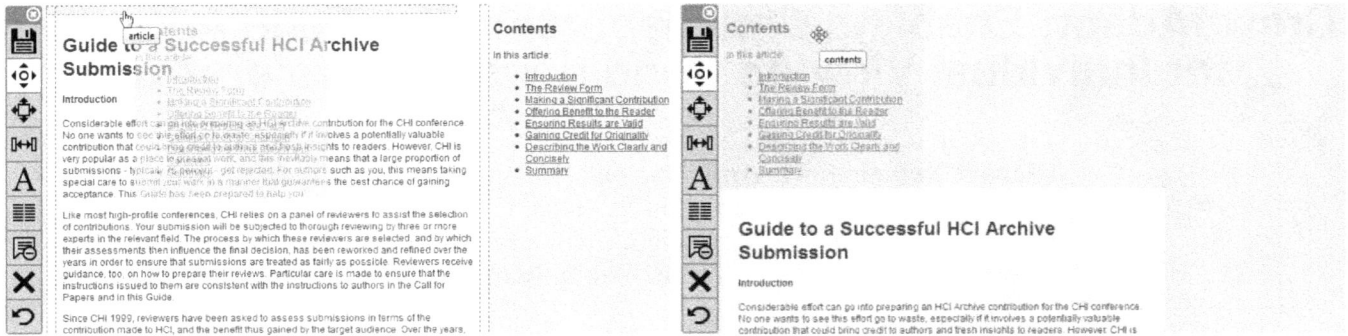

Figure 2: Demonstrating CrowdAdapt's move operation (before and after) for re-anchoring the sidebar element as an example.

to enable crowdsourced adaptation of existing web sites. Recently, we have started to address the technical challenges of designing a model, architecture and runtime environment capable of supporting the dynamic definition and deployment of web site adaptations in a safe and efficient manner [14]. In this paper, we present *CrowdAdapt*, a context-aware web design tool that we developed based on these building blocks to enable and test our concept of crowdsourced adaptation. Our specific combination of end-user development and crowdsourcing for context-aware adaptation is novel and marks an important step forward in research on mixed-initiative interfaces [4]. Specifically, CrowdAdapt is able to aggregate crowd-generated layouts designed for different window and screen sizes to provide an adaptive layout solution catering for a large variety of viewing conditions. We present one experiment in detail in which CrowdAdapt was used in a real-world setting for the CNN web site (Fig. 1), one of the world's most popular news web sites according to the Alexa ranking[1].

An important scenario that we wanted to enable using our approach is the adaptation to large, high-resolution displays that the majority of web sites still fail to support [13]. This is surprising given the fact that average screen sizes and resolutions have dramatically increased over the past few years. For web design, however, wide-screen contexts present a new setting in need of interface design guidelines and flexible layout solutions to make appropriate use of the greater screen real estate and increasingly horizontal screen distances. Typical design issues with current web layouts at larger viewing sizes are that background rather than content often fills the screen in the case of static layout, or that the text spreads across the entire screen width in fluid layout. This means that screen real estate is potentially wasted, or that readability is impacted due to excessively long lines of text. Our vision is that crowdsourced adaptation will alleviate the problems in such cases. For example, one of our study participants used CrowdAdapt to reduce the need for scrolling for the static, fixed-width layout of CNN at larger window sizes by adjusting the spatial layout and size of the headline, image and story areas (Fig. 1). We do not want to make a case for this particular layout, but instead use it as an example of a crowd-generated layout that illustrates the potential of crowdsourced adaptation.

_____
[1] http://www.alexa.com/siteinfo/cnn.com

In the following, we present the key components of CrowdAdapt. For each component, we will discuss both the implemented functionality and the key design challenges that had to be addressed. This is followed by a description of our experiment based on the CNN web site and a discussion of the results obtained from user evaluations.

CROWDADAPT

The key idea behind CrowdAdapt is to allow end-users to adapt the interface to their specific use context if it is insufficiently supported by the current web page design. Drawing from individual user contributions allows the system to build an adaptive layout solution that caters for a wide variety of device characteristics and user preferences. At the same time, the design task can be kept rather simple since each user only has to think in terms of their own setting. CrowdAdapt provides a visual design environment that augments web pages loaded in the browser to allow users to customise the layout. The changes are then deployed on a server in the form of a new layout template which will be automatically downloaded and applied in subsequent visits of the same user. Moreover, the layouts are automatically shared with other users so that new visitors using the same, or a similar, device can directly benefit from the adaptations. CrowdAdapt supports two deployment modes so that it can either be bundled directly with a web site or be installed separately as a browser plugin. The first deployment scenario does not require separate infrastructure and allows contributors to share their customisations with other users of the same site. Also other users require no additional software for viewing the site in a shared layout, which may be preferred by those primarily in the role of the consumer. The second scenario follows the popular example of userscripts.org, where a large collection of scripts for augmented browsing based on plugins such as Greasemonkey is self-maintained by an active user community. The CrowdAdapt plugin allows users, not only to create new adaptations for any web site they would like to customise even if the web site provider does not directly support this, but also to obtain adaptations contributed by plugin users for other sites.

Direct Manipulation Toolkit

The core of CrowdAdapt is the direct manipulation toolkit running on the client to provide the user with a set of visual tools for customising the interface directly in the browser.

There were three major challenges in developing this component. First, we had to decide on the concrete set of adaptation operations that would be required to adjust interfaces to different conditions. Second, all operations had to be designed with non-technical end-users in mind. Finally, each adaptation must yield a valid manipulation of the interface in order to keep the underlying implementation intact.

The current set of 7 adaptation operations were derived from an analysis of the differences between web page layouts at different viewing sizes and the changes required to make effective use of both small and large-screen settings [13]. The example web sites that we considered for the analysis ranged from news web sites, blogs, wikis and forums to other types of applications such as web mail and social media sites such as Facebook and Twitter that are typically used by active user communities for both the consumption and sharing of content. The defined operations, especially when used in combination, cater for a wide range of adaptations, but also reflect what is technically feasible without imposing particular web design conventions. Note that we refer to web page "elements" in terms of the rendered interface. At the hypertext level, elements refers to the HTML DOM elements part of the `body` which includes both simple elements, such as headings `h1` to `h6`, or container elements such `div` and `span` which may nest other elements.

The two main operations are "move" and "resize". Move repositions web page elements in the document via drag-n-drop. Elements can be freely positioned in the page or re-anchored and snapped to other elements by dropping on either edge of the target (Figure 2). Resize scales elements in horizontal and/or vertical direction by dragging the edges or corners as known from common window managers. While the actions can be controlled via additional handles that are dynamically displayed for in-place element manipulation, the remaining operations trigger a context-sensitive popup menu on the selected element. The "spacer" operation increases or decreases the space around an element via "+" or "-" menu options. The "hide" function toggles the visibility of an element or restores previously hidden ones via the menu. Alternatively, "collapse" replaces an element with a placeholder link to allow users to later unfold the content. Both of these operations are especially useful for adaptation to smaller screen sizes, but also as intermediate design steps when bigger changes are performed to a more complex layout. The "font size" operation increases or decreases the text height. Moreover, the "multi-column" operation controls the number of columns used for content layout, which is particularly useful for large-screen settings. While only one tool can be active at a time, operations can be subsequently combined with each other as well as reverted via an undo command.

Each of the operations updates the CSS and/or the HTML DOM as required, which is straightforward in most cases. For example, for freely moving or resizing elements, only the CSS position and dimension properties are adjusted. Similarly, the spacer operation controls the CSS margin and multi-column layout is based on the new CSS3 properties[2]. On the other hand, for re-anchoring moved elements and in order to support element nesting and maintain the z-index, the HTML DOM is also updated by internally moving the dragged element node either before or after the drop target. Hiding an element again just toggles the CSS display property, which is sufficient to prevent that the inner content is loaded by the client in future visits. While these design decisions generally help to maintain the functionality of the web interface, it is still possible to break JavaScript that refers to page elements via the DOM element path rather than the ID if the element was moved to a new position.

CrowdAdapt does not require manual configuration for every web site. By default, operations can be invoked on all page elements with ID so that a unique reference to the respective DOM node can be maintained. This is usually feasible because the main web site components are typically labelled for CSS and programmatic access via JavaScript anyway. However, CrowdAdapt can be configured by both web developers and users. For example, web developers may extend, or constrain, the scope of adaptations by including, or excluding, certain web page elements based on jQuery selectors[3]. Users can configure the toolkit to automatically deactivate text selection, links to other pages and embedded objects such as videos or Flash animations in order not to accidentally trigger associated actions while customising the web interface.

Adaptation Engine
While the toolkit operations allow users to fit the interface to their individual viewing condition, the actual context-awareness comes from the adaptation engine which is responsible for managing the overall adaptive interface solution based on crowd contributions. With each manipulation of the web interface, CrowdAdapt learns a new adaptation rule for the current context and user. For example, as the user increases the width of the main content container to 1600 pixels on a Full HD display, CrowdAdapt internally generates a new design instruction similar to the one below which describes the adaptation based on CSS3 media queries[4].

```
@media only screen
  and (min-width: 1870px)
  and (max-width: 1970px)
  and (device-width: 1920px)
  and (orientation: landscape) {
  #main { width: 1600px; }
}
```

Based on the user interaction and according to the respective adaptation operation, the adaptation rules are generated in three steps. First, the context information is automatically collected in terms of the window size, screen resolution and orientation of the client device. CrowdAdapt then approximates the window size using min/max values based on a configurable 100 pixel threshold to match similar viewing conditions. Finally, the actual adaptation rule is composed of the condition that triggers the adaptation with respect to the client context and the design rule that alters the original layout to better fit the new condition. All manipulations are recorded

---

[2]http://www.w3.org/TR/css3-multicol

[3]http://api.jquery.com/category/selectors
[4]http://www.w3.org/TR/css3-mediaqueries

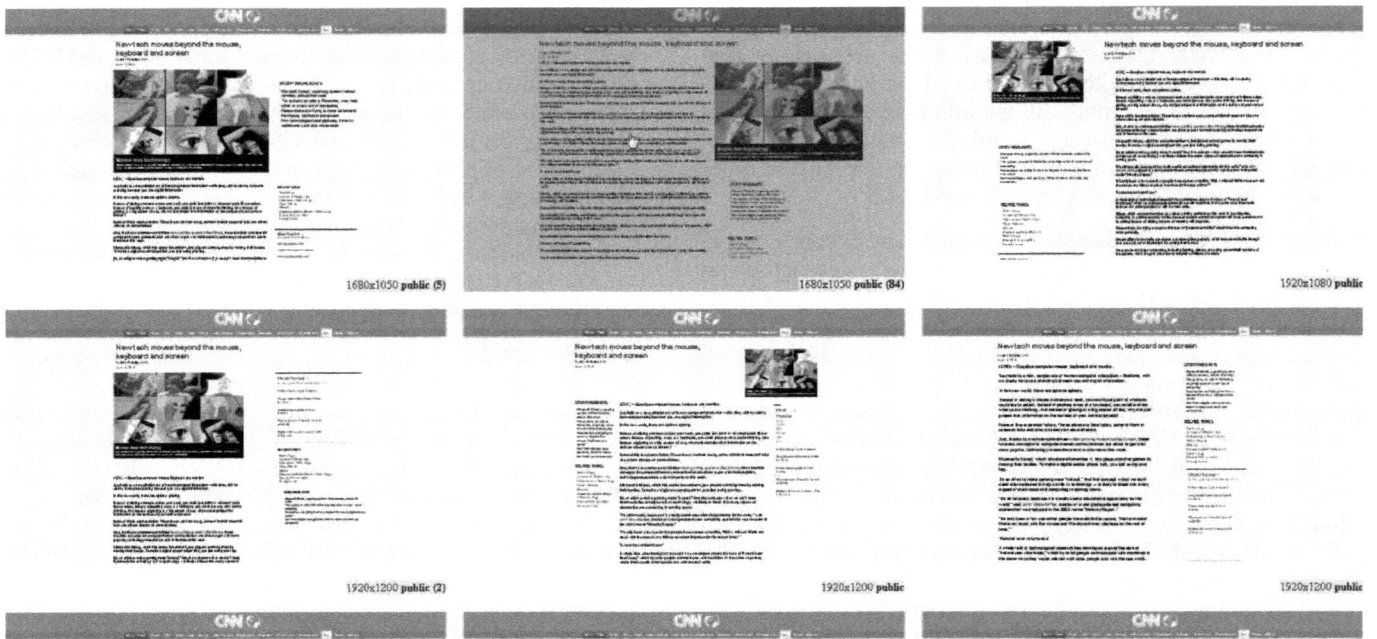

Figure 3: The in-built review and rating system allows end-users to preview adaptations and select the preferred layout.

on the client-side and sent to the server in suitable 30-second intervals as well as when the "save" function is used. In addition, the user is asked to save changes before navigating to a different site or closing the CrowdAdapt toolkit or browser window in order to confirm the changes. All generated design rules together then define the set of adaptations that describe the custom web interface similar to a new layout template.

By default, adaptations are strictly collected per URL path. However, many modern web sites dynamically generate pages with different content from a single URL based on different query strings. This enables reuse of adaptations between pages based on naming conventions. Alternatively, CrowdAdapt can be configured by the host site to aggregate page-specific adaptations based on URL pattern matching, which may be required for web sites that use URL rewriting. The same feature can also be exploited for web sites that consist of many individual HTML documents that essentially share the same elements due to similar structure and layout. While CrowdAdapt's support for generalising adaptation rules across web pages and sites is still rather limited, the basic mechanisms and the means for configuration already provide a relatively flexible solution that works well with many existing web applications due to the fact that the underlying content engines typically generate pages based on a fixed set of common templates. Nevertheless, generalisability is a hard problem due to the lack of standards in web interface implementations. The discussion later in this paper will look at possible ways in which CrowdAdapt could be extended to provide more advanced support for reusing adaptation rules.

Deployment and Review System

Since the main goal of CrowdAdapt is to collectively improve the adaptability of a web site for different viewing situations, we decided that the adaptations created by one user are automatically shared with other users of the web site. While many different schemes are possible, the deployment of new adaptations is therefore kept rather straightforward and is in fact mostly done automatically by CrowdAdapt, but still regulated by the end-users as follows.

- When a new user visits the web site, CrowdAdapt dynamically determines the client context and fetches all adaptations that potentially match the user's setting. If no adaptations are available for the current context, the original layout will be used, but the user will be asked to customise the interface. Otherwise CrowdAdapt automatically applies the currently best-matching adaptation.

- The adaptations created or adopted by a user are automatically reused in subsequent visits of that user to seamlessly restore the custom interface without user invocation.

CrowdAdapt allows adaptations to be previewed and selected like different "themes" for the web site as illustrated in Figure 3. It can also be configured to always ask users before potentially matching crowdsourced adaptations are applied. Initially, custom layouts are ranked in terms of similar window and screen sizes, but the initial ranking is then influenced by user ratings so that matching adaptations will be ranked higher the more positive votes they receive.

Implementation

The core client-side functionality is implemented based on the popular jQuery JavaScript framework[5] and its UI behaviours in combination with a PHP/MySQL server backend. To embed the tools in an existing web site, it is sufficient

---

[5] http://jquery.com

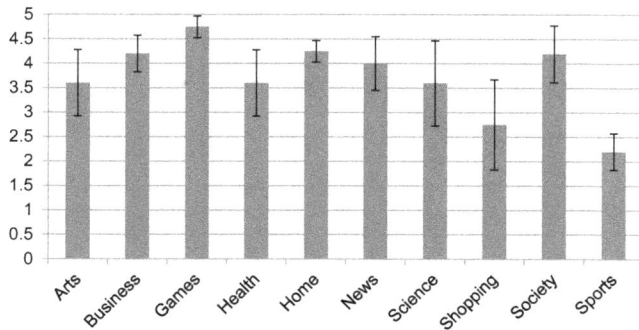

(a) Average ratings (1=poor, 5=excellent)

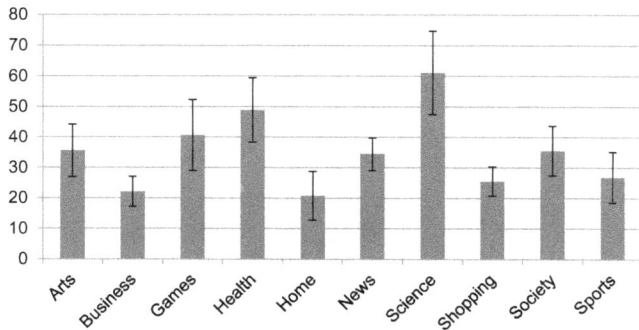

(b) Average DIV-ID ratios (higher is usually better)

Figure 4: Compatibility tests for 50 Alexa Top Sites

to link CrowdAdapt as an external JavaScript source and configure the adaptation engine with database settings. Crowd-Adapt was developed and tested primarily with Firefox and requires version 3.6 or higher. However, in some versions, the multi-column function showed unpredictable behaviour so that elements could not be activated and modified after additional columns had been added. The CrowdAdapt plugin is an extended version of the script that additionally builds on Greasemonkey for Firefox to get access to any web page loaded in the browser. More configuration, e.g. for including or excluding certain page elements from the adaptation process and URL pattern matching, is usually optional, but may be required for some web sites as described earlier.

CrowdAdapt was tested on several popular sites. We carried out a study on 50 top sites from 10 different genres (Arts, Business, Games, Health, Home, News, Science, Shopping, Society, Sports) as ranked by Alexa[6]. Note that Alexa ranks top sites according to popularity and traffic. Demonstrating compatibility of CrowdAdapt for a selection of Alexa sites therefore means that many millions of users would benefit. CrowdAdapt was loaded into each site and the performance and compatibility assessed for two adaptation scenarios, namely small and large screens. A 5-point scale from $1 = poor$ for sites that showed major issues to $5 = excellent$ if all adaptations were successfully stored and reapplied was used for the rating. In addition, we computed the ratio of page elements that can be adapted without manual configuration.

As shown in Fig. 4, most ratings were around 4=good with an average of 3.7 (sd=1.6, mode=5) across all categories. CrowdAdapt worked best with Business, Games, Home, News and Society sites (all above 4). By far the lowest ratings of 2.2 on average (sd=0.8, mode=3) showed in the Sports genre due to fixed-size, graphics-heavy designs of sites such as ESPN that are difficult to adapt without also editing background images etc. On average, 35% of DOM elements (sd=21.4) could be adapted using our ID-based approach with good results for the majority of sites. However, our tests revealed conflicts in some cases.

For example, due to how our proof-of-concept implementation prepares elements for move and resize, the move tool seemed very slow on Facebook and not always working correctly when trying to customise the position of elements. Facebook generates lots of IDs for many small components, such as posted comments which are, by default, all processed as potential drop targets. We were able to achieve a high performance when excluding unnecessary classes of DOM elements from customisation. Another example is Twitter where our tools generally worked well, but their Bootstrap UI toolkit[7] provides its own functionality to control layout based on a responsive grid, which might contradict Crowd-Adapt rules. However, sites that employ responsive design are still relatively rare at this stage and also not our primary target, as they already make sure that the layout adapts to different screen sizes. Nevertheless, CrowdAdapt could be extended to better integrate with such frameworks. To enable also others to experiment with this, more information and the CrowdAdapt source code are available online[8].

EVALUATION

In a first experiment, we focused on how crowdsourced adaptation based on CrowdAdapt may be used to improve the reading experience in large-screen contexts for text-heavy sites such as CNN (Figure 1). CrowdAdapt was embedded in an example news article and configured so that the main article and sidebar content could be adapted. The site's header, top navigation bar and footer content were specifically excluded from customisation as this may be in the interest of the web site provider and also helped focus the user attention on the article layout. All adaptation operations were available except for the multi-column feature which we removed from the experiment due to browser compatibility issues. The adaptation engine was configured to partition contexts into widescreen and other screen formats. Similar to reports from DisplaySearch[9], widescreen here refers to HD resolutions of 1280x720 pixels and more, and 16:10 window size ratios. Our evaluation was guided by three questions:

- Are the proposed design tools usable and complete to support individual requirements and preferences?

- How would end-users make use of the system when designing for their viewing conditions?

---

[6] http://www.alexa.com/topsites

[7] http://twitter.github.com/bootstrap
[8] http://dev.globis.ethz.ch/crowdadapt
[9] http://www.displaysearch.com

- Could crowdsourced evaluation based on CrowdAdapt overall enable a better user experience?

We aim to show the general potential of CrowdAdapt to be useful based on a qualitative analysis of the adaptations produced by the crowd. At the same time, its functionality and the feasibility of our design decisions concerning the adaptation tools and automatic deployment of new adaptations are assessed based on questionnaire feedback.

Method

To make for a controlled experiment while evaluating Crowd-Adapt in its anticipated setting, the experiment was divided into two phases. Initially, the original layout was used as the basis for the experiment. In a second phase, this was changed to the best-ranked crowdsourced layout at this stage. With these two stages, we wanted to explore the design space based on different starting points and generally see whether users would appreciate layouts designed by other users and perceive them as an improvement over the original layout. Each new participant to the experiment was randomly given one of three tasks illustrated in Figure 5. Once they finished a task and submitted their responses, they were asked to work on additional ones as they liked. In the design task, participants were asked to customise the layout of the news article for their viewing situation and reading preferences and to provide feedback on the tools. Layouts were automatically shared if the design task was completed with questionnaire feedback. In the second task, participants compared and rated three layouts in random order—the original layout, a random matching adaptation not designed by them and the currently best-ranked matching adaptation. Ratings were collected in three steps where each step showed two previews for comparison, allowing users to focus on the differences between only two layouts at a time. The last task was specifically designed to test crowdsourced layouts when applied to the news article and collected user feedback in terms of reading comfort and efficiency. Participants were first asked to read the article and then to answer five questions on the text. Questions had to be answered by clicking on the respective text paragraph that contained the answer, rather than typing the answer directly since this required visual search and depends on layout quality as well as memory. In addition, the times for reading and answering were measured separately. The first task therefore assessed the direct manipulation tools, while the other tasks concerned the perceived quality and functionality of crowd-generated layouts and ensured that user feedback would not only be based on aesthetic considerations.

Results

Over a 10 day period, 93 participants who frequently consume online news on sites such as CNN were recruited via internal and public mailing lists, student forums, as well as social bookmarking sites Reddit and digg. The majority of participants compared layouts, 28 contributed a customised layout to the experiment and 42 provided reading feedback.

We registered 53 viewing contexts for the design and evaluate tasks combined. Screen sizes ranged from 1200 to 2560 pixels for the width and from 768 to 1920 pixels for the height.

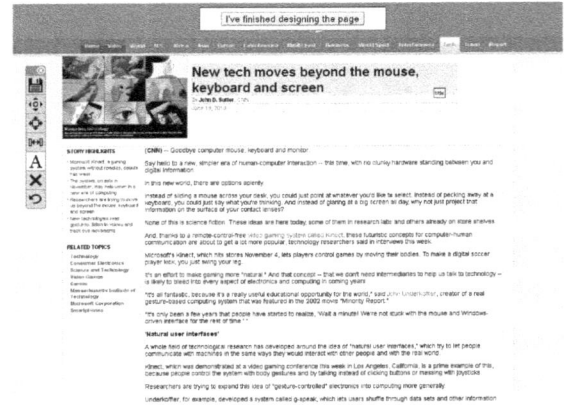

(a) Design task

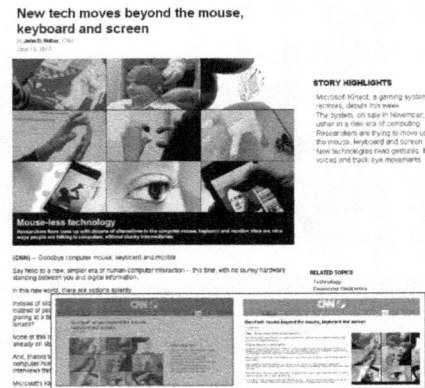

(b) Compare task

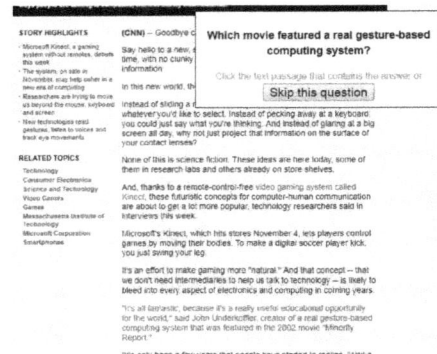

(c) Evaluate task

Figure 5: Showing the design task, the compare task for rating and the evaluate task for testing the layouts.

16 participants browsed in fullscreen and the rest in window mode (using less than 95% of the screen). From the 48 participants (91%) that had a high-resolution, wide-format display, 77% browsed in widescreen mode. Despite the small number of participants browsing in fullscreen, the median window size[10] was still 1417x912 pixels and the majority of users viewed the web site at a resolution of 1680x1050 pixels. This

---

[10]For the few users that resized the window during the task, we used the final window size as the basis for our analysis.

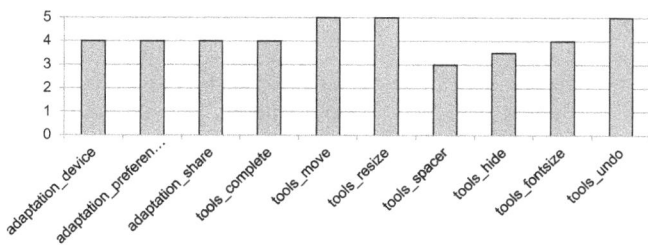

Figure 6: Median ratings of design tools (1=worst, 5=best)

means that the "average" viewing condition was significantly larger than the "standard" resolution of 1024x768 pixels assumed by the original design of the web site.

Design task As shown in Figure 6, the design feedback showed a very positive assessment of CrowdAdapt's features when rating questionnaire statements concerning the design tools and support for sharing (consistent median of 4 on a 5-point Likert scale; 1 = *strongly disagree*, 5 = *strongly agree*). Participants therefore felt they were able to adapt the layout to fit their viewing conditions (*adaptation_device*) and preferences (*adaptation_preferences*). In addition, they felt that the new design should be the default layout for their viewing conditions and could also be better for other users (*adaptation_share*). Overall, the set of adaptation operations seemed well-suited to the adaptation scenario. Participants expressed that the tools allowed them to perform most of the changes they wanted (*tools_complete*) and the usefulness of each individual tool was rated positively. Participants most appreciated the move and resize tools (*tools_move* and *tools_resize*) and liked the tool for changing the font size (*tools_fontsize*). There was a neutral rating for the spacer operation (*tools_spacer*) which was also not used so much although essential for smaller optimisations concerning the spacing between nested DOM elements. The moderate rating for the hide tool (*tools_hide*) is not surprising given the experiment focus on large-screen adaptation. Finally, participants welcomed the undo tool (*tools_undo*). In particular, participants from the widescreen group, noted the absence of the multi-column operation we removed due to browser compatibility issues ("A function to create new text columns would be useful"). There were no notable differences otherwise.

The set of 28 adaptations we received spanned 8 different screen sizes. The median window size was 1345x945 (min = 1107x579, max = 1903x1071) and the majority of participants (16) designed for widescreen contexts at a median resolution of 1920x1080 (min = 1280x800, max = 2560x1600), which was not anticipated by the original design. In the first parallel design phase, we could see a variety of adaptations of the original layout of which we show a selection in Figure 7. The vast majority of changes concerned the story image and article text. On average, the image was reduced to 84% of its original size of 640x436 pixels, while the original text width of 434 pixels was in all widescreen settings increased, on average by 168%. As a result, the image was often scaled down and in one case even cropped by resizing it to show only part of the original picture for which we present an example in Figure 7b. Four adaptations were completely text-oriented, in two cases even discarding the image. Moreover, the original

(a) Rough redesign of the layout with minor design problems

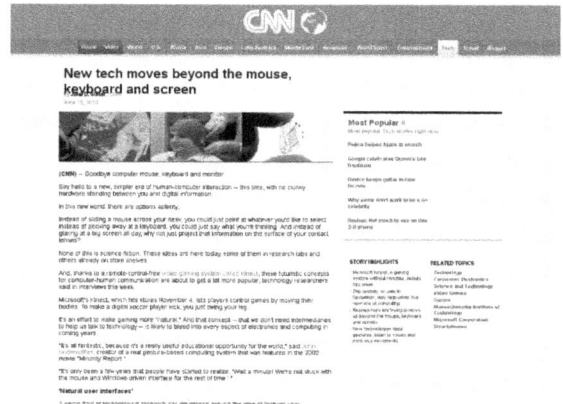

(b) Similar to Figure 7a, but the image was cropped and resized and sidebar elements better aligned

(c) Iteration of crowdsourced layout in Figure 1b showing minor changes to secondary elements to optimise space usage

Figure 7: Selection of crowdsourced layouts for widescreen (screenshots scaled at target window width)

font size of 14 pixels was increased in half of the adaptations designed for widescreen settings.

In terms of the position of elements, the sidebar content, originally aligned left of the article text, was moved to the right of the screen in 74% of all contributed layouts. One participant also moved the image to the right which resulted in a lot more visible text on the first screen. By the end of our experiment, this contribution was the highest-ranked crowdsourced layout overall (Figure 1b). Also worth mentioning is the fact that 30% of crowdsourced layouts aligned the container with the entire content on the left-hand side of the screen, which is in contrast to the original centred layout.

Seven contributions showed minor design problems in terms of overlapping page elements. Figure 7a is a concrete example of this as it shows smaller issues in the bottom-right corner. However, some of the designs were also quite similar and so it happened that, similar to Figure 7b, other crowdsourced layouts provided an alternative with no design problems. As expected, participants designing based on a matching crowdsourced layout usually did not change the core layout aspects, but focused on finer details such as the position and size of secondary elements to win extra space for the article text. For example, Figure 7c shows an incremental adaptation that was created based on the best-ranked, best-matching crowdsourced layout from the first phase (Figure 1b). We can see that the participant who customised based on this layout could afford to pay more attention to detail as they repositioned the author and date of the article in the page and emphasised the story highlights by moving it on top of other elements in the sidebar and increasing the font size. Generally, we could observe the trend that designing based on a crowdsourced layout overall afforded less changes by participants.

Compare task In terms of ratings, we registered 143 direct comparisons until the end of our study period. Layouts with design problems received almost no votes and were therefore eliminated without administrative effort. The "best" crowdsourced layout won 41 times against all other layouts including the original design. The original design, on the other hand, was preferred 67 times to all user contributions. While not all crowdsourced adaptations were considered an improvement, crowd-generated layouts achieved best results for larger screen contexts that were poorly supported by the original design. There was little improvement over the original design for the smaller resolutions for which it was created, but this does not mean that crowdsourced versions were inferior. The overall trend in the widescreen group was positive and the ratings generally in favour of crowd-generated layouts, especially in the second stage where iterative design was allowed and achieved potentially higher quality of results.

We will now focus on the highest-ranked crowdsourced layout for the rest of the discussion. The ratio between this custom layout and the original design was 3 to 4, indicating the promising result that crowdsourced adaptation was considered an improvement in 43% of direct comparisons.

Evaluate task The positive trend also showed in the reading times and feedback we collected on the original and crowdsourced layout. Overall, there was a 25% performance gain for the crowdsourced layout, where reading was on average 40 seconds faster compared to the original layout. The majority of participants found it easy to read the text using either layout (mode 4 on a 5-point Likert scale from 1 = *strongly*

disagree, 5 = *strongly agree*) and the crowdsourced layout received higher ratings in terms of a comfortable reading experience (mode 4 as opposed to 2). The fact that users did not feel efficient with either layout (mode 2) is surprising given the improvement in task performance, but could still be explained by some of the design critiques both layouts received. For example, participants from the widescreen group commented on the original layout that "reading the text with big white margins to the left and right of it that are broader than the text itself is not so comfortable". On the other hand, the crowdsourced layout was generally received quite positively (e.g. "Matches the expected layout of a newspage"), but also received critiques such as "The whole text seemed very long to read, could have organized better to view everything in a single page instead of scrolling down".

In summary, the results of our experiment suggest that crowdsourced adaptation based on a system like CrowdAdapt has the potential to improve the browsing experience and could be appreciated. The overall feedback on the tool support and the idea of sharing customised layouts was very positive. In line with other experiments [12], the quality of crowd-generated layouts seemed generally better in the second, iterative rather than the parallel, design mode. Layouts with minor design problems and radically different contributions, such as the ones focusing on the text only, were generally outvoted, which is good as they may also not be in the interest of web developers. While an administrative component could be added to the approach to give more control to web developers, or trusted users, so that their approval or rejection have significant impact on the ranking of crowdsourced adaptations, a review phase based on the one implemented in the evaluate task might be sufficient for step-wise roll-out and a pilot-and-push workflow even without such a component.

DISCUSSION AND RELATED WORK
This paper has investigated the idea of crowdsourced adaptation with the focus on the technical tools. A major premise of the techniques developed as part of this work is that they integrate well with common web architecture and widespread technologies. In consequence, a significant amount of our work went into developing methods and tools that are compatible with state-of-the-art web development practices so as to increase compatibility with existing application code and reduce the manual work required of developers in order to build on our solution. CrowdAdapt's operations were carefully engineered to handle possible edge cases by building on web standards and training on different sites. However, our goal was not to aim for completely automatic solutions. Rather, we argue that the control should always remain with web developers. We make use of crowdsourcing primarily as a tool for developers to receive design feedback and elicit context-specific design requirements for many different viewing conditions and individual user preferences. Using crowdsourcing for these aspects is viable, as it keeps developers informed about new requirements as they emerge.

Unlike much of the research on crowdsourcing [9], our focus is *not* on paid crowd work via Amazon Mechanical Turk. Instead, we build on frequent visitors and the chance that especially power users could have a particular interest in customising the layout for their own use context. By making the new layout available to other users, one user can benefit directly from another user's customisations. Therefore, the amount of pages a new user needs to customise can be substantially reduced. As we promote sharing and reuse within the web site community, our approach is designed to directly benefit the same group of users that also contribute, which was shown to raise motivation to participate [17].

Compared to previous approaches, we see the following three advantages for crowdsourced adaptation as far as the underlying techniques are concerned.

First, in contrast to previous model-based approaches, our approach does not require or impose a certain web design method such as WebML [6] and also no specific models of the user interface [5]. Since our adaptation techniques build directly on the final web interface, it is not relevant how the interface was developed as long as it can be represented in HTML and rendered in web browsers. This also means that no interface generation or transformation processes are involved. Interface generation usually starts from a model, then using a rule-based approach or machine learning to build a representation from which the user interface can be generated. Typical examples of interface generation approaches are PUC [15] and Supple [7]. On the other hand, interface transformation refers to approaches where existing representations of a user interface are mapped to models from which a new interface can be generated. Interface transformation therefore usually consists of three steps: reverse engineering [1], model transformation [11] and interface generation. This is described in detail for the CAMELEON reference framework [5] which formed the basis of many model-based user interface approaches such as MARIA [16]. In contrast to interface generation and transformation, crowdsourced adaptation directly starts from an existing final interface rather than a model or more abstract representation, and also does not require any intermediate representations. As a consequence, there is no need for reverse engineering and other model transformation techniques.

Second, our approach is tailored to the adaptation of web interfaces, whereas the majority of approaches such as PUC, Supple and MARIA aim to be comprehensive and handle web interfaces just like another output channel. However, such general approaches to adaptive user interfaces usually require proprietary user interface descriptions at a more abstract level. As a consequence, different user interface description languages have been proposed that are, however, not native to the web and therefore increase the threshold for being picked up by web developers. We therefore argue that our focus on the adaptivity of web interfaces is not a limitation, but rather an advantage since it means that we can directly build on and complement, rather than replace, established web standards and technologies.

Third, while previous adaptive interface techniques required complex constraint solving algorithms and additional server-side infrastructure to support web environments [18], we leverage native browser support and, in particular, new fea-

tures of HTML5 and CSS3 that make it possible that much of the adaptation process can now run directly on the client-side. This client-side adaptation approach therefore also requires less technical overhead compared to previous, commonly proxy-based, approaches.

From the initial experiments with CrowdAdapt, we learned that the sharing of customised layouts between users in similar contexts generally makes sense and could be appreciated. However, we need to point out several limitations to the experiment and our current implementation of the approach.

First, the question of whether crowd-generated layouts are "good" deserves special attention. A short, but fair, answer is: "it depends". Many customised layouts met the preferences of other users, but could still be criticised from a professional user interface design perspective. Important is that users must have felt that their customisations improved their viewing situation and that even our simple in-built voting system and the pilot testing among participants eliminated "bad" layouts in the majority of cases. The results also indicate that the iterative task design similar to [12] and task splitting using a variant of the well-established *find-fix-verify* pattern [2]—for our purposes with a combined *find-fix* phase in the design task and a two-step *verify* stage in the compare-evaluate cycle for minor and major testing of crowdsourced adaptations—helped improve the quality of results. Additional means might be required to handle cases in which the crowd agrees on a new, potentially better, layout, that was, however, not requested by a frequent visitor and might even contradict how some users are used to working with the site.

Moreover, there is an interesting interplay between personalisation and adaptation to device that involves several factors which were difficult to isolate in the experiment. Clearly, the preferred adaptation at a particular moment may no longer be preferred later on, as this depends on many factors including the task at hand. Our experiment was driven by the task of improving the CNN layout for readability. Personalisation was therefore not the main goal, although it is still a factor in end-user customisation. An important aspect of our online experiment was to see the variety of use contexts, especially in large-display settings, and how they impact the use of CrowdAdapt. We have considered a controlled lab study modelled on top of our experiment to reassess some of the findings. While this is likely to increase the validity of results, it will require significant resources to emulate the different viewing conditions and might only provide little new insight. We therefore accepted the necessary tradeoffs, but paid great attention to the experiment design. Note that, as CrowdAdapt targets spatial adaptations to better fit different screen sizes, it may be combined with other customisation tools that usually target personalisation of design and content (colours, language, etc.) rather than adaptation to device.

Finally, our use of CrowdAdapt explored how crowd-generated layouts could be used "as is". The focus was on looking at how both developers and end-users could potentially benefit from using basic forms of crowdsourced adaptation, but the features and workflow could be extended to further improve crowd work. Ideally, one would want to allow end-users to apply several fixes that may come from multiple crowd-generated layouts. While this could also be the result of a longer iterative design process, we could develop additional tools for directly picking different aspects from layouts and merging the underlying adaptations into a new template. This is feasible since, in our approach, adaptations are managed for each interface component based on jQuery selectors and could be applied selectively rather than as a whole. In our experiments, the ID-based adaptation approach worked fairly well for reusing adaptations across different news pages, wikis and blogs. However, we are aware of more advanced DOM structure-based similarity measures used in systems such as PageTailor [3], which could also be added to the approach. It could also be interesting to use data mining in CrowdAdapt, e.g., for supporting users when they customise the interface similar to [4] by suggesting changes done by other users in matching contexts, and also to learn a model of common adaptations. This could be done similar to [10], but our particular goal would then be to produce design patterns for different web site genres and use contexts.

CONCLUSION

This paper explored a crowdsourcing approach to achieving a higher degree of adaptivity of existing web interfaces and supporting a variety of device settings and user preferences. Future work could be based on the technical tools presented in this paper and take the ideas further. For example, an interesting direction could be to specifically design for certain groups of users and to take cultural aspects as well as special needs into account. CrowdAdapt could be refined to support this by adjusting the operations and extending the context model with more user-related aspects. Another direction could expand on the ideas of community-based design and allow end-users, not only to adjust the layout, but to get more creative and also provide additional content and functionality. The fact that our tools allow for the integration with existing web interfaces as well as different deployment modes could enable also other researchers to experiment with such ideas.

Acknowledgements
We would like to thank Rob Miller and Fabio Paternò for their helpful comments on earlier versions of this paper. This work was supported by the Swiss NSF (grant nr. 200020_134983).

REFERENCES
1. Bellucci, F., Ghiani, G., Paternò, F., and Porta, C. Automatic Reverse Engineering of Interactive Dynamic Web Applications to Support Adaptation across Platforms. In *Proc. IUI* (2012).

2. Bernstein, M. S., Little, G., Miller, R. C., Hartmann, B., Ackerman, M. S., Karger, D. R., Crowell, D., and Panovich, K. Soylent: A Word Processor with a Crowd Inside. In *Proc. UIST* (2010).

3. Bila, N., Ronda, T., Mohomed, I., Truong, K. N., and de Lara, E. PageTailor: Reusable End-User Customization for the Mobile Web. In *Proc. MobiSys* (2007).

4. Bunt, A., Conati, C., and McGrenere, J. Supporting Interface Customization using a Mixed-Initiative Approach. In *Proc. IUI* (2007).

5. Calvary, G., Coutaz, J., Thevenin, D., Limbourg, Q., Bouillon, L., and Vanderdonckt, J. A Unifying Reference Framework for Multi-Target User Interfaces. *IWC 15* (2003).

6. Ceri, S., Daniel, F., Matera, M., and Facca, F. M. Model-driven Development of Context-Aware Web Applications. *TOIT 7*, 1 (2007).

7. Gajos, K. Z., Wobbrock, J. O., and Weld, D. S. Improving the Performance of Motor-Impaired Users with Automatically-Generated, Ability-Based Interfaces. In *Proc. CHI* (2008).

8. Hattori, G., Hoashi, K., Matsumoto, K., and Sugaya, F. Robust Web Page Segmentation for Mobile Terminal Using Content-Distances and Page Layout Information. In *Proc. WWW* (2007).

9. Kittur, A., Nickerson, J. V., Bernstein, M. S., Gerber, E., Shaw, A. D., Zimmerman, J., Lease, M., and Horton, J. The Future of Crowd Work. In *Proc. CSCW* (2013).

10. Kumar, R., Talton, J. O., Ahmad, S., and Klemmer, S. R. Bricolage: Example-Based Retargeting for Web Design. In *Proc. CHI* (2011).

11. Limbourg, Q., and Vanderdonckt, J. Multipath Transformational Development of User Interfaces with Graph Transformations. In *Proc. HCSE*. Springer, 2009.

12. Little, G., Chilton, L. B., Goldman, M., and Miller, R. C. Exploring Iterative and Parallel Human Computation Processes. In *Proc. CHI Extended Abstracts, HCOMP Workshop* (2010).

13. Nebeling, M., Matulic, F., and Norrie, M. C. Metrics for the Evaluation of News Site Content Layout in Large-Screen Contexts. In *Proc. CHI* (2011).

14. Nebeling, M., and Norrie, M. C. Tools and Architectural Support for Crowdsourced Adaptation of Web Interfaces. In *Proc. ICWE* (2011).

15. Nichols, J., Chau, D. H., and Myers, B. A. Demonstrating the Viability of Automatically Generated User Interfaces. In *Proc. CHI* (2007).

16. Paternò, F., Santoro, C., and Spano, L. MARIA: A Universal, Declarative, Multiple Abstraction-Level Language for Service-Oriented Applications in Ubiquitous Environments. *TOCHI 16*, 4 (2009).

17. Rashid, A. M., Ling, K. S., Tassone, R. D., Resnick, P., Kraut, R. E., and Riedl, J. Motivating Participation by Displaying the Value of Contribution. In *Proc. CHI* (2006).

18. Schrier, E., Dontcheva, M., Jacobs, C., Wade, G., and Salesin, D. Adaptive Layout for Dynamically Aggregated Documents. In *Proc. IUI* (2008).

ACCESS: A Technical Framework for Adaptive Accessibility Support

Michael Heron
Canterbury Christ Church University
Department of Computing
Canterbury, CT1 1QU
michael.heron@canterbury.ac.uk

Vicki L. Hanson
University of Dundee
School of Computing
Dundee, DD1 4HN
vlh@computing.dundee.ac.uk

Ian W. Ricketts
University of Dundee
School of Computing
Dundee, DD1 4HN
ricketts@computing.dundee.ac.uk

ABSTRACT
In this paper we outline ACCESS – an open source, cross-platform, plug-in enabled software framework designed to provide a mapping between user needs and system configuration. The framework inverts the responsibility for making system configuration changes so that it lies with the computer rather than the user. In turn, the responsibility for identifying when changes should be made is delegated onto the plug-ins that have been incorporated into the framework. User feedback is solicited by a simple reinforcement mechanic through which individuals can like or dislike adaptations that are made. User interaction adjusts the probabilities that plug-ins will be selected in future, and also allows for plug-ins to adjust their own algorithms in line with user preferences. Results of experimental testing are encouraging, and show strong support for the perceived benefit, tractability and appropriateness of the framework.

Author Keywords
Accessibility; Human Factors; Adaptive Interfaces; Software Framework

ACM Classification Keywords
H.5.2 [**Information Interfaces and Presentation**]: User Interfaces – *input devices and strategies, user-centred design, Assistive technologies for persons with disabilities*

General Terms
Design; Human Factors

INTRODUCTION
In this paper we describe the design of ACCESS (Accessibility and Cognitive Capability Evaluation Support System), a software framework aimed at addressing a number of substantial problems associated with supporting novice users with special interaction needs.

Modern operating systems have numerous accessibility tools built into them, and these tools are often of very high

quality. Windows 7 for example comes complete with settings for altering mouse speed, keyboard repeat and de-bounce rates, magnifiers for the partially sighted, and tools to allow those with movement impairments to use the keyboard rather than the mouse for cursor control. It also comes with a screen reader and an on-screen keyboard for those who cannot use a traditional input device. The range of tools offered support a wide range of physical impairments, and by virtue of being part of the operating system themselves they are tightly integrated into the user experience.

However, the complexity of an average control panel for most operating systems is problematic for users who are unfamiliar with the impact of changes, and the jargon used. [5] and [14] have identified several considerable problems with user configuration of systems. Novice users often lack awareness that the options are available, often lack the knowledge of how to change the options, and often lack the confidence to make the changes that they know how to make. Additionally, some users may be operating under restricted circumstances which frustrate their ability to change settings at all.

The control panel of any modern operating system is an unknown quantity for substantial numbers of novice users [6] and in many cases they are unaware of some of its options. Upon being presented with a window from a relevant control panel, the user is presented with a combination of jargon, range of choices, and lack of clear guidance as to when an option has use to a particular individual. The result is an environment for configuration that puts at a disadvantage those users who would most benefit from the availability of accessibility support.

While these are not insoluble problems and many tools have been tested to provide adaptable corrections to a user's experience [9, 15, 16, 17], they suffer from being tightly bound to both the deployment context and the specific interaction difficulty that they are designed to address. Approaches such as used in SUPPLE [2] offer significant opportunities, but are difficult to integrate into the traditional workflow of software engineering. Additionally the choice of implementation language has significant consequences for any attempt to take a more holistic approach to the development of adaptive interfaces.

[18] argues that the shifting nature of information services demands a new approach to usability, one that he refers to as 'ubiquitous accessibility'. Through the Raising the Floor initiative[1], progress is being made to incorporate these principles into the world wide web. [18] also argues that there are benefits to be reaped from the common, collaborative development of a technical core which allows for user interface 'micro adaptations' to be 'plugged into' a common framework and invoked as needed on behalf of the user.

Currently developers must make a choice between gaining control of the underlying input streams of an operating system, or developing in a language that allows for high degrees of platform independence through the use of a virtual machine. Creating an accessibility application that can support a user across multiple platforms and multiple methods of input is currently an extremely difficult task.

VIRTUAL MACHINES AND THE DEPLOYMENT CONTEXT

The choice of language in which a tool will be implemented has implications for how straightforward it will be to develop and port to different platforms and contexts. Abstracted programming languages such as Java and C# do not execute directly on the underlying operating system. Instead, they are compiled into a form of bytecode and this bytecode is then executed on a virtual machine. The virtual machine interprets the bytecode, and makes requests of the underlying operating system to handle the functionality. This offers developers a tremendous benefit in that their programs become *platform independent* - provided an operating system has a supported virtual machine, the bytecode will run without modification for the majority of straightforward applications.

However, the nature of this architecture means that developers are writing software for the virtual machine and not the operating system upon which the software runs. This necessitates that programs have little direct interaction with the operating system. Most languages offer classes for abstracting platform specific interactions such as saving files or storing preferences. Unfortunately these are generalised implementations and simplify many of the details so as to ensure consistency between platforms. The result of this is that only functionality that is commonly supported on deployment platforms can be made available via the virtual machine.

This is an important limitation, and the developers of such languages have also provided mechanisms for accessing platform specific features. For example, it is possible through the System class on Java to execute any arbitrary command line instruction. This can be used to invoke installed applications or access shell tools and pipe their

responses back into the Java program. However, when this is done platform independence is lost as a result of the need to correctly handle the complexities associated with operating system differences.

One very simple example of where this becomes a problem is in the directory structures on Windows and Linux based systems. The Linux directory structure has a distribution specific role for each of its directories and subdirectories, with physical layout of drives being of secondary importance. The emphasis on Windows in comparison is that individual drives are the focus of directory management.

Invoking an external application on Linux then is likely to require locating the appropriate binary in /usr/ or /bin/, and then executing it through the shell to start it up. The same task on Windows will require a different path because of the differences in the directory structures. As such, between any given Linux and windows application, the developer must support two different directory structures in order to invoke an external application even if we can assume that the same application is available.

A second, more substantial difference is in how different platforms handle storing of data files. Windows applications primarily function through database entries in the registry, whereas Linux applications use flat text files located in a particular directory. Thus, changing a particular system preference on Windows is mostly done through a consistent interface, whereas changing the same system setting on Linux requires locating the appropriate configuration file and making the adjustment to the text within. These are not simply philosophical differences – they have a major impact on the way in which applications must interact with the underlying system. The registry permits for values to be queried and set if you have access to the correct identifiers, whereas text-file configuration requires parsing the file in code and then committing the change to the underlying system. Moreover, these systems are not consistent even within different versions of the operating systems themselves. The location of files can change between versions of an operating system, or be made entirely obsolete.

These problems exist regardless of which kind of programming language is used. C and C++ do not have to mediate through a virtual machine, but in order to make these systems work on multiple platforms they must instead go through a manual process of 'porting' in which incompatibilities between one platform and another are resolved.

Other issues are introduced when developers need access to parts of the operating system that the virtual machine does not support. Java and the .NET virtual machines do not permit access to low-level IO streams – if you need access to these, you must write in a language that is closer to the operating system. The only way to get access to keyboard

---
[1] http://raisingthefloor.org/

and mouse input through the virtual machine is to link it up to an active GUI window. The input is available only when that window is active, and when the window is minimised or invisible, the input data is no longer available. As such, getting access to user input across an entire operating system – a task which is core to many kinds of accessibility solutions – is something that cannot be done within the confines of the virtual machine. If these kinds of interactions are routinely required, then a virtual machine gets in the way of productive development. Platform specific development is often tied directly into the context and making a program work on another operating system is a challenging and specialised task. The burden of knowledge on a developer is considerable – it is not simply a case of changing function names or constant values, sometimes it requires significant re-architecting of how an application functions. Windows has an event hook structure that can be overriden, whereas Linux doesn't have this structure and thus requires another approach such as continual polling of the keyboard port.

However, where virtual languages do excel is in their flexibility for routine software development, and in the amount of support and expertise already available. Java and C# are languages that are routinely used for teaching programming, and almost all developers (novice or otherwise) will have some exposure to the way in which they work.

Non-virtualized languages have one facility that virtual languages don't – they can access underlying input streams and other low-level operating system functionality. That which is impossible in pure Java (getting access to keyboard and mouse input across the entire operating system) is easily achievable in C provided the developer understands the way that the underlying event hook architecture works.

For the development of accessibility software, this means that the choice of implementation language involves a tradeoff between access to input streams and flexibility of deployment as well as the ease with which software can be developed and deployed.

A HYBRID APPROACH

The approach that has been taken in ACCESS is to create a hybrid system, which is a solution that has been employed in other contexts with success (for example in the Java3D API). The majority of the framework is written in Java which allows for portability and tractability for developers. Those parts of the system that cannot be implemented in Java have instead been delegated to small daemon programs that are executed as part of the framework's initialization. Communication between these daemons and the framework itself is handled via socket communication, allowing bidirectional input and output. Sitting between these daemons and the framework is an operating system context – a class which implements the API of the framework.

Figure 1 shows the outline of the framework – elements in dark grey are written in C, and the rest is written in Java. JNI[2] is used where appropriate to handle the invocation of external functionality, but its use is confined to the operating system context.

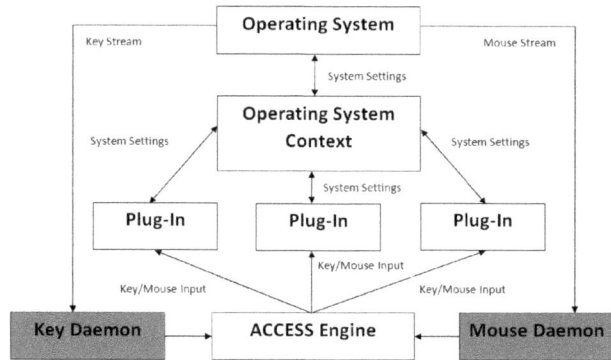

Figure 1 - ACCESS Framework Architecture

This architecture allows for the majority of the framework to be developed in a cross-platform way, and minimizes the development cost required to deploy ACCESS on another platform. In order to port the framework, two things must be done – an operating system context must be written to implement the set of functionality supported by the framework, and a key/mouse daemon must be written and deployed.

The task of implementing an operating system context may involve the development of other programs, but these can be handled independently and without reference to the rest of the framework. As an example, to handle some of the Windows functionality, ACCESS incorporates a DLL that handles functionality such as querying open windows and interacting with the registry. The operating system context then uses this DLL to implement certain aspects of its API. The API enumerates the possible operating system options (though functions such as setMouseTrails or setKeyRepeatRate), and the operating system context uses the DLL to handle the appropriate interaction with the registry to make this happen. Examples of this currently supported include changing of key repeat rates, key debounce rates, pointer speed and pointer precision. New options can be added to the framework in a matter of minutes due to the high level of abstraction between the framework and the underlying DLL files that handle the complexities of configuration.

The framework then does not remove the need for people to understand the inner workings of the registry, and does not remove the need to use pointers or system input hooks.

---

[2] Java Native Interface – a mechanism available in Java to use native code as if it was developed in Java. It is tremendously powerful, but it removes the portability of a java application.

However, the framework design ensures that these parts of the system are kept entirely separate from the parts that an accessibility researcher would work with on a day to day basis. While novice programmers would be limited to the expressive potential provided by the framework, they can work productively within these constraints to accomplish their goals. Several example of plug-ins that do just that are discussed in a later section.

All of this must be implemented to create a deployment of the framework on a new operating system, but sometimes this task is simpler than requiring a complex interrelationship of different objects and external applications. Much can be accomplished using Linux shell commands and this obviates the need of extra coding . Windows XP requires a DLL file to get the current window title, but it can be done on Linux and OS X through the use of the *xprop* command line tool. Much of the complexity of changing system preferences on OS X can be handled through the use of Applescript. In this way, each context can make use of the underlying platform in the way that is simplest and most appropriate. The framework puts no requirements on how particular functionality is to be implemented within a context, and so it can be done using the best tool for the job. All that is required is that the parameters, type, and content of returned values of the operating system context methods are kept consistent.

In this way, plug-ins written for the framework will function in an equivalent way on all platforms for which a context has been written.

ACCESS ACCESSIBILITY PLUG-INS
The majority of the work that developers do within the framework is handled via plug-ins. These are small, conceptually simple Java classes that make use of the provided API to listen for user interactions and then make changes to the underlying system based on analysis of those interactions. This is done in a period known as a 'tick', the length of which is configurable upon installation of the framework. The majority of plug-ins for ACCESS have no interface with which the user can interact[3] and operate invisibly in the background until they make a change to the user's system.

A developer may be interested in providing accessibility support for mouse interaction, and so the plug-in they develop will register an interest in mouse events. Inside the plug-in the developer can perform whatever calculations that they feel are appropriate based on the mouse-input that is provided by the framework. When an opportunity to improve the user's operating context is identified, the plug-ins can register themselves as being interested in making a change to the underlying operating system. Every five

minutes, the framework polls all registered plug-ins, and one of these plug-ins is then selected semi-randomly and then allowed to make a change to the user's operating context. Changes are generally small and incremental, such as adjusting the delay between which double-clicks must be registered or altering the speed of the mouse pointer. A plug-in requires no knowledge of which context is being used, the setup and selection of the appropriate context is handled by the framework itself.

The expressiveness of the kind of changes that can be made are, at time of writing, limited to what was needed to support the plug-ins that were developed as part of the exploratory research. They are currently able to change pointer size, pointer speed, pointer precision, size of pointer trails, double click delays, keyboard de-bounce rates, and keyboard repeat rates. They can also capture user input and replay it back so that it interacts with user interface elements. They have access to low level data streams for mouse and keyboard, and can also query the current working application and user login information. They can communicate with external applications through the use of sockets.

When a plug-in has made a correction, it presents a description of what it has done to the user and provides the opportunity for the user to indicate their approval or disapproval of the change that was made. Only two options are presented when a plug-in is selected to make a corrective action: 'I like this' or 'I don't like this'.

The provision of these two options ensures tractability – users do not need to know the range of configuration options available to them, and they do not need to understand when an option is of value. The goal in ACCESS is to remove as much of that complexity as is possible, rendering the decision down to a flat like or dislike choice.

Each plug-in must implement a pre-defined interface and then be added to the list of plug-ins loaded by the framework. Plug-ins sit passively in the framework, and the methods that draw in user input are called only at predetermined points in the framework's lifecycle. Each plug-in is responsible for setting and manipulating its own internal state, and interpreting user corrections with regards to its internal trigger values.

The framework also provides support for plug-ins to register themselves as listening on a socket. This allows for individual applications, such as the testing application developed as part of this project, to communicate with individual plug-ins and provide information that cannot otherwise be algorithmically detected. While it is not possible for the framework to simplify socket development on a client application, within the context of a plug-in the framework manages the multi-threading, instantiation and management of sockets and connections. All a plug-in must to to gain access to a socket is to implement a method

---

[3] The framework does include functionality for deploying plug-ins that can be invoked, but these are not the focus of this paper.

that defines a port for the socket, and then implement a method to interpret the string data that comes in.

PLUG-IN WEIGHTINGS

At the core of the user interaction loop in ACCESS is a system of operant conditioning. This is based on an adjustment of internal weightings modified by liking or disliking the operating system changes that have been made by a plug-in.

When the time comes to choose a plug-in to make a correction, the Framework constructs a roulette wheel[4] of the plug-ins that have registered an interest in making a change. This wheel is constructed based on the *weightings* of each plug-in. The wheel is then spun to choose which plug-in is permitted to make its chosen correction. Lowering the weighting of a plug-in then will reduce the chance it will be selected in any given wheel.

The opportunity to rate a plug-in is provided after it has made its correction to the underlying system. The user is provided with the information about the change that has been made and asked to either 'like' or 'dislike' the change. The option to rate remains in place for a number of ticks - if the plug-in has not been conditioned after the preset number of ticks, consent is silently assumed but no adjustments are made to the internal weightings of the plug-in. Disliking a change will revert the operating system to its state before the change was made and reduce the weighting of the-plug-in. Liking will commit the change and increase the weighing of the plug-in accordingly. The flow of this is shown in Figure 2.

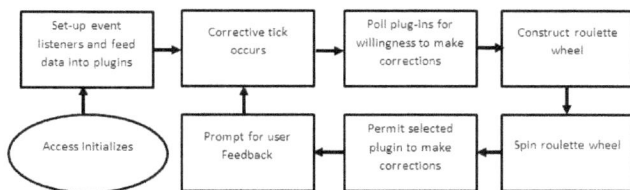

Figure 2 - User Interaction Loop

When the rating is applied, the Framework will also pass on details of the rating to the plug-in itself. Plug-ins can then use this information to adjust their own internal values to make them more or less sensitive as is appropriate. A plug-in interested in detecting when a mouse is shaken for example can make its calculations more or less sensitive based on user feedback. As user feedback is recorded over time, a user influences which plug-ins have impact on their operating environment by directly modifying the chance they perform corrective action.

---

[4] A roulette wheel in this context is a selection regime common in genetic programming techniques – the weighting of each plug-in is used to provide a structure that selects elements by virtue of probability. The lower the weighting, the less chance a plug-in will be selected.

It is important to appreciate however that binary choices lack expressiveness. Core to this design is the hypothesis that granularity of user opinions can be adequately captured via analysis of a series of binary data points. Repeated ratings result in greater impact on selection weighting for a plug-in, and internally a plug-in can provide whatever analysis is required for its own context sensitive reconfiguration. The framework however does not present the results of this analysis to the user – the user's only decision is to say whether they liked a change that was made, or they didn't.

ACCESS PLUG-INS

For the research that generated this paper a total of nine plug-ins were written. Seven of these were experimentally trialed. Our goal for the testing was to assess the viability of the approach as a mechanism for correcting interaction difficulties rather than looking to provide support for the real-word appropriateness of any specific plug-in. The approach used to test these was to conduct a study in two parts, both conducted with the context of a single experimental session. In the first part, the DoubleClick plug-in was tested in isolation. For the second, all plug-ins were tested as a full suite. The intention was to provoke user interaction complications to assess if the framework in conjunction with a suite of plug-ins could correct a user's computer experience in a way that was seen as appropriate and non-intrusive by the user. The tasks were designed to stress areas in which users are known to have interaction difficulties, and did not represent a realistic view of regular user interaction. Tasks included double-clicking on stationary and moving targets, keeping the pointer within moving targets, and simple quiz that involved looking between the screen and a provided sheet of paper before hitting the correct moving or stationary button.

The participants in these studies consisted of 15 males and 23 females, ranging in age from 60 to 80 (Mean=67.89, SD=6.02), all recruited through the SiDE User Pool at the University of Dundee[5]. The user pool is an opt-in register of older adults interested in participating in computing research at the university. All participants were native English speakers with no reported disabilities. Each participant was given a £20 voucher in exchange for their volunteered time. To quantitatively assess the framework, we employed a number of metrics. First, we examined the number of successful interactions as well as the time to complete these interactions. We also obtained self-reported measures of ease of use, difficulty of the tasks, helpfulness and non-intrusiveness of the plug-ins and the appropriateness of configurations. While the results of this study fall outside the scope of this paper, they are discussed in full in [6].

---

[5] http://side.computing.dundee.ac.uk/

A brief outline of the mechanics of each of these plug-ins is provided in this paper to show the flexibility of the framework and some of the ends to which it has currently been put. The code for all of these plug-ins is available on the project website[6] or those who wish to examine the structure and algorithms in more depth.

DoubleClick

Double clicking is known to be an area in which users have interaction difficulties, and the literature on the topic is considerable [1, 13]. The DoubleClick plug-in keeps track of difficulties in registering a double click as defined in the operating system settings. When a click is registered, the plug-in makes a note of the time it was recorded. When a second click is registered, it makes a note of the time that was recorded, and then compares the difference between the two time periods. If the time elapsed is greater than a full second, then the plug-in interprets this as two intentional single clicks. If the time elapsed is lower than this but greater than the threshold for a double click set in the operating system, then it registers this as an intended but failed double click. Each time this condition is triggered, the internal counter for the plug-in is increased by one. If it passes a threshold of two within a polling period, a correction is made.

When the first click is registered, a limit is placed on mouse-movement within the framework with regards to assessing whether or not a double click was intended. Movement of more than 10 pixels in any direction between the first and second click removes a pair of clicks from consideration as an intended double click.

PointerSize and MouseTrails

The intention behind both of these plug-ins is to resolve pointer location difficulties, some of which are highlighted in [10] and [12].

Both of these plug-ins share a core of code. They only differ in what their intended corrections are when difficulties are identified. In both cases, they implement three metrics for identifying when users are having issues locating their mouse cursor:

1. When the user moves the mouse to the top left hand corner, this counts as a lost cursor.
2. When the user moves the mouse sharply from side to side, this counts as a lost cursor.
3. When the user moves the mouse in spirals around the screen, this counts as a lost cursor.

For occasional loss of a mouse cursor, these are quick and effective workarounds. All are however sub-optimal. The first solution suffers in situations where the resolution of the screen extends beyond the monitor bounds (as is often the case with incorrectly configured equipment) because the

mouse cursor will often disappear off the screen entirely. The second and third strategies require the user to catch the movement of the cursor and such movement is not always immediately apparent. This is especially true in situations where that motion may be obscured by other movement or noisy, low contrast backgrounds.

For more pronounced problems with locating the mouse, there are accessibility solutions available in the operating system itself.

- The mouse cursor can be made bigger
- The mouse cursor can be given a trail when it is moved
- The mouse cursor can be made to 'pulse' when a particular key is pressed and held.

These two plugins were developed to pick up upon users having difficulty in mouse location by analysing mouse movements to pick up on the three compensatory behaviours outlined above. They differ only in the corrective action they make. The first plug in, PointerSize, will increase the size of the cursor when its internal thresholds are triggered. It will increase the cursor size each time it encounters a problem until the maximum cursor size has been reached, at which point it will cease to present itself for corrective actions. The second plug in, MouseTrails, will instead switch on the mouse trails. If mouse trails are already enabled, it will increase the length of those trails until the maximum has been reached. As mouse trails are not available on a Macintosh, this plug-in is Windows only.

To identify rapid shaking of a mouse, the plug-ins create an array of direction changes within a single mouse motion. Firstly, an array of co-ordinates is collapsed into an array of directions from previous to current and this array is then flattened down into an array that contains only direction changes. From the flattened array, each pair of directions is assessed in turn for 'abruptness'. Northeast and east have an abruptness of one, while east and west have an abruptness of three. The abruptness of each pair of points is calculated. The algorithm for determining mouse shake then is:

- Accumulate co-ordinates across a sustained mouse motion. If there are less than 50 data points, discard.
- Flatten the array
- Add the abruptness of each direction change to a counter
- Calculate the percentage of co-ordinates in the original array that registered a direction change
- Average the abruptness over the entire motion.
- Multiply the average of the abruptness by the percentage of direction changes.

If from this algorithm we get a value over five, this is interpreted as a mouse shake within the plug-in. This

---

[6] https://github.com/drakkos/ACCESS

algorithm was developed via observation of users during a number of pilot studies for the research.

Spirals are detected using a similar mechanic – the array of points to be analysed is first flattened, and then the distance between each pair of directions is calculated. The following algorithm was then used to identify a spiral:

- Get the distance between current and previous directions
- If this distance is counter clockwise, then the current direction is set to false.
    - Otherwise, if it is clockwise, it is set to true.
    - If it is neither, continue with the next pair of points.
- If the distance between two points is greater than 2 then continue with the next pair of points.
- If the last direction is the same as the current direction, add one to the internal counter
- Set the last direction to be the current direction
- If the counter is greater than or equal to four, then a spiral has been detected.

As with the shake detection, this algorithm was developed as a result of observation of users during the pilot studies conducted prior to the actual research.

The last of the metrics for identifying a lost pointer is much simpler – if the mouse cursor moves within 20 pixels of the top left hand corner, the lost cursor counter is incremented by one.

All three of these metrics are analysed, and if more than two incidents are encountered during a tick of the framework, the plug-in will register its interest in making a correction – increasing the pointer size for the PointerSize plug-in, and enabling or lengthening mouse trails for the MouseTrails plug-in.

DoubleBack

DoubleBack identified doubling-back behavior of mouse motions (when the course of a motion abruptly changed at the end of an interaction), and adjusted the speed of the mouse as a correction. The design of the plug-in is to compensate for 'overshoot' in mouse positioning, as discussed in [8] and [19].

The DoubleBack plug-in looks to determine if the last few moments of a mouse interaction were of a different average direction than the main body of the movement. It does this by separating out an array of co-ordinates into two parts – the head and the tail. The tail consists of the last ten co-ordinates of the movement, and the head consists of everything else. If either part of the motion has less than ten entries, this is discarded as being too short for meaningful analysis. If the difference between the two averaged directions is equal to or greater than one, it counts this as an attempt to double-back and thus increments the internal counter accordingly. If the counter reaches five during a tick of the framework, then the plug-in will reduce

the speed of the cursor to attempt to correct difficulties in target acquisition.

MissedClicks

Several of the tasks in the experimental trials involved clicking on moving targets. MissedClicks identified when users had difficulty in clicking a moving testing target, and enabled pointer precision when this scenario was encountered. Some examples of situations in which this can be problematic are outlined in [3] and [4]

The testing application sent an inform to the framework via a socket whenever the participant missed a target. This information was then passed on to the MissedClicks plug-in which incremented an internal counter by one. When the counter reached ten over the course of the exercise, the plug-in would enable pointer precision.

This particular plug-in is not cross platform because it is dependent on an external application to trigger the socket communication, but it does show some of the flexibility of the framework even when confined to a single operating system context. The relatively complex tasks of pulling in user input, modifying system settings, and communicating via applications and plug-ins is all handled by implementing stub methods, and none of the code associated with any of these methods is complex.

InputRecorder

The last of the plug-ins that were experimentally trialed was the InputRecorder, and this functioned silently and invisibly in the background recording user system interactions. It did this as logs of input events rather than as a video, since in this way it could be made to 'play back' a user's interactions and have them trigger appropriately with the operating system. This allows for the logs of user interactions to be used to fine-tune the framework performance since it is possible to use actual experimental interactions and analyse the impact of changes made to the plug-in algorithms. Of course, once the behaviour of the framework differs from that observed during the trial it is no longer possible to precisely replicate a session, but smaller segments of input can be extracted to create small, 'interaction vignettes'.

The plug-in works both as an invokable plug-in (this provides the control panel for loading and replaying user interactions) and as an invisible plug-in that starts recording on the basis of a command issued over a socket. All user input from that point on is recorded and saved to disk. When it is to be played back, the framework makes use of the Robot class of Java, feeding back the input data with the delays indicated in the logs.

BENEFITS OF THE FRAMEWORK

EXPERIMENTAL VALIDATION

The tool has been experimentally evaluated. It was found that the tool will pick up the need for corrective activity, and will make corrections in a way that is evaluated by participants as understandable, appropriate and non-intrusive. Quantitative measures of performance were increased through application of the tool (statistically significant at $p < 0.05$ as determined by a Student's T-Test in most cases), and participants self-reported a statistically significant improvement in terms of computer responsiveness and perceived easiness of the tasks that they performed.

The full outline of these results represents a substantial amount of content due to the relative complexity of the experimental setup and the process that was used to evaluate the plug-ins, but they are fully outlined in [6].

Lowered burden of knowledge on developers
It seems unreasonable to expect that individuals who wish to provide accessibility support need to first navigate the low level IO layers in order to develop even simple tools. As discussed above virtual languages simplify much programming but they simultaneously make it difficult for developers to act within an OS wide context without traversing somewhat esoteric territory. Inexperienced developers are often faced with the prospect of developing outside of their comfort zone in order to implement even trivial accessibility functionality. Such tools are almost always developed in isolation without consideration given for what other equivalent tools they may be competing against for system resources.

Usually the actual 'core' functionality is at least moderately straightforward - the code for identifying mouse shake as discussed above involves calculations on points in a 2D co-ordinate space. This is as simple as performing arithmetic on data elements in an array. It is not the accessibility functionality that takes up the greatest developer burden - it's the architecture needed for that functionality to be incorporated into the operating system.

Within the ACCESS Framework, the architecture for OS communication is provided, and developer applications (the plug-ins) are completely passive - they receive information from the framework at pre-defined points of time and may or may not act upon that information as they choose. How a plug-in manages its own internal data structure is of no concern to the ACCESS Framework - a plug-in may be a single class, or a far more complex package of interrelated units. They can use all of the tools of OO design to properly package their functionality. All that matters is that there is an ACCESS class that implements a simple set of defined behaviours and beyond that point the plug-in acts like a black box.

Lowered burden of knowledge on users

This paper has focused primarily on the technical benefits that come from having a consistent software framework for accessibility. However, this is a tool designed for end-users as well as developers, and technical benefits are not sufficient to persuade an end user that they should use a tool.

[14] identified some of the key problems with existing accessibility tools, as outlined in the introduction. These fall primarily into two main categories – users lack the capability or knowledge to make substantial changes, or users lack the confidence to make the changes. These are two areas in which this Framework is aimed at improving the user experience.

Resolves user confidence issues

Many users often lack confidence in their actions when working with computers, and will often blame themselves for faults which more correctly belong with a badly designed application [11]. Many accessibility solutions have a subtle impact that cannot be immediately observed (changing a key de-bounce rate, or slightly altering the speed of a mouse), and the lack of direct, obvious feedback on what has happened is an additional factor in the lack of confidence individuals display.

The ACCESS Framework attempts to resolve this issue by reducing the question down to 'do you like the change that has been made'. There is no need for complex analysis of potential impact, just a statement of preference as to the way their system is currently functioning. Where those changes are invisible, the framework suggests that the user simply try out the change for a while - time is permitted to experiment. The framework will silently assume consent after a certain amount of time has passed and in cases where the user cannot detect the impact of a change, they can simply allow the framework to commit the alteration without having to make a specific decision about something they cannot judge.

Resolves lack of knowledge issues

Many useful accessibility tools built into an operating system are left underutilized because users simply do not know they are there. The ACCESS Framework resolves this problem by moving the responsibility for detecting the applicability of an accessibility option to a plug-in. Only when a plug-in determines that support is required will a change be made to the user's system. In this way, a user does not have to be concerned with how to access the functionality – the functionality is provided when a need is externally identified.

This also resolves the problems of those who may be operating without the capability of making a change – those who have mouse interaction problems may not be able to navigate to the appropriate part of the operating system because of their impairments (As discussed in [20]). As with those who lack the knowledge to make an accessibility change, the provision of support when the need is identified also improves the situation for those who cannot access the underlying functionality.

LIMITATIONS AND ISSUES
Technically the system functions as has been described above – it has been developed and tested across multiple

platforms, and the core design of the framework demonstrates low structural coupling and high conceptual cohesion. Design patterns have been incorporated as and when they contribute to improvements in the software architecture. However, leaving aside the technical considerations, the framework does bring up several important ethical issues.

The first of these lies in the issue of user trust - specifically, how far should users trust the engine. It could be argued that the primary mechanism of 'change and then consent' used by the tool raises concerns. It is a violation of user norms for a system to make a change to the system and only then seek consent, and that is what the framework does – consent for changes is assumed and then confirmed. The issue here is in soliciting honesty in user feedback – it's important in the design to not to anthropomorphize the framework in such a way that it appears as if the feedback is anything other than cool, dispassionate assessment of corrective activity.

The assumption of consent in the framework allows for users to first assess what actual impact a change will have before they confirm or deny it. In order to do this the system has to assume responsibility over the change and the user's operating context. One potential solution to this is to adopt instead a system of 'consent then reinforce' in which a plug-in would indicate its intention to make a change and require the user to sign off on it. However, follow-up focus groups of research participants felt that this made the tool too intrusive and clunky. This option is a setting that can be toggled on deployment, although by default it is not switched on. These two objections have a third factor that acts as an additional imperative for resolution - that of the power present in plug-ins. It is trivial within the ACCESS Framework to develop a comprehensive, hidden key-logger for example - one that can keep track of application context and mouse input. Of a necessity, the framework must expose information that can be damaging to privacy. While some mechanisms could be applied to counteract this - such as scrambling the actual values of keys pressed - they all carry with them a cost in terms of potential accessibility functionality – tools such as [16] for example would not be possible under such a regime.

Additionally there are some technical limitations with the framework as it stands in its current version which limits accessibility support to the altering of control panel settings in the operating system. The inability to make changes in real time is an important restriction, but one that will be addressed in future developmental phases. Within the limitations as they currently exist, the tool can perform some relatively complex adjustments for any applications that can make a socket connection with the framework. Information can be sent and received via these sockets, including application specific information required for effective configuration.

FURTHER WORK

The experimental results for the framework are promising [6], but have thus far been conducted only within research scenarios. Additionally, the expressiveness of the framework is currently limited to that needed to permit the proper functioning of the plug-ins addressed during the research. A substantial part of the future research into this tool will be to develop a larger library of plug-ins and to expand the feature-set of the tool. Additionally, research will focus on ensuring that the framework works correctly across multiple operating systems and contexts, as well as across multiple streams of input - support for both the WiiMote and the Microsoft Kinect platform are planned extensions to the tool, and future versions of the tool designed to adaptively address the issue of accessibility in games [7] are planned.

CONCLUSION

Developing accessibility software requires a disproportionate knowledge of programming considering the often simple functional requirements being met. The ACCESS Framework has been developed as a way to lower the barrier of participation with regards to individuals being able to develop genuinely useful accessibility and cognitive support tools. In addition, with no additional work on the part of an accessibility developer, these tools will work on multiple operating systems with equivalent functionality.

Virtualized programming languages have enabled platform independence in a low cost way for developers. While their limitations do not impact on most routine application development, they are extremely problematic for accessibility developers due to the way they increasingly abstract the program code away from the underlying operating system. The ACCESS Framework has been written to resolve this issue as outlined in this paper – the primary technique used is a hybrid approach whereby platform specific elements are implemented in a non-virtualized language such as C. The actionable code developed by individual accessibility researchers is implemented in Java. The framework itself handles interrelating all of these parts, instantiating the correct context, handling socket based communication, and providing access to the Framework API to each individual plug-in. Plug-ins are thus reduced to being small, conceptually simple implementations of stub functions.

The plug-ins discussed in this paper are collected here to show some of the details of their implementation as they relate to the framework itself. A full code accounting of these plug-ins is available at the project website (https://github.com/drakkos/ACCESS).

ACKNOWLEDGEMENTS

The research described in this paper was conducted as part of an IBM Open Collaborative Research project between IBM Research and the University of Dundee. Additional funding was provided by a Royal Society Wolfson Merit

Award to the second author and by grant RCUK EP/G066019/1 "RCUK Hub: Inclusion in the Digital Economy".

Special acknowledgements go to Dr. Norman Alm, Professor Peter Gregor, Professor Alan Newell, and Dr. Janet Hughes, all of the University of Dundee, for their suggestions, advice and guidance. Thanks go to Dr. Shari Trewin of IBM and Pauline Belford for their very helpful feedback and suggestions.

REFERENCES

[1] Dickinson, A., Eisma, R. & Gregor, P. Challenging interfaces/redesigning users. *SIGCAPH Comput. Phys. Handicap.* 61-68 (2002).

[2] Gajos, K. Z., Weld, D. S. & Wobbrock, J. O. Automatically generating personalized user interfaces with supple. *Artif. Intell.* **174**, 910-950 (2010).

[3] Hajri, A. A., Fels, S., Miller, G. & Ilich, M. Moving target selection in 2D graphical user interfaces. In *Proceedings of the 13th IFIP TC 13 international conference on Human-computer interaction - Volume Part II*, INTERACT'11, 141-161 (Springer-Verlag, Berlin, Heidelberg, 2011).

[4] Hasan, K., Grossman, T. & Irani, P. Comet and target ghost: techniques for selecting moving targets. In *Proceedings of the 2011 annual conference on Human factors in computing systems*, CHI '11, 839-848 (ACM, New York, NY, USA, 2011).

[5] Hawthorn, D. How universal is good design for older users? In *CUU '03: Proceedings of the 2003 conference on Universal usability*, 38-45 (ACM, New York, NY, USA, 2003).

[6] Heron, M.J., Hanson, V.L, & Ricketts, I. (2013*).* Accessibility Support with the ACCESS Framework. *The International Journal of Human Computer Interaction.* Seattle, Washington. Doi: 10.1080/10447318.2013.768139

[7] Heron, M. Inaccessible through oversight: the need for inclusive game design. *Computer Games Journal* **1** (2012).

[8] Hwang, F., Keates, S., Langdon, P. & Clarkson, P. Movement time prediction for tasks assisted by force-feedback. In *: Designing a More Inclusive World: the 2nd Cambridge Workshop on Universal Access and Assistive Technology*, 143-152 (2004).

[9] Koester, H. H., Lopresti, E. & Simpson, R. C. Toward automatic adjustment of keyboard settings for people with physical impairments. *Disabil Rehabil Assist Technol* **2**, 261-274 (2007).

[10] Money, A., Fernando, S., Lines, L. & Elliman, T. Developing and evaluating web-based assistive technologies for older adults. *Gerontechnology* **8**, 165-177 (2009).

[11] Newell, A. F., Dickinson, A., Smith, M. J. & Gregor, P. Designing a portal for older users: A case study of an industrial/academic collaboration. *ACM Trans. Comput.-Hum. Interact.* **13**, 347-375 (2006).

[12] Paradise, J., Trewin, S. & Keathes, S. Using pointing devices: difficulties encountered and strategies employed. In *Proceedings of 3rd International Conference on Universal Access and Human-Computer Interaction* (2005).

[13] Sayago, S. & Blat, J. About the relevance of accessibility barriers in the everyday interactions of older people with the web. In *Proceedings of the 2009 International Cross-Disciplinary Conference on Web Accessibililty (W4A)*, W4A '09, 104-113 (ACM, New York, NY, USA, 2009).

[14] Trewin, S. Configuration agents, control and privacy. In *CUU '00: Proceedings on the 2000 conference on Universal Usability*, 9-16 (ACM, New York, NY, USA, 2000).

[15] Trewin, S. An invisible keyguard. In *Assets '02: Proceedings of the fifth international ACM conference on Assistive technologies*, 143-149 (ACM, New York, NY, USA, 2002).

[16] Trewin, S. Automating accessibility: the dynamic keyboard. In *Assets '04: Proceedings of the 6th international ACM SIGACCESS conference on Computers and accessibility*, 71-78 (ACM, New York, NY, USA, 2004).

[17] Trewin, S., Keates, S. & Moffatt, K. Developing steady clicks: a method of cursor assistance for people with motor impairments. *Assets '06: Proceedings of the 8th international ACM SIGACCESS conference on Computers and accessibility* 26-33 (2006).

[18] Vanderheiden, G. C. Ubiquitous accessibility, common technology core, and micro assistive technology: Commentary on "computers and people with disabilities". *ACM Trans. Access. Comput.* **1**, 1-7 (2008).

[19] Wobbrock, J. O., Fogarty, J., Liu, S. Y. S., Kimuro, S. & Harada, S. The angle mouse: target-agnostic dynamic gain adjustment based on angular deviation. In *Proceedings of the 27th international conference on Human factors in computing systems*, CHI '09, 1401-1410 (ACM, New York, NY, USA, 2009).

[20] Zajicek, M. Older adults: Key factors in design. In *Future Interaction Design*, 151-176 (Springer London, 2005).

An Environment for Designing and Sharing Adaptation Rules for Accessible Applications

Raúl Miñón
School of Informatics,
University of the Basque
Country
Manuel Lardizabal 1, E-20018
Donostia, Spain
raul.minon@ehu.es
+34 943015590

Fabio Paternò
ISTI-CNR
Via Moruzzi 1, 56124 Pisa, Italy
fabio.paterno@isti.cnr.it
+39 050 3153066

Myriam Arrue
School of Informatics,
University of the Basque
Country
Manuel Lardizabal 1, E-20018
Donostia, Spain
myriam.arrue@ehu.es
+34 943015590

ABSTRACT
In this work we present a design space for adaptation rules for applications accessible to people with special needs, and an environment supporting the sharing of such rules across various applications. The adaptation rules are classified according to the target user disabilities, as well as other relevant criteria useful to ease their integration in other design tools.

Author Keywords
Accessibility; Adaptation Rule; Model-Based UI; Design Space;

ACM Classification Keywords
H.5.2 [Information Interfaces and Presentation]: User Interfaces—User-centered design; interaction styles; theory and methods

INTRODUCTION
Besides satisfying different countries' legislations and expanding the target user groups, the development of accessible applications must be addressed in order to allow people with special needs to enjoy the same experience as everyone else. For this purpose, accessibility guidelines, such as the WCAG 2.0 [14], must be fulfilled. Unfortunately, there are many developers that do not consider these rules and, in consequence, many users cannot access the resulting applications. Additionally, some accessibility guidelines are adequate for a specific group of users, while they are not very appropriate for others.

One promising approach to deal with these problems is Model-Based User Interfaces design, since it enables the possibility of generating different Final User Interfaces (FUI) from logical descriptions independent of the programming language and the user platform. In addition, this approach also allows modifications of the FUI with limited effort. Thus, the FUI can be easily adapted to the specific user's capabilities. The required standards and accessibility guidelines can be included in the generation process of the FUI. The integration of accessibility requirements at design time in the UI development process of the Cameleon Reference framework [1] was proposed in [7]. However, that approach does not consider context-aware adaptation rules. The MyUI Toolkit [10] provides design patterns for building adaptive UIs. Nevertheless, this toolkit neither provides a mechanism for sharing these patterns to other MBUI design tools nor consider explicitly key aspects of the users with disabilities, such as the assistive technology required.

A Global Public Inclusive approach [13] has been proposed for automatically providing disabled users with a solution able to enhance their interaction with different public services. In contrast, in our solution the designer takes part in the adaptation process in order to identify the most relevant adaptation rules.

General design spaces for considering multiple dimensions of context-aware adaptations and a reference framework for classifying adaptation rules in different domains have already been proposed [2] [4]. In our case, we focus on interface adaptations for improving overall accessibility, which is not sufficiently covered in the previously mentioned research works. We also propose an environment to support sharing of adaptation rules across various design tools, so that accessibility issues can be considered in a more convenient manner.

More specifically, the objective of this paper is twofold: to define a design space able to include a comprehensive set of adaptation rules for accessible applications and to design a repository for compiling many different adaptation rules devoted to people with special needs. For this purpose, we have classified the gathered adaptation rules according to the user disability and other relevant aspects. The resulting repository will enable third-party designers that use model-based UI approaches to easily integrate the available adaptation rules with their tools, either at design time or at run-time.

The paper is organized as follows; section 2 discusses the considered key concepts that structure the design space; subsequently, section 3 describes the design of the repository; afterwards, section 4 illustrates the architecture of the environment and explains the integration process; and finally, section 5 provides conclusions and indications for future work.

DIMENSIONS OF THE DESIGN SPACE

There are some important concepts that can influence the adaptation process, such as, the target user, the granularity level, whether the adaptation aims to generate an adapted or an adaptive UI, and the considered abstraction level of the UI. In this work, these concepts are used to structure a design space able to indicate the different types of adaptations for enhancing the user interfaces devoted to people with disabilities. Figure 1 illustrates the proposed design space populated with different examples, which cover all possible values of the dimensions proposed. For some dimensions it is possible to define an ordering (Granularity Level and Abstraction Level), while for others (User Disability and Adaptation Type) we just indicate the set of possible values.

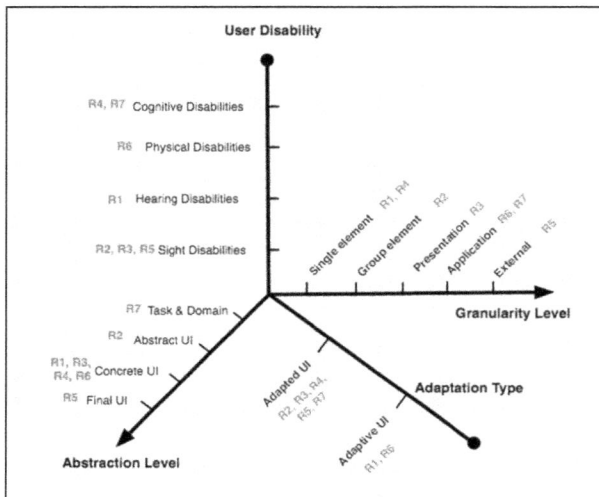

Figure 1. The design space proposed with the adaptation rules exemplified related with each concept.

The concepts considered in the design space are discussed in the rest of this section.

Target Users. It is well known that people with different capabilities require different types of interactions and, as consequence, different types of adaptations. Thus, users are classified in terms of disabilities in order to select the most appropriate adaptation rules for them. In this paper, some disabilities have been considered to test the design space. The disabilities are mainly based on the WCAG 2.0 guidelines [14] and belong to four general categories: Sight Disabilities including low vision, blindness, colour blindness, photosensitivity and eyestrain; Hearing Disabilities including deafness and mild-deafness; Physical

Disabilities including limited-movement, key-board only users, Parkinson and paraplegia; and Cognitive Disabilities including decline in maintaining attention, learning disabilities, language disabilities and reduced memory capacity. With this disabilities classification, the adaptation rules can be related to a general category such as the rule 4 or to a specific disability such as the rule 7.

The information for defining relationships between adaptation techniques and considered disabilities has been collected from various specific research works: adaptations techniques devoted to users with motor impairments were collected from [3], techniques focused on cognitive and sensory impairments were taken from [5], [8] and [11], and the information in [6] led us to techniques for visual impairments.

The following examples define an adaptation rule for some specific disabilities: Rule 1 is related to mild-deafness and Rule 2 to blindness. The rules are structured in terms of events, conditions, and actions describing their effects.

Rule 1 (deaf target group):

Event: the noise of the environment changes to a value higher than 25 decibels.

Condition: the user has a mild-deafness disability.

Action: every video has to be changed to a video with subtitles.

Description: when the noise level in the environment is increased over 25 decibels, subtitles are added to each video element.

Rule 2 (blind target group):

Event: the user accesses an application with many interaction elements.

Condition: the user is blind

Action: an application table of content is created to easily access each interaction element.

Description: if a UI contains many interaction elements, a blind user needs a mechanism to identify and easily access each element.

Granularity levels. Adaptation can have an impact at different granularity levels of the user interface: Application, Presentation, Group of Elements and Single Element. Another level denominated External is also considered to refer to adaptations that go further the current application. For example, some cases require that an assistive technology be launched.

These granularity levels are helpful to identify the most suitable order of execution for the adaptation rules required, since it is possible to follow a policy indicating to apply first the adaptation rules related to higher granularity levels and then the others. Thus, for example, if there is one rule changing a group of elements, and a rule changing only one of such elements, following this policy the change specific to the single element is not lost.

The following examples define an adaptation rule for specific granularity levels: Rule 3 is related to presentation level, Rule 4 to single element level and Rule 5 to external level.

Rule 3 (presentation granularity level):

Event: the user interface is activated.

Condition: the user is colour-blind.

Action: change the foreground colour to black and the background colour to white in order to provide a high-contrast UI.

Description: This rule is triggered when the UI is activated; then, it checks if the user has the colour-blind disability; finally, the action part changes the UI background and foreground colours to colours more appropriate for the user disability.

Rule 4 (single element granularity level):

Event: the UI contains an element with a timeout.

Condition: the user has a cognitive disability.

Action: remove the timeout or increase the time limit considerably if it is really necessary.

Description: this rule satisfies the WCAG 2.0 [14] success criterion 2.2.1: *"Cognitive limitations may require more time to read content or to perform functions such as filling out on-line forms. If Web functions are time-dependent, it will be difficult for some users to perform the required action before a time limit occurs"*

Rule 5 (external granularity level):

Event: the user interface is activated.

Condition: the user has low vision.

Action: activate a screen magnifier.

Description: this rule activates an assistive technology when the user has low vision.

Adapted UIs and Adaptive UIs. Adapted users interfaces are interfaces that are adapted at design time and are instantiated at run-time. In the case of people with special needs, they are focused on tailoring the most adequate user interface for the specific capabilities of the user. Thus, when users with disabilities interact with the UI, it is totally adapted to their needs. These UIs are valid when the context of the user is static. However, when the context (considered as user, platform, environment and social relations) is dynamic, for example when the user is walking or the noise of the environment is increased, sometimes the UI interface needs to be adaptive in order to change according to the surrounding context. One example of adaptation performed when the context changes is the change of UI modality. This dimension is necessary to identify in the design space both types of adaptations, the ones that are defined at design-time and those obtained at run-time.

The following example, Rule 6, defines an adaptation rule for adaptive UI.

Rule 6 (adaptive UI):

Event: the user begins to move.

Condition: the user has paraplegia AND the UI is not rendered with the vocal modality.

Action: the user interface is changed to the vocal modality.

Description: this rule is triggered when the user begins to move and a change in the context is detected. It checks if the user has Paraplegia and if the UI modality is not vocal. Finally, an equivalent UI with the vocal modality is provided.

Attributes / Rules	Adapted/ Adaptive	Disability Category	Granularity Level	Abstraction Level	Assistive Technology
Rule 1	Adaptive	Hearing Disabilities	Single element	CUI	NONE
Rule 2	Adapted	Sight Disabilities	Group element	Abstract	NONE
Rule 3	Adapted	Sight Disabilities	Presentation	CUI	NONE
Rule 4	Adapted	Cognitive Disabilities	Single element	CUI	NONE
Rule 5	Adapted	Sight Disabilities	External	FUI	Magnifier
Rule 6	Adaptive	Physical Disability	Application	CUI	Speech Recogniser
Rule 7	Adapted	Cognitive Disabilities	Application	Task & Domain	NONE

Table 1. The meta-information associated with each rule.

Abstraction Level. The consideration of the abstraction level in the design space is useful to provide the designers with the possibility of integrating the required adaptations in their applications at the level of generality preferred. Thus, if there was a specific requirement derived from an adaptation rule, the designer can perform the necessary changes in the first phases of the design process, which require less effort in making modifications. For instance, if an adaptation rule requires splitting the UI for a cognitive impairment person in various UIs, it is better for the designers to know it when they are defining the task model instead of knowing it when all the design of the UI is implemented and then considerable effort is required to update it.

According to the Cameleon Reference Framework [1], there are four different abstraction levels in the development process of model–based User Interfaces: Task and Domain, Abstract User Interface, Concrete User Interface and Final User Interface. The adaptations can be applied at each of these different levels. For instance, adaptation rules related to task sequencing must be considered at the Task & Domain level, whereas adaptation rules related with some specific UI modality must be considered at the Concrete UI level.

The following example, Rule 7, defines an adaptation rule for the task abstraction level.

Rule 7 (task abstraction level):

Event: the application contains too many different interaction elements for performing different tasks at the same time.

Condition: the user has problems in maintaining attention.

Action: the UI is organised in such a way that only one task is shown in every moment.

Description: showing many options and interaction elements can be confusing for users with problems in maintaining attention. This rule aims at simplifying the UI so users can efficiently perform tasks.

DESIGN OF THE ADAPTATION REPOSITORY
The repository stores the different adaptation rules modelled with some meta-information in order to select and classify them adequately. The necessary meta-information is:

Rule ID. A unique identifier.

Source. The adaptation rule's path and name.

Adapted/Adaptive. This value indicates if the adaptation rule is devoted for adapted UI or for adaptive UI.

Disability. This attribute is composed of a set of values that indicate the disabilities addressed with the adaptation rule.

Granularity Level. This value specifies the granularity level.

Assistive Technology. This value indicates if the adaptation rule requires any specific assistive technology to work. Although the assistive technology is not a dimension in the design space, it is useful to include it in the meta-information for practical purposes.

Abstraction Level. This value indicates the abstraction level associated with the adaptation.

Table 1 provides the meta-information associated with each example rule included in the previous section. In order to specify the rules we have used the AAL-DL [12] language since it fulfils our requirements. This language allows modelling of adaptation rules following an ECA approach (Event-Condition-Action). The event part identifies when the adaptation rules have to be applied, such as when the UI is activated or when a change in the context is detected. The condition part filters the rules for specific situations, target groups or contexts. Finally, the action part specifies necessary changes in the UI.

ARCHITECTURE OVERVIEW AND INTEGRATION PROCESS
As previously mentioned, the repository allows the integration of adaptation rules devoted for people with disabilities in Model-Based User Interface tools. These adaptation rules can be integrated both at design time and at run-time. At design-time it allows designers to obtain the necessary adaptation rules for specific groups of people with disabilities at the different abstraction levels, whereas the run-time approach provides support for context-aware UIs. Figure 2 illustrates the adaptation process, divided into several steps. We include a normalization step because we want to provide the possibility of supporting various model-based languages and their supporting tools, but we cannot implement transformations for all of them. Thus, we have a normalization step that transforms them to the MARIA language. MARIA [9] was selected as underlying language, because it implements every levels of the Cameleon Framework both at design-time and at run-time. Additionally, it is compliant with the language AAL-DL [12], which was selected for the implementation of the adaptation rules as mentioned in the previous section. Below these steps are explained in detail:

Step1: the Model-Based UI (MBUI) design tool performs a query to the *Adaptation environment* sending two parameters, the MBUI specification and the filter. The filter contains the user disability. The MBUI design tool can access the repository through a web service integrated in the system.

Step 2: the *Adaptation environment* receives the query and sends it to the *Request Parser* module. This module identifies the User Interface Description Language (UIDL) used, the **abstraction level of the UI** and the **disability** selected by the designer. The *Request Parser* module sends this information to the *UIDL Normalization* module.

Step 3: the *UIDL Normalization* module transforms the received UI to the MARIA language.

Step 4: after the UIDL normalization, the *Adaptation Manager* module selects the adaptations rules dedicated to the disability selected and the UI abstraction level. As mentioned in the previous section, the adaptation rules are stored in the *Adaptation Repository*, therefore, this module establishes communication with it to obtain the rules. It is worth to point out that the designer can access the *Adaptation environment* when considering every abstraction level of the UI development process to obtain the available adaptation rules of the corresponding level. Once the adaptation rules are selected, the module orders the adaptation rules to solve conflicts between them. For this purpose, as previously stated, the **granularity level** of the adaptation rule is a key concept. Firstly, the ones with the granularity level with the *external* value will be applied; then, the rules with the *application* value; after that, the rules with the *presentation* value; subsequently, the ones with the *group of elements* value; and finally, the rules with the *single element* value.

Step 5: having the rules selected with the adequate order, the *Adapter* module applies the adaptation rules to the UI specification. The result of this step provides a UI specification adapted to the user disabilities.

Step 6 and Step 7: the UI adapted is transformed into the original model-based language by means of the *UIDL Inverse Normalization* module and it is returned to the corresponding MBUI design tool. Then, the MBUI design tool is able to generate FUIs adapted to the user disabilities.

Step 8: as previously mentioned, the repository also provides support for context-aware UIs. The designer of the application will be able to decide whether enable this support or not. If he/she does not want to enable it, the process finishes in the previous step. Otherwise, the MBUI design tool sends to the *Adaptation environment* the MBUI specification and the context information in order to apply the context-aware adaptation rules. The MBUI design tool needs to integrate a specific code to detect changes in the context. Then, each time the context changes the FUI will be adapted if necessary.

Step 9: the repository receives the new query and sends it to the *Request Parser* module.

Step 10: the *UIDL Normalization* module transforms again the received MBUI specification to the MARIA language.

Step 11: the context-aware adaptation rules related to the context information are selected and, as in the Step 4, the adaptation rules selected are ordered.

Step 12: the necessary context-aware adaptations are applied to the MBUI specification through the *Adapter* module.

Step 13: the MBUI specification is transformed into the original model-based language.

Step 14: the context-aware MBUI specification generated is returned to the MBUI design tool, which will then be able to generate the context-aware FUI.

Thus, when the process is finished, users with specific disabilities will interact with a FUI adapted to their needs.

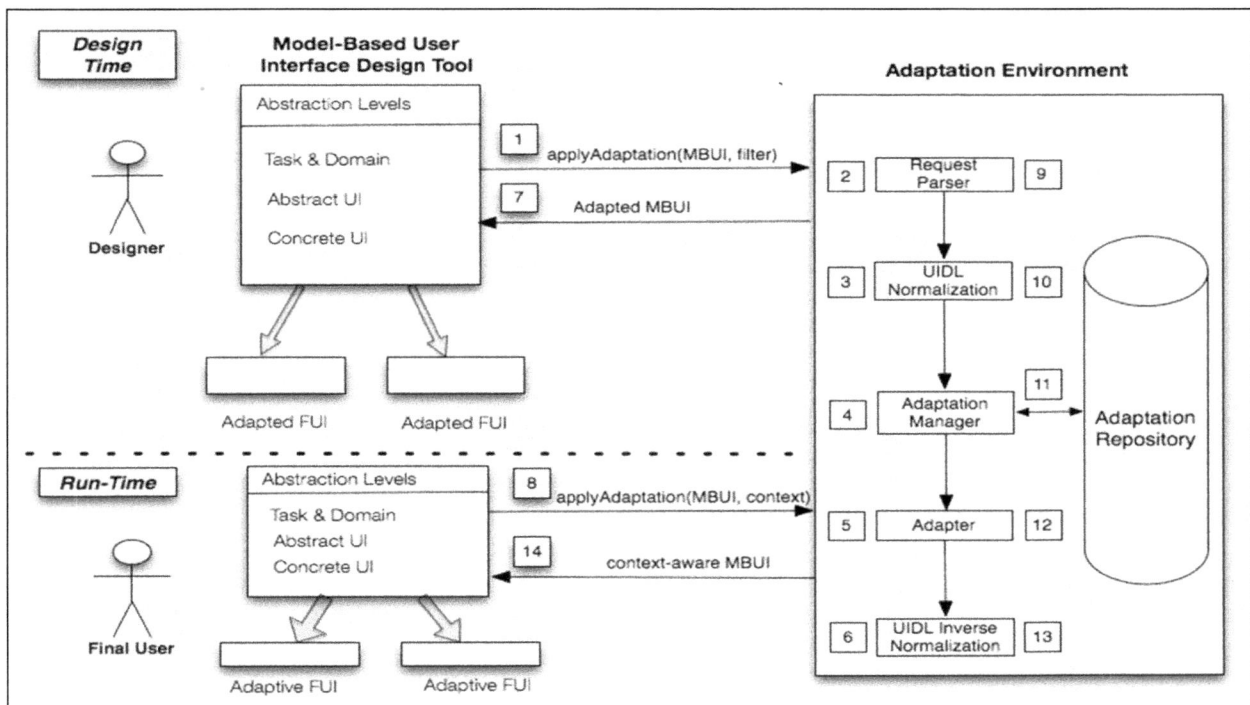

This FUI will also be able to support changes in the surrounding context improving the interaction and the experience of the user through an accessible context-aware FUI.

CONCLUSIONS AND FUTURE WORK

The main contribution of this work is to provide a design space structured with the key concepts that must be exploited when considering adaptations for people with disabilities. In addition, we present examples covering the different dimensions of the design space in order to better understand it and ease the integration of different types of adaptations in other model-based approaches.

Moreover, we describe the design of a repository and the necessary meta-information to share and access these adaptation rules, and describe an architecture to support the interaction with the repository, both at design-time and at run-time. This repository facilitates the integration of adaptation rules in other applications.

In future work, we will explore adaptation to support combination of different disabilities. Furthermore, we will investigate further mechanisms in order to solve possible conflicts among the rules.

ACKNOWLEDGMENTS

This research work has been partly funded by the Spanish Ministry of Science and Innovation ModelAcces project (grant TIN2010-15549), the Department of Education, Universities and Research of the Basque Government (grant IT395-10) and by the EU FP7 STREP SERENOA project (http://www.serenoa-fp7.eu). In addition, Raúl Miñón holds a Ph.D. scholarship and a scholarship for performing a research stay in a foreign country from the Research Staff Training Programme of the Department of Education, Universities and Research of the Basque Government.

REFERENCES

1. Calvary, G., Coutaz, J., Bouillon, L., Florins, M., Limbourg, Q., Marucci, L., Paternò, F., Santoro, C., Souchon, N., Thevenin, D., Vanderdonckt, J. 2002. The CAMELEON reference framework, 2002. Deliverable 1.1, CAMELEON Project. http://www.w3.org/2005/Incubator/model-based-ui/wiki/Cameleon reference framework

2. Coutaz, J., Calvary, G. HCI and Software Engineering for User Interface Plasticity. In *Human-Computer Interaction Handbook: Fundamentals, Evolving Technologies, and Emerging Applications*, Third Edition, Julie A. Jacko (Ed.), 2012, 1195-1220

3. Gajos, K.Z., Weld, D.S., Wobbrock, J.O. Automatically Generating Custom User Interfaces for Users with Physical Disabilities. In *J. Artificial Intelligence*, 2010, Elsevier, Vol. 174, N.12-13, 910-950.

4. Genaro Motti, V., A computational framework for multi-dimensional context-aware adaptation. In *Procs. of the 3rd ACM SIGCHI symposium on Engineering interactive computing systems*, 2011. ACM, 315-318.

5. Kurniawan, S. H., King, A. D., Evans , G., Blenkhorn, P. L. Personalising web page presentation for older people. In *Interact. Comput.*, 2006, ACM, 18, 3, 457-477.

6. Lunn, D., Bechhofer, S., Harper, S. The SADIe transcoding platform. In *Proceedings of the 2008 international cross-disciplinary conference on Web accessibility, W4A 2008*, 128-129. ACM Press.

7. Miñón, R., Moreno, L., Abascal, J. A Graphical Tool to Create User Interface Models for Ubiquitous Interaction Satisfying Accessibility Requirements. In *Universal Access in the Information Society*, 2012, Springer, 1-13. http://link.springer.com/article/10.1007/s10209-012-0284-x#

8. National Institute on Aging and National Library of Medicine. Making Your Web Site Senior Friendly: A Checklist. , NIH & NLM, 2002, http://www.nlm.nih.gov/pubs/checklist.pdf

9. Paternò, F., Santoro, C., Spano, L.D. MARIA: A Universal Language for Service-Oriented Applications in Ubiquitous Environment. In *ACM Transactions on Computer-Human Interaction*, 2009, Vol.16, N.4, 19:1-19:30.

10. Peissner, M., Häbe, D., Janssen, D., Sellner, T. MyUI: generating accessible user interfaces from multimodal design patterns. In *Procs. of the 4th ACM SIGCHI symposium on Engineering interactive computing systems*, 2012. ACM, 81-90.

11. Richards, J.T., Hanson, V.L. Web Accessibility: A Broader View. In *Procs. of the 13th Int. conference on World Wide Web, WWW 2004*, ACM Press , 72-79.

12. Serenoa Project, AAL-DL: Semantics, Syntaxes and Stylistics, http://www.serenoa-fp7.eu/wp-content/uploads/2012/07/SERENOA_D3.3.1.pdf

13. Vanderheiden, G.C., Treviranus, J. Creating a Global Public Inclusive Infrastructure. In *Procs. of HCI Internationanl, 2011* (5), LNCS 6765, Vol. 5, 517-526.

14. W3C, WAI, Web Content Accessibility Guidelines (WCAG) Overview, 2012, http://www.w3.org/WAI/intro/wcag.php

A Constructive Approach for Design Space Exploration

Anke Dittmar
Dept. of Computer Science
University of Rostock
A.-Einstein-Str. 22
D-18051 Rostock, Germany
anke.dittmar@uni-rostock.de

Stefan Piehler
Dept. of Computer Science
University of Rostock
A.-Einstein-Str. 22
D-18051 Rostock, Germany
stefan.piehler@uni-rostock.de

ABSTRACT

The co-evolution of different kinds of external representations is essential in Human-Centered Design. It helps design teams to interleave different design activities and to view a design problem from different perspectives. The paper investigates a coupling of representations for Design Rationale, formal HCI models, and prototypical implementations for a more effective co-exploration of problem and design spaces with both analytical and empirical means. Deliberated underdesign and parallel, model-guided prototyping are proposed techniques to systematically integrate exploratory design steps into evolutionary prototyping. The general approach is instantiated with QOC diagrams, HOPS models, and Java implementations. HOPS models are used for two purposes: to create 'throw-away extensions' of an existing prototype and to specify design goals and constraints. The animation tool allows designers to explore and to reflect the model-guided prototypes. A case study demonstrates the applicability of the approach. Implications for related design practices are discussed.

Author Keywords

External design representations; design space exploration; model-guided prototyping; underdesign.

ACM Classification Keywords

H.5.2 Information Interfaces and Presentation (e.g. HCI): Miscellaneous: D.2.2.Software Engineering: Design Tools and Techniques – user interfaces.

General Terms

Design Rationale; HCI modeling; Prototyping.

INTRODUCTION

The design of interactive artifacts requires a broad spectrum of skills. Interaction designers need to understand the activities of people and the contexts. They need to know the possibilities offered by technologies. They need to develop and evaluate alternative designs and iterate until a good solution is found that support people in their activities [5]. External

representations such as temporal notations, sketches, and the artifact under development are ubiquitous in this process [13]. Externalizations can be shared, negotiated, and agreed on between members of a design team [15]. In creative processes, they help to shape new ideas. Schön's concept of the designer's 'reflective conversation' with the material [25] is of particular interest in HCI.

The nature of the applied methods, notations, and tools has a profound impact on the produced externalizations [13] and how they 'talk back'. For example, formal temporal notations allow to express the fine details of a systems' behavior and to develop tools for model animation and model checking. Sketches, as another example, are valuable because of their ambiguity that supports the generation of new ideas by leaving a lot to the imagination [6]. Human-Centered Design approaches support the use of different external representations to enable design teams to address design questions from different perspectives and to include many stakeholders in this process. What material is used and how it is used tells much about the participants' skills and the underlying design understanding. For example, a co-evolution of design goals and descriptions representing possible solutions and emerging constraints shows an acceptance of design problems as being ill-structured. Frequent moves between descriptions of current and envisaged situations support the idea of design as intervention in a complex situation. As a last example, the co-development of technical system specifications and representations which are comprehensible for many stakeholders (e.g. usage scenarios and prototypes) supports the idea of participatory design.

Although it is well-accepted in Human-Centered Design that a co-evolution of external representations is necessary to interleave different design activities in a flexible way as recommended e.g. in [18][1], the effective coupling of such representations remains problematic. It can be too loose but also too stringent. Existing artifacts for Design Rationale, for example, do not relate solution construction and argumentation sufficiently [17]. In contrast, the mappings between task models, abstract user interface models, and implementations in model-based design approaches are often too rigid to enable reflection of an interactive application with respect to different usage situations [10],[12] or to support ad hoc im-

---

[1]The star life cycle [18] is an evaluation-centered process model that minimizes the ordering of design activities. One can move freely between the different activities, but needs to evaluate the results after each step.

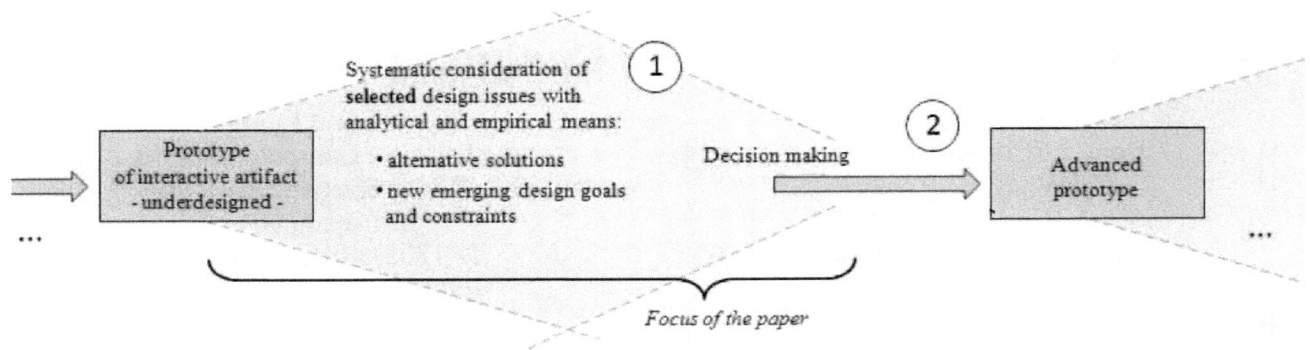

Figure 1. Positioning of the proposed approach.

plementations of application parts that may not require additional specification activities.

This paper aims at providing design teams with an approach to intertwine exploratory, analytical, empirical, and implementation activities more effectively. In particular, it investigates a convenient coupling of three different kinds of design representations: representations for Design Rationale (DR), formal HCI models, and prototypical implementations. In the proposed approach, prototypes are partial implementations of interactive artifacts under development that have to be improved in further iterative steps. DR representations help to analytically explore and evaluate alternative solutions to design issues that are not considered so far in a prototype. Formal models serve as the 'glue' between DR diagrams and prototypes. The contribution of the paper is twofold.

- It is demonstrated that formal modeling techniques in interactive system design are useful for coupling different design representations in order to facilitate an intertwined exploration and examination of the problem space and the design space with both analytical and empirical means.

- New usage scenarios for formal HCI models are suggested. Formal models are mainly used in transformation processes (e.g. model-driven approaches) and for reasoning about the systems' behavior under different constraints (e.g. resource-based approaches). In this paper, their application for 'sketching' possible design solutions is especially investigated.

The general approach is explained in more detail in the following section. It is then instantiated with QOC diagrams (*Q*uestions, *O*ptions, and *C*riteria) [21], HOPS models (*H*igher *O*rder *P*rocesses *S*pecifications) [12], and Java implementations. HOPS models are used to formalize structural and behavioral aspects of design ideas and constraints that are documented in a QOC diagram. They also describe mappings to Java code. The HOPS notation and the corresponding tool have been revised and extended to support parallel model-guided prototyping, a technique aimed at highlighting and analyzing possible effects of the different design options on the existing prototype. The example study in the second part of the paper illustrates the main ideas of the approach, the representations in use, how they are coupled and how their creation and use is supported by tools. A discussion of consequences

of the suggested approach for related design practices, and an analysis of related work concludes this paper.

SUPPORTING DESIGN SPACE EXPLORATION

The ideas that are introduced in this paper support an overall evolutionary design process. Prototypes are considered as 'workpieces' from which the interactive artifacts are gradually shaped in iterative steps. Evolutionary prototyping is especially recommended when the requirements of an application cannot be fully understood in advance.

This paper contributes to an integration of evolutionary and exploratory prototyping as illustrated in figure 1. The arrows and the boxes indicate the evolution of the prototypical implementation over time. It is assumed that the prototype is deliberately unfinished with respect to design issues that can be considered as 'wicked problems'. In their seminal paper [23], Rittel and Webber characterize wicked problems as having no definite formulation and no 'best' solution. In addition, every implemented solution has consequences that have to be taken into consideration. Well-defined and soluble problems, in contrast, are called 'tamed problems' (e.g. some mathematical problems). One reason why we are often confronted with wicked problems in the design of interactive artifacts is to be found in the fact that stakeholders typically have different perspectives and interests. Rittel and Webber point out that "part of the art of dealing with wicked problems is the art of not knowing too early what type of solution to apply" [23].

The terms 'underdesign' and 'underdesigned prototype' are used in this paper to emphasize that design teams deliberately have to avoid premature commitments to solutions of those parts of a design problem that are not well understood or negotiated yet. Fischer et al. use the same term to describe their approach to end user development: "To accommodate unexpected issues at use time, systems must be 'underdesigned' at design time... Instead of designers aiming at designing complete solutions for users at design time, underdesign aims to provide social and technical instruments for the owners of problems to create the solutions themselves at use time" [16]. Although this paper does not consider the design-use gap of systems explicitly, our approach is embedded in evolutionary prototyping and acknowledges the above ideas. The term 'designer' refers, in the context of this paper, to the members in multidisciplinary teams.

The focus of the paper is on the exploration steps (depicted by the encircled number 1 in figure 1). In each such step, alternative solutions to one or more open design issues are developed and documented in a systematic way. By applying analytical DR techniques, the alternatives are assessed against design goals and constraints. The elaboration and reduction of design ideas can optionally be guided by formal models that allow to express certain aspects of design issues, goals, constraints, and solutions in a more precise way. These models, corresponding notations and tools are the basis for parallel model-guided prototyping, a technique that is introduced to describe possible refinements or enrichments of prototypical implementations at a conceptual level and to facilitate, by model animation, their exploration and reflection with empirical means. The examples given in the paper often explore behavioral aspects.

Formal models have a central role in the proposed approach. They are 'constructive' descriptions of elements in DR diagrams that can be connected to prototypes. Hence the title of the paper. This coupling of different design representations as well as the above mentioned related design techniques (underdesign and parallel model-guided prototyping) allow a stepwise co-exploration of the problem space and the design space. New design issues and constraints may emerge in this process. Benyon et al. point out that "prototypes are first and foremost a way of involving people and clients in evaluating design ideas" [5]. Model-guided prototypes in our approach are the 'throw-away extensions' of an existing prototype that help many stakeholders to elaborate and reflect alternatives on how to advance this prototype. A more integrated and better-informed decision making process is possible.

The implementation of design decisions is indicated by the arrows and by the encircled number 2 in figure 1. These steps are not discussed in detail in this paper. It is assumed though that they also include design activities to implement obvious solutions to problems that do not have to be embedded in argumentation processes (referred to above as tamed problems).

TOOLS FOR EXPLORATION

To make the general approach more feasible, it is instantiated in the following with QOC diagrams, HOPS models, and Java prototypes. QOC was chosen because it is a widely known notation for Design Rationale. HOPS allows to model interactive systems from a users' perspective and in a notation that is partly familiar from task modeling (e.g. [22]). Model composition and mappings between HOPS models and Java code are essential for implementing the constructive approach for design space exploration. The object-oriented programming language Java provides convenient means to underdesign prototypes (e.g. abstract classes).

Design Rationale with QOC Diagrams

"Design Rationale in the most general sense is an explanation of why an artifact is designed the way it is" [20]. The QOC notation (Questions, Options, and Criteria) is a semiformal notation to embed design space exploration and evaluation into collaborative argumentation processes [21]. QOC diagrams are structure-oriented representations of the Design

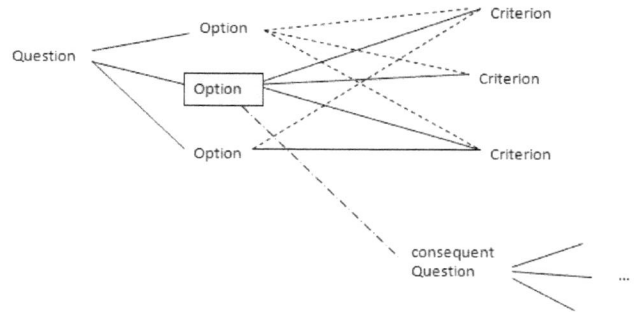

Figure 2. Schematic representation of QOC diagrams.

Rationale of artifacts that position them in relation to alternative solutions [20].

Figure 2 schematically shows the elements of QOC graphs and how they are related. Question nodes (shortly Q-nodes) refer to design issues with no obvious or no best solution. It is pointed out in [3] that they "are crucial in providing an appropriate structure for the space of options" which are represented by option nodes (shortly O-nodes). Criteria describe design goals as well as constraints and are represented by C-nodes in the graphs. They are used to assess options and to facilitate a decision on which option to choose (drawn in a box). A solid line between an O-node and a C-node denotes that the option supports the achievement of the criterion, a dashed line denotes that it is hindered. Arguments in the form of theories, empirical data, analogies, ad hoc theories etc. back up the assessments of options. In figure 3, Argument 1 is the reason why Option 2 is seen to be better than Option 1. Argument 2 questions the assessment of Option 2. Argument 3 supports Argument 1 while Argument 4 challenges it.

QOC diagrams facilitate problem analysis and structuring, idea generation and decision making. Case studies such as [2] demonstrate how different viewpoints of stakeholders can be integrated and shared. However, as in other DR approaches, the argumentation processes are isolated from activities to construct solutions [17]. Later in this section, we suggest to optionally attach HOPS models to Q-, O-, and C-nodes of a diagram to alleviate this problem. Arguments are not formalized. The next section gives a short introduction to the concepts of HOPS and tool-supported modeling techniques that are relevant in the context of this paper.

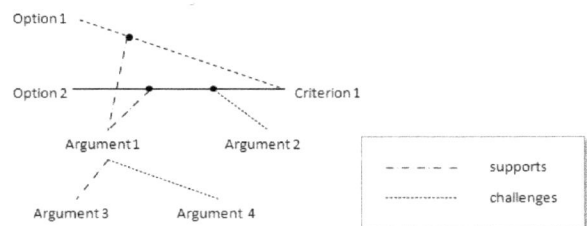

Figure 3. Relations between arguments and assessments of options with respect to criteria.

Formal Modeling with HOPS Models

HOPS (*Higher Order Processes Specifications*) is a specification formalism with high-level concepts for describing interaction from different viewpoints and at different levels of abstraction [12]. In HOPS, systems are considered as sets of interacting sub-systems which can exist independently. Essential modeling concepts are processes, operations, components, and sub-processes. A HOPS model is a process that specifies the behavior of a system by a set of operation sequences. Operations are seen as the smallest units of behavior in a specific modeling context. HOPS is a textual notation and offers sub-processes and corresponding temporal equations as a means to structure behavioral descriptions (e.g. in a hierarchical way). In the equations, temporal operators are used as they are known from process algebras and applied, for example, in CTT [22] and other task modeling approaches.

Listing 1. Specification of a basic HOPS process.

```
1 PROCESS Light
2 OPS on(), off(),
3 SUB PROCESSES
4   Light IS (on() [] off())*,
5 END PROCESS
```

Listing 1 shows the basic process `Light` which knows two operations, `on` and `off`. Its behavior is specified by arbitrary sequences of these operations (* denotes the iterative operator, [] the alternative one).

Model Composition

In order to describe more complex behavior, HOPS processes contain components representing sub-systems of the system under consideration. Components are processes themselves, and hence, higher-order processes not only supply hierarchically structured descriptions of systems but enable a distributed description of emerging behavioral constraints, across different levels of abstraction and in partly redundant models. On the one hand, the behavior of a higher-order process P is based on and constrained by the concurrent behavior of its components (bottom-up control). On the other hand, P controls how the components interact with each other (top-down control). The operations defined by P either abstract from (optionally conditioned) sequences of operations from components or they describe new behavior that emerges from the interaction. The components' operations that are bound to operations of P are controlled by this higher-order process, all other operations are not controlled by P and visible in the behavioral description of P.

An example of a higher-order process is given in listing 2. Process *TrafficLight* models traffic lights as compositions of three instances of the above given light process (lines 2-5). Three operations (lines 6-13) and two sub-processes (lines 15-17) are defined to explain their functioning. A traffic light can be switched on and off. If it is switched on it iteratively runs through a sequence of four light configurations. Operation `next` has an integer parameter that is used to specify this higher-order operation in terms of conditioned sequences of operations of the light components. Each such sequence describes a valid configuration of the single lights. A traffic light with the top and the bottom light on, for example, would not

be valid behavior. Sub-process `On` serves to describe valid sequences of parameterized `next` operations (lines 16-17) and their possible interruption by switching off the traffic light (; denotes the sequential operator).

Listing 2. Higher-order process with three components.

```
1  PROCESS TrafficLight
2  BASIC COMPS
3    t : Light,          // top light
4    m : Light,          // middle light
5    b : Light,          // bottom light
6  OPS
7    next(s:INT)
8      COND (s==0) IS t.on() ; m.off() ; b.off()
9      COND (s==1) IS t.on() ; m.on() ; b.off()
10     COND (s==2) IS t.off() ; m.off() ; b.on()
11     COND (s==3) IS t.off() ; m.on() ; b.off(),
12   switchOff() IS t.off() ; m.off() ; b.off(),
13   switchOn(),
14 SUB PROCESSES
15   Off IS switchOn() ; On(0),
16   On(i:INT) IS
17     (next(i) ; On((i+1)%4)) [] (switchOff() ; Off)
18 END PROCESS
```

Applications of Model Composition in the Approach

Model composition is essential for the implementation of the proposed approach. It is used for three main purposes. First, it combines models of the existing prototype and possible refinements or extensions. Second, model composition helps to implement parallel, model-guided prototyping. And third, it supports the assessment of design solutions against criteria. The first two points will be explained in more detail later. The traffic light example is continued now to show how model composition serves the third mentioned purpose. The model in listing 3 translates assumptions about the use of traffic lights into valid operation sequences (lines 4-5).

Listing 3. Expected Use of traffic lights.

```
1 PROCESS ExpectedUse
2 OPS red(), red_yellow(), green(), yellow(),
3 SUB PROCESSES
4   ExpectedUse IS
5     (red() ; red_yellow() ; green() ; yellow())*,
6 END PROCESS
```

Listing 4. Model composition to assess a system design.

```
1  PROCESS AssessTrLight
2  BASIC COMPS
3    s: Off>>TrafficLight,
4    e: ExpectedUse,
5  OPS
6    red()         IS e.red() ; s.next(0),
7    red_yellow()  IS e.red_yellow() ; s.next(1),
8    green()       IS e.green() ; s.next(2),
9    yellow()      IS e.yellow() ; s.next(3),
10 SUB PROCESSES
11   AssessTrLight IS
12     (red() [] red_yellow() [] green() [] yellow())*,
13 END PROCESS
```

In listing 4, process `AssessTrLight` composes the model of the traffic light system (listing 2) that is assumed to be switched off initially (line 3) and the above usage model (line 4). The operations of this process bind all operations of the expected use and map them to (parameterized) `next` operations of the traffic light system (lines 6-9). The temporal

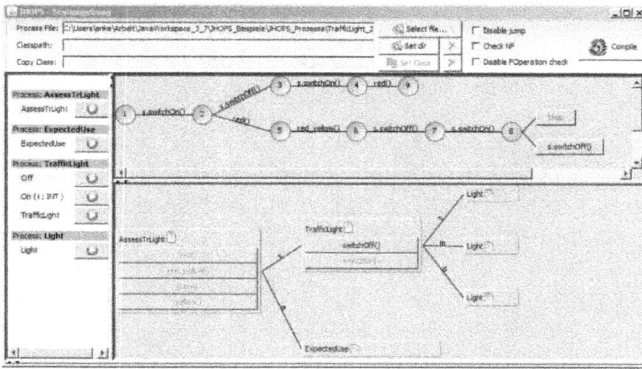

Figure 4. Animation of `AssessTrLight`: **after the execution of** $\langle switchOn, red, red\_yellow, switchOff, switchOn \rangle$ **only operation** `switchOff` **is enabled and not, as expected, operation** `green`.

equation (lines 11-12) does not induce further constraints on the order of the components' operations. According to this composition, process `TrafficLight` (in state `Off`) facilitates the expected use if every valid operation sequence of process `ExpectedUse` can be obtained from at least one valid sequence of `AssessTrLight` with removed component operations `s.switchOn()` and `s.switchOff()`. In the example, there are inconsistencies between expectations and system behavior. While it is expected that traffic lights go through red, red-yellow, green and yellow phases cyclically, the considered system starts after each switching off/on operation with the red phase. This mismatch can be investigated by the HOPS tool.

Model Animation - The HOPS Tool
The HOPS tool makes possible to explore the behavior of models by their interactive animation. Figure 4 shows a screenshot of an animation session of the above process `AssessTrLight`. On the left-hand side of the depicted window, a user can choose the (sub-)process which (s)he wants to explore in an interactive session. The central part of the window shows the actual state of the session. In the animation tree (top part), each path represents an already executed operation sequence (a prefix of a valid operation sequence of the process). The end node of the actual path has buttons attached which represent all enabled operations for the next animation step. The mentioned mismatch becomes apparent in the depicted situation. To continue the animation, the user activates an operation either from the animation tree or from the component tree which is represented in the bottom part. Component trees visualize both the hierarchical structure of processes and the distribution of control over their components. In figure 4, all bound operation of components (represented by the tree nodes) are hidden. The other operations are represented either by enabled buttons, if the operations can be executed in the next step, or by disabled buttons otherwise.

Model-Guided Prototyping with Java and HOPS
The HOPS notation allows mappings between HOPS processes and Java classes. When animating a model the HOPS

tool also activates the representations that are mapped to elements of the formal model. By this means, model-guided prototyping is facilitated. The specification examples in this paper are written in HOPS 3. In this version, the idea of model-guided prototyping is better supported by enabling additional mappings between Java events and HOPS operations[2]. Model-guided prototyping is illustrated and discussed in detail in the case study section. But before turning to it, the coupling between the different representations in use is explained in the next section.

Coupling the Representations
The coupling between QOC diagrams, HOPS models and prototypical implementations in Java is suggested as follows. A prototype is assumed to be deliberately underdesigned with respect to a number of design issues. Some of them are addressed by key questions of a QOC diagram. Corresponding Q-nodes can be enriched by HOPS models (Q-Models). Their purpose is to connect the questions to the existing prototype and to selectively model those aspects that need further elaboration. HOPS models can be attached to options that are not followed by further questions in the diagram in order to specify, at a conceptual level, possible solutions on how to refine or extend the prototype (O-models). HOPS models can also be used to formalize aspects of design goals/constraints (C-models).

Figure 5 is a schematic illustration of the coupling. It shows the Q-, O-, and C-models in boxes and links them by their position to elements of a QOC diagram. The coupling between options and the current prototype is achieved by model composition. Each Q-model is a component of its associated O-models (1). Hence, operations in O-models can build on the operations in Q-models and their mappings to the prototype. In addition, existing C-models are components of related options as well (2). O-models can furthermore be connected to additional prototypical implementations to provide during model animation a more convenient visualization of the ideas.

The designer's decision on how to advance the existing prototype is supported by parallel model-guided prototyping. As indicated in figure 5, it is implemented by the dynamic composition of the currently selected O-models (4) of all key questions (3). In the following section, the ideas are applied to a small case study.

A CASE STUDY
In the example, a system is to be designed that allows users to steer a simulated vehicle. The vehicle has a left motor and a right motor, each with a speed range from say -100 rpm to +100 rpm. If both motors would run with the same positive/negative speed the vehicle would move forward/backward (with full power if the speed is 100/-100). With one motors' speed being $+x$ and the other $-x$ ($1 \le x \le 100$) the vehicle would turn left and right on the spot respectively. For other speed pairs the vehicle travels on a circular path.

---

[2]New to HOPS 3 are also internal components and conditioned definitions of higher-order operations (see e.g. operation `next` in listing 2).

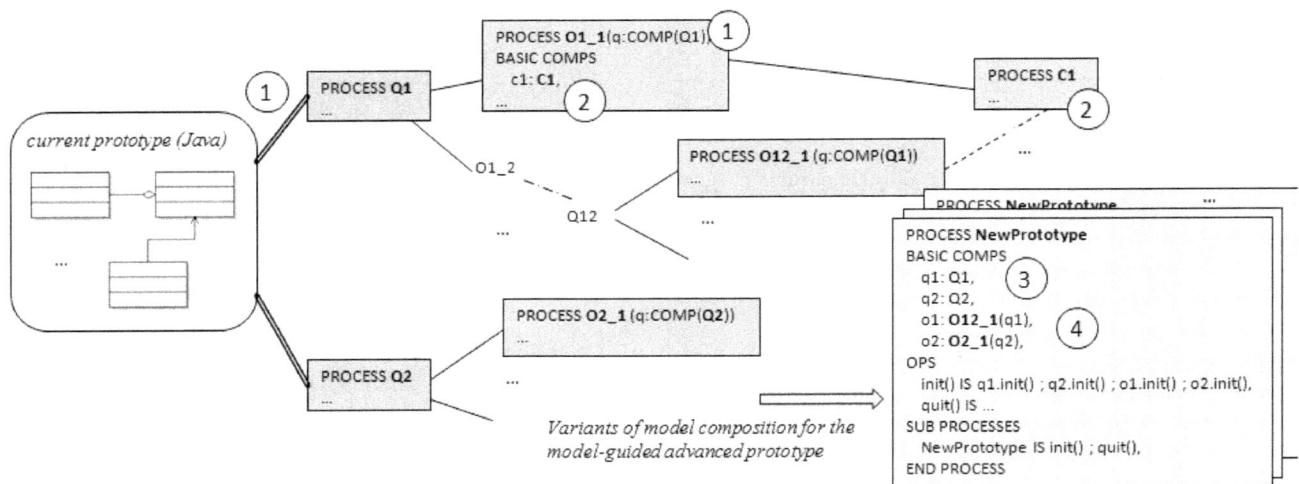

Figure 5. Coupling of representations by model composition in HOPS.

The purpose of the case study is to illustrate the overall approach and the suggested coupling of design representations. The chosen example is convenient for several reasons. First, it shows an underdesigned prototype, second, the considered design issue is easy to explain and understand but a wicked problem, third, formal models for the alternative solutions are concise and can be presented in the format of a paper, and forth, it demonstrates corresponding parallel model-guided prototyping to explore the alternatives in a way that is accessible to many stakeholders.

Design Issue and Q-Model

Let us assume that there already exists an implementation of the vehicle with an interface to move it. The current prototype may also allow users to switch between different background images. The vehicle moves in an 'urban' or in a 'natural' area. The open issue we want to consider in the case study concerns the design of the user interface part for controlling the vehicle. How should the motors be controlled by the user? There is no simple answer to this question.

Figure 6 depicts a Q-model that focuses on those aspects of the current Java prototype that seem to be relevant to explore the design issue. The prototype is represented by a screenshot and a class diagram fragment. On the right-hand side of the figure, the HOPS model is to be seen that specifies the connection to the prototype by mapping the process `VehicleControl` to the Java class `Vehicle` and by mapping HOPS operations to methods of this class. The mappings are indicated by dotted lines. During an animation session of Q-model `VehicleControl`, the execution of the HOPS operation `init()` would also start the Java prototype. The execution of HOPS operation `setMotors(l,r)` in the animation tool would set the motor values in the prototype and the vehicle would move correspondingly. Finally, operation `quit()` would quit the Java application as well. However, the animated model only partly controls the associated prototype. For example, users can switch between the urban and the natural area in the Java prototype, but this interaction is not described in the model because it is not seen as relevant with respect to the focused design issues.

QOC Diagram: How should the motors be controlled?

Figure 7 shows a QOC diagram for the current design issue. The key question (with HOPS model `VehicleControl`, figure 6) provides the context for two options: both motors use the same control instance (O11) or they are controlled independently (O12). These options are the basis for consequent questions (Q3 and Q2) that help to structure the design space in a hierarchical way and to group related options. All in all, five alternative solutions are described and evaluated (O21, O22, O31, O41, and O42, all depicted in dotted boxes). Take note that a more differentiated assessment of O11 with respect to C2 was made by evaluating the options of its follow-up question. Each of the five options is enriched by an O-model. In the following, three such models are discussed in more detail. Two of them have similar O-models but differ in their accompanying Java representation as will become more apparent in corresponding model-guided prototyping sessions. For reasons of brevity, none of the criteria was formalized in the example. The assessment of a system design by C-models was already discussed in a previous section (incl. listings 3,4).

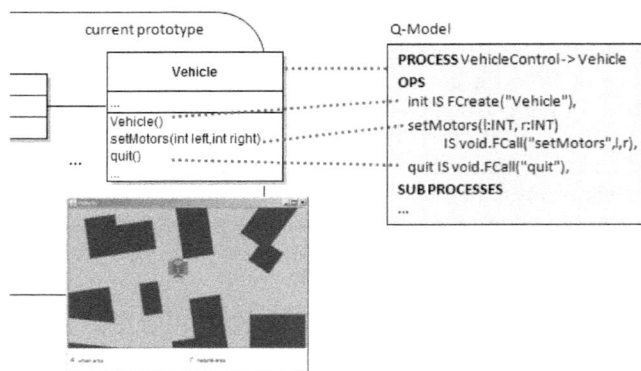

Figure 6. Current prototype and a Q-model.

54

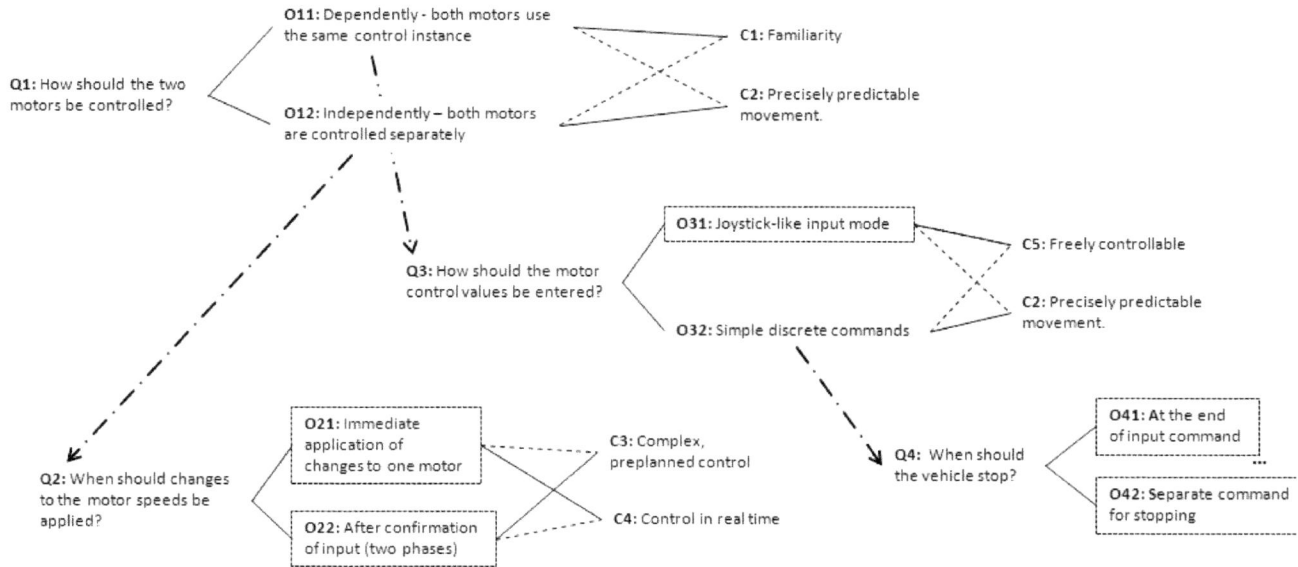

Figure 7. QOC diagram of the case study. The key question is: How should the two motors be controlled?

O-Models

O-models, in the case study, represent alternative conceptual user interface designs to steer a simulated vehicle. Examples are given in listing 5 and listing 6. The specification for option O42 in listing 5 suggests simple discrete commands for driving the vehicle forward or backward and turn it to the left or to the right (HOPS operations `forward`, `backward`, `turnLeft`, `turnRight`). Each movement has to be finished with the stop-command (HOPS operation `stop`). The behavioral specification is to be found in lines 8-11.

Listing 5. O-model of option O42 in figure 7.

```
1  PROCESS O42 (q: COMP(VehicleControl))
2  OPS
3      stop() IS q.setMove(0,0),
4      forward() IS q.setMove(60,60),
5      turnLeft() IS q.setMove(-60,60),
6      ...
7  SUB PROCESSES
8      O42 IS init() ;
9          (( ( forward() [] backward() [] turnRight()
10             [] turnLeft())
11          ; stop())* [> quit()),
12 END PROCESS
```

The solution in listing 6 describes a two-phases independent control of both motors with HOPS operations `adjustLeft`, `adjustRight`. The adjusted values are set for the motors when they are confirmed (HOPS operation `start`).

Model-Guided Explorative Prototyping

In [11], model-guided prototyping is introduced as a technique where the use of a prototypical implementation is partly controlled by the animation of a formal model describing selected aspects of the prototype. In our approach, Q-models focus on those aspects of the evolutionary Java prototype that need further elaboration in the next design step. Q-models include mappings to the prototype and are components of their related O-models (see figure 5). Hence, O-models can access the current prototype via the components' operations and extend it at a conceptual level. For example, operations `stop`, `forward`, `turnLeft`... in listing 5 (lines 3-6) and operations `start` and `stop` in listing 6 (lines 8-9) are defined by means of operations from the Q-component (named by `q`).

Listing 6. O-model of option O22 in figure 7.

```
1  PROCESS O22 (q: COMP(VehicleControl))
2  VAR
3      left:INT=0,
4      right:INT=0,
5  OPS
6      adjustLeft(i:INT) IS left.set(i),
7      adjustRight(i:INT) IS right.set(i),
8      start() IS q.setMove(left,right),
9      stop() IS q.setMove(0,0),
10     init(), quit(),
11 SUB PROCESSES
12     O22 IS init() ; ((AdjustLeftOrRight*
13         ; start() ; stop())* [> quit()),
14     AdjustLeftOrRight
15         VAR i:INT,
16         IS (read("Left: ",i) ; adjustLeft(i))
17             [] (read("Right: ",i) ; adjustRight(i)),
18 END PROCESS
```

Figure 8 illustrates how the animation of O-models guides the exploration of the corresponding extended prototype. In the background, it shows the HOPS tool with the actual state of the animated O-model O42 (figure 7, listing 5). The so far executed scenario $\langle init, backward, stop, forward, stop, turnLeft, stop \rangle$ and the operations that are enabled in the next animation step are presented in the top part of the main panel. The prototype is to be seen in the foreground of the figure. The user can control the vehicle by activating enabled HOPS operations, all other interactions with the prototype are not controlled by the HOPS model because they are not in the current focus of interest.

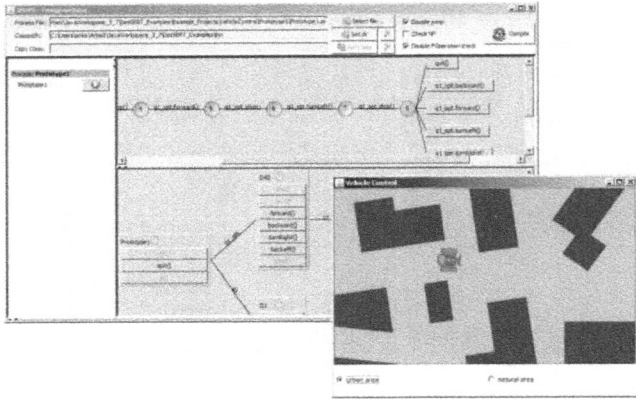

Figure 8. Animation run of the O-model in listing 5: HOPS operations `forward`, `backward`, `turnLeft`, `turnRight`, **and** `stop` **steer the vehicle in the current prototype.**

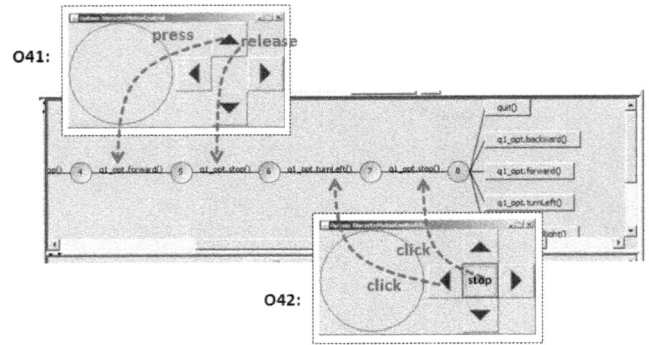

Figure 9. Effects of the different event mappings from listing 7 on the interaction with the model-guided prototypes for O41 and O42. Both O-models have the same underlying specification given in listing 5.

Extended Support for Model-Guided Prototyping

The models that are assigned to options in the QOC diagram of figure 7 provide precise descriptions of alternative user interfaces for the vehicle control, partly with subtle differences only. They can easily be modified and the effects on the prototype can be reflected in further animation sessions with the HOPS tool. As explained earlier, HOPS models can also be used to formalize aspects of design goals and constraints. For example, strategies for steering the vehicle in 'urban' areas and in 'natural' areas could be formalized.

Listing 7. O-model fragments of O41 and O42 (figure 7) with different event mappings.

```
1  PROCESS O41 (q: COMP(VehicleControl))
2          -> options.DiscreteMotorControl
3  OPS
4     init() IS FCreate(q)
5            ; FSetEventManager("setEventManager"),
6     forward() IS q.setMove(60,60) ; void.FCall("north"),
7     ...
8  EVENT MAPPINGS
9     northButton : mousePressed(BUTTON1)  -> forward,
10    eastButton  : mousePressed(BUTTON1)  -> turnRight,
11    northButton : mouseReleased(BUTTON1) -> stop,
12    eastButton  : mouseReleased(BUTTON1) -> stop,
13    ...
14 END PROCESS
15
16 PROCESS O42 (q: COMP(VehicleControl))
17         -> options.DiscreteMotorControlStop
18 OPS ...
19 EVENT MAPPINGS
20    northButton : mouseClicked(BUTTON1) -> forward,
21    eastButton  : mouseClicked(BUTTON1) -> turnRight,
22    stopButton  : mouseClicked(BUTTON1) -> stop,
23    ...
```

O-models are abstract specifications of alternative solutions and sometimes it is useful to enrich them by additional prototypical representations (Java). If we look closer at the options O41 and O42 in the example, we will find out that the specification in listing 5 may work for both options. A user of the application 'tells' the car repeatedly that it has to move forward/backward or to turn to the left/right, and then to stop. However, the idea of option O41 is that the user presses a 'button' to move the vehicle and stops it by releasing this 'button'. Option O42 suggests a separate command for stopping.

In contrast to earlier versions, HOPS 3 not only allows to map sequences of Java methods to HOPS operations (and to execute them during model animation), but it is also possible to map events of a Java application to HOPS operations. This supports a prototypical implementation of abstract ideas and a more convenient use of the still model-guided prototype.

Listing 7 shows parts of the enriched O-models for options O41 and O42. For example, process `O41` is mapped to the Java class `DiscreteMotorControl` (lines 1-2) which implements a 'rough' GUI for the suggested vehicle control (without implementing behavioral aspects). The process specifications also contain mappings from events to HOPS operations (lines 8-12 and 19-22). Figure 9 visualizes effects of the different event mappings on the model-guided prototypes for both options. If, for example, the forward-button in the prototypical GUI of model O41 is pressed in an animation session, HOPS-operation `forward` is executed and the vehicle moves forward. Operation `stop` is executed when the user releases this button again. When animating model O42, the user would have to click the forward-button, and then the stop-button to achieve the same effect. The HOPS operations could also be activated from the animation tree (center of the figure), but to experience this more abstract interaction with the vehicle control may not be sufficient in this case.

Tool Support for Parallel Prototyping

The suggested coupling of design representations is supported by a tool that allows to develop QOC-like graphs and to attach HOPS models in the way described above. The designer's decision process on how to advance the existing prototype is supported by parallel model-guided prototyping. It is implemented by the dynamic composition of the currently selected O-models of all key questions that was described earlier (see figure 5). Figure 10 shows the editor for QOC-like graphs in the background. For each key question, an option can be selected. Here, option O22 was chosen (1) and the HOPS animator was started for the actual model of the advanced prototype (2). The animation includes a GUI representation of the suggested control with sliders for the speed values of both motors, a start button and a stop button (3).

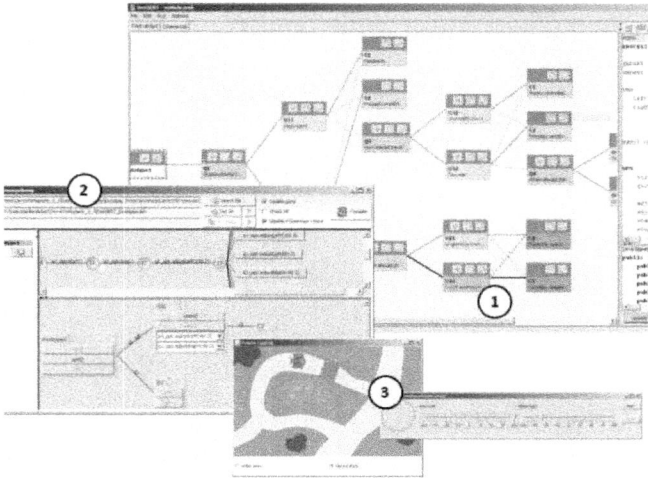

Figure 10. Tool support for parallel prototyping - current animation: option O22 in figure 7.

DISCUSSION AND RELATED WORK

The proposed approach assumes that interactive artifacts are gradually shaped by looking at them 'through the lenses' of different external representations in an evolutionary and participatory design process. It is further assumed that the way the representations can be coupled has a profound impact on how design teams intertwine their activities, and hence, an impact on the quality of the artifacts. The paper distinguishes between 'tamed' and 'wicked' design problems [23]. Problems of the second type need to be examined in a systematic way. On the one hand, it is necessary to provide the different stakeholders with representations that support a collaborative argumentation process. On the other hand, the participants need to use their specific skills to progress the development process. While QOC diagrams and prototypes, in the suggested coupling, support argumentation and empirical testing, HOPS models and Java code are more specific means to work towards design solutions via specification steps.

Bellotti et al. identify four different areas for modeling in HCI: system modeling, cognitive user modeling, interaction modeling, and describing design spaces explicitly [4]. Other areas such as context modeling are discussed in the literature. In engineering interactive systems, we may find three fundamental ways to use formal models. First, formal models can be transformed. Model-based approaches, as an example, apply transformations on conceptual models (e.g. task models) to get system specifications [7], [22]. Second, formal models can be run simultaneously to prototype a system (e.g. [1]). Third, formal specifications of interactive devices[3] can be reflected against models of the application context (e.g. by model checking as in [8] or by model animation as in [12]). Formal models are also central in the suggested approach where they play different roles (Q-models, O-models, C-models). However, in contrast to other approaches, they do not present complete system specifications, but are partial descriptions of alternative extensions of an already existing pro-

totype. Especially O-models are used, in a way, as 'sketches' to explore selected aspects of a systems' behavior. Corresponding model-guided prototypes make visible even subtle variants in such models that are difficult to deal with at an analytical level only or difficult to communicate in natural language. Examples were given in the paper.

The idea of developing and examining alternative solutions by parallel, model-guided prototyping is supported, for example, by findings in [14]. Dow and colleagues have shown that parallel prototyping helps to avoid design fixations. The need of computational tools for manipulating solution variations is discussed in [26].

Of course, many authors suggest to integrate different design representations in order to mitigate the limitations of single approaches. For example, task models and scenarios are related to QOC diagrams in [19]. QOC diagrams were used in the case study in [4] to integrate knowledge from the different participants of the multidisciplinary design team and to establish a mutual understanding between them. However, the authors also point out that 'culture clashes' due to different professional backgrounds influence the receptivity and that a revision of design assumptions is necessary for effective collaboration[4]. They argue, for example, that the conventional notion in the software engineering community "...that formal methods are only useful if used within a structured development context from the beginning of a project, through refinement, to implementation" restricts their applicability [4].

A consequence of coupling the representations as suggested in this paper will be an adaptation of prevalent usage practices. Prototypes need to be deliberately underdesigned to avoid premature design commitments and take into consideration emerging design issues and constraints. Options in QOC diagrams can also be expressed and explored in prototypes as demonstrated in the case study. Formal models are not required to be complete specifications and can be used to 'sketch out' possible enhancements of prototypes and so on. On the one hand, designers are more responsible for taking reasonable steps in the design process. On the other hand, the suggested approach supports a (systematic) transfer of knowledge between different design perspectives and helps to overcome some problems of the single approaches. To give two examples, the formal specification of design options and optional implementation steps may help to limit the design rationale to a reasonable number of alternatives. The separation of O-models describing selected aspects of a system design and C-models describing assumptions about the application context may help to increase the designers' consciousness about their use of design representations[5].

---

[3]Typically, an interactive artifact is specified in terms of user actions and information resources.

[4]Carroll sees fragmentation as an "ironic downside of the inclusive multidisciplinarity of HCI". Researchers and practitioners are challenged by a huge scope of concepts and approaches. One possible consequence is that individuals or groups deliberately isolate from some of the field's activity and knowledge [9].

[5] In [24] dangerous effects are discussed when representations "pass through different groups and are used for different purposes". For example, descriptions *of* work can easily become descriptions *for* work if they are directly interpreted as system specifications.

CONCLUSIONS

A constructive approach for design space exploration was introduced. It encourages design teams to become familiar with different design representations in order to reflect more effectively the inevitable tensions between design goals and alternative solutions. The interactive artifact under design emerges from the coupling of such representations in an appropriate intertwining of exploratory, analytical, empirical, and implementation design activities. In future work, we would like to investigate more sophisticated strategies to underdesign prototypes. Another interesting question concerns a more differentiated treatment of design options (e.g. a distinction between alternatives and variations).

ACKNOWLEDGMENTS

The first author wishes to thank Stéphane Chatty for comments on earlier drafts of this paper. Our thanks go to Martin Evert, Johann-P. Wolff, and project course 23149(2012). Thanks to Stefan Dittmar for the graphics of the example.

REFERENCES

1. Barboni, E., Ladry, J.-F., Navarre, D., Palanque, P., and Winckler, M. Beyond modelling: an integrated environment supporting co-execution of tasks and systems models. In *Proc. of EICS '10*, ACM (2010), 165–174.

2. Bellotti, V. Integrating theoreticians' and practitioners' perspectives with design rationale. In *Proc. of INTERACT '93*, CHI '93, ACM (1993), 101–106.

3. Bellotti, V., Maclean, A., and Moran, T. Generating good design questions. Tech. rep., 1991.

4. Bellotti, V., Shum, S. B., MacLean, A., and Hammond, N. Multidisciplinary modelling in HCI design... in theory and in practice. In *Proc. of CHI '95*, ACM Press/Addison-Wesley Publishing Co. (1995), 146–153.

5. Benyon, D., Turner, P., and Turner, S. *Designing interactive systems: people, activities, contexts, technologies*. Addison-Wesley, 2005.

6. Buxton, B. *Sketching User Experiences: Getting the Design Right and the Right Design*. Morgan Kaufmann Publishers Inc., 2007.

7. Calvary, G., Coutaz, J., Thevenin, D., Limbourg, Q., Bouillon, L., and Vanderdonckt, J. A unifying reference framework for multi-target user interfaces. *Interacting with Computers 15* (2003), 289–308.

8. Campos, J., Doherty, G., and Harrison, M. Including User Behavior as Model Checking Analysis. Tech. Rep. DI-CCTC-09-17, University of Minho, Braga, 2009.

9. Carroll, J. Introduction: Toward a Multidisciplinary Science of Human-Computer Interaction. In *HCI models, theories, and frameworks: Toward a multidisciplinary science*, J. Carroll, Ed. Morgan Kaufmann, 2003, 1–10.

10. Cass, A. G., and Fernandes, C. S. T. Using Task Models for Cascading Selective Undo. In *TAMODIA*, vol. 4385 of *Lecture Notes in Computer Science*, Springer (2006), 186–201.

11. Dittmar, A., and Forbrig, P. Selective Modeling to Support Task Migratability of Interactive Artifacts. In *INTERACT (3)*, vol. 6948 of *Lecture Notes in Computer Science*, Springer (2011), 571–588.

12. Dittmar, A., and Harrison, M. D. Representations for an iterative resource-based design approach. In *Proc. of EICS '10*, ACM (2010), 135–144.

13. Dix, A., and Gongora, L. Externalisation and design. In *Proc. of DESIRE '11*, ACM (2011), 31–42.

14. Dow, S. P., Glassco, A., Kass, J., Schwarz, M., Schwartz, D. L., and Klemmer, S. R. Parallel prototyping leads to better design results, more divergence, and increased self-efficacy. *ACM Trans. Comput.-Hum. Interact. 17*, 4 (2010), 18:1–18:24.

15. Dubberly, H., and Evenson, S. On modeling: The analysis-systhesis bridge model. *interactions 15*, 2 (2008), 57–61.

16. Fischer, G., Giaccardi, E., Ye, Y., Sutcliffe, A. G., and Mehandjiev, N. Meta-design: a manifesto for end-user development. *Commun. ACM 47*, 9 (2004), 33–37.

17. Fischer, G., Lemke, A., McCall, R., and Morch, A. Making Argumentation Serve Design. In *Design Rationale: Concepts, Techniques, and Use*, T. Moran and J. Carroll, Eds. Lawrence Erlbaum Associates, Inc., 1996.

18. Hix, D., and Hartson, H. *Developing User Interfaces: Ensuring Usability Through Product and Process*. Wiley, New York, 1993.

19. Lacaze, X., Palanque, P., Barboni, E., and Navarre, D. Design Rationale for Increasing Profitability of Interactive Systems Development . In *Encyclopedia of Human Computer Interaction* . 2005.

20. Lee, J., and Lai, K. What's In Design Rationale. In *Design Rationale: Concepts, Techniques, and Use*, T. Moran and J. Carroll, Eds. Lawrence Erlbaum Associates, Inc., 1996.

21. MacLean, A., Young, R. M., Bellotti, V. M. E., and Moran, T. P. Questions, options, and criteria: elements of design space analysis. *Hum.-Comput. Interact. 6*, 3 (1991), 201–250.

22. Paterno, F. *Model-Based Design and Evaluation of Interactive Applications*. Springer, 2000.

23. Rittel, H. W. J., and Webber, M. M. Dilemmas in a General Theory of Planning. *Policy Sciences 4* (1973), 155–169.

24. Robinson, M., and Bannon, L. Questioning representations. In *Proc. of ECSCW'91* (1991), 219–233.

25. Schön, D. *The reflective practitioner: How professionals think in action*. New York, Basic Books, 1983.

26. Terry, M., Mynatt, E. D., Nakakoji, K., and Yamamoto, Y. Variation in element and action: supporting simultaneous development of alternative solutions. In *Proc. of CHI '04*, ACM (2004), 711–718.

IOWAState: Models and Design Patterns for Identity-Aware User Interfaces Based on State Machines

Yann Laurillau
University of Grenoble, UPMF, CNRS, LIG Laboratory
110 av. de la Chimie, Domaine Universitaire, BP 53, 38041 Grenoble cedex 9, FRANCE
{first name}.{last name}@imag.fr

ABSTRACT

The emergence of interactive surfaces and technologies able to differentiate users allows the design and development of Identity-Aware (IA) interfaces, a new and richer set of user interfaces (UIs). Such user interfaces are able to adapt their behavior depending on who is interacting. However, existing implementations, mostly as software toolkits, are still ad-hoc and mostly based on existing GUI toolkits which are not designed to support user differentiation. The problem is that the development of IA interfaces is more complex than the development of traditional UIs and still requires extra programming efforts. To address these issues, we present a set of implementation models, named IOWAState models, to specify the behavior as state machines, the architecture and the components of IA interfaces. In addition, based on our IOWAState models and a classification of IA user interfaces, we detail a set of design patterns to implement the behavior of IA user interfaces.

Author Keywords

Identity-aware user interfaces; Interactive surfaces; Software design patterns; Architecture model; State machine model.

ACM Classification Keywords

H.5.2. User Interfaces: Graphical User Interfaces, Interaction styles, Prototyping, User-Centered design. H.5.3. Group and Organization Interfaces: Web-based interaction. D.2.2. Design Tools and Techniques: User interfaces.

INTRODUCTION

Research on multi-touch interactive surfaces, in particular interactive tabletops, is now well established in the fields of Human-Computer Interaction (HCI) and of Computer-Supported Cooperative Work (CSCW). The directness of interaction and the multiuser capabilities of tabletops may explain the growing interest for these systems. Currently, several technological solutions are available [12,32] including commercial ones [9,17]. Among these

technologies, few are able to differentiate users touching the surface [9,16,24,32].

In conjunction with the growing number of technological solutions allowing user identification and differentiation (e.g., [1,16]), work is done on the development of identity-aware (IA) user interfaces, taking advantage of user differentiation and showing the capabilities and benefits of such UIs (e.g. [26,27]). For instance, SIDES [25] is an IA multi-user tabletop-based interactive system designed to develop effective social skills. It shows that such category of technology is helpful for a therapeutic purpose considering teenagers with Asperger's syndrome. In particular, IA widgets requiring synchronous actions were key in its success.

As Identity-Aware User Interfaces (IAUIs) are more complex than traditional and single-user interfaces, their development is still challenging. We identify several issues:

Lack of implementation models and guidelines: developing IAUIs requires extra programming efforts due to the lack of models and of capitalization of best practices (e.g. guidelines, design patterns). We observed that existing IA applications are mostly developed from scratch and, similarly to the development of multi-touch gesture-based interactive systems, developers must deal with low-level events.

User interfaces' behavioral model split across the code: traditional UI toolkits (e.g. Java's Swing), including UI toolkits that support user differentiation (e.g. DiamondSpin [28] toolkit is based on Java's Swing), massively rely on the well-known callback-based programming model: developers have to write a bunch of callbacks to handle each input event for each UI component. Thus, they must maintain the state of the UI component across these callbacks which usually leads to produce "spaghetti" of code [21].

Dealing with concurrent inputs and differentiated outputs: although a traditional UI receives and deals with events generated by the same user, an IAUI has to manage input events generated by different users due to simultaneous actions, sometimes concurrent. Furthermore, such an UI must maintain a much more complex state model in order to produce consistent and customized outputs.

At implementation level, although most of the work done focuses on technical issues to allow user differentiation such as dedicated software toolkits, we investigate the building of software models that would help and drive the development of IAUI components. In particular, we investigate the use of state machines as a means to address the two last issues.

This paper is structured as follows. First, we introduce an example to illustrate IAUIs. Then, we present the IOWAState models, our first contribution: a set of models to specify the behavior, the main components and the architecture of IAUI components. Based on our IOWAState models, we detail our second contribution, seven design patterns to implement the behavior of IAUI components, and our methodology. We conclude with a discussion and perspectives.

ILLUSTRATIVE EXAMPLE

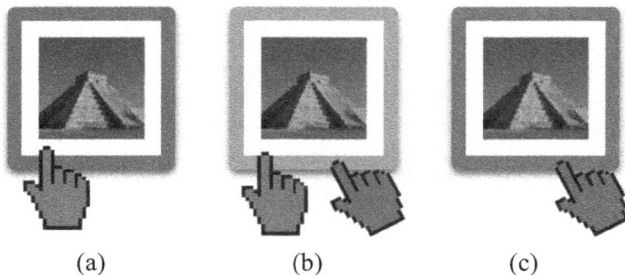

(a)   (b)   (c)

Figure 1: Cooperative gesture to transfer ownership [18].

Let us consider the following scenario: two users, Green and Blue, are interacting simultaneously on a user-differentiating multitouch surface, manipulating digital artifacts (widgets, images, shapes, etc). Some are public while others are private. Thanks to user differentiation, supporting privacy, private artifacts are accessible by their owner only. However, user Green wants to give an image he/she owns to user Blue. Thanks to user differentiation, the users Green and Blue just have to accomplish a cooperative gesture [18] to transfer ownership. As shown in Figure 1, having first activated ownership transfer mode, (a) user Green touches the image he/she wants to relinquish; (b) user Blue touches Green's image to indicate that he/she will be the next owner; (c) ownership is granted to user Blue when user Green releases his/her finger from the surface. This example is used further in the part about design patterns.

BACKGROUND AND RELATED WORK

As underlined in introduction, multi-touch technologies, especially interactive surfaces, are intensively studied and are now well known in our research communities. Therefore, in this paper we concentrate on IA User Interfaces and on development tools supporting user differentiation.

Identity-aware user interfaces

In the 90's, researchers started to investigate the development of groupware using a single and shared display: Single Display Groupware systems (SDG) are ancestors of actual research on interactive surfaces such as tabletops: co-located users were able to interact simultaneously using multiple input devices [29]. Therefore, assigning an input device per user allows user identification and thus the development of identity-aware applications. The most basic example is multi-pointers on a shared display: each user owns a pointer and is allowed to manipulate simultaneously the shared UI elements displayed on the screen. In particular, MMM [4], Pebbles [22], and Kidpad [10] are usually considered in the literature as the very first systems implementing and illustrating the concept of SDG. These systems are the first to take advantage of user identification to develop identity-aware interfaces.

Proxy-Sketch [1] is another example of identity-aware interface dedicated to the creation of GUI prototypes. User identification is used to associate owners to content. It also supports casual observers (i.e. not logged in) that prevent from accidental changes.

Idlenses [27] is an identity-aware interaction technique that revisits magic lenses to provide a moveable personal area. Once identified, users benefit of personal tools that support access control to restricted and personal data, personalized actions such as automatic filling of web forms with personal data, a private clipboard, etc.

Tse et al. [30] have investigated multi-user and multimodal identity-aware interactive systems for gaming, based on DiamondTouch [9]. The underlying mechanism for multimodal fusion uses user identification to link speech with gesture.

To capitalize the work done in this area, Ryall et al. [26] propose the conceptual iDwidgets framework. The authors define identity-aware widgets (i.e. called iDwidgets for identity-differentiated widgets) as an extension of "*the widget concept by including identity as an input parameter, which lets us customize interactions in a variety of ways*". For instance, an identity-aware paintbrush tool will adapt its color or stroke size according to the user.

Toolkits supporting user differentiation

In order to facilitate the development of identity-aware interfaces and widgets, several toolkits have been designed and developed to support user differentiation.

The very first toolkits used peripherals as a means to differentiate users. The implicit user differentiation mechanism was "*one input device, one user; one user, one input device*". For instance, Multiple Input Devices (MID) [13] is a software library built on top of Java. In order to support multiple mice, MID revisits the underlying Java event mechanism. Therefore, it allows developers to implement identity-aware interfaces based on the mouse ID. Such a piece of information is implemented as an extra attribute of event objects.

SDGToolkit [31] is an extension of MID as it supports multiple keyboards. At UI level, the toolkit provides mechanisms to support orientation in tabletop setups. This toolkit is built on top of the .NET framework and is written in C#. Similarly to MID, events generated by input devices are associated to devices based on a device ID. It allows the use of standard widgets provided by the .NET framework to develop identity-aware interfaces as well to develop its own identity-aware widgets from scratch. This toolkit gave rise to IdenTTop [24], adding support for any multi-touch devices and support for a Polemus motion tracker. In addition, IdenTTop proposes a development framework for identity-aware applications based on a set of software components.

For touch surfaces, especially DiamondTouch [9], DiamondSpin [28] is the most well-known toolkit. It is built on top of Java and extends Java's Swing GUI toolkit to support widget orientation. User identification is achieved using a similar mechanism as SDGToolkit: events generated by touches are associated to users by the way of a specific attribute: a user ID. In particular, the toolkit provides identity-aware frames (DSFrame component) allowing users to customize the appearance: a frame can be rotated, zoomed or resized. Similarly to SDGToolkit, it allows developers to reuse standard Java's Swing components in a DSFrame. Compared to DiamondSpin, the GIL Library (gil.imag.fr) is another toolkit based on DiamondTouch but built on top of Tcl/Tk

While the java-based T3 toolkit focuses on high-resolution tabletop interfaces using wireless pens as devices for user identification [32], TouchID [16] goes beyond user identification as it investigates user-, hand-, and handpart-aware tabletops. Similarly to SDGToolkit and IdenTTop, TouchID is build on top of the .NET framework and based on the Microsoft Surface touch table [17].

IOWASTATE MODELS
As our model is intended for the design and the implementation of Identity-Aware UIs (IAUI), the IOWAState model encompasses three modeling primitives:

- A behavior model based on standard state machine models to describe the behavior of an IAUI. As detailed further, we used this modeling primitive to identify recurrent behavior patterns. In particular, we highlight how user differentiation is achieved in terms of state machine.

- A component model that identifies the main components of an IAUI and their relationships. In particular, this model highlights how we handle multiple state machines in order to allow parallel or concurrent user actions on an IAUI.

- An architecture model to describe the structure of an IAUI component. It illustrates how low-level events are processed to produce high-level events and are propagated to sub-components.

In the following, as the IOWA component model is based on the Model-View-Controller (MVC) design pattern, we will refer to it.

IOWA Behavior model
We chose to model and implement the Model part using hierarchical state machines (HSM), a derivative of finite state machines (FSM). Since Newman's work [23], user interfaces are often specified using state machines [15,21,33]. In addition, several works have demonstrated the feasibility and the benefits implementing state machine-based UIs [1,5,14].

As state machines are well suited to specify mode-driven interactions, we allow the Model to encompass several state machines, one per user, and support their parallel execution. Indeed, collaborative settings such as tabletops enable the interleaving modal actions.

In addition, using state machines facilitated the comparison of identity-aware widget's implementations and helped us to identify classes of identity-aware widgets based on their implementation model.

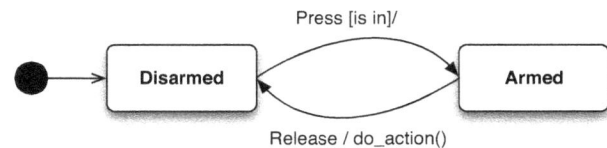

Figure 2: Example of state model of a button.

A state machine is a combination of states and transitions connecting states. Using UML statecharts, transitions are labeled according to the following syntax: *trigger* [*guard*] / *effect*. *Trigger* is an event name, *guard* is a set of conditions and *effect* is an action executed when the transition is triggered. Figure 2 shows a classic state model of a button constituted of two states: disarmed: the button is raised; armed: the button is pushed. Such a state model responds to the press and release events. For instance, if the active state is "Armed" while a release event occurs, the *do_action()* is fired and the button goes in the "Disarmed" state.

Finally, the main advantage of Hierarchical State Machines is to facilitate the control of the state explosion problem as it allows the refinement of states as finite state machines. Indeed, specifying a state model using HSMs is a top-down approach like problem solving: an overall state model is decomposed into FSMs as problems are decomposed into smaller problems. For instance, HSMs are part of UML to specify state machines.

IOWA Component model
The IOWA component model slightly differs from the MVC design pattern as an IOWA Component inherits from an IOWA StateMachine (i.e. Model) and an IOWA UI (i.e. View). The main advantage is to present a component that looks externally as a whole, hiding the model and view

parts, while preserving modularity and loose coupling between the View and the Model.

In order to support the design of IAUIs, user differentiation is first achieved at the Model level. As shown in Figure 3, the Model is an instance of an IOWA StateMachine that describes the behavior of an IAUI, as explained in the previous part, with an IA state machine. Such a state machine is hierarchical as each state (i.e. IOWA State) may be described as a hierarchy of states. Transitions between states are triggered by events sent through a *post()* operation. Events are propagated in the state hierarchy. As events carry the identity of the user (i.e. user ID) who performs the associated action, this mechanism allows the design of IA state machines.

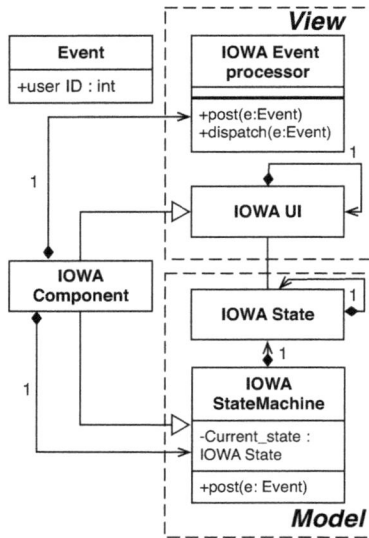

Figure 3: IOWAState's component model.

In order to support the interleaving of different user's actions and concurrent actions, although an IOWA Component is already statemachine, an IOWA Component may handle a set of IOWA StateMachines, one per user. Indeed, each event received by an IOWA Component and processed by the *post()* operation is dispatched to the state machine associated with the user ID that produces such an event.

An IOWA State component is responsible for handling high-level events supplemented with a user ID and achieving user-differentiation. Indeed, depending on the event type and the user ID, an IOWA State component verifies conditions on transitions associated to it: if a condition is verified, this component indicates to the related IOWA StateMachines component what the new state is.

As part of the View, an IOWA UI produces an output representation to the user. It defines the look and feel of an IAUI. In this model, similarly to HsmTk [5], an IOWA UI is a composition of IOWA UIs, one per state. For input events, an IOWA UI is associated with an IOWA Event Processor

that receives low-level events and produces high-level events sent to the IOWA Component through a *post()* operation. Such an IOWA Event Processor may be seen as a pipeline of event filters.

IOWA Architecture model

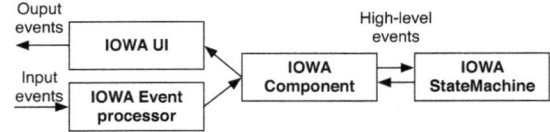

Figure 4: IOWAState's architecture model.

As shown in Figure 4, the IOWA architecture model is layered according to the MVC design pattern. As explained previously, an IOWA UI and an IOWA Event Processor constitutes the View while an IOWA StateMachine constitutes the Model. They are assembled to constitute an event processing chain that processes user' input events and generates an output representation. As an IOWA Component may be a composition of sub-IOWA Component, in addition to the dispatch of events to the state machine, the IOWA Event Processor dispatches events to the sub-components. Furthermore, the state machine may generate events that are also dispatches to the sub-components.

IMPLEMENTING IOWASTATE MODELS

The IOWAState Models, in particular the IOWA behavior model, may be directly specified with an object-oriented programming language that allows a one-to-one correspondence between the IOWAState Models and the implementation. We chose such an approach because, as underlined in introduction, IAUIs are more complex to design and to implement than traditional single-user UIs. The implementation step is usually complex as existing toolkits that support user differentiation mostly rely on usual WIMP toolkits (e.g. Java's Swing). To address this issue, in particular about the implementation of state machines, existing works advocate a developer-centric approach claiming a tight integration of models with dynamic programming languages [2,5,11]. Indeed, a state machine leads to produce code easier to read and to maintain. In addition, it supports a better reusability and extensibility as we may easily add, remove or modify states and transitions thanks to the inheritance mechanism supported by object oriented programming languages.

In order to demonstrate the validity of our IOWAState models, without giving implementation details, we implemented eight very different IAUI components. Although existing implementations focus on customization of appearance [16,24,28,30,32] (e.g. orientation to a particular user), we focus on component's behavior in terms of internal/external functionality and group input [26]. Precisely, in order to cover the largest range of IAUI component classes as identified by Ryall et al. [26], the components we implemented are taken and adapted from [18,19,20,26].

For instance, one of the eight components we implemented is a multi-user slider having a differentiated behavior, performing the same action (i.e. selecting a value) whoever the user is. However, it behaves with different styles depending on the user's identity. For instance, one user may slide the cursor from tick to tick and select a value on a discrete scale, another user would slide the cursor continuously.

Another example is a cumulative voting component allowing different users clicking on a same button to perform an action. Achieving the action requires a minimum number of users performing the interaction.

The height IAUI components we implemented are developed in Python, to be used with a Diamondtouch device [9]. In order to be independent from any GUI toolkit and their associated programming paradigm, we used basic graphic primitives to draw the components (i.e. OpenGL rendering engine). In order to support identity-awareness, we rely on the user-differentiation mechanism provided by the Diamondtouch device [9], able to differentiate up to four users. The low-level events sent by the device are supplemented with a user ID represented as an integer value in a range of 0-3. It allowed us to implement an event loop that sends high-level events supplemented with a user ID to the user interface and thus to our IAUI components.

DESIGN PATTERNS

Methodology

In order to identify recurring design patterns for IAUIs, we defined and followed a twofold method. The first part of this method consists in analyzing and in reverse-engineering the source code of existing identity-aware widgets to detect recurring implementation patterns. The second part of this method consists in developing identity-aware widgets using state machines to model and implement widget's behavior. We chose to reuse and adapt existing identity-aware widgets that are the ones described in the previous section. Obviously, these developments are on our IOWA state models.

Code-based analysis of existing IA widgets

Concomitantly with the development of the eight widgets detailed in the previous section, we analyzed the code of a set of existing prototypes that includes IA widgets. We focused on prototypes developed with toolkits allowing user identification: SDG [31], DiamondSpin [28], T3 [32], TouchID [16] and GIL [3]. We did not consider the IdenTTop toolkit [24] because the code is not publicly available. Although several IA widgets and the related source code are available online, we also requested additional examples from the authors of the DiamondSpin and GIL toolkits.

We analyzed seven IA widgets taken from SDG, DiamondSpin, and GIL. We found no relevant widget for the T3 and TouchID toolkits. The source code was reversed engineered to identify implementation patterns of identity-aware widgets. First, we carefully examined the code as follows: (1) identification of callbacks or related methods managing user input events supplemented with a user ID; (2) identification of attributes used to store the component state; (3) identification of control structures that use the user ID to update the attributes related to the component state. Then, we modeled IA widgets using state machine representations. In order to verify our models, we compared the models at runtime. In order to classify state machines and to derive patterns, based both on our developments and on the analysis of existing components, we focused on similarities and differences in terms of states (e.g. associated states) and transitions (i.e. conditions).

The IA widgets and IA interaction techniques we analyzed are:

- From SDG toolkit, a multi-user button (SDGButton) allowing two interaction modes: (1) restricted interaction to the first user pushing the button (one-user-at-a-time); (2) cumulative effect; a multi-user check button (SDGCheckButton) that paints parts of its border with the color related to the users that checked it; a multi-user slider with multiple cursors (SDGTrackBar), one per user.

- From DiamondSpin toolkit: an identity-aware and moveable menubar (DSMenuBar); a multi-user chess board [8] (RealTimeChess); a RingMenu.

- From GIL toolkit: a cooperative design application to assemble shapes in order to design a building.

Design patterns

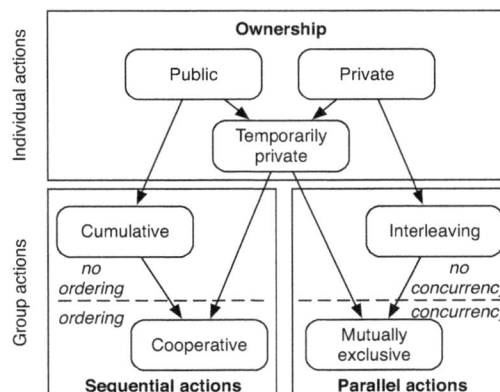

Figure 5: Design pattern graph.

As shown in Figure 5, our method leads us to identify three categories of patterns related to:

- *Individual actions*: these patterns deal with ownership, i.e. how a UI component is owned by one or multiple users. We identify three kinds of ownership: (a) public UI components that are free and not owned; (b) private UI components that are owned by one or multiple users and that can exclusively be used by the owners; (c) temporarily UI components that are free UI components owned for a limited amount of time.

- *Group actions to achieve a sequence of actions*: these patterns identify UI components that require multiple users to achieve a group action: (a) cumulative UI components that take into account the number of users whatever the sequence of action is; (b) cooperative UI components that imply a well-defined and ordered sequence of actions.

- *Group actions allowing parallel execution of actions*: we identify two situations: (a) the interleaving of actions with no concurrency; (b) mutually exclusive UI components to deal with concurrency.

In the following, we detail each design pattern using Borchers' pattern language [6]. In addition, illustrations of state machines are given using UML statecharts.

Public IAUI

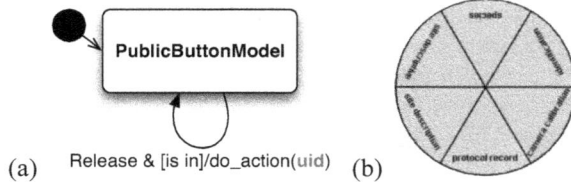

(a)   Release & [is in]/do_action(uid)   (b)

**Figure 6: (a) SM model for Public IAUI;
(b) TeamTag centralized control [19].**

Context: in order to achieve an individual task, different users simultaneously interact with a same UI element (e.g. a button) of the shared workspace to issue a command that acts on an artifact associated with her/him.

Problem: First, traditional widgets are single-user and do not support simultaneous actions. Secondly, the display may offer a limited amount of space: replicated UI elements would clutter the interacting space and would waste pixels. Thirdly, simultaneous but opposite actions on a same UI element would produce an inconsistent visual representation or have no effects: for instance, a user is pressing his/her finger on a button that should look armed while another user releases his/her finger on the same button that should look disarmed.

Solution: a single instance of an identity-unaware state machine composed of a single state would support simultaneous actions: transitions are labeled without uid-based conditions. Thus, user differentiation is achieved by an external function triggered when an action is performed on the UI (i.e. associated to the triggered state transition such as the function do_action(**uid**) shown in Figure 6 (a)). Such a function takes the user id associated to a user event as an argument: different actions are executed according to the user id.

To support presentation consistency for simultaneous actions, a unique output representation is coupled with the state machine because the state machine is composed of a single state.

Examples: TeamTag's IA controls [19] (Figure 6 (b)).

Private IAUI

Context: an interactive surface is partitioned into shared and private territories, allowing users to interact with private artifacts located in their private territory and to perform individual tasks.

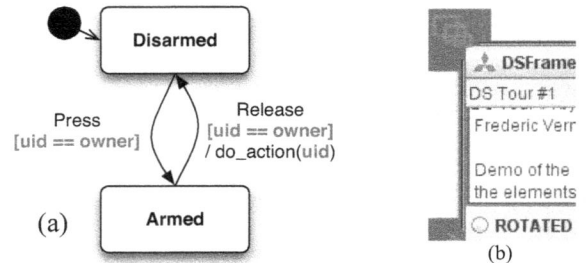

**Figure 7: (a) SM model for Private IAUI;
(b) Swing widgets in a DSFrame [28].**

Problem: an interactive surface is naturally a public shared resource as everything is visible and potentially free, including private territories. Tacit social rules are the most common mechanism that preserves private territories.

Solution: an IAUI exclusively associated to an owner, based on his/her user id, prevents other users to interact with such private UI elements. All transitions of the state machine associated with the private IAUI must be labeled with uid-based conditions: when an event is received, a transition is triggered if the user ID carried by the event matches the owner ID (e.g. condition [uid == owner] as shown in red in Figure 7 (a)). We may consider that an owner is associated to such an IAUI element at instantiation time.

Examples: Swing widget in a DSFrame [28] (Figure 7 (b)), IdLenses [27].

Temporarily Private IAUI

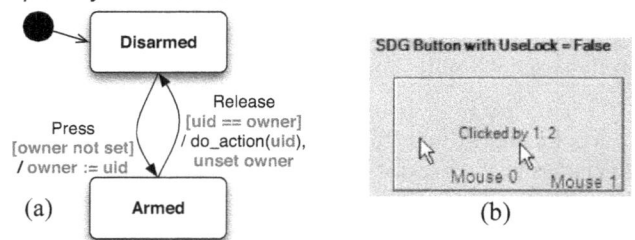

**Figure 8: (a) SM model for Temporarily Private IAUI;
(b) Single-user lock SDGButton [31].**

Context: different users simultaneously access to a shared and free UI element such as a widget or an artifact (e.g. digital photo).

Problem: although some UI elements are public and freely available, some UI elements may only support interactions for one user at a time.

Solution: an IAUI element temporarily owned by the current user interacting with the IAUI: ownership is granted to the very first user that interacts with the IAUI element; ownership is released when the user action is completed. To support such mechanism, the state machine associated to a temporarily private IAUI element should be designed based on two categories of transitions: transitions labeled (a) without and (b) with uid-based conditions. The first category allows any user to take ownership on a free IAUI element (e.g. condition [owner not set] as show in red in Figure 8 (a)): when this kind of transition is triggered, the current user is then marked as the current owner of the IAUI element he/she is manipulating (e.g. effect owner := uid as shown in green in Figure 8 (a)). Therefore, the IAUI element is considered as private. Similarly to Private IAUI, the remaining transitions are related to the second category (e.g. condition [uid == owner] as shown in red in Figure 8(a)). However, when triggered, at least one transition of the second category must release ownership (e.g. effect unset owner as show in green in Figure 8 (a)).

Examples: DSMenuBar [28], Single-user lock SDGButton [31] (Figure 8 (b)).

References: PUBLIC IAUI, PRIVATE IAUI.

Cumulative IAUI

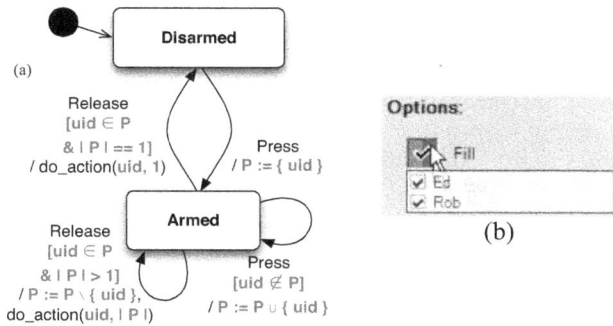

Figure 9: (a) SM model for Cumulative IAUI; (b) Cumulative SDGCheckButton [31].

Context: different users are interacting with the same UI element to perform a group and synchronized action.

Problem: the UI element must consider how many users (i.e. critical mass) are interacting to achieve a group action (e.g. majority). Furthermore, this UI element must remember who is interacting to take into account each user only once: for instance, a user touching a button with two different fingers must be counted as a single touch.

Solution: an IAUI element that maintains a list of users already interacting with it. This list is updated when transitions of the associated state machine are triggered. Three categories of conditions are observed:

- Conditions verifying if a user is not already in the list to avoid duplicate entries (e.g. condition [uid ∉ P] as shown in Figure 9 (a)). Consequently, for transitions that verify such a condition, the associated action consists in adding the new interacting user to the list (e.g. condition [P := P ∪ {uid}] as shown in Figure 9 (a)).

- Conditions verifying if a user is already on the list (e.g. condition [uid ∈ P] as shown in Figure 9 (a)) when the user interaction is completed. Consequently, for transitions that verify such a condition, the associated action consists in removing the associated user from the list (e.g. condition [P := P \ {uid}] as shown in Figure 9 (a)).

- Conditions verifying if no more users are interacting with the IAUI element to maintain state consistency (e.g. condition [|P| > 1] where |P| denotes the cardinality of set P as shown in Figure 9 (a)). Such a condition can be seen as threshold to reach in order to select a state transition in case of alternatives.

Although a Public IAUI element responds to individual actions, a Cumulative IAUI element responds to group actions. Similarly, there is no owner associated with it.

Examples: SDGButton [31] (Figure 9 (b)), Voting button [20], SIDES [25], SDGTrackBar [31].

References: PUBLIC IAUI.

Cooperative IAUI

Context: different users are interacting with the same UI element to perform a synchronized group action, involving a limited number of users. Achieving the group action requires to execute actions in a certain order (i.e. ordered sequence of actions). Depending on the number of users or depending on who is interacting, the UI element behaves in different ways (modes).

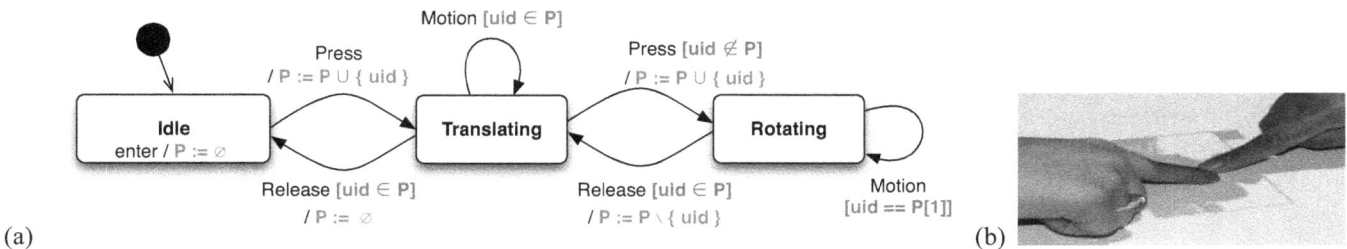

Figure 10: (a) SM model for Cooperative IAUI; (b) Cooperative gesture [17].

Problem: the UI element must consider how many users are interacting to achieve a group action. Furthermore, this UI element must remember who is interacting to take into account each user only once. As the UI element behaves differently depending on who is interacting, several states must be considered to represent the sequence of actions.

Solution: an IAUI element's state machine composed of an ordered set of states. This set corresponds to the ordered sequence of actions that the users must execute to achieve the group action. Each state is associated to different behaviors of the IAUI element. User differentiation is performed to (1) limit the number of users interacting with the IAUI element using a list similarly to a Cumulative IAUI element; (2) to associate a user for different modes of interaction using uid-based conditions (e.g. condition [uid == P[1]] as shown in red in Figure 10 (a)). As the number of users allowed to interact with a Cooperative IAUI element is limited, such a component may be seen as Temporarily private IAUI element.

Examples: Cooperative gesture [18] (Figure 10 (b)), Rotating shape (Figure 1).

References: TEMPORARILY PRIVATE IAUI, CUMULATIVE IAUI.

Interleaving IAUI

Context: different users are simultaneously interacting in a shared workspace on different artifacts. Some of the users may execute destructive actions (e.g. delete).

Problem: using a global mode (i.e. the same mode for all) in a shared workspace does not support parallel moded interactions. For instance, if one person is in an erasing mode, other persons cannot be in a different mode such as drawing: once the erase mode is activated, the next selected stroke would be erased.

Solution: an IAUI component's state machine managing a set of multiple instances of the same sub-state machine that are running in parallel (Figure 11 (a)). The master state machine intercepts the events and, as a proxy, dispatches events to each instance. Each instance is owned (i.e. private) by a user (e.g. conditions [uid == user_N] on transitions as shown in red in Figure 11 (a)) and is responsible for the management of moded interactions. Such a mechanism allows the interleaving of actions and

avoids concurrent actions, even for destructive actions.

Examples: DTMap [26] (Figure 11 (b)).

References: PRIVATE IAUI.

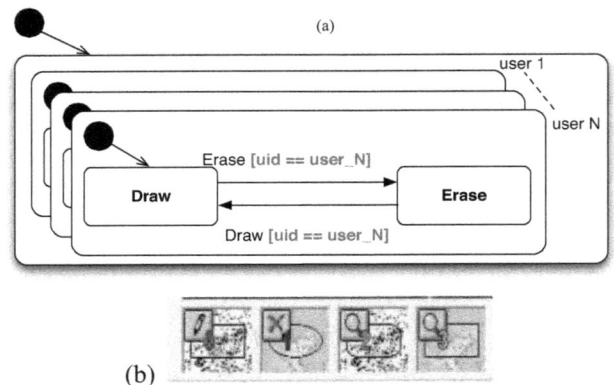

(b)

Figure 11: (a) SM model for Interleaving IAUI; (b) DTMap.

Mutually exclusive IAUI

Context: Two users are interacting simultaneously with the same UI component.

Problem: a user must wait for the first user already interacting to end up taking his/her turn and then accomplish his/her own action.

Solution: similarly to an Interleaving IAUI component, a Mutually exclusive IAUI component is based on a master state machine that manages several sub-state machines running in parallel. In addition, each sub-state machine implements an Idle/Active mechanism: the idle state is reached when a user is not interacting; the active state is reached when a user is interacting. For the latter, two sub-states are considered in order to support mutual exclusion and the fact that a user must wait his/her turn: two sub-sub-states are considered as show in Figure 12 (a): an operative state that locks the IAUI component (i.e. ownership taken) until the interaction is ended up (i.e. ownership released); a non-operative state that corresponds to a stand-by period.

Examples: Waiter's Diamondspin mechanism [28], RingMenu [8] (Figure 12 (b)).

References: TEMPORARILY PRIVATE IAUI, INTERLEAVING IAUI.

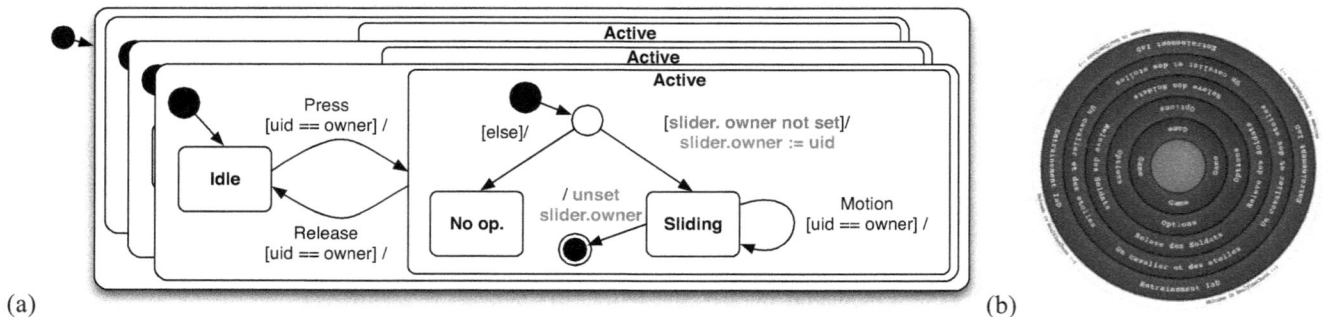

(a)   (b)

Figure 12: (a) SM model for Mutually exclusive IAUI; (b) RingMenu [7].

DISCUSSION

IOWA models

As a first evaluation, we instantiated the IOWAState models to develop eight very different IAUI components. As a second evaluation, we used our models as a framework to analyze existing implementations and to identify recurring patterns. Of course, a long-term evaluation would be clearly appropriate for a good understanding of the strengths and weaknesses of our models. In particular, we currently use our models to implement a serious game, based on a DiamoundTouch device, for the learning of cooperative practices for engineering tasks.

As the IOWA models are based on HSMs to specify the behavior of IAUIs, our approach is similar to SwingState [2], StateStream [11] or HsmTk [5] models and implementations. Although these works target single-user interfaces, our models are designed to support IA user interfaces. In particular, an IOWA component supports simultaneous user inputs and an ownership mechanism in order to allow the development of Private and Temporarily private IAUIs. In addition, our models are designed to support the parallel execution of HSMs within a MVC-like architecture in order to allow the development of Interleaving and Mutually exclusive IAUIs. The IOWA architecture model is designed to allow compositions of state machines. However this point is out of the scope of this article.

Compared to existing IA toolkits [15,23,28,32,33] widely based on a callback-based programming model inherited from traditional GUI toolkits, since our models are based on HSMs to specify the behavior of IAUIs, our several developments show it can be easily translated into code in order to produce code easier to read and to maintain, avoiding the use of a specialized and additional language. Furthermore, as we adopted an object-oriented programming approach for the implementation of the IOWAState models, we observed that the inheritance mechanism facilitates the reuse of existing HSMs. It also facilitates the creation of new behaviors with minor modifications of existing HSMs. It seems an interesting property to investigate further in order to address state explosion.

Currently, as explained previously, a first limit of our approach is the lack of long-term evaluation. Particularly, we consider another long-term evaluation with Master students following computer engineering courses, asked to implement IAUIs based on our models. Focusing only on IAUI's behavior constitutes another limit. Investigating how our models are extensible to support user-differentiation at presentation level must be considered further. Finally, we do not address the combination of two IAUI components, in particular two IAUI components having conflictual behaviors.

Design patterns

In terms of evaluation, according to [7], a pattern follows a lifecycle model composed of several steps. Currently, our patterns have reached step #5 "Pattern Gestalt" for which readers review the patterns. This article contributes to this step. The next step must be "Popular acceptance". Contributing to the evaluation as well as demonstrating the completeness of our patterns, our pattern classification covers the classification of the IDWidgets framework [26] related to behavior, and coherently integrates cooperative gestures [18]. In addition, we go one step further towards software implementation of IAUIs as we provide and detail seven design patterns. Furthermore, although CSCW literature considers UI elements' ownership as private or public, we identify a new and intermediate situation of ownership: temporary ownership.

Complementary to the conceptual IDWidgets framework [26] providing classes of IAUI widgets, our pattern classification is at implementation level and identifies classes of identity-aware user interactions. Except the fact that our patterns should reach step "Popular acceptance" (step #7), an unanswered issue is the completeness of our design patterns and the related classification. Particularly, our patterns focus on behavior only and patterns for user-differentiated presentations should be investigated further.

CONCLUSION

Focusing on the design and development of Identity-Aware User Interfaces, this article presents two main findings. First, the IOWAState models revisit the MVC architecture model to rely on hierarchical state machines in order to support identity awareness, simultaneous user inputs, and to help developers to produce code easier to read and to maintain. Another significant contribution is a classification of IAUIs based on a set of seven design patterns to specify the behavior of IAUIs using state machines.

As a perspective, we need to investigate rules to combine several IAUI components. Indeed, combining two IAUI components may lead to the combination of conflictual HSMs such as a Private IAUI component embedding a Public IAUI component. In terms of implementation, we need to investigate alternative programming languages to Python to demonstrate the generative power of the IOWAState models. Finally, we plan to extend our patterns and the state machine approach to single-user multi-touch user interfaces.

ACKNOWLEDGMENTS

This work is funded by the FI MSTIC University Joseph Fourier Grenoble 1 (TIGRE project). To Renaud Blanch for advice and hints he gave about HSMs and the permission to use his HSM-based SWIT toolkit.

REFERENCES

1. Annett, M., Grossman, T., Wigdor, D., and Fitzmaurice, G. Medusa: a proximity-aware multi-touch tabletop. In *Proc. of UIST 2011*, ACM Press (2011), 337–346.

2. Appert, C., and Beaudouin-Lafon, M. SwingStates: adding state machines to the Swing toolkit. In *Proc. of UIST 2006*, ACM Press (2006), 319–322.

3. Bérard, F., and Laurillau, Y. Single User Multitouch on the DiamondTouch: From 2x1D to 2D. In *Proc of ITS 2009*, ACM Press (2009), 1–8. http://gil.imag.fr

4. Bier, E., and Freeman, S. MMM: A User Interface Architecture for Shared Editors on a Single Screen. In *Proc. of UIST 1991*, ACM Press (1991), 79–86.

5. Blanch, R., and Beaudouin-Lafon, M. Programming rich interactions using the hierarchical state machine toolkit. In *Proc. of AVI 2006*, ACM Press (2006), 51–58.

6. Borchers, J. A pattern approach to interaction design. In *Proc of DIS 2000*, ACM Press (2000), 369–378.

7. Brown, W., Malveau, R., McCormick, H., Mowbray, T., and Thomas, S.W. The Software Patterns Criteria (1998), http://www.antipatterns.com/whatisapattern/

8. Chaboissier, J., Isenberg, P., and Vernier, F. RealTimeChess: lessons from a participatory design process for a collaborative multi-touch, multi-user game. In *Proc. of ITS 2011*, ACM Press (2011), 97–106.

9. Dietz, P., and Leigh, D. DiamondTouch: A multi-user touch technology. In *Proc. of UIST 2001*, ACM Press (2001), 219–226.

10. Druin, A., Stewart, J., Proft, D., Bederson, B., and Hollan, J. KidPad: a design collaboration between children, technologists, and educators. In *Proc. of CHI 1997*, ACM Press (1997), 463–470.

11. de Haan, G., and Post, F. StateStream: a developer-centric approach towards unifying interaction models and architecture. In *Proc of EICS 2009*, ACM Press (2009), 13–22.

12. Han, J. Y. Low-cost multi-touch sensing through frustrated total internal reflection. In *Proc of UIST 2005*, ACM Press (2005), 115–118.

13. Hourcade, H.P., and Bederson, B. Architecture and implementation of a java package for multiple input devices (MID). *Univ. of Maryland Human–Computer Interaction Lab. (HCIL)*. Tech. report no. 99–08 (1999).

14. Kin, K., Hartmann, B., DeRose, T., and Agrawala, M. Proton: multitouch gestures as regular expressions. In *Proc. of CHI 2012*, ACM Press (2012), 2885–2894.

15. Letondal, C., Chatty, S., Phillips, G., André, F., and Conversy, S. Usability requirements for interaction-oriented development tools. *Psychology of Programming*, Maria P. D. Pérez and M.B. Rosson (2010), 12–26.

16. Marquardt, N., Kiemer, J., Ledo, D., Boring, S., and Greenberg, S. Designing user-, hand-, and handpart-aware tabletop interactions with the TouchID toolkit. In *Proc. of ITS 2011*, ACM Press (2011), 21–30.

17. Microsoft Surface, www.microsoft.com/surface/

18. Morris, M.R., Huang, A., Paepcke, A., and Winograd, T. Cooperative gestures: multi-user gestural interactions for co-located groupware. In *Proc. of CHI 2006*, ACM Press (2006), 1201–1210.

19. Morris, M.R. TeamTag: exploring centralized versus replicated controls for co-located tabletop Groupware. In *Proc. of CHI 2006*, ACM Press (2006), 1273-1282.

20. Morris, M. R. Designing Tabletop Groupware. In *Adjunct Proc. of UIST 2005*, ACM Press (2005).

21. Myers, B.A. Separating application code from toolkits: eliminating the spaghetti of callbacks. In *Proc. of UIST 1991*, ACM Press (1991), 211–220.

22. Myers, BA, Stiel, H., and Gargiulo, R. Collaboration using multiple PDAs connected to a PC. In *Proc of CSCW 1998*, ACM Press (1998), 285–294.

23. Newman, W.M. A system for interactive graphical programming. In *Proc. of AFIPS 1968*, ACM Press (1968), 47–54.

24. Partridge, G.A., and Irani, P.P. IdenTTop: a flexible platform for exploring identity-enabled surfaces. In *Ext. Abstr. of CHI 2009*, ACM Press (2009), 4411–4416.

25. Piper, A.M., O'Brien, E., Morris, M.R. and Winograd, T. SIDES: A cooperative tabletop computer game for social skills development. In *Proc. of CSCW 2006*, ACM Press (2006), 1–10.

26. Ryall, K., Esenther, A., Forlines, C., Shen, C., Shipman, S., Morris, M.R., Everitt, K., and Vernier, F. Identity-differentiating widgets for multiuser interactive surfaces. *IEEE Comput. Graph. 26*, 5 (2006), 56–64.

27. Schmidt, D., Chong, M.K., and Gellersen, H. IdLenses: dynamic personal areas on shared surfaces. In *Proc. of ITS 2010*, ACM Press (2010), 131–134.

28. Shen, C., Vernier, F., Forlines, C., and Morris, M.R. DiamondSpin: an extensible toolkit for around-the-table interaction. In *Proc. of CHI 2004*, ACM Press (2004), 167–174.

29. Stewart, J., Bederson, B., and Druin, A. Single display groupware: a model for co-present collaboration. In Proc. of CHI 1999, ACM Press (1999), 286–293.

30. Tse, E., Greenberg, S., Shen, C., Forlines, C., and Kodama, R. Exploring true multi-user multimodal interaction over a digital table. In *Proc. of DIS 2008*, ACM Press (2008), 109–118.

31. Tse, E., and Greenberg, S. Rapidly prototyping Single Display Groupware through the SDGToolkit. In *Proc. of AUIC 2004*, Australian Computer Society (2004), 101–110.

32. Tuddenham, P., and Robinson, P. T3: A toolkit for high-resolution tabletop interfaces. In *Ext. Abstr. of CSCW 2006*, ACM Press (2006), 2237–2242.

33. Wellner, P. Statemaster: A UIMS based on statechart for prototyping and target implementation. In *Proc. of CHI 1989*, ACM Press (1989), 177–182.

Guidelines for Integrating Personas into Software Engineering Tools

Shamal Faily
Department of Computer Science
University of Oxford, Oxford OX1 3QD, UK
firstname.lastname@cs.ox.ac.uk

John Lyle
Department of Computer Science
University of Oxford, Oxford OX1 3QD, UK
firstname.lastname@cs.ox.ac.uk

ABSTRACT

Personas have attracted the interest of many in the usability and software engineering communities. To date, however, there has been little work illustrating how personas can be integrated into software tools to support these engineering activities. This paper presents four guidelines that software engineering tools should incorporate to support the design and evolution of personas. These guidelines are grounded in our experiences modifying the open-source CAIRIS Requirements Management tool to support design and development activities for the EU FP7 *webinos* project.

Author Keywords

Personas; Design Rationale; CAIRIS; CAQDAS; XML

ACM Classification Keywords

H.5.2 User Interfaces: User-centered design

General Terms

Human Factors; Design.

INTRODUCTION

Personas – behavioural specifications that embody the goals and needs of archetypical users – have been a popular technique in user-centered design practice since they were first introduced over 10 years ago [4]. Personas were introduced to deal with developer biases arising from the word *user*. Such biases lead programmers to bend and stretch assumptions about what users should do. By building systems with only specific users in mind, developers only have to focus on those requirements necessary to keep these users happy. The idiosyncratic detail associated with personas also makes them communicative to a variety of different technical and non-technical stakeholders.

In recent years, interest in personas and the personification of archetypical users has extended to the software engineering communities. For example, Constantine [3] describes how models of user roles, which are analogous to personas, can drive visual interface design, while Roberts [17] claims that

personas can supplement UML models by contextualising descriptions of user roles. Surprisingly, however, despite several proposals for integrating personas methodologically with software engineering [1, 2, 15], there has been little work describing how software engineering tools should be augmented to support their creation, usage, and on-going maintenance. We believe this is unfortunate. From a user-centered design perspective, it may be acceptable to create and use personas without the use of software. However, from an engineering perspective, personas may be intricately woven into the traceability of different models, and justify design decisions at many levels of abstraction. Failure to properly specify, validate, or maintain personas may lead to precisely the sort of problems they were originally designed to address. Consequently, while personas are not rigorously specified, they are still models that contribute to the engineering of interactive systems.

It seems reasonable that personas be accorded the same level of tool-support as other software design models. However, to date, the focus of software engineering tools has been to support the design and development of software, not user-centered design artifacts like personas. This means we need to understand how personas can be integrated into software tools to ensure they help, rather than hinder, software engineering practice.

In this paper, we present four guidelines that enable software engineering tools to support the creation, use, and on-going evolution of personas. After describing the related work that motivated our work, we briefly introduce the open-source CAIRIS software tool, and the EU FP 7 *webinos* project that formed our context of study. We then present four guidelines based on our experiences using personas to support the design and development of the *webinos* platform. We conclude by discussing some of the consequences of our work.

RELATED WORK

Despite their value in supporting the design and development process, there is a surprising lack of both literature and software tools for supporting the creation, analysis, and on-going management of personas. One of the few current examples of software for persona creation and management is *Persona* [13] from Mariner Software. This tool manages information about personas, and predicts their behaviour. However, the tool itself is designed to support creative writing so some of its capabilities, such as re-using hero and villain archetypes, are of limited use to software design. Moreover, while the tool's capabilities for exploring persona relationships may have some value when designing collaborative systems, engineers may prefer to focus on explicit aspects of these interactions using more formal, UML based models.

The software engineering community have long argued that personas can be used to bridge usability and software engineering processes. For example, recent work by Schneidewind et al. [18] argued that personas can support all stages of the requirements engineering process, from requirements elicitation with use cases through to requirements validation. This is made possible because the purposes of personas, such as modelling and prioritising, align with different requirements engineering activities that require insights about users. However, while personas help support these activities, their effect may be marred without effective tool-support. For example, Schneidewind et al. claim that personas help prioritise requirements because they help understand the requirements of use case actors. However, the needs of personas may conflict, and such conflicts may not be immediately obvious from descriptions and use cases alone. It is, therefore, necessary to view the different relationships personas have with different design models, and ensure both personas and associated models are shared between team members and other stakeholders.

One of the few examples of software that integrates personas with different software design models is CAIRIS (Computer Aided Integration of Requirements and Information Security) [6]. CAIRIS is an open-source Requirements Management tool that was initially designed to support the specification of interactive secure systems. In addition to managing requirements models such as use cases and goal models, CAIRIS also manages the data associated with several security and usability engineering models, such as risks, scenarios, and personas. CAIRIS complements the use of specific security, requirements, and usability engineering techniques. If these techniques were properly applied, then models arising from them could be directly entered or imported into CAIRIS. The implications of personas in a system's design would then be amenable to some automated analysis. For example, [7] illustrates how the alignment between personas, scenarios, and risk analysis models can be used to visualise both the security and usability impact of different scenarios to personas.

As a product of 'autobiographical' design research [16], CAIRIS had previously been used in several projects where a single designer was responsible for eliciting all of the data managed by the tool. However, on larger projects, designers collecting data may not be the same people responsible for building or using personas. In such situations, designers may be uncomfortable using personas if the data upon which they are based is unavailable. For example, in a recent study examining how designers use personas, Matthews et al. [14] found that many designers find personas too abstract, and instead prefer using the data upon which these are based. Such data allows designers to make their own sense of user data. This suggests that if software tools are to adequately support personas, they also need to support the qualitative data analysis processes that create them. However, to date, Computer Aided Qualitative Data Analysis (CAQDAS) software tools,

techniques, and general insights for carrying out qualitative data analysis, e.g. [11] remain largely restricted to academic researchers rather than software engineers.

INTEGRATING PERSONAS INTO WEBINOS

To understand how personas can be integrated into software tools, we customised CAIRIS for the EU FP 7 *webinos* project [22]. This project integrated the use of personas with its design and development activities.

webinos is a software infrastructure (*webinos*) for running web applications across different device platforms [10]. The project team was drawn from 24 organisations across Europe, including universities, network providers, handset and car manufacturers, mobile software houses and market analysts.

To understand the expectations of prospective *webinos* users and application developers, ten personas was created. These personas were created by a team of five designers, drawn from across the *webinos* consortium; this team was responsible for not only creating the personas, but also maintaining them throughout the life of the project. To create the personas, the designers elicited factoids about prospective users from a variety of data sources. Affinity diagramming was used to categorise these factoids into clusters of potential behaviour. These clusters were structured using argumentation models [19] to motivate individual persona characteristics. More information about process used to create these personas, and the personas themselves, can be found in [20]. Once the personas had been created, the designers entered the persona argumentation structures and narratives into CAIRIS. These designers were also responsible for maintaining the personas throughout the project.

In addition to personas, scenarios were also created by project team members to envisage how *webinos* might be used, and describe some of the unintended consequences that might arise as a result. The design team incorporated and, where necessary, revised these scenarios based on the different personas. These scenarios were then entered into CAIRIS, together with related use cases and requirements for different functional areas of *webinos* [21].

As the project progressed, personas were used to motivate more detailed design and implementation activities. Personas played an important role in supporting an architectural risk analysis of the *webinos* software platform [9], and were used by developers to motivate new feature requests, e.g. [12]. When necessary, new personas were also created. For example, one persona was created for a 5 year old child to understand how he might interact with a *webinos*-enabled travel game for young children.

GUIDELINES

Based on our experiences customising CAIRIS for *webinos*, we have elicited the following four guidelines for developers wishing to integrate personas into their own software engineering tools.

- *Make persona characteristics explicit*
  Software Engineering tools should make the rationale for

persona characteristics available from the interfaces where persona narratives are displayed.

- *Integrate qualitative data analysis*
  Software Engineering tools should provide the analytical support necessary to create and maintain personas.

- *Facilitate persona interchange*
  Software Engineering tools should serialise personas in a format that encourages interchange and maintenance by developers that may be using different tools.

- *Revision control personas*
  Software Engineering tools should facilitate the revision control of personas.

We motivate and demonstrate these guidelines in the following sub-sections.

Make persona characteristics explicit

Personas were a new concept to most people on the project, with some developers being hesitant to trust what they considered to be fictional narratives. This meant that the analysis underpinning the personas needed to provide rationale for their descriptions, at the point when this rationale might be needed.

We believed that aligning the narrative of persona characteristics with their argumentation models would provide this missing rationale. However, questions about these characteristics and their validity still arose when interacting with personas using CAIRIS. To address this, we decided to link context-specific argumentation models within the persona dialog controls. Each persona dialog contained folders for the persona's activities, attitudes, aptitudes, motivations, and skills; these were based on behavioural variable types suggested by [5]. We added a context-sensitive menu to each folder to allow the visualisation of all the characteristic argumentation models associated each behavioural variable type.

Figure 1 illustrates the visualisation of the argument underpinning the persona characteristic 'Contextual variety encourages rather than discourages user-centeredness'. Based on Toulmin's model of argumentation, the white boxes act as the grounds for the characteristic's claim, while the blue boxes act as warrants connecting the grounds to the characteristic. The link to the data source document is indicated by the grey boxes linking the grounds and warrant objects. Finally, the dotted box shows a qualifying term indicating how confident the analyst is about this characteristic.

Applying this guideline helped the team identify personas that were overly general or ambiguous. In a number of cases, we identified personas that were built incorrectly by developers and analysts, who wrote the person narratives before following the argumentation process; this effectively bypassed the prescribed processes for creating personas. The argumentation model visualisation was useful in spotting and correcting such personas by drawing attention to the fallacies underpinning the personas' characteristics and, together with the

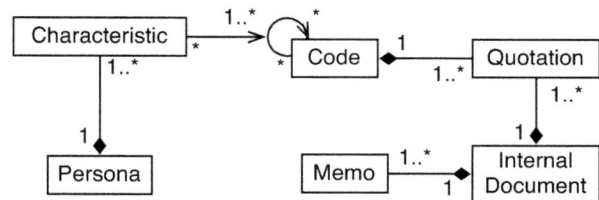

Figure 2. Meta-model of a persona's qualitative data analysis elements

personas' designers, walking through how the prescribed process — and the argumentation models in particular — identified these fallacies, while also eliciting new characteristics about the persona.

Integrate qualitative data analysis

The argumentation models provided some assurance about a persona's characteristics, but useful insights which arose while creating the personas were lost once the personas were created. To capture such insights, it is not enough for tools for interact with persona data - they need to support the analytical processes necessary to create and maintain them as well.

The Persona Case framework set out in [8] provided an approach for qualitatively analysing this data and, based on this analysis, developing new persona characteristics. This framework, however, assumed that a dedicated CAQDAS tool was available to carry out this analysis. Unfortunately, financial constraints meant that the potential commercial tools could not be used, and no suitable open-source alternative was available. Consequently, we decided to update CAIRIS to incorporate all the elements necessary to support qualitative data analysis while conforming to the framework described by [8].

To examine the efficacy of this integration, we used CAIRIS and the Persona Case framework to augment an existing persona with new characteristics. This persona (Jimmy) was based on application developer, which was a key audience for *webinos*. The empirical data upon which Jimmy's characteristics were based were collected was selected during three focus group sessions organised for potential *webinos* application developers. Focus group participants were recruited based on characteristics they shared with Jimmy.

The class diagram in Figure 2 shows the concepts incorporated into CAIRIS' data model and interfaces. The focus group reports were imported into CAIRIS as *internal documents*. The reports were qualitative coded, and text segments were annotated as *quotations* that were categorised according to a specific categorical *code*. Alternatively, where text segments raised particular questions or insights then these could be annotated with *memos*. Conceptual relationships between codes could be modelled, where each relationship corresponded to a persona *characteristic*. The Persona Case framework requires the quotations associated with each code to be both further categorised and labelled according to the role it plays in each characteristic's argumentation model.

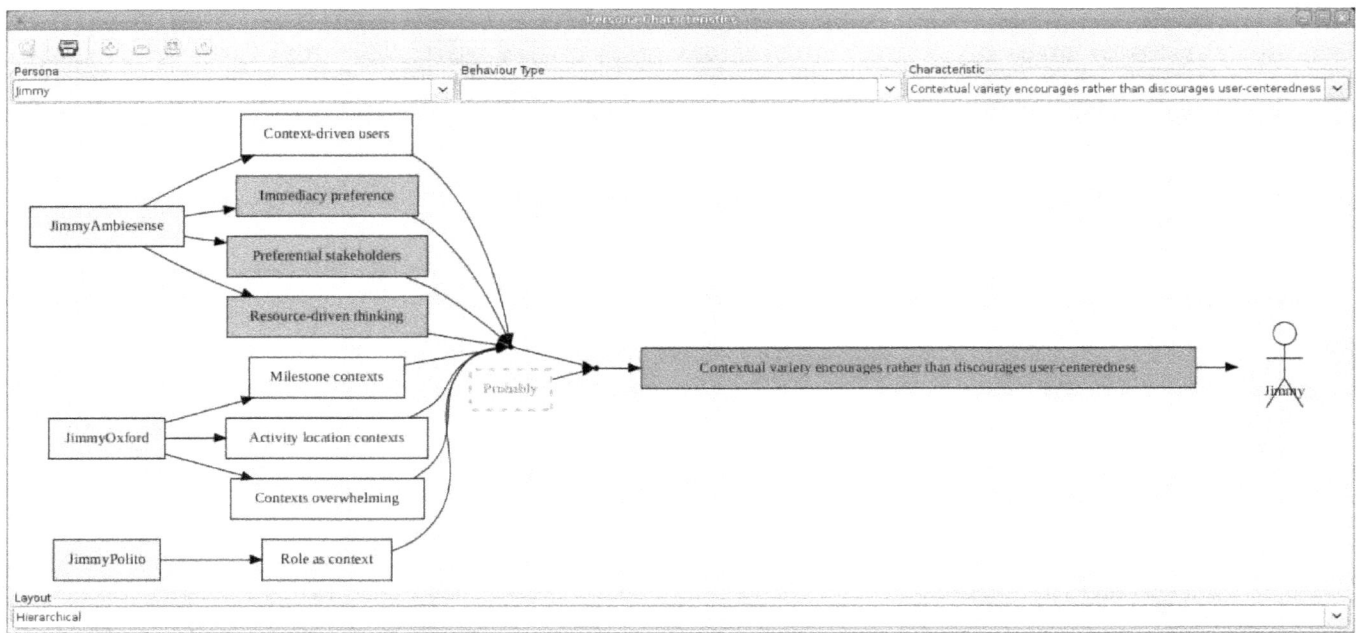

Figure 1. Visual model of a persona characteristic's grounding

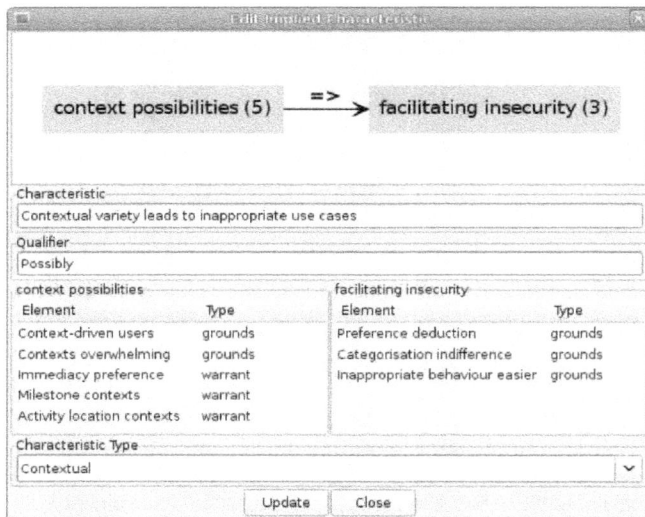

Figure 3. Details of qualitative grounding of a persona characteristic

To support the specification of this information, interfaces were added not only for adding and managing codes, quotations, and code relationships but also, as Figure 3 shows, the role each quotation played in a characteristic's argumentation model.

Facilitate persona interchange

Making CAIRIS available to everyone on the project made model interchangeability a concern. CAIRIS facilitated model interchange using XML; models would be exported to XML on one running instance of CAIRIS, and imported on another. Due to the complexity of the underlying CAIRIS database, which contained over 320 tables, the *webinos* mod-

els were spread across multiple XML documents; each document was structured according to a Document Type Description (DTD). These DTDs structured elements according to different model categories. For example, requirements model elements were structured according to a 'goals' DTD, while usability model elements such as personas and scenarios were structured based on a 'usability DTD'. Because there were dependencies between different XML documents that could not be easily resolved, these needed to be imported into CAIRIS in a particular order to ensure referential integrity in the database was maintained.

Developers were comfortable using XML to exchange models, but not all developers wanted to use CAIRIS. CAIRIS, however, played an important role is analysing the impact of different models on persona characteristics and vice-versa. Therefore, to ensure that team members would maintain personas, model interchangeability had to be supported at the level of personas, rather than at the coarse grained levels of the DTD. To do this, we modified the DTD for CAIRIS 'usability' elements to make the exchange of personas easier. An excerpt of the revised usability DTD is visualised in Figure 4. Class names correspond with element names, and the left-right order in the diagram indicates the order of elements within the DTD. Our aim in modifying this DTD was to allow personas and all their supplemental data to be externalised in a single XML document. We also wanted to make the structure of these documents as close as possible to CAIRIS' conceptual model of personas. This meant that, while the DTD was sub-optimal when compared to XML schema validation, it was easier for most team members to understand and maintain.

We believe this approach to persona interchange was successful because, while CAIRIS was only consistently used by a

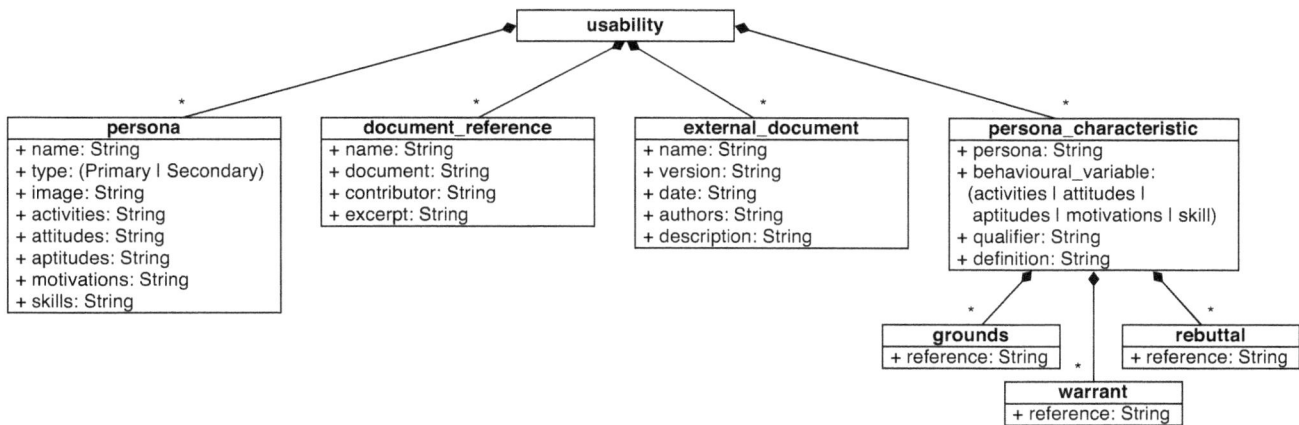

Figure 4. Class diagram of persona DTD structure

few team members, the personas still continued to be maintained and used. This is because scripts were created to export the CAIRIS models to the project wiki for easy viewing. If changes were necessary, the XML models could be edited directly using simple text editors.

Revision control personas

The interchangeability of personas raised questions about how they should be treated with respect to other design models. We were concerned not only with the traceability of personas with other models, but also how these would be maintained as *webinos'* design evolved. This was particularly important when personas were used to discuss implementation specific features, e.g. [12]. Consequently, if personas were to be accorded the same consideration as other models by the project team they would need to be placed under revision control. This is because the other design models were already under revision control and made openly available as a GitHub project [23].

We implemented this guideline in two ways. First, as described in the previous section, each persona and its associated qualitative data was stored in a single XML document. However, because some persona argumentation elements were used to ground multiple personas, importing individual persona XML files would lead to the import of duplicate data, thereby breaking the CAIRIS database's entity integrity. Therefore, the import logic was modified to ensure such duplicates would not be added. Second, the persona files were stored in a single directory on GitHub, and the model *build* script was revised to import each individual persona into the CAIRIS database. This meant personas would be kept in one place for ease of access, and any syntactical errors in the XML documents, or referential integrity errors resulting from problematic traceability links, could be addressed while models were being imported into CAIRIS.

CONCLUSION

In this paper, we illustrated how personas could be better supported with software engineering tools, and presented four guidelines based on our experiences modifying CAIRIS for

the *webinos* project. As a result, we believe this paper makes three important contributions.

First, we have drawn attention to the need for tool-support for personas, and discussed the consequences of this need remaining unaddressed. We hope others in the community share our concerns and will be inspired to join us by continuing work in this area.

Second, we have provided practical examples of how software tools can be augmented to better support personas when engineering interactive systems. The need for supporting persona interchangeability and revision control may seem self-evident, but our work has demonstrated how such guidelines can be implemented. We are conscious of the limitations of these guidelines, which are grounded only in the experiences in a single project. However, as a large-scale project, we believe that these experiences can be generalised.

Third, we believe these guidelines raise broader methodological questions. For example, our approach for revision controlling personas was appropriate for *webinos* as all source data had been anonymised. However, such an approach may not be appropriate when working with sensitive data that needs to be anonymised or access controlled. While such concerns are orthogonal to this paper, provisioning CAIRIS for the creation and maintenance of personas highlighted issues that might otherwise have remained unaddressed.

ACKNOWLEDGMENTS
The research described in this paper was funded by EPSRC *EUSTACE* project (R24401/GA001), and EU FP7 *webinos* project (FP7-ICT-2009-05 Objective 1.2).

REFERENCES
1. Behrenbruch, K., Atzmüller, M., Evers, C., Schmidt, L., Stumme, G., and Geihs, K. A personality based design approach using subgroup discovery. In *Proceedings of the 4th international conference on Human-Centered Software Engineering*, HCSE'12, Springer-Verlag (Berlin, Heidelberg, 2012), 259–266.

2. Castro, J. W., Acuna, S. T., and Juristo, N. Integrating the personas technique into the requirements analysis

activity. In *Proceedings of the 2008 Mexican International Conference on Computer Science*, IEEE Computer Society (2008), 104–112.

3. Constantine, L. Users, Roles, and Personas. In *The persona lifecycle: keeping people in mind throughout product design*, J. Pruitt and T. Adlin, Eds. Morgan Kaufmann, 2006, ch. 8, 498–519.

4. Cooper, A. *The Inmates Are Running the Asylum: Why High Tech Products Drive Us Crazy and How to Restore the Sanity (2nd Edition)*. Pearson Higher Education, 1999.

5. Cooper, A., Reimann, R., and Cronin, D. *About Face 3: The Essentials of Interaction Design*. John Wiley & Sons, 2007.

6. Faily, S. CAIRIS web site. `http://github.com/failys/CAIRIS`, March 2013.

7. Faily, S., and Fléchais, I. Towards tool-support for Usable Secure Requirements Engineering with CAIRIS. *International Journal of Secure Software Engineering 1*, 3 (July-September 2010), 56–70.

8. Faily, S., and Fléchais, I. Persona cases: a technique for grounding personas. In *Proceedings of the 29th international conference on Human factors in computing systems*, ACM (2011), 2267–2270.

9. Faily, S., Lyle, J., Namiluko, C., Atzeni, A., and Cameroni, C. Model-driven architectural risk analysis using architectural and contextualised attack patterns. In *Proceedings of the Workshop on Model-Driven Security*, ACM (2012), 3:1–3:6.

10. Fuhrhop, C., Lyle, J., and Faily, S. The webinos project. In *Proceedings of the 21st international conference companion on World Wide Web*, WWW '12 Companion, ACM (New York, NY, USA, 2012), 259–262.

11. Lewins, A., and Silver, C. *Using software in qualitative research : a step-by-step guide*. SAGE, Los Angeles, 2007.

12. Lyle, J. JIRA Issue WP-596: Single authentication for peer-to-peer service sharing. `http://jira.webinos.org/browse/WP-596`, 2012 November.

13. Mariner Software. Persona. `http://www.marinersoftware.com/products/persona`, March 2013.

14. Matthews, T., Judge, T., and Whittaker, S. How do designers and user experience professionals actually perceive and use personas? In *Proceedings of the 2012 ACM annual conference on Human Factors in Computing Systems*, CHI '12, ACM (2012), 1219–1228.

15. Moundalexis, M., Deery, J., and Roberts, K. *Integrating human-computer interaction artifacts into system development*, vol. 5619 LNCS. Springer, 2009.

16. Neustaedter, C., and Sengers, P. Autobiographical design in hci research: designing and learning through use-it-yourself. In *Proceedings of the Designing Interactive Systems Conference*, DIS '12, ACM (2012), 514–523.

17. Roberts, D. Coping with complexity. In *Human-Centered Software Engineering: Integrating Usability in the Software Development Lifecycle*, A. Seffah, J. Gulliksen, and M. C. Desmarais, Eds. Springer, 2005, ch. 11, 201–217.

18. Schneidewind, L., Horold, S., Mayas, C., Kromker, H., Falke, S., and Pucklitsch, T. How personas support requirements engineering. In *Usability and Accessibility Focused Requirements Engineering (UsARE), 2012 First International Workshop on* (2012), 1–5.

19. Toulmin, S. *The uses of argument*, updated ed. Cambridge University Press, 2003.

20. webinos Consortium. User expectations on privacy and security. `http://webinos.org/content/webinos-User_Expectations_on_Security_and_Privacy_v1.pdf`, February 2011.

21. webinos Consortium. Updates on Requirements and available Solutions. `http://www.webinos.org/wp-content/uploads/2012/09/Updates_on_Requirements_and_available_Solutions_v1.1_public.pdf`, August 2012.

22. webinos Consortium. webinos web site. `http://webinos.org`, March 2012.

23. webinos Consortium. webinos design data repository. `https://github.com/webinos/webinos-design-data`, March 2013.

A Methodology for Generating an Assistive System for Smart Environments Based on Contextual Activity Patterns

Michael Zaki
Rostock University
Albert Einstein-Str.22, Rostock
michael.zaki@uni-rostock.de

Peter Forbrig
Rostock University
Albert Einstein-Str.22, Rostock
peter.forbirg@uni-rostock.de

ABSTRACT

Despite the existence of various approaches addressing the development of nowadays interactive systems, smart environments impose an additional set of challenges for the designer. The main tenet of those environments is to deliver proper assistance to resident users who are performing their daily life tasks. However, an assistive system to be deployed in a smart environment has to meet some crucial requirements in order to successfully accomplish its mission. Thus, a well-defined development methodology for the generation of such a system to be employed in a given smart environment is highly beneficial. In this paper, we present a development methodology enabling the generation of tailored (user-specific) assistive user interfaces based on contextual activity patterns. We illustrate step by step the various stages by which the development of a supportive system for smart environments has to pass.

Author Keywords

smart environment, task models, contextual activity patterns, team patterns, dialog graphs, assistive user interface.

ACM Classification Keywords

H.1.2. Human centered Computing; H.5.2. User Interfaces-User-centered design; H.5.5. Modeling

General Terms

Design, Human Factors

INTRODUCTION AND RELATED WORK

Smart environments gained a lot of attention in the last decade. The main concept of those environments has been well described by [7] as they define a smart environment to be "*a small world where different kinds of smart devices are continuously working to make inhabitants' lives more comfortable*". Several prototypical smart environments exist nowadays. For example in [8], the authors introduce the MavHome project which aims to create a home acting like an agent. The main idea of MavHome is to recognize patterns in the inhabitant's history and which can serve as a basis for a prediction algorithm making it feasible to react upon the activity the system believes the user is performing. Also the iRoom [17] is an example of a smart meeting room, where the two problems of user interfaces distribution and personalization have been addressed and the room is adopting a human-system explicit interaction technique.

Smart environments impose several technical challenges on different layers [2]. However, in the context of our work we focus on the characteristics of the assistive system that should be developed for such environments and the requirements that should be satisfied in order to provide an optimal assistance to the environment's inhabitants. Those system requirements can be briefly described in the following:

1) Is unambiguous

One of the main characteristics of a usable system is to make it feasible for the user to perform the tasks using the introduced system in a very similar way he/she used to perform them without any intervening assistance. Taking this criterion into consideration leads to an unambiguous system which does not require the user to waste time and effort to adapt to the system providing the desired assistance.

2) Provides personalized assistance

Since the main tenet of a given smart environment is to offer the optimal assistance to every user performing a set of tasks in the environment, then each user should feel that the system is designed only for him/her and is totally compatible with his/her personal profile. In other words, providing personalized and user-tailored support opens the gate for a seamless usage and a maximum benefit of the system designed. Thus, a user model is required to adjust the behavior of the system to cope with the specific needs of each user.

3) Enables centralized control and feedback

It can be very distracting to the user if the system starts to react in an unexpected manner. An unsuitable system intervention may result from an erroneous inference of the activity of the user for example. Therefore, a methodology should be adopted in order to enable the user to adjust the system's behavior whenever such cases are encountered. The user should be able to provide feedback to the system about the assistance offered and its' suitability.

4) Offers hybrid interaction technique

The many advantages provided by the implicit interaction technique and especially in the smart environments field can be very tempting. This is due to the fact that the user does not have to bear extra tasks in order to ask the system for the desired assistance. Schmidt [19] defines implicit interaction to be *"an action performed by the user that is not primarily aimed to interact with a computerized system but which such a system understands as input"*. However, from usability point of view, the user's satisfaction can be negatively influenced if he/she feels controlled by the environment instead of controlling it. Moreover, if the system does not successfully infer the activity the user is performing, the environment may react in an unexpected way and disturbs the user. Therefore, there is a continuous need for giving the user the opportunity to interact in an explicit way (through a user interface) with the system. Thus, a hybrid interaction technique encapsulating the desired equilibration between the explicit and the implicit interaction paradigms is needed. According to [13], even if it is possible to interact using only one interaction technique, both paradigms are needed to implement a robust and usable system.

5) Is extensible

Last but not least is the system's extensibility. Even if our development methodology is comprehensible enough to consider the different user characteristics and criteria, it is still possible that after the system's deployment in the environment, new set of properties appear to which the system should be adaptable. The system's extensibility is its' ability to adapt to the newly discovered properties and user preferences in a seamless and effective way.

To design a usable, unambiguous and user-acceptable supportive system, the set of services and assistances provided should be accessed in a user-friendly way. Thus, the design of our system should be based on a thorough understanding of the nature of activities the user usually performs in a given environment. Therefore, it is very beneficial to gradually derive the skeleton of our system from a convenient human behavior model encapsulating the tasks the user wants to execute.

Several techniques for modeling the human behavior can be employed for this purpose [25], [14], [15]. For example the planning domain definition language (PDDL) [25] is used in to model human behavior in the environment as the atomic actions are defined as PDDL operators having environmental preconditions and effects. Despite the fact that PDDL allows hierarchical modeling of actions, the notion of time is missing. To the best of our knowledge, PDDL does not provide information about the tasks' execution order or temporal interrelation. For the purpose of our work, task models [15] seem to be a proper starting point for the development of our assistive system. Task models are basically a hierarchical description and representation of the tasks a user has to perform in order to achieve a desired goal. Various notations for task models exist (HTA [3], GOMS [6], CTT [16], UAN [12]…etc.). Among those notations, CTT is the most commonly used, due to its graphical representation as well as the existence of temporal operators between subtasks on the same abstraction level allowing to determine the logical execution sequence in which the tasks should be performed.

For our approach, the smart environment domain should be thoroughly investigated in order to extract the activity patterns which are compiled and represented in the form of task models. In [27] activity patterns are defined to be *"A sequence of actions the user usually follows in order to perform a given activity in the environment"*. While the term "pattern" was initially introduced in urban architecture by C. Alexander [1], patterns have known their way to the software engineering as well as the human computer interaction (HCI) area. The gang of four [11] adopted the concept of patterns in the software engineering field by introducing them as recurring solutions for common software design problems. Given the brilliant success of the concept of reuse provided by patterns in software engineering area, HCI researchers started also to investigate their domain to extract beneficial patterns. Borchers [5] defines HCI design patterns to be *"a structured textual and graphical description of a proven solution to a recurring design problem"*. Various HCI patterns collections and languages have been compiled (e.g. [21], [22] and [23]).

Activity patterns are the basis of the development of interactive applications in smart environments according to our methodology. They are basically adaptable task models very similar to the so-called task patterns. The notion of task patterns was introduced by [4] where they identified reusable structures or templates and suggested their usage in the application's design process. Afterwards, this idea was extended in [20] where the authors suggested using patterns as generic reusable task fragments serving as building blocks for the creation of task models. They also introduced domain variables as placeholders to integrate the context of use. However, task patterns have usually been collected to denote a reusable solution for modeling the interaction of the user with the system in a given recurrent situation. On the contrary, the activity patterns we compile are extracted from the user's daily life in smart environments without yet interacting with the assistive system we strive to implement.

The paper is further structured as follows: In the next section, we start by having an overview of our approach and the proposed methodology for generating individualized assistive user interfaces. Afterwards, the two main components of the suggested methodology, namely the contextual activity patterns and the model-based user interface generation flow are thoroughly discussed and illustrated. Finally, in the last section we conclude the paper and highlight the main contribution presented by our work.

A METHODOLOGY FOR GENERATING PERSONALIZED ASSISTIVE USER INTERFACES

As already discussed, a set of crucial requirements have to be satisfied by a suitable assistive system offering optimal support to smart environments inhabitants. A thorough analysis of those requirements enables us to determine the frame of the assistive system that is suitable to be deployed in smart environments. To guarantee a high level of assistance without taking control from the user, we suggest a mixture of explicit and implicit interaction paradigms forming a hybrid user-system interaction technique. In more details, a personalized user interface is dedicated to each user in the environment. Then, the system aims to implicitly recognize the user activity taking advantage of the various sensors available in the room and thus adapts the user's personal user interface accordingly. Consequently, each user has the opportunity to explicitly access the environment's services which are relevant to the tasks currently being performed by the user. In that way, the user is not bothered with a crowded user interface encapsulating services which are irrelevant to the activity he/she performs. Instead, only services which are bound to the user's goal are displayed.

The methodology we propose is composed out of two main components which are the collection of contextual activity patterns and the user interface generation development flow. In the following, those two components are discussed in further details. It is noteworthy to mention that in the context of our work we focus on the domain of smart meeting rooms; however the proposed methodology can be generalized for all smart environments types.

I. A Collection of Contextual Activity Patterns

For the required system to be inspired from the original way users used to perform a given activity in the environment, it is highly desirable to base its development upon a human behavior model encapsulating the tasks carried out by the user and which the system aims to support. We make the same assumption which is stated in [24] and which denotes that the behavior of a given user in the environment can be approximated to the role he/she has to play. A thorough investigation of smart meeting rooms enables us to extract a set of various goals for which a group of people would gather in a meeting room. By a further analysis of those team goals, the required individual goals to be played by the different actors can be identified. For example, in the case of a conference session scenario, three distinguishable roles are recognized, namely *"Presenter"*, *"Listener"* and *"Chairman"*. Through the observation of several conference sessions, patterns of user behavior are detected. In other words, there is usually a precise logic sequence of actions a given user in the environment follows whenever he/she is playing one of the existing roles. We refer to this repetitive sequence of actions executed in order to perform a given activity and achieve a precise goal as "activity pattern". In Fig.1, a task model in CTT notation illustrating a graphical description of the tasks contained within the activity pattern corresponding to the role to be played by a given listener is depicted.

Figure 1: Task within activity pattern for Role "Listener"

The two main advantages of compiling those activity patterns is to first, provide the designer with reusable adaptable building blocks fostering the modeling process of the human behavior in smart meeting rooms, and second to derive the final assistive system based on those patterns. However, according to [9] in order to truly reflect the way the tasks are performed in the room, those tasks have to be modeled in combination with the environmental conditions under which their execution is feasible. Therefore, we strive to compile the so-called contextual activity patterns ranging from repetitive task templates to complete repetitive roles (as in Fig.1), where the environmental constraints are as well encapsulated.

In the literature, patterns authors used various notations to document their patterns. The chosen notation is usually suitable to the nature of patterns and the way they should be applied. Nevertheless, in 2003 the CHI Workshop [10] participants tried to address the pattern notation inconsistency problem in the HCI area and as an outcome, they provided the pattern language markup language (PLML) to standardize the way different patterns languages and collections should be formalized. In the context of our work, the contextual activity patterns are intended for reuse by the designers and are supposed to be integrated to the task models carrying the tasks to be performed by the different users. Thus, the solution suggested by those patterns should be understandable to both, humans and machines. Therefore, we split the notation used to store our patterns into two main parts:

a) Descriptive Information

This part contains all descriptive information about the pattern. It is structured according to PLML and gives the developer the needed knowledge about the name of the pattern, when to use it, in which context and a graphical description of the solution and the related environmental dependencies. Fig.2. presents an illustrative example of the descriptive information for the "Present Slides" pattern. As visualized, the solution provided by the pattern, the environmental dependencies as well as the execution constraints are graphically described for the designer [26].

b) Machine-readable solution

The solution encapsulated by the contextual task patterns is stored in XML format. The environmental pre and post-conditions are encapsulated in the interchangeable machine readable solution. Thus, the solution can be directly integrated in the existing task model.

77

patternID	1
Name	Present Slides
Problem	Use the projector and the presenter device in order to present some slides to the audience.
Situation	A given user in the environment has to present some slides on the canvas. This may be needed in a conference session, lecture or a discussion.
Solution	The actor who is performing this task needs to iterate over all the slides of his/her presentation and to explain them one by one. As a pre-request, he/she should be located in the presentation area, having the slides to be presented stored on his/her presenter device which is connected to the projector in use. The number of projectors needed depend on the presentation mode (e.g.: the smart room gives the user the opportunity to use only one projector for his presentation, or alternatively several ones in case the slides should be presented on more than one canvas. Only in case the presenter is deaf, he/she can use a text to speech converter to present the slides to the audience.
Related Patterns	Deaf Output Accessibility
Diagram	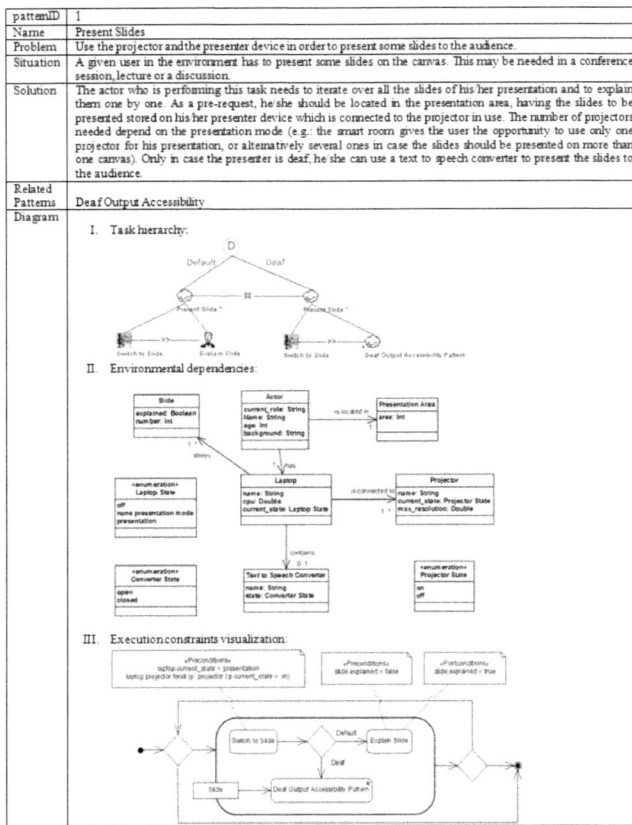

Figure 2: "Present Slides" contextual activity pattern

II. Model-based user interface generation flow

As previously described, our starting point is the analysis of the human behavior in smart meeting rooms. In the previous subsection, we presented the contextual activity patterns which can help the developer building the required models in the analysis level. In this subsection, we discuss a suggested flow for the generation of assistive user interfaces based on the existing task models and which is depicted in Fig.3. The obtained user interfaces have to render the set of services which are relevant to the activity inferred by the room based on the observation of the user in the environment using the existing sensors. Thus, whenever the room detects that the user has successfully performed a task and is currently executing another one, the dedicated user interface must be updated accordingly.

We divide the generation process of the desired user interfaces over three time frames which are "Design phase", "Deployment phase" and "Runtime phase". At design phase, the developer manually engineers step by step the task models collected in the analysis stage in order to gradually integrate the functional requirements to be satisfied by the system under design and then finally adds the required technical design decisions and non-functional requirements. In other words, this phase is the bridge between the initial state where the tasks are performed without any external support and the final state in which it

is specified the way tasks are performed using the designed assistance. The resulting task model is a detailed model based on which the design of the system is feasible. Thus, by "design phase" we refer to the transition of the task model from the analysis to the design stage. It is noteworthy to mention that at this phase, the developer only knows the smart environment type for which the application is to be tailored, (e.g. smart meeting room) but he/she is not aware of the exact room or concrete environment in which the system is to be deployed. This has the advantage of designing an application which can then be configured to suit various smart meeting rooms. Afterwards, at deployment phase, the system has to be manually configured to exactly fit to the environment in which the application is being planted. This manual configuration takes place only once and should be accomplished by the system's expert through a wizard where he/she gives as input the specific settings of the environment. In case of a smart meeting room where different presentations and talks are to be given, such settings can be for example the number of projectors, screens or lamps in the room. Finally, at runtime phase, the resident actors can connect to the application in order to be offered the different kinds of support provided by the system. To guarantee a user-specific assistance, a user profile for each resident actor has to be collected. Therefore, through a wizard each user is asked a set of questions tailoring the assistance to be compatible with his/her exact needs. This enables us to provide personalized assistance as required. Then, well-defined heuristics [28] are followed to automate the transformation process for the resulting individualized task model to the so-called dialog graph [18]. Dialog graphs define a sequence of user interactions, or an activity chain that has to be followed to achieve a desired goal. They present in an abstract way the transitions between the different views included in the final user interfaces.

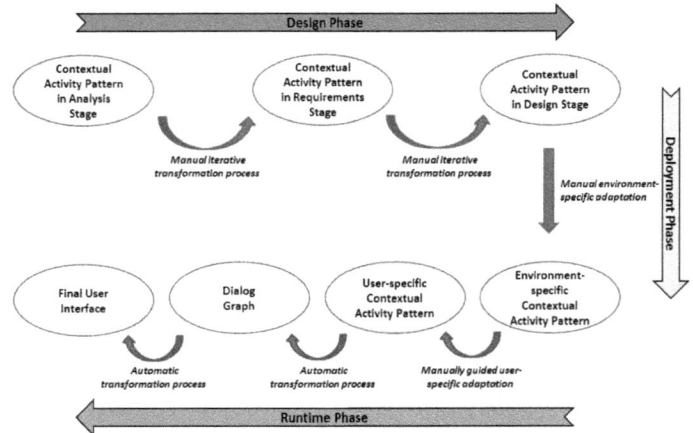

Figure 3: Flow for model-based generation of assistive user interface

Initially, dialog graphs consider only explicit transitions between the different views, where the user presses a given button on the interface in order to get directed to another view. However, as already described in our case, it should be possible to also change the view if the room recognizes that the preconditions of a new task have been satisfied. For example, after a presenter is finished with his talk, he may go back to the seats zone to listen to the next talk. In that case, the new position of the user is an indicator for another role he/she is about to play. Thus, a need for expressing implicit transitions between the different views in dialog graphs rises. Therefore, we extended the dialog graphs by the implicit sequential transition and the implicit concurrent transition. The interested reader is referred to [28]. Fig.4. pictures a dialog graph representing the different views to be displayed to an actor playing the role "presenter".

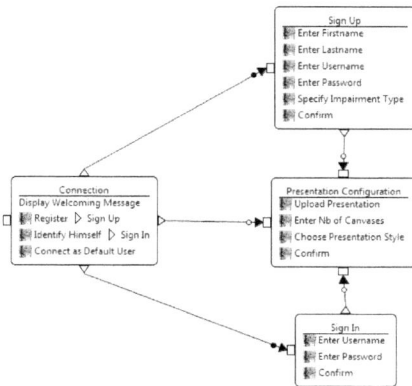

Figure 4: Dialog graph for a presenter

In the previous figure, an explicit sequential transition (noted by a black ellipse and a black triangle) exists between the "Connection" and the "Sign Up" views. This transition is triggered by pressing the button "Register". On the other hand, an implicit sequential transition (noted by a white ellipse and a black triangle) exists between the "Sign Up" and the "presentation configuration" views. This transition is triggered if the localization sensors detect that the user is standing in the presentation zone. Finally, mapping rules are guiding an automatic transformation of the generated dialog graph to a final user interface displayed for the user. Fig.5 depicts an example of such an assistive user interface. Through this interface, the presenter is offered the opportunity to configure the room according to the presentation style in which he/she would like to present the slides of the talk as well as the number of canvases that should be used. Moreover, the application has to provide the users with a centralized control over the system running in the room. Therefore, we additionally collected a set of team patterns. A team pattern is a task model similar to the one illustrated in Fig.1 in which the cooperative tasks to be carried by the users as a team are shown. This team pattern will be displayed to the room's responsible. Each cooperative task included in the team pattern is actually linked to several tasks in the individual activity patterns. Thus, whenever the room detects that the preconditions for the bound individual tasks are met, it is

assumed that the linked cooperative task is currently being executed. The room's responsible can then manually edit the team pattern and change the team task performed. Accordingly, the bound individual activity patterns will be updated. Thus, an erroneous recognition of the user activity by the room can be adjusted. In Fig.6, an animated team pattern for a "Watching video" session is shown. This session represents the situation when a group of people gather to watch a movie or a documentary for example. As visualized, the task "Enter Room" is enabled which means that the corresponding preconditions are satisfied. However, the other tasks are yet still in the disabled mode.

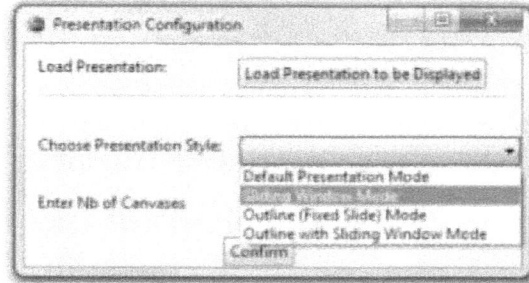

Figure 5: Presentation configuration assistive user interface

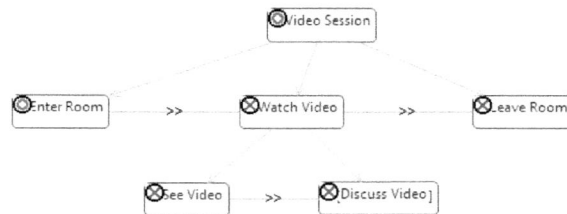

Figure 6: "Video Session" team pattern

CONCLUSION

In this paper we provided a methodology for the generation of assistive user interfaces for smart environments. We started by highlighting the main challenges and requirements that should be satisfied by an assistive system to be deployed in this kind of environments. We made it clear that there is an emerging need for an equilibrated and hybrid interaction technique to be employed in order to provide a robust system offering the needed assistance without taking the control from the user. Additionally, the need for an unambiguous system offering personalized assistance and receiving feedback from the user about the current state has been discussed. Afterwards, we suggested a methodology to be followed when the designer strives to design an application for smart environments meeting the mentioned requirements. Two main components have been presented, first the contextual activity patterns which are repetitive sequences of actions the user performs and which are stored in combination with their environmental dependencies and second, a model-based user interface generation flow where we discussed in details its various steps over the design, deployment and runtime phases.

REFERENCES

1. Alexander, C., S. I., Silverstien,M., 1977. A Pattern Language. In: Towns, Buildings,Construction, <u>Oxford University Press</u>.
2. Augusto, J. Nakashima, H. and Aghajan, H. Ambient Intelligence and Smart Environments: A State of the Art, *Handbook of Ambient Intelligence and Smart Environments, (2010)*.
3. Annett,J. and Duncan,K.D. Task Analysis and Training Design, Occupational Psychology, Volume 41, pp. 211-221, 1967.
4. Breedvelt-Schouten, I.M., Paternò, F., and Severijns, C. 1997. Reusable structures in task models. *In Proceedings of DSV-IS : 225-239.*
5. Borchers,J., 2001. A pattern approach to interaction design, DIS '00 Proceedings of the 3rd conference on Designing interactive systems: processes, practices, methods, and techniques. ISBN: 1-58113-219-0: 369-378.
6. Card,S, Moran.T, and Newell,A. , The psychology of Human Computer Interaction, Lawrence Erlbaum, pp. 357-366, 1983.
7. Cook, D. and Das, S. (2004). Smart Environments: Technology, Protocols and Applications (Wiley Series on Parallel and Distributed Computing).
8. Cook, D.J.; Youngblood, M.; Heierman, E.O., III; Gopalratnam, K.; Rao, S.; Litvin, A.; Khawaja, F., "MavHome: an agent-based smart home," *Pervasive Computing and Communications, 2003. (PerCom 2003). Proceedings of the First IEEE International Conference on* , vol., no., pp.521,524, 23-26 March 2003
9. Dittmar, A. and Forbrig, P. Higher-Order Task Models, Interactive Systems. Design, Specification, and Verification, Lecture Notes in Computer Science series, Volume 2844, pp. 219-230, 2003.
10. Fincher,S. Perspectives on HCI patterns: concepts and tools (introducing PLML). In Workshop at CHI 2003.
11. Gamma,E., H.,R., Johnson, R., Vlissides, J., 1994. Design Patterns: Elements of Reusable Object-Oriented Software. *Reading, Mass., Addison-Wesley.*
12. Hartson,R. and Gray,P. , Temporal Aspects of Tasks in the User Action Notation, Human Computer Interaction, Volume 7, pp. 1-45, 1992.
13. Ju, W. and Leifer, L. (2008). The design of implicit interactions: Making interactive systems less obnoxious.
14. Matessa, M. (2004) An ACT-R modeling framework for interleving templates of human behavior. In proceedings of the *26th Annual Conference of the Cognitive Science Society* (pp. 903-908) . August 4-7, Chicago, USA
15. Paterno, F. Task Models in Interactive Software Systems. IN HANDBOOK OF SOFTWARE ENGINEERING AND KNOWLEDGE, World Scientific Publishing Co.
16. Paterno, F., M,C., Meniconi, C., 1997. ConcurTaskTrees: A diagrammatic Notation for Specifying Task Models, in INTERACT 97, IFIP TC13: 362-369.
17. Ponnekanti, S. R., L. A. Robles and A. Fox (2002). User Interfaces for Network Services: What, from Where, and How. Proceedings of the Fourth IEEE Workshop on Mobile Computing Systems and Applications, IEEE Computer Society.
18. Schlungbaum, E. and Elwert, T. (1996). Dialogue graphs-a formal and visual specification technique for dialogue modelling.
19. Schmidt, A. (2000). "Implicit Human Computer Interaction Through Context." Personal and Ubiquitous Computing 4.
20. Sinnig, D. (2004) The Complicity of Patterns and Model-Based Engineering, Master Thesis in the Department of Computer Science, Concordia University, Montreal (Canada).
21. Tidwell, J. (1999). Common Ground: A Pattern Language for Human-Computer Interface Design. Available at http://www.mit.edu/~jtidwell/interaction_patterns.html (last accessed: 2013.03.25).
22. Tidwell, J. (2004). UI Patterns and Techniques. Available athttp://time-tripper.com/uipatterns/index.php (last accessed: 2013.03.25).
23. Welie, M. (2004). Patterns in Interaction Design. Available at http://www.welie.com/ (last accessed: 2013.03.25).
24. Wurdel, M., Sinnig, D., Forbrig, P., 2008. CTML: Domain and Task Modeling for Collaborative Environments. *J.UCS 14: 3188-3201.*
25. Yordanova, K., "Modelling Human Behaviour Using Partial Order Planning Based on Atomic Action Templates," *Intelligent Environments (IE), 2011 7th International Conference on* , vol., no., pp.338,341, 25-28 July 2011 doi: 10.1109/IE.2011.27
26. Zaki, M., Bruening, J., and Forbrig, P. Towards contextual task patterns for smart meeting rooms. In Pervasive and Embedded Computing and Communication Systems (PECCS), SciTePress, isbn = 978-989-8565-00-6, pp. 162-169, 2012.
27. Zaki, M. and Forbirg,P., Towards the Generation of Assistive User Interfaces for Smart Meeting Rooms based on Activity Patterns, AMI, Springer, isbn = 978-3-642-34897-6, pp. 288-295, 2012.
28. Zaki, M. and Forbrig, P Making Task Models and Dialog Graphs Suitable for Generating Assistive and Adaptable User Interfaces for Smart Environments. In Pervasive and Embedded Computing and Communication Systems (PECCS), SciTePress, 2013.

Verification of interactive software for medical devices: PCA infusion pumps and FDA regulation as an example

Paolo Masci, Paul Curzon
Michael D. Harrison
Queen Mary University of London
United Kingdom
{paolo.masci,pc,mdh}@eecs.qmul.ac.uk

Anaheed Ayoub, Insup Lee
University of Pennsylvania
Philadelphia, PA, USA
{anaheed,lee}@seas.upenn.edu

Harold Thimbleby
Swansea University
United Kingdom
h.thimbleby@swansea.ac.uk

ABSTRACT

Medical device regulators such as the US Food and Drug Administration (FDA) aim to make sure that medical devices are reasonably safe before entering the market. To expedite the approval process and make it more uniform and rigorous, regulators are considering the development of reference models that encapsulate safety requirements against which software incorporated in to medical devices must be verified. Safety, insofar as it relates to interactive systems and its regulation, is generally a neglected topic, particularly in the context of medical systems. An example is presented here that illustrates how the interactive behaviour of a commercial Patient Controlled Analgesia (PCA) infusion pump can be verified against a reference model. Infusion pumps are medical devices used in healthcare to deliver drugs to patients, and PCA pumps are particular infusion pump devices that are often used to provide pain relief to patients on demand. The reference model encapsulates the Generic PCA safety requirements provided by the FDA, and the verification is performed using a refinement approach. The contribution of this work is that it demonstrates a concise and semantically unambiguous approach to representing what a regulator's requirements for a particular interactive device might be, in this case focusing on user-interface requirements. It provides an inspectable and repeatable process for demonstrating that the requirements are satisfied. It has the potential to replace the considerable documentation produced at the moment by a succinct document that can be subjected to careful and systematic analysis.

Author Keywords

Software Engineering Methods and Processes - Formal; Model-Based System Development.

ACM Classification Keywords

D.2.4. [Software/Program Verification];
D.2.2. [Design Tools and Techniques: User Interfaces]

INTRODUCTION

Many interactive systems are safety critical in the sense that user action may have consequences that will compromise safety (i.e., cause damage or harm). An important aspect of the engineering of interactive computer systems is to provide appropriate processes and evidence that systems are designed to satisfy the various requirements that have been established to reduce the risk of products causing such harm. This paper addresses the engineering problem by describing a formal technique that supports proof that user interface related safety requirements are satisfied in a specified interactive systems design. The medical domain is chosen to demonstrate the approach.

In many countries, medical equipment undergoes a degree of scrutiny prior to being placed on the market. This scrutiny is required by regulators to provide confidence that the device is safe and fit for purpose, and (through the statutory role of regulation) to manage potential litigation if defects are later discovered. Currently, device approval is not standardised across nations, and how the approval process should be carried out [18, 19] continues to be a matter for debate. Current approaches to medical device regulation typically combine premarket review and post-market surveillance. As part of the premarket review, manufacturers are required to "demonstrate the safety and effectiveness of a device" prior to introduction to market. Post-market surveillance involves the development of monitoring mechanisms to identify potential safety issues with deployed devices — in some cases these issues only become apparent after the device has been in service for several years with a large user population.

The level of scrutiny imposed by regulators in the premarket review depends on risks in device use. The US Food and Drug Administration (FDA), which is taken as a benchmark by many other countries, e.g., in Japan and China [10], has identified three main risk classes of medical devices. *Class I* medical devices are low risk devices subject only to "general controls" [23] for example relating to misbranding. An example of a Class I device is a syringe. *Class II* medical devices are medium risk devices that require general controls (the same as Class I devices) plus "special controls" such as verification of mandatory performance and safety requirements. External infusion pumps, used as examples in the paper, belong to this class. *Class III* medical devices are high risk devices that support or sustain human life and are of substantial importance in preventing impairment of human health. Examples include implantable devices such as pacemakers. These devices require general controls and "premarket approval". This involves submitting sufficient engineering and clinical evaluation evidence that the device can be safely deployed in its intended context. Most marketed medical devices are classified as Class II devices [24] because medical devices can be considered as Class II by regulators when manufacturers can demonstrate substantial equivalence to already legally marketed devices. A new device is substantially equivalent to a legally marketed device when it has the same intended use and either the same technological characteristics or different technological characteristics that do not raise new questions of safety and effectiveness. The manufacturer can satisfy the regulator by demonstrating that the new device is at least as safe and effective as the already marketed device. This review process is described in the *Premarket Notification document* [25], known as 510(k) clearance.

The FDA's Centre for Devices and Radiological Health (CDRH), which is responsible for medical device review, is fairly small and needs to review a large number of devices each year [29]. Recent figures suggest that over five thousand new devices require 510(k) clearance each year. 510(k) applications must be substantively reviewed within 90 calendar days of the date at which they were filed [27]. Device approval is entirely based on written documents and does not involve any direct evaluation of the product. The typical size of a 510(k) submission is tens of thousands of printed pages.

The FDA is currently reviewing the 510(k) clearance process because a number of unexpected incidents have involved cleared medical devices. There are a growing number of device recalls issued over the last few years for dangerous or defective products that could cause serious health consequences or death [3].

Several incidents have been due to external drug infusion pumps, most commonly a result of (i) "software errors" and (ii) "human factors errors" (e.g., use errors) [26].

To promote a more rigorous analysis of infusion pumps, the FDA is running a pilot project, the *Generic Infusion Pump* (GIP) [2], that aims to demonstrate how systematic and rigorous model-based analysis can be applied to software for infusion pumps. The idea is to specify safety requirements for broad classes of infusion pumps, such as Patient Controlled Analgesia and Insulin pumps. As part of the GIP project, Kim et al [9] have demonstrated how a model-based development approach can be used to implement software for the controller of a Patient Controlled Analgesia (PCA) pump verified against the Generic PCA (GPCA) safety requirements provided by the FDA. This paper, in contrast, focuses on the user interface module of a commercial infusion pump of the

PCA family. It takes a different approach with a focus on user interface requirements, by creating a model from the software of an existing product and then verifying this model against the required safety requirements to verify the interactive behaviour of the already implemented software.

The *contributions* of this paper are: (i) a verification approach, based on reverse engineering and model refinement that allows the verification of interactive software incorporated in user interfaces of medical devices (such as infusion pumps) against given safety requirements; (ii) a tool-neutral formalisation of selected GPCA safety requirements; (iii) an example based on a commercial PCA infusion pump, where PVS [14] (a higher-order logic based verification system) is used to verify a reverse engineered version of the software incorporated in the pump user interface against the GPCA safety requirements.

The structure of the paper is as follows. After discussing related research, the verification approach is presented. It combines reverse engineering and model refinement. A formalisation of the GPCA safety requirements provided by the FDA is developed in a form suitable for use with refinement approaches. The PVS verification system is then used to specify and verify the interactive behaviour of a commercial PCA pump against the formalised safety requirements. This leads to a discussion of the utility of the approach within the current regulatory and production cycles of medical devices. Finally conclusions are drawn.

RELATED WORK
The work described in this paper brings together a number of threads of previous research.

The verification of interactive systems against requirements has been performed both informally using techniques such as heuristic evaluation [13] and formally using model checking techniques [7]. Indeed the models that are behind the concrete models described in this paper were originally developed for model checking analyses using MAL and NuSMV. Other work checking properties of interactive behaviour includes the use of PVS to analyse predictability in number entry [11, 12]. The use of finite state machines to describe interactive systems has a very long history originating in the early 1980s. Notable in this history has been the work of Degani [6] and Thimbleby [21].

The original GPCA safety requirements [2] were also formalised in [9]. In that work, the authors verified the controller of the GPCA model provided by the FDA against the GPCA safety requirements. They used an approach based on model transformations and manually translated the safety requirements into properties of the controller of a formalisation of the GPCA model. Here, in contrast, (i) an approach is used based on refinement — this makes it possible to specify safety requirements independently of the model to be verified; and (ii) verification of the user-interface related GPCA safety requirements is carried out on the user interface of a commercial PCA pump, thus demonstrating that formal verification can be used effectively even if software has been already developed and the model (if there was any) is not available.

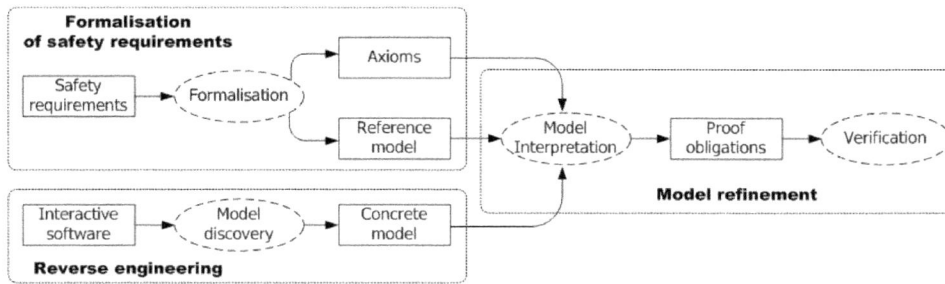

Figure 1. Approach based on reverse engineering and model refinement.

A refinement approach similar to that used in our work has been used in [16] for redeveloping core parts of a commercial air traffic information system. The functional requirements of the system were given as a VDM specification, and the original development produced a single large specification that was hard to comprehend and analyse. Event-B and the Rodin platform were used for creating an abstract specification that captured the core functionalities of the system. This abstract specification was then gradually refined to a distributed model that allowed reasoning about the consistency of the specification. This work shares with ours the use of a verification approach based on refinement for the verification of an already implemented system. However, in their work refinement is used just for reasoning about the consistency of the specification. In our work, in contrast, refinement is used to verify the interactive behaviour of an existing user interface against safety requirements independently provided by regulators.

Bowen and Reeves [5] presented a refinement approach for user interface design. Their work specifically targets the design of user interface layouts. Presentation Interaction Models (PIMs) are used to describe the user interface layout in terms of its component widgets. They use a mixture of formal and informal refinement for turning the initial specification into its implementation. Their work targets the verification of user interface layout. With this perspective, their approach could be used in a complementary way to ours, which is concerned with the verification of user interface behaviour.

THE VERIFICATION APPROACH
The verification approach combines reverse engineering and model refinement (see Figure 1). The verification process starts with two independent branches:

- *Formalisation of safety requirements*: An abstract representation of safety requirements is created that highlights relevant functionalities of the implemented software to be verified. This abstract representation is specified by means of properties (axioms) of a model, hereafter called the *reference model* of the user interface.

- *Reverse engineering*: An accurate model of the behaviour of interactive software incorporated in the device user interface is obtained through systematic exploration of the user interface functionalities and analysis of specification documents (e.g., user manuals). This accurate model will be referred to as the *concrete model* of the user interface.

Model refinement merges these two branches together. Model refinement relates the semantics of two models (the reference model and the concrete model in this case) and shows that the behaviour of the two models is constrained by the refinement relation. A technique called *model interpretation* is used in this work to perform refinement. Model interpretation transforms axioms of the reference model into proof obligations for the concrete model. Discharging these proof obligations makes it possible to demonstrate that the concrete model meets given safety requirements.

Formalisation of safety requirements. Safety requirements are typically provided within a document written in natural language. The approach translates the informal description into a specification by identifying key notions and relationships in the textual description. This identification process is based on heuristics [28], and can be performed either manually, or semi-automatically through natural language processing techniques. Here, a manual identification is performed as it is sufficient to demonstrate the approach. The aim of the formalisation is to create a model (the *reference model*) that will form the basis for the analysis of the implemented software. The reference model encapsulates the semantics of the requirements and can provide guidance when performing verification of the final implemented software, as a systematic comparison against the reference model helps to understand the correspondence between functionalities of the user interface behaviour and the safety requirements.

Reverse engineering. Reverse engineering makes it possible to create a detailed model (the *concrete model*) of a product (interactive software in this case) that can be used for analysis or re-engineering. Techniques that are suitable for reverse engineering a user interface include *model-discovery* [22] and *interaction walkthrough* [20]. Both techniques develop a *parallel system* from the concrete implementation by exploring implemented functionalities systematically. These approaches can be applied either by the development team (in this case compiled or source code would probably be the starting point), or by independent third parties (in this case the final product would probably be the starting point).

Model refinement. Refinement is a formal process that makes it possible to relate the semantics of two models and show that the behaviour of the two models are constrained by the refinement relation. This form of refinement is usually referred to as "structural" or "vertical" refinement, and the refinement relation is usually called the *glueing invari-*

ant. Safety requirements can be verified by this means. The reference model is used as the source model. The concrete model obtained through reverse engineering is used as the target model. The refinement relation connects the reference model to the concrete model. This makes it possible to translate axioms of the reference model (which encapsulate the semantics of given safety requirements) into safety properties for the concrete model. These safety properties of the concrete models are called *proof obligations*, and they are to be verified in order to demonstrate that the safety requirements are met.

The next sections illustrate the approach in more detail. First, a tool-neutral formalisation based on predicate logic is presented of the GPCA safety requirements relating to usability. The reverse engineering and refinement-based verification approach are then demonstrated using PVS [14]. The analysis is performed on the user interface of a commercial PCA infusion pump [4].

FORMALISATION OF THE GPCA REQUIREMENTS

The FDA has released a draft document [2] that includes safety requirements for PCA pumps.

Patients interact with the PCA pump with the help of a single button. This can be used by them to request an additional pre-specified amount of pain relief medication called a "bolus." The pump is pre-programmed by a clinician by specifying the infusion parameters within hard limits, usually preset by a technician, as appropriate for the class of treatment. PCA pumps, particularly epidural pumps, are small and can be carried conveniently by patients outside hospitals without clinical supervision.

The GPCA safety requirements are designed to mitigate identified hazards [2] for the software of PCA pump controllers. However, out of 97 GPCA requirements, we found that almost half of them can be actually related to user interface functionalities. These requirements have been designed by the FDA to be easily translated into a specification in either a programming language or formal language.

The first step in our formalisation process is to extract those terms that specify functionalities of the reference model that are relevant to the semantics of the safety requirement. The second step is to translate the semantics of each safety requirement into a logic formula. This translation step defines relational constraints that must be verified to meet the corresponding safety requirement. This systematic process leads to the creation of a model (the *reference model*) given as an abstract state machine — each extracted term defines a state transition function of the reference model, and each safety requirements is a property (axiom) of the reference model.

The formalisation of selected GPCA safety requirements provided by the FDA is now illustrated. In some cases the formalisation is based on our understanding of their semantics. A further process would be required in which the formalisation is validated with the FDA. In some cases there appears to be overlap or duplication between requirements. This process of formalisation and negotiation is valuable in bringing clarity to established safety requirements. Classical logic operators such as ∧ (conjunction), ∨ (disjunction), ⇒ (implication) are used to establish logic relations.

R1. *Clearing of the pump settings and resetting of the pump shall require confirmation.* (GPCA safety requirement 2.2.3 about user input [2])

This safety requirement is designed to mitigate some hazards that arise when clinicians or patients change infusion settings inadvertently. The terms that are extracted from the requirement are: **clearing settings**, **resetting pump**, and **require confirmation**. **R1** is ambiguous because the English "and" could mean a logical or, a logical and, or requiring the actions in a sequence. Further enquiries with the FDA confirmed the interpretation "or." The following formalisation reflects the concepts described in the requirement:

$$(clearing\_settings \lor resetting\_pump) \Rightarrow require\_confirmation$$

The formalisation also begs important questions that are not explicit in the requirement. For example, does resetting the pump imply changing the settings? Can settings be cleared if they have already been cleared? Can the pump be used if the settings are cleared? Analysis by the manufacturer during this process would enable them to probe other features of their design, which while not being crucial to safety would allow them to improve the design's usability.

R2. *To avoid accidental tampering of the infusion pump's settings such as flow rate/vtbi[1], at least two steps should be required to change the setting.* (GPCA safety requirement 2.1.1 about user interface resistance to tampering and accidents [2])

This safety requirement is designed to mitigate hazards that result from accidental or intentional tampering with pump settings without authorisation. The formalisation of this requirement introduces the following terms: **changing settings** and **require two steps**:

$$changing\_settings \Rightarrow require\_two\_steps$$

Although there may be a relation between the "two steps" requirement for **R2** and the "confirmation" requirement mentioned in **R1**, this relation is not explicit in the GPCA safety requirements. To leave room for different interpretations, *require_two_steps* is introduced instead of reusing the term *require_confirmation* from requirement **R1**.

R3. *The pump shall issue an alert if paused for more than t minutes.* (GPCA safety requirement 2.2.2 about user input [2])

This safety requirement is designed to mitigate situations where the infusion settings are inadvertently changed. The relevant terms are: **issue alert**, **paused more than t minutes**. The second term embeds two notions: the pump is paused, and the pump state has been the same for at least a given period of time. These terms keep the specification as general as possible, avoiding the necessity to be too specific about the meaning of "more than" — does it mean strictly greater

---

[1]VTBI stands for "volume to be infused" and is the limit of the total dose the pump will provide.

than ($>$) or greater than or equal ($\geq$)? During interactive data entry this distinction may make a difference. The philosophy followed here is that the formalisation must not add more constraints in this phase than those described in the safety requirement. Given that the safety requirement is not specific about the meaning of "more than", the same should be true for the formalisation. The natural language description of the requirement need to be modified if "more than t minutes" needs to be more specific. The developed formalisation follows.

$$paused\_more\_than\_t\_minutes \Rightarrow issue\_alert$$

R4. *If the pump is in a state where user input is required, the pump shall issue periodic alerts/indications every t minutes until the required input is provided.* (GPCA safety requirement 2.2.1 about user input [2])

This safety requirement is designed to mitigate situations in which incomplete infusion parameters have been entered. The relevant terms are: **user input required**, **periodic alerts every t minutes**, **required input provided**. The terms extracted in this requirement can be phrased for reuse: the statement "*until the required input is provided*" can be rephrased into the equivalent statement "*if the required input is provided then the periodic alerts/indications are cancelled.*" This rephrasing makes it possible to reuse **required input provided**, and leads to the identification of a new term **alert cancelled**. This reformulation does not change the semantics of the requirement — it is not adding additional constraints, and makes explicit an implicit relation between two concepts described in the same requirement. The requirement can be formalised as follows:

$$(user\_input\_required \Rightarrow periodic\_alerts\_every\_t\_minutes) \land$$
$$((periodic\_alerts\_every\_t\_minutes \land required\_input\_provided)$$
$$\Rightarrow alert\_cancelled)$$

R5. *The flow rate for the pump shall be programmable.* (GPCA safety requirement 1.1.1 about flow rate infusion control [2])

This safety requirement is designed to mitigate hazards that result from incorrectly specified infusion parameters (e.g., flow rate too high or too low). To keep the formalisation general a single notion is introduced, **flow rate programmable** which allows different definitions of "programmable", e.g., a sequence of button clicks (this is the typical solution for the current generation of infusion pumps), wireless communication from the pharmacy, or voice activation controls (these functionalities are envisaged in future generations of infusion pumps). The specific definition will be given when mapping functionalities of a real device to the identified concept. This requirement is thus formalised as follows:

$$flow\_rate\_programmable$$

The rest of the paper uses the formalisation of the GPCA safety requirements to verify the interactive behaviour of a commercial PCA pump [4]. The requirements are translated into a PVS [14] specification. The PVS theorem prover is then used to verify that a concrete user interface model maintains a defined refinement relation with the reference model.

VERIFICATION OF A COMMERCIAL PCA PUMP

The logic-based formalisation of the GPCA safety requirements is used to develop a PVS specification of the reference model. The specification is given as a set of properties (axioms) over the model. This development approach guarantees that the reference model meets the formalised requirements.

The PVS specification language builds on classical typed higher-order logic with the usual base types (e.g., `bool`, `nat`, `integer` and `real`), function type constructors `[A -> B]` (predicates are functions with range type `bool`), and abstract data types. The language supports *predicate subtyping*, which is a powerful mechanism to express complex consistency requirements.

PVS specifications are organised into modules called *theories* that describe types, axioms, definitions and theorems. Theories can be parametric in types and constants, and they can use definitions and theorems of other theories by importing them. PVS provides a pre-defined built-in prelude, and a number of loadable libraries of standard definitions and proved facts that can be used when developing new theories.

PVS has an automated theorem prover that can be used to interactively apply powerful inference procedures within a sequent calculus framework. The primitive inferences procedures include, among others, propositional and quantifier rules, induction, simplification using decision procedures for equality and linear arithmetic, data and predicate abstraction.

Formalisation of safety requirements

The extracted terms identified in the previous section define the transition functions (hereafter *function recognisers*) of the reference model. Function recognisers can be specified in PVS using uninterpreted predicates. For example the predicate `require_confirmation?` translates the recogniser *require_confirmation*. By this means GPCA safety requirements can be expressed as axioms of the reference model. As an illustration a complete example for safety requirement **R1** is given here. The specification and verification of the other requirements can be done similarly but are not included for lack of space. The reference model is specified in theory `reference_model_th` given in Listing 1.

Listing 1. The Reference Model

```
reference_model_th: THEORY BEGIN
ui_state: TYPE
st,st0,st1: VAR ui_state

clearing_settings?(st): boolean
resetting_pump?(st): boolean
require_confirmation?(st): boolean

%-- requirement R1
R1(st): boolean =
  (clearing_settings?(st) OR resetting_pump?(st))
    => require_confirmation?(st)

R1_Axiom: AXIOM
  (init?(st) => R1(st)) AND
  ((R1(st0) AND R1_trans(st0, st1)) => R1(st1))
END reference_model_th
```

The state of the reference model is defined with an uninter-preted type, ui_state. Two logical variables, st0 and st1, identify the current state and the next state of the reference model respectively. A third logical variable, st, identifies a generic state of the reference model. When using theory interpretation, these logical variables of the reference model can be mapped to one or more states of the concrete model. Because of this, at this stage it is not necessary to specify how many distinct states are needed to express the requirement.

Safety requirements are specified as axioms of the reference model. Given that the safety properties are to be verified in a theorem prover, a sensible choice is to specify axioms in a form that supports structural induction. Structural induction proves a predicate R modelling a safety property as follows: (i) R must hold for the initial system state (base case); (ii) if R holds in a state $st0$, then R holds also for any state $st1$ resulting from $st0$ by applying any transition function (inductive step). This is illustrated in the specification of R1_axiom in Listing 1 for safety requirement **R1**. In the PVS specification, init? identifies the initial system state; R1_trans is the set of transitions; R1 translates the logic-based formalisation of requirement **R1** into a predicate.

Reverse engineering

A reproduction of the layout of the particular PCA pump [4] considered in this work is shown in Figure 2. A detailed model of the interactive behaviour of a commercial volu-metric infusion pump that shares many of the characteristics of this device is described in [7]. The model has been obtained by reverse engineering the pump using interaction walkthrough [20]. The model is specified using a "layered" approach to enable specification reuse. The inner "pump" layer abstracts the behaviour of the controller for devices of the same class. The middle "device" layer is specific to the device being modelled and describes its user interface be-haviour. The outer "activity" layer (which is not needed here) describes intended user activities. The original model is given in Modal Action Logic (MAL) [17] and is available in the Minho repository (**http://hcispecs.di.uminho.pt**).

This MAL specification has been translated into PVS higher order logic. The use of PVS is motivated by the fact that (i) PVS has a mechanism (*theory interpretations* [15]) for per-forming model refinement, and (ii) PVS has an expressive specification language which allowed us to create a specifi-cation that can be mapped easily to the original MAL model. Other tools that support refinement like Rodin [1] have a less rich specification language, and translating the original MAL specification would have been less straightforward. A frag-ment of the MAL specification is sufficient to illustrate the verification approach. Relevant excerpts of the developed PVS model that translate those fragments are now illustrated.

The state of the inner "pump" layer is specified in theory pump_th with a new PVS record type, pump as shown in Listing 2. The type has four fields: powered_on? is a Boolean field modelling whether the pump is turned on; infusing? is a Boolean field modelling whether an infu-sion is running; infusionrate is a bounded non-negative real number modelling the actual rate pumped by the device;

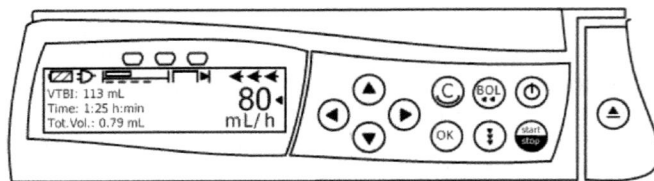

Figure 2. Reproduction of the layout of the commercial PCA pump user interface analysed in this work.

and time is a bounded non-negative real number modelling the time left to complete the programmed infusion.

Listing 2. The 'pump' layer

```
pump: TYPE =
[# powered_on? : boolean,
   infusing?   : boolean,
   infusionrate: {x: nonneg_real | x < maxrate},
   time        : {x: nonneg_real | x < maxtime} #]
```

The state of the user interface is specified in theory concrete_model_th with a new PVS record type, concrete_state given in Listing 3. The type includes the following fields: device of type pump holds the state of the inner "pump" layer; the enumerated type displaymode identifies the current display mode of the user interface; disprate models the rate displayed by the user interface and has type irates, a record with two fields — val, a real number, and vis, a Boolean that models whether the rate is visible on the user interface; entrymode, an enumerated type that models two generic user interface modes — interac-tive data entry mode (an interactive mode where the user en-ters the infusion parameters) or in confirm mode (where the interface requires input from the user); two fields prevdm and prevem that store the previous display mode and entry mode (this information is used for the functionalities of but-tons like clear that need to restore the previous display and entry modes); timeout, a field holding the timer counter used in various user interface modes; btnpressed, an enu-merated field that stores information about the button being clicked — this is used to support modelling of key *press & hold* interactions.

Listing 3. The 'device' layer

```
concrete_state: TYPE =
[# device      : pump,
   displaymode : dispmode,
   disprate    : irates,
   entrymode   : emode,
   prevdm      : dispmode,
   prevem      : emode,
   timeout     : nonneg_real,
   btnpressed  : btnID #]
```

Actions are specified as transition functions over states of the user interface (concrete_state). An example of an ac-tion is on. This describes the behaviour of the *on* button that toggles the pump on and off. The behaviour of *on* and *clear* is now illustrated as they are relevant to requirement **R1**.

Button *on* can be used to reset the pump settings. When the device is powered off, interactions with the *on* button involve button clicks (a button click turns on the pump). When the device is powered on, pressing and holding down the button for more than 3 seconds turns the pump off. When the *on* button is initially pressed, the user interface enters a confirmation mode and a countdown elapses while the button is continuously held down. A way to model this functionality is to split the specification of transition function on into two parts: one for *key pressed* actions (on_pressed, as shown in Listing 4), and the other one for *key released* actions (on_released, as shown in Listing 5).

A detailed illustration of function on_pressed given in Listing 4 is now provided. The argument, p, of the function is a device state. The type of p is a subtype of concrete_state obtained through predicate per_press_on. The predicate translates a MAL "permission", that is the condition under which the action can be applied. The use of permissions is useful to enforce legal sequences. In this case, for instance, the permission states that the press action for button *on* can be performed only if another button is not already pressed. This reflects the actual behaviour of the pump user interface, which disables pressing multiple-keys simultaneously. The return type of on_pressed is concrete_state. The body of the function is thus defined. The button overloads the on and off functionalities. Therefore a distinction is made for the two cases. If the device is powered on (the condition is encoded in the Boolean field powered_on? of the device layer device(p)) and the user interface is not showing a power off confirmation message (condition NOT msg_turningoff? in Listing 4) then the user interface enters a confirmation mode where the power off message is shown. A timer is also started that expires in 3 seconds. The user interface stays in this confirmation mode as long as the *on* button is pressed and held down continuously (condition msg_turningoff?(..) AND timeout(p)-1>0 in Listing 4). When the timer expires, the pump powers off.

Listing 4. Specification of the *on* button pressed action

```
on_pressed(p: (per_press_on))
 : concrete_state =
IF device(p)'powered_on?
 THEN
   COND
   NOT msg_turningoff?(displaymode(p))
   -> display_poweroff_confirmation(p, 3),
   msg_turningoff?(displaymode(p))
     AND timeout(p) - 1 > 0
   -> decrement_poweroff_timer(p),
   msg_turningoff?(displaymode(p))
     AND timeout(p) - 1 <= 0
   -> power_down(p)
   ENDCOND
 ELSE power_up(p) ENDIF
```

The specification of function on_released is given in a similar way. The *on* button can be released only after being pressed (subtype (per_release_on) for the argument p). The body of the function specifies that the action restores the previous user interface state if the power off countdown was started. Otherwise, the function just resets the action permissions (function restore_permission).

Listing 5. Specification of the *on* button released action

```
on_released(p: (per_release_on))
  : concrete_state =
IF device(p)'powered_on?
  AND msg_turningoff?(displaymode(p))
 THEN restore_prevmode(p)
 ELSE restore_permission(p) ENDIF
```

Button *clear* can be used to clear settings. Interactions with the *clear* button involve button clicks while the pump is turned on. The cases given in Listing 6 describe the behaviour of the button: (i) if the user interface is in interactive data-entry mode, a *clear* button click zeroes the value on the display and moves the pump into a confirmation mode; (ii) if the user interface is alarming, a *clear* button click clears the alarm; (iii) if the user interface is displaying the main menu and the device is not infusing, then the *clear* button makes it possible to clear the infusion parameters; (iv) if the device is not infusing then the *clear* button makes it possible to navigate in reverse order the bootstrap sequence of the user interface screens (main screen, main menu, use last therapy, and new patient). When in confirmation mode, if the user interface is left idle for predefined time periods then the user interface enters an alert mode. An excerpt of the PVS specification for click actions of button *clear* (clear_clicked) is given in Listing 6. A detailed description is omitted from this paper due to lack of space.

Listing 6. Specification of the *clear* button

```
clear_clicked(p: (per_click_clear))
  : concrete_state =
IF disprate?(displaymode(p))
    AND entrymode(p) = dataentry
 THEN clear_display(p,cm_timeout)
ELSIF mainmenu?(displaymode(p))
        AND entrymode(p) = nullemode THEN COND
  device(p)'infusing? = FALSE
   -> display_last_therapy(p, tm_timeout),
  device(p)'infusing? = TRUE
   -> display_mainscreen(p,0) ENDCOND
ELSIF %.. additional conditions omitted
```

Model refinement

Model refinement can be implemented in PVS through theory interpretations [15]. It is a way to give semantics to uninterpreted terms by mapping them to concrete expressions. In this case the reference model is interpreted using the concrete model. Given that the reference model is an abstract state machine specified in terms of function recognisers, the interpretation consists of mapping functionalities of the concrete model into those function recognisers. With this approach, axioms of the reference model are turned into proof obligations for the concrete model. Discharging these proof obligations makes it possible to show that the behaviour of the concrete model is *consistent* with the behaviour of the reference model. The reference model is verified against the safety requirements by construction — safety requirements are properties (axioms) of the model. Therefore the verification of proof obligations corresponds to demonstrating that the concrete model meets the same safety requirements.

Theory interpretation is now applied to refine function recognisers used for the axiom (R1_axiom) that specifies safety requirement **R1**. The syntax for specifying a theory interpretation in PVS is that of a PVS theory importing clause (keyword IMPORTING followed by the theory name) with actual parameters (a list of substitutions provided within double curly brackets).

For R1_axiom, an interpretation must be provided for the following types and constants (Listing 7): the reference model state (ui_state) is interpreted with a pair of concrete user interface states in this case (the current and the next device state); the uninterpreted constant init? is interpreted with the predicate concrete_init? that identifies the initial state of the concrete model; R1_trans is interpreted by enumerating all actions (transition functions) of the user interface:

Listing 7. Theory interpretation for requirement R1 (part 1 of 4)

```
IMPORTING reference_model_th {{
ui_state := [concrete_state, concrete_state],
init? := LAMBDA (st: [concrete_state,
                      concrete_state]):
    concrete_init?(st`1),
R1_trans := LAMBDA (st, st_prime:
                    [concrete_state,
                     concrete_state]):
    (per_click_clear(st`1) AND
      st_prime`1 = clear_clicked(st`1)) OR %...
```

The interpretations of the function recognisers "*clearing settings*," "*resetting pump*" and "*require confirmation*" in terms of the concrete model are as follows.

Clearing settings. The PCA pump under analysis makes it possible to clear settings with the *clear* button in the following situations (Listing 8): (i) when the user is entering infusion parameters (i.e., the outer layer of the concrete model is in dataentry mode), irrespective of whether or not the device is infusing; (ii) from the main menu, when the pump is not infusing (i.e., the outer layer of the concrete model is in mainmenu mode and the infusing? field of the inner layer is *false*). This mapping relation is specified in terms of the theory interpretation parameters:

Listing 8. Theory interpretation for requirement R1 (part 2 of 4)

```
clearing_settings?
 := LAMBDA (st: [concrete_state, concrete_state]):
    (dataentry?(entrymode(st`1))
     OR (mainmenu?(displaymode(st`1))
       AND NOT infusing?(device(st`1))))
      AND per_click_clear(st`1)
        AND st`2 = clear_clicked(st`1),
```

Resetting pump. The pump under analysis can be reset either by clicking the *clear* key or by pressing and holding down the *on* key for more than three seconds (Listing 9). The following situations can be identified: (i) the *clear* key can be used to reset the infusion parameters to their default settings from the main menu when the pump is not infusing; (ii) the *on* key can be clicked and held down in any situation for turning off the pump and hence reset the infusion status and parameters to

their default values. This mapping relation can be specified as follows in the theory interpretation parameters:

Listing 9. Theory interpretation for requirement R1 (part 3 of 4)

```
resetting_pump?
 := LAMBDA (st: [concrete_state, concrete_state]):
    (per_click_clear(st`1)
     AND st`2 = clear_clicked(st`1)
      AND mainmenu?(displaymode(st`1))
       AND NOT infusing?(device(st`1)))
    OR (per_press_on(st`1)
         AND st`2 = on_pressed(st`1)),
```

Require confirmation. The PCA pump under analysis has predefined confirmation screens. In the developed model, they correspond to states where field entrymode is confirmmode shown in Listing 10. The mapping relation that completes the specification of the theory interpretation parameters is therefore the following:

Listing 10. Theory interpretation for requirement R1 (part 4 of 4)

```
require_confirmation?
 := LAMBDA (st: [concrete_state, concrete_state]):
    entrymode(st`2) = confirmmode }}
```

The theory interpretation given in Listing 7, 8, 9, and 10 generates the proof obligation named type check condition (TCC) shown in Listing 11. The TCC must be discharged to show that **R1** is satisfied.

Listing 11. Proof obligation generated from R1

```
% Mapped-axiom TCC generated
IMP_reference_model_th_R1_Axiom_TCC1: OBLIGATION
FORALL (st, st0, st1:
        [concrete_state, concrete_state]):
 (concrete_init?(st`1) => R1(st)) AND
  ((R1(st0) AND
     ((per_click_clear(st0`1)
       AND st1`1 = clear_clicked(st0`1))
      OR %... ))) => R1(st1));
```

This proof obligation is simply the interpretation of axiom R1_Axiom and can be proved with the PVS theorem prover. In the following we illustrate how we discharged the above proof obligation in PVS. The verification was almost automatic, and a similar verification approach has also been used to discharge proof obligations generated for other axioms.

Proving the axiom. The proof of the induction base was automatically discharged by PVS in seconds with grind, a predefined decision procedure of PVS that repeatedly applies definition expansion, propositional simplification, and type-appropriate decision procedures. The verification of the inductive step was discharged with a small amount of manual intervention. More in details, a direct application of grind was initially not successful because expansions and substitutions automatically performed by the strategy were leading to unreachable device states (e.g., device infusion when turned off). This is not a weakness of the theorem prover or a mistake in the specification, but a lack of conditions in the permissions – the subtyping constraints imposed in the permission of the transition functions were not accurate enough. Manual case-splitting allowed us to diagnose the combination of cases leading to the unreachable states. A small number of additional subtyping conditions were thus included in the permission of transition functions to avoid these combination of cases. After the modification, `grind` automatically proved the inductive step.

DISCUSSION

The review process of medical devices is a dialogue between manufacturers and regulators. The verification approach illustrated here aims to make this dialogue precise and inspectable, as manufacturers can specify in a precise way what a requirement means with respect to the behaviour of their device user interface — the "interpretation" phase within our approach. Additionally, manufacturers can also provide a mathematical proof that the behaviour of the device user interface is always compliant to the provided interpretation.

The possibility to provide different interpretations is a flexibility that both regulators and manufacturers are willing to have, because they need to take into account different trade-offs in different systems, and want to leave space for innovation. The validity of the interpretation is negotiated during the review process.

The presented approach relies on reverse engineering. As such, the produced model may contain mistakes, and therefore have a behaviour that is slightly different from the original device. The impact of mistakes in the reverse engineering process can be mitigated through validation of failure traces on the original device – this way false positives can be identified and the model adjusted. When the verification of a safety requirement succeeds, a successful trace should be generated and validated against the original device — this way false negatives can also be identified.

Within production and regulatory cycles, the presented approach can be used in several ways.

(1.) It can be used to generate supporting evidence for human factors claims, for example, as part of a safety case [8]. For example a claim that a clinician will not be able to enter an incorrect infusion rate may be supported in part by providing evidence that the device requires confirmation whenever any number entry is completed.
(2.) It can be used to develop user interface reference models that characterise the key features of broad classes of devices.
(3.) It can be used to identify the source of user interface problems (e.g., during forensic engineering investigations) by checking the device systematically against the reference model and encapsulated requirements.
(4.) It can be used to understand how to *fix* design problems, e.g., when a device is recalled or fixed in the field. Analysing these requirements and the match to the reference model is formative in that failure of a requirement will lead to suggestions about how the design could be improved.

Before the techniques described here can be used as part of a regulatory process, the community, both regulators and manufacturers, must be convinced that the process of learning these skills and applying them is justified. At one level this process can only be achieved through successive generations of the process to demonstrate both the savings in terms of documentation and the clarity and inspectability of the result. Further work also needs to be done to automate these processes, rendering the requirements and reference models as libraries and automating the means of refining the reference models to the concrete models and proving the resulting refined requirements.

CONCLUSIONS

There are a number of obstacles to developing systems from models. The classical model based design process lacks flexibility, failing to address the iterative and experimental approach that is usually the practice of developers, particularly in relation to the interactive system. In practice a process of refinement closer to reverse engineering, as described in this paper, enables a developer to assess the extent to which requirements are satisfied in a design. Reference models, that describe the generic classes of systems, are useful because, typically, there are many products that are designed to satisfy a similar set of requirements and to support a similar set of activities.

This paper describes and illustrates a method of assessing the extent to which a design satisfies requirements. The method is of broad applicability but is clearly relevant to the case of interactive systems where a particular class of requirements must be satisfied. This paper demonstrates that verification approaches based on model refinement are applicable to this situation by using a specific class of medical devices that are subject to regulatory control. Safety requirements, as specified in FDA draft regulatory material, have been translated into a logic-based formal representation using function recognisers. These function recognisers are used as the basis for a reference model generic to a class of systems, in this case PCA pumps. It describes how, using a process akin to interaction walkthrough, a concrete model can be constructed using PVS and that the function recognisers can be linked to this concrete model using a refinement relation. Finally, it has been demonstrated by illustration that these formalised requirements can be re-expressed as theorems and proved of the PVS concrete model.

The contribution of this work is that it demonstrates a concise and semantically unambiguous approach to representing what a regulator's requirements for a particular device might be. It provides an inspectable and repeatable process for demonstrating that the requirements are satisfied. It has the potential to replace the considerable documentation produced at the moment by a succinct document that can be subjected to careful and systematic analysis. The challenge of this work is to facilitate these techniques so that their use as part of the everyday development of interactive software can be clearly justified. Formal approaches raise and address subtle consequences of a design that require a systematic approach; in other words, a formal approach like the one we outline is necessary. Using a formal development process rigorously enough in principle for regulatory use relies on advanced formal skill levels that are unlikely to be familiar to industrial developers. It is therefore a matter of priority to develop good formally-based tools that work effectively in real environments.

Acknowledgements

CHI+MED (EPSRC EP/G059063/1), NSF CNS-1035715, and NSF CNS-1042829.

REFERENCES

1. Event-B and the Rodin Platform.
   `http://www.event-b.org/`.

2. The Generic Patient Controlled Analgesia Pump Hazard Analysis and Safety Requirements.
   `http://rtg.cis.upenn.edu/gip.php3`.

3. *Medical Devices and the Public's Health: The FDA 510(k) Clearance Process at 35 Years*. Institute of Medicine, 2011.

4. B-Braun Melsungen AG. Perfusor Space and Accessory: Instruction for Use.

5. Bowen, J., and Reeves, S. Refinement for user interface designs. *Formal Aspects of Computing 21*, 6 (2009).

6. Degani, A. *Taming HAL: Designing Interfaces Beyond 2001*. Palgrave Macmillan, 2004.

7. Harrison, M., Campos, J., and Masci, P. Reusing models and properties in the analysis of similar interactive devices. *Innovations in Systems and Software Engineering* (2013), 1–17.

8. Kelly, T. *Arguing safety – a systematic approach to managing safety cases*. PhD thesis, Department of Computer Science, University of York, 1998.

9. Kim, B., Ayoub, A., Sokolsky, O., Lee, I., Jones, P., Zhang, Y., and Jetley, R. Safety-assured development of the GPCA infusion pump software. In *Proceedings of the ninth ACM international conference on Embedded software*, EMSOFT '11, ACM (New York, NY, USA, 2011), 155–164.

10. Liu, G., Fukuda, T., Lee, C., Chen, V., Zheng, Q., and Kamae, I. Evidence-Based Decision-Making on Medical Technologies in China, Japan, and Singapore. *Value in Health 12, Supplement 3*, 0 (2009), S12–S17.

11. Masci, P., Rukšėnas, R., Oladimeji, P., Cauchi, A., Gimblett, A., Li, Y., Curzon, P., and Thimbleby, H. On formalising interactive number entry on infusion pumps. *ECEASST 45* (2011).

12. Masci, P., Rukšėnas, R., Oladimeji, P., Cauchi, A., Gimblett, A., Li, Y., Curzon, P., and Thimbleby, H. The benefits of formalising design guidelines: a case study on the predictability of drug infusion pumps. *Innovations in Systems and Software Engineering* (2013), 1–21.

13. Nielsen, J., and Molich, R. Heuristic evaluation of user interfaces. In *Proceedings of the SIGCHI Conference on Human Factors in Computing Systems*, CHI '90, ACM (New York, NY, USA, 1990), 249–256.

14. Owre, S., Rajan, S., Rushby, J., Shankar, N., and Srivas, M. PVS: Combining Specification, Proof Checking, and Model Checking. In *Computer-Aided Verification, CAV '96*, no. 1102 in Lecture Notes in Computer Science, Springer-Verlag (1996), 411–414.

15. Owre, S., and Shankar, N. Theory Interpretations in PVS. Tech. Rep. SRI-CSL-01-01, Computer Science Laboratory, SRI International, Menlo Park, CA, 2001.

16. Rezazadeh, A., Evans, N., and Butler, M. Redevelopment of an Industrial Case Study Using Event-B and Rodin. In *BCS-FACS Meeting - Formal Methods In Industry* (December 2007).

17. Ryan, M., Fiadeiro, J., and Maibaum, T. Sharing actions and attributes in modal action logic. In *Proceedings of the International Conference on Theoretical Aspects of Computer Software*, TACS '91, Springer-Verlag (London, UK, UK, 1991), 569–593.

18. Schoonmaker, M. The U.S. Approval Process for Medical Devices: Legislative Issues and Comparison with the Drug Model, March 2005. CSR Report for Congress.

19. Sorrel, S. Medical device development: U.S. and EU differences. *Applied Clinical Trials Online* (August 2006).

20. Thimbleby, H. Interaction walkthrough: evaluation of safety critical interactive systems. In *Proceedings of the 13th international conference on Interactive systems: Design, specification, and verification*, DSVIS'06, Springer-Verlag (Berlin, Heidelberg, 2007), 52–66.

21. Thimbleby, H. *Press On: Principles of Interaction Programming*. Mit Press, 2010.

22. Thimbleby, H., and Gimblett, A. User interface model discovery: Towards a generic approach. In *Proceedings ACM SIGCHI Symposium on Engineering Interactive Computing Systems — EICS 2010*, G. Doherty, J. Nichols, and M. D. Harrison, Eds., ACM (2010), 145–154.

23. US Food and Drug Administration. General Controls for Medical Devices, 2009.

24. US Food and Drug Administration. Learn if a Medical Device Has Been Cleared by FDA for Marketing, 2009.

25. US Food and Drug Administration. Premarket Notification (510k), 2009.

26. US Food and Drug Administration. Total Product Life Cycle: Infusion Pump - Premarket Notification [510(k)] Submissions - Draft Guidance, April 2010.

27. US Food and Drug Administration. FDA and Industry Actions on Premarket Approval Applications (PMAs): Effect on FDA Review Clock and Goals, October 2012.

28. Vadera, S. and Meziane, F. From English to formal specifications. *The Computer Journal 37*, 9 (1994).

29. Zuckerman, D., Brown, P., and Nissen, S. Medical device recalls and the FDA approval process. *Archives of Internal Medicine 171*, 11 (2011), 1006–1011.

Modelling Safety Properties of Interactive Medical Systems

Judy Bowen
The University of Waikato
New Zealand
jbowen@cs.waikato.ac.nz

Steve Reeves
The University of Waikato
New Zealand
stever@cs.waikato.ac.nz

ABSTRACT

Formally modelling the software functionality and interactivity of safety-critical devices allows us to prove properties about their behaviours and be certain that they will respond to user interaction correctly. In domains such as medical environments, where many different devices may be used, it is equally important to ensure that all devices used adhere to a set of safety, and other, principles designed for that environment. In this paper we look at modelling important properties of interactive medical devices including safety considerations mandated by their users. We use ProZ for model checking to ensure that properties stated in temporal logic hold, and also to check invariants. In this way we gain confidence that important properties do hold of the device, and that models of particular devices adhere to the properties described.

Author Keywords

Formal models; LTL, interactive systems; medical devices; safety properties

ACM Classification Keywords

D.2.4 Software/Program Verification

General Terms

Reliability; Verification

INTRODUCTION

Safety-critical interactive devices are becoming increasingly mainstream due to their proliferation within the medical domain. As more and more devices are introduced to support patient care and the delivery of medication, so the need to ensure their correctness, robustness and usability increases. Research in the area of software engineering for interactive systems is increasingly focussing on this important area [13, 3, 7] as the number of adverse incidents relating to these devices continues to grow [8].

Formally modelling interactive systems (including medical devices) has been shown to be effective in identifying potential problems both with underlying functionality [5] and usability [1] as well as providing the ability to identify consistency issues with documentation and user manuals [3]. While

the work in this paper can be generalised to any interactive system, here we focus on a particular category of safety-critical interactive devices, that of medical devices (specifically our examples focus on infusion and syringe pumps).

In order to provide safety[1] guarantees to hospitals and other medical institutions who are typically using many different devices provided by different manufacturers it may not be enough to ensure that behaviour meets the requirements specified by the manufacturer. We also need to ensure that devices meet specific safety criteria identified by the hospital. In this paper we build on our previous work of modelling both these, and other interactive systems [2] by using temporal logic and invariants in the ProZ tool (a part of the ProB tool [12]) to analyse existing models to check for such properties

We begin by giving an overview of the models used and a small example of the types of properties, both temporal and invariant, we can investigate using ProZ. We then give some instances of actual properties we can check of the T34 Syringe pump [4] and discuss the benefits and challenges provided by this approach and the ProZ tool.

MODELS

Our requirements for modelling interactive medical devices are the ability to describe both system functionality and interface/interaction in an unambiguous manner. That is we require a language with formal syntax and semantics and an associated logic which enables us to use model-checking and/or theorem proving to prove properties about our models, and hence our interactive systems.

In order to capture all of the necessary aspects (functional and interactive) we use the following models and formal notations:

- Presentation models
- Presentation interaction models (PIMs)
- Z specification
- Presentation model relation (PMR)

We give a brief description of each of these next.

---

[1]Note: in this paper we use "safety" more in its common, informal and wide-ranging sense of "safe to use", rather than the formal, precise sense of properties associated with trace semantics *etc.*, though the two meanings necessarily should and do overlap.

Presentation Models

The interactive medical devices we are dealing with are modal devices. That is they have a fixed set of widgets (unlike interactive software systems which may have multiple windows, dialogues *etc.* each with their own set of widgets) but the behaviour of these widgets is dependent on the mode the device is in. Presentation models are used to describe interaction and interactivity of such modal devices by way of describing the different modes of the device, the widgets of the device, and the behaviour of the widgets in each of the modes. Each mode is described in a component presentation model and the total system is then the concatenation of these component models.

Figure 1 shows the Niki T34 Syringe pump, a device commonly used to deliver pain-relief medication in hospitals and respite care homes [4]. This device has ten widgets, which in-

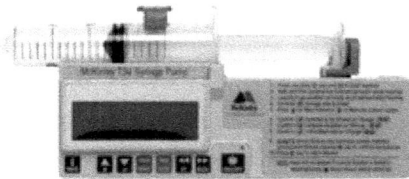

Figure 1. T34 Syringe Pump

clude the display screen, eight soft keys and an audible alarm. It has fourteen different modes. In each mode the behaviours exhibited by the widgets may be different (and in some modes widgets may have no behaviour at all). As an example, the component presentation model for the *SetDuration* mode of this device is as follows:

SetDuration is:
>   *(Display, Responder, (S_ShowDuration, S_IncDuration, S_DecDuration)),*
>   *(OnOffSK, ActionControl, (I_Init)),*
>   *(InfoSK, ActionControl, (I_Info)),*
>   *(YesStartSK, ActionControl, (S_SetDuration, I_RateConfirm)),*
>   *(NoStopSK, ActionControl, (I_SetVolume)),*
>   *(UpPlusSK, ActionControl, (S_IncDuration)),*
>   *(DownMinusSK, ActionControl, (S_DecDuration)),*
>   *(LeftFFSK, ActionControl, ()),*
>   *(RightBackSK, ActionControl, ()),*
>   *(AudibleAlarm, Responder, (S_Timeout))*

The presentation model uses labels for behaviours which denote whether or not the behaviour is linked to the underlying functionality of the device (these are called S-behaviours and names are prefixed with S_) or to interaction (these are the I-behaviours whose names are prefixed with I_). The meanings of the S-behaviours are given by the operations in the Z specification and those of the I-behaviours are given by the transitions of the PIM. We discuss these next.

PIMs

Presentation interaction models (PIMs) are based on finite state automata describing the navigational possibilities of an interactive system or device. Each state is associated with a component presentation model (as such the PIM is an abstraction of the behaviour of the entire system), *i.e.* there is a state for each mode of the device. Transitions between states are labelled with I-behaviours, so for each component presentation model every I-behaviour is associated with a transition. For the example shown in figure 1 the state representing *SetDuration* will have four outgoing transitions labelled *I_Init*, *I_Info*, *I_RateConfirm* and *I_SetVolume* respectively, and these transitions are the formal meanings of the four I-behaviours.

Figure 2 shows the entire PIM for the T34 syringe pump. The combination of presentation model and PIM models all behaviours of the device available through user interaction as well as availability of these behaviours (*i.e.* which mode the pump needs to be in for a given behaviour to be available as well as how to navigate to that mode).

As can be seen from figure 2 although the device is small with only a limited number of widgets it has a complex PIM. As this represents the navigational possibilities of the T34 and shows availability of behaviours (via the link to the presentation models) a user of this device needs to have a mental model which matches the PIM in order to successfully use it. It is clear, therefore, that even small devices like the T34 can be challenging for users.

The PIM is described using the μ-Charts language [15] which allows a generalisation of finite state automata and has both a visual syntax (the state transition diagram as shown in figure 2) and a semantics given in the Z specification language [14, 9]. We use a tool, called ZooM [16], to create the Z semantics (as a Z specification) that gives the formal meaning of a given μ-chart.

Z Specification

We use Z in entirely conventional ways to model the functional (as opposed to the interactive) part of the system. So, the state of the system is described, as usual, by Z state schemas. These give the names and types of the parts of the state that can be observed, which we call *observations*, together with predicates which express properties of and constraints on and between these observations.

Together the observations and predicates model allowable states of the underlying functionality of the system being modelled. Further, we have operation schemas which describe, in terms of changes to observations, how the state of the system changes from one state to another. These operation schemas give a formal meaning to the S-behaviours of the PMs, and the mapping between S-behaviours and Z operation schemas is given (as mentioned below) by a PMR (in a similar way, as explained above, the transitions in the PIM give a formal meaning to the I-behaviours of the PMs—so everything in the model has a completely formal meaning).

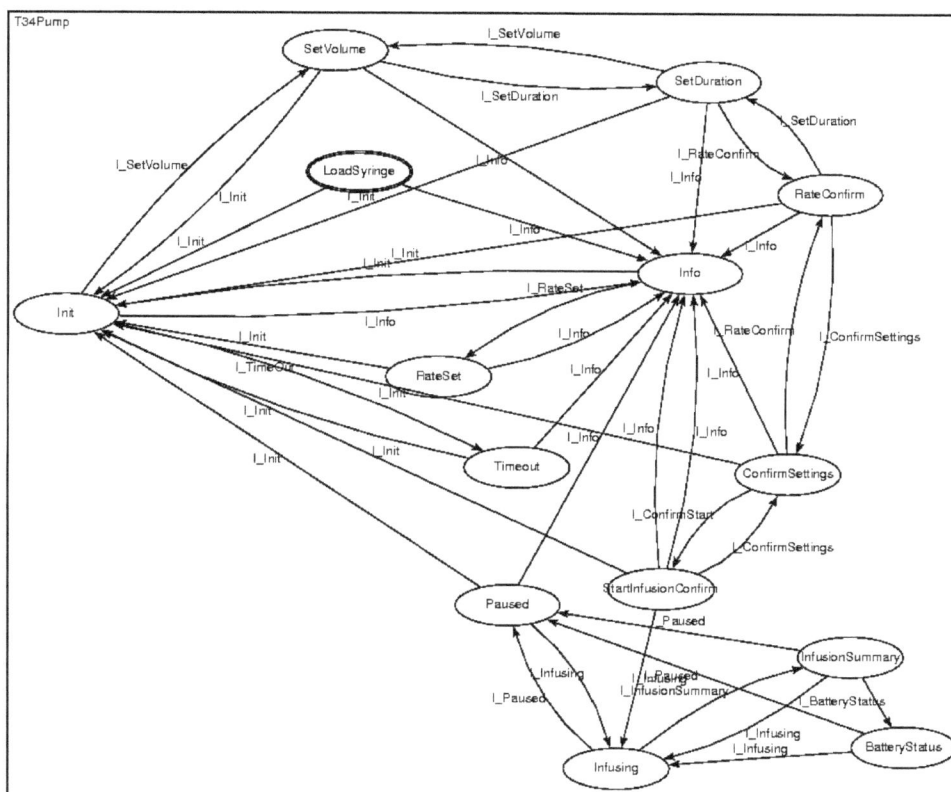

Figure 2. T34 PIM

PMR

Finally, in order to link the Z specification with the presentation model we create a relation between the S-behaviours of the presentation model and the operations of the Z specification. That is, for every S-behaviour there is a corresponding operation in the Z specification which gives its meaning. Figure 4 shows how the models and techniques applied in this paper fit together.

PROZ

We use ProZ [10], which is an extension of ProB [12] that supports Z specifications, to investigate our models. It can be used for general animation during design and testing and usability phases of model building, but also for the formal activities of model checking and LTL predicate testing. Leuschel and Plagge have shown that using ProZ and LTL is faster and more complete than previous model-checking approaches for Z [11]. ProZ works, basically, by exploring the state space of the model as follows. It first initialises the model by invoking a user-specified initialisation operation, and this puts it into its initial state. In this state, as in any other that is subsequently reached, it uses the operations that are enabled in the state to generate a collection of new states. It then repeats this activity with the newly created states, and so on.

The user has control over the order in which states are visited, being given the choice of either depth-first or breadth-first visiting. Once a state is generated one of the enabled operations in that state is used, generating another new state, and so on.

Once that sequence comes to an end (because a state is generated in which no operations are enabled) then the process returns to the very first state generated and a second operation is applied to it, generating another new state and so on. Clearly, this order of developing and searching the state space can lead to problems if a sequence being generated never ends (or is very long) because the rest of the state space is never (or hardly) visited.

In the breadth-first order, all operations that are enabled in a state are used, generating a collection of new states, then all operations that are enabled are applied to the first state in the new collection, then all operations enabled are applied to the second state in the new collection and so on. This order has the advantage that the search does not dash off down a single sequence of states, but it does mean that arriving at a state of interest, while always possible (which it is not with depth-first search) might take longer than one is prepared to wait, or longer than resources allow.

So, each ordering has its good and bad points. ProZ also allows a mixed order which (according to some user-supplied parameters) allows some depth-first searching to take place, followed by some breadth-first and so on.

This searching is at the heart of ProZ. Whether checking the validity of a temporal predicate, or checking that the state of the system never falsifies an invariant (much more on all this below), traversing the state space is the central concern. Much development has gone on (and still is going on) to make

```
\begin{schema}{ConfirmDuration}
\Delta T34State
\where
systemReady = no\\
hoursduration > 0 \lor minutesduration > 0\\

% A simplification for time model checking
infusionrate' = infusionrate\\
%infusionrate' = 60 * vtbi \div (60 * hoursduration + minutesduration)\\
\Xi BatteryState\\
\Xi Syringe\\
\Xi KeyPad\\
\Xi TechMenu\\
\Xi Program\\
\Xi VTBI\\
\Xi Duration\\
systemReady' = no
\end{schema}

% Again, ignore for time passing model checking

%\begin{schema}{IncreaseRate}
%\Delta T34State\\
```

Ln 512, Col 14

State Properties	Enabled Operations	History
invariant_ok	InitialiseSyringe	ConfirmVTBI
PerCent = (0 .. 100)	ConfirmVTBI	InitialiseSyringe
hours = {-1,0,1,2}	DecreaseDuration	SyringeConfirmation(BDPlastipak,yes)
minutes = {-1,0,1,2,3,4,5,6,7,8,9,10,11,12,	ConfirmDuration	INITIALISATION(yes,90,BDPlastipak,yes,0,10
seconds = {-1,0,1,2,3,4,5,6,7,8,9,10,11,12,		SETUP_CONSTANTS((0 .. 100),{-1,0,1,2},{-1
tenthmillilitres = (-100 .. 1000)		
tenthmillilitresperhour = (0 .. 10000)		
tenthmillimeters = (0 .. 1000)		
barrelOK = yes		
batteryCharge = 90		
brand = BDPlastipak		
collarOK = yes		
hoursduration = 0		
infusionrate = 10		
keypadlocked = yes		
minutesduration = 1		
plungerOK = yes		
plungerPosition = 50		
programlocked = yes		
secondsduration = 0		
size = 10		
syringeOK = yes		
systemReady = no		
techmenulocked = yes		
volumeLeft = 10		
vtbi = 10		

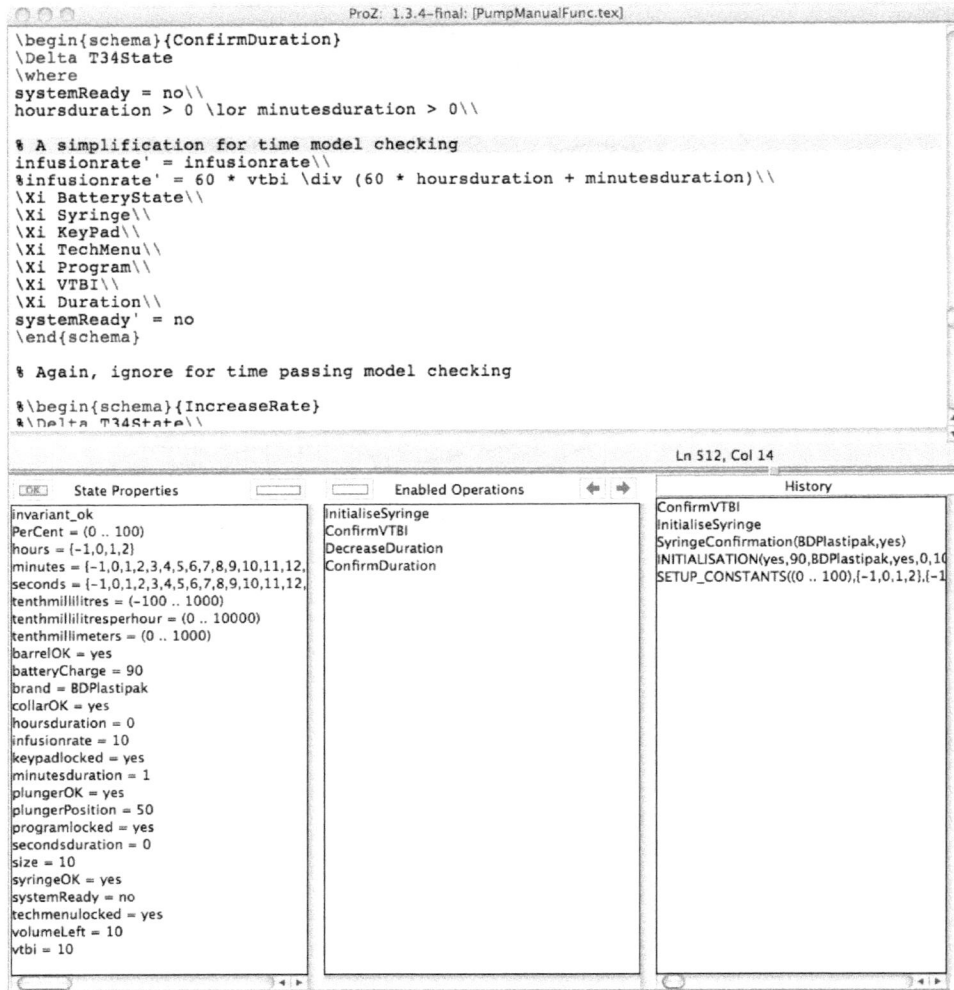

Figure 3. ProZ animation of functional specification

the searching more efficient and more effective. This is a huge undertaking and goes far beyond the subject of this paper. We are users of this technology, not developers of it.

A screenshot of a Z specification in ProZ during a modelling session is given in figure 3.

LTL AND INVARIANTS IN PROZ

LTL

ProZ provides support for linear temporal logic (LTL) model checking using an extension of LTL called LTL^e and Past-LTL [11]. LTL^e supports propositions on transitions as well as states.

Atomic propositions can be used to check if an operation is enabled in a state. For our Z semantics for PIMs this means checking whether transitions (which are given meaning via operation schemas) are enabled. Transition propositions can be used to check for the next enabled operation in the path as well as arguments to that operation. The following temporal operators are supported in ProZ (where f and g are predicates):

Temporal operators (future)
G *f*: "globally"
F *f*: "finally"
X *f*: "next"
f **U** *g*: "until"
f **W** *g*: "weak until"
f **R** *g*: "release"

In addition, past temporal operators which are the dual to the future operators given above (apart from "weak until") are supported (**H, O, Y, S, T** respectively). Logical constants and operators supported are:
true and *false*
not: negation
&, *or* and => : conjunction, disjunction and implication

As an example consider the μ-chart (representing the PIM of a simple interactive device) given in figure 5. The system consists of a single observation called *cSimpleExample* which represents the current active state of the μ-chart. Each transi-

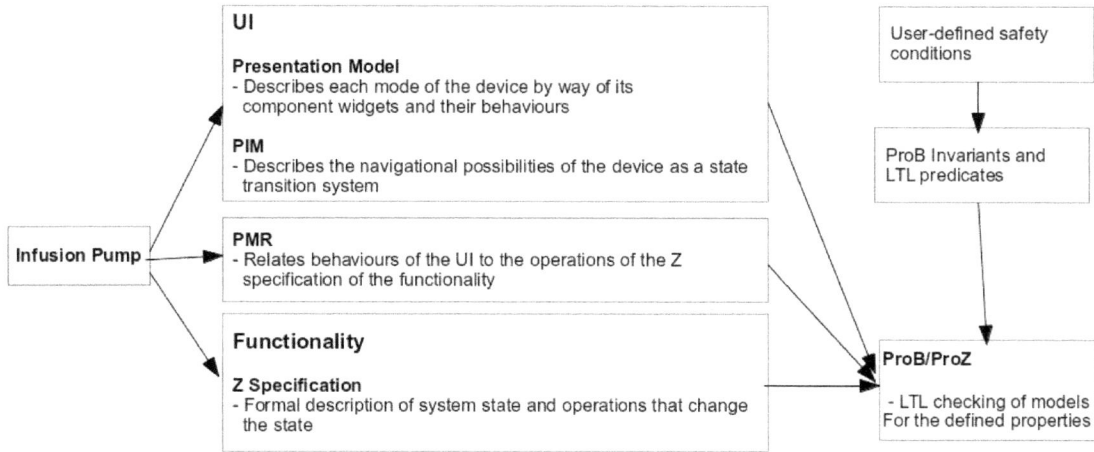

Figure 4. Overview of Process

tion is described as an operation where given a particular start state and the relevant input signal (to match the guard on the transition) the μ-chart moves into the end state defined by the transition.

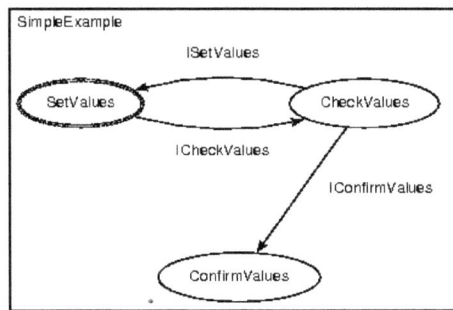

Figure 5. Simple PIM Example

For example, the following operation schema represents the transition from the *SetValues* state to the *CheckValues* state in figure 5:

$$
\begin{array}{l}
\underline{\quad \delta SimpleExamplecSetValuesCheckValues \quad} \\
SetValues \\
CheckValues' \\
iSimpleExample? : \mathbb{P}\,Signal \\
active : \mathbb{P}\,MicroState \\
oSimpleExample! : \mathbb{P}\,outputISimpleExample \\
\hline
SimpleExample \in active \\
SICheckValues \in iSimpleExample? \\
oSimpleExample! = \{\}
\end{array}
$$

The schema naming is an artefact of the translation tool which prefixes the name of the chart to each transition and adds an alpha character label to each transition. Here *SetValues* and *CheckValues* are schemas representing the μ-chart in the corresponding state, the prime decoration on *CheckValues* means that the all of the observations are similarly primed, which means that this is their value after the operation. We can read

the above to mean that if an input signal *SICheckValues* (the transition guard) is in the input set for the chart when it is in the *SetValues* state then the state of the chart will change to *CheckValues*. The other two transitions shown in figure 5 are similarly represented.

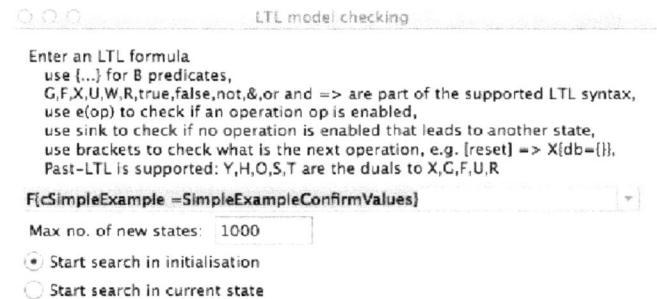

Figure 6. ProZ LTL Checker

We can now use ProZ's LTL checker to check a temporal proposition such as:

$$\Diamond cSimpleExample = ConfirmValues$$

That is we can check that the model will eventually be in the state *ConfirmValues*. Figure 6 shows the syntax used in the ProZ LTL checker. We can choose to either start the check from the initialisation state (as we have in this example) or from the current state, assuming we have animated part of the specification to move to a different state. Unsurprisingly, the checker returns a result of FALSE (we say unsurprisingly as from the μ-chart shown in figure 5 we can see that it is possible to loop between the *SetValues* and *CheckValues* states without ever reaching the *ConfirmValues* state. In addition to giving the FALSE result, ProZ also provides a counter-example in its *history list* (which shows operations and states visited in order from bottom to top). Figure 7 shows the history which tells us that after setup and initialisation the model-checker has performed the *deltaSimpleExamplecSetValuesCheckValues* operation followed by the *deltaSimpleExamplebCheckValuesSetValues* operation which represents the loop transitions between these two states and therefore provides a counter example for our proposition.

Figure 7. History with Counter-Example

Of course if we want to make sure that it is possible for the model to reach the *ConfirmValues* state (even though it is not guaranteed that it will ever be in that state) then we can check a different proposition. We use negation with the *finally* predicate to state the following:

$$not \Diamond cSimpleExample = ConfirmValues$$

which states that there is no path in the model which leads to the *ConfirmValues* state. When we check this with the LTL checker it returns FALSE which shows us that it is indeed possible to reach this state. Again we can check the traces in the history listing which gives the counter-example showing how this is possible.

Checking a Temporal Safety Property of the T34 Model

Within clinical environments, or other settings where similar safety-critical devices are used, procedures and guidelines are developed to support best-practice. As such in order to manage the number and diversity of devices in use safety properties can be described which are used to support integration of new and existing devices and also to understand which settings are appropriate for which devices. As an example we can consider a set of safety properties that should be applied to all infusion and syringe pumps.

For example, we might want to ensure that immediately prior to starting an infusion the user can review the settings (rate, time *etc.*) to ensure they are correct, and if necessary change them. This provides a final safety check before the infusion begins. Given this safety property we return to our models of the T34 syringe pump and show how we can incorporate this and check for satisfiability. We begin by identifying the relevant states of the model. In the PIM we have a state called *StartInfusionConfirm* which represents the mode of the pump where all set values are displayed. To ensure the safety property holds this state should be immediately before the *Infusing* state in the transition system, that is, we cannot move into a state *Infusing* for the first time except from the state *StartInfusionConfirm*. We use the *release* operator **R** of LTL for this. Release can be described as follows:
A **R** *B* holds, if whenever ¬ *B* occurs at a state on the path, *A*

occurs before, that is *A* occurs before the first state at which *B* is violated.

For our safety property we can define *A* as an expression describing the PIM being in the state *StartInfusionConfirm* and *B* as an expression describing the PIM **not** being in the state *Infusing*. The double negation then gives our intended meaning. In ProZ we then select the CheckLTLFormula option and enter:
$\{cT34 = sT34StartInfusionConfirm\}$
R
$\{not(cT34 = sT34Infusing)\}$

and get the result:
"Formula TRUE.
No counterexample found"

which shows that the model satisfies the given property.

Rather than just checking that the state prior to *Infusing* has a particular name (where in this case we know that this indicates the required behaviour) it is more useful to check that a state has a particular behaviour. So we might check instead that if the model is in the state prior to *Infusion* then a particular operation is enabled which has the desired behaviour.

Recall that the Z specification gives the meanings of the behaviours and the PMR relates these to the S-behaviours of the presentation models. In this way the PIM abstracts away both the details of the presentation models and the S-behaviours. Implicit to the PIM is that for any state representing a model containing S-behaviours there are self-loop transitions on the state guarded with those S-behaviours (loop transitions because they have no effect on the interactive state of the pump only the functionality). If we add these back into the model then we can perform a test as described.

We still use the *release* operator, but instead of just checking for a particular state prior to infusing, we check that an operation is enabled, *i.e.* the operation which displays all of the values assigned to time, rate, vtbi *etc.*

Checking for Livelock

As another example of some testing using LTL, we consider a process to check that, unless it was intended, no state is a dead end even though it is always possible to "do something" when we are in it, *i.e.* that no state is a livelock.

The example is important for our PIMs because they use the "do nothing" semantics for μ-charts, which means that all states, when confronted with a signal that the writer has not explicitly taken account of in a given state, simply "do nothing", which means formally that there is a transition, labelled with the signal in question, which has the state concerned as both its start and end state. Sometimes this sort of transition is called a self-loop. So, for a PIM, we cannot detect deadlocks, *i.e.* the situation where there are no transitions out of a state, because all states have, at least, these self-loops. No state has no transitions coming from it.

We want a process which we can follow in order to detect any such livelock states, *i.e.* states where the only transitions are self-loops. Of course, it might be that the model *should* have a livelock state. But, since this is unusual, having a process to find these (so that we can check to see whether or not we really meant them to be livelocks) is clearly useful and should be part of a model investigation.

For a small PIM we can simply look at the chart and see live-locks. For realistic devices, though, such visual inspection is likely to be error prone. So, some uniform process that is guaranteed to find such states is needed.

Our proposal for this is as follows. In ProZ there is a special value in the LTL it uses—*sink*. This is a predicate that is true of a state if it contains only outgoing transitions that are self-loops. We want to check that no state is a state that has *sink* true of it. If such a state is found, we want a trace which takes us to such a state. So, we actually want to check the predicate *not*(*sink*) on all paths through the chart. This means that we check the predicate $\mathbf{G}(not(sink))$ starting from the start state. If the LTL checker tells us (eventually) that this predicate is true then we know that no state has only self-loops, and that therefore the PIM is free from (possibly worrying) livelocks. However, if during its search the checker finds a state where *not*(*sink*) is false the it has clearly found a livelock state. The trace then leads us to this state, and we can direct our attention to it and, basically, ask the question: did we mean this to be a livelock?

Having found one such state, we can temporarily introduce a "dummy" transition from the state in question to a "dummy" state, so that the state in question is no longer livelocked and hence *sink* will not be true of it, and re-run the checker on this modified PIM. The state found previously will now no longer cause the LTL formula to be false, but the next state in the PIM (if any) which is a livelock state will now make the formula false, and so we will again have our attention directed at a livelock state. This can then be discounted from future searches by adding a "dummy" transition to the "dummy" state, and the process can be repeated. Once the checker finds no states that make the checking formula $\mathbf{G}(not(sink))$ false, then we know we have considered all the possible livelock states. The PIM can then be returned to its proper form by deleting the "dummy" state and all the transitions that go to it.

Invariants

Not all of the properties we want to check are temporal. For example, limits set on infusion values, such as rate or volume to be infused, are invariant. To check invariants in ProZ we add a schema called *Invariant* to our specification which contains the necessary predicate(s). Invariants are checked against the functional specification of the system model as they are properties of the system that change due to operations on the state of the system.

If we return again to the small example given in figure 5, the functional specification of the system describes the state of the system with two observations *time* and *volume*, one for time and one for volume respectively (here both are simplified to be values belonging to the set of natural numbers) as follows:

$$\boxed{\begin{array}{l} ExampleSystem \\ \hline volume : \mathbb{N} \\ time : \mathbb{N} \end{array}}$$

Various operations are described which can set the values for the volume and time observations as well as increment the existing values. *IncVolumeOperation* is described as:

$$\boxed{\begin{array}{l} IncVolumeOperation \\ \Delta ExampleSystem \\ \hline volume' = volume + 1 \\ time' = time \end{array}}$$

$\Delta ExampleSystem$ means that we have two copies of the *ExampleSystem* observations, those that exist before the operation and those that exist after the operation (which are denoted with the $'$ symbol). So the specification states that after the operation has occurred the value of *volume* will have increased by one while the time observation *time* will remain unchanged.

Now we can add an invariant schema which gives the condition we want to ensure is maintained irrespective of the state of the system or any operation that occurs. It is reasonable to set upper limits on the volume of any drug that can be infused in order to prevent overdosing patients. For this example we will just state that we want the value of *volume* to remain below a fixed level which we declare as *maxVol* (and which for this example has a value of 20).

$$\boxed{\begin{array}{l} Invariant \\ \hline volume : \mathbb{N} \\ \hline volume < maxVol \end{array}}$$

Although it appears we are declaring a *new* observation called *volume* in this schema this is not the case as the ProZ invariant definition requires the inclusion of a subset of the existing state variables. So *volume* here is the observation *volume* declared in *ExampleSystem*.

We can now check that this invariant is maintained in a couple of different ways. First we can model-check the specification whereby ProZ will search the state-space for invariant violations. Figure 8 shows the result of performing this check on our example, which is that the invariant has been violated. If we examine the history list again we can also see the sequence of operations which led to the invariant being violated—in this case an invocation of *SetVolumeOperation* with the value 3 followed by 17 invocations of *IncVolumeOperation*. We can also animate the model by stepping through enabled operations one at a time. If at any point the invariant is violated a green label containing the text 'OK' which is located above the state properties turns red and the text reverses to read 'KO'. Thus we can manually recreate the invariant violation discovered by the model checker by repeatedly selecting *IncVolumeOperation*. Note that once the invariant has been violated *IncVolumeOperation* is not disabled as there is nothing in the predicate of the operation schema itself that checks the new value of *volume* against *maxVol*, *i.e.* it is not a precondition of this operation.

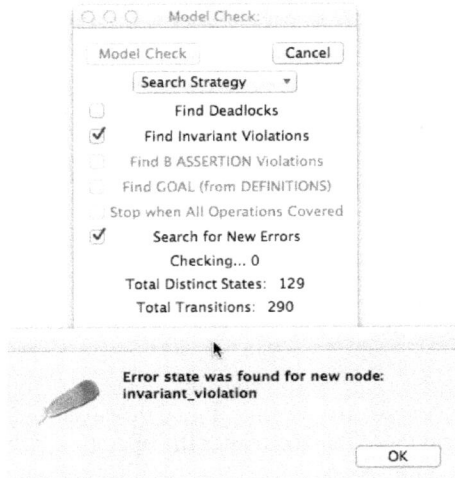

Figure 8. Model Checking finds Invariant Violation

Having discovered the violation we can then refer to the original property from which the rule is derived to understand the consequences of the violation for this device (we cannot assume that such a violation means that the device is "wrong" or not safe to use but we must understand what affect the violation has on the use of the device in its intended environment.)

For example within its set of safety properties a hospital may want to set conditions on the maximum allowable infusion rates for *specific* drugs. These can be described as invariants which we can add to the relevant models. The model of the T34 however can violate such an invariant as it has no constraints on volumes of individual medications. However a model of the Alaris Volumetric Pump with the GuardRails software [6] would not violate such an invariant as it has this functionality included. This may guide practitioners to use the T34 and Alaris pumps in different medical settings depending on the requirement to adhere to this safety property. So, the results of the modelling and invariant checking can be used to support reasoned decision making.

Using Invariants to Check Boundary Values

One notorious place where models of systems go wrong is at the boundaries of data values. The question of whether upper and lower bounds on values are properly respected and properly handled arises frequently, and so it is something that clearly needs to be checked where possible. The volume example shown previously is an example of this.

In the T34 model we model the passing of time by an operation called *Tick* (which we assume models the underlying clock within the pump measuring time). So, once the pump is given the command to start infusion, the clock measures the passing seconds and causes the duration to decrease appropriately. Once the duration is zero, the infusion stops. As the seconds pass the duration has to properly keep track of the hours and minutes and seconds remaining. Clearly there are several boundaries to be checked here, the most important being to check that the pump always reaches exactly zero, *i.e.* we ask, are there any sort of rounding errors that cause zero to

be "jumped", which in turn cause the pump not to stop when it should?

We can put several predicates into the *Invariant* schema which give conditions that should be true of all states as time passes, *i.e.* as the device performs its *Tick* operation. Let us assume that the model has observations of the remaining seconds, minutes and hours, given by *seconds*, *minutes* and *hours* respectively. Then, for example, we need the following to be true for all states: $hours \geq 0 \wedge minutes \geq 0 \wedge seconds \geq 0$.

We have a similar property to check when we set the duration of an infusion. Does time work properly during the set up phase? Again at the minutes, hours and seconds boundaries does, for example, decreasing the duration for one minute give us valid times? Assume that we have the following observations as components of the duration we are setting: *secondsduration*, *minutesduration* and *hoursduration*. Also assume that we have an invariant that says each of these values must always be greater than or equal to zero. Now consider part of an operation *DecreaseDuration* which when invoked decreases the minutes-to-go by one. An obvious way to do this is given by the predicates:

$$minutesduration \geq 1 \Rightarrow$$
$$(minutesduration' = minutesduration - 1 \wedge$$
$$hoursduration' = hoursduration)$$
$$minutesduration = 0 \Rightarrow$$
$$(minutesduration' = 59 \wedge$$
$$hoursduration' = hoursduration - 1)$$
$$secondsduration = secondsduration'$$

but model checking shows that the hours observation can become negative, and thus the invariant is violated. This is because when the minutes and hours components are zero then this operation sets the minutes component to 59 (correctly) but also decreases the hours component. We might consider the following as a way of fixing this:

$$(minutesduration \geq 1 \Rightarrow$$
$$(minutesduration' = minutesduration - 1 \wedge$$
$$hoursduration' = hoursduration)$$
$$(minutesduration = 0 \wedge hoursduration \geq 1) \Rightarrow$$
$$(minutesduration' = 59 \wedge$$
$$hoursduration' = hoursduration - 1)$$
$$secondsduration = secondsduration'$$

Well, no—since although we have correctly "caught" the previous error with the extra antecedent and implication in the second predicate, model checking again says that *hoursduration* can become negative. This is because we have not said what value the hours component should be after the operation when minutes and hours are both zero before the operation. In Z this means that the hours component can take on any value (the operation does not constrain it). In fact, of course, this is not only an error because the hours component can become negative, but more generally because it can become any value—clearly moving from zero to five would also be an error. To finally correct this we add a further constraint which fixes what *hoursduration* should be after the operation if is was zero before it:

98

$$(minutesduration \geq 1 \Rightarrow$$
$$(minutesduration' = minutesduration - 1 \land$$
$$hoursduration' = hoursduration)$$
$$(minutesduration = 0 \land hoursduration \geq 1) \Rightarrow$$
$$(minutesduration' = 59 \land$$
$$hoursduration' = hoursduration - 1)$$
$$(minutesduration = 0 \land hoursduration = 0) \Rightarrow$$
$$(minutesduration' = 0 \land hoursduration' = 0)$$
$$secondsduration = secondsduration'$$

The other extreme (in terms of boundaries) concerns the maximum duration for an infusion. Here a question to ask is: when the duration for an infusion is being set up, is it possible to go over 24 hours, and if so, does the way time is recorded allow for this properly? The point here is that we have probably made efforts to model valid times, *e.g.* 23:46:34 is a valid time but 24:23:12 is not since, as a time as shown by a clock, this should be 00:23:12. While we have probably got this right, have we allowed for the fact that an infusion might be set to run for 24 hours and 24 minutes, in which case how is that duration recorded? Clearly, when we are setting up the duration we *should* allow 24:24:00 to be set, even though that is not a valid (clock) time. So, in fact, the recording of duration and the recording of actual time passing are not quite the same, and what is more these two things interact.

So, whatever the upper limit for duration of infusion is, our model needs to check that no state exceeds it (which might happen during duration set up). Different devices cope with this in different ways. The Alaris Volumetric pump for example can be set for infusions greater than 24 hours. During the setting phase it displays actual time (*e.g.* 26:40:32 to represent 26 hours, 40 minutes and 32 seconds) but during infusion it displays "24 +" until the time left to infuse drops below 24 hours and then it reverts to showing actual time in hours, minutes and seconds again.

MODELLING AND TESTING CONSIDERATIONS

In common with all other modelling methods, once we start to consider large, realistic systems we come across the practical problem of checking properties within a feasible time or using feasible amounts of storage. The main thrust of research in this area is, of course, in improving the algorithms behind, and the implementation of, model checkers (like ProB). This, though, is not the point of this paper—to reiterate, we are *users* of model checking technology, not developers of it. However, even as users we can use some simple techniques for shrinking the size of our problems so that they can be dealt with within acceptable physical limits. One example of this, which often arises with the sorts of devices that we are concerned with in this paper, is to do with the modelling of time passing or duration of various physical operations (like how long an infusion should take). Because time is usually measured in seconds (as in the example in the previous section), or perhaps even fractions of a second, in order to get an acceptable precision in delivering drugs, and because the duration of an operation (like an infusion) might stretch over hours, the size of the possible state space to be checked once time is involved can quickly because too large for various technologies to handle.

There are some straightforward ways of shrinking the state space, for the purposes of model checking, that we might use. For example, if a duration might stretch over 24 hours, we might model check on a duration that has two hours as its maximum. This makes the state space far smaller, but does not mean we miss checking things like behaviour at boundaries (*i.e.* negative duration—likely to be an error), normal operation, and going beyond the upper boundary of duration. This then means that we can still check (as in a previous section above) that errors are caught, time "roll over" behaves correctly at upper boundaries and so on—while making the model small enough that checking is feasible.

We can also make sure that operations which do not have anything to do with the time component of the model are, temporarily, ignored, which again means that our state space is smaller. We do this in our models by partitioning the state space into smaller component state spaces (this is standard Z practice, in fact, and helps with comprehension of the models), making sure that time is modelled in a state schema which mentions no other observations. Then, (again as standard Z practice) any operation which has (and can have) no effect on time is easily identified since it will have a constraint in its predicate part which says that for this operation the time component does not change. Formally this will be stated by having the predicate $\Xi Time$ in any such operation, assuming that the time component of the state space is modelled by a state schema call *Time*. Then, when we run our model checker we can comment out all operations that have $\Xi Time$ in their predicate parts since we know that they can have no effect on the time component of the model and hence when we are checking properties of time they can have no bearing on our results.

CONCLUSION

In this paper we have shown how temporal logic and invariants describing safety properties of interactive medical devices can be investigated within the ProZ tool. We have given examples of checking for such properties against a model of the T34 syringe pump and discussed some of the results and challenges we have encountered using this approach.

We believe that using techniques such as these, and other model-checking functionalities, contributes to supporting safer use of interactive medical devices. That is we can use such techniques not just to help develop better and safer systems (where such techniques are most typically used) but also, as we have shown here, to investigate existing devices to ensure they can be safely used within the clinical setting.

Future Work

Another area we have been investigating is the effect of different environments on the use of interactive medical devices. In particular what factors need to be taken into consideration when making decisions about using devices in different locations (such as emergency rescue helicopters). As we begin to identify the important factors and their effects we can then investigate how (and if) we might describe these in the same way as the safety properties discussed in this paper. That is we can investigate if a similar approach will be helpful in managing the challenges that moving locations present.

REFERENCES

1. Blandford, A., Buchanan, G., Curzon, P., Furniss, D., and Thimbleby, H. Who's looking? Invisible problems with interactive medical devices. In *Proceedings of the First International Workshop on Interactive Systems in Healthcare*, ACM Special Interest Group on Computer-Human Interaction (USA, 2010), 9–12.

2. Bowen, J., and Reeves, S. Formal models for user interface design artefacts. *Innovations in Systems and Software Engineering 4*, 2 (2008), 125–141.

3. Bowen, J., and Reeves, S. Modelling user manuals of modal medical devices and learning from the experience. In *Proceedings of the Fourth ACM SIGCHI Symposium on Engineering interactive Computing Systems (Copenhagen, Denmark, June, 2012). EICS '12*, ACM, New York, NY (2012).

4. Caesarea Medical Electronics. Niki T34 syringe pump instruction manual. *ref. 100-090SS Edition* (2008).

5. Campos, J., and Harrison, M. Modelling and analysing the interactive behaviour of an infusion pump. *ECEASST 11* (2011).

6. Alaris Guardrails Suite - For medication safety and quality auditing, http://www.carefusion.co.uk/medical-products/infusion/alaris-system/guardrails_suite.aspx, 2010.

7. Engineering and Physical Sciences Research Council. CHI+MED: Multidisciplinary computer-human interaction research for the design and safe use of interactive medical devices, EPSRC reference: EP/G059063/1, 2011.

8. Group, A. F. C. I. W. Infusion working groups summary. *Association for the Advancement of Medical Instrumentation, Healthcare Technology Institute* (2001).

9. ISO/IEC 13568. *Information Technology—Z Formal Specification Notation—Syntax, Type System and Semantics*, first ed. Prentice-Hall International series in computer science. ISO/IEC, 2002.

10. Plagge, D., and Leuschel, M. Validating Z specifications using the ProB animator and model checker. In *IFM*, J. Davies and J. Gibbons, Eds., vol. 4591 of *Lecture Notes in Computer Science*, Springer (2007), 480–500.

11. Plagge, D., and Leuschel, M. Seven at one stroke: LTL model checking for high-level specifications in B, Z, CSP, and more. *STTT 12*, 1 (2010), 9–21.

12. ProB, http://www.stups.uni-dusseldorf.de/prob, 2012.

13. Rajkomar, A., and Blandford, A. Understanding infusion administration in the ICU through distributed cognition. *Journal of Biomedical Informatics 45*, 3 (2012), 580 – 590.

14. Reeve, G. *A Refinement Theory for μCharts*. PhD thesis, The University of Waikato, 2005.

15. Reeve, G., and Reeves, S. μ-Charts and Z: Hows, whys, and wherefores. In *IFM* (2000), 255–276.

16. Zoom, http://sourceforge.net/projects/pims1/files/?source=directory, 2012.

Applying theorem discovery to automatically find and check usability heuristics

Andy Gimblett
Future Interaction Technology Lab
Swansea University
a.m.gimblett@swansea.ac.uk

Harold Thimbleby
Future Interaction Technology Lab
Swansea University
h.thimbleby@swansea.ac.uk

ABSTRACT

Theorem discovery is a novel technique for the automatic analysis of statespace-based models of user interfaces, in which possible sequences of user actions are systematically computed and compared for equivalence, or close equivalence, of effect. Using this technique, we noticed a previously undetected problem with the behaviour of many widely-used inexpensive off-the-shelf interactive devices. Specifically, on many calculators, pressing the decimal point key has no effect on the display, thus unnecessarily breaking the well known usability heuristic that an interactive system should provide appropriate feedback to the user, and potentially causing unnecessary confusion that may lead to error. While this insight is interesting in itself, it is also of significance as a simple but nonetheless non-trivial example of the power and potential of theorem discovery as an analytical technique, not least because the problem—obvious once pointed out—has apparently remained undetected and unremarked upon for many years.

Author Keywords

Theorem discovery; discovery tools; interaction programming; structural usability

ACM Classification Keywords

H.5.2 (D.2.2, H.1.2, I.36) User Interfaces: Theory and methods

General Terms

Algorithms; Human Factors; Verification

1. INTRODUCTION

The problem of analysing user interface (UI) behaviour is an unsolved and interesting one. One possible technique, described and illustrated in this paper, is to automatically and systematically look for sequences of user input that are equivalent in their effects on the system, or nearly so. Equivalences of this kind can embody interesting behavioural properties (one such equivalence plays a central role in this paper), and we believe that sequences of actions that are nearly equivalent are potential sources of confusion for the user, who may

believe they are exactly equivalent, unaware of the discrepancies. Potential applications are wide; in particular, for safety-critical devices, actual differences between sequences that seem the same to the user may have adverse consequences.

The scope of our current approach is reactive devices with discrete interfaces and finite state spaces, subject to some assumptions: the system responds (almost) immediately to user actions; the responses are manifested in the system's (and its UI's) state; silent or external actions which modify the state may be included in the model. Clearly many non-trivial devices satisfy these assumptions. Our models are directed graphs whose nodes represent (sets of) system states, and whose edges represent user actions. This class of model is easily comprehended, and is not particularly specialised or esoteric, but we show here that such models may be readily used to gain real insights into UI behaviour which might otherwise go unnoticed.

This paper's contributions are threefold. First, we identify a previously unnoticed design defect with a wide range of desktop calculator devices—a defect which seems minor but which, we argue, is in fact potentially serious, and of interest precisely *because* it has gone unnoticed for so long. Second, building on [10], we describe a novel analytical technique, theorem discovery, and its application to the calculator; theorem discovery is readily understood and easily applied but (as we show) has great potential as a tool for user interface analysis. Third, building on [2] we describe the application of model discovery to this example; in particular, we introduce and discuss a novel extension related to the production of non-deterministic models.

1.1 Motivation

The use of formal methods needs no justification here, but we are particularly motivated by high mortality rates associated with preventable errors in hospitals, about 10% of which are caused by calculation error—potentially (we argue) aggravated by poor user interfaces that do not adequately support clinicians in performing their tasks, such as accurate drug dose calculations. A recent retrospective study estimates England has 12–15,000 preventable adult deaths per year [3], which scales to a figure of 14–18,000 for the UK as a whole, and a simple estimate of £1Bn per year in additional hospital costs [1]—and this is just direct hospital costs, ignoring other problems such as economic costs for families. We know from our own studies that nurses miss approximately 4% of the numerical data entry errors they make [12].

It appears that: there is considerable scope to improve healthcare; IT could be a large part of that improvement process; and even "small" (by conventional standards) contributions to user interface design may have a very worthwhile impact in improving outcomes for patients. Elsewhere we have therefore explored and shown the benefits of using conventional formal methods in the design of medical devices [4], but this paper seeks to push the methodological boundaries further.

Our goal is more dependable user interfaces: ones suitable and appropriate for human users interactively controlling mission-critical systems. Yet the methods that might support this—formal methods on the one hand, and HCI on the other—are ill-suited to the task and have virtually no overlap: formal methods are analytic, rigorous and mathematical, whereas HCI is human, subjective, and empirical. If we are to make progress and create methods that work in practice, we need to address some or all of the following key issues:

- Formal methods (particular in the wild) are difficult to use, and not widely adopted; we need popular formal methods, or a way of avoiding formalisation [7]. User interfaces are rarely formalised, and programs implementing them use imperative style, side-effects, complex timing (event queues, etc.), and low level error management, all of which are difficult to formalise. Often a UI's success depends on unformalised features, such as the user's ability to track mode. UIs are usually extremely complex, and implemented on top of interacting APIs with unknown provenance; these APIs, even for routine tasks such as number entry, are unformalised and usually surprisingly bug ridden [9]. Hence even if formal methods are used for UIs, the UI is not properly checked. Many UIs have a large hardware component, and are subject to unspecified hardware-oriented interactions (e.g. key bounce, display size limitations).

- Even though safety critical applications usually have UIs, the main thrust of HCI addresses user experience, satisfaction, etc.—properties that are not readily formalised, and not related to dependability, arguably the main concern of formal methods.

- Finally, there is little economic pressure to improve dependability: it is invisible throughout design and deployment, to consumers, developers and regulators. Computers are fast and fun, and investment in rigorous development to avoid rarely experienced defects is not cost effective, particularly if legal safeguards can reduce liability.

That list of issues suffices to motivate the present paper, and our emphasis on 'lightweight' techniques for the rigorous analysis of running systems; we recommend [6] for more on formal methods, though we are unaware of similar critiques of HCI.

2. CASE STUDY: THE CASIO HS-8V

As a case study to introduce our methods we choose a device which is sufficiently complex to exhibit interesting properties, but also familiar enough that we need not explain its intended

Figure 1: Casio HS-8V: actual device and simulation

behaviour, use requirements, and so on, and that is of a class which has been very widely studied in the psychological, HCI and programming literature; arguably, we should find nothing new of note.

The Casio HS-8V is a popular desktop calculator of a very familiar kind: it has a keypad for entry of decimal digits, a screen with space for numbers up to eight digits long, basic arithmetic operations such as addition and multiplication, and a simple memory facility. Devices like this are common in healthcare where they are routinely used for drug dosage calculations, and so their correct use and operation is clearly critical; as such they are potentially interesting examples for researchers concerned with general methods of improving the safe use of interactive devices. Note that there is nothing particularly special about the HS-8V, and we do not seek to single it out for attention in and of itself: we see exactly the same behaviour and issues described here on a wide range of desktop and scientific calculators, from many different manufacturers including Canon, Citizen, HP, and Sharp, and generic brands; the HS-8V is simply the instance we happened to study in detail first.

We built an HS-8V simulation using Mathematica, and used model discovery [2] to extract models of some aspects of the simulation's behaviour; [11] introduces the simulation and the models, as the subject of a social-network based analysis. Figure 1 shows the device and our simulation, and figure 2 shows a graphical view of typical models we produced and subsequently analysed.

This simulation-based approach has both limitations and advantages. It would, obviously, be ideal in practice (but not necessarily for a research programme) to perform model discovery directly on a running device or at least its underlying software, but as this was not feasible we took the simulation approach. The device is small enough that we can be confident that the simulation is accurate to a point where it potentially provides useful insights into the actual device behaviour, and indeed this has been the case: we found some surprising results that are valid in general, and readily checked by hand to be valid for the HS-8V in particular. More usefully, we have shown our techniques scale to a real

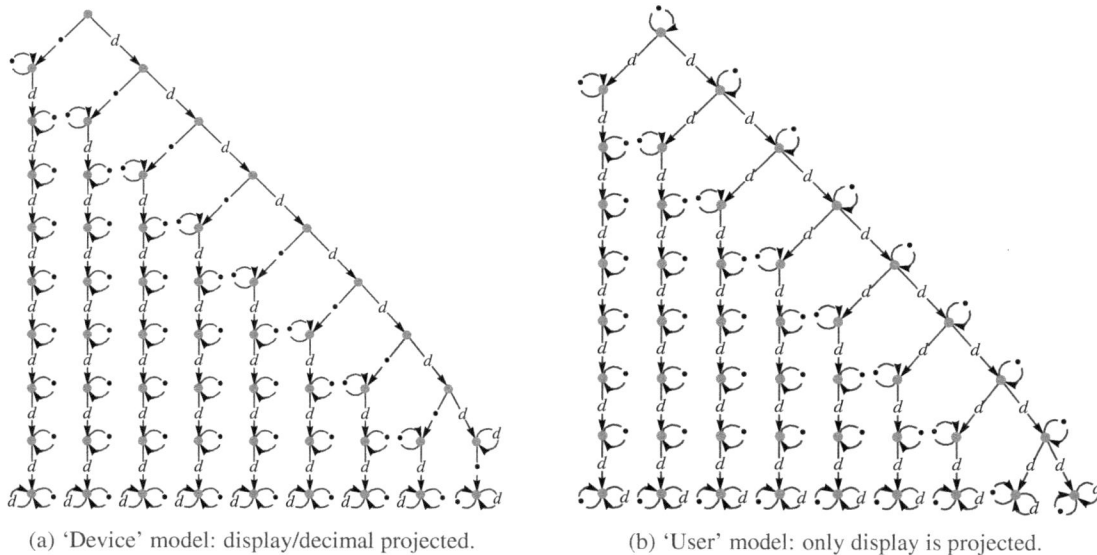

(a) 'Device' model: display/decimal projected.　　　　(b) 'User' model: only display is projected.

Figure 2: Two models of number entry on the Casio HS-8V desktop calculator.

level of complexity, and therefore are likely to have wider applications in user interface software development.

What did we find in our analysis? When the HS-8V is switched on, although the user has keyed nothing it displays ▨, as noted in [11]. Now, if the user subsequently keys ⊡0⊡ or ⊡•⊡, the display remains unchanged. Therefore with a display of ▨, the user cannot tell if they (or somebody else) has previously keyed ⊡0⊡ or ⊡•⊡; if they then press ⊡5⊡ (say) the resultant number could be either 0.5 or 5.0.

What theorem discovery showed us is that *whenever* the user keys a decimal point, the display remains unchanged: the ⊡•⊡ key *never* changes the display at all! This was so surprising that we assumed there was a bug in our model or analysis, but on inspection the observation was found to be true, not only of the model but also of the actual device. (We describe the theorem discovery process and its application to the HS-8V—and some other theorems we discovered—in section 4.)

That the display remains unchanged is not only surprising, but also quite worrying. We knew before we started that if the user keys a second decimal point the display would be unchanged: that is, the HS-8V ignores syntax errors, and elsewhere we have argued the dangers of this design defect [9]. In particular, the HS-8V gives the user no clue how many decimal points (0 or more) have been keyed, nor even whether the ⊡•⊡ was the last key pressed; thus, the feedback usability heuristic [5] is broken. Going deeper, if the HS-8V had a ⊡DEL⊡ key, its use would be unpredictable. (Indeed, the HP EasyCalc 100 also always displays a decimal point, and *does* have a delete key which behaves unpredictably as a consequence.) In short: a class of user error is undetected by the HS-8V, is undetectable by the user (the HS-8V display gives inadequate feedback), and even if errors were correctable, correction would be unpredictable. Since users may make er-

rors from slips or key bounce, we would argue that this type of design is unsatisfactory, particularly as the device may be used in safety critical environments.

Our approach has *automatically* found a design defect we had overlooked. Since we (and everyone else for maybe 50 years) had previously overlooked this defect, it is hard to imagine performing experiments that would have uncovered it. Having discovered it, it is easy to propose solutions and, for example, plan A/B empirical studies: which designs do users prefer, and which lead to fewer errors?

3. MODEL DISCOVERY OF THE HS-8V

We built our models using the basic technique of model discovery as described in [2], but with some special considerations and extensions tailored to the application, which we now describe.

First, we faced the problem that the full state space for the calculator is about 10^{17} states, as there is a display of 8 decimal digits, a memory of 8 decimal digits, and a few modes. This is too large to generate an explicit model for, and such a model would anyway be computationally expensive to analyse—certainly beyond our current theorem discovery implementation. Instead, we focussed on a particular aspect of interest to us, i.e. number entry, by ignoring the arithmetical/operational keys (⊡+⊡, ⊡=⊡, ⊡M+⊡, etc.); going further, we have good reason to believe that every non-zero digit behaves the same way, and therefore used ⊡1⊡ as a proxy for all non-zero digits (displayed in figure 2 as d). Our final alphabet of user actions for model discovery thus consisted of only ⊡1⊡ and ⊡•⊡. (We also produced and analysed some models where ⊡0⊡ and ⊡AC⊡ were included, but we do not discuss them here.)

We produced two models, distinguished by the state projection used, and pictured in figure 2. In the first, which we call

103

the 'device' model, we project the full internal state of the simulation, including not only the display but also a value indicating whether the decimal key has been pressed recently; in the second, which we call the 'user' model, we project only the display contents: what the user can see.

Finally, we applied a novel extension to model discovery, which has not been described previously. The basic operation of model discovery is to have a queue of (state, action) pairs, and to repeatedly pick out a pair, reset the device to the given state, apply the given action, and see where it takes you. Our novel extension is to add pairs whose actions are *compound*, i.e. sequences of atomic user actions, where previously only atomic actions have been used. In particular, we hard-coded that at every state, four actions would be explored: $\boxed{1}$, $\boxed{\bullet}$, $\boxed{1}\,\boxed{\bullet}$, and $\boxed{\bullet}\,\boxed{1}$. Note that the effects of these compound actions appear in the model in 'small step' form, where every intermediate state/edge visited during the compound action is added to the model (if not already present)—there are no edges labelled $\boxed{\bullet}\,\boxed{d}$, for example. By differentiating between the effect of a $\boxed{1}$ on its own, and a $\boxed{1}$ which immediately follows a $\boxed{\bullet}$, we are able to probe our simulation (modulo the abstraction used) for non-determinism.

As can be seen from figure 2(b), this strategy was successful in the case of the 'user' model. Consider the root/initial state, at the top of the figure: here $\boxed{\bullet}$ induces a self-loop (the display is unchanged by that action), and we have two edges labelled d, leading non-deterministically to those parts of the model in which $\boxed{\bullet}$ was previously pressed (left-hand branch) and those parts where it was not (right-hand branch). This pattern is repeated to the right: *each* left-hand branch is a world where $\boxed{\bullet}$ has just been pressed, and only $\boxed{1}$ has any effect on the model; and each right-hand branch is a world where $\boxed{\bullet}$ is yet to be pressed. Without compound actions, model discovery as described in [2] could not possibly produce such a model, as it only allows one outgoing edge per action per state.

That a compound action (such as, in this case, $\boxed{\bullet}\,\boxed{1}$) adds a new state or edge to the model during the model discovery process should, arguably, raise a warning: it indicates either that the abstraction/projection being used is poor (i.e. it is collapsing too many states together), or that an observer (e.g. the end user) cannot predictably differentiate between states that should rightfully be distinct. In the case of the HS-8V user model, this non-determinism is bound up in the fact that $\boxed{\bullet}$ never changes the display, as exposed to us via theorem discovery—but an earlier warning, during model discovery, could have been salient. Finally, note that the 'device' model is deterministic: the compound actions, though explored, never add any new states or edges in that model.

4. THEOREM DISCOVERY

Theorem discovery, introduced in [10] is based on a simple core concept: given a state machine which notionally represents a model of some user interface (its states are system states and its edges user actions), we systematically compute *strings* of actions, and the *effects* of those strings over the

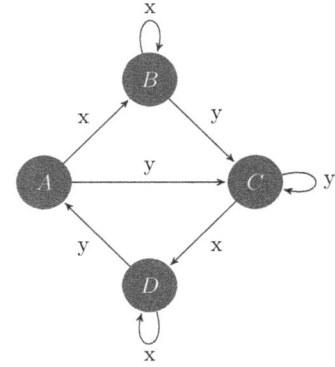

Figure 3: A finite state machine

whole model, and look for equivalences between the effects (and thus, in some sense, the strings). The key question is: what exactly do we mean by the 'effect' of a string of actions 'over the whole model'? How are such effects to be represented and computed?

Consider the simple machine in figure 3; we have four states labelled, $\{A, B, C, D\}$ and an alphabet of two actions $\{x, y\}$. Writing $[\![x]\!]$ and $[\![y]\!]$ for the effects of the actions x and y over the whole model, we can represent those effects very easily in various ways, e.g. as functions from state to state:

$$\begin{array}{ll} [\![x]\!](A) = B & , \quad [\![y]\!](A) = C \\ [\![x]\!](B) = B & , \quad [\![y]\!](B) = C \\ [\![x]\!](C) = D & , \quad [\![y]\!](C) = C \\ [\![x]\!](D) = D & , \quad [\![y]\!](D) = A \end{array}$$

Or, more concisely as ordered lists of destination states, where source state is encoded as list position:

$$[\![x]\!] = \langle B, B, D, D \rangle \quad , \quad [\![y]\!] = \langle C, C, C, A \rangle$$

Or (as described in detail in [8]), as adjacency matrices:

$$[\![x]\!] = \begin{pmatrix} 0 & 1 & 0 & 0 \\ 0 & 1 & 0 & 0 \\ 0 & 0 & 0 & 1 \\ 0 & 0 & 0 & 1 \end{pmatrix}, \quad [\![y]\!] = \begin{pmatrix} 0 & 0 & 1 & 0 \\ 0 & 0 & 1 & 0 \\ 0 & 0 & 1 & 0 \\ 1 & 0 & 0 & 0 \end{pmatrix}$$

All of these representations are easily extended to deal with strings of actions, and the appropriate representation for the effect of a given string is easily computed by composition of the values for the string's components (e.g. in the matrix case by multiplication); for example:

$$\begin{array}{llll} [\![x]\!](A) = B & \wedge & [\![y]\!](B) = C & \Rightarrow & [\![xy]\!](A) = C \\ [\![x]\!](B) = B & \wedge & [\![y]\!](B) = C & \Rightarrow & [\![xy]\!](B) = C \\ [\![x]\!](C) = D & \wedge & [\![y]\!](D) = A & \Rightarrow & [\![xy]\!](C) = A \\ [\![x]\!](D) = D & \wedge & [\![y]\!](D) = A & \Rightarrow & [\![xy]\!](D) = A \end{array}$$

So xy takes you from A to C, from B to C, etc., as is easily checked by inspection. Or, again, we might write:

$$[\![xy]\!] = \langle C, C, A, A \rangle$$

Now, checking such effect representations for equality is obviously trivial.

(Note: this machine is deterministic, so there is one destination for each action in each state; non-deterministic machines

104

require sets of destination states, so to be fully general we should write $[\![xy]\!] = \langle \{C\}, \{C\}, \{A\}, \{A\} \rangle$; of course, this is easily programmed—and happens to be trivially handled by the matrix representation.)

Given that we can represent and compute effects in this way, it is then straightforward to construct an algorithm which computes equivalence theorems. In essence, the algorithm systematically computes ever-longer strings of actions and their effects, grouping the strings into equivalence classes by effect. When a string is added to an existing class (rather than forming a new one), the algorithm reports an equivalence theorem between that string and the canonical/first member of the class it's been added to. Such an algorithm is described in [10]; that version happens to be written in terms of the matrix representation, whereas our implementation (in Haskell) uses a list based representation internally, and allows a variety of input formats. Running that theorem discovery implementation on the example above, we find five equivalence theorems, two of which (again, readily checked by inspection) are: $[\![xx]\!] = [\![x]\!]$ and $[\![xyy]\!] = [\![yy]\!]$.

4.1 Theorem discovery of the HS-8V

Here we introduce two notations: $\boxed{x}^{\,y}$ for y presses of the key $\boxed{x}$, and $\equiv$ for effect equivalence, so $x \equiv y$ means $[\![x]\!] = [\![y]\!]$. We define $\boxed{x}^{\,0} \equiv \mathbb{I}$, where $\mathbb{I}$ is the identity/empty action (which causes no change of state at all).

Running theorem discovery on the HS-8V 'user' model, we found two theorems. First, we have that $\boxed{\bullet} \equiv \mathbb{I}$. This is the "decimal point key does nothing" theorem discussed in section 3, and it manifests in figure 2(b) as the $\bullet$-labelled self-loops on every state. Second, we have that $\boxed{1}^{\,9} \equiv \boxed{1}^{\,8}$. This clearly reflects the display size of the calculator: once you've entered eight digits, further keypresses have no effect. This theorem manifests in figure 2(b) as the d-labelled self-loop on the leaf state at the very bottom-right. This raises the question: why isn't there a similar theorem corresponding to each of the other leaf states, all of which have a d-labelled self-loop? The answer is that any such theorems would differ from this one only in that they would contain a $\boxed{\bullet}$ somewhere—and as $\boxed{\bullet} \equiv \mathbb{I}$, they are automatically pruned without being reported.

Running theorem discovery on the 'device' model yielded 17 theorems, which may be grouped into two families. First, we have 9 theorems which, taken together, mean "after pressing the $\boxed{\bullet}$ key once, subsequent presses of it have no effect":

$$\forall\, 0 \leq n \leq 8 : \boxed{\bullet}\,\boxed{1}^{\,n}\,\boxed{\bullet} \equiv \boxed{\bullet}\,\boxed{1}^{\,n}$$

Second, we have 8 theorems which, taken together, mean "after 8 digits have been entered, subsequent keypresses have no effect":

$$\forall\, 1 \leq n \leq 8 : \boxed{1}^{\,n}\,\boxed{\bullet}\,\boxed{1}^{\,(9-n)} \equiv \boxed{1}^{\,n}\,\boxed{\bullet}\,\boxed{1}^{\,(8-n)}$$

(Both of these may be generalised to all $n > 0$ given the 8-character limit of the display.) Now, neither of these insights is particular deep or surprising, but they do accurately reflect two aspects of the device which we would expect to be true. Note that because $\boxed{\bullet}$ is *not* the identity in the 'device' model, that key plays a more active role here, yielding families of theorems whose interpretation required thoughtful consideration. The question of how to make such interpretations in general and automatically is obviously a challenging one, however.

5. DISCUSSION

A "small" problem was unnoticed for years and is easy to fix; it is tempting to dismiss it as trivial. We would disagree. The problem, however rare and unrecognised, can have major consequences, and the techniques we used to find the underlying design problems are easily used to find related problems in other systems, whether retrospectively or during production.

Although mode confusion such as decimal point confusion is a known design problem, there is no empirical data available on whether adverse incidents are caused by confusion with displaying a decimal point regardless of how many have been keyed by the user. One can envisage usability experiments to quantify error rates, and a sufficiently long experiment would obviously establish $p > 0$. One would then reflect on the cost/benefit ratios to decide whether to implement an improved design.

The following examples suggest that the benefits of avoiding the design problem are so considerable that it is irrelevant to ask for a specific value of p before weighing up the trivial additional cost of fixing it. From [12] we know that "trivial" keying errors *do* occur; these examples (listed below) we argue, show that they may have devastating consequences.

1. The 1992 Air Inter Flight 148, that crashed killing 87 people (9 survived), was caused by an autopilot mode confusion between 33 being entered and displayed in a way that could mean either $3.3°$ or $3,300$ feet. The apparently safe height of $3,300$ feet was in fact a steeply descending flight path angle.

2. After an unblemished career, the nurse Kimberly Hiatt calculated a drug dose (of CaCl) ten times too high. The patient, a baby, subsequently died, though possibly from other complications. Hiatt subsequently took her own life, and the Nursing Commission therefore terminated their investigation. Because of that decision, we have no idea how the out by ten error was made, but the cause could have been a misplaced decimal point during a dosage calculation.

3. Vicente *et al.* [13] reports a incident consistent with a nurse entering 1 instead of 5, resulting in a fatal five times overdose of morphine; they estimate the probability of this sort of error as 1 in 33,000 to 1 in 338,800 (a large range of uncertainty because of problems with obtaining accurate data) and accounting for between 65–667 deaths per year in the US.

There are cases of improved designs—they just need reproducing. For example, the Apple iPhone calculator displays ▮0 with no decimal point when it is switched on or cleared (by pressing $\boxed{\text{C}}$). The calculator doesn't show a decimal point until one is keyed—though like the HS-8V a second or subsequent decimal point has no effect (i.e. the syntax error is ignored). The question is why isn't every calculator implemented properly?

6. RELATED WORK

Theorem discovery may be seen as a 'dual' to model checking: in model checking we have a model and properties we wish to check are true in that model; here, we have a model and compute properties which *are* true in that model. This approach is more prospective and exploratory by nature—though we can envisage using the two in combination in a regression testing scenario, where theorem discovery looks for properties, which are then identified as desirable or not and subsequently checked for using model checking.

More generally, many approaches (Petri nets, CSP, state-charts, etc.) can formalise UI features, and are able (to varying degrees) to address usability and safety issues, but usually as part of an approach in the style criticised in section 1.1; our approach is distinctive in two key ways. First, although we can check user interfaces implement required properties, a distinctive benefit is we can *discover* new properties that may be relevant to the application but which had not been previously considered. Second, the techniques are simple and based in practical programming rather than in advanced mathematics; they are very accessible to competent programmers.

7. FUTURE WORK

Theorem discovery as described here concerns only (strict) equivalence of effects; however, we envisage and are exploring a number of variations and extensions to this basic setting. One such variant is *partial equivalences*, where we report effects which are nearly, but not quite, equal—representing areas of potential mode confusion and surprise for the user [10]. We have also started exploring so-called *metatheorems*, computed from sets of the basic equivalences described in this paper; for example, if we have some sequence y such that for all actions x it is the case that $xy \equiv \mathbb{I}$ then y is, in some sense, an undo. Going further, the question of how to *automatically* interpret families of theorems in the way shown in section 4.1 is clearly a challenging one.

We have applied theorem discovery to "flat" statespace-based models of interactive systems, which may readily be obtained from a running system via model discovery or computed statically from some other suitable model of the system's behaviour. The essential idea of theorem discovery is, however, more general, and could be applied to many other kinds of model.

8. CONCLUSIONS

Interactive number entry is ubiquitous, and used in many safety critical applications; in this paper we have drawn attention to a small but (we argue) significant and common defect which has gone unremarked for many years.

More generally, we proposed theorem discovery as a process to uncover unknown user interface properties. An important feature of our approach is it permits conventional software development processes to be used, whether or not they are underpinned by a formal methods approach: after all, all the work reported in this paper was performed *after* a product had been fully implemented. The new insights can then lead to an iterative improvement of the user interface, complementing conventional empirical methods, and indeed raising new design tradeoffs that may beg deeper empirical investigation.

9. REFERENCES

1. K. G. M. M. Alberti. Medical errors: A common problem. *British Medical Journal*, 322:501, 2001.

2. A. Gimblett and H. Thimbleby. User interface model discovery: towards a generic approach. In *Proceedings 2nd ACM SIGCHI symposium on Engineering Interactive Computing Systems (EICS'10)*, pages 145–154, 2010.

3. H. Hogan, F. Healey, G. Neale, R. Thomson, C. Vincent, and N. Black. Preventable deaths due to problems in care in English acute hospitals: a retrospective case record review study. *BMJ Quality & Safety*, 21:737–745, 2001.

4. P. Masci, R. Rukšėnas, P. Oladimeji, A. Cauchi, A. Gimblett, Y. Li, and P. Curzon. The benefits of formalising design guidelines: A case study on the predictability of drug infusion pumps. *Innovations in Systems and Software Engineering*, in press.

5. J. Nielsen. *Usability Engineering*. Morgan Kaufmann Publishers Inc., 1993.

6. D. L. Parnas. Really rethinking 'formal methods'. *Computer*, 43(1):28–34, Jan. 2010.

7. D. A. Schmidt. On the need for a popular formal semantics. *ACM Comput. Surv.*, 28(4es), Dec. 1996.

8. H. Thimbleby. User interface design with matrix algebra. *ACM Transactions on Computer-Human Interaction*, 11(2):181–236, 2004.

9. H. Thimbleby and P. Cairns. Reducing number entry errors: Solving a widespread, serious problem. *Journal Royal Society Interface*, 7(51):1429–1439, 2010.

10. H. Thimbleby, J. Gow, and P. Cairns. Automatic critiques of interface modes. In *Proceedings Interactive Systems, Design, Specification, and Verification 12th. International Workshop — DSVIS 2005*, LNCS 3941, pages 201–212, 2006.

11. H. Thimbleby and P. Oladimeji. Social network analysis and interactive device design. In *Proceedings ACM SIGCHI Symposium on Engineering Interactive Computing Systems (EICS'09)*, pages 91–100, 2009.

12. H. Thimbleby, P. Oladimeji, and A. Cox. Number entry interfaces and their effects on errors and number perception. In *Proceedings IFIP Conference on Human-Computer Interaction — Interact 2011*, volume IV, pages 178–185, 2011.

13. K. J. Vicente, K. Kada-Bekhaled, G. Hillel, A. Cassano, and B. A. Orser. Programming errors contribute to death from patient-controlled analgesia: case report and estimate of probability. *Canadian Journal Anethesia*, 50(4):328–332, 2003.

Combining Static and Dynamic Analysis for the Reverse Engineering of Web Applications

Carlos Eduardo Silva
Departamento de Informática/Universidade do
Minho & HASLab/INESC TEC
Braga, Portugal
cems@di.uminho.pt

José Creissac Campos
Departamento de Informática/Universidade do
Minho & HASLab/INESC TEC
Braga, Portugal
jose.campos@di.uminho.pt

ABSTRACT

Software has become so complex that it is increasingly hard to have a complete understanding of how a particular system will behave. Web applications, their user interfaces in particular, are built with a wide variety of technologies making them particularly hard to debug and maintain. Reverse engineering techniques, either through static analysis of the code or dynamic analysis of the running application, can be used to help gain this understanding. Each type of technique has its limitations. With static analysis it is difficult to have good coverage of highly dynamic applications, while dynamic analysis faces problems with guaranteeing that generated models fully capture the behavior of the system. This paper proposes a new hybrid approach for the reverse engineering of web applications' user interfaces. The approach combines dynamic analyzes of the application at runtime, with static analyzes of the source code of the event handlers found during interaction. Information derived from the source code is both directly added to the generated models, and used to guide the dynamic analysis.

Author Keywords

Static Analysis; Dynamic Analysis; Web applications.

ACM Classification Keywords

H.5.2. Information Interfaces and Presentation (e.g. HCI): User Interfaces; D.2.7. Software Engineering: Distribution, Maintenance, and Enhancement—*Restructuring, reverse engineering, and reengineering.*

General Terms

Human Factors; Reliability.

INTRODUCTION

Reverse engineering techniques can be useful for both testing and maintaining a software system [4]. For interactive computing systems, reverse engineering can be used to extract information about the structure of the user interface as well as its behavior. This can be achieved either by looking at the

code (static analysis), or by analyzing the running application (dynamic analysis).

Regarding web applications, static analysis faces problems related to the highly dynamic nature of the user interfaces. In many situations, the relation between user interface controls and the corresponding event handlers is only defined at runtime. Even the structure of the user interface might be defined dynamically at runtime, with only a basic skeleton defined statically in the code. Additionally, the diversity of technologies that are available to program such systems (both server-side and client-side), makes it difficult to develop a generic approach.

Dynamic analysis solves some of these issues by analyzing the actual running systems. However, it faces problems of its own. On the one hand, the behavior of the applications depends on both the internal state of the interactive computing system, and on the inputs provided. There is the risk that relevant parts of the user interface might be left unexplored. On the other hand, what is observed is the behavior of the application. The reasons for that behavior have to somehow be inferred. In any case, using dynamic analysis alone, the resulting model will likely be incomplete. It might miss relevant aspects of the user interface, and it will be ambiguous regarding what conditions trigger which alternative behaviors.

In this paper we report on work that aims to develop an hybrid approach to the reverse engineering of web applications. The approach takes advantage of the fact that information about the code behind a given user interface is available through the browser. Using a dynamic reverse engineering approach, a first model of the user interface is obtained. Then, by static analysis of the event handlers attached to each user interface control, relevant conditions over the input values in the user interface are determined. This provides two benefits. It supports completing the model by determining which input values should be provided so that all user interface behaviors are observed. It supports disambiguating the model by making explicit the conditions that lead to each alternative behavior of the user interface.

The paper is structured as follows: the next section provides an overview of the state of the art of Reverse Engineering applied to interactive computing systems; after that, an example application is described which will be used to illustrate the approach; the following section analyses the application emphasizing the dynamic analysis' shortcomings when attempting to reverse engineer its user interface; our proposal to solve these problems is then presented; the paper concludes with a discussion and conclusions on our approach.

STATE OF THE ART

As stated above, the two main approaches for Reverse Engineering are: static analysis and dynamic analysis. When both approaches are combined, we talk of hybrid analysis techniques. This section presents a brief review on the use of these techniques to reverse engineer user interfaces.

Static Analysis

Static analysis performs a system's analysis without executing it. This is achieved through the analysis of the source code or the binaries of the system. Examples of static analysis tools usually involve targeting a specific language. For instance, Bouillon et al. [3] reverse engineer simple HTML pages; Staiger [15] is targeted at C/C++ applications that use user interface libraries like Qt or TK; Guha et al. [6] use static control flow analysis on JavaScript applications; Ko et al. [7] use static analysis on JavaScript applications to search for missing feedback in applications; Bellucci et al. [2] perform static analysis of HTML and CSS to support adaptation of Web Applications across platforms, the approach addresses architectural aspects keeping the same JavaScript between the adaptations.

In an attempt to be more generic, and thus reduce the effort of changing the target application's programming language/framework, Silva et al. [14] separate the parser and Abstract Syntax Tree (AST) analyzer from the rest of their tool (GUIsurfer). This enables them to reverse engineer Java/Swing and GWT applications, but also WxHaskell applications, with minimal adaptation to the tool.

When attempting to adapt the GUIsurfer approach to other web based technologies [13], however, problems arose related to the highly dynamic nature of the code. For example, the binding of event handlers to controls is, in many cases, done at execution time only. Indeed, when considering interactive applications, one of the main problems with static analysis approaches is identifying the binding of event handlers to user interface controls. The fact that there are many different ways to perform this binding, makes it hard to determine such binding from a purely static analysis of the code. In the case of web applications, this problem is exacerbated by the dynamic nature of the code. Indeed, Mesbah et al. [10] affirm that reverse engineering Ajax based on static analysis is not feasible.

Dynamic Analysis

Dynamic analysis aims to obtain a model of a system from observation of its runtime behavior. Several authors have studied its applicability to interactive systems. Memon' et al. [9] describe an application called GUI Ripping which consists of a dynamic process that traverses a Graphical User Interface (GUI) by opening all its windows and extracting all the widgets and their information. Amalfitano et al. [1] use dynamic analysis to create Finite State Machines (FSMs) from Rich Internet Applications (RIAs). Crawljax is a tool that crawls Ajax based Web applications analyzing dynamically state changes and creates a FSM [10]. Morgado et

al. [11] describe the ReGUI tool that automatically extracts structural and behavioral information from a GUI, producing a wide variety of views and formats of the data, thus enabling different types of analysis.

While this type of approach solves the problem faced by static analysis with dynamically generated user interfaces, it can only observe the behavior of the interface, and has problems with determining the logic behind that behavior, and with guaranteeing that all relevant behavior has been observed.

Hybrid Approaches

Hybrid approaches try to take advantage of the best feature of both static and dynamic analysis. For example, Systa [16] gathers both dynamic views (using a customized JDK debugger) and static views (parsing Java byte code), and afterwards improves them by merging aspects from both types of views. Li and Wohlstadter [8] describe an hybrid approach that enables runtime maintenance of GUIs. This tool was developed for Java/Swing applications and its focus is on supporting changes to elements of the user interface at runtime, while our focus is on creating models that describe the user interface. This is also the goal of Gimblett and Thimbleby [5] which *discover* a model of an interactive system by simulating user actions. Models created are directed graphs where nodes represent system states and edges correspond to user actions. The approach is dynamic but it also considers access to application source code.

AN ILLUSTRATIVE EXAMPLE

In order to illustrate both the limitations of static and dynamic approaches in the reverse engineering of web applications, and our proposal for an hybrid approach, a small illustrative example will be used. This is a contacts agenda application enabling users to maintain a list of contacts.

Figure 1 shows a subset of the frames of the application. We are specifically focusing on the "Find" functionality of the application (on the left side of Figure 1) which allows a user to search for contacts in his/her contact list. As illustrated in the figure, clicking the "Search" button can lead to three different frames. Two of them are warnings, stating no text was entered or no contact was found. The third one is the main window with the found contacts selected. The results will depend on the list of contacts of the user, the text entered in the textbox and the state of the two checkboxes for "Match Case" and "Whole Words". The other two buttons ("Cancel" and "Show") are currently not being considered for simplification.

The "Search" button has an event handler which triggers the *search* function, presented in JavaScript in Figure 2. The function starts by analyzing if there is any text in the inputBox, and in case there is not, it creates an alert with the text "No text entered". If there is text, the findContacts function is invoked with three parameters: the text input by the user, and the states of the matchCase (mC) and wholeWords (wW) checkboxes (note that this function can be defined in the client or in the server). Afterwards, the function checks if there was any result returned from that function. In case there was a result, it updates the contacts list, and closes the frame. The

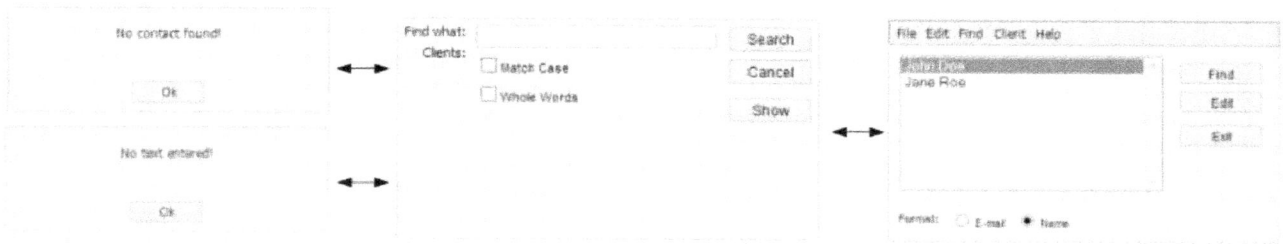

Figure 1. Subset of the frames of the Contacts Agenda applications

```
1   function search(){
2       fInput=document.getElementById("fInput").value;
3       if(fInput!=""){
4           var mC = document.getElementById("mC").checked;
5           var wW = document.getElementById("wW").checked;
6           var res = -1;
7           res = findContacts(fInput, mC, wW);
8           if(res>-1){
9               contactsListUpdate(res);
10              findExit();
11          }
12          else {
13              customAlert("No contact found!");
14          }
15      }
16      else {
17          customAlert("No text entered!")
18      }
19  }
```

Figure 2. Search function

user is thus returned to the mainForm frame (depicted in the top left of Figure 1). Otherwise, an alert is raised with the text "No contact Found".

ANALYSIS

The contacts application is an Ajax application, thus using both HTML, CSS and JavaScript to code the client side and, in this particular case, PHP to code the server side. Therefore, a purely static analysis would have to take into consideration these four languages in order to get some sound results. Not only is that a problem, but we also need to take into consideration the highly dynamic possibilities of JavaScript, as already discussed.

Analyzing the application in a purely dynamic analysis, solves the problems above. On the one hand, we do not have to deal with all the different technologies that might be used to develop web applications. On the other hand, we are able to observe the effect of the event handlers at runtime regardless of how they are registered. Using this type of approach we are able to identify the different states of the interface, but the question remains of how to infer which conditions govern the different behaviors of the application.

As an example, we built a state machine of our application using a dynamic analysis tool (Crawljax). Figure 3 presents a manually enhanced version of the resulting finite state machine. For readability purposes states have been decorated with the names of the corresponding frames, and state tran-

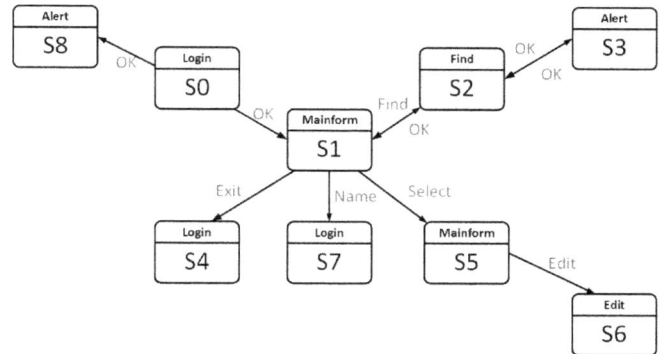

Figure 3. State Diagram based on a model extracted with Crawljax

sitions with the names of the controls (in this case, buttons) responsible for causing them. While this information is not present on the original diagram generated by the tool, that diagram can be interactively explored and such information obtained.

Only a subset of the state machine is important for this analysis: the *find* frame (S2), the *mainform* frame (S1) and the "No contact found" alert (S3). Other frames (and corresponding states) of the application are not further discussed for simplification purposes. The model suffers from a number of shortcomings that we will discuss below.

Model disambiguation problems

When interacting with the application, and as can be seen in Figure 1, clicking on the Search button can lead us to a number of different frames. Through dynamic analysis we were able to (at least partially) identify this situation. As depicted in Figure 3, we were able to determine that we can go from S2 (the Find frame) to either S1 (the Main frame) or S3 (an Alert Frame).

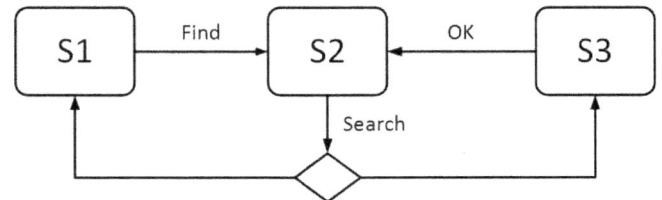

Figure 4. State diagram with buttons information

Figure 4 depicts a subset of the overall state machine with

only the states relevant to our analysis present, and the choice points more clearly identified. The problem is that, while the state diagram shows that when we click the Search button two possible next takes can be reached (S1 and S3), it says nothing about what conditions determine the behavior of the interface. In practice the model that is generated is ambiguous and needs further work.

It should be noted that while we could think of analyzing the inputs used in each case to infer the missing conditions, we could still have the same inputs going to different states, depending on what the state of the system (i.e. the current contacts list). A possible solution can be explored of using machine learning as seen in [12]. However such methods involve previous background knowledge including the encoding of the patterns for the disambiguation. Our proposal is to disambiguate the models through the static analysis of the events that trigger new states in the application.

Input space definition problems

Another aspect that becomes clear in Figure 4 is that one frame is missing from the model. In this case the "no text entered" alert was not found through dynamic analysis. This happened due to the test cases used during the dynamic exploration. A more thorough analysis, with more execution traces, would be needed to have found it.

Indeed, a common difficulty in dynamic analysis is choosing the inputs that should be used to explore the application. Normally, fully automatic dynamic approaches use random input generators or machine learning to define the inputs. Semi-automatic approaches usually rely on the tool's user to ascertain possible input values that are interesting for their intended analysis. In any case, unless knowledge about the application can be obtained and used, it is not possible to be sure that all relevant path in the behavior of the system have been covered.

Our proposal is to identify relevant input values by analyzing the conditions present in the event handlers associated with user actions.

PROPOSAL

As stated, in order to solve the two problems identified above, we propose to include an element of static analysis in the dynamic exploration of the user interface, thus creating an hybrid approach. Through dynamic analysis we are able to identify the event handlers that are associated with each user interface control. By analyzing the source code of the event handlers that trigger the state changes in the application, we are able to add more information to the dynamic exploration process, thus solving the disambiguation problem.

Hence, the process consists of a dynamic crawler that, for each identified frame, performs static analysis using a process which can be defined as follows:

1. Identify the user interface controls of the frame.

2. Discover which event handlers are associated with the controls.

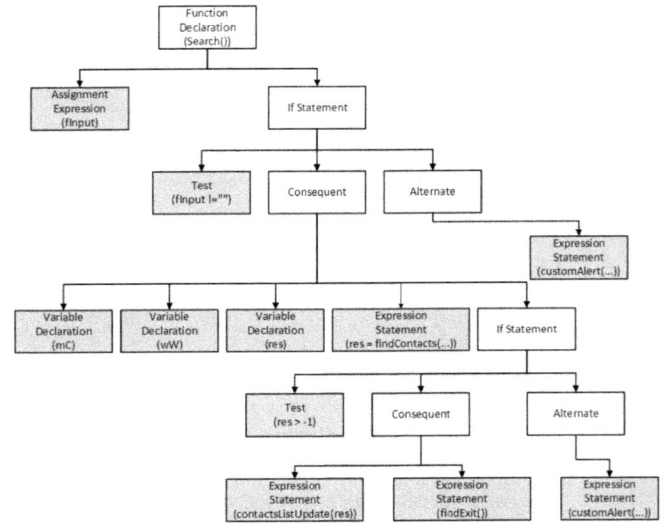

Figure 5. Abstract Syntax Tree for the Search function

3. Analyze the conditions of the discovered event handlers to determine if all behaviors have been analyzed.

4. Set up additional test cases as needed.

Identifying the user interface controls is something already done by a typical dynamic analysis tool. The event handlers can then be easily identified. Since this is done at runtime, we avoid the problems associated with the dynamic binding of event handlers. Note that although this example only uses synchronous calls to the application logic, asynchronous calls (cf. Ajax) can also be dealt with since we have access to the asynchronous request handler. Then, for each handler function, we create an Abstract Syntax Tree (AST) that represents it. Using the AST we analyze the conditions of the event handlers. Two type of variables are relevant. Variables whose value is obtained from input controls (input variables), and variables whose value is obtained from functions of the applications' logic (synthesized variables).

Enough test cases must be generated that all possible behaviors of the handler (branches of the AST) are executed. Regarding input values, this is achieved by identifying which input values must be used during the dynamic exploration. Regarding synthesized variables, determining what input values will cause the application layer to generate appropriate synthesized values is in most cases not easily achieved. This will be discussed below.

A simplified version of the AST for the search function is depicted on Figure 5. Analyzing it, we can see that it starts by assigning the variable findInput from the DOM. Afterwards we get a condition that tests if the variable is an empty string or not. Since this variable is directly associated with an input control we can manipulate, we add test cases for both an empty and an non empty string to the execution traces. And since in the automatic test we had not tested the empty string, we are able to to find a state that was not previously discovered. We called the new state SY, which is an alert of "No

110

text entered".

The next condition is related to a variable named *res*. Unlike the previous analysis, here the variable is not associated with a control we might manipulate but with the *findContacts(...)* function. Hence, it is a synthesized variable. We know that two different states can potentially be reached depending on the value of *res*, as the variable is used in a condition that changes the event flow. In order to fully test the behavior of the system we must, thus, find a way to establish which branch leads to which state (in this case S1 or S3, but note that the dynamic analysis could have not yet found all the possible states, as illustrated above), and that depends on the value of the synthesized variable.

Three alternative solutions can be considered:

1. We can use a debugger to analyze the values of the variable. For instance, in JavaScript we are able see the variables' values at each point using tools like Firebug. Despite being the simplest solution, we have a problem in that our execution traces might not cover all possible behaviors (e.g., if a contact is never found, we will never have the *res* variable positive and will never observe that, in that case the flow goes to S3). Moreover, using a third party debugger to inspect the variables would turn the approach to a semi-automatic process.

2. We can use code injection to change the event handler so that it generates predefined values. In the case of the example, for example, this will be a new function that is exactly the same as the Search function depicted in Figure 2 but has another line after line 7 setting the *res* value so that each of the conditional flows is executed. Hence, in one execution trace we would have assigned *res* to a random negative value and on the other to a random positive value.

   This approach has the problem that changing the event handler's result might have unexpected effects in the application.

3. If we have access to the source code on the server side, we are able to perform the instrumentation as in the previous approach but in this case in the actual source code of the applications, thus changing the actual application code and not having to worry about problems with having changed the event handler. Besides requiring access to the server side code, a further problem with this approach is that after changing the source code, we would have to rerun the application for the instrumentation to be applied.

Since we want to keep our analysis as dynamic as possible we have opted to implement the second choice of dynamically changing the event handlers to functions with the instrumented code.

Returning to the example, after analysis of both conditions it was then feasible to build a more detailed state diagram, like the one presented in Figure 6, where we can see which conditions were responsible to trigger which state transitions.

We can summarize the whole process as follows:

1. Use a dynamic approach to start creating the state diagram

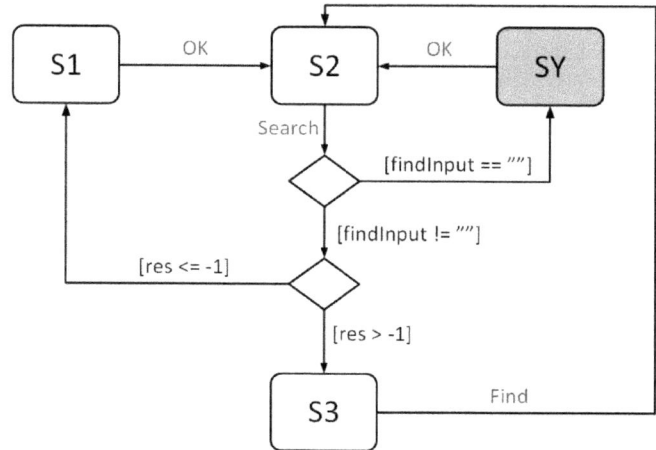

Figure 6. Complete state diagram for the Search function

2. For each state analyze the interaction widgets for the corresponding listeners

3. For each listener create an AST of the corresponding function

4. Analyze the method conditions:

   (a) Analysis which variables are used in the conditions

   (b) From those variables discover which ones are input variables (that we can control during dynamic exploration) and which are synthesized variables.

   (c) For input variables test conditions by testing the different input possibilities in the application. If test cases were missing create new test cases.

   (d) For synthesized variables alter the listener in runtime to a new function with instrumented code testing the conditions.

5. The final states are compared according to the DOM

6. Perform conditions pruning to eliminate conditions where all alternatives lead to the same state (a case that did not appear in our example, but might nevertheless happen in practice).

With such a process we are able to build state diagrams that represent the behavior of Web applications GUIs with more detail such as the one depicted in Figure 6. The added detail shows why interactions with the same widgets can lead to different states.

DISCUSSION

When comparing our analysis to other approaches to reverse engineer Web Applications we believe that we can cover more applications than previous static analysis work on Ajax Web applications such as in Guha et al. [6] and Ko et al. [7]. Moreover, we can add more detail to dynamic analysis approaches of Web applications as we see in Amalfitano et al. [1] and Mesbah et al. [10].

In terms of hybrid approaches the most similar to our approach is Systa's [16]. The main differences are that while

Systa's approach enables a static analysis of the application both before, during and after the dynamic analysis, our approach is done only during the dynamic analysis. Moreover, Systa's approach implies a full static analysis of the application. While that may be feasible on Java, it is not in Web applications since not only are the client side part based on a wide variety of different frameworks, we may also not have access to the server side of those applications. Li and Wohlstadter's approach [8] has a different focus which aims to use static analysis to propagate the changes made on the dynamic view, thus mapping widgets with code. Gimblett and Thimbleby's approach [5] is based on a semi-automatic process and hence not directly comparable. Finally, comparing our work with that of Morgado et al. [12] which use machine learning to perform disambiguation of the models, an hybrid approach has the advantage of not requiring previous background knowledge of the application and its domain.

A tool that automates the proposed approach is currently being developed. The tool uses Selenium to interact with the web application under analysis, and is able to differentiate, at each point, between visible and non-visible widgets, since only visible widgets are relevant for the analysis. Furthermore, the tool is able to extract a JavaScript AST for each of the event handlers registered in the widgets. This information will then be used to guide the reverse engineering process as proposed above.

CONCLUSION

Developing an understanding of an implemented web application is a complex task which can be aided by reverse engineering techniques. In this paper we have discussed the shortcomings of traditional reverse engineering techniques when applied to web applications. An approach to integrate static and analysis techniques has been presented, and illustrated with an example. By mixing the two techniques we are able to explore the best of dynamic analysis, while incorporating knowledge about the code into the models. This has enabled us to construct a more complete model of the user interface.

ACKNOWLEDGMENTS

This work is funded by ERDF - European Regional Development Fund through the COMPETE Programme (operational programme for competitiveness) and by National Funds through the FCT - Fundação para a Ciência e a Tecnologia (Portuguese Foundation for Science and Technology) within project FCOMP-01-0124-FEDER-015095. Carlos Eduardo Silva is further funded by the Portuguese Government through FCT, grant SFRH/BD/71136/2010.

REFERENCES

1. Amalfitano, D., Fasolino, A. R., and Tramontana, P. Reverse Engineering Finite State Machines from Rich Internet Applications. In *Proc. 15th WCRE*, IEEE Computer Society (2008), 69–73.

2. Bellucci, F., Ghiani, G., Paternò, F., and Porta, C. Automatic reverse engineering of interactive dynamic web applications to support adaptation across platforms. In *Proc. IUI '12*, ACM Press (2012), 217–226.

3. Bouillon, L., Limbourg, Q., Vanderdonckt, J., and Mirchotte, B. Reverse engineering of web pages based on derivations and transformations. In *Proc. LA-Web '05*, IEEE Computer Society (2005), 3–.

4. Eilam, E. *Reversing: Secrets of Reverse Engineering*. Wiley, 2005.

5. Gimblett, A., and Thimbleby, H. User Interface Model Discovery : Towards a Generic Approach. In *Proc. EICS '10*, ACM Press (2010), 145–154.

6. Guha, A., Krishnamurthi, S., and Jim, T. Using static analysis for Ajax intrusion detection. In *Proc. 18th WWW '09*, ACM, Ed., ACM Press (2009), 561–570.

7. Ko, A. J., and Zhang, X. Feedlack detects missing feedback in web applications. In *Proc. CHI '11*, ACM Press (2011), 2177–2186.

8. Li, P., and Wohlstadter, E. View-based maintenance of graphical user interfaces. In *Proc. 7th AOSD '08*, ACM Press (2008), 156–167.

9. Memon, A., Banerjee, I., and Nagarajan, A. GUI ripping: reverse engineering of graphical user interfaces for testing. In *Proc. 10th WCRE '03*, IEEE Computer Society (2003), 260–269.

10. Mesbah, A., Bozdag, E., and van Deursen, A. Crawling AJAX by Inferring User Interface State Changes. In *Proc. ICWE '08*, IEEE Computer Society (2008), 122–134.

11. Morgado, I. C., Paiva, A. C. R., and Faria, J. a. P. Dynamic Reverse Engineering of Graphical User Interfaces. *International Journal On Advances in Software 5*, 3 (2012), 224–236.

12. Morgado, I. C., Paiva, A. C. R., Faria, J. P., and Camacho, R. GUI reverse engineering with machine learning. In *Proc. RAISE '12*, IEEE Computer Society (2012), 27–31.

13. Silva, C. E. Reverse engineering of rich internet applications. Master's thesis, Escola de Engenharia, Universidade do Minho, 2009.

14. Silva, J. C., Silva, C. E., Gonçalo, R., Saraiva, J., and Campos, J. C. The GUISurfer tool: towards a language independent approach to reverse engineering GUI code. In *Proc. EICS '10*, ACM Press (2010), 181–186.

15. Staiger, S. Static Analysis of Programs with Graphical User Interface. In *Proc. CSMR '07*, IEEE Computer Society (2007), 252–264.

16. Systa, T. On the relationships between static and dynamic models in reverse engineering Java software. In *Proc. 6th WCRE 1999*, IEEE Computer Society (1999), 304–313.

Timisto: A Technique to Extract Usage Sequences from Storyboards

Joël Vogt[1,2] **Kris Luyten**[2] **Mieke Haesen**[2] **Karin Coninx**[2] **Andreas Meier**[1]

[1]Department of Informatics
University of Fribourg, 1700 Fribourg,
Switzerland
{joel.vogt, andreas.meier}@unifr.ch

[2]Hasselt University - transnationale Universiteit
Limburg - IBBT Expertise Centre for Digital Media
Wetenschapspark 2, 3590 Diepenbeek, Belgium
{kris.luyten, mieke.haesen, karin.coninx}@uhaselt.be

ABSTRACT

Storyboarding is a technique that is often used for the conception of new interactive systems. A storyboard illustrates graphically how a system is used by its users and what a typical context of usage is. Although the informal notation of a storyboard stimulates creativity, and makes them easy to understand for everyone, it is more difficult to integrate in further steps in the engineering process. We present an approach, "Time In Storyboards" (Timisto), to extract valuable information on how various interactions with the system are positioned in time with respect to each other. Timisto does not interfere with the creative process of storyboarding, but maximizes the structured information about time that can be deduced from a storyboard.

Author Keywords

Design Methods;Analysis Methods;

ACM Classification Keywords

H.5.2 User Interfaces (D.2.2, H.1.2, I.3.6): User-centered design; I.2.4 Knowledge Representation Formalisms and Methods (F.4.1): Temporal logic

INTRODUCTION

Engineering an interactive software system is essentially a creative activity that needs input from both technical and non-technical people. Current notations and tools often follow a strict *separation of concern* strategy in which members of such a team use the notations and tools they are accustomed with [3]. Given the wide diversity of notations and tools, synchronizing the various efforts is cumbersome [7]. Informal design artifacts are very accessible to non-technical people and often only require pen and paper [4, 13]. Storyboarding is such an informal technique that is frequently used for the design of interactive systems [14] and that will be the basic notation for the contributions described in this paper. The

focus in this paper is on the extraction of both a comprehensible and formal specification of time based on informal storyboard drawings. With this piece of work we strengthen the link between the valuable informal artifacts that help us to understand the requirements and the users point of view and the engineering artifacts that are used to construct the interactive software system. As such this piece of work contributes to the engineering process to create interactive systems, more specifically helps to connect informal and formal artifacts.

We use McCloud's works on comics [9, 10] as a reference framework for analyzing storyboards. Like comics, storyboards are a visual form of storytelling. Images of imaginary or real things such as places, people or ideas are used to illustrate and convey ideas. Furthermore, drawing comics or storyboards is inherently spatial. The physical space that is used by sequences of drawings often visualizes the progression of the story in time. The sequence of images, their size, and the distance between images help the reader to move through time by moving through space. Panels have a special role in comics. They are snapshots that explicitly show moments of the story. The story evolves between the panels and is developed further in the reader's imagination. Figure 1 presents a storyboard that describes an interactive setup for an exhibition.

Unlike textual descriptions of scenarios or engineering models, understanding storyboards comes naturally to people because images do not require specific knowledge to decode [9]. A limitation of storyboards for further usage in an engineering process is that they are informal and subjective and often are still a subject to discussion. There is no explicit model that is agreed upon, and the information in storyboards is therefore not accessible to computers. Further comments or graphical annotations may be added to improve understanding among members of the design team [4, 16]. Without formal semantics, the content remains difficult if not impossible to process by a computer [12]. Providing tool support that would allow to automatically infer new information from the knowledge base or transform model to other modeling languages is therefore complex and not possible [4, 8, 12, 13]. There is already a lot of temporal information available in storyboards that can be extracted. Although this information is often incomplete or even subject to

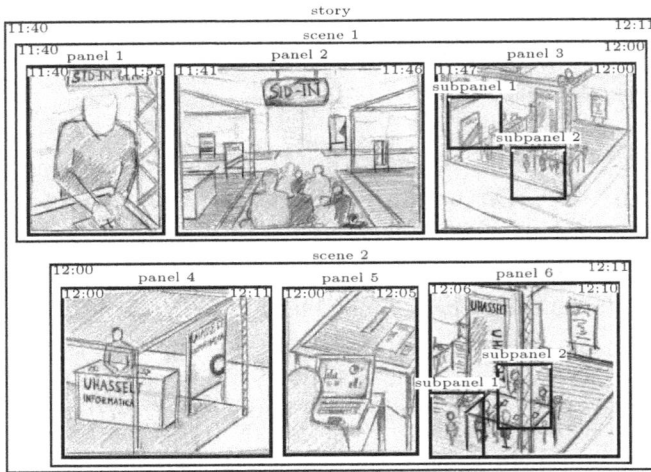

Figure 1: A storyboard presenting an interactive multi-touch system for exhibitions or fairs in seven panels.

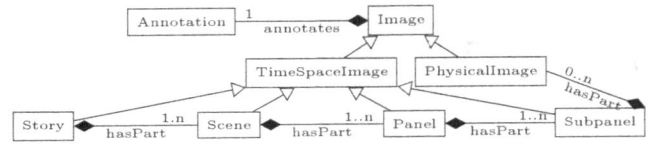

Figure 2: A storyboard contains images to visualize time and physical items. The passage of time is visualized by the structure of the storyboard and the size of images

change, most of the expected behavior of the software can be deduced from a storyboard. Notice we make the assumption a storyboard is sufficiently detailed to get a detailed overview of how a system works.

Storyboarding is a technique that is used in various domains to provide initial ideas and requirements. For example storyboards are a common tool in media production [6] and animations [15]. However, the applications form these domains are not designed to be integrated within an engineering process. We found the essential bit to connect storyboards with other software engineering artifacts, is the ability to extract temporal information from storyboards in a machine-understandable way. Haesen et al explored the technique of storyboarding as part of the engineering process [4, 8], but to our knowledge there is no well-defined way to translate system behavior as described in a storyboard in such a way it can be adopted by other software engineering artifacts such as a process model. We argue that the behavior of interactive software equals the set of ordering that can be found in a storyboard.

We present Timisto, an approach to extract useful temporal information from a storyboard. Our approach does not restrict designers' creativity since we do not interfere with the storyboarding activity itself, but rather helps designers to make precise statements about the time in a storyboard. After the storyboard has been created, our tool asks to annotate it with absolute time stamps. We use absolute time stamps for two reasons: first it fits with the storyboarding concept in drawing a concrete example so we handle the annotations accordingly. Second, using relative timings requires translating this information to more precise timing information which can be cumbersome. Third, using absolute timings avoids disagreement and misunderstandings, since relative timing annotations might be interpreted differently by the team

members. Notice that our approach translates these timings to relative timings afterward and encodes them using Allen's temporal interval algebra [1]. The temporal information is used to map the content of the storyboard onto a timeline that visualizes the passage of time in storyboard. This visual depiction of the timeline helps designers and users to analyze how an interactive system behaves over time according to the storyboard.

STORYBOARD LANGUAGE

Our interpretation of storyboards is strongly inspired by McCloud's work on comics [9, 10]. McCloud defines comics as a "sequential art" or more verbosely as "juxtaposed pictorial and other images in deliberate sequence" [9]. By defining a storyboard language we want to clarify the way a storyboard provides information by means of images and structure. This combination of images and structure is very powerful to specify temporal information in storyboards.

A storyboard can be compared to a comic and basically presents images that are shown in a sequential order. These images are called *panels*. The meaning of the term panel will be explained below, but first we will give an example of a storyboard and its panels. The storyboard in Figure 1 presents an interactive multi-touch system for exhibitions or fairs in seven panels. On the one hand, the system presented by the storyboard provides information to visitors of the booth at the exhibition. On the other hand, it allows visitors to enter their personal data in order to be contacted by the exhibitor afterwards. Panel 1 zooms in to the multi-touch system and its users, panels 2, 3 and 6 provide an overview of the booth at the exhibition and panels 4 and 5 visualize the representative of the booth behind a desk, collecting information of the visitors that was entered into the multi-touch system. Besides the aforementioned structure that is clearly visualized by the panels in a storyboard, other information can also be inferred from a storyboard. To make use of this inferred information for specifying temporal information in tool support, we propose to annotate basic elements of a storyboard. These annotations concern *scenes* (a group of related panels), *panels* (images in a storyboard) and *subpanels*. The relationship between them is shown in the storyboard model depicted in Figure 2. The characteristics of the storyboard's structural elements can be summarized as follows:

Scene : A storyboard is drawn as one or more scenes

by physically grouping panels of a storyboard that are related to each other in time or in space. In some comics, the author tries to fit all panels of one scene to a page in order to improve the readability of a comic. However, authors of comics can also present two different scenes in successive panels, just to emphasize significant distances between time or space [11].

Panel : A panel is a window into a moment of the story, that shows what is happening during that time. The size of a panel often refers to the time the panel takes. Inside a panel, an actor performs an action during that moment that implies the advancement of time. An action is visually depicted as "motion" or "sounds". Although it is difficult to visually present motions or sounds in still images, there are several techniques to realize this [9]. Panels also steer the reader's interpretation of the story with the angle through which the reader views the story, the level of detail and the placement of objects within the panel.

Subpanel : According to McCloud, a panel with more than one action implies more than one moment. A subpanel captures a specific action inside a panel, thus mostly shows one or more users performing an action. For each action that occurs in a panel a separate subpanel is used.

TIME AND SPACE IN STORYBOARDS

The way time is visualized in a storyboard is not precise enough when concrete information about the passage of time is needed. Truong et al. [16] found that explicit depictions of time can affect a reader's understanding of a story. They argue that "time passing was a significant element needed to understand particular storyboards" [16].

The Timisto Approach

The Time In Storyboards (Timisto) approach builds on the findings of Truong et al. to add an additional layer of precise temporal information on existing storyboards: (1) we extract temporal relations from a storyboard based on structure and content in combination with annotations for more precision and (2) when these temporal relations are incorrect we provide feedback to the user.

For example, panel 1 in Figure 1 can be annotated with specific timestamps that show it lasts from 11:40AM to 11:55AM. During that time the exhibitor checks the multi-touch system and observes the newly arrived visitors. Panel 2 starts at 11:41AM, when the group of visitors arrives at the exhibition, and ends at 11:46AM. In panel 3, booth visitors interact with the multi-touch table: one group from 11:47AM to 11:55AM and a second group from 11:53AM until 12:00PM. These interactions represent two sub panels of panel 3. Panel 3 therefore lasts from 11:47AM to 12:00PM. Timestamps are provided by users and designers to discuss the progression of the story. These values are estimates and the precise timing is not important. What is important however are the temporal relationships between elements in the storyboard that users implicitly describe through the precise time stamps. For example, in panel 1 the exhibitor observes a group of visitors, who just arrived in panel 2. After having arrived, visitors gather around the multi-touch table in panel 3. This means that the action of observing visitors occurs when new visitors arrive. Furthermore, visitors must first arrive before they can access the multi-touch table. With the precise timestamps, such temporal relationships between different parts of the storyboard can be automatically inferred.

Allen's Temporal Interval Algebra

We make use of *Allen's temporal interval algebra* [1] to describe temporal relationships in storyboards. This algebra has thirteen disjoint relationships. The five basic relationships are *before*, *equals*, *overlaps*, *meets* and *during*. The relationships *starts* and *finishes* are two special cases of *during*. Each relationship has an inverse relationship (except for *equals*). The temporal relationships between the first three panels of Figure 1 that were informally introduced for the example in the pervious section, are as follows: "Exhibitor observes" (Panel 1) *overlaps* "Visitors arriving" (Panel 2). "Visitors arrive" (Panel 2) *before* "Gathering around the multi-touch table" (Panel 3). Allen's temporal relationships are transitive: "Exhibitor observes visitors" *before* "They gather around the multi-touch table". Allen's temporal interval algebra is suitable for specifying time in storyboards, because it is a generic algebra and usuable within most application domains. Furhtermore, Allen's temporal algebra works with relative time.

Temporal Domain Ontology for Storyboards

We developed our ontology specifically to accommodate the extra information we encode with respect to the Web Ontology Language (OWL)-Time ontology, being the storyboard structure. Since both use Allen's temporal interval algebra as the foundation for time specification, full equivalence is guaranteed with OWL-Time ontology. Before explaining how the actual extraction of temporal information is done, we define *five* interval types that need to be considered for storyboards:

- **Temporal interval:** A temporal interval defines the time span of each interval with *from* and *to*, i.e. the time beginning and the end of the interval i, where $from(i) \leq to(i)$. If an interval contains other intervals, its *from* value is set to that of its first ancestor and the *to* value to that of its last ancestor. The *hasPart* relationships, respectively *partOf* refer to the the physical nesting of their annotations on the storyboard. The relationships *hasPart* and *partOf* are strictly between intervals of lower, respectively higher granularity on the storyboard. Furthermore, each interval is unique and it is assumed that all intervals are known.

- **Story Interval:** A story interval represents the time of the entire story. It consists of the sequence of scenes that lead up to one or more actor achieving their goal and ending the story. A story interval states *how long* a story took.

- **Scene Interval:** A scene interval represents the time of a scene. In the storyboard, a scene is most likely a group of panels on a page or a very large panel. Figure 1 contains two scenes. The first scene informs the reader that the main setting is an exhibition and the actors are an exhibitor and visitors. It shows a newly arrived group of visitors who gather around a multi-touch table. The second scene shows the exhibitor using a remote monitoring tool to analyze how the multi-touch table is used.

- **Task Interval:** A task interval is the time during which one or more subjects perform one or more actions to reach a goal. A task interval is associated with one or more panels. A task interval describes *during* what time someone did something at a location. *Where* is described by a location ontology. In the first panel of Figure 1, the main task of the exhibitor is to watch newly arrived visitors. His goal is provide information to visitors if they have questions.

- **Action Interval:** An action describes the time of an image that visualizes motion or sound that advance the story in time. An action states *when* a subject does a task. The type of action is described by another ontology. *Who* is described for example in a persona. Again in the first panel of Figure 1, the action of the exhibitor is watching newly arrived visitors to be able to assist if needed.

VISUALIZING TIME IN A STORYBOARD

In this section, we discuss the Timisto application that was developed to provide tool support for the Timisto approach and explain how the precise time information can be used to visualize the passage of time in the storyboard as a timeline.

Specifying the Time with the Timisto Application

Our tool allows users to draw annotations on digital images of storyboards and specify time of the annotation. The annotations delimit the structure and layout of the storyboard and specify the kind of structural element, i.e. scene, panel or subpanel, of each annotation, as shown in Figure 2.

The time of an annotation specifies the duration of that image, which is stored as a temporal interval. The Timisto application keeps a list that associates structural elements of the storyboard language to interval types. The storyboard is represented as a story interval. An annotation of a scene is represented as a scene interval, an annotation of a panel as a task interval and an annotation of a subpanel as an action interval. This assignment can be made automatically, since the structure of the storyboard represents the structure of time.

Function createTimeLine(interval,addLane)

```
1   levels ← {{},{},{},{}}, level ← 0;
2   begin
3       if addLane then
4           lane ← {};
5           add(levels[level],lane)   // Add propagated lane;
6       else
7           lane ← last(levels[level])   // Use existing lane;
8       end
9       descendants ← {};
10      cType ← descendantTypeConstraint(interval);
11      if cType ≠ null then
12          descendants ← ∀i ∈ cType: hasPart(interval,i);
13      end
14      sort(descendants);
15      foreach descendant ∈ descendants do
16          level++;
17          createTimeLine(descendant,addLane);
18          add(lane,descendant);
19          conflict ← ∀i ∈ descendants : overlaps(descendant,i) ∨ contains(descendant,i) ∨ equals(descendant,i);
20          if |conflict| > 0 then
21              lane ← {};
22              add(levels[level − 1],lane);
23              addLane ← True    // Propagate new lane;
24          else
25              addLane ← False   // Set existing lane;
26          end
27          level--;
28      end
29   end
```

Time Extraction and Visualization Algorithm

In this section we present the algorithm we designed for extracting temporal relations from a storyboard and, simultaneously, creating a graphical overview of these temporal relationships. For the sake of reproducibility, we provide an in depth description of the algorithm alongside an example of execution of the algorithm. In the spirit of RepliCHI[1] and Executable Papers[2], we will provide a publicly accessible executable demo of this tool through the SHARE environment [2].

Based on the precise time information, the Timisto application can render a timeline of the storyboard to visualize the passage of time. It will split the storyboard in subparts according to the temporal interval types linked to annotations and present a graphical timeline with these subparts of the storyboard ordered on top of the timeline. We believe this is an important feature of our approach, since during storyboarding a visual and detailed representation of the temporal relationships within a storyboard also informs the creators of the storyboard. It allows for additional adjustments and to detect ambiguities with respect to time during the storyboarding phase.

The createTimeLine function receives an temporal interval, interval and a boolean value, addLane, that states if a

[1] http://replichi.org/
[2] http://www.executablepapers.com/

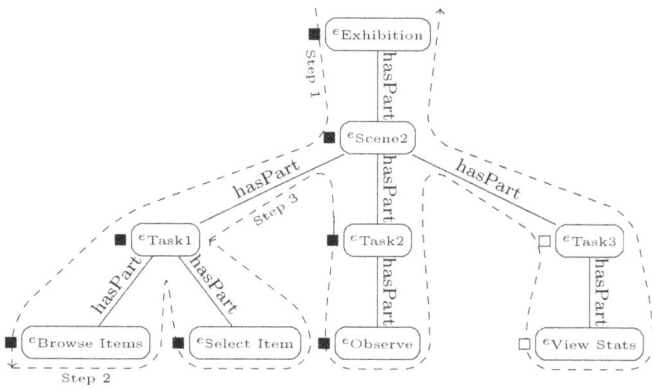

Figure 3: Interval hierarchy for scene 2 in Figure 1. The dashed line shows how createTimeLine places intervals on the timeline. The square left of an interval shows the value of addLane. Full square: a new lane is added. Empty square: existing lane is used

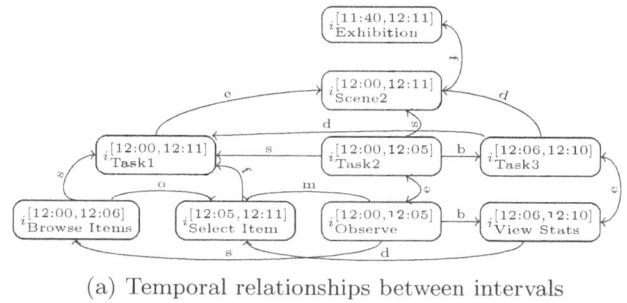

(a) Temporal relationships between intervals

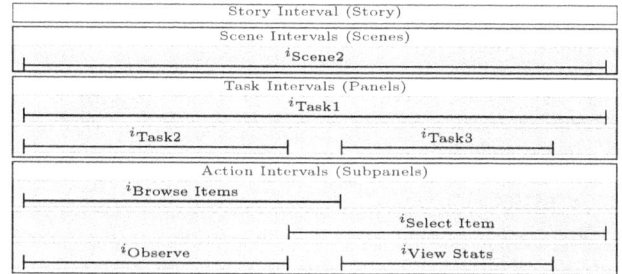

(b) Timeline visualizes temporal relationships

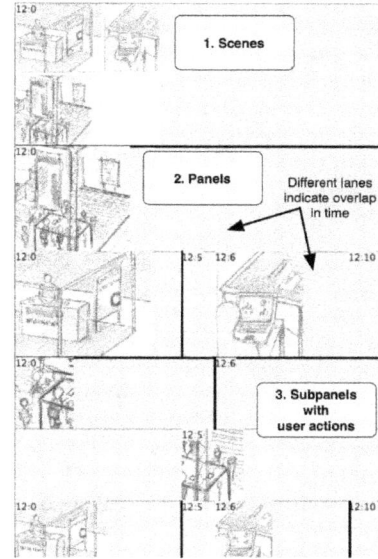

(c) Replacing intervals with images

Figure 4: Visualizing the time of scene 2 as a timeline

new lane for its direct descendants has to be created or an existing lane can be used. A lane is one horizontal layer that can be seen in Figure 4c, so it is a graphical division that represents a timeline for a specific level of detail. To create a timeline, the first argument is the topmost temporal, i.e. the story interval, and addLane is set to true to add a new lane to each level. createTimeLine first prepares a lane in the timeline on which direct descendants of interval will be placed. Next, it processes the direct descendants of interval in chronological order. For each direct descendant, createTimeLine is called, with addLane as argument. descendant is then added to the previously prepared lane. The algorithm then verifies if the descendant right of interval, which will be processed in the next iteration, overlaps with the current descendant. If there is no overlap, that interval can be placed on the same lane as descendant and addLane is set to false. However if the next direct descendent overlaps with descendant, subsequent direct descendants will be placed on a new lane below. Because the time of an interval depends on its first, respectively last descendent, a new lane is also propagated to lower levels by setting addLane to true. The recursive implementation of createTimeLine means that a temporal interval is only added to the timeline after all of its descendants are added. The first temporal interval to be added is therefore the first action interval that starts the storyboard. The timeline is finally rendered by substituting temporal intervals with their annotations. Consider timeline in Figure 4c. It was rendered by annotating the structure of the second scene in Figure 1 and specifying the time in each image. This information is stored as a temporal interval hierarchy, shown in Figure 3. createTimeLine was called with the values interval $= i_{Exhibition}$ and addLane = true as arguments. The dashed line with arrow in Figure 3 shows the order in which createTimeLine traverses the interval hierarchy to place each interval in the right order and level on the timeline.

- **Step 1** createTimeLine is called with interval $= i_{Exhibition}$, and addLane = true, causing a new lane to be added to each level except for the story level. $i_{Exhibition}$ will not be placed on the timeline, because it is not called $i_{Exhibition}$. createTimeLine first sorts the direct descendants of interval, before increasing level by one and calling itself recursively for each descendant. For i_{Scene2}, it adds a lane to the task level, and for i_{Task1} to the action level.

- **Step 2** An interval is added by the createTimeLine for its parent interval. $i_{BrowseItems}$ is added first,

117

then $i_{SelectItem}$. Because createTimeLine for i_{Task1} detects an overlap between its two descendants, it adds $i_{SelectItem}$ onto a new lane. createTimeLine for i_{Task1} exits and is added to the task level.

- **Step 3** However, it overlaps with its sibling i_{Task2}. A new lane is therefore added to the task level. Furthermore, addLane is set to true, to add a lane for the descendant of i_{Task2}, $i_{Observe}$. $i_{Observe}$ is added to the new lane of the action level, and then i_{Task2} is added to the new lane of the task level. Because i_{Task3} does not intersect with i_{Task2}, it will also added to the same level. addLane is set to false, causing the first descendant of i_{Task3} to be added to the same lane as $i_{Observe}$.

Once the timeline contains all intervals (Figure 4), they are replaced with their corresponding annotated image, as shown in Figure 4c.

CONCLUSION

In this paper we introduced Timisto, an essential part to enable correct and consistent integration of storyboards with other engineering artifacts. A storyboard contains a lot of important time-related information on the usage of an interactive system, which was not accessible up until now. Timisto extracts temporal information from a storyboard as a set of temporal relationships that reflect the temporal behavior that should also be represented by the other software models leading to an interactive system, such as process models. Our algorithm uses simple straight-forward annotations on top of a storyboard and generates temporal relations that adhere Allen's temporal interval algebra, a widely accepted algebra for specifying relative time. Our approach has several benefits: it provides an accessible way for non-engineers to describe the time-related aspects of an interactive system. It provides a visual overview of the temporal information in a storyboard. Figure 4 presents such a timeline and shows both the hierarchy (containment in time), overlaps and sequences are easy to read from this visualization. Temporal relationships *meets* and *before* that correspond to sequential events are placed in chronological order. Events that occur in parallel, related by *overlaps*, *equal* and *during* (with the special cases *starts* and *finishes*), are placed on separate lanes. Especially encompassing user interface description languages such as UsiXML [5] can take advantage of our work to connect with the early, informal stages in the engineering cycle. We are currently planning an integration with UsiXML by integration our algorithm with the StoryBoardML language devised by Luyten et al. [8].

The focus in this paper is on the extraction of both a comprehensible and formal specification of time based on informal storyboard drawings. With this piece of work we strengthen the link between the valuable informal artifacts that help us to understand the requirements and the users point of view and the engineering artifacts that are used to construct the interactive software system.

REFERENCES

1. Allen, J. F. Maintaining knowledge about temporal intervals. *Communications of the ACM 26*, 11 (1983), 832–843.

2. Gorp, P. V., and Mazanek, S. Share: a web portal for creating and sharing executable research papers. *Procedia CS 4* (2011), 589–597.

3. Haesen, M., Coninx, K., Van den Bergh, J., and Luyten, K. Muicser: A process framework for multi-disciplinary user-centred software engineering processes. In *EICS*, Springer (2008), 150–165.

4. Haesen, M., Van den Bergh, J., Meskens, J., Luyten, K., Degrandsart, S., Demeyer, S., and Coninx, K. Using storyboards to integrate models and informal design knowledge. *MDDAUI* (2011), 87–106.

5. Jean Vanderdonckt, J., Beuvens, F., Melchior, J., and Tesoriero, R., Eds. *UsiXML*. W3C Working Group Submission, 2010. http://www.lilab.be/W3C/.

6. Jones, M. Getting started with celtx: Scriptwriting and pre-production. *Screen Education*, 46 (2007), 196.

7. Lindland, O. I., Sindre, G., and Solvberg, A. Understanding quality in conceptual modeling. *Software, IEEE 11*, 2 (1994), 42–49.

8. Luyten, K., Haesen, M., Ostrowski, D., Coninx, K., Degrandsart, S., and Demeyer, S. D. On stories, models and notations: Storyboard creation as an entry point for model-based interface development with usixml. In *USIXML*, ACM (2010).

9. McCloud, S. *Understanding comics : the invisible art*. HarperPerennial, New York, 1994.

10. McCloud, S. Reinventing comics: How imagination and technology are revolutionizing an art form. *Perennial, New York* (2000), 118–122.

11. McCloud, S. *Making comics : storytelling secrets of comics, manga and graphic novels*. Harper, New York, 2006.

12. Meyer, B. On formalism in specifications. *Software, IEEE 2*, 1 (1 1985), 6–26.

13. Ozenc, F. K., Kim, M., Zimmerman, J., Oney, S., and Myers, B. How to support designers in getting hold of the immaterial material of software. In *CHI '10*, ACM (2010), 2513–2522.

14. Rogers, Y., Sharp, H., and Preece, J. *Interaction Design: Beyond Human-Computer Interaction*. John Wiley and Sons Ltd, 2011.

15. Smith, J., Osborn, J., and Team, A. C. Adobe creative suite 5 design premium digital classroom. *Beograd: Mikro knjiga* (2010).

16. Truong, K. N., Hayes, G. R., and Abowd, G. D. Storyboarding: an empirical determination of best practices and effective guidelines. In *DIS '06*, ACM (New York, NY, USA, 2006), 12–21.

Design for Human Interaction: Communication as a Special Case of Misunderstanding

Patrick G. T. Healey
Queen Mary University of London,
Cognitive Science Research Group,
School of Electronic Engineering and Computer Science,
Mile End Road,
London E1 4NS
ph@eecs.qmul.ac.uk

KEYNOTE TALK ABSTRACT

In order to engineer effective and usable interactive computing systems we need to consider not just the human-system interface but the human-human interface. The success of many technologies depends not just on how easy they are to understand and operate but also on how effectively they integrate with the wider ecology of our interactions with others. This point has been made especially clearly by ethnomethodological studies of the use of technology in workplace contexts (e.g. Heath and Luff, 2000). It also helps to explain why, for example, the evolution of video and music technology has been driven as much by ease of sharing as it has been by image or audio quality and why some technologies, such as SMS messaging succeed despite having a poor human-system interface. As Kang (2000) succinctly put it "The killer application of the internet is other people" (p.1150, cited in Bargh and McKenna 2004).

If technology acts, by accident or by design, as an interface between people then we might try to generalise human-system approaches to design by treating them as the basic building blocks of the larger human-system-human interface. This talk will argue, however, that this kind of 'scaling-up' approach is insufficient. In particular, the generalization of human-system models to contexts which involve multiple participants leads us to ignore some critical processes that underpin the effectiveness of human-human interaction. More specifically, a focus on the cognitive, behavioural or communicative capabilities of individual human beings does not provide an adequate understanding of how different people co-ordinate their

[1]. Note that most reviewers will use a North American/European version of Acrobat reader, which cannot handle documents containing non-North American or non-European fonts (e.g. Asian fonts). Please therefore do not use Asian fonts, and verify this by testing with a

understanding of what they are doing through communication.

This line of argument suggests that in addition to understanding the broader social context of interactive systems we can also benefit from focusing on the specific low level mechanisms that underpin human interaction. The recurrent need to co-ordinate understanding amongst multiple participants, across a variety of contexts, highlights the importance of the processes by which people collaborate to detect and recover from misunderstandings using whatever resources are to hand (Sacks, Schegloff, and Jefferson, 1974; Clark 1996, Healey, 2008).

This approach can feed into the design of interactive systems in a number of ways. It moves our understanding of human interaction beyond 'informational bandwith' and 'psychological bandwith' approaches. It brings into focus co-ordination processes that are often impeded even by tools that are specifically designed to support human communication. This can provide new ideas for design, a diagnostic process for requirements gathering and formative analysis and comparative metrics for assessing how a technology impacts on the success of communication (Healey, Colman and Thirlwell, 2005).

Author Keywords
Design, Human Interaction, Miscommunication, Repair.

ACM Classification Keywords
Design, Human Factors.

General Terms
Human Factors; Design; Measurement.

REFERENCES

1. Bargh, J.A., McKenna, K.Y.A. (2004): The Internet and Social Life. Annual Review of Psychology, 672 vol. 55, pp. 573–590.

2. Clark, H. H. (1996). Using language. Cambridge University Press.

3. Healey, P.G.T. and Colman, M. and Thirlwell, M. (2005) Analysing Multi-Modal Communication:

Repair-Based Measures of Human Communicative Co-ordination. In Natural, Intelligent and Effective Interaction in Multimodal Dialogue Systems", van Kuppevelt, J. and Dybkjaer, L. and Bernsen, N. (eds.). Dordrecht: Kluwer Academic pages 113-129.

4. Healey, P. G. T. (2008). Interactive misalignment: The role of repair in the development of group sub-languages. In R. Cooper & R. Kempson (Eds.), Language in flux. Kings College Publications.

5. Heath, C. and Luff, P. (2000) Technology in Action. Cambridge: Cambridge University Press.

6. Sacks, H., Schegloff, E., & Jefferson, G. (1974). A simplest systematics for the organization of turn-taking for conversation. Language, 50(4), 696–735.

Crowdsourcing User Interface Adaptations for Minimizing the Bloat in Enterprise Applications

Pierre A. Akiki, Arosha K. Bandara, and Yijun Yu
Computing Department, The Open University
Walton Hall, Milton Keynes, United Kingdom
{pierre.akiki, a.k.bandara, y.yu}@open.ac.uk

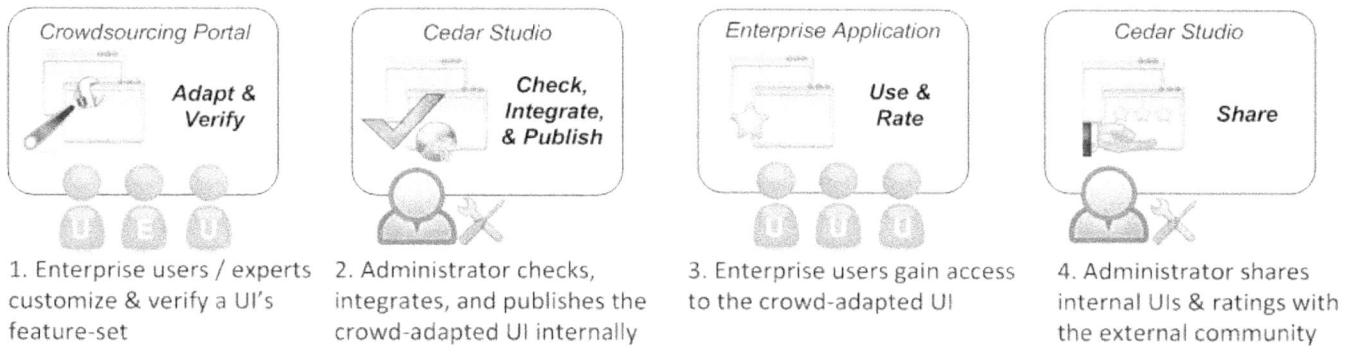

Crowdsourcing Portal	Cedar Studio	Enterprise Application	Cedar Studio
Adapt & Verify	Check, Integrate, & Publish	Use & Rate	Share
1. Enterprise users / experts customize & verify a UI's feature-set	2. Administrator checks, integrates, and publishes the crowd-adapted UI internally	3. Enterprise users gain access to the crowd-adapted UI	4. Administrator shares internal UIs & ratings with the external community

Figure 1. Our Process for Crowdsourcing Enterprise Application User Interface Adaptations

ABSTRACT

Bloated software systems encompass a large number of features resulting in an increase in visual complexity. Enterprise applications are a common example of such types of systems. Since many users only use a distinct subset of the available features, providing a mechanism to tailor user interfaces according to each user's needs helps in decreasing the bloat thereby reducing the visual complexity. Crowdsourcing can be a means for speeding up the adaptation process by engaging and leveraging the enterprise application communities. This paper presents a tool supported model-driven mechanism for crowdsourcing user interface adaptations. We evaluate our proposed mechanism and tool through a basic preliminary user study.

Author Keywords

Crowdsourcing; Adaptable user interfaces; Bloated UI; Enterprise applications; Model-driven engineering

ACM Classification Keywords

[Software Engineering]: D.2.11 Software Architectures - Domain-specific architectures; D.2.2 Design Tools and Techniques - User interfaces; [Information Interfaces and Presentation]: H.5.2 User Interfaces – User-centered design

General Terms

Design; Human Factors

INTRODUCTION

The term "Bloat" [14] is used when referring to an excess of features in software applications leading to a diminished user experience [15]. Although enterprise applications (e.g., enterprise resource planning (ERP) systems, online retail stores, etc.) present the users with a large set of features, each user tends to use a different subset of them. This variation in user needs makes the concept of "Bloat" highly applicable to enterprise applications. Adapting a user interface's feature-set to the needs of individual users could greatly decrease its visual complexity [13].

The concept of crowdsourcing UI adaptations has been used by the gaming community to allow gamers to customize the user interface of a game level and share it with the rest of the community [9]. Leveraging this concept for enterprise applications could be beneficial when considering the large communities and commercial interests in these applications. We differentiate between the following two types of crowdsourcing for adapting enterprise application UIs:

- *Enterprise Crowdsourcing*: Allows internal enterprise staff members to adapt user interfaces

- *Community Crowdsourcing*: Leverages the external communities that use the same enterprise system

A combination of both types could be used for gaining the widest possible benefit from the crowd. An overview of our proposed process is illustrated in Figure 1 and will be further explained in the paper.

The model-driven approach to UI development [7] provides an interesting foundation for dealing with bloated UIs. We previously presented a mechanism called Role-Based User

Interface Simplification (RBUIS) [2] that provides the ability to minimize a UI's feature-set by assigning roles to tasks in task models hence achieving a multi-layer user interface design [19]. In RBUIS, roles are usually assigned by enterprise administrators using the *Cedar Studio* IDE and the end-users are given the ability to provide their feedback on the adaptations presented by the system. RBUIS is based on the CEDAR architecture [1], which promotes the use of interpreted runtime models for developing adaptive enterprise application user interfaces.

In this paper, we extend RBUIS by allowing end-users to perform the adaptation through a web-based feature-set editing tool, which can be made available online for enterprise community members. We should note that the technique presented in this paper complements RBUIS from the following perspectives: (1) End-users can adapt the feature-set using a simple tool without attaching the adaptations to user roles, afterwards administrators could attach the UI adapted by the crowd to one or more enterprise roles. This helps administrators in delegating some of the adaptation effort to the crowd. (2) The proposed technique is potentially helpful with non-role-based enterprise tools (e.g., word processors, spreadsheet managers, etc.) where the user could apply one of the crowd-adapted user interfaces based on a given context.

We consider the following criteria to be important in any approach targeting crowdsourcing enterprise application user interface adaptations:

- An web-based visual tool that allows various enterprise stakeholders (e.g., end-users, experts, etc.) to easily adapt the feature-set of user interfaces
- The ability to check whether the selected user interface features are consistent with the unselected ones according to the inherent dependencies
- A means for end-users to evaluate the usability of the crowd-adapted user interfaces
- Catering for enterprise privacy concerns by allowing administrators to control the UIs that are made available to the internal users and the ones that are shared with external communities

This paper makes the following contributions:

- A tool supported technique for crowdsourcing the adaptation of enterprise application UIs addressing the previously listed criteria
- An evaluation of the tool and technique through a basic online user study (with some limitations) that provided encouraging results in terms of the perceived usability and measured efficiency and effectiveness

RELATED WORK

This section briefly discusses existing works that target the minimization of the UI feature-set to fit various needs and the crowdsourcing of UI adaptations for engaging online software communities in the adaptation process.

Several research works target the adaptation of the UI feature-set such as: "*multi-layered UI*" [19], "*training wheels UI*" [8], "*two-interface design*" [13], "*MANTRA*" [5], etc. Yet, although crowdsourcing has been targeted by researchers for various purposes (e.g., performing expert work [10], human centered tasks such as image selection [4], etc.) few research works target crowdsourcing as a means for UI adaptation that engages and leverages the user communities behind software applications.

A primary advantage of our technique over existing works targeting the crowdsourcing of UI adaptations is the use of a model-driven approach that allows automatic model-checking to determine whether removing a feature affects other remaining features. This dependency is determined through the temporal operators in ConcurTaskTrees (CTT) [18] that are used to represent a UI's task model. Other researchers [3] have used a similar approach for checking CTTs for task dependency but our technique can be demonstrated by an algorithm (Appendix).

Adaptable Gimp [12] is presented as a socially adaptable alternative of the GNU image manipulation program Gimp. Adaptable Gimp allows the community to customize its UI by creating task-sets in a wiki. The work stresses on the importance of user feedback but no mechanism is provided for the users to evaluate the crowd-adapted UIs. Also, even though Gimp has a WIMP style UI, the adaptation focuses on a list of actions in the toolbar. Other research on UI adaption similarly focuses on drop-down menus [13]. Our aim is to be able to adapt any parts of the UI. Also, privacy concerns in terms of managing the adopted and shared UIs are not an issue in non-enterprise tools such as Gimp but our approach addresses these concerns by allowing administrators to control parts of the process.

Another approach [17] allows HTML based UIs to be adapted by users through a toolkit with a predefined set of adaptation operations. The changes are stored in a central repository as Cascading Style Sheets (CSS), which could be applied for other users with similar needs. This approach has several downsides: (1) It is technology dependent since the toolkit only works with HTML based web-pages whereas a model-driven approach provides technology independence. (2) Storing the customizations as CSS files makes operations such as model checking difficult.

One approach [16] attempts to involve the application's user community in the initial user interface design process by crowdsourcing the engineering of UIs. Although this approach has its advantages it does not tackle multi-context UI adaptation, which occurs at a post development stage.

The following section explains the steps, illustrated in Figure 1, of our process for crowdsourcing UI adaptations.

Figure 2. User Interface Task Model (Left) and Concrete UI Model (Right) created using Cedar Studio (Excerpt)

PROCESS OF CROWDSOURCING UI ADAPTATIONS

User interfaces can be represented in *Cedar Studio* on the levels of abstraction given by the CAMELEON reference framework [7]. The excerpt in Figure 2 shows two of these levels namely the task model (left) and the concrete UI (CUI) model (right) representing an "*Item Maintenance*" UI that is common in ERP systems. *Cedar Studio* stores the UI models in a relational database, which could serve as a repository for sharing these UIs among various enterprise stakeholders who can adapt the feature-set. The following subsections explain our process for crowdsourcing the adaptation of enterprise application UIs (Figure 1).

Step 1: Enterprise Stakeholders Adapt and Verify the UI

The adaptation process starts with enterprise stakeholders adapting a UI and executing an automatic verification to check whether the adaptation creates any conflicts. The stakeholders could be internal employees primarily wishing to adapt the UI for their personal use or external experts willing to contribute their experience to the community.

Any stakeholder can adapt UIs by using our web-based visual feature-set editing tool shown in Figure 3. Internal employees could connect the tool to their local enterprise database, whereas external experts could connect it to an online repository setup by the community for collaboration. The tool loads the task model as a tree structure (Figure 3 – Left), and dynamically renders the CUI using HTML (Figure 3 – Right). Stakeholders wishing to adapt the UI's feature-set could simply check/uncheck the selected task in the tree or click on the check/delete buttons next to each CUI element. Upon removing a parent task, the tool will automatically remove all of its subtasks. A description is given to the adapted UI to indicate the purpose of the adaptation (e.g., task, user's computer literacy, device, etc.).

The dependency between features could create conflicts when removing some while keeping others. For example, a conflict could happen if "Field A" was removed but "Field

B" depends on it to calculate its value. The solution for such conflicts would be either removing or keeping both features. Upon completing the adaptation, it is possible to automatically verify the outcome. This verification relies on Algorithm 1 (Appendix) for checking if the removed tasks affect any other remaining tasks. Errors similar to the one shown in Figure 3 would be displayed with the option of reversing the action by re-enabling the disabled feature or fixing it by disabling any dependent features.

If the stakeholder adapting the UI is an internal employee, he or she will gain direct access to the adapted UI through the enterprise application. On the other hand UIs adapted by external experts remain in the online repository to be accessed by administrators from different enterprises. As the next subsections explain, due to business related usability and privacy matters, administrators are able to control the internally/externally adapted UIs that are made available to the enterprise employees and the internally adapted UIs that are shared with external communities.

Step 2: Administrator Checks, Integrates, and Publishes the Crowd-Adapted User Interface

The administrator of an enterprise application checks if the adapted UI matches the description given in the previous step. In case the UI had been adapted by one of the internal employees then the administrator would have access to it through *Cedar Studio* from the local database. Yet, if the UI was adapted by an external expert the administrator could download it using *Cedar Studio* from the online repository in XML format and import it to the local database.

Afterwards, the administrator associates the crowd-adapted UI with one or more enterprise roles (e.g., accountant, novice user, etc.). *Cedar Studio* automatically performs the role allocation to integrate the UI with our Role-Based User Interface Simplification mechanism (RBUIS).

Finally, the administrator publishes the crowd-adapted UI internally for the enterprise employees to use.

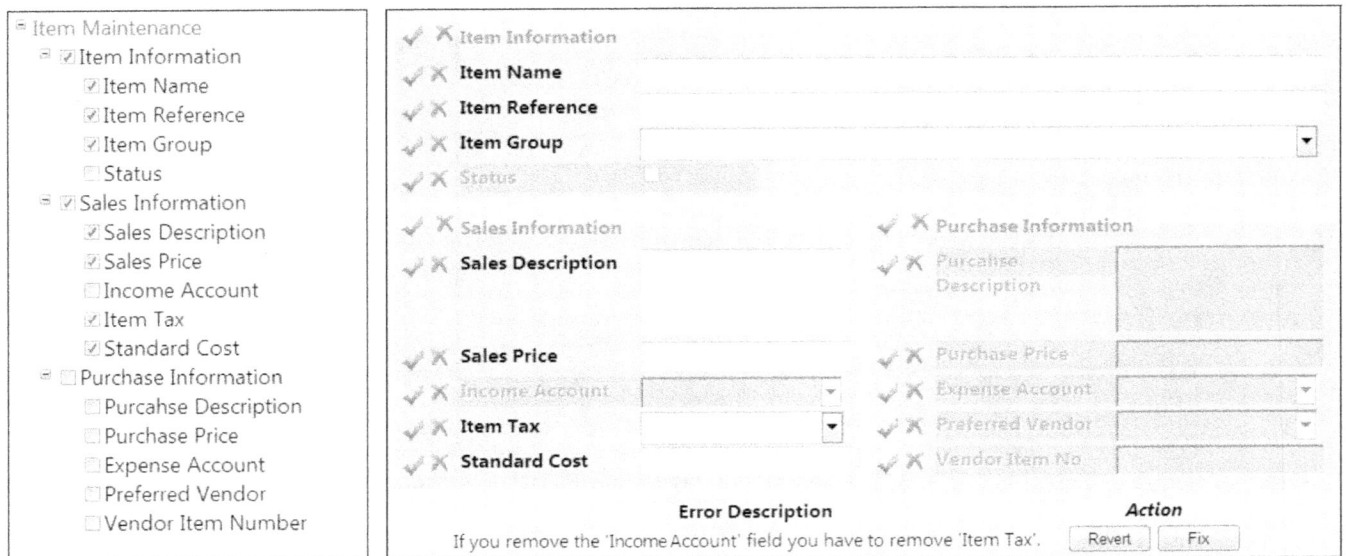

Figure 3. Our Web-Based Visual Feature-Set Editing Tool for Supporting Crowdsourcing User Interface Adaptations

Step 3: Enterprise Users Use and Rate the Adapted UI

After the administrator checks, integrates, and publishes the crowd-adapted UI, enterprise users with the appropriate roles will gain access to it. Although the crowd-adapted UI is ideally intended to provide a better user experience, the quality of the adaptation is always a concern. Hence, an end-user evaluation mechanism is needed to determine the adaptations that truly enhance usability for a given context.

After using the crowd-adapted user interface the users will be prompted to rate their user experience. One possible option to consider is the System Usability Scale (SUS) [6], which provides ten Likert-scale questions that could be converted into one numeric score.

Step 4: Administrators Share Internally-Adapted UIs and Internal Ratings

Due to privacy matters, some enterprises might decide not to share all the internally-adapted UIs and ratings. Hence, administrators are given control over which internally-adapted UIs and internally given ratings to share with the external communities.

In case the administrator decides to share an internally adapted UI, *Cedar Studio* could be used to upload the UI to an online repository alongside a description indicating the purpose of the adaptation. We should note that internally created enterprise roles are not shared with external communities due to their highly specific enterprise nature. Hence, the description fits as a substitution for these roles. Furthermore, ratings for internally or externally adapted UIs could be uploaded and aggregated with the rating data in the online repository to allow the external communities to benefit from this quality metric when searching for an adapted user interface that fits a particular context.

PRIVACY CONCERNS AND BUILDING COMMUNITIES AROUND ENTERPRISE APPLICATIONS

As we previously mentioned some enterprises might have privacy concerns regarding sharing some UIs, which have been internally adapted, with possible business competitors. Yet, this does not neglect the benefits of crowdsourcing UI adaptations. External experts could still contribute adapted UIs to online repositories for enterprises to benefit from.

Experts in commercial (e.g., SAP, Dynamics, etc.) as well as open-source (e.g., Compiere, A1, etc.) enterprise systems already contribute both knowledge and functionality to the enterprise communities. These experts contribute their knowledge to forums and gain a higher status (e.g., Microsoft MVP) in particular enterprise communities. Also, they contribute functionality by extending open-source applications and creating add-ons for commercial ones.

Enterprise applications already have numerous community networks (e.g., SAP Community Network [20]) where experts contribute their experience by helping other community members in solving enterprise application problems. Therefore, similar networks could be created for crowdsourcing the adaptation of enterprise application UIs. These networks could provide access to the feature-set editing tool (Figure 3), which could store the adapted user interface in the network's database thereby making the adaptations accessible online to any registered member.

Enterprises could also have an incentive for selling some proprietary adapted UIs on one of the enterprise application stores (e.g., Microsoft Dynamics Marketplace [21]). Some enterprises could even specialize in adapting and selling UIs for widely adopted enterprise systems. We should note that UIs developed with *Cedar Studio* could be easily shared in XML format due to their relational data nature.

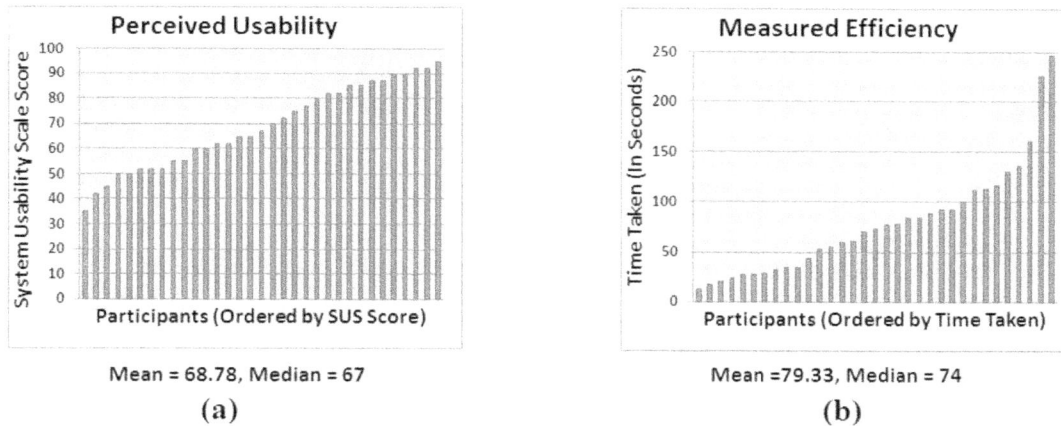

Figure 4. Results of the Study Conducted for Evaluating the Web-Based Visual Feature-Set Editing Tool

EVALUATION STUDY

In order to evaluate the approach that we are proposing in this paper, we made our feature-set editing tool available online and asked participants to adapt the feature-set of an "*Item Maintenance*" user interface as illustrated in Figure 3.

We used Amazon Mechanical Turk for crowdsourcing the adaptation task to 33 participants who were selected based on their Mechanical Turk experience and performance (>5000 hits and >95% accuracy). We diversified the sample by classifying participants into groups based on computer literacy. The participants were asked to rate their computer literacy through a series of questions based on an existing test [11]. The answers allowed us to classify participants as intermediate (13) and expert (20) computer users.

The participants were asked to minimize the feature-set based on given textual requirements describing the fields to be removed. After performing the adaptation, participants were asked to answer the System Usability Scale (SUS) questions to evaluate the usability of the tool. The task model resulting from the adaptation was stored alongside the time it took each participant to perform the adaptation. The stored information helps in assessing the efficiency and effectiveness of the participants when using the tool.

The results of the study are illustrated in Figure 4. Based on the given SUS scores (Figure 4 – a), with a mean score of 68.78, we can say that the participants perceived the system to be usable. Also, the participants were able to accomplish the given task successfully and efficiently with a mean time of 79.33 seconds (Figure 4 – b).

This basic preliminary study provides encouraging results in terms of the overall perceived usability and efficiency by participants with various computer skills. Yet, we should indicate that the study has some limitations in terms of the simplicity of the considered example and the selected participants. When the participants were asked if they would use such a tool in practice the majority agreed, nevertheless we are aware that Mechanical Turk participant could create some bias in terms of providing the researchers with the answers that they want to hear. Therefore, we are merely considering this study as a basic initial indicator and a pilot for future lab-based studies. In future studies we will consider more sophisticated examples from a specific enterprise application and we will recruit participants from the selected application's end-user community to test the tool. Based on the results of future studies we will be able say whether extending the tool can be worthwhile and possibly identify the new features that it should include.

CONCLUSIONS AND FUTURE WORK

In this paper we presented an approach for crowdsourcing UI adaptations by targeting the minimization of a UI's feature-set to reduce the "bloat" in enterprise applications.

Our approach relies on model-driven UI construction and making UIs available for the crowd to adapt through a web-based editing tool. To cater for privacy and quality concerns of enterprises, administrators are given a role in the adaptation process for controlling the externally adapted UIs that are published to the enterprise and the internally adapted ones that are shared with external communities. We argue that such concerns should not prevent online communities from forming around the proposed approach.

Our tool was evaluated through a preliminary online user-study that provided encouraging results in terms of perceived usability, and measured efficiency and effectiveness. Yet, we indicated the limitations in this study and our aim to overcome them in future lab-based studies.

In the future we could extend our web-based feature-set editing tool to support the adaptation of concrete UI widget properties (e.g., size, location, etc.). Also, we will test our tool with a real-life application by crowdsourcing UI adaptations to the application's relevant online community.

ACKNOWLEDGMENT

This work is partially funded by ERC Advanced Grant 291652.

125

REFERENCES

1. Akiki, P.A., Bandara, A.K., and Yu, Y. Using Interpreted Runtime Models for Devising Adaptive User Interfaces of Enterprise Applications. ICEIS'12, SciTePress (2012), 72-77.

2. Akiki, P.A., Bandara, A.K., and Yu, Y. RBUIS: Simplifying Enterprise Application User Interfaces through Engineering Role-Based Adaptive Behavior. EICS'13, ACM (2013), *Forthcoming*

3. Bergh, J., Sahni, D., and Coninx, K. Task Models for Safe Software Evolution and Adaptation. TAMODIA'09, Springer (2010), 72-77.

4. Bernstein, M.S., Brandt, J., Miller, R.C., and Karger, D.R. Crowds in Two Seconds: Enabling Realtime CrowdPowered Interfaces. UIST'11, ACM (2011), 33-42.

5. Botterweck, G. Multi Front-End Engineering. Model-Driven Development of Advanced User Interfaces. Springer (2011), 27-42.

6. Brooke, J. SUS: A Quick and Dirty Usability Scale. Usability Evaluation in Industry, Taylor and Francis (1996), 189-194.

7. Calvary, G., Coutaz, J., Thevenin, D., Limbourg, Q., Bouillon, L., and Vanderdonckt, J. A Unifying Reference Framework for Multi-Target User Interfaces. Interacting with Computers, 15, 3, Elsevier (2003), 289-308.

8. Carroll, J.M. and Carrithers, C. Training Wheels in a User Interface. Communications of the ACM 27, 8, ACM (1984), 800-806.

9. Gajos, K. Automatically Generating Personalized Adaptive User Interfaces. Stanford University (2008). http://www.youtube.com/watch?v=ODrE7SodLPs.

10. Heimerl, K., Gawalt, B., Chen, K., Parikh, T.S., and Hartmann, B. CommunitySourcing: Engaging Local Crowds to Perform Expert Work via Physical Kiosks. CHI'12, ACM (2012), 1539-1548.

11. Kay, R.H. A Practical Research Tool for Assessing Ability to Use Computers: The Computer Ability Survey (CAS). JRCE 26, 1, IACE (1993), 16-27.

12. Lafreniere, B., Bunt, A., Lount, M., Krynicki, F., and Terry, M.A. AdaptableGIMP: Designing a Socially-Adaptable Interface. UIST'11, ACM (2011), 89-90.

13. McGrenere, J., Baecker, R.M., and Booth, K.S. An Evaluation of a Multiple Interface Design Solution for Bloated Software. CHI'02, ACM (2002), 164-170.

14. McGrenere, J. and Moore, G. Are We All In the Same "Bloat"? Graphics Interface, A.K. Peters (2000), 187-196.

15. McGrenere, J. "Bloat": The Objective and Subject Dimensions. CHI'00, ACM (2000), 337-338.

16. Nebeling, M., Leone, S., and Norrie, M. Crowdsourced Web Engineering and Design. Web Engineering. Springer (2012), 31-45.

17. Nebeling, M., Leone, S., and Norrie, M. Crowdsourced Web Engineering and Design. ICWE'12, Springer (2012), 31-45.

18. Paternò, F., Mancini, C., and Meniconi, S. Concur TaskTrees: A Diagrammatic Notation for Specifying Task Models. INTERACT'97, Chapman & Hall (1997), 362-369.

19. Shneiderman, B. Promoting Universal Usability with Multilayer Interface Design. CUU'03, ACM (2003), 1-8.

20. SAP Community Network. http://scn.sap.com/welcome.

21. Microsoft Dynamics Marketplace. http://dynamics.pinpoint.microsoft.com/en-GB/home.

APPENDIX

Algorithm 1. Conflict Checking for Feature-Set Minimization Based on CTT Temporal Constraints

```
// m = number of unselected tasks, n = number of conflicting tasks
// CON = Constant, POL = Polynomial, c1 … c9 = cost1 … cost9
                    [] CheckForConflicts(TaskModel TM) // Running Time = O(m)
                       {//Get the unselected tasks and their relevant relationships
CON  c1   O( )       UnselectedTasks[] ← Select * From TM.Tasks Where Selected == false
CON  c2   O( )       UnselTaskRelationships[] ← Select * From TM.Relationships as R
.    c2   O( )       Where (Select TaskID From UnselectedTasks).Contains(R.SourceTaskID)
.    c2   O( )       || (Select TaskID From UnselectedTasks).Contains(R.TargetTaskID)
.    .    .          //CTT Rel. types that indicate dependency between tasks (TA & TB)
CON  c3   O( )       RemoveTAIfTBIsRemoved[] ← { Concurrency with Info. Exchange }
.    c3   O( )       RemoveTBIfTAIsRemoved[] ← { Concurrency with Info. Exchange,
.    c3   O( )                                   Enabling, Enabling with Info. Exchange }
CON  c4   O( )       ConflictingTasks ← [];
POL  c5   O(m)       foreach uTask in UnselectedTasks
.    .    .                  //Get the conflicts created by unselecting the task
CON  c6   O( )               ConflictingTasks ← Select * From TM.Tasks as T Where
.    c6   O( )               (Select SourceTaskID From UnselTaskRelationships
.    c6   O( )               Where TargetTaskID == uTask.TaskID
.    c6   O( )               && RemoveTAIfTBIsRemoved.Contains(RelType)).Contains(T.TaskID)

.    c6   O( )               ||(Select TargetTaskID From UnselTaskRelationships
.    c6   O( )               Where SourceTaskID == uTask.TaskID
.    c6   O( )               && RemoveTBIfTAIsRemoved.Contains(RelType)).Contains(T.TaskID)
CON  c7   O( )       return ConflictingTasks
```

Supporting Elastic Collaboration: Integration of Collaboration Components in Dynamic Contexts

Jordan Janeiro
Delft University of Technology
2628 BX, Delft, Netherlands
j.janeiro@tudelft.nl

Stephan Lukosch
Delft University of Technology
2628 BX, Delft, Netherlands
s.g.lukosch@tudelft.nl

Stefan Radomski
TU Darmstadt
D-64289, Darmstadt, Germany
radomski@cs.tu-darmstadt.de

Mathias Johanson
Alkit Communications
SE-43137, Möndal, Sweden
mathias@alkit.se

Massimo Mecella
Sapienza - Università di Roma
I-00185, Rome, Italy
mecella@dis.uniroma1.it

Jonas Larsson
Volvo Construction Equipment
SE-63185, Eskilstuna, Sweden
jonas.jl.larsson@volvo.com

ABSTRACT

In dynamic problem-solving situations, groups and organizations have to become more flexible to adapt collaborative workspaces according to their needs. New paradigms propose to bridge two opposing process and ad-hoc perspectives to achieve such flexibility. However, a key challenge relies on the dynamic integration of groupware tools in the same collaborative workspace. This paper proposes a collaborative workspace (Elgar) that supports the Elastic Collaboration concept, and a standard interface to realize the integration of groupware tools, named Elastic Collaboration Components. The paper illustrates the use of such flexible collaborative workspace and the use of groupware tools in a machine diagnosis scenario that requires collaboration.

Author Keywords

Elastic Collaboration; Collaborative Workspaces; Collaboration Component Integration; Groupware Integration; Engineering

ACM Classification Keywords

H.5.3 [Information Interfaces and Presentation]: Group and Organization Interfaces; D.2.11 [Software Engineering]: Software Architectures

INTRODUCTION

In dynamic problem-solving situations, groups and organizations have to adapt working processes and environments to match changing technologies, customer demands and unexpected events. Process-aware systems do not represent a suitable approach to support such situations due to the rigidity of processes. Processes-oriented approaches are suitable for highly specified and repetitive activities and not for situations that require adaptations often. As an alternative, organizations use loosely-coupled groupware tools in an ad-hoc manner to support the evolving needs of dynamic situations. However, such tools require users to coordinate efforts or to become aware of executed and future activities. User may adapt groupware to a situation but may lack of guidance during work processes.

New emerging paradigms propose to bridge process and ad-hoc perspectives [7, 2] by building flexible collaborative workspaces that support a range of profiles: from highly structured (prescription) to highly unstructured (ad hoc). As means of flexibility users assess a situation and choose a profile of the workspace that suits them better.

A key challenge of flexibility relies on the availability of groupware tools within the same collaborative workspace and the possibility of their integration. In such systems, profiles needs to integrate and provide groupware tools accordingly. In the case of a process-aware systems approach, the system needs to compose tools in the structure of a process for guided usage. In the case of the ad-hoc approach, the system needs to structure a virtual repository by which users search, select and integrate tools.

This paper presents an approach to integrate groupware tools, through Elastic Collaboration Components, into a collaborative workspace that supports Elastic Collaboration. The elastic collaboration reflects the flexibility for users to adapt the system to different application scenarios and requirements. The architecture of the workspace relies on a software component approach that provides interfaces to integrate both web-based and native applications, exchanging data over a dedicated communication channel. The novelty of the approach lies in the ability to integrate Elastic Collaboration Components of different natures into a common user interface, for specific collaborative tasks. The paper discusses the use of the approach instantiating three different collaboration components: a collaborative sensor analyser, a collaborative notepad and a multimedia communication tool.

PROBLEM ANALYSIS

Volvo Construction Equipment is a construction machine manufacturer, currently investing resources on the next generation of machines to further increase their availability. The company envisions that teams of geographically dispersed engineers, connected through collaborative workspaces, are able to diagnose machines remotely. For that purpose, wheel loaders are developed with services that deliver telemetric data (data streams) in real-time to engineers for fault-tracing purposes.

This scenario allows for exploring new forms of collaboration in dynamic problem-solving processes. In some cases for the same process, engineers shall (i) follow standard diagnosis processes, using prescribed groupware tools and (ii) select freely and make use of several decision-making, coordination, analytics and communication components to overcome unexpected situations that are not documented in processes. However, current collaborative workspaces are not flexible enough to support prescription of tools in a process form and ad-hoc selection and configuration of tools. For example, Activity Explorer [9] focus on ad-hoc collaboration, in which users exchange shared objects (e.g. files, e-mail or chat entries) through groupware tools in the context of a task spontaneously. However, the system does not implement guidance mechanisms throughout formal processes, delegating to users the identification of processes and coordination of activities. Bernstein [2] initially proposed a system that bridges different interaction support types (Specificity Frontier). It handles the execution of business processes (highly specified) and a minimal set of loosely-coupled tools (highly unspecified). However, the approach does not specify a scalable mechanism to extend the system with additional tools or well-defined tool interfaces to enable data exchange between them.

Dashboards are often used as flexible workspaces to support user-centric customization. Through the workspace, users are able to select and include tools of their preference, according to their needs. In the context of collaborative software development, some dashboard solutions support distributed teams on use of several production, management and awareness tools [3, 12]. Though [6] focuses on understanding user-based dashboard customization, dashboards often lack of guiding mechanisms for users and a high flexibility for users in customizing dashboards with tools, may compromise the realization of structures to facilitate guidance of repetitive tasks, captured in a process.

ELASTIC COLLABORATION

Elastic Collaboration is an approach that supports different types of interaction support in collaboration [7]. In this approach, there is a concept of a spectrum that embraces two opposite types of collaboration: *unstructured collaboration* and *structured collaboration*. Each type occupies a place in the extreme parts of the spectrum, and the spaces in between have characteristics that combine a certain degree of both, as illustrated by Figure 1. Delimited subspectra represent a specific interaction support type, according to the collaboration characteristics of the spectrum. The Figure 1 shows two op-

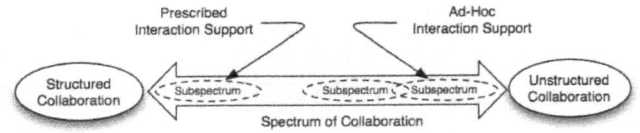

Figure 1. Interaction support types in the spectrum of collaboration.

posite types of interaction support: *ad-hoc interaction support* and *prescribed interaction support*.

Ad-Hoc interaction support implements the concept of unstructured collaboration, in which computer-mediated collaboration within a team naturally emerges and is not guided by prescription. It suits teams that do not need guidance and coordination during collaboration. In Ad-Hoc Interaction Support, users dynamically agree upon the usage of collaboration components for a specific purpose. Collaborative workspaces implementing this approach enable users to customize their workspace by adding components and requesting participation from other users. Here, the team monitors their activities and coordinate the usage of components based on their needs. This approach is based on traditional dashboard systems [8]. However the emphasis of this approach is to use dashboard components as collaboration components and not only focus on, e.g. awareness tools [3].

Prescribed Interaction Support implements the concept of structured collaboration. In such a type of collaboration, facilitators plan the sequence of collaboration activities based on experience, and by each activity they suggest the use of tools. By implementing such a concept, Prescribed Interaction Support guides users on the usage of collaboration components. Guidance is described as a collaboration process, which represents a sequence of collaborative activities, each associated with a collaboration component. In prescribed interaction support, the collaboration process is described in design time and coordinates the collaborative activities that a team executes. This interaction support is based on process-aware systems [4], in which processes are described to coordinate users in accomplishing established goals. However, the emphasis of prescribed interaction support is to provide guidance to users in collaborative activities through components, and not to guide the execution of process activities individually [11] or to require a facilitator to enable and disable tools at specific moments [5].

During collaboration, users are able to transit between interaction support types described in the spectrum. Users may decide by themselves on the interaction support to use according to their needs.

ARCHITECTURE OF ELGAR

As means to implement the interaction support types in a single environment, this paper proposes the Elgar (*ELastic GroupwARe*) system, a web-based collaborative workspace that supports Elastic Collaboration. Elgar provides the software infrastructure to describe groupware tools as software components and integrate them. Currently Elgar supports two interaction types represented as sub spectra in Figure 1: prescribed interaction support and ad-hoc interaction support. In

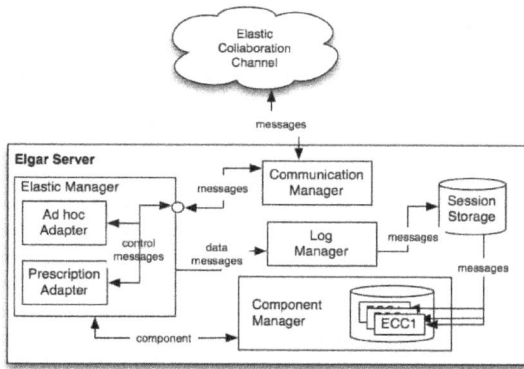

Figure 2. Architecture of the Elgar from the server-side perspective.

prescribed interaction support, groupware tools are integrated through a process language that provides user guidance. In ad-hoc interaction support, the system expects users to select and appropriate groupware tools according to their needs.

Figure 2 depicts the system's architecture and explains the role of each entity in the integration.

In Elgar, an *Elastic Collaboration Component* (ECC) represents a web-based user interface front end for a groupware tool, inspired on *portlets*. An ECC wraps the logic of a tool, extending it to become compliant with the system. Developers of groupware tools need to implement an ECC to use their applications as part of the Elgar system.

Subsequently, developers have to register ECCs within the system to make them available for use. This is through the *Component Manager*. The registration process is simple, requiring the developer to upload the ECC to the server. From this moment, the retrieval of an ECC is possible through the Component Manager.

Session Storage is an important part for ECCs; it contains all data exchanged by instances of a component, and actions performed by users during the usage of the system and the components. Session Storage represents a semi-structured data model that does not set apart the data and the schema. By implementing the Session Storage as such, ECCs evolve the data model of the collaborative workspace dynamically. Every ECC extends the Session Storage with specific component's data. In Figure 3, the Base Model represents base concepts that ECCs may use, e.g. ideas of possible problems occurring with a wheel loader. By registering new ECCs in Elgar, each extends the Base Model with their own data model (Extended Models), e.g. the set of sensor names that indicate a wheel loader's problem.

The *Communication Manager* handles the communication between clients and between clients and the server. The Communication Manager is based on a publish/subscribe mechanism over the HTTP protocol. It creates a reserved channel called *Elastic Communication Channel*. Either clients or server may publish in the channel or subscribe to the channel. The server in particular, monitors the Elastic Communication Channel and records all messages transmitted through it, for

future analysis of collaboration behaviour. The Communication Manager forwards a copy of all incoming messages to the *Log Manager*, which in turn prepares messages to a logging format.

In the system, each sub spectra is implemented as a specific *adapter*. Elgar offers two adapters initially: the *Ad-Hoc Adapter*, associated with the Ad-Hoc interaction support and the *Prescription Adapter*, associated with the Prescribed interaction support.

The *Ad-Hoc Adapter* handles the instantiation of ECCs in the client. The adapter draws the user interface of a web portal that contains instances of ECCs. The user interface of this adapter is based on a grid layout and, like in a matrix, the adapter snaps instances of ECCs in intersections of row and columns. Through its user interface, users instantiate ECCs by selecting them from a menu. The Ad-Hoc Adapter contacts the server requesting a component and starts the procedures to create an instance of the selected component and draw its user interface. The adapter also manages the removal of ECCs from the user interface. Whenever users choose to close an ECC instance, the adapter runs modifications in the user interface.

The *Prescription Adapter* also handles the instantiation of ECCs in the client, like the previous adapter. However, it differs in the management of the user interface and the communication with the server. This adapter implements the user interface of a web portal but it only instantiates the set of ECCs associated to a process activity at a time. Upon a request, the Prescription Adapter retrieves ECCs for an activity from the server. The adapter instantiates the ECCs, draws its user interface and provides instructions to the user about the usage of the component to accomplish the activity.

The *Elastic Manager* implements the collaboration spectrum and handles the transition between different types of interaction support. This manager acts as a container of types, loading and unloading them upon user request.

In Elgar, there are two types of messages: control messages and data messages. Adapters use control messages to encapsulate all function requests, e.g. request ECCs of a process activity or request of an ECC selected by the user, whereas ECCs use data messages to exchange data between their instances. Only the Elastic Manager is able to processes both message types, delegating them to the proper manager: it forwards control messages to adapters and it forwards data messages to the Log Manager.

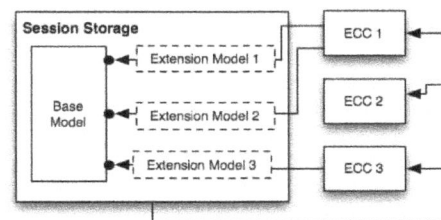

Figure 3. Session Storage: A dynamic extensible data model.

Although not representing a mashup environment, the implementation of Elgar addresses some design guidelines for mashup tools, such as WYSIWYG mechanisms and non-programmers support [1]. Elgar supports data exchange between ECCs through WYSIWYG mechanisms and enables users to customize the collaborative workspace layout by arranging ECCs. Elgar is also designed and implemented to support engineers, considered often times non-programmers, to facilitate the customization of the workspace by integrating ECCs.

ARCHITECTURE OF ELASTIC COLLABORATION COMPONENTS

The challenge to predict integration of groupware tools in upfront, makes straightforward to design and build such tools as loosely-coupled software components. The implementation of groupware as components facilitate users to dynamically compose heterogeneous tools in the collaborative workspace, without additional integration efforts. For example, during a machine diagnosis process, engineers need to link sensor measurements, displayed by a tool, to discussions of possible solutions and their consequences for the machine, generated by another tool. This example illustrates that both tools were designed independently and their interoperability becomes feasible due to implementation of agreed interfaces.

In the context of Elgar, ECCs have to implement a set of standard interfaces and compulsory functionalities to support such interoperability through data sharing between components.

ECCs exchange data with local and remote instances of ECCs, the Elgar server and local native applications. Communication with these entities occurs through either user interface (UI) or channel events. The first type of event regards local data exchange between active instances of an ECC in Elgar. Users trigger such events when they drag and drop data between ECC's instances. The second type of event regards remote communication between instances of ECCs or between an ECC and the Elgar server. ECCs trigger these events when they broadcast messages through the Elastic Collaboration Channel.

An ECC has to implement four interfaces to handle the events regarding data exchange: Channel Event Handler, User Interface Event Handler, Input Projection and Output Projection. The first two interfaces have to be implemented in the client side of the component and the last two interfaces are registered by the component at the server side. With the Input Projection extracting the ECC's initial state from the Session Storage and the Output Projection updating the Session Storage while the ECC is in use.

The Channel Event Handler shall implement functions that transmit messages from an instance of an ECC type to the Elastic Collaboration Channel and process incoming messages from the Elastic Collaboration Channel. The Channel Event Handler has to differentiate between two types of messages: data exchange messages and initialization messages. The first type refers to data messages generated by other ECC instances, e.g. the instance of a Sensor Analyser ECC

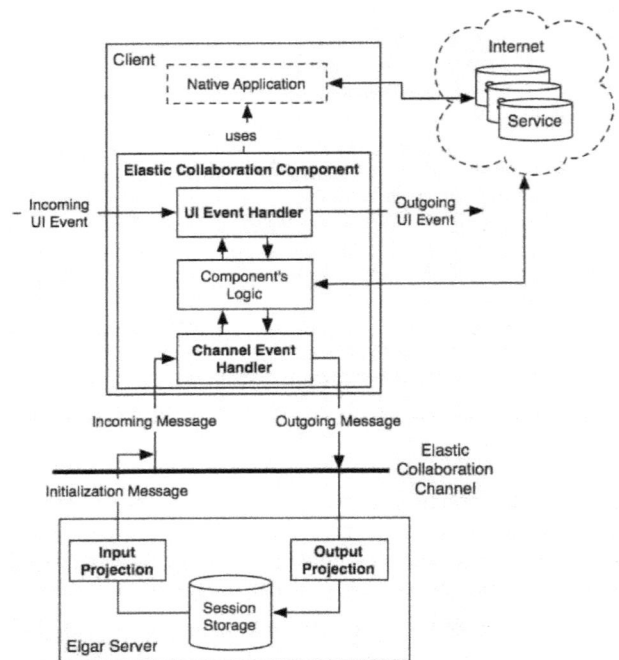

Figure 4. Architecture of an elastic collaboration component.

broadcasts a user's sensor query to all other instances. The other type of message refers to data generated by instances of ECCs previously. In prescribed collaboration users navigate through a set of ECC instances, prescribed in a process description. In this case, users load and unload ECC's instances in the client according to their needs. The initialization data aims at retrieving exchanged data between instances while the instance is unloaded. An instance requests initialization data to the Elgar server as soon as a user loads it. For example, whenever a user loads the instance of a Sensor Analyser ECC, it requests all queries issued by other instances previously in a session.

In ad-hoc collaboration, users instantiate ECCs according to the problem-solving situation. For a matter of quick data integration, ECCs exchange data through user interface events, in this case Incoming UI Events represent drop events and Outgoing UI Events represent drag events. ECCs implement mechanisms that handle such events through the UI Event Handler. This handler constantly monitors both events (drag and drop) and whenever one of them is detected, the component invokes internal functions to process them. For example, an instance of a Sensor Analyser ECC invokes its UI Event Handler interface when a user drags a sensor query displayed in the list of a component and another instance of the Sensor Analyser ECC invokes its handler whenever the user drops the sensor query in it.

Such a data exchange approach evolves incrementally. As soon as an ECC needs to process different types of dragged or dropped data, developers need to extend the functionalities of the ECC, implementing new UI Event Handlers. For example, a developer implements a new handler for the Sensor Analyser ECC to process text input as sensor annotations, in addition to query input. This design decision avoids developers to predict all types of front end user interface data exchange in design time, such as in [10].

ECCs have to implement two server-side interfaces: Input Projection and Output Projection. These interfaces implement mechanisms for an ECC to retrieve or store data on the server side. Input Projection retrieves data from the Session Storage concerning the ECC's data model whereas the Output Projection records data exchanged by instances of ECCs. The Input Projection is only invoked upon a user's request to load a component. An Output Projection is invoked whenever the Elgar server detects incoming messages from the instances of ECCs.

Some ECCs need the support of local native applications to implement their functionality, e.g. audio-visual conference and screen sharing components. This approach is used because current web-based applications cannot implement mechanisms to consume and produce real-time streams of data. Therefore, in this case ECCs represent unser interface front ends that delegate to the local native applications the handling of streams.

INSTANCES OF ELASTIC COLLABORATION COMPONENTS

To solidify our claim of integration of heterogeneous components, the following describes the implementation of three groupware tools according the ECC architecture, deployed in the Elgar system.

Collpad

Collaborative Notepad (Collpad) is a multi-role ECC that allows its users to share their ideas and create text structures, based on lists, collaboratively. The component supports engineers in documenting ideas of possible problems, solutions for given problems, description of consequences for both problems and solution, and to sketch action plans for a wheel loader's diagnosis process. Such tool is important to create collaborative documentation during the problem-solving scenario, described in this paper previously. The component allows users to define the topic of a certain discussion and provide contributions focusing on the topic. A contribution can either be a category or ideas.

The component's instance sends contributions through the Elastic Communication Channel whenever a user writes them locally. The Channel Event Handler wraps the content of a contribution in a (outgoing) message to the channel. As soon as the message reaches the clients, the local Channel Event Handlers of Collpad ECC decodes the message and adapts the component's instance to include a contribution. In parallel, the server invokes the Output Projection of the component to store it in the Session Storage.

If a user loads for the first time an instance of the Collpad ECC, the component sends a special message to the Elgar server. The server invokes the Input Projection of the ECC that retrieves the contributions exchanged by all instances of the component in that collaboration session and wrap them in the initialization message.

In addition, users share contributions by directly moving them between components, in a WYSIWYG approach. The UI Event Handler of the Collpad ECC transforms contributions, arriving from the channel or added by the user, in draggable objects. Such approach allows users to drag and drop ideas between Collpad ECC instances for quicker organization and contextualization.

Visual Query and Visualization Tool

The Visual Query and Visualization Tool (V2QT) is an ECC that enables engineers to visually pose continuous queries (CQs) over machine sensor measurements. V2QT handles query request and response and displays results in a time-oriented graph. Users gain insights, through the V2QT, over possible anomalous equipment behaviours, e.g. the main hydraulic pressure is above a threshold.

V2QT is not a collaborative query editor but it creates awareness among users regarding all issued queries in a problem-solving process. Whenever a user sends a query to the DSMS, the Channel Event Handler encapsulates a copy of it in a message and transmits to all instances of the V2QT, through the Elastic Collaboration Channel. The instances receive the message and adapt the V2QT local history of queries. In parallel, the Elgar server invokes the V2QT's Output Projection to store the issued query. The goal of such mechanism is to make a team of engineers aware of individual analysis of a wheel loader's sensor measurements.

Users may combine the Collpad with the V2QT to annotate results of a graph. In this case, both components have to implement UI Event Handler to enable inter-component data exchange. The Collpad's UI Event Handle shall implement the drag event of ideas and the V2QT's UI Event Handler shall implement the logic for annotating values of graphs whenever a user drops a contribution on it.

Confero

Confero is a commercial multimedia communication tool, supporting synchronous multipoint audio-visual communication, shared whiteboard, text messaging, application and file sharing.

In the context of the Elgar system, Confero ECC provides interpersonal and machine-person multimedia communication, delivered as real-time media streams. Through this ECC, users can join the audio conference channel, assigned to a specific problem-solving session, or invite other users to join an audio channel. In addition, Confero ECC broadcasts video streams from machines, associated to a problem-solving session, to a team of engineers engaged in the session. Such streams are important for trained engineers to recognize malfunctioning signs based on sounds emitted by machines. This way engineers can recognize and solve a problem quickly, avoiding further sensor measurement analysis.

The implementation of Confero as an ECC is different from the two previous ECCs. It has two parts, as described in the Figure 4: the ECC and the local native application. The main functionality of the Confero ECC is to manage participants of an audio session. The component uses the Channel Event

Handler to keep a distributed list of participants. Whenever engineers join or leave the session, the instance of a Confero ECC broadcasts (through the Elastic Collaboration Channel) the engineer's identification and the action (join or leave) to all instances. Upon receiving the message, the ECC instance updates an internal list of participants accordingly. In parallel, the Elgar server receives a copy of the message storing the action in the Session Storage (Output Projection). The implementation of Confero ECC is based on HTML and Javascript languages, imposing technological constraints for the component to handle audio-visual streams. Therefore, this ECC delegates the implementation to a dedicated local native application.

CONCLUSION AND FUTURE WORK

This paper introduces a novel architecture for a collaborative workspace (Elgar) that supports a new emerging paradigm (Elastic Collaboration). Elastic Collaboration embraces two opposite interaction support types, prescribed and ad hoc. The first one refers to the prescription of groupware tools in a process-oriented manner whereas the second relies on users for the ad-hoc selection of tools.

In addition, the paper proposes a standard definition of groupware tools, named Elastic Collaboration Component (ECCs). Such definition requires tools to implement a set of interfaces that target data integration problems between ECCs in a collaborative workspace. By implementing the set of interfaces, it becomes feasible to integrate a variety of web-based heterogeneous ECCs, inclusive the ones that depend on local native application, e.g. audio-visual data streams. Finally, the paper discusses the implementation of ECCs for three groupware tools in the context of the wheel loader's diagnosis scenario: a collaborative notepad to document the discussion about a machine diagnosis situation (Collpad), a visual query editor and visualization tool to analyse sensor measurements (V2QT) and an interpersonal and machine-person multimedia communication (Confero).

Future research aims at the evaluation of the Elgar system, and the three proposed ECC instances, in a wheel loader diagnosis scenario, with engineers. The goal of the evaluation is to understand the reasons and the moments in which engineers choose for a certain type of interaction support and the context in which they switch from one interaction support to the other. For that purpose the experiments will use visual records of interaction with Elgar and the analysis of activity logs.

ACKNOWLEDGEMENTS

This work has been partially supported by the FP7 EU Large-scale Integrating Project SMART VORTEX co-financed by the European Union. For more details, visit http://www.smartvortex.eu/. We thank our colleague Stefan Knoll for valuable discussions related to this work.

REFERENCES

1. Aghaee, S., Nowak, M., and Pautasso, C. Reusable decision space for mashup tool design. In *Proceedings of the 4th ACM SIGCHI symposium on Engineering interactive computing systems*, ACM (2012), 211–220.

2. Bernstein, A. How can cooperative work tools support dynamic group process? bridging the specificity frontier. In *Proceedings of the 2000 ACM Conference on Computer Supported Cooperative Work*, ACM (2000), 279–288.

3. Biehl, J. T., Czerwinski, M., Smith, G., and Robertson, G. G. Fastdash: a visual dashboard for fostering awareness in software teams. In *Proceedings of the SIGCHI Conference on Human Factors in Computing Systems*, CHI '07, ACM (New York, NY, USA, 2007), 1313–1322.

4. Dumas, M., Van Der Aalst, W., and Ter Hofstede, A. *Process-Aware Information Systems*. Wiley Online Library, 2005.

5. Ellis, C. A., Barthelmess, P., Chen, J., and Wainer, J. Person-to-person processes: Computer-supported collaborative work. *Process-Aware Information Systems* (2005), 37.

6. Grammel, L., Treude, C., and Storey, M.-A. Mashup environments in software engineering. In *Proceedings of the 1st Workshop on Web 2.0 for Software Engineering*, Web2SE '10, ACM (New York, NY, USA, 2010), 24–25.

7. Janeiro, J., Lukosch, S., and Brazier, F. Elastic collaboration support: from workflow-based to emergent collaboration. In *Proceedings of the 17th ACM international conference on Supporting group work*, ACM (2012), 317–320.

8. Marcus, A. Dashboards in your future. *interactions 13*, 1 (Jan. 2006), 48–60.

9. Muller, M. J., Geyer, W., Brownholtz, B., Wilcox, E., and Millen, D. R. One-hundred days in an activity-centric collaboration environment based on shared objects. In *Proceedings of the SIGCHI Conference on Human Factors in Computing Systems*, CHI '04, ACM (New York, NY, USA, 2004), 375–382.

10. Nestler, T., Namoun, A., and Schill, A. End-user development of service-based interactive web applications at the presentation layer. In *Proceedings of the 3rd ACM SIGCHI symposium on Engineering interactive computing systems*, EICS '11, ACM (New York, NY, USA, 2011), 197–206.

11. Oberweis, A. Person-to-application processes: Workflow management. *Process-Aware Information Systems* (2005), 21–36.

12. Treude, C., and Storey, M. Awareness 2.0: staying aware of projects, developers and tasks using dashboards and feeds. In *Software Engineering, 2010 ACM/IEEE 32nd International Conference on*, vol. 1, IEEE (2010), 365–374.

Visualization of Physical Library Shelves to Facilitate Collection Management and Retrieval

Matthew Jervis
Department of Computer Science
The University of Waikato
Hamilton, New Zealand
mjervis@cs.waikato.ac.nz

Masood Masoodian
Department of Computer Science
The University of Waikato
Hamilton, New Zealand
masood@cs.waikato.ac.nz

ABSTRACT

Electronic cataloguing systems are used by libraries to provide search mechanisms for finding books in their collections. These systems provide limited, if any, tools for browsing content electronically in a manner similar to browsing books on physical library shelves. Furthermore, library patrons often struggle to physically locate and retrieve books, even after they have found what they are looking for using library catalogue systems. A number of prototype technologies have been developed in recent years to assist library users with the task of locating books. These systems are, however, rather limited in their functionality, and generally do not provide tools for remote browsing of library shelves. In this paper we introduce Metis, a system designed to allow virtual viewing of collections, and to assist with physical retrieval of books using a range of desktop and mobile computing devices.

Author Keywords

Physical libraries; virtual libraries; digital libraries; books; tangible interaction; browsing; search; retrieval.

ACM Classification Keywords

H.5.2 Information interfaces and presentation: User Interfaces—*Physical user interfaces*; H.3.7 Information Storage and Retrieval: Digital Libraries—*Browsing, search and retrieval*

INTRODUCTION

Many libraries hold millions of items in their collections, and use classification methods such as Dewey Decimal scheme for the management of their collections. Cataloguing tools also exist to facilitate search and retrieval of material from libraries. Despite these developments, however, many libraries suffer from a range of problems that make their use less than ideal. For instance, classification schemes are not entirely adequate for organising and retrieving library material [8], and many patrons find them difficult to understand and can't always translate items' call number to their corresponding shelf location [15]. Even when users find the shelf where

the searched item is supposed to be, it may be misplaced or completely missing. It is not, therefore, surprising that finding library material tends to be a tedious and time-consuming task [4, 7, 20].

Although a number of systems have been proposed [4, 6, 14, 18, 20] to assist library patrons with locating and retrieving physical material, none of them provide a completely satisfactory solution to these problems. They also fail to address another problem with existing library cataloguing software, which although provide search functionality, tend not to support browsing of the library collection very effectively. This is something which is also lacking from digital libraries [2]. The ability to browse related books is an important affordance provided by library shelving of books, which support browsing and serendipitous discovery of material by placement of related items in close proximity to each other [21, 19].

In this paper we describe a prototype system that we have developed to monitor placement of library items (e.g., books) on physical shelves, and use this to provide virtual viewing of library shelves to users. This virtual viewing can be combined with search functionality provided by existing cataloguing software to support digital browsing of library collections.

RELATED WORK

There are a number of prototype systems that attempt to solve some of the problems associated with physical libraries. These systems can generally be divided into two categories, computer vision-based and RFID-based systems.

Computer vision-based approaches process images coming from one or more cameras (fixed or mobile) in order to determine the locations of books and detect user interactions with them. For instance [6] describes a system that uses a mobile camera to detect tags placed on book spines to track their positions. Similarly, [3] uses mobile phone camera and other sensors (e.g., accelerometer, digital compass, etc.) to update book positions in the library database and to provide information about selected books on the user's phone. These systems, however, have a major limitation in that they do not continually update their database of book locations in real time. Therefore, if a book is removed from a shelf, this action is not be detected until the next time that shelf is scanned.

Most vision-based systems also take an augmented reality approach in their information feedback to the user. For instance ShelfTorchlight [13] combines book detection using a mobile phone camera with in-place information display using a mobile projector. Similarly, [14] describes a system that augments users' browsing of physical books by projecting the cover of a selected book over the top of the physical books on the shelf. These systems tend to require the user to carry a mobile device as well as perhaps a mobile projector, to access libraries; thus limiting their potential use. All vision-based systems also suffer from a range of problems associated with them (e.g., items being out-of-sight, bad lighting, etc.).

RFID-based systems, on the other hand, use RFID tags to determine the location of items being tracked. For example, [18] describes a system that uses RFID tags with photosensors to determine the positions of items on a shelf, and then projects information using a handheld projector over the items. A more advanced system has been developed by Choi et al. [4] in which items and shelves are tagged with RFID tags. Item positions are determined by scanning the shelf with an RFID tag reader that reads the item and shelf tags. The system then determines which shelf tag each item is closest to and stores this mapping in a database. Typically there will be multiple items associated with a shelf tag. Each shelf tag also has an LED associated with it, and when a user wants to retrieve a book the LED of the appropriate shelf can be lit. However, in this case the LED only shows the general location of a book on the shelf, not its exact location. This is similar to finding the right shelf in a conventional library, as opposed to finding the right book on the shelf. Furthermore, this system also requires constant scanning of the shelves to keep the mappings of books and shelves up-to-date, otherwise if a book is moved between scans the move will not be detected.

Another sophisticated system is proposed by Satpathy and Mathew [20] to help users find items in libraries, through a combination of guidance provided using PDAs (e.g., positing of the appropriate shelf, and approximate position of an item on it), and on shelf LEDs to show the correct shelf when the user is in range, and the position of the book on the shelf. However, while Satpathy and Mathew describe the functionality of such a system, and discuss a user study that confirms the potential benefits of its functionality, the user study was conducted using an analog method and the implementation of the system is not discussed.

METIS
We have developed a system called Metis[1] which aims to overcome technical limitations of the proposed systems described in previous section, as well as providing other functionality not supported by these systems.

Unlike the RFID and vision-based approaches described above, Metis takes an alternative approach and makes use of wired communication that requires physical contact between the shelves and the items on them. This is achieved using a method of physical connection and a communication protocol that provides the ability to dynamically detect and identify item nodes.

The design of Metis is similar to that of the SOPHYA [11] document management system. SOPHYA technology can be used to determine the positions of document containers

---

[1]Greek Titan goddess of counsel, advise, and wisdom.

(e.g., folders, binders, and archival boxes) within storage locations such as filing cabinets. To provide this capability, document containers are augmented with electronic circuitry which gives each of them a unique ID. The storage locations are also augmented with electronic circuitry that includes a linear array of conductive pads. When containers are placed in a storage location such as a filing cabinet, conductive pads on the bottom of the container contact one or more pads of the storage location. Through the electrical connection that this makes, the storage location is thus able to read the unique ID of the container. By using the information about which pads a given container is in contact with, it is possible for the storage location to accurately determine the exact location of each container, as well as the sequential ordering of all the containers within it. SOPHYA uses the Dallas-Maxim 1-wire protocol [12] to support communication between containers and storage locations.

The design of Metis provides a novel application of the technology underlying SOPHYA. It assumes that library material (e.g., books) are augmented to act like SOPHYA containers, while the augmented shelves behave like storage locations in SOPHYA. This design allows the shelves to communicate with the books placed on them to determine their locations. This information can in turn be used to identify the position of each book in relation to other books on the shelve to create an ordered list of books.

However, to make it possible to utilise the SOPHYA technology for Metis, we have had to update the design of its low-level architecture to improve scalability (i.e. from managing limited number of office document containers, to extremely large number of library collections) and incorporate other output display mechanisms (to be discussed later). Furthermore, we have also had to design new physical hardware to allow for the application of the system in this new domain, as well as developing new software application to take advantage of features provided by Metis.

ARCHITECTURE OF METIS
The architecture of Metis is based on the SOPHYA architecture described in [11], and is divided into four main parts:

Physical interface: comprises the physical library items, the shelves, the electronic circuitry, and the low-level software used to provide position determination and tangible user interaction functionality (e.g., to control buttons, LEDs, etc.). The physical interface component will be discussed further in the next section.

Middleware: is responsible for aggregating the position information coming from the shelves and communicating this to the library management system.

Library management system: is where the position information is combined with other information such as the library catalogue and loan records. This is also where the unique identifiers given to each book by their attached circuitry is mapped to electronic information in the library catalogue. The library management system component also manages the communication between the client application software and the underlying components of Metis.

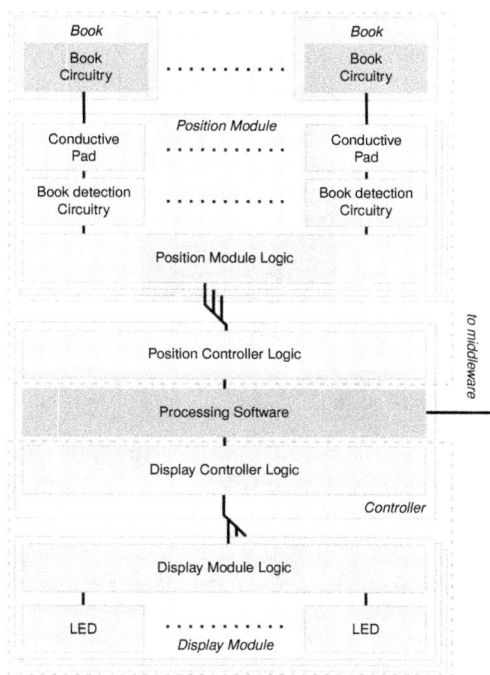

Figure 1. The physical interface sub-architecture of Metis.

Client application software: is developed for the specific needs of different groups of users (e.g., library patrons, or staff in charge of acquisition, cataloguing, shelving, etc.). These client applications will be detailed later in this paper.

Physical Interface Sub-Architecture

The architecture of the physical interface, as shown in Figure 1, has been adapted from the architecture proposed for SOPHYA in [11] and expanded to add support for visual output. It has two independent components, as shown by the dashed outlines in the figure. The first component (shown at the top) is responsible for determining the positions of library material such as books on a given library shelf, and passing this information to higher-layer software. The second component (shown at the bottom) is responsible for controlling the user interaction elements such as position display devices (e.g., LEDs or LCD panels) of the shelf. The reason for this split is to allow mounting the two components on physically separate parts of the shelf.

Each of the two components of this architecture has two main parts: control logic and a number of modules. The modules are, for instance, responsible for implementing the book detection circuitry (in the case of the position component) or the output display (in the case of the display component). The number of modules used can be varied depending on the size and number of shelves. The modules connect via a bus network (e.g., I^2C [17]) to a controller, which interfaces between them and the processing software layer.

Each controller is given a unique ID number. Each module connected to a controller also has a unique number within the scope of that controller, along with each conductive pad within a module which has its own unique number as well.

Therefore, every possible position can be given a globally unique ID based on this hierarchy by concatenating the controller ID, module number, and contact pad number. In a simple implementation which has a one-to-one mapping of one LED per each contact pad, each LED is given a number corresponding to its contact pad. As a result each position and its associated LED is uniquely identifiable at the software layer.

This hierarchical architecture allows it to be scaled to support arbitrarily large collection of items which most libraries need to accommodate. For example, each library shelf may comprise a number of position modules connected to a shared bus, and the same for display modules. These buses, along with those of a number of nearby shelves would connect to the same control logic and processing software unit. Since the majority of the processing is performed in these units, the communication between them and the middleware is minimal, involving only updates when items change state (i.e., are added, removed, or moved) and communications from the middleware when the display for a given item needs to be activated. Therefore, a very large number of these units could communicate with a single middleware server, and if necessary (for example in a very large library) the middleware can be further broken down with different parts of the library having separate middleware servers.

METIS HARDWARE PROTOTYPE

The hardware design of Metis has required careful consideration to allow physical storage and retrieval of material placed on shelves. Libraries deal with a range of physical material in their collection, including books, periodicals such as journals and magazines, archival boxes, etc. Of these, books are the most challenging type of items to augment with electronic circuitry that supports the previously discussed position detection method while still allowing them to be placed on shelves in the conventional manner (i.e., spine facing out). Book spines provide useful visual, as well as textual, information to the patrons, and include library information such as call number labels. Although the easiest solution would be to attach the tracking circuitry to the spine of books and place them on the shelves with the spine touching the back of the shelves where conductive pads could be placed, this would hide the spines and make the browsing of library books on the shelves difficult.

Therefore, a number of other design alternatives were considered, including the placement of circuitry underneath the cover and running conductor strips over the cover of the book, having a folding flap that the book sits on, or putting the books inside augmented book jackets. All these alternatives, however, have problems associated with them, including books falling inside the shelves and losing contact, flaps wearing out, books being misplaced in wrong jackets, etc. We therefore decided to choose the spine option, and place the circuitry with its contacts on the lower part of the spine.

While having the contacts on the spine of the book makes sense in terms of placement on the book, it does however necessitate having some form of an edge at the front of the shelf with the position modules mounted on it in order that they can make contact with the books as they are placed with the

Figure 2. A prototype Metis bookshelf.

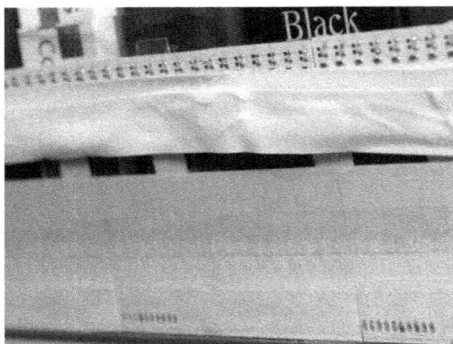

Figure 3. A close-up of the display component of the bookshelf.

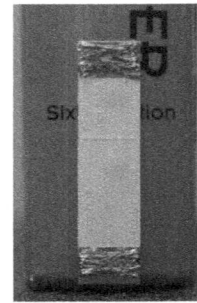

Figure 4. A book with Metis circuitry attached.

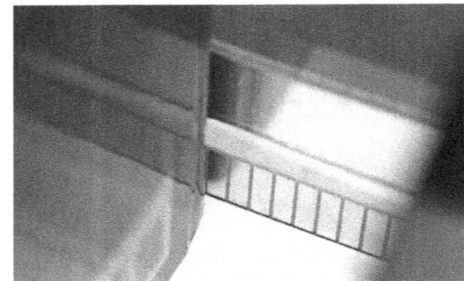

Figure 5. The position module with contact pads inside the bookshelf.

spines facing out. Additionally, the shelf is mounted such that it is slightly tilted to form a shallow gradient, so that books slide toward the front of the shelf and as a result some weight is placed on the the spine to ensure that contact is made.

Figure 2 shows an implementation of a Metis bookshelf using this design, with several books. Figure 3 gives a close-up view of the display component of the shelf, which can be used to indicate to users the positions of selected books. Although this prototype uses a series of LEDs as the display component, other display options such as LCD panels could easily be used when more advanced display capabilities are needed.

The circuitry used for the items being managed is the same as that of the containers of the SOPHYA system described in [11]. As with SOPHYA the Dallas-Maxim 1-wire protocol [12] is used for communication between the shelves and the items on them. A single DS2401 1-wire silicon serial number IC [5] gives each item a unique ID. The item circuitry, which comprises the DS2401 and the contacts used for communication with the shelves, is assembled on a single 0.2mm thick PCB that is attached to the spine of the book (see Figure 4).

The position and display modules are also assembled on the printed circuit board, and these share the same circuit board layout (except that position modules have contacts, whereas display modules have LEDs). Each module consists of a PIC18F2620 microcontroller [16] and sixteen contacts (see Figure 5) or LEDs. The modules connect to their respective controllers using an I^2C bus. The microcontroller of the position modules executes firmware that continuously polls its

conductive pads in turn, reading the ID of any item contacting them, and passes this to the position controller on the position I^2C bus. Conversely, the display module firmware allows the display controller to set the state of its LEDs individually by writing to it via the display I^2C bus.

The position and display controllers are connected to a computer or embedded system that processes the raw information from them and transforms this to information such as addition/removal events, which are then passed to the middleware. This processing software also receives commands for the LEDs from the middleware and passes these to the appropriate display controller.

Managing Other Library Material

The hardware described here has been designed to deal mainly with the management of books on shelves that resemble conventional library shelves. The width of individual items in such settings can vary, and of course there is a minimum width that augmented systems are able to deal with. Vision-based systems need to be able to detect the spine of individual items clearly, while RFID-based systems are limited in their precision as discussed earlier. The minimum item width that Metis can deal with is limited to the width of individual conductive pads that can be manufactured (e.g., 1cm).

Other library content such as current magazines and periodicals (rather than archived collection of magazines and periodicals kept in boxes) that are placed on display shelves differently can also be readily managed using a modified version of Metis. These types of items are often placed on shelves with their cover facing up rather than their spine. Furthermore, with these currently used items only their availability, and not their exact ordering on the shelf, is important to the users. A modified version of Metis based on unordered SOPHYA [9],

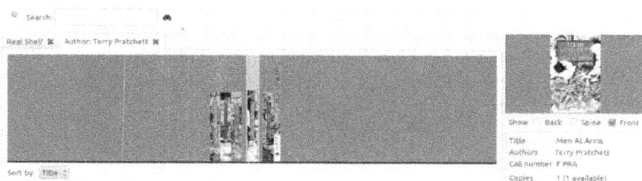
Figure 6. A Metis client application displaying the results of a search.

Figure 7. A Metis client application displaying the books on the shelf as they are physically ordered.

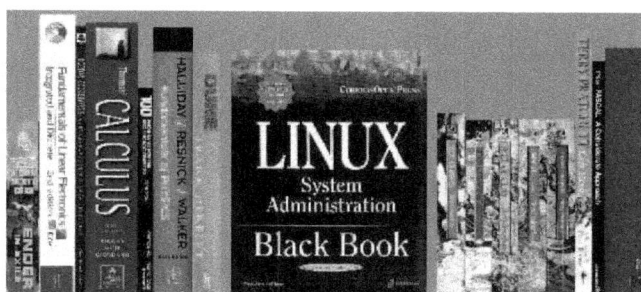
Figure 8. A Metis client application demonstrating the bifocal zoom.

which integrates seamlessly with its ordered version, can be used to link with the version of Metis hardware introduced in this paper without any difficulty.

CLIENT APPLICATION SOFTWARE

The underlying Metis technology described above is generic enough to be used for development of a range of client applications serving different types of users' needs. This has been taken into account when designing the architecture of Metis to separate the client applications layer from the hardware specific layers.

We are in the process of developing several demonstrative client applications. The first of these applications attempts to solve one of the problems with existing systems that tend to ignore the need to support remote browsing of library material as discussed earlier.

The basic concept for this client application is to combine the library material tracking information obtained from Metis with the library catalogue information about that material, in order to provide a dynamic virtual view of the collection of the material as it is stored on physical library shelves. This capability can then be utilised, along with the existing search capabilities of conventional library catalogue software, to present to users their search results as they appear on physical library shelves. In essence, this is like allowing the user to remotely look at the library shelves where the individual searched items exist.

Figure 6 shows the results of a library search carried out using the client application. Initially all the items resulting from a search are shown together on a "composed" shelf. This search shelf is a non-real "composed" shelf, as it is composed of items that may be on different physical shelves in the library. Clicking on the spine of an item on the search shelf shows the cover of that item and its metadata on the right hand side of the screen. Using this application, library catalogue searches can be performed using any metadata fields or by cross-referencing metadata of an already selected item (e.g., all the books by the author of a selected book).

It is also possible to move from the view of the composed shelf to views of the physical shelves containing the items from the composed shelf. Right-clicking on an item on the search shelf displays a context menu, from which it is possible to choose to get a virtual view of the physical shelf on which the selected item is located. Figure 7 shows the view of the physical shelf resulting from clicking on the selected item shown in Figure 6.

Furthermore, users can create their own self-composed shelves by placing items of interest on them. These self-composed shelves can have items placed on them by the user dragging and dropping items from the view of other shelves. This is similar to creating a short-cut to each of those items.

A range of other functionality can be added to this client application to enhance the capabilities of the virtual view of the physical and composed shelves. One such functionality which we have added is a bifocal zoom technique [1] for viewing of shelves. This functionality allows viewing details of items of interest (i.e., focus) while providing a peripheral view of related items on the shelf (i.e., context). Figure 8 shows bifocal zoom being used to view contents of a shelf.

Also since it is possible to open a number of virtual views of physical and composed shelves simultaneously, the client application allows different ways of stacking them on the screen by moving them around. It would, therefore, be possible to use a bifocal zoom mechanism, not only within a shelf (as shown above), but also between shelves by reducing the size of the open context shelves (i.e., shelves other than the shelf where the focus of view is).

Support for Ubiquitous Access

In a world where people daily use different types of devices to access information, it is important to design software applications that work seamlessly across a range of heterogeneous devices. Libraries need to support a diverse group of users who may wish to access their systems from different locations (e.g., remotely, while on the move, from the library) using different devices (e.g., smart phones, tablets, PCs, etc.).

To support these possibilities our objective is to design client software that share similar interfaces components across different devices to allow seamless access to Metis. The graphical shelf visualization interface component described above can be easily ported to different device environments with varying display screen sizes. In addition to our client ap-

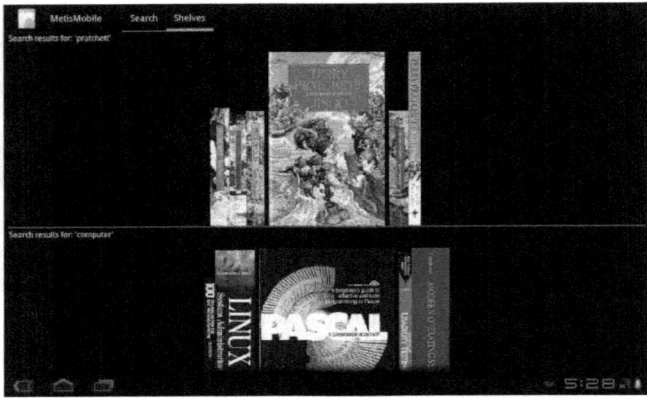

Figure 9. A mobile Metis client application for Android-based tablets.

plication for conventional desktop or laptop computers we have also developed an application for mobile devices such as smart phones and tablets. Figure 9 shows a screenshot of this client on an Android-based tablet. This application supports multi-touch interaction with Metis virtual library shelves using bifocal zoom, etc. The current version of the client supports a similar feature set to the desktop client described above. Future plans for this client include adding support for displaying maps depicting the library shelves and the locations of books in these, and adding the ability to read book barcodes using the camera of the tablet in order to provide functionality such as adding scanned books to self-composed shelves, providing the user with metadata about scanned books, and enabling searching for related books (e.g., those by the same author).

CONCLUSIONS

This paper introduced the Metis library collection management system, and described several prototype client applications developed to provide virtual views of physical library shelves to facilitate remote browsing of library content.

Although we are yet to carry out a formal user study of Metis, a user study of the related (though different) SOHPYA system [10] has shown that users are able to learn and use such a physical content management system without any difficulty. We aim to conduct an evaluation of Metis in the near future.

REFERENCES

1. Apperley, M., Tzavaras, I., and Spence, R. A bifocal display technique for data presentation. In *Proc. of Eurographics 82* (1982), 27–43.

2. Buchanan, G. R. The fused library: integrating digital and physical libraries with location-aware sensors. In *Proc. of JCDL '10*, ACM (2010), 273–282.

3. Chen, D. M., Tsai, S. S., Girod, B., Hsu, C.-H., Kim, K.-H., and Singh, J. P. Building book inventories using smartphones. In *Proc. of MM '10*, ACM (2010), 651–654.

4. Choi, J., Oh, D., and Song, I. R-LIM: an affordable library search system based on RFID. In *Proc. of ICHIT '06*, IEEE Computer Society (2006), 103–108.

5. Dallas Semiconductor/Maxim. DS2401 Data Sheet. `datasheets.maxim-ic.com/en/ds/DS2401.pdf`, 2006.

6. de Ipiña, D. L., Mendonça, P. R. S., and Hopper, A. Trip: A low-cost vision-based location system for ubiquitous computing. *Personal and Ubiquitous Computing 6*, 3 (2002), 206–219.

7. De Rosa, C., Cantrell, J., Cellentani, D., Hawk, J., Jenkins, L., and Wilson, A. Perceptions of libraries and information resources. A report to the OCLC membership, OCLC Online Computer Library Center Inc., 2005.

8. Gorman, M. The longer the number, the smaller the spine. *American Libraries 12*, 8 (1981), 498–499.

9. Jervis, M., and Masoodian, M. Digital management and retrieval of physical documents. In *Proc. of TEI '09*, ACM (2009), 47–54.

10. Jervis, M., and Masoodian, M. Evaluation of an integrated paper and digital document management system. In *Proc. of INTERACT 2011*, Springer-Verlag (2011), 100–116.

11. Jervis, M. G., and Masoodian, M. SOPHYA: a system for digital management of ordered physical document collections. In *Proc. of TEI '10*, ACM (2010), 33–40.

12. Linke, B. Overview of 1-Wire® Technology and Its Use. `pdfserv.maxim-ic.com/en/an/AN1796.pdf`, 2008.

13. Löchtefeld, M., Gehring, S., Schöning, J., and Krüger, A. Shelftorchlight: Augmenting a shelf using a camera projector unit. In *Workshop Proc. of Ubiprojection '10* (2010).

14. Matsushita, K., Iwai, D., and Sato, K. Interactive bookshelf surface for in situ book searching and storing support. In *Proc. AH '11*, ACM (2011), 2:1–2:8.

15. McKay, D., and Conyers, B. Where the streets have no name: how library users get lost in the stacks. In *Proc. of CHINZ '10*, ACM (2010), 77–80.

16. Microhip Technology, Inc. PIC18F2525/2620/4525/4620 Data Sheet. `ww1.microchip.com/downloads/en/devicedoc/39626b.pdf`, 2004.

17. NXP Semiconductor. UM10204: I^2C-bus specification and user manual. `www.nxp.com/documents/user_manual/UM10204.pdf`, 2007.

18. Raskar, R., Beardsley, P., Dietz, P., and van Baar, J. Photosensing wireless tags for geometric procedures. *Communications of the ACM 48*, 9 (2005), 46–51.

19. Rice, R., McCreadie, M., and Chang, S. *Accessing and browsing information and communication*. MIT Press, 2001.

20. Satpathy, L., and Mathew, A. P. RFID assistance system for faster book search in public libraries. In *Extended abstracts of CHI '06*, ACM (2006), 1289–1294.

21. Svenonius, E. *The intellectual foundation of information organization*. MIT Press, 2000.

Cedar Studio: An IDE Supporting Adaptive Model-Driven User Interfaces for Enterprise Applications

Pierre A. Akiki, Arosha K. Bandara, and Yijun Yu
Computing Department, The Open University
Walton Hall, Milton Keynes, United Kingdom
{pierre.akiki, a.k.bandara, y.yu}@open.ac.uk

ABSTRACT

Support tools are necessary for the adoption of model-driven engineering of adaptive user interfaces (UI). Enterprise applications in particular, require a tool that could be used by developers as well as I.T. personnel during all the development and post-development phases. An IDE that supports adaptive model-driven enterprise UIs could further promote the adoption of this approach. This paper describes *Cedar Studio*, our IDE for building adaptive model-driven UIs based on the CEDAR reference architecture for adaptive UIs. This IDE provides visual design and code editing tools for UI models and adaptive behavior. It is evaluated conceptually using a set of criteria from the literature and applied practically by devising example adaptive enterprise user interfaces.

Author Keywords

IDE; Model-driven engineering; Adaptive user interfaces; Enterprise applications; User interface simplification

ACM Classification Keywords

[Software Engineering]: D.2.11 Software Architectures - Domain-specific architectures; D.2.2 Design Tools and Techniques - User interfaces; [Information Interfaces and Presentation]: H.5.2 User Interfaces – User-centered design

General Terms

Design; Human Factors

INTRODUCTION

The model-driven approach to UI development can serve as a basis for devising adaptive UIs for enterprise applications due to the possibility of applying different types of adaptations on the various levels of abstraction [2].

Yet, practically implementing adaptive model-driven UIs requires tools that support the creation of the necessary UI models and adaptive behavior. Existing tools lack many features required for supporting adaptive model-driven enterprise user interfaces. From a model-driven engineering perspective, such tools should be able to support the

modeling, generation, and synchronization of all the levels of abstraction. Also, these tools should provide the ability to devise the adaptive behavior both visually and through code to support developers and I.T. personnel. Furthermore, an IDE style UI could provide the necessary ease-of-use for managing the complex user interface and adaptive behavior artifacts of large-scale enterprise applications.

This paper provides an overview of *Cedar Studio*, our Integrated Development Environment (IDE) that supports the development of adaptive model-driven enterprise application user interfaces based on the CEDAR reference architecture, which promotes the use of interpreted runtime models instead of code generation [1]. CEDAR is based on the: CAMELEON reference framework [4], Three Layer Architecture [11] and Model-View-Controller paradigm [12]. The UI and adaptive behavior models created using *Cedar Studio* are stored in a relational database, which provides an easier means for managing these artifacts at runtime. CEDAR's implementation is offered as a service consumed by *Cedar Studio* and technology specific APIs, which allow more enterprise applications to integrate with our solution. APIs can be devised for any presentation technology (e.g., HTML, Swing, etc.) and used in combination with *Cedar Studio* for developing adaptive UIs. The adaptations currently supported by *Cedar Studio* are primarily focused on UI simplification, which we define as a mechanism for increasing usability through adaptive behavior by providing users with a minimal feature-set and an optimal layout based on the context-of-use (user, platform, and environment). These adaptations are part of our Role-Based UI Simplification (RBUIS) mechanism [2].

Cedar Studio provides developers and I.T. personnel with an ease of access to all the visual design and code editing tools in one place. Currently, it supports visual design tools for the following artifacts: (1) *Task Models*, (2) *Domain Models*, (3) *Abstract UI (AUI) Models*, (4) *Concrete UI (CUI) Models*, and (5) *Goal Models*. Also, it supports automatic generation and synchronization between various levels of abstraction (Task Model, AUI, and CUI) and offers the possibility of making manual changes at any level. Additionally, *Cedar Studio* supports a combination of visual design and code editing tools that are necessary for implementing adaptive UI behavior including: (1) *Visual Adaptive Behavior Workflows* and (2) *Dynamic Scripts* for optimizing a UI's layout, (3) *Visual Role Assignments* and (4) *Code-Based Rules* for minimizing a UI's feature-set to a particular context, and (5) *SQL-based Model Constraints* for verifying manually created models.

Cedar Studio is meant to be used during various phases of the software lifecycle (development, deployment, and post-deployment). The UI models are created at development time and the adaptive UI behavior could be added at deployment time according to the needs of each enterprise.

The remainder of this paper is structured as follows: The next section briefly describes the gaps in existing tools. Then, we present the features of *Cedar Studio* and the process of using it for devising adaptive model-driven enterprise application UIs. Afterwards, we assess *Cedar Studio* based on criteria from the literature [18]. Finally, we give the conclusions and state our future work.

RELATED WORK

This section provides a brief overview of existing software tools that target model-driven and adaptive user interfaces.

Some tools supporting the development of model-driven UIs such as UsiComp [10], Xplain [9], Damask [14], and Gummy [15] are early stage research prototypes that do not provide an IDE style UI that generally helps developers and I.T. personnel in managing a large number of artifacts (e.g., UI models, code files, etc.) for real-life enterprise applications. Other similar tools such as SketchiXML [5], IdealXML [17], GraphiXML [16] just target specific phases of the UI construction process. MASP [7] provides tool support for devising adaptive UI layouts for home systems but does not provide a canvas-style visual design tool for devising WIMP style concrete UIs. Some approaches such as Supple [8] partially implement model-driven engineering of user interfaces, which is reflected in the accompanying tools that do not support all the levels of abstraction. *Cedar Studio* was developed in the form of an IDE that is aimed at providing integrated features and full support for the model-driven approach to user interface development.

There are commercial tools for supporting model-driven UI construction. Leonardi [24] is a UI design tool owned by the W4 company. Since Leonardi is a rapid application development tool, it limits its UI representation to the CUI level of abstraction. Additionally, various frameworks and tools (e.g., OpenXava [25], Himalia [26], etc.) provide different model-driven approaches for constructing UIs. Yet, the tight coupling of these tools with programming languages (e.g., Java, .NET, etc.) discourages their adoption as a generic solution. The UIs created with *Cedar Studio* are technology independent and are interpreted by separate APIs that could target any presentation technology.

A survey [21] on model-driven engineering tools for developing UIs included: ACCELEO, AndroMDA, ADT, AToM3, DSL Tools, Kermeta, ModFact, Merlin, MDA Workbench, MOFLON, OptimalJ, QVT Partners, SmartQVT, and UMLX. The models generated by these tools are static hence only adaptable at design-time whereas *Cedar Studio*

is intended to support both user interface and adaptive behavior models that can be interpreted at runtime.

The next section presents *Cedar Studio* and explains how it can be used for simplifying UIs using adaptive behavior.

CEDAR STUDIO FEATURES AND PROCESS

This section presents the features of *Cedar Studio*, and explains the process of using this tool to devise adaptive model-driven UIs. *Cedar Studio* allows the process to start at any level of abstraction but we only demonstrate it starting from the task model due to space limits.

Task Models

The task model design tool, illustrated in Figure 1, supports visual composition of task models using ConcurTaskTrees (CTT) [20]. The importance of this tool is that it provides designers with the ability to visually design task models and allocate roles to them through the dialog shown in Figure 2 while maintaining the ability to allocate roles through more general code-based rules using a code editor. This visual and code-based combination for applying RBUIS in enterprise scenarios could enhance the *expressive match* denoting the closeness between the means for applying design choices and the problem at hand [19].

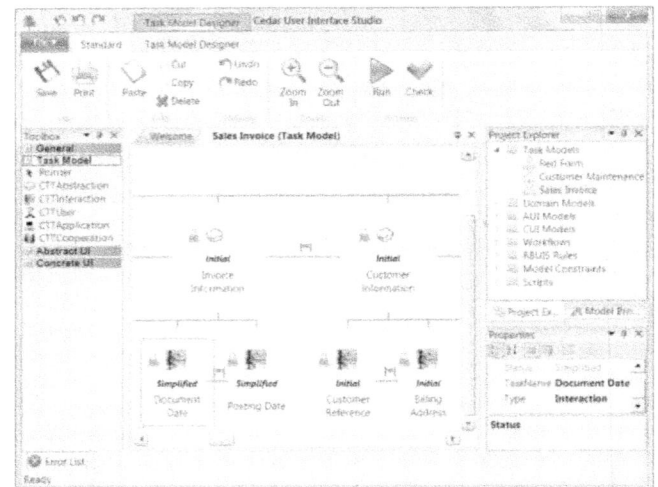

Figure 1. Task Model Design Tool

This tool supports a tree layout algorithm that can automatically adjust the presentation of large task models. Visual and code-based support is provided for the simplification process through role allocation to tasks. The lock-shaped button on each task allows a visual allocation of access rights using the UI shown in Figure 2. A default policy ("*All-Roles*") is implicitly assigned to grant access to all the roles on any given task. This policy could be overridden by explicitly assigning roles from different groups (Figure 2 - a) to each task. The concrete operation (e.g. hide, disable, etc.) and the ability to reverse it by the user are specified for each role (Figure 2 - b). A task can inherit or override roles assigned to its parent task

(Figure 2 - c). The order of each role can be changed to indicate its priority. An assignment can be made to indicate the priority source (Figure 2 - d).

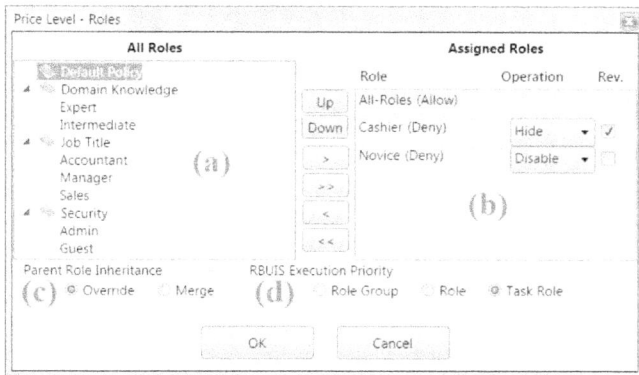

Figure 2. Visual Role Allocation on Tasks

The allocation of roles to tasks can also be done through SQL-based rules. RBUIS rules are written in the form of an SQL condition conforming to our meta-model [2]. This condition is assigned roles and allocated to the task models on which it should be executed. *Cedar Studio* provides an editor for RBUIS rules and the ability to validate the SQL syntax and display errors in the "*Error List*".

Due to possible human errors in the allocation of roles to tasks, model verification is required. The example SQL-based constraint illustrated in Figure 3 retrieves all the tasks not accessible by any user in the system. These tasks are then displayed in the "*Error List*" as errors or warnings. Furthermore, the SQL syntax itself can be validated in a similar manner to how RBUIS rules are validated.

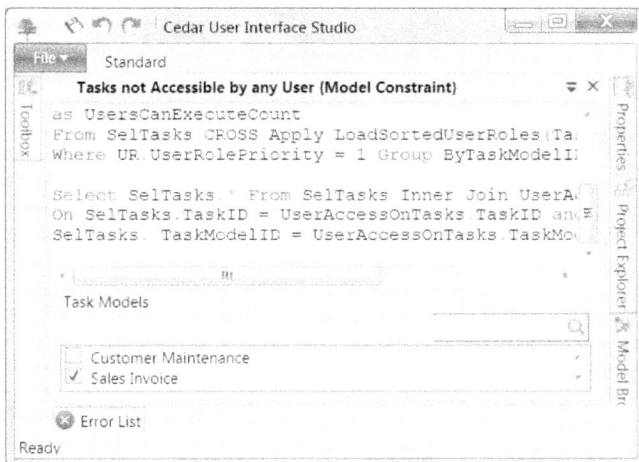

Figure 3. Model Checking Constraints Code Editor

The second level of abstraction, namely AUI models can be automatically generated from task models. It is possible to visually override the default mapping using the UI shown in Figure 4 by allocating each task one or more AUI elements. This option spares the designers from having to individually add, delete, or modify elements on the canvas.

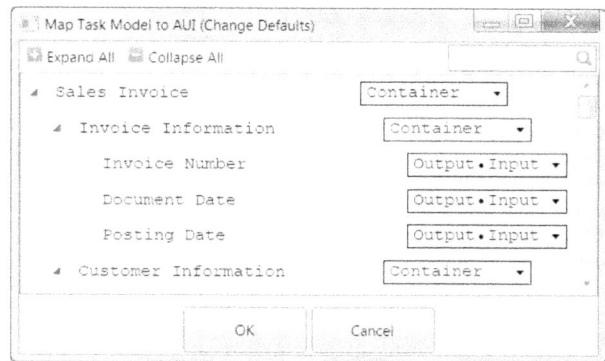

Figure 4. Mapping Task Model to AUI

Abstract User Interface Models

The generated AUI is easily modifiable through the visual design tool illustrated in Figure 5. Simplicity is the main advantage of this tool that supports the specification of AUIs with basic building blocks on a flow-style layout canvas, which could be used by non-technical designers.

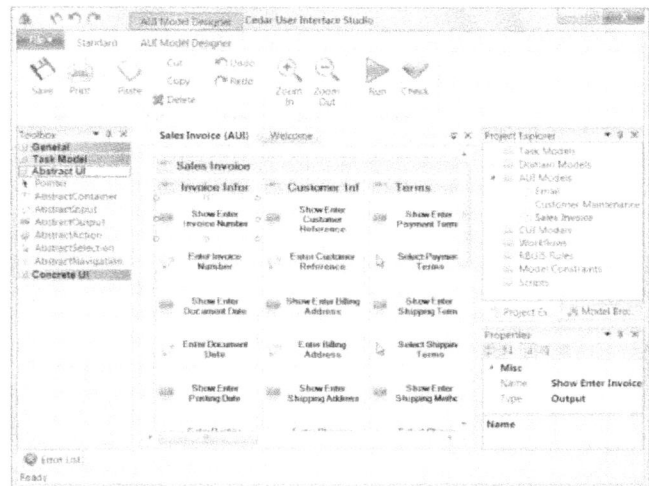

Figure 5. Abstract User Interface Design Tool

Since AUI models are a modality independent representation, the design canvas shows each element as a box with a name, icon, and color. This tool allows AUI containers to be nested within one another and provides an easy-to-use flow style for visually manipulating the AUI elements. The properties box allows the modification of an element's properties including its type. As suggested in existing literature [22], placeholder elements are used upon deletion to maintain the mapping between the models. The type of the placeholder can be switched to an AUI element type without affecting the mapping. New elements can be added from the toolbar and manually mapped to their related tasks in the task model.

CUI models can be automatically generated from AUI models similarly to how AUI models are generated from task models. An interface, similar to the one in Figure 4, is also provided for manually adjusting the default mappings.

Concrete User Interface Models

The input of the human designer is highly desirable for achieving higher usability [22] through the manipulation of concrete objects rather than just an abstract representation [6]. Providing a robust CUI design tool helps designers in providing their input on the look on feel of the UI. Visual user interface builders provide a graphical means for expressing graphical concepts thereby providing a low threshold due to the reduction of the learning curve [18].

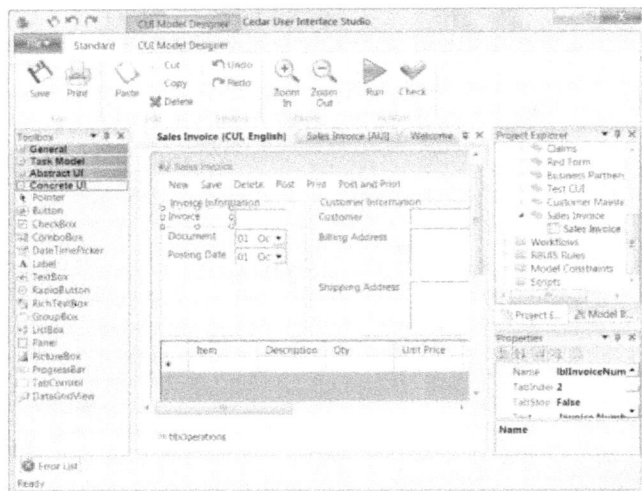

Figure 6. Concrete User Interface Design Tool

Cedar Studio provides a feature-rich CUI design tool (Figure 6) by seamlessly integrating and extending the "*Windows Forms*" design tool of "*Visual Studio .NET*". This design tool has been time tested through its usage in developing UIs for many enterprise applications. Similar to that of the AUI, the CUI design tool supports placeholders upon deletion in addition to complete deletion of elements which could be manually replaced and mapped to the AUI model. A rich toolbar is provided including both basic (e.g., date-time picker) and advanced (e.g., data grid) widgets required by enterprise applications.

Adaptive Behavior Workflows

Workflows are common in enterprise applications for representing business rules. Our approach takes advantage of workflows to represent adaptive behavior both visually and through code. This approach gives the opportunity for both developers and I.T. personnel to implement this behavior through a straight forward visual canvas (Figure 7 - a). Similar to the task model design and role assignment tool, the visual and code-based combination also enhances *expressive match*. Furthermore, *expressive leverage* by promoting reusability [19] is achieved by supporting the integration of reusable visual components and scripts.

Workflows can be assigned roles and the CUI models to be executed on. We integrated the "*Windows Workflow*" design tool of "*Visual Studio .NET*". This tool provides a rich set of visual programming constructs (Figure 7 - b),

which can be dynamically extended with custom activities (Figure 7 - c) written in "*C#*" or "*VB.NET*". One of the extensions we have built supports calling adaptive behavior written in the scripting language "*Iron Python*". *Cedar Studio* stores workflows in an XML format that allows any workflow to be dynamically loaded and executed.

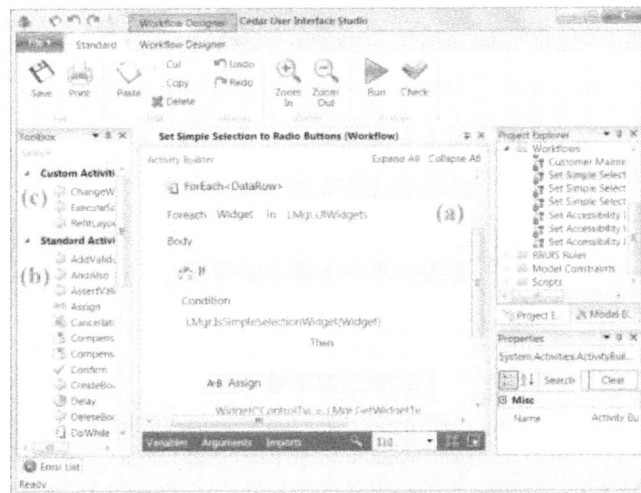

Figure 7. Adaptive Behavior Workflow Design Tool

Cedar Studio supports an "*Iron Python*" script editor. Scripts are created separately and can be called from within any workflow by selecting the script, specifying the method to call, and passing it the appropriate parameters. The entire process is done visually through the workflow design tool.

Testing Adapted UIs from within Cedar Studio

Cedar Studio provides developers with the ability to run the devised UIs with and without adaptations using "*Run*" and "*Run As*" commands respectively. By combining this feature with the previously described design tools, we achieved *flexibility* in terms of supporting rapid design changes that can be performed and evaluated by the developers [19].

The "*Run*" command simply executes the initial version of the UI whereas "*Run As*" prompts the developer to enter a user identifier and executes the UI version corresponding that user's roles. This functionality allows developers to test UIs and adaptive behavior from within the IDE.

The UI illustrated in "Figure 8 – Left" represents a fully-featured "*Sales Invoice*", which is one of the cases we used for testing RBUIS and *Cedar Studio*. We considered a role called "*Cashier*" requiring a simplified version of this UI.

By allocating the role "*Cashier*" to the appropriate tasks, applying the necessary adaptive behavior workflows, and running the UI with a user allocated the role "*Cashier*", the version illustrated in "Figure 8 – Right" will be displayed.

When the user's role is modified (e.g., *Cashier* to *Manger*, *Novice* to *Expert*, etc.), the adaptation will dynamically change according to the new role. This conforms to the concept of multi-layer interface design [23].

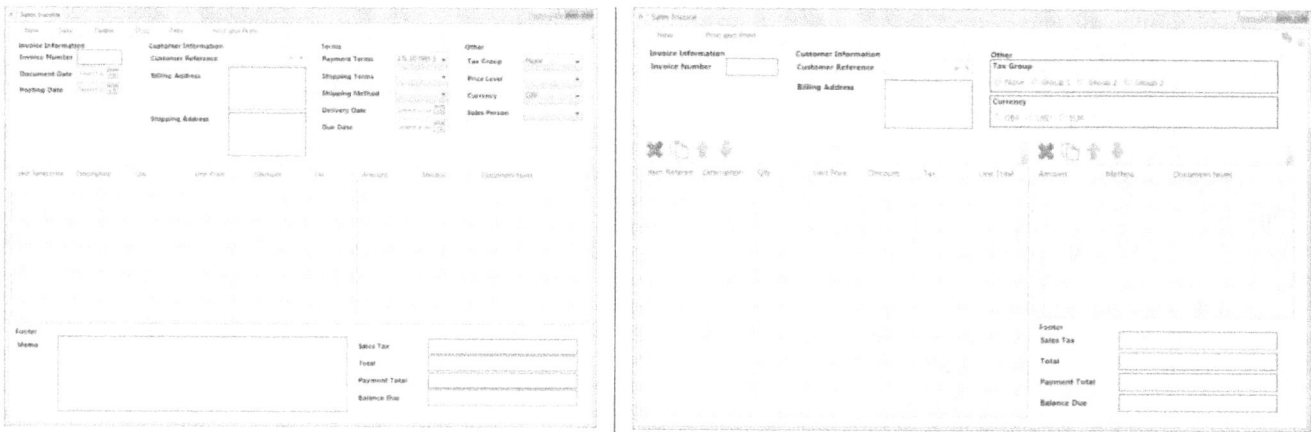

Figure 8. Sales Invoice Initial Version (Left) and Simplified Version (Right)

ASSESSING CEDAR STUDIO

Cedar Studio was practically assessed by constructing a few enterprise resource planning (ERP) UIs, such as the one shown in Figure 8, and basic adaptive behavior. One of the main observed strengths of using *Cedar Studio* in practice is in its design tools (AUI, CUI, and Workflow) that are based on existing mature *Visual Studio* components. The task model design tool can be developed further to reach the same level of maturity and the code editors can be enhanced by adding intelligent-sense. In the future this assessment will be expanded and applied in an industrial scenario.

In the previous sections we described the advantages of *Cedar Studio* in terms of criteria such as *flexibility, expressive match*, and *expressive leverage*. In this section, we assess *Cedar Studio* based on another set of criteria recommended for user interface development tools [18]:

- **Threshold and Ceiling**: The "*threshold*" represents the difficulty in learning and using the tool, and the "*ceiling*" relates to how advanced the tool's outcome can be. An ideal tool would have a low threshold and a high ceiling.

- **Path of Least Resistance**: Developers should be guided to construct the UI in an appropriate manner by making the right approach easier to follow than the wrong one.

- **Predictability**: Any automated approach provided by the tool should be predictable to the developers using it.

- **Moving Targets**: The tool should be able to keep up with the rapid developments in user interface technology.

Upon designing and developing *Cedar Studio* we tried to meet the above mentioned criteria as much as possible.

It might not be feasible to achieve low threshold and high ceiling in all cases. This is due to the learning curve created by any additional features that would allow the tool to produce a more advanced outcome. Yet, we aimed towards achieving a proper balance between *threshold* and *ceiling*. We integrated automated generation and synchronization between models (*low threshold*), alongside the possibility of conducting manual adjustments (*high ceiling*).

Furthermore, if developers understand the semantics of the model they can use the visual design tools to produce an advanced outcome (*medium threshold / high ceiling*). In the cases where coding could be used a visual design tool alternative was provided (e.g., *Visual Workflows* instead of *Scripts, Visual Role Assignments* instead of *RBUIS Rules*) or the language the most familiar to developers was chosen (e.g., SQL instead of OCL for *Model Verification*).

The *path of least resistance* is maintained by allowing developers to easily apply the model-driven approach. The automated generation of models representing the various levels of abstraction and the mapping between them saves the time of having to perform the model design and mapping manually. The automatic generation preserves *predictability* by allowing developers to customize the default mappings between the different model elements (e.g., abstract input to text box). Furthermore, the support for visual adjustment and resynchronization provides an easy way to customize what was automatically generated.

Concerning the *Moving Targets* criteria, the model-driven approach supported by *Cedar Studio* was initially created to absorb the effect of changes in technology and requirements. The model-driven approach allows our IDE to be independent from presentation technologies and to evolve more easily alongside them. If new techniques for building UIs or even new UI types emerge in the future, models are a good approach to cope with such change since it is possible to rely on the existing abstract representations to regenerate different types of concrete user interfaces.

CONCLUSIONS AND FUTURE WORK

This paper presented an overview of *Cedar Studio*, an IDE for developing adaptive model-driven enterprise application user interfaces. *Cedar Studio* supports model-driven UI development, based on the CEDAR architecture, through a set of visual design and code editing tools that can be used by both developers and I.T. personnel. Additionally, *Cedar Studio* supports integrated testing of the devised adaptive behavior by running the developed UI from within the IDE itself. The supported adaptive behavior is primarily targeted at the simplification of enterprise UIs by minimizing the feature-set and optimizing the layout based on the context-of-use. We evaluated *Cedar Studio* conceptually based on a set of criteria suggested by the literature and practically by developing example adaptive enterprise application UIs.

Currently, the user interface models (Task, AUI, and CUI) are supported by visual design tools. We plan on extending *Cedar Studio* with a code view for each of these models for supporting XML-based representations, which could make it easier to define and manage larger models. UI description languages (UIDL) provide technology independent XML-based representation for user interfaces. One promising UIDL to consider is UsiXml [13]. Also, we intend to extend an early-stage tool that we developed in the spirit of *Cedar Studio* for engaging user communities in the adaptation process [3]. We intend to evaluate *Cedar Studio* with an industrial case study. The study would involve asking both developers and I.T. personnel to use the tool for developing real-life user interfaces and providing their feedback on how *Cedar Studio* and the model-driven approach compare to their traditional development techniques and tools.

ACKNOWLEDGMENTS
This work is partially funded by ERC Advanced Grant 291652.

REFERENCES
1. Akiki, P.A., Bandara, A.K., and Yu, Y. Using Interpreted Runtime Models for Devising Adaptive User Interfaces of Enterprise Applications. ICEIS'12, SciTePress (2012), 72-77.

2. Akiki, P.A., Bandara, A.K., and Yu, Y. RBUIS: Simplifying Enterprise Application User Interfaces through Engineering Role-Based Adaptive Behavior. EICS'13, ACM (2013), *Forthcoming*.

3. Akiki, P.A., Bandara, A.K., and Yu, Y. Crowdsourcing User Interface Adaptations for Minimizing the Bloat in Enterprise Applications. EICS'13, ACM (2013), *Forthcoming*.

4. Calvary, G., Coutaz, J., Thevenin, D., Limbourg, Q., Bouillon, L., and Vanderdonckt, J. A Unifying Reference Framework for Multi-Target User Interfaces. Interacting with Computers 15, 3, Elsevier (2003), 289-308.

5. Coyette, A. and V, J. A Sketching Tool for Designing Anyuser, Anyplatform, Anywhere User Interfaces. INTERACT'05, Springer-Verlag (2005), 12-16.

6. Demeure, A., Meskens, J., Luyten, K., and Coninx, K. Design by Example of Graphical User Interfaces Adapting to Available Screen Size. Computer-Aided Design of User Interfaces VI, Springer, (2009), 277-282.

7. Feuerstack, S., Blumendorf, M., Schwartze, V., and Albayrak, S. Model-based Layout Generation. AVI '08, ACM (2008), 217-224.

8. Gajos, K.Z., Weld, D.S., and Wobbrock, J.O. Automatically Generating Personalized User Interfaces with Supple. Artificial Intelligence, Elsevier (2010), 910-950.

9. García Frey, A., Calvary, G., and Dupuy-Chessa, S. Xplain: An Editor for Building Self-Explanatory User Interfaces by Model-Driven Engineering. EICS'10, ACM (2010), 41-46.

10. García Frey, A., Céret, E., Dupuy-Chessa, S., Calvary, G., and Gabillon, Y. UsiComp: An Extensible Model-Driven Composer. EICS'12, ACM (2012), 263-268.

11. Kramer, J. and Magee, J. Self-Managed Systems: an Architectural Challenge. FOSE'07, IEEE (2007), 259-268.

12. Krasner, G.E., Pope, S.T. A Description of the Model-View-Controller User Interface Paradigm in the Smalltalk-80 System. JOOP 1, 3, SIGS (1988), 26-49.

13. Limbourg, Q. and Vanderdonckt, J. USIXML: A User Interface Description Language Supporting Multiple Levels of Independence. ICWE'04 Workshops, Rinton Press (2004), 325-338.

14. Lin, J. and Landay, J.A. Employing Patterns and Layers for Early-Stage Design and Prototyping of Cross-Device User Interfaces. CHI'08, ACM (2008), 1313-1322.

15. Meskens, J., Vermeulen, J., Luyten, K., and Coninx, K. Gummy for Multi-Platform User Interface Designs: Shape me, Multiply me, Fix me, Use me. AVI'08, ACM (2008), 233-240.

16. Michotte, B. and Vanderdonckt, J. GrafiXML, a Multi-target User Interface Builder Based on UsiXML. ICAS'08, IARIA (2008), 15-22.

17. Montero, F. and López-Jaquero, V. IdealXML: An Interaction Design Tool. Computer-Aided Design of User Interfaces, Springer (2007), 245-252.

18. Myers, B., Hudson, S.E., and Pausch, R. Past, Present, and Future of User Interface Software Tools. TOCHI 7, 1, ACM (2000), 3-28.

19. Olsen, Jr., D.R. Evaluating User Interface Systems Research. UIST'07, ACM (2007), 251-258.

20. Paterno, F. Model-based Design and Evaluation of Interactive Applications. Springer-Verlag (1999).

21. Pérez-Medina, J.-L., Dupuy-Chessa, S., and Front, A. A Survey of Model Driven Engineering Tools for User Interface Design. Task Models and Diagrams for User Interface Design. Springer (2007), 84-97.

22. Pleuss, A., Botterweck, G., and Dhungana, D. Integrating Automated Product Derivation and Individual User Interface Design. VaMoS'10, Universitat Duisburg-Essen (2010), 69-76.

23. Shneiderman, B. Promoting Universal Usability with Multi-Layer Interface Design. CUU'03, ACM (2003), 1-8.

24. LEONARDI. http://www.leonardi-free.org.

25. OpenXava. http://www.openxava.org.

26. Himalia.net. http://bit.ly/HimaliaDotNet.

Tool Support for Automated Multi-device GUI Generation from Discourse-based Communication Models

Roman Popp, David Raneburger and Hermann Kaindl
Institute of Computer Technology, Vienna University of Technology
Gusshausstrasse 27-29, 1040 Vienna, Austria
{roman.popp, david.raneburger, hermann.kaindl}@tuwien.ac.at

ABSTRACT

Automated generation of graphical user interfaces (GUIs) from models is possible, but their usability is often not good enough for real-world use, in particular not for small devices. Also automated tailoring of GUIs for different devices is still an issue. Our tools provide such tailoring for different devices through automatic optimization of corresponding optimization objectives under given constraints. Currently, two different optimization strategies are implemented, with their focus on tapping and vertical scrolling on touchscreen, respectively. The constraints (relevant properties such as screen size and resolution) are to be provided by the users of our tools in device specifications. Through our tool support, WIMP (window, icon, menu, pointer) GUIs can be generated at a decent level of usability nearly automatically, in particular for small devices. This is important due to the more and more widespread use of smartphones.

Author Keywords

Discourse-based Communication Model; Multi-device GUI generation; Unified Communication Platform

ACM Classification Keywords

D.2.2. Design Tools and Techniques: User Interfaces

INTRODUCTION AND RELATED WORK

A formal demonstration of a previous version of our tools for GUI generation at ACM IUI'09 [4] was based on technology as published, e.g., in [6, 7, 12]. At this time, the tools were able to generate GUIs, but with no particular emphasis yet on device tailoring. Related improvements and new techniques can be found, e.g., in [8, 13, 14, 18, 19, 20, 21]. This formal demonstration of our tool support for automated GUI generation has special emphasis on multi-device generation and the tailoring involved, which is new compared to the one at ACM IUI'09 [4].

The current version of our tools is able to automatically optimize GUIs for objectives fitting a given device (such as

scrolling on a touchscreen). In this course, constraints given by the device are taken into account as well. Through such tailoring for given devices, a decent level of usability of the generated GUIs can be achieved, especially for small devices like current smartphones, whose market share is still growing. These tools are part of our Unified Communication Platform (UCP).[1]

Most of the other tools for design-time generation of GUIs are based on task models. The MARIA Environment (MARIAE) uses ConcurTaskTree (CTT) models and provides tool support for the development of multi-modal UIs, employing Web services [10]. UsiXML supports UI development at design-time based on task models as well, providing an elaborate tool chain [23]. UsiComp uses UsiXML for the specification of the involved models and supports the development and modification of models at design- and run-time [5]. None of these tools provides automated optimization, however.

As a running example in this paper, we use a simple bike rental application. Since for such an application mobile use is prevalent, we show generated GUIs for a smartphone.

The remainder of this paper is organized in the following manner. First, we provide some background material, in order to make it self-contained. The core of the paper presents a typical scenario of use of our tools for generating GUIs tailored for tablet computer and smartphone, respectively. Finally, we discuss our approach more generally and provide an outlook on future work.

BACKGROUND ON THE MODELING APPROACH

Discourse-based Communication Models [3] specify high-level communicative interaction between a user and the application, primarily based on discourses in the sense of dialogues. Such models are device- and modality-independent. A small excerpt of the Communication Model of a simple bike rental application is shown in Figure 1, more precisely its Discourse Model part. This excerpt models the interaction between the user and the system during the collection of registration data (i.e., username / password and personal details).

The basic building blocks of Discourse Models are Communicative Acts, depicted as rounded rectangles in Figure 1, with the information on their type given in bold face (Open-Question, Answer, Request, etc.). Each Communicative Act

---

[1]More information can be found at **http://ucp.ict.tuwien.ac.at**.

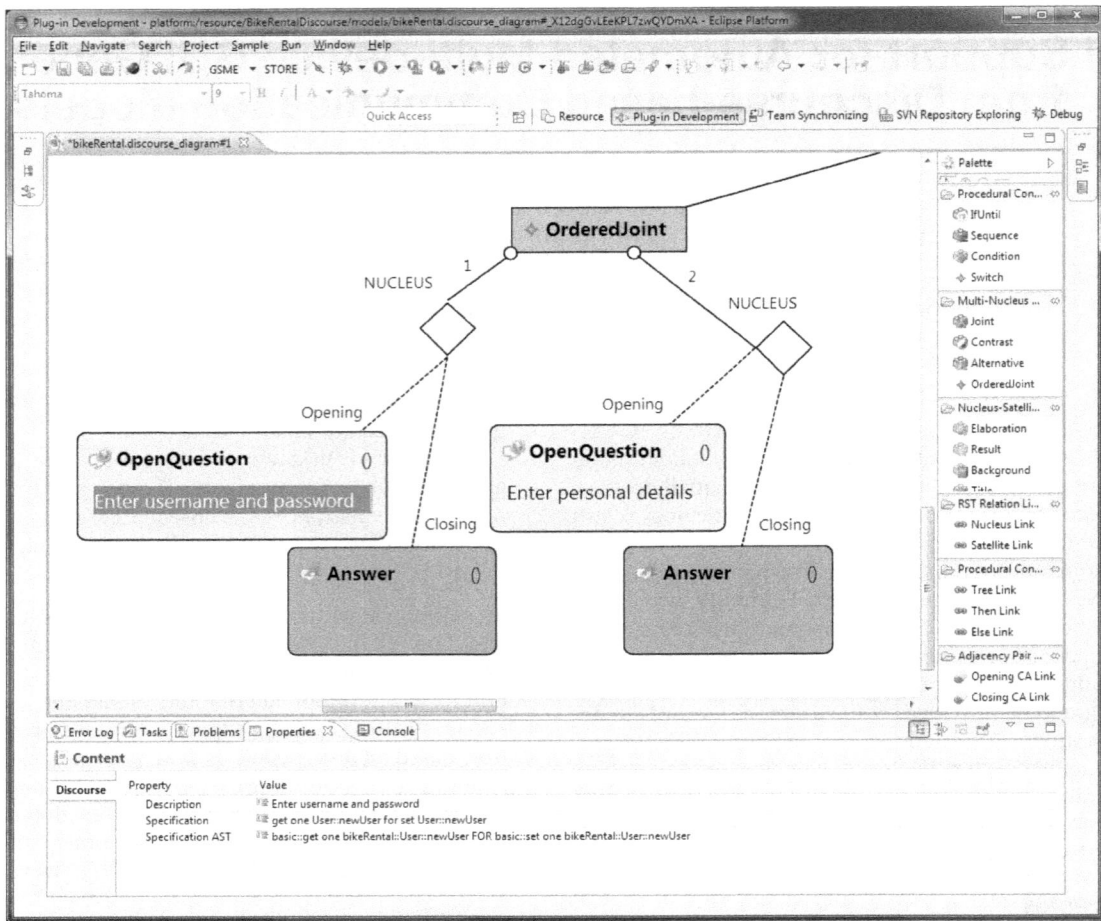

Figure 1. Communication Model Editor

is assigned to an agent, represented through its fill color (green / dark for User, and yellow / light for System). *Adjacency Pairs* model typical turn-takings in a conversation (e.g., Question–Answer or Offer–Accept /Reject). Such Adjacency Pairs are represented through diamonds as shown in Figure 1 and relate one opening and zero to two closing Communicative Acts.

Additional Discourse Relations, like the *OrderedJoint* relation, can be used to link such Adjacency Pairs and to model more complex interaction. The OrderedJoint relation, as depicted in Figure 1 links two or more Adjacency Pairs and specifies that all of them may be executed concurrently, but not in reverse order. If all branches can be executed through the same presentation unit (e.g., a screen), the placement of the related widgets is according to the defined order, from top left to bottom right (as usual in Western cultures). If this is not possible, e.g., the screen is too small, the OrderedJoint relation defines the sequence of executing the branches, e.g., the sequence of the corresponding screens of a GUI.

A Discourse Model refers to a so-called Domain-of-Discourse Model, which specifies the concepts that the two interacting agents can "talk about". A Domain-of-Discourse Model can be specified by an Ecore diagram. More precisely,

the connection between the Discourse and the Domain-of-Discourse Model is established through the propositional content specified for a Communicative Act. Only the content of opening Communicative Acts has to be specified, because the content of the closing Communicative Acts can be derived automatically from the content of the corresponding opening ones. The graphical representation actually just contains an easily readable shortcut, as shown in the lower part of the rounded rectangle. In addition, the propositional content refers to the so-called Action-Notification Model, which specifies Actions and Notifications to be performed by the interacting parties (for more details see [11, 14]).

HOW TO GENERATE GUIS TAILORED FOR SMART-PHONE AND TABLET COMPUTER

The tools presented in this paper support specifying Discourse-based Communication Models and automatically transform them into device-tailored HTML GUIs at design-time, e.g., for smartphones and tablet computers. The process for such automated GUI generation starts with modeling the interaction using our Discourse-based Communication Models as sketched above. Our generator tool can automatically transform such a Communication Model to a User

146

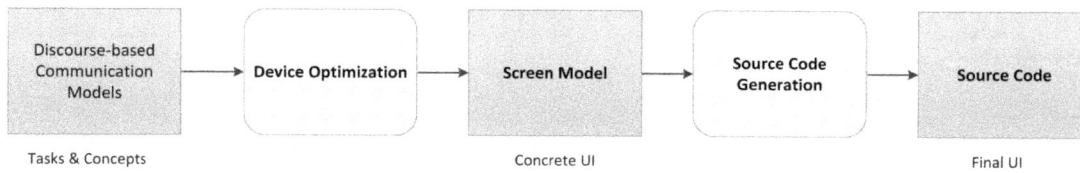

Figure 2. UCP:UI Transformation Approach

Interface Model (Screen Model [19]), which is on the Concrete User Interface Level of the Cameleon Reference Framework [2]. This transformation is more complex than usual, since it includes optimization for device-tailoring (as initially presented in [20] using specific optimization objectives for avoiding scrolling). Finally, the generator tool produces the source code for our runtime environment. Figure 2 illustrates our transformation process starting from a given Discourse-based Communication Model. More details on this process are available in [19].

Editor for Discourse-based Communication Models

For specifying such Discourse-based Communication Models, we have developed our own editor based on the Eclipse Modeling Framework[2]. This editor consists of three parts, one for the Discourse Model, one for the Domain-of-Discourse Model and one for the Action-Notification Model. For specifying Domain-of-Discourse Models, we make use of the standard ecore editor provided by EMF. For Discourse Models and Action-Notification Models, however, we have developed graphical editors ourselves.

In this paper we focus on the Discourse Editor as the most elaborate one, which also serves for combining the three kinds of models. Figure 1 shows a screen shot with a part of the Discourse Model for our bike rental example as explained above. The designer can work on such model diagrams via direct manipulation.

The right side of Figure 1 shows the tool palette of our editor, which allows the designer to add new elements to a Communication Model per drag & drop. The properties of each element can be configured in the EMF properties view shown at the bottom of Figure 1.

Bodgan et al. [1] already employed an early version of our Discourse Editor a few years ago in a study with end users. It provided an innovative interface for end-user development, which became *end-user modeling* instead of programming.

Checking the Models and Configuring Generation

Our tool performs integrity checks to detect and localize certain errors in the involved models [22]. Such checks are applied automatically on the Communication Model and the transformation rules before the generation is started, and on the generated Behavioral and Structural Screen Model during the generation process. They can also be triggered manually by the designer.

We support the overall configuration of generation options and the input of additional information (e.g., device specification) through the GUI depicted in Figure 3. The view of the "General" tab visible in Figure 3 allows for the specification of the Communication Model to transform, which transformation steps to execute, where to save the intermediate (Behavioral and Structural) Screen Model and where to find the implementation classes for the Domain-of-Discourse Model. The view of the "Discourse –>Structural UI" tab allows for providing the device-specification and application-specific transformation rules, as well as the selection of an optimization strategy. The view of the "UI Code Generation" tab allows for the selection of the target-toolkit (e.g., HTML), the specification of an application-specific style sheet, base package name and source folder for the final GUI code. The view of the "Runtime" tab allows for the specification of the partner service that represents the application logic, and the view of the "Common" tab allows saving the launch configuration.

GUI Generation using Model Transformation

A model-transformation engine developed by ourselves performs the model-driven transformation of our Communication Models into Screen Models [13]. The major reason for developing our own engine was the need for certain tool features that we employ for achieving tailored (graphical) UIs in more specific situations (e.g., a specific small device). This involves firing more specific rules in addition to the standard, more general ones, without having to discard the latter. To enable optimization for device-tailoring, comparing alternatives is mandatory [17]. Therefore, our (fully implemented) transformation engine for declarative rules is specifically designed for model-driven UI generation and optimization [13].

Our optimization approach is essentially a heuristic search of alternative models generated in this way, additionally taking constraints into account [20]. The interaction designer has to provide the search constraints in the form of a so-called device specification (in addition to the models mentioned above). It contains information about the given device that is important for the GUI to be generated, e.g., its screen size and resolution. An excerpt of the properties defined in our device specification is shown in Table 1.

Table 1. Device characteristics that influence the optimization

Device Characteristic	Value Type
Screen width	Pixel
Screen height	Pixel
Dots per inch (dpi)	Integer
Max. horizontal scroll length	Integer
Max. vertical scroll length	Integer

---

[2] http://www.eclipse.org/modeling/emf/

147

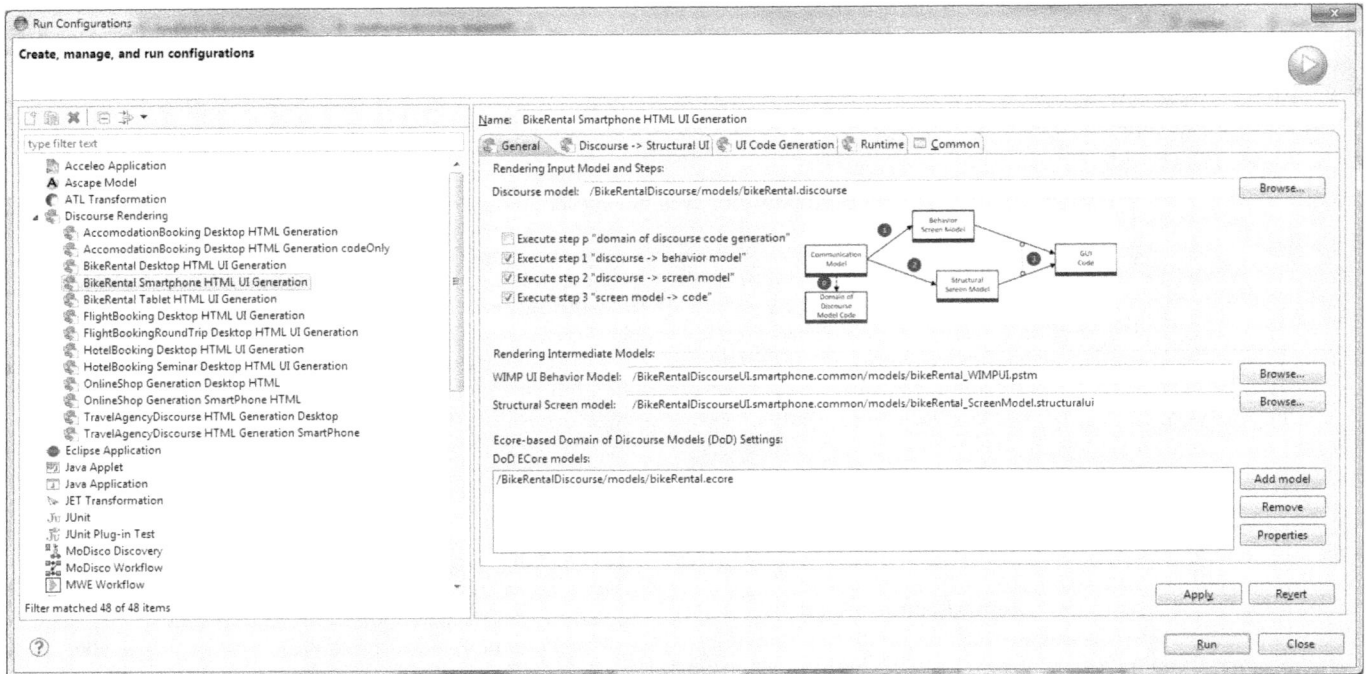

Figure 3. Editor for Configuring the GUI Generation

In addition to such physical properties, our approach takes application-tailored device specifications into account [8]. A touchscreen may be used with different pointing granularity, depending on whether it is to be used by an application with a finger vs., e.g., a mouse.

Originally, our optimization approach as published in [20] targeted (only) optimization objectives for minimizing scrolling. While this is a good strategy for PCs to be used with a mouse, on current smartphones with touchscreens used with fingers, (vertical) scrolling may even be a preferable interaction technique. Now our approach can optimize for such a strategy as well (as an alternative choice for the designer).

This can be achieved through a simple trick with the device specification, where a multiple of the (vertical) size of a given device is specified as the maximum (vertical) scroll length, see Table 1. In effect, the screen width and height together with the maximum vertical and horizontal scroll lengths define the screen real estate available for widget layout. E.g., maximum vertical scroll length of 5 and horizontal scroll length of 1 mean that the GUI height may be up to 5 times the actual screen height (e.g., for the same smartphone 360×2400 instead of 480).

Apart from implementing this unique optimization approach, our GUI generation strictly distinguishes between static and dynamic aspects. Our model-driven engine transforms a Discourse-based Communication Model to a so-called Structural UI Model, which contains all the structural information of the resulting GUI. The Structural UI Model is weaved with a Behavioral UI model generated according to [12, 18]. The layout of the GUI is determined heuristically according to [21] and represented in the Screen Model.

The generation of the Structural UI Model actually happens in two interleaved transformation steps [8], where the first step applies rules to Discourse Model elements that generate an overall GUI structure by use of pattern matching. These rules generate abstract widgets like labels for headings and placeholders for data of the propositional content. They also associate parts of the propositional content with the generated placeholders. The second step executes content transformation rules within the context of the rules of the first step. This embedding allows the selection of abstract widgets for the resulting Structural UI Model depending on the content type, the content's referring Communicative Act type and the current context the Communicative Act is embedded in, as defined by the enclosing rule [8].

Source Code Generation & Runtime

The source code for the dynamic and the structural parts of the Screen Model is generated independently of each other. For the dynamic part a UI Controller is generated by using xPand. For the structural part velocity templates for HTML pages are generated. The runtime is built according to the MVC pattern, where the velocity templates are a main part of the View component, and the generated UI Controller is the Controller of the MVC pattern. The MVC Model represents the application logic.

During runtime, a Java-based Web server such as Apache Tomcat receives the HTTP requests and the UI Controller decides which page has to be presented. The corresponding velocity template is filled dynamically with the values received from the application logic to create the HTML page.[3]

---

[3]Examples of such device-tailored GUIs can be seen at **http://ontoucp.ict.tuwien.ac.at/UI/FlightBooking**.

148

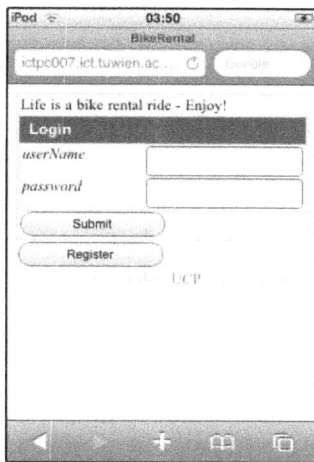

Figure 4. Screen for user login

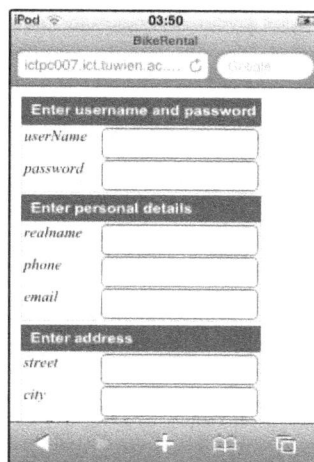

Figure 5. Screen for user registration

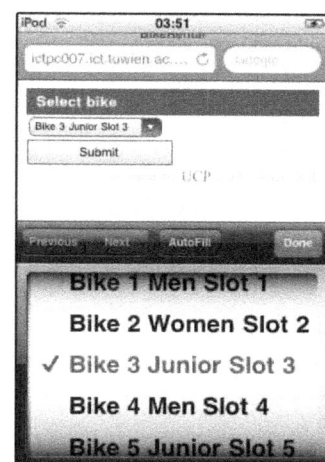

Figure 6. Screen for bike selection

Of course, other front-end technologies could be generated instead of HTML (and earlier versions of our tools did that, e.g., for Java Swing [15]).

Figures 4, 5 and 6 show screens for the running example generated for an iPodTouch (which are the same on an iPhone up to version 4S).

Manual Customization

We did not apply any manual customization to the generated GUIs presented in Figures 4, 5 and 6. The texts in these screens are taken from the propositional content descriptions in the Communication Model (e.g., the headings) or Domain-of-Discourse element attributes (e.g., the labels for the text boxes). These texts can be customized to provide a clear and consistent wording throughout the application.

We also refrained from adapting the style of the resulting GUI, which uses the default styles specified in the transformation rules. However, our tool supports style customizations through an application-specific style sheet.

DISCUSSION AND ON-GOING WORK

Surprisingly, it has turned out to be easier generating GUIs with good usability for small screens than for larger devices. The counter-intuitive reason is that the smaller screens are more constraining. However, we have to compare with GUIs human designers may produce, and these face the same constraints. While our optimization search can deal with these constraints well enough, for larger screens today's approaches to automated GUI generation lack other criteria such as esthetics, which human designers obviously can deal with much better.

In general, fully-automated UI generation typically results in UIs with rather low usability [9]. The use of default styles and the application of layout heuristics alone do typically not lead to an appealing esthetic appearance of the resulting GUI. Manual style and layout customizations can remedy this problem. More advanced manual adaptations (of models) by designers according to [16] are in progress.

CONCLUSION

In summary, we demonstrate our tool support for automated multi-device GUI generation from Discourse-based Communication Models. These tools allow specifying communication on a high level and automated generation of WIMP UIs. These are specifically tailored for different devices through optimization techniques taking device constraints into account.

ACKNOWLEDGMENTS

Part of this research has been carried out in the OntoUCP project (No. 809254/9312) funded by the Austrian FIT-IT Program and Siemens AG Österreich; another part in the CommRob project partially funded by the EU (contract number IST-045441 under the 6th framework programme); and another part in the GENUINE project (No. 830831) funded by the Austrian FFG. We also thank Points Management GmbH for sponsoring part of this research in the context of a project partially funded by the Austrian FFG.

REFERENCES

1. Bogdan, C., Kaindl, H., Falb, J., and Popp, R. Modeling of interaction design by end users through discourse modeling. In *Proceedings of the 2008 ACM International Conference on Intelligent User Interfaces (IUI 2008)*, ACM Press: New York, NY (Maspalomas, Gran Canaria, Spain, 2008).

2. Calvary, G., Coutaz, J., Thevenin, D., Limbourg, Q., Bouillon, L., and Vanderdonckt, J. A unifying reference framework for multi-target user interfaces. *Interacting with Computers 15*, 3 (2003), 289–308.

3. Falb, J., Kaindl, H., Horacek, H., Bogdan, C., Popp, R., and Arnautovic, E. A discourse model for interaction design based on theories of human communication. In *Extended Abstracts on Human Factors in Computing Systems (CHI '06)*, ACM Press: New York, NY (2006), 754–759.

4. Falb, J., Kavaldjian, S., Popp, R., Raneburger, D., Arnautovic, E., and Kaindl, H. Fully automatic user

interface generation from discourse models. In *Proceedings of the 13th International Conference on Intelligent User Interfaces (IUI '09)*, ACM Press: New York, NY (2009), 475–476.

5. García Frey, A., Céret, E., Dupuy-Chessa, S., Calvary, G., and Gabillon, Y. Usicomp: an extensible model-driven composer. In *Proceedings of the 4th ACM SIGCHI Symposium on Engineering Interactive Computing Systems*, EICS '12, ACM (New York, NY, USA, 2012), 263–268.

6. Kavaldjian, S., Bogdan, C., Falb, J., and Kaindl, H. Transforming discourse models to structural user interface models. In *Models in Software Engineering, LNCS 5002*, vol. 5002/2008. Springer, Berlin / Heidelberg, 2008, 77–88.

7. Kavaldjian, S., Falb, J., and Kaindl, H. Generating content presentation according to purpose. In *Proceedings of the 2009 IEEE International Conference on Systems, Man and Cybernetics (SMC2009)* (San Antonio, TX, USA, Oct. 2009).

8. Kavaldjian, S., Raneburger, D., Falb, J., Kaindl, H., and Ertl, D. Semi-automatic user interface generation considering pointing granularity. In *Proceedings of the 2009 IEEE International Conference on Systems, Man and Cybernetics (SMC 2009)* (San Antonio, TX, USA, Oct. 2009).

9. Meixner, G., Paternò, F., and Vanderdonckt, J. Past, present, and future of model-based user interface development. *i-com 10*, 3 (November 2011), 2–10.

10. Paternò, F., Santoro, C., and Spano, L. D. Exploiting web service annotations in model-based user interface development. In *Proceedings of the 2nd ACM SIGCHI Symposium on Engineering Interactive Computing Systems*, EICS '10, ACM (New York, NY, USA, 2010), 219–224.

11. Popp, R. A unified solution for service-oriented architecture and user interface generation through discourse-based communication models. Doctoral dissertation, Vienna University of Technology, Vienna, Austria, 2012.

12. Popp, R., Falb, J., Arnautovic, E., Kaindl, H., Kavaldjian, S., Ertl, D., Horacek, H., and Bogdan, C. Automatic generation of the behavior of a user interface from a high-level discourse model. In *Proceedings of the 42nd Annual Hawaii International Conference on System Sciences (HICSS-42)*, IEEE Computer Society Press (Piscataway, NJ, USA, 2009).

13. Popp, R., Falb, J., Raneburger, D., and Kaindl, H. A transformation engine for model-driven UI generation. In *Proceedings of the 4th ACM SIGCHI Symposium on Engineering Interactive Computing Systems*, EICS '12, ACM (New York, NY, USA, 2012), 281–286.

14. Popp, R., and Raneburger, D. A High-Level Agent Interaction Protocol Based on a Communication Ontology. In *E-Commerce and Web Technologies*,

C. Huemer, T. Setzer, W. Aalst, J. Mylopoulos, N. M. Sadeh, M. J. Shaw, and C. Szyperski, Eds., vol. 85 of *Lecture Notes in Business Information Processing*. Springer Berlin Heidelberg, 2011, 233–245. 10.1007/978-3-642-23014-1_20.

15. Raneburger, D. Automated graphical user interface generation based on an abstract user interface specification. Master's thesis, Vienna University of Technology, Vienna, Austria, 2008.

16. Raneburger, D. Interactive model driven graphical user interface generation. In *Proceedings of the 2nd ACM SIGCHI Symposium on Engineering Interactive Computing Systems (EICS '10)*, ACM (New York, NY, USA, 2010), 321–324.

17. Raneburger, D., Popp, R., and Kaindl, H. Model-driven transformation for optimizing PSMs: A case study of rule design for multi-device GUI generation. In *Proceedings of the 8th International Joint Conference on Software Technologies (ICSOFT'13)*, SciTePress (July 2013).

18. Raneburger, D., Popp, R., Kaindl, H., and Falb, J. Automated WIMP-UI behavior generation: Parallelism and granularity of communication units. In *Systems, Man, and Cybernetics (SMC), 2011 IEEE International Conference on* (Oct. 2011), 2816–2821.

19. Raneburger, D., Popp, R., Kaindl, H., Falb, J., and Ertl, D. Automated Generation of Device-Specific WIMP UIs: Weaving of Structural and Behavioral Models. In *Proceedings of the 3rd ACM SIGCHI Symposium on Engineering Interactive Computing Systems*, EICS '11, ACM (New York, NY, USA, 2011), 41–46.

20. Raneburger, D., Popp, R., Kavaldjian, S., Kaindl, H., and Falb, J. Optimized GUI generation for small screens. In *Model-Driven Development of Advanced User Interfaces*, H. Hussmann, G. Meixner, and D. Zuehlke, Eds., vol. 340 of *Studies in Computational Intelligence*. Springer Berlin / Heidelberg, 2011, 107–122.

21. Raneburger, D., Popp, R., and Vanderdonckt, J. An automated layout approach for model-driven WIMP-UI generation. In *Proceedings of the 4th ACM SIGCHI Symposium on Engineering Interactive computing systems*, EICS '12, ACM (New York, NY, USA, 2012), 91–100.

22. Raneburger, D., Schörkhuber, A., Kaindl, H., and Falb, J. UI Development Support through Model-integrity Checks in a Discourse-based Generation Framework. In *Proceedings of the First International Workshop on Combining Design and Engineering of Interactive Systems through Models and Tools (ComDeisMoto)* (2011).

23. Vanderdonckt, J. M. Model-driven engineering of user interfaces: Promises, successes, and failures. In *Proceedings of 5th Annual Romanian Conf. on Human-Computer Interaction*. Matrix ROM, Sept. 2008, 1–10.

Engineering Adaptive User Interfaces
for Enterprise Applications

Pierre A. Akiki
Computing Department, The Open University
Walton Hall, Milton Keynes, United Kingdom
pierre.akiki@open.ac.uk

ABSTRACT

The user interface (UI) layer is considered an important component in software applications since it links the users to the software's functionality. Enterprise applications such as enterprise resource planning and customer relationship management systems have very complex UIs that are used by users with diverse needs in terms of the required features and layout preferences. The inability to cater for the variety of user needs diminishes the usability of these applications. One way to cater for those needs is through adaptive UIs. Some enterprise software providers offer mechanisms for tailoring UIs based on the variable user needs, yet those are not generic enough to be used with other applications and require maintaining multiple UI copies manually. A generic platform based on a model-driven approach could be more reusable since operating on the model level makes it technology independent. The main objective of this research is devising a generic, scalable, and extensible platform for building adaptive enterprise application UIs based on a runtime model-driven approach. This platform primarily targets UI simplification, which we defined as a mechanism for increasing usability through adaptive behavior by providing users with a minimal feature-set and an optimal layout based on the context-of-use. This paper provides an overview of the research questions and methodology, the results that were achieved so far, and the remaining work.

Author Keywords

Adaptive user interfaces; Simplification;
Enterprise applications; Model-driven engineering

ACM Classification Keywords

[Software Engineering]: D.2.11 Software Architectures - Domain-specific architectures; D.2.2 Design Tools and Techniques - User interfaces; [Information Interfaces and Presentation]: H.5.2 User Interfaces – User-centered design

INTRODUCTION

Enterprise applications (e.g., enterprise resource planning, customer relationship management, etc.) generally serve

various purposes in an enterprise's functional business areas such as: Accounting, finance, marketing, inventory, etc. The heavy dependence on these applications drives business owners to ask for UIs that maximize employee efficiency and effectiveness. Yet, as existing research [22] and industry reports [17] have shown, enterprise applications are regarded as lacking in usability and incapable of catering for the variety in user needs. Adaptive behavior has been suggested as a means for enhancing usability [6] and some works particularly suggested applying it to enterprise application UIs [22]. Also, it has been used for tailoring UIs based on several aspects such as: "Accessibility" [14], "Culture" [20], "Natural Context" [7], etc.

A model-driven development approach could form a basis for devising adaptive UIs due to the ability of representing UIs on multiple levels of abstraction that can be loaded and adapted at runtime. The CAMELEON reference framework [9] represents UIs on multiple levels of abstraction: (1) *Tasks Models* can be represented as ConcurTaskTrees [19] and *Domain Models* as UML class diagrams, (2) *Abstract User Interface* (AUI), represents the UI independent of any modality (e.g., Graphical, Voice, etc.), (3) *Concrete User Interface* (CUI), represents the UI as concrete widgets (e.g., Buttons, Labels, etc.), and (4) *Final User Interface* (FUI), is the running UI rendered in a presentation technology.

The primary objective of this research is devising a generic, scalable, and extensible platform for building adaptive enterprise application UIs based on a runtime model-driven approach. The main target of this platform would be UI simplification, which we defined [2] as a mechanism for increasing usability through adaptive behavior by providing users with a minimal feature-set and an optimal layout based on the context-of-use (user, platform, environment).

The remainder of the paper is organized as follows: The next section states and explains the proposed research questions. Then, the related work is briefly discussed and evaluated in the context of the research questions. Later, the research methodology is explained. Afterwards, the results that the research has yielded so far are presented. Finally, the conclusions are given and the remaining work is stated.

RESEARCH QUESTIONS

This work will answer the following main research question from which three sub-questions were derived:

How can adaptive UI behavior be leveraged for simplifying enterprise applications in order to increase their usability?

Software companies attempt to develop user interfaces that are capable of accommodating the vast majority of an application's target users. Due to the differences in end-user needs, when user interfaces are concerned one does not fit all. For example, if a UI is developed with full functionality it might be over-bloated for basic users. Yet, removing functionality would prevent advanced users from fulfilling their tasks. Also, certain CUI related choices (e.g., type of widgets, layout grouping, etc.) might allow some users to perform their tasks more efficiently in certain contexts-of-use (e.g., a different widget grouping for a mobile phone UI than for a desktop UI, novice users could have widget preferences such as radios over combos, etc.). Another, scenario involves daily tasks that require the use of functionality scattered across multiple UIs. Monitoring user behavior could allow this functionality to be grouped under one UI to make the fulfillment of daily tasks more efficient.

Identifying the various user needs, especially for generic enterprise applications, would be difficult to do at design time. Furthermore, developing and maintaining multiple editions of the same UI is costly especially for enterprise applications comprising thousands of user interfaces. The simplification theme targeted in this research is meant to address the existing variety in the needs of enterprise users by leveraging adaptive user interfaces. The following sub-questions elaborate more on the research specifics.

1. *What is an effective way to automatically simplify individual enterprise application user interfaces based on each end-user's needs?*

2. *What is an effective way to compose new user interfaces at runtime from existing ones based on user behavior?*

3. *What will be the impact of the devised simplification mechanism on the end-users' satisfaction and efficiency?*

RELATED WORK
Based on the previously presented research questions, this section discusses the related work in terms of the ability to:

- Minimize a user interface's feature-set and optimize its layout at runtime

- Decompose existing user interfaces into smaller parts at runtime and use those parts to recompose new UIs

Several existing works discuss adapting the feature-set of UIs such as: "Multi-layered UI" [21], "training wheels UI" [10], and "two-interface design" [18]. Yet, these works are theoretical and there is still a need for a tool supported solution that allows developers to minimize a UI's feature-set in practice at runtime based on the users' needs.

Other works use different approaches to target layout adaptation. The Comet [8] is introduced as a set of widgets that support UI plasticity but only target the adaptation of individual widgets and not the entire layout. Supple [14] is

a system capable of generating UIs adapted to each user's motor abilities by treating UI generation as an optimization problem. Yet, Supple does not support the various possible levels of abstraction thereby preventing designer input from being made at the CUI level making it difficult to adopt for enterprise applications. Another adaptation approach [5] defines content personalization at design-time, which is stated to be a major limitation. MASP [7] targets ubiquitous UIs in smart environments and promotes runtime modeling of UIs. MASP relies on code for devising the UI and uses a box-based layouting tool to segment the UI for runtime manipulation. This technique does not make it possible to simplify the UI at the widget level since the manipulation is done on the segments that group multiple widgets. It also does not allow new UIs to be created at runtime since the adaptations expect a code-based UI as input.

Graceful degradation is used as a method for supporting UIs on multiple devices [13] and could be used for decomposing/recomposing UIs. Yet, this method's main limitation lies in its design-time application that relies on designer annotations hence it would not work when the adaptations are only known at runtime. An interesting approach would be to combine annotations with automated procedures based on user behavior. Another approach called (de)composition seems to complement some aspects of the graceful degradation process [16]. It aims towards supporting reusability at a high level design without the need for applying constant copy and paste operations. The authors mention the applicability of (de)composition both at design/run-time but all the given examples were restricted to design-time. Decomposing/Composing UIs at runtime would also require adapting the functionality behind the UI.

RESEARCH METHODOLOGY
Easterbrook et al. [11] differentiate between "*knowledge*" and "*design*" research questions. They note that knowledge questions focus on "*the way the world is*", whereas design questions focus on establishing "*better ways to do software engineering*". Empirical research is usually the path chosen by researchers posing knowledge questions as opposed to an engineering approach taken for design questions.

This research follows an engineering approach containing a mixture of both design and knowledge questions. The design questions aim towards coming up with an effective technique for developing enterprise UIs with simplification capabilities based on existing research work. On the other hand, the knowledge question aims towards answering how this technique would perform in a practical scenario.

Several engineering techniques will be employed in this research to answer sub-questions 1 and 2. The proposed techniques include modeling, implementing support tools and prototypes, and conducting performance evaluations.

Surveys will be used for the preliminary investigations whereas lab based usability studies will be conducted for confirmatory validation purposes to answer sub-question 3.

RESULTS

This section discusses the parts of the research that have been accomplished so far.

CEDAR Architecture

The CEDAR architecture [1], illustrated in Figure 1, serves as a reference for devising adaptive model-driven enterprise application UIs. This architecture is based on the: (1) Three Layer Architecture [15] (*Adaptive System Layering*), (2) CAMELEON reference framework [9] (*UI Abstraction*), and (3) Model-View-Controller paradigm (*Implementation*). CEDAR promotes the use of interpreted runtime models instead of code generation for providing more flexibility in performing advanced UI adaptations at runtime. A practical implementation [1] based on CEDAR showed that runtime UI rendering does not negatively impact performance. A major part of CEDAR has been implemented to support our UI simplification mechanism described in the next section.

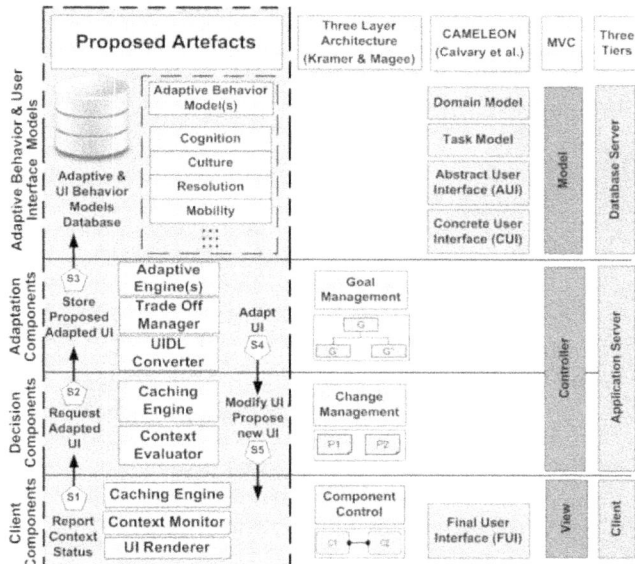

Figure 1: The CEDAR Architecture

Role-Based UI Simplification (RBUIS)

Role-Based UI Simplification (RBUIS) [2] is a mechanism that merges role-based access control (RBAC) [12] with adaptive behavior for simplifying UIs. In RBUIS, *roles* are divided into groups representing the aspects based on which the UI will be simplified such as computer literacy, job title, etc. RBUIS supports *feature-set minimization* by assigning roles to task models for providing users with a minimal feature-set based on the context-of-use. The assignment could be done by I.T. personnel but there is also a potential for engaging end-users in the process [3]. *Layout optimization* is supported by assigning roles to workflows that represent adaptive UI behavior visually and through code and can be applied on CUI models. Furthermore, RBUIS promotes user feedback for refining the adaptation operations. Hence, users are allowed to reverse feature-set minimizations and

layout optimizations, and to choose possible alternative layout optimizations. A user-study [2] showed that applying RBUIS enhances the usability of complex user interfaces.

(a) Initial Item Maintenance UI

(b) Simplified Item Maintenance UI

Figure 2: User Interface Simplification with RBUIS

The example illustrated in Figure 2 demonstrates how RBUIS can be applied to simplify UIs by minimizing the feature-set (sales information and delete button are removed in this case) and optimizing the layout (combo-boxes are substituted with radio-buttons in this case). Additionally, the example shows a chameleon icon in the corner of the simplified UI (Figure 2 – b). This icon allows users to view a list of adaptations on which they can provide feedback. The change between versions (a) and (b) is based on the set of roles representing different aspects such as computer literacy, job title, etc. When an enterprise user logs into the system and activates a UI, the version that is loaded on the screen is dynamically adapted according to the roles that have been assigned to the session's user identifier.

Cedar Studio

The *Cedar Studio* IDE [4] provides tool support for building enterprise applications based on the CEDAR architecture. *Cedar Studio* allows developers and I.T. personnel to apply RBUIS using a set of visual design and code editing tools that support the creation of UI models and adaptive behavior. Automatic generation between the levels of abstraction (Task, AUI, and CUI) is supported with the possibility to make manual changes at any level. The CUI designer of *Cedar Studio* is shown in Figure 3.

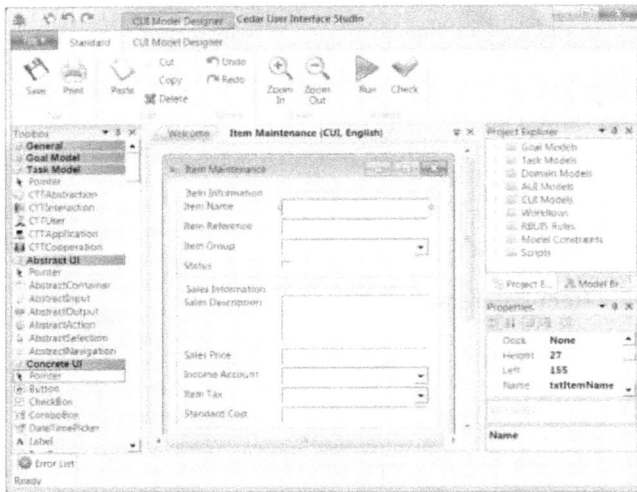

Figure 3: The Cedar Studio IDE

CONCLUSIONS AND REMAINING WORK

This paper presented an overview of an ongoing PhD work on simplifying enterprise application user interfaces through engineering adaptive behavior. The proposed research questions and methodology were explained and the results obtained so far were presented.

In order to fully answer the research questions some work still has to be done. A technique complementary to RBUIS will be proposed to answer the second question on composing new UIs at runtime by monitoring user behavior. This technique will provide the ability to combine features from multiple UIs into a new UI to make it easier to accomplish tasks that require partial features from different UIs. This process has to take into consideration both the layout and the code-behind in order to maintain the UI's functionality. A comprehensive performance study will be conducted to test the entire simplification technique in an industrial scenario. Additionally, more lab studies will be conducted to test the usability of the produced outcome using several example UIs from existing enterprise applications.

ACKNOWLEDGMENTS
This PhD is funded through a three year studentship granted by the Computing Department at The Open University U.K.

REFERENCES

1. Akiki, P.A., Bandara, A.K., and Yu, Y. Using Interpreted Runtime Models for Devising Adaptive User Interfaces of Enterprise Applications. ICEIS'12, SciTePress (2012), 72-77.

2. Akiki, P.A., Bandara, A.K., and Yu, Y. RBUIS: Simplifying Enterprise Application User Interfaces through Engineering Role-Based Adaptive Behavior. EICS'13, ACM (2013), *Forthcoming*.

3. Akiki, P.A., Bandara, A.K., and Yu, Y. Crowdsourcing User Interface Adaptations for Minimizing the Bloat in Enterprise Applications. EICS'13, ACM (2013), *Forthcoming*.

4. Akiki, P.A., Bandara, A.K., and Yu, Y. Cedar Studio: An IDE Supporting Adaptive Model-Driven User Interfaces for Enterprise Applications. EICS'13, ACM (2013), *Forthcoming*.

5. Bacha, F., Oliveira, K., and Abed, M. A Model Driven Architecture Approach for User Interface Generation Focused on Content Personalization. RCIS'11, IEEE (2011), 1-6.

6. Benyon, D. Adaptive systems: a solution to usability problems. User Modeling and User-Adapted Interaction 3, 1 Springer (1993), 65-87.

7. Blumendorf, M., Lehmann, G., and Albayrak, S. Bridging Models and Systems at Runtime to Build Adaptive User Interfaces. EICS'10, ACM (2010), 9-18.

8. Calvary, G., Coutaz, J., Dâassi, O., Balme, L., and Demeure, A. Towards a New Generation of Widgets for Supporting Software Plasticity: The "Comet". Eng. HCI and Interactive Systems. Springer (2005), 306-324.

9. Calvary, G., Coutaz, J., Thevenin, D., Limbourg, Q., Bouillon, L., and Vanderdonckt, J. A Unifying Reference Framework for Multi-Target User Interfaces. Interacting with Computers 15, 3, Elsevier (2003), 289-308.

10. Carroll, J.M. and Carrithers, C. Training Wheels in a User Interface. CACM 27, 8, ACM (1984), 800-806.

11. Easterbrook, S., Singer, J., Storey, M.-A., and Damian, D. Selecting Empirical Methods for Software Engineering Research. Guide to Advanced Empirical Software Engineering, Springer (2008), 285-311.

12. Ferraiolo, D.F., Sandhu, R., Gavrila, S., Kuhn, D.R., and Chandramouli, R. Proposed NIST Standard for Role-Based Access Control. TISSEC, ACM (2001), 224-274.

13. Florins, M. and Vanderdonckt, J. Graceful Degradation of User Interfaces as a Design Method for Multiplatform Systems. IUI'04, ACM (2004), 140-147.

14. Gajos, K.Z., Weld, D.S., and Wobbrock, J.O. Automatically Generating Personalized User Interfaces with Supple. Artificial Intelligence, Elsevier (2010), 910-950.

15. Kramer, J. and Magee, J. Self-Managed Systems: an Architectural Challenge.FOSE'07, IEEE (2007), 259-268.

16. Lepreux, S., Vanderdonckt, J., and Michotte, B. Visual Design of User Interfaces by (De)Composition. DSV-IS'07, Springer-Verlag (2007), 157-170.

17. Lykkegaard, B. and Elbak, A. IDC - Document at a Glance - LC52T. International Data Corporation (2011).

18. McGrenere, J., Baecker, R.M., and Booth, K.S. An Evaluation of a Multiple Interface Design Solution for Bloated Software. CHI'02, ACM (2002), 164-170.

19. Paterno, F. Model-based Design and Evaluation of Interactive Applications. Springer-Verlag (1999).

20. Reinecke, K. and Bernstein, A. Improving Performance, Perceived Usability, and Aesthetics with Culturally Adaptive User Interfaces. TOCHI 18, ACM (2011), 1-29.

21. Shneiderman, B. Promoting Universal Usability with Multi-Layer Interface Design. CUU'03, ACM (2003), 1-8.

22. Singh, A. and Wesson, J. Evaluation Criteria for Assessing the Usability of ERP Systems. SAICSIT '09, ACM (2009), 87-95.

Using Differential Formal Analysis for Dependable Number Entry

Abigail Cauchi
Swansea University
Swansea
abigail@cauchi.net

abstract
ABSTRACT
User interfaces that employ the same display and buttons may look the same but can work very differently depending on how they are implemented. In healthcare, it is critical that interfaces that look the same *are* the same. Hospitals typically have many types of similar infusion pump, with different software versions, and variation between pump behavior may lead to unexpected adverse events. For example, when entering drug doses into infusion pumps that use the same display and button designs, different results may arise when pushing identical sequences of buttons. These differences arise as a result of subtle implementation differences and may lead to under-dose or over-dose errors.

This work explores different implementations of a 5-key interface for entering numbers using a new user interface analysis technique, *Differential Formal Analysis*.

Using Differential Formal Analysis different 5-key interfaces are analysed based on log data collected from 19 infusion pumps over a 3 year period from a UK hospital. The results from this analysis is domain specific to infusion pumps. A comparison is made between domain specific results and generic results from Differential Formal Analysis performed using random data.

Author Keywords
Number Entry; Stochastic Simulation; Medical Devices; Differential Formal Analysis

ACM Classification Keywords
H.5.2. User Interface: Input devices and strategies

INTRODUCTION
Number entry is required for almost all clinical procedures (e.g., radiation treatment, drug infusion, patient records). Software errors and HCI options can have a significant impact on dependability (i.e., the ability of the clinician to successfully enter the number intended). We are concerned with quantifying error magnitudes in relation to number entry of prescribed *values*: for example an error that is 1% out is less

Permission to make digital or hard copies of all or part of this work for personal or classroom use is granted without fee provided that copies are not made or distributed for profit or commercial advantage and that copies bear this notice and the full citation on the first page. To copy otherwise, or republish, to post on servers or to redistribute to lists, requires prior specific permission and/or a fee.
EICS'13, June 24–27, 2013, London, United Kingdom.
Copyright 2013 ACM 978-1-4503-2138-9/13/06...$15.00.

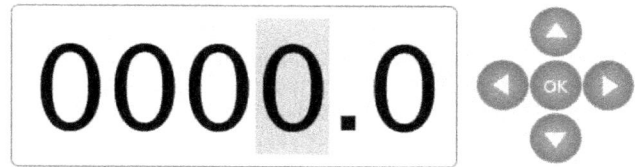

Figure 1: A typical 5-key user interface layout. Here the cursor is shown in the right-most position, and in this case the display format is suitable for entering times, 0 minutes to 999:59 hours. Some 5-key interfaces omit the OK button as its use can be implied by the user performing any action with a non-arrow button.

significant than an error that is out by a factor of ten. This is not however the only role that numbers can play in a medical context. Numbers are also used in healthcare as *identifiers* such as patient identifiers, and here different techniques (such as checksums) should be used — an error of 1%, unless detected, will be a completely different patient. An approach beyond the scope of the present work is entering numeric values of *standard* values, which are both identifiers and numeric values (*e.g.* a menu of 10, 20, 50mg).

An observation that motivated this work is that infusion pumps with 5-key number entry systems with interfaces that *look* the same do not *behave* the same. A 5-key number entry system, shown in figure 1, uses ▲ ▼ ◄ ► and OK keys to set a number. The keys ◄ and ► move the cursor to select a digit and the keys ▲ and ▼ change the value of the highlighted digit. The OK key is pressed to confirm the number.

Consider entering a dose of 950mL into two current infusion pumps with 5-key number entry systems, the BBraun Infusomat Space and Zimed AD. Starting with both devices showing **0**, the underline indicating the digit highlighted by the cursor, keying in the same plausible key sequence ◄ ▲ ▲ ▲ ▲ ▲ ◄ ▼ on both devices simultaneously results in the the Zimed AD display showing **950** and the BBraun Infusomat Space display showing **000.1**. This behaviour is illustrated in figure 2, that shows how the displays of both devices change on each key press.

Both devices work the same until the final key press, ▼. At this point, the two number entry systems are implemented to do different things, hence the different values. The difference in results between the two devices could have significant impact if, for example, a clinician trained on one device transfers to using the other. We do not need to assert one or the other

Key Press	Zimed AD	BBraun Infusomat Space
	0	0
◄	00	00
▲	10	10
▲	20	20
▲	30	30
▲	40	40
▲	50	50
◄	050	050
▼	950	000.1

Figure 2: A key sequence being input into Zimed AD and BBraun Infusomat SpaceThis table shows the change in displays after pressing the key in the "Key Press" column. In the first row there is no key press to show the starting displays of the two devices.

device is better, but clearly the *difference* is hazardous and any hospital is unwise to have both devices when they are so different.

AIMS AND GOALS

It is evident that standardisation is essential for such safety critical interfaces and the objectives of this work are (*i*) to present a validated method for finding the most dependable user interface between interfaces that are very similar (*ii*) to present finely-grained requirements for dependable number entry systems for safety critical use, particularly in the medical domain.

BACKGROUND

KLM and GOMS, and their variants, [1] are well-established evaluation methods that are useful for obtaining a measure of time to perform a specified goal. These techniques generally assume no user errors and evaluate unit tasks (CogTool is a tool that partly automates this process). In contrast, the approach described in this paper is specifically concerned with user error and how to design to manage it better. A task like "enter a number" is not considered to be a unit task. The user may make errors within the task and this requires careful analysis. The focus of our analysis is error rates rather than time. Making a user interface safer, and finding out how to make them safer, is more important than making them faster. In the design of safety critical number entry systems, the safest design is not necessarily the fastest or most appealing to users. In safety critical domains, having a design that reduces errors is desirable, however, design is a trade-off and an appropriate balance between speed and safety is required.

In [6] a lab study compared two different styles of number entry interfaces using the criteria of speed and accuracy. The study indicated that error rates in lab experiments are low, and undetected error rates (i.e., errors nurses make that they do not notice) are even lower. We are interested in choosing the best implementation of a 5-key interface so that human error is as low as reasonably practical. Since the differences in interface designs are subtle implementation differences in interfaces, it is not practicable to find the best design using lab studies because of the very low error rates.

Fields [4] explores the consequences of different kinds of error being made, based on a similar classification to ours. He developed a finite state transition notation for describing task models that can be combined with a device model. Combined models were then analysed using off-the-shelf model checking technology to analyse the effect of executing tasks on the device. He also defined patterns of user error that could be introduced into the model based on a similar classification to ours (e.g., omission or repetition of action). The consequences of the introduced errors could then be investigated via model checking. An issue that arises is how to determine which errors are likely to occur in practice and so worth considering the weights of proposed design changes. Fields considers exploring underlying cognitive causes, an approach further considered by, for example, Rukšėnas *et al.* [3]. Our work here offers a different solution—to consider sensitivity analysis.

The work presented in this paper complements [5], which defined the property *predictability* of a user interface in higher order logic, and explored how such a property can be verified on real systems through automated reasoning tools. The predictability property tests whether an expert user can tell what state the device is in from the perceptible output of the system, and hence accurately predict the consequences of an action from that state—normal human users can do no better. The analysis was performed on the formalisation of two real devices, and showed that devices, when closely examined, have many boundary cases where interactive functionality seems awkward. Here we explore the impact of errors, and assess in a systematic way if variations in the design of the numeric entry system can reduce harm when errors are made.

Medical device logs have been analysed in [7]. Lee *et al.* present valuable insight into how infusion pumps are used in hospitals, how we can gain insight into hospital infrastructure from analyzing logs, how much it costs for nurses to attend to alarms over a period of a year and other interesting findings from logs that can significantly improve healthcare systems. In this work, there is a different focus on retrieving information from logs. The concern here is to use medical device logs to answer very specific empirical questions to tailor the Differential Formal Analysis method to the medical domain.

5-Key number entry case study

The case of 5-key number entry systems is used throughout. Empirical evidence shows that across different number entry layouts, people are less prone to keying in erroneous numbers on 5-key layouts [6] and the small amount of buttons for number entry makes the device cheaper, which is a benefit for manufacturers.

Design choices subtly affect the result that a key sequence has on the display. The main 5-key variants are described here since this terminology will be used throughout the paper:

- **Left or Right Start** – In the starting screen, is the cursor on the left or on the right?

- **Cursor Wraparound** – When the cursor is at a display edge (leftmost or rightmost position), what happens when going beyond that edge? Does it wraparound to the opposite edge or stay at that edge?

- **Digit Wraparound** – When reaching the minimum or maximum number for a particular digit (0 or 9) what happens when attempting to go beyond it? Does it wraparound to the other edge or stay on the same number?

- **Arithmetic** – Another option for going beyond the edge for a particular digit is doing simple arithmetic operations. If at 9 and up is pressed does it show 0 and add 1 to the next digit? (Therefore having a display showing the value 10?)

- **Block errors** – If a user action does not change the interface, block interaction and alert the user.

WORK IN-PROGRESS

The analytical method, Differential Formal Analysis I presented in [2], distinguishes between different implementations of one type of interface. In [2] trials were run on 28 different 5-key interface implementations. The method simulates users of number entry tasks injecting all combinations of keystroke errors (omission, repetition, transposition and substitution) with a fixed probability p per keystroke. The analysis using the Differential Formal Analysis process makes a number of predictions and raises a number of questions that require validation through empirical data.

The analysis method [2] simulates number entry tasks over random numbers. However, it is clear (see [8]) that the distribution of numbers used in infusion pumps is not uniformly random. An analysis of the frequency of digits shows that the digit 0 is about three times more likely to appear than any other digit, the digit 5 is another commonly used digit and numbers such as 4 and 7 appear far less frequently. Ongoing work in my thesis focuses Differential Formal Analysis on the medical domain by using number distributions that coincide with those that frequently occur in a hospital context using 5-key interfaces. In [8] the analysis is performed on logs retrieved from an infusion pump with a number keypad style of number entry interface. The Differential Formal Analysis process is tailored for medical devices by implementing the results from the empirical findings of the 5-key device log study.

Another important empirical question raised by [2] is about the strategy users take to input numbers. From the keystroke logs of BBraun Infusomat Space pumps, I have analysed strategies medical practitioners use to enter numbers in 5-key interfaces. The Differential Formal Analysis process was tailored to implement these strategies to obtain results, specifically for the medical domain.

RESULTS

Running Differential Formal Analysis ranks designs according to their sensitivity to keystroke error. In figure 3, the results from a random trial of 28 different 5-key number entry designs are plotted. The probability per keystroke error is

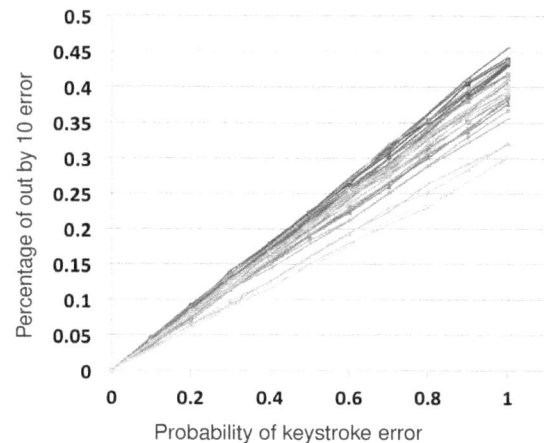

Figure 3: This graph shows probability per keystroke error against percentage of out by 10 errors from a trial with 1 million random numbers. The lower the gradient of the line, the better the design.

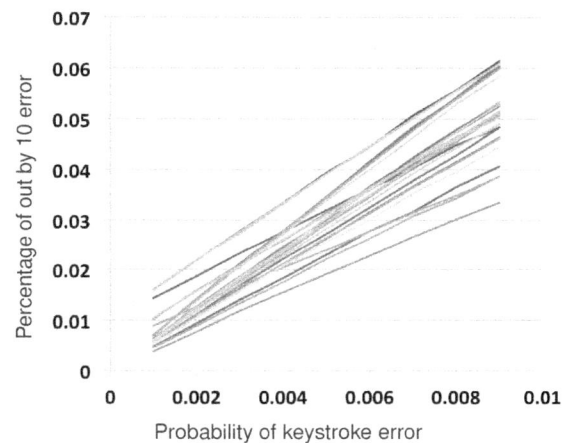

Figure 4: This graph shows probability per keystroke error against percentage of out by 10 errors from an empirically informed trial using 1 million numbers.

variable in this plot since we do not have the empirical data of the exact value. We see that in the plot of probability per keystroke error against the percentage of out by 10 error, the different designs do not interleave, implying that what the actual value of the probability per keystroke error is, is not required.

Figure 4 shows a similar plot to figure 3 but this plot is generated after the Differential Formal Analysis process was empirically informed with data from medical device logs of devices used in a hospital. There is interleaving present between some of the designs however, the best designs are consistently best throughout the various probability per keystroke error.

Figures 5 and 6 are two similar bar charts generated from results of running Differential Formal Analysis on random data and tailoring it to the medical domain respectively. The bar graphs show the aggregate gradients of the slopes seen in figures 3 and 4 depending on when the feature is on or off.

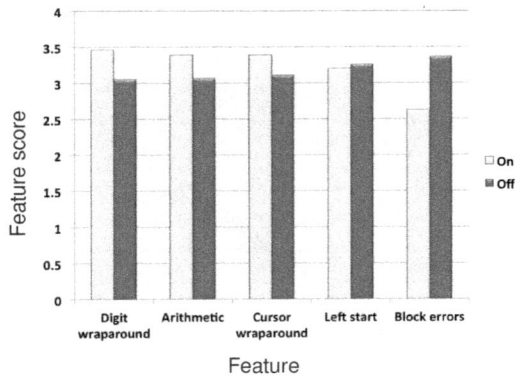

Figure 5: This bar chart shows whether features are better on or off from a random number analysis. A lower score means that the feature is better

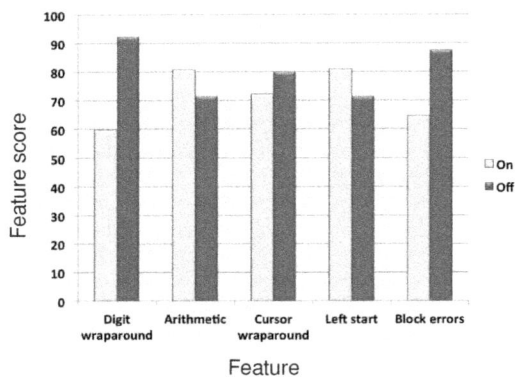

Figure 6: This bar chart shows whether features are better on or off from an empirically informed trial. A lower score means that the feature is better.

The lower the the bar is, the better, since a lower gradient in the previous graphs indicate a better design.

The best design from the random trials has no digit wraparound, no arithmetic, no cursor wraparound, right start and blocks errors. The worst design has digit wraparound, arithmetic, cursor wraparound, right start and no error blocking. The empirically informed Differential Formal Analysis showed higher out by 10 error rates and although the feature analysis seems different to the random trials, the only difference between the best and worst design is the arithmetic feature. In the empirically informed analysis, the best design has arithmetic enabled.

CONCLUSIONS

Number entry systems have been highly overlooked and research into how to make more dependable safety critical systems is minimal. Previous work has focussed on finding out which number entry system button layout is better through running empirical trials. In this work we see that within the same button layout style, there are various possibilities in how the interface can be programmed.

Differential Formal Analysis is a new methodology that should be used to complement user trials for more rigorous evaluation of safety critical number entry systems. Subtle interaction design choices in number entry lead to drastically different outcomes, it is crucial that these choices are explored and implement a design which is resilient to human error.

The issues and process presented are globally important and it is critical that we, as a community, get it right. Although these are clearly human-computer interaction issues, the presented approach which focusses on *safe* design, is not conventional and further work is necessary to bridge the gap between human-computer interaction and *safe* human-computer interaction.

ACKNOWLEDGMENTS
Special thanks goes to Professor Harold Thimbleby and Professor Michael Harrison for their help, advice and support for this work, and other colleagues whose feedback has been invaluable. This work is funded as part of the CHI+MED: UK EPSRC Grant Number EP/G059063/1 (see: www.chi-med.ac.uk).

REFERENCES
1. Card, S. K., Newell, A., and Moran, T. P. *The Psychology of Human-Computer Interaction*. L. Erlbaum Associates Inc., Hillsdale, NJ, USA, 2000.

2. Cauchi, A., Gimblett, A., Thimbleby, H., Curzon, P., and Masci, P. Safer "5-key" number entry user interfaces using differential formal analysis. In *Proceedings of the 26th Annual BCS Interaction Specialist Group Conference on People and Computers*, BCS-HCI '12, British Computer Society (Swinton, UK, UK, 2012), 29–38.

3. Curzon, P., Rukšėnas, R., and Blandford, A. An approach to formal verification of human-computer interaction. *Formal Aspects of Computing 4*, 19 (2007), 512–550.

4. Fields, R. E. *Analysis of erroneous actions in the design of critical systems*. DPhil thesis, University of York, 2001.

5. Masci, P., Rukšėnas, R., Oladimeji, P., Cauchi, A., Gimblett, A., Li, Y., Curzon, P., and Thimbleby, H. On formalising interactive number entry on infusion pumps. In *FMIS2011, the 4th Intl. Workshop on Formal Methods for Interactive Systems* (2011).

6. Oladimeji, P., Thimbleby, H., and Cox, A. Number entry interfaces and their effects on error detection. In *Proceedings of the 13th IFIP TC 13 international conference on Human-computer interaction - Volume IV*, INTERACT'11, Springer-Verlag (Berlin, Heidelberg, 2011), 178–185.

7. Thimbleby, H., Lee, P., and Thompson, F. Analysis of infusion pump error logs and their significance for healthcare. *British Journal of Nursing 21* (2012), 12–22.

8. Wiseman, S., Cox, A., and Brumby, D. Designing for the task: what numbers are really used in hospitals? In *Proceedings of the 2012 ACM annual conference extended abstracts on Human Factors in Computing Systems Extended Abstracts*, CHI EA'12, ACM (New York, NY, USA, 2012), 1733–1738.

The CoGenIVE Concept Revisited: A Toolkit for Prototyping Multimodal Systems

Fredy Cuenca
Hasselt University – tUL – iMinds
Expertise Centre for Digital Media, Diepenbeek, Belgium
fredy.cuencalucero@uhasselt.be

ABSTRACT

Many specialized toolkits have been developed with the purpose of facilitating the creation of multimodal systems. They allow their users to specify certain tasks of their intended systems by means of a visual language instead of programming code. One of these toolkits, CoGenIVE, was developed in our research lab, and despite of its successful application in many internal projects, it gradually fell into disuse. The rethinking of CoGenIVE unveiled the existence of important gaps hindering a fuller understanding of these toolkits for rapid prototyping of multimodal systems. This paper aims to remedy some of these gaps with the proposal of: (a) the architecture of a toolkit for rapid prototyping of multimodal systems, (b) a scale for measuring the support for implementation provided by a toolkit, and (c) a classification of a representative set of existing toolkits.

Author Keywords

User interface toolkits; Visual languages;

ACM Classification Keywords

H.5.m. Information Interfaces and Presentation (e.g. HCI): Miscellaneous

INTRODUCTION

A multimodal system is a computer system capable of collecting the information provided by the user through multiple input modes, combining these inputs in order to interpret the user's intent, and responding to the user through multiple output modes. Users can enter information into a multimodal system through speech, touch, handwriting, hand gestures or facial expressions; the system can respond the user with images, audio, synthesized voice or haptics. Its capability to decode user commands whose information is carried by several input signals is what distinguishes a multimodal system from a traditional WIMP system.

The implementation of a multimodal system is time-consuming and therefore expensive. Thus, several specialized toolkits have been developed with the purpose of facilitating the implementation of multimodal systems. These toolkits enable their users to specify certain functionality of the intended multimodal system by means of a visual language instead of programming code.

These so-called toolkits for rapid prototyping of multimodal systems started to be proposed since more than a decade ago, e.g. ICon [4], MEngine [1], OpenInterface [7], Squidy [9], HephaisTK [5]. During that period, we successfully developed a toolkit specifically designed to facilitate the development of multimodal virtual environments. Indeed, CoGenIVE [3] was internally used by many PhD students to create the interactive virtual worlds needed for their research projects. However, the lack of proper maintenance and its narrow scope made it fall into disuse, as did other toolkits. The analysis of this situation revealed that there are still gaps that hinder a fuller understanding of different toolkits for rapid prototyping multimodal systems. Some of these gaps include: (a) the lack of a broad description covering the structure and behavior of all the existing toolkits, which may be caused by the many differences among them, (b) the absence of a scale for measuring the support for implementation provided by a toolkit, which is pivotal to determine whether the proposal of a new toolkit advances the state-of-the-art or not, and (c) the shortage of cross-evaluations, which are always useful to classify apparently distinct elements, thus allowing their organized study.

The overarching goal of the research under discussion is the implementation of a visual language for modeling multimodal interaction, and of its supporting toolkit. This new language must rectify the shortcomings experienced with CoGenIVE's visual language: excessive notation, complex semantics, inability to model concurrency, and lack of underlying formalism. The first stage of this research is devoted to providing the theoretical background that fills the aforementioned gaps, this being the theme of the present paper.

TOOLKIT FOR RAPID PROTOTYPING OF MULTIMODAL SYSTEMS

A toolkit for rapid prototyping of multimodal systems consists of a framework and a graphical editor. The framework can be approached as a server offering some functionality to a client application. This application has to be developed without support from a toolkit. It has to implement the application-specific functionality of the intended multimodal system.

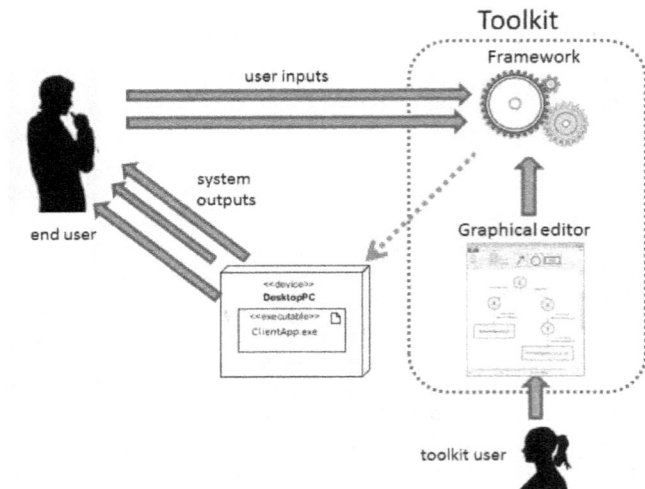

Figure 1. Architecture of a toolkit for rapid prototyping of multimodal systems.

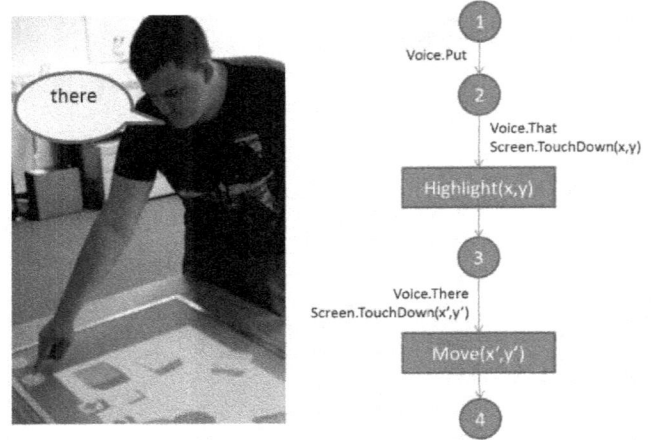

Figure 2. Left. End user interacting with a multimodal system. Right. Visual model used for specifying human-machine interaction.

Based on the study of several toolkits, the services usually provided by their frameworks include the recognition of user inputs, the identification of the user's intent, the identification of the system's state, and/or the dissociation of the system's response through multiple outputs. These services aim at extending the functionality of a client application so that it can handle multimodal input/output. The visual models depicted with the graphical editor of a toolkit are intended to specify how to intermix the services incorporated in the framework of a toolkit with the subroutines of a client application. These specifications are depicted by the user of a toolkit (who can also be the programmer of the client application), and are to be interpreted by its framework.

Once the framework and the client application are up and running, the end user is able to issue multimodal commands to an enhanced client application, which may not be originally capable of supporting multimodal interaction (Figure 1). Therefore, the client application is not the final system but a prototype: a partial implementation that needs to be supplemented by a toolkit so that its prospective users can have a means for experimenting, evaluating and/or redefining the intended system.

For illustrative purposes, consider a multimodal system whose users are allowed to utter a voice command 'zoom here' while touching a specific point on the screen to indicate the region to zoom in (left side of Figure 2). Prototyping such a system with the support of a toolkit entails the implementation of the GUI that the end user will interact with, and the subroutine(s) required to scale a specific region of this GUI. The particular behavior of the GUI and the specific scaling algorithms must be implemented (probably with a textual programming language) as part of a client application. This client application does not need to detect voice commands or touchscreen events. It neither has to verify the temporal co-occurrence of the speech input 'here' and the touch on the screen –required to zoom in on a region of the GUI. Both functionalities can be delegated to the framework through a visual model like the one shown on the right side of Figure 2.

This model specifies that the detection of the speech input 'zoom' followed by the simultaneous detection of the speech input 'here' and a touch on the screen will cause the execution of the subroutine *ZoomAt*, implemented in the client application. The use of visual models is due to the fact that their creation and maintenance is faster and easier than the edition of programming code.

A SCALE FOR MEASURING THE GAINS OFFERED BY A TOOLKIT

The more services a toolkit offers to its users, the less programming workload they will experience. Thus, the support for implementation provided by a toolkit depends on the functionalities that are pre-programmed in its framework. The study and testing of several toolkits revealed that the services commonly incorporated in their frameworks are:

Recognition of user inputs The framework incorporates software for recognizing a wide assortment of triggering events issued from several hardware devices.

Identification of the user's intent The framework can detect the occurrence of a multimodal command. Since the services offered by a system are requested through the issuing of multimodal commands, their detection reveal the user's intent. This process entails the recognition of patterns of events, i.e. sets of user events occurring in a particular order.

Identification of the system's state The framework can accurately determine the current state of the system after any arbitrary sequence of events. This permits prototyping systems that issue context-dependent responses.

Dissociation of the system's response The framework can concurrently launch several subroutines of the client application, and synchronize their execution.

The aforementioned functionalities are the ones used to describe the architecture of a multimodal system. Indeed, these match with the functions in charge of the recognizers, fusion engine, dialog manager and fission component of a multi-modal system respectively [2] [6].

We propose to express the support provided by a toolkit as a set of the aforementioned functionalitites. For instance, the support of CoGenIVE is {recognition of inputs, identification of the user's intent, identification of the system's state}, meaning that CoGenIVE releases its users from programming these functionalities. Then, the set containing all the possible combinations of the aforementioned functionalities is the scale of measurement we are proposing.

Heuristics to uncover framework's capabilities

The study and testing of several toolkits show that they all incorporate software for detecting the inputs coming from a myriad of hardware devices. This implies that their users do not have to implement algorithms for event recognition in their client applications. Rather, they can delegate the recognition of user inputs to the framework of a toolkit, as seen in Figure 1.

Regarding the identification of the user's intent, the detection of the system's state, and the dissociation of a response, these functionalities are not always pre-programmed in all the studied toolkits. Fortunately, it is possible to infer whether these services are provided by a toolkit or not, by examining its visual language.

The toolkits capable of detecting multimodal commands allow their users to specify composite events in their visual models. For instance, Figure 2 shows a composite event made up of two elements, *Voice.Here* and *Screen.TouchDown*, linked by a relation of simultaneity. The way a composite event is depicted, and the relations allowed among its constituent events, vary from toolkit to toolkit. In any case, the presence of composite events in a visual model is necessary to indicate the framework those sets of events whose perception (in a particular order) reveals that the user is requesting some service from the system.

The toolkits that can assume the responsibility of handling context-dependent human-machine dialogs always allow the depiction of the system's state in their visual models. This possibility enables users to specify multimodal systems that respond differently to the same command, depending on the state of the multimodal system. The model depicted in Figure 2 shows that both the perceptibility and response of the system to a multimodal command depends on its current state, e.g. once in state 2, the system will only respond to the designation of a target area, and will ignore other commands. The dissociation of the system's response involves the concurrent activation of several synthesizers, and the coordination of their outputs. We found that toolkits whose visual models are variations of state diagrams (e.g. Figure 2) cannot be used to specify concurrency and synchronization. This limitation stems from the fact that state diagrams only experience one transition at a time, and thus only one subroutine can be executed in a given moment. However, toolkits capable of interpreting visual models based on Petri nets (e.g. PetShop [8]) allow for modeling both concurrent execution of subroutines and synchronization of events.

	Recognition of inputs	Identification of multimodal commands	Identification of the system's state	Dissociaton of responses
ICon	✓	✗	✗	✗
OpenInterface	✓	✗	✗	✗
Squidy	✓	✗	✗	✗
MEngine	✓	✓	✓	✗
CoGenIVE	✓	✓	✓	✗
HephaisTK	✓	✓	✓	✗
PetShop	✓	✓	✓	✓
Hinckley	✓	✓	✓	✓

Figure 3. Checkmarks are used to indicate the services offered by different toolkits to their users. Under this criterion, toolkits can be clustered into three groups.

EVALUATION AND COMPARISON OF TOOLKITS

Cross-evaluations of toolkits for rapid prototyping of multimodal systems are few and difficult to conduct. This may be caused by the abundant differences among these toolkits: they offer different features, target different domains, operate with different programming paradigms and/or expect different skills from their users. However, despite of these numerous differences, some similarities can be observed when identifying the functionalities of their frameworks. The evaluation of several toolkits uncovered the existence of three classes of toolkits (Figure 3).

Toolkits in the first class are called *flow-based* toolkits. They incorporate software for event recognition, thus releasing their users from implementing this functionality. The visual models depicted with the editors of these toolkits resemble block diagrams. They specify the transformations experienced by the data flowing from the input devices to a client application. ICon [4], OpenInterface [7], and Squidy [9] are some examples of flow-based toolkits.

In addition, a second group of toolkits allow the specification of composite events and the depiction of the system state. Therefore, their users can delegate the detection of multimodal commands, and the execution of pertinent context-dependent responses to their frameworks. These toolkits are called *state-based* toolkits because of the resemblance of their visual models with state diagrams. Examples of this type of toolkits include MEngine [1], CoGenIVE [3] and HephaisTK [5].

Finally, the third class of toolkits also facilitates the dissociation of the system's response through multiple outputs. These toolkits use Petri nets as visual models. The tokens allow modeling concurrent activities, and the transition rule serves as a synchronization mechanism. These toolkits are called *token-based*, Petshop being [8] its most prominent example.

The clustering observed in Figure 3 suggests that the services a toolkit can offer to its users are restricted by the formalism (block diagrams, state diagrams or Petri nets) on which its visual language is based. This observation must be taken into account by those developing a toolkit for rapid prototyping, in order to avoid unwanted limitations of their intended toolkits after the implementation of its visual language.

161

CONCLUSIONS

In this paper, we propose novel theoretical tools intended for improving the understanding of toolkits for prototyping of multimodal systems, and allowing their precise evaluation and objective comparison. Our proposal includes: (a) the architecture of a toolkit for rapid prototyping of multimodal systems, (b) a scale for measuring the support for implementation provided by a toolkit, and (c) a classification of a set of toolkits based on the support they offer.

In the proposed architecture, a toolkit for rapid prototyping of multimodal systems can be approached as a server intended to extend a client application with multimodal features.

Regarding the measurement scale, we proposed to measure the support for implementation provided by a toolkit in terms of the services it provides. The services used to evaluate the capabilities of a toolkit, are the ones that describe the architecture of a multimodal system, namely, the recognition of user inputs, the identification of the user's intent, the identification of the system's state, and the dissociation of a response through multiple output modes [2] [6]. A reference scale where the gains provided by a toolkit can be measured on is necessary to determine whether the use of a particular toolkit can lead to a higher reduction of the programming workload, which is the primary goal of these toolkits. Without such scale, it is also hard to assess whether new or improved toolkits are advancing the state of the art or not. In our opinion, this is a challenge that the community has not yet solved.

By comparing several toolkits, we noticed that they can be clustered into three groups called flow-based, state-based and token-based toolkits. Toolkits within each group do not only offer the same services to their users, but also exhibit resemblance in their visual languages.

FUTURE WORK

A potentially successful way to continue this research may consist of (a) the creation of a simple textual programming language for specifying composite events, (b) the creation of a simple textual programming language for specifying the execution of concurrent and synchronized actions, and (c) the development of a graphical editor that allows representing human-machine dialogs as state diagrams whose arcs will be annotated with the utterances of the languages mentioned in (a) and (b). The utterances of (a) will specify the composite events that will cause a system transition, and the utterances of (b), the actions to be performed during this transition. A state diagram enhanced with the languages (a) and (b) will give us the following advantages: First, the possibility to specify composite events with a textual notation rather than with a graphical one, will lead us to more concise models, which are probably easy to read, maintain, and extend. Second, the inability of CoGenIVE's visual language for specifying the concurrent execution of many subroutines will be overcome by annotating the arcs of a state diagram with the utterances of the textual language described in (b). Third, readers in general will not have to accomplish the undesirable task of inferring the semantics of CoGenIVE's visual language from informal descriptions of running examples. The semantics of a state diagram can be concisely and formally described with a set of mathematical formulas.

ACKNOWLEDGMENTS

This research was funded by the BOF financing of Hasselt University. We want to thank our UHasselt colleagues of the HCI group for the discussions about and feedback on this research.

REFERENCES

1. Bourget, M. Designing and prototyping multimodal commands. In *Proc. of INTERACT'03* (2003).

2. Bui, T. *Multimodal Dialogue Management - State of the Art*. PhD thesis, University of Twente, 2008.

3. De Boeck, J., Vanacken, D., Raymaekers, C., and Coninx, K. High level modeling of multimodal interaction techniques using NiMMiT. *Journal of Virtual Reality and Broadcasting 4*, 2 (2007).

4. Dragicevic, P., and Fekete, J. Icon: Input device selection and interaction configuration. In *ACM UIST 2002* (2002).

5. Dumas, B., Lalanne, D., and Ingold, R. Description Languages for Multimodal Interaction: A Set of Guidelines and its Illustration with SMUIML. *Journal of Multimodal User Interfaces 3*, 3 (2010).

6. Dumas, B., Lalanne, D., and Oviatt, S. Multimodal interfaces: A survey of principles, models and frameworks. In *Human Machine Interaction*, Springer Verlag (2009).

7. Lawson, L., Al-Akkad, A., Vanderdonckt, J., and Macq, B. An open source workbench for prototyping multimodal interactions based on off-the-shelf heterogeneous components. In *Proc. of the 1st ACM SIGCHI Symposium on Engineering Interactive Computing Systems EICS 09* (2009).

8. Navarre, D., Palanque, P., Ladry, J., and Barboni, E. ICOs: A Model-Based User Interface Description Technique dedicated to Interactive Systems Addressing Usability, Reliability and Scalability. *ACM Transactions on Computer-Human Interaction 16*, 4 (2009).

9. Werner, K., Raedle, R., and Harald, R. Interactive Design of Multimodal User Interfaces - Reducing technical and visual complexity. *Journal on Multimodal User Interfaces 3*, 3 (2010).

Addressing Dependability for Interactive Systems: Application to Interactive Cockpits

Camille Fayollas

ICS-IRIT, University of Toulouse, 118 Route de Narbonne, F-31062, Toulouse, France
LAAS-CNRS, University of Toulouse, 7 avenue du colonel Roche, F-31400 Toulouse, France
fayollas@irit.fr

ABSTRACT

Most of the work done for improving interactive systems reliability is based on methods and techniques to avoid the occurrence of faults. The goal of most of such techniques is to remove software defects prior to deployment. However, it has been proved that regardless of the approaches that are setup, system crashes may still occur at runtime. One of the potential sources of such crashes is natural faults triggered by alpha-particles from radioactive contaminants in the chips or neutron from cosmic radiation. This phenomenon appears with a higher probability while flying in the high atmosphere, which is the case for aircrafts. Safety-critical systems need to cope with this type of fault to be dependable.

The main goal of this PhD is to provide means and methodology to build dependable interactive systems using interactive cockpits as a case study. The work presented in this doctorial consortium paper gives an excerpt of the solution proposed to build dependable interactive systems. This approach is a two-fold solution to deal with both (i) software faults prior to operation by using zero-default development dedicated to interactive systems and (ii) natural faults by embedding fault-tolerant mechanisms in the interactive system.

Author Keywords

Dependability; WIMP interfaces; Widgets; Fault-tolerance; Formal description techniques; Interactive cockpits; Critical systems.

ACM Classification Keywords

H.5.2. Information interfaces and presentation (e.g., HCI): User Interfaces; C.4. Performance of Systems.

INTRODUCTION

Interactive systems surrounding us have increasingly evolved these last few years. Besides the classical WIMP interaction techniques using a mouse and a keyboard, post-WIMP interaction techniques using tactile interfaces are nowadays very common. When it comes to safety-critical interactive systems, such as interactive cockpits, this evolution is slower due to the safety-critical nature of the system. A safety-critical system is a system in which any failure or error has the potential to lead to loss of life or injuries to human beings [5] while a system is called critical when the cost of a potential error is much higher than the cost of development [11]. The complexity and quantity of data being manipulated, the high number of commands to trigger and the amount of systems to be controlled call for the use of sophisticated interaction techniques in most of safety-critical or critical interactive systems. This is the case in new interactive cockpits (e.g. with Airbus A380) where integration of control and command takes place through interactive applications and interaction techniques as in any other interactive context (web applications, games, mobile devices ...). Nevertheless, it is worth noting that currently this interactive approach is only used in avionics for non-critical functions. The challenge is now to extend it to critical functions.

This doctoral consortium submission describes a PhD subject and its current development, describing a solution to provide dependable [3] and safe interactive systems for interactive cockpits. To build reliable interactive systems, we proposed a two-fold approach relying on (i) fault-prevention using a formal description technique dedicated to the description and design of interactive systems [4,10] and (ii) fault-tolerance using classical fault-tolerant mechanisms [14,13,7].

PROBLEM STATEMENT

Building reliable interactive systems is a difficult task due to their very specific nature. Interactive systems belong to the class of reactive systems because of their event driven nature. Their main specificity remains the human operator which implies several constraints: users can behave in an unexpected and unpredictable way and the information must be presented in such a way that it can be perceived and interpreted correctly. Lastly, interactive systems require addressing simultaneously hardware and software aspects (e.g. input and output devices together with their device drivers). Due to these specificities, standard software engineering approaches cannot be applied for building reliable interactive systems and a lot of work has been carried out to address this challenge. Nevertheless, most of this work has been focusing on removing software default during the system development.

Yet, such complex system can be subject to faults and empirical studies have demonstrated that software crashes may occur even though the development of the system has been extremely rigorous. One of the many sources of such crashes is called natural faults [3] triggered by alpha-particles from radioactive contaminants in the chips or neutron from cosmic radiation. A higher probability of occurrence of faults concerns systems deployed in the high atmosphere (e.g. aircrafts) or in space. A simple example of these natural faults can be an unexpected bit flip.

Such faults demonstrate the necessity to go beyond classical fault avoidance techniques at development time. In the area of dependable computing, five different ways to increase a system dependability have been identified [3]:

- *Fault avoidance:* preventing the occurrence or introduction of faults by construction (usually by using formal description techniques and proving safety and liveness properties).

- *Fault removal*: reducing the number of faults that can occur (by verification of properties).

- *Fault mitigation*: reducing the severity of faults (by adding barriers or healing behaviors).

- *Fault forecasting*: estimating the number, future incidence and likely consequences of faults (usually by statistical evaluation of the occurrence and consequences of faults).

- *Fault tolerance*: avoiding service failure in the presence of faults (usually by adding redundancy, multiple versions and voting mechanisms).

My PhD study focuses on both software faults during development and natural faults during operation that cannot be predictable or avoidable. These types of faults bring us to choose fault-avoidance to prevent software faults during development and fault-tolerance to allow service delivery even in the presence of unavoidable natural faults.

CONTEXT

Interactive cockpits

Our study is based on the example of Airbus cockpits, in particular the A380 cockpit. The interactive Control and Display System (CDS) of the Airbus A380 (see Figure 1) is composed of 2 input devices called KCCUs (Keyboard and Cursor Control Unit) and 8 output devices called DUs (Display Unit). Only some of the 8 DUs allow the crew to use the interactivity, the other ones are only used for displaying information.

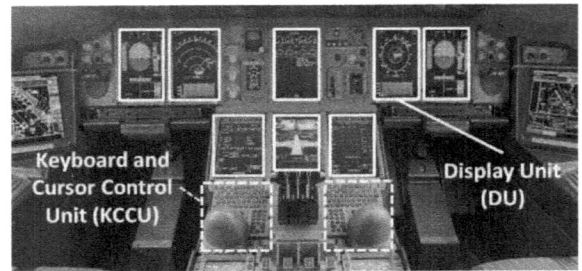

Figure 1. Airbus A380 interactive cockpit

The type of interactive applications that can be proposed in the new generation of interactive cockpits is based on ARINC 661 specification [2]. This specification describes the interactive system architecture as well as the communication protocol between the various components of an interactive cockpit (see Figure 3):

- *Input and output devices*: KCCUs (Keyboard and Cursor Control Unit) and LCD screens. These devices allow the crew members to interact with the application.

- *Window and widgets managers*: composed of an event manager, a display manager and a set of interactive elements called widgets distributed in a set of windows which will be rendered on the LCD screens.

PushButton RadioButton EditBoxNumeric

Figure 2. Examples of widgets

The widgets (see Figure 2) are the basic interactive components such as PushButtons dedicated to commands triggering, RadioButtons dedicated to selection of one option among a set of available one or EditBoxNumeric dedicated to entering numeric values.

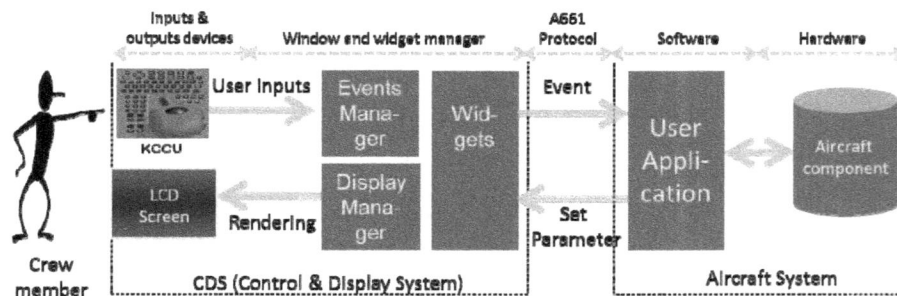

Figure 3. Simplified architecture compliant with ARINC 661 specification.

The CDS manages information for two types of clients:

- *Aircraft systems*: information to and from aircraft systems flows through dedicated so-called User Applications (UAs) which are applications featuring a graphical user interface for a given avionic function. They process the event notifications sent by the widgets (and might trigger commands on the physical aircraft components). They can also update the widgets (by calling update methods called SetParameters) in order to provide feedback to the flight crew according to state changes which occurred in the aircraft systems.

- *Crew members*: they have the responsibility of flying the aircraft by monitoring the aircraft systems through the LCD screens and controlling the aircraft system through input devices. They interact with the displayed widgets. For instance, they can click on a button in order to trigger a command, enter a numeric value in an EditBoxNumeric to send a value to an avionic function.

Main hypotheses and functional failures to cover

The focus of the work carried during the PhD is on the dependability of interactive systems, more precisely, the CDS dependability as a computer-based system. To concentrate on this issue, we assume the following:

- Human-errors are considered out of scope. This is indeed a very strong hypothesis but operator reliability can be considered as independent as it does not influence the occurence of natural faults. Furthermore, a lot of work has been done to prevent human-made faults during operation [6,8,12].

- The communication between the CDS and aircraft system is reliable. The data transfer is without corruption and this can easily be achieved using conventional reliable protocols on a FIFO communication channel. Communication between the different components is also reliable.

- The displays of the CDS are reliable, graphical commands sent to the LCD screen are always correctly displayed.

- The KCCU is sending reliable data to the server.

To ensure the correct service of the interactive system during operation, we have to make sure it correctly processes input events from crew members and correctly renders parameters received from the avionics systems. This made us targeting at managing three possible functional failures:

- *Erroneous display*: Incorrect display of data received from functional core (e.g. a widget receives the value 20 to render and displays another value);

- *Erroneous control*: Transmission of a different action from the one done by the user (e.g. user click on Button1 but the event Click-Button2 is sent to the application);

- *Inadvertent control*: Transmission of an action without any user's action (e.g. an event click is sent to the application without user action on the input devices).

PROPOSED APPROACH

To deal both with software faults such as development faults and physical faults such as natural and unpredictable ones, we propose a two-fold approach based on:

- *A zero-default approach*: to deal with software faults prior to operation, we propose the use of a formal description technique, associated with analysis for validation and verification, for designing and describing the interactive system.

- *A fault-tolerant computing approach*: to deal with natural faults that can't be avoided, we propose the introduction of fault-tolerant mechanisms in the interactive system associated with correspondent fault-tolerant architectures.

A zero default approach

We proposed to describe our system using a formal description technique dedicated to the specification and verification of interactive systems: the Interactive Cooperative Objects (ICO) [10,4]. In the domain of safety critical systems, the use of a formal description technique is very valuable as it provides non-ambiguous complete and concise models. The use of a formal description technique can be considered as a zero-default development approach if it is widened with formal analysis for verification and validation which can be done with the ICO formalism as it is Petri Net based.

A fault-tolerant computing approach

In the area of dependable computing, many approaches have been investigated to provide fault-tolerance mechanisms. We propose to embed one of the different fault-tolerance mechanisms into our system: the self-checking mechanism [9,15]. This mechanism can be roughly described as two pieces of the software, the first one being the classical component (functional component) and the second one being here to check its execution (monitoring component). We first proposed to introduce this mechanism into the basic component of the interaction: the widgets [14,13]. As every part of the interactive system has to be covered, we are now proposing to extend this mechanism to the other components of our interactive system (e.g. the window and widgets manager, the software part of the aircraft system …). Due to their composition and role differences, these components call for a different implementation of the self-checking mechanism [7]. The use of a software fault-tolerant mechanism such as the self-checking mechanism needs to take into account error confinement areas to separate the two pieces of software by isolating the functional component from its monitoring component. To solve this issue, we propose to implement our system using the confinement facilities provided by a specific run-time support [7], namely the ARINC 653 operating system kernel [1].

PHD PROGRESS AND FUTURE WORK

This doctoral consortium paper presents the current work which has been focusing on defining the theoretical aspects of the study such as the two folds of our approach. This work has been carried out during the first year of my PhD and permitted to propose an approach to deal with the dependability of safety-critical interactive systems, and particularly the dependability of interactive aircraft cockpits. The proposed approach is composed of two steps which are (i) the use of a formal description technique to describe our system together with analysis for validation and verification to build fault-free software and (ii) the embedding of fault-tolerant mechanisms in our system. The approach describes in this doctoral consortium paper was published in an international workshop on reliable computing [7].

As I am starting my second year, we are currently working on the application of the self-checking mechanism on every components of the interactive application. Furthermore, we are currently studying an aircraft function as a case study. With this mindset, we are developing a realistic platform to be able to test our approach on this very case study. The implementation of this realistic case study aims at proving the efficiency of our approach. We also plan to study the usability of our dependable interactive system to make sure that the added mechanisms do not affect the usability of the system.

The final goal pursued in this work is to provide means and methodology to build dependable interactive systems using interactive cockpits as a case study.

ACKNOWLEDGMENTS

I would like to thanks my supervisors: Prof. Philippe Palanque, Prof. Jean-Charles Fabre and Yannick Deleris.

This work is partly funded by Airbus under the contract R&T Display System X31WD1107313.

REFERENCES

1. ARINC 653 Avionics Application Software Standard Interface. ARINC Specification 653. Airlines Electronic Engineering Committee July 15, 2003.

2. ARINC 661 Cockpit Display System Interfaces to User Systems. ARINC Specification 661. Airlines Electronic Engineering Committee 2002.

3. Avizienis, A., Laprie, J.-C., Randell, B., Landwehr, C. Basic concepts and taxonomy of dependable and secure computing. In IEEE Trans. on Dependable and Secure Computing, vol.1, no.1, pp. 11- 33, Jan.-March 2004.

4. Barboni, E., Conversy, S., Navarre, D., Palanque, P. Model-Based Engineering of Widgets, User Applications and Servers Compliant with ARINC 661 Specification. DSVIS 2006. LNCS n°4323, pp. 25–38.

5. Bowen J. and Stavridou V. Formal Methods, Safety-Critical Systems and Standards. Software Engineering Journal, 8(4):189–209, July 1993.

6. Dearden, A. M and Harrison, M. D. Formalising human error resistance and human error tolerance. Proceedings of the Fifth International Conference on Human-Machine Interaction and Artificial Intelligence in Aerospace. 1995. EURISCO.

7. Fayollas C., Fabre J-C., Navarre D., Palanque P. and Deleris Y. Fault-Tolerant Interactive Cockpits for Critical Applications: Overall Approach. 4th International Workshop on Software Engineering for Resilient Systems (SERENE 2012), LNCS, Springer Verlag. pp. 134-155.

8. Hollnagel, E. Barriers and Accident Prevention. 2004. Ashgage.

9. Laprie, J-C., Arlat, J., Béounes, C., Kanoun, K. Definition and Analysis of hardware and software Fault-Tolerant Architectures, IEEE computer, vol.23, no.7, pp.39-51, 1990.

10. Navarre, D., Palanque, P., Ladry, J., and Barboni, E. ICOs: A model-based user interface description technique dedicated to interactive systems addressing usability, reliability and scalability, ACM TOCHI, 2009, V. 16, 4, pp. 1-56.

11. Palanque P. & Bastide B.. A Formalism for Reliable User Interfaces. Workshop Software Engineering / Human Computer Interaction associated with the IEEE / ICSE 16 conference. Sorento, Italy 16-21 May 1994.

12. Palanque P. & Basnyat S. Task Patterns for Taking into account in an efficient and systematic way both standard and erroneous user behaviours. 6th International Conference on Human Error, Safety and System Development, Springer Verlag pp. 123-139.

13. Tankeu-Choitat, A., Navarre, D., Palanque, P., Deleris, Y., Fabre, J.-C., Fayollas, C. Self-checking components for dependable interactive cockpits using formal description techniques. In Proc of 17th IEEE Pacific Rim International Symposium on Dependable Computing (PRDC 2011) Pasadena, California, USA.

14. Tankeu-Choitat A., FabreJ-C., Palanque P., Navarre D., Deleris Y. Self-Checking Components for Dependable Interactive Cockpits. 13th European Workshop on Dependable Computing (EWDC 2011), Pisa, ACM DL.

15. Yau S.S, R.C Cheung, "Design of self-Checking Software", proc. Int. Conf. on Reliable Software, Los Angeles, CA, USA, IEEE Computer Society Press, 1975, pp. 450-457.

A Context-aware Dialog Model for Multi-device Web Apps

Javier Rodríguez Escolar

Fundación CTIC Centro Tecnológico, Parque Científico y Tecnológico de Gijón
c/ Ada Byron, 39 Edificio Centros Tecnológicos, 33203 Gijón - Asturias - España
Javier.rodriguez@fundacionctic.org

ABSTRACT

Model-Based User Interface Design (MBUID) consists of a step-wise method that structures the development of User Interfaces (UIs) based on models. According to this method, developers focus on creating a UI model, that is an abstract representation of it, and delegate the UI code generation process to automatic tools that take into account platform peculiarities. This paper explores the applicability of MBUI techniques to context-aware Service Front Ends (SFEs), i.e. UIs of web services that react to context changes. For this purpose, it introduces a context-aware dialog model that captures the adaptable behavior of a UI depending on variations of the context of use, a standard-based notation to represent it, and an open-source development environment that supports this development method.

Author Keywords

Connection-awareness, context awareness, dialog, model-based design of user interface, navigation, SCXML.

ACM Classification Keywords

D.2.2 [**Software Engineering**]: Design tools and techniques – *User Interfaces*. H.5.2 [**Information Interfaces and Presentation**]: User Interfaces – *Graphical User Interfaces, Group and organization interfaces*.

General Terms

Design, Languages.

INTRODUCTION

A context-aware Service Front End (SFE) aims at providing a User Interface (UI) of a Web application that exhibits some capability to be aware of the context and to react to its changes in a continuous manner. Consequently, the UI should be tailored to the user (e.g., abilities, preferences), to the platform (e.g., operating system, device), and to the environmental conditions (e.g., noise, light), thus improving user experience in comparison to fixed SFEs. The development of context-aware SFEs is a very complex process since it considers multiple aspects of the context of use. In order to address the complexity of manual dealing of tasks related to that problem, Model Based Design of User Interfaces (MBUID) makes the development process more structured by identifying high-level models, which allow designers to specify and analyze interactive software applications

from an abstract level rather than starting immediately to address the implementation level. This allows them to concentrate on important aspects without being immediately confused by many implementation details [2].

One important factor in MBUID is to precisely define each part of the development process in an independent way, thus establishing a clear separation of concerns in the definition of the applications. In MBUID, dialog (or navigation) models are traditionally in charge of the specification of those dynamic aspects related to the user-device interaction. That means determining how to react in response to user events, which consequently implies defining the possible transitions among the different UIs and to define when to execute functions belonging to the semantic core of the application. This paper argues that a dialog model intended to facilitate the creation of context-aware UIs also needs to include advanced mechanisms to handle context variations. For instance, if the user's device has a low battery level, it would be convenient to provide her with a predefined UI version that optimizes the consumption of computational resources. Analogously, if the light conditions are poor, it would be suitable to provide her with a UI version that facilitates the visualization under such conditions (e.g., by increasing font size, by changing the layout); if the network connection speed is too slow (or even unavailable), an alternate UI could be provided instead (e.g., by providing previously gathered information and informing the user she might be visualizing outdated data).

DEFINITION OF THE PROBLEM

Different research works have relied on MBUID to automatically create SFEs. However, some shortcomings have been identified when it comes to define dialog models to guide the automatic generation of such SFEs:

- Dialog models are embedded in presentation [12].
- Efforts have been done in defining task and domain models. Still creating SFEs requires deeper research in the creation of models at low levels of abstraction [7].
- Dialog models should be considered at different levels of abstraction. Moreover, the development process might be started from the dialog models rather than from the task models [10].
- The creation of SFEs requires dialog models to be prepared to handle context information [8].
- Dialog models should provide clear handles where to consider device constraints, e.g., for splitting [4].
- Dialog models could be considered for various levels of fidelity [3].

Some works have studied how task and domain models could be transformed into a dialog model [7,9]. Unfortunately, the process is not trivial and the lack of a standard notation to define both of them makes it even more difficult. Some research efforts have been focused on the resolution of the problem for desktop Web applications: *State-WebCharts* [11], *Spring Web Flow* [5]. However, the existing scientific research in this field lacks advanced mechanisms to handle context awareness, which is relevant to mobile Web development due to the variability of the context and of software tools supporting application development. In addition, the automatic creation of modern Web UIs for multiple devices requires further considerations imposed by the incoming standards regarding mobile Web development, such as:

- Enabling users to interact with Web applications and documents even when their network connection is unavailable. HTML5 offers the possibility of creating offline applications. This means not only to consider the connection modality (online/offline) in dialog models, but also to guarantee the synchronization between client and server side dialogs when changing from offline to online or vice versa. Note that in some scenarios, it is not possible to offer the same user experience to the user when there is no connection available.

- Managing bi-directional communications with servers. This is a key issue in the provision of fresh and up-to-date context data from the server to the client. To accomplish this goal, the *WebSocket* API is being standardized by W3C.

- Managing dynamic context information coming from hardware sensors installed in the device as reflected in the W3C Device APIs Working Group.

- Handling not only physical multi-touch interface events, but also higher-level events as defined in the W3C Web Events Working Group.

MAIN MOTIVATIONS

The goal of the dissertation is to demonstrate that a context-aware defined dialog model is necessary to guide the automatic generation of multi-device Web UIs that are able to be aware of the context and to react to its changes in a continuous way. To this purpose, the research aims at providing a dialog model to guide the generation of context-aware Web applications for multiple devices.

The resolution of the aforementioned problem has an important impact on end users and SFEs developers. End users could benefit from personalized UIs tailored to their specific context of use. Developers could benefit from a mechanism to automatically generate context-aware Web applications, thus improving their efficiency and reducing the time-to-market of these applications.

RESEARCH METHODOLOGY

The research methodology is structured as follows (Fig. 1): The concerns of the existing dialog models (with respect to SFEs of Web applications) guide the definition of this work statement and they are the main input for the state-of-the-art analysis. This analysis identifies a set of shortcomings, which will be taken into account in eliciting requirements. These requirements will guide the fulfillment of the work statement and they will be used to validate its results.

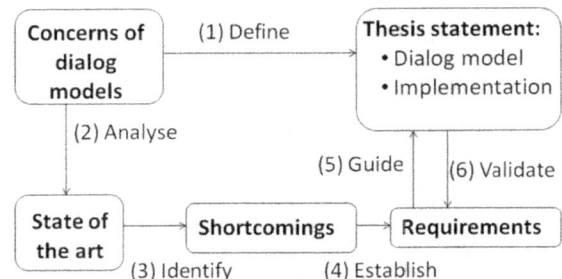

Figure 1. Diagram of the research methodology.

PRELIMINARY RESULTS

So far, a first version of a context-aware dialog model intended to represent Web application flows has been created and it will be enhanced by means of continuous iterations. In order to represent the aforementioned model, a standard-based notation has been defined. Finally, the proposal has been implemented as part of the Controller layer of an open source framework intended to facilitate the creation of mobile Web applications. The following subsections explain further details about the ongoing work in this research.

Proposed dialog model

The proposal is to create a dialog model based on the state machine concept. For that purpose, three types of states are distinguished. An *ApplicationState* represents the whole application and is composed of *UseCaseStates*, which represent specific use cases within the application flow. They are composed by a set of *ViewStates* and the navigation flow among them. *ViewStates* represent concrete UIs (e.g. web pages). The basic elements to drive the flow from one state to another are called *transitions* and its main function is to decide the next state to be visited in response to *events*. The proposed model considers two types of transitions. *Global transitions* are shared by a set of states, while *local transitions* are restricted to the current state. *Events* are in charge of triggering transitions. Two types of events are distinguished. *User events* are generated as a result of the interaction between the user and the device. *Context events* are generated due to the occurrence of any context variation. One of the keys to properly manage the flow of device independence applications is the definition of *conditions* that indicate if a transition should be triggered or not. The establishment of guard-conditions depending on the delivery context information is a crucial aspect in this research. Finally, *actions* represent specific tasks that are susceptible of being executed as a result of a *transition*.

One of the first dynamic properties of the context considered in the creation of the proposed dialog model is the status of the network connection, since it has an immediate repercussion on the Web contents to be delivered. In this research, we refer to *connection-aware Web applications* as those applications created to be consumed from a Web browser and which are able to provide an optimized user experience regardless of the network status. So far, we consider two different statuses: online and offline. An *online* status indicates a state of connectivity between the client and the server, while an *offline* status reflects that there is no connection between them. The assumption of a constant online status is not always admissible and users are increasingly demanding rich Web applications, which can provide a minimum functionality even when a wireless connection is not available. The web development community usually refers to this kind of software as *offline applications*.

In order to cover connection-aware applications, the proposed dialog model includes specific mechanisms to handle variations in the network status. First of all, each *StateChart* is associated to a *DataModel*, which is composed of multiple *DataElements*. Each *DataElement* is defined by its storage (note that the information might be stored at client side, at server side or both), its scope (session or application) and a set of synchronization policies that indicate how to carry out the synchronization between the data stored at client side and the data stored at server side. Apart from that, a specific *Synchronization action* has been included in order to force synchronization tasks when a connection change *event* (e.g. from offline to online mode) is detected. Moreover, *ViewStates* needs to define not only its URL, but also whether if its contents can be statically cached for its usage in offline mode or not.

The selected notation for the representation of the aforementioned dialog model has been created as an extension to the State Charts eXtensible Markup Language (SCXML) [1] defined by W3C. The SCXML specification considers the possibility of including new attributes and elements in non-scxml namespaces. In order to indicate the SCXML processor how to handle those elements and attributes out of the SCXML namespace, the specification proposes the use of the *exmode* attribute inside the *scxml* element. Taking advantage of the extensibility of SCXML, we propose to add a new set of elements and attributes for being able to model context-aware mobile Web applications according to the proposed dialog model.

Implementation of software support
In order to validate the viability of the method, the Controller layer of MyMobileWeb (MMW) [6] has been implemented: MMW is an open-source standards-based platform that simplifies the agile development of mobile Web applications in an effort to optimize the user experience. MMW provides an implementation of the MVC design pattern as follows:

- *Model*: the data model managed by applications is separated in two aspects: application data (bound to the specific application scenario) and context information. In order to extract context information, the platform is able to interoperate with any Device Description Repository (DDR) implementing the W3C DDR Simple API. In addition, MMW provides standard-based JavaScript components to extract dynamic capabilities from the device sensors.

- *View*: the platform uses IDEAL2, an XML-based authoring language to describe UIs in an abstract manner targeted to multiple delivery contexts. IDEAL2 is intended to provide a description of the views of the Web applications.

- *Controller*: prior to the development of this work, MMW managed the navigation flow in a programmatic way by means of Java handlers. As part of this research work, the author has implemented a new flow engine, which provides the developers with the possibility of specifying the navigation flow by means of the above-mentioned context-aware dialog model expressed in a declarative manner through an extended version of the SCXML notation. The new flow engine is in charge of deciding what actions to execute according to both context and user events. When the context of use is considered jointly as a combination of user, platform, and user [2], this flow engine could also regulate the priority in considering which entity is considered in which order, for instance the user first, then the platform.

In order to model the controller layer, the platform maintains one machine state per user as part of the session information. Each time the user interacts with the application or a context event takes place, a client-side controller is invoked. If there were no network connection, the client-side controller would locally manage the event and determine the local version of the contents to be provided. If there is network connection, then an HTTP request is sent to the server. In the case of context events, this request includes the name of the event (e.g. *FromOfflineToOnline*). In the case of user interactions, this request includes both the UI component ("control", in the terminology used in MMW) which the user has interacted with, and the event generated as a consequence of the interaction. Using this information, the platform automatically creates a new event containing both the type of interaction (e.g. *click*, *drag*, etc.) and the control which has raised it (e.g. *button*, *label*, etc.). This event is then propagated to the state machine processor, which acts accordingly.

The implementation of the SCXML processor uses the Commons SCXML library, an open-source Java SCXML engine. This library provides its own implementation of the Java object model for SCXML and a custom parser. Note that in the definition of the application flow it is possible to establish transition conditions which make reference to the Model, including context information.

CONCLUSION AND FUTURE WORK

This work proposes the creation of a specific context-aware dialog model to facilitate the development of multi-device Web UIs. The preliminary results obtained are encouraging. However, there is still the need of a formal validation in order to demonstrate that the expressiveness of the proposed dialog model is sufficient to define context-aware applications at the dialog model and concise enough in order to not increase the complexity of the method in comparison with other approaches. The research work will be validated by means of two types of validation: internal and external. The internal validation of the thesis will be carried out by providing a standard-based implementation of the proposed dialog model and assessing it against the identified requirements. In this sense, the current implementation needs to be refined in order to cover further requirements for the dialog model. The external validation will be considered based on user testing through experimental studies related to the provided implementation once it has been completed.

ACKNOWLEDGMENTS

The research is being performed thanks to the participation of the author in different projects and activities:

- MyMobileWeb: an open source project intended to facilitate the creation of mobile Web applications funded by Ministerio de Industra, Turismo y Comercio (MI-TyC) within the framework of The National Plan for Scientific Research, Development and Technological Innovation 2008-2011 and by the European Regional Development Fund (ERDF).

- Serenoa: a European project aimed at developing a novel, open platform for enabling the creation of context-sensitive SFEs. This project has received funding from the European Commission's Seventh Framework Programme under grant agreement n° 258030 (FP7-ICT-2009-5).

- W3C Model-Based User Interfaces Working Group: as part of the Ubiquitous Web Activity, its mission is to develop standards as a basis for interoperability across authoring tools for context aware Web UIs.

REFERENCES

1. Barnett, J. et al.: State Chart XML (SCXML): State Machine Notation for Control Abstraction. W3C Working Draft, 16 February 2012, http://www.w3.org/TR/2012/WD-scxml-20120216/.
2. Cantera Fonseca, J.M., González Calleros, J.M., Meixner, G., Paternò, F., Pullmann, J., Raggett, D., Schwabe, D., and Vanderdonckt, J. *Model-Based User Interface Incubator Group*, Final Report. 4 May 2010. Available at http://www.w3.org/2005/Incubator/model-based-ui/XGR-mbui/.
3. Coyette, A., Kieffer, S., Vanderdonckt, J. Multi-Fidelity Prototyping of User Interfaces, *Proc. of IFIP Conf. on Human-Computer Interaction INTERACT'2007*. Lecture Notes in Computer Science, Vol. 4662. Springer-Verlag, Berlin, 2007, pp. 149-162.
4. Florins, M., Montero, F., Vanderdonckt, J., Michotte, B. Splitting Rules for Graceful Degradation of User Interfaces, *Proc. of ACM Conf. on Advanced Visual Interfaces AVI'2006*. ACM Press, New York, 2006, pp. 59-66.
5. Mak, G., Long, J., Rubio, D., Mak, G., Long, J., Rubio, D. *Spring Web Flow. Spring Recipes*. Apress, 2010, pp. 249-295. Project web site: http://www.springsource.org/spring-web-flow
6. MyMobileWeb Project web site, http://mymobileweb.morfeo-project.org.
7. Montero, F., López-Jaquero, V. Comprehensive Task and Dialog Modelling, *Proc. of Int. Conf. on Human-Computer Interaction: Interaction Design and Usability*. Lecture Notes in Computer Science, Vol. 4550. Springer-Verlag, Berlin, 2007, pp. 1149-1158.
8. Vanacken, L. Multimodal selection in virtual environments: Enhancing the user experience and facilitating development. PhD Thesis. University of Hasselt, Diepenbeek, 2009.
9. Van den Bergh, J. and Coninx, K. From task to dialog model in the UML, *Proc. of Tamodia'2007*. Lecture notes in Computer Science, Vol. 4849. Springer-Verlag, Berlin, 2007, pp. 98-111.
10. Winckler, M., Trindade, F., Stanciulescu, A., and Vanderdonckt, J. Cascading Dialog Modeling with UsiXML, *Proc. of Int. Workshop on Design, Specification, and Verification of Interactive Systems DSV-IS'2008*. Lecture Notes in Computer Science, Vol. 5136. Springer-Verlag, Berlin, 2008, pp. 121-135.
11. Winckler, M. and Palanque, P. StateWebCharts: a formal description technique dedicated to navigation modelling of web applications, *Proc. of Int. Workshop on Design, Specification, and Verification of Interactive Systems DSV-IS 2003*. Lecture Notes in Computer Science, Vol. 2844, Springer-Verlag, Berlin, 2003, pp. 61-76.
12. Zhang, Gefei and Hölz, M. Aspect-Oriented Modeling of Web Applications with HiLA, *Proc. of the 11th International Conference on Current Trends in Web Engineering*. Lecture Notes in Computer Science, Vol. 7059, 2012, pp. 211-222.

UISKEI++: Multi-Device Wizard of Oz Prototyping

Vinícius C. V. B. Segura
vsegura@inf.puc-rio.br

Simone D. J. Barbosa
simone@inf.puc-rio.br

Departamento de Informática
Pontifcia Universidade Católica do Rio de Janeiro
Rio de Janeiro, RJ, Brazil

ABSTRACT

Low-fidelity prototyping is an inexpensive and quick alternative for exploring different design solutions. And with Wizard of Oz experiments, one can present an interactive — yet unfinished — prototype to the final user, who can see how the system is planned to work. Combining low-fidelity prototyping with Wizard of Oz can be a low cost and time-efficient way to prototype both the user interface and the interaction. This would be particularly useful in the case of prototyping for multiple devices, since different solutions need to be developed and tailored to suit each device's characteristics. This proposal discusses plans for developing a tool to provide multi-device prototyping support through the incorporation of different abstraction levels and support for Wizard of Oz experiments.

Author Keywords

sketch-based user interface design; model-based user interface design; low-fidelity prototyping; multi-device prototyping; Wizard of Oz;

ACM Classification Keywords

H.5.2. Information Interfaces and Presentation (e.g. HCI): User Interfaces

General Terms

Human Factors; Design;

INTRODUCTION

During early user interface (UI) design, different design solutions should be explored and iteratively refined. To evaluate initial solutions without committing to any particular one, successful designers tend to use low-fidelity prototyping, due to its low creation and modification costs. In addition to being inexpensive, low-fidelity prototyping also allows designers to collect invaluable user feedback on the proposed solutions early in the design process [9], thus helping to increase the overall quality of the final product. These characteristics make it a very popular design "tool" [17]. However, there is a pressing need to support designers in prototyping the UI

behavior as well. As stated by Bailey and Konstan, "low-fidelity tools, however, are ineffective for helping a designer explore and communicate behavioral design ideas while high-fidelity tools require a designer to invest too much time and effort, impeding the early exploration of the design space." [1]

In parallel, the recent advent of multitouch mobile phones and tablets is causing multi-device systems to become more common, ubiquitous even. Many systems must be developed in different versions to fit in specific devices. Even when using a responsive approach, we need to prototype how they will look in each device. UI designers and developers now face the challenge of choosing the right set of features for each device while maintaining enough consistency across versions to build a coherent ecosystem.

To address the complex challenge of supporting multi-device low-fidelity prototyping, we propose UISKEI++, an evolution of UISKEI (User Interface SKetching and Evaluation Instrument) [21, 24, 25]. UISKEI++ will enable designers to work at multiple abstraction levels (analogous to the Cameleon framework[1]) and to conduct multi-device Wizard of Oz experiments. The combination of low-fidelity prototyping and the Wizard of Oz technique offers UI designers and developers an inexpensive way to compare not only the interface, but also the UI interactive behavior, across different versions of a same system in multiple devices.

This paper is divided as follows. In the next section, we will introduce some related work regarding multi-device prototyping and Wizard of Oz tools. Then, we present our ideas about UISKEI++, discussing the planned new features and how we envision to develop and evaluate them. We conclude this work with some final remarks.

RELATED WORK

Several tools have been developed to support multi-device prototyping, for desktop, mobile and/or voice UIs. Yet, few of them offer related models at different levels of abstraction or solutions that allow conditionals when expressing UI behavior, which is essential not only for increasing the depth of the early evaluation, but also for providing a more complete specification and code skeletons when moving from design to development.

DAMASK [12, 13], for example, allows desktop, mobile, and voice UI prototypes to be simultaneously created. It relies on design patterns to keep the different devices synced, since

---

[1] `http://giove.isti.cnr.it/projects/cameleon.html`

changes in one device prototype are automatically reflected in the others. However, it can only define navigational actions and cannot express conditionals to the interaction. Another limitation is that the simulation runs inside a browser. Therefore it does not have a device-specific application and it cannot handle device-specific events.

De Sá and Carriço [5] developed a tool divided into a desktop and a PDA version. The desktop part allows sketching the user interface, while the PDA part visualizes the prototype. However, the behavior is again limited to marking clickable hotspots in the prototype for navigational purposes. An interesting feature is the possibility to update and rearrange the sketches and prototypes directly on the PDA.

Even though Vellis and colleagues have recently proposed a model-based approach to UI development [27], as it extends UsiXML[2] for polymorphic UI specification, it focuses more on the development of the actual system than on early prototyping, thus failing to achieve the degree of design-development balance we envision.

GAMBIT [19, 20] aids the design process by providing a collaborative whiteboard for design sessions. It allows multiple users with different devices to share a common workspace in a large display. At this time, it does not create an actual prototype — its current purpose is to allow the design team to discuss different ideas.

Regarding Wizard of Oz prototyping, several systems focus on only one kind of interaction or device. SketchWizard [4] was developed as a Wizard of Oz tool for pen-based interaction. It therefore aims to support prototyping pen-based user interfaces, and not to handle multiple devices or different interaction techniques. Moreover, it does not allow behaviors to be defined prior to the simulation.

ActiveStory Touch [8] only focuses on multi-touch interfaces. Similar to DAMASK, the simulation is executed over a web server, and it is not device-specific. However, it uses the Gesture Toolkit (based on the Silverlight API) to detect common gestures, such as dragging, swiping, pinching, tapping, double-tapping, and lassoing, which may limit its wider application.

DART is a "design environment for augmented and mixed-reality systems" with support for Wizard of Oz [6]. It works with Macromedia Director to integrate video, tracking devices, and other sensors within media applications. It stores the data collected during the experiments so they can be replayed later. One interesting characteristic is that the "wizard" can play different roles, being able to act as a controller, moderator, or supervisor.

Linnell and colleagues [14] are developing a Wizard of Oz tool specifically for the Android operating system. Their application builds prototypes based on screen images. So, if a screen has different states, the designer must provide different screens for each state (which means that the application also generates different images for each screen). Only navigational actions are supported, but they can also be triggered by a GPS location or a timed event.

A different approach can be seen in SKEMMI [10, 11]. Instead of sketching or building the interface by adding elements from a library, it uses a dataflow approach. The designer adds components and establishes connections between output and input ports. This approach is in line with its biggest concern: a runtime infrastructure for allowing seamless integration and off-the-shelf components reuse.

UISKEI++

UISKEI is a pen-based software for early UI low-fidelity prototyping, written in C# and currently under development at PUC-Rio. Built to provide a paperless early prototyping experience, it allows the designer[3] to sketch both the UI and its behavior. The behavior is defined by an <Event, Condition(s), Action(s)> (ECA) structure. Besides supporting navigation actions (as most prototyping tools do), UISKEI also supports state changing and message issuing actions. The ECA structure facilitates behavior definition by non programmers. With the original UISKEI, we aimed to satisfy the McGee and colleagues' requirements to a successful design tool: "Therefore, to be successful, a multimodal interface design tool must be easy to learn, require little programming expertise to use, and support the rapid creation, testing, and modification of interface designs. These requirements form the basis of any user interface prototyping tool targeted towards interface designers." [16]

UISKEI++ will build on this, aiming to support multi-device prototyping and incorporating two features: multiple abstraction levels (interaction and concrete user interface) and Wizard of Oz experiments. In the following sections, we present the novel features in UISKEI++, our development approach, and how we will evalute the tool.

Novel features
Multiple Abstraction Levels. One of the main difficulties faced when prototyping for multiple devices is maintaining consistency across different versions of the system [12, 15]. This involves adapting the interaction and the user interface to the device at hand, since screen size, screen resolution, distance between user and screen, and interaction paradigm may change. To address this issue, UISKEI++ will represent a project using different abstraction levels. At the lower abstraction level — the concrete or UI level — the designer will build the user interface, choosing the elements (widgets) that compose it. At the higher abstraction level, a model will represent the interactive solution being designed. We chose MoLIC (Modeling Language for Interaction as Conversation) [2], a modeling language designed to support the semiotic engineering of HCI [26]. It represents the conversational exchanges and turn taking in the conversation between designer and user, via abstractions of UI elements. With this model, designers will be better equipped to compare solutions across devices, despite device-specific characteristics. This could facilitate multi-device prototyping, and ultimately produce a more consistent solution and thus a coherent ecosystem.

---

[2]USer Interface eXtensible Markup Language **www.usixml.org**

[3]The term "designer" will be used to refer to UISKEI++'s user, who can be either a UI designer or a developer.

In UISKEI++, we propose to create the interaction model automatically, while the designer is building the UI and defining its behavior in one device. Thus, once the sketch is completed at the concrete level, the underlying model will have already been built. The designer will then be able to analyze the model and compare different solutions at this higher abstraction level. Changes at the abstract level will also be reflected at the concrete level. If something is represented in or removed from MoLIC models, the designer will be notified of this change at the concrete level.

Multi-device Wizard of Oz. Having defined (some of) the prototype UI and behavior, the designer may wish to test the prototype with the final user. UISKEI's current *simulation mode* already allows the final user to test an interactive prototype based on the pre-defined ECAs. UISKEI++ will extend this simulation in two ways. First, we will enable Wizard of Oz experiments [3], to allow modifications in the project to occur during the simulation (a user test session). The Wizard of Oz module will grant the designer (playing the wizard role) greater flexibility and the capacity to handle unplanned interaction paths. The earlier the evaluation (the more incomplete the ECA model is), the more valuable the Wizard of Oz module, since the wizard will be able to complete the behavior model "on demand", according to the user's actions. Second, we will extend UISKEI's behavior definition to incorporate different types of events, such as touch or body gestures found in natural user interfaces (NUIs).

The implementation of the Wizard of Oz will occur in three phases. We will start by supporting a single device/single user simulation session. Then, we will scale up to a multiple devices/single user setup. Finally, we will incorporate multiple devices/multiple users testing.

Development and Evaluation

The UISKEI++'s desktop editor will continue to be developed in C#, using Microsoft Visual Studio 2012. We also plan to have Windows 8 and Android applications running on tablets, smartphones, and large displays. The applications running on these devices will only receive an image from the *wizard* application and send the events — such as pointer movements, taps or body gestures — that the device can handle. All the simulation and interpretation of the events will take place on the wizard's side. A similar approach, using VNC,[4] was implemented by Linnell and colleagues [14] for the Android operating system.

The usability and communicability [18] of UISKEI++ will be evaluated with UI designers and developers. A set of design tasks will be given to study participants, whose interaction with UISKEI++ will be captured in video. In a post-test session, the evaluator will conduct an interview and ask the participant to fill in a Likert-scale questionnaire to help assess the quality of the tool along different dimensions related to usability (such as efficiency, efficacy, and satisfaction) and to the cognitive dimensions of notations (expressiveness, viscosity, and so on) [7]. We will also compare UISKEI++ with

---

[4]Virtual Network Computing, `http://en.wikipedia.org/wiki/Virtual_Network_Computing`

the existing prototyping tools using a questionnaire similar to the one developed for assessing UISKEI [22, 23, 25].

FINAL REMARKS

In this paper, we have presented the intended evolution of UISKEI from a single-device prototyping tool to UISKEI++, a multi-device Wizard of Oz + prototyping tool.

The new features of the tool will address two main research questions. First, *"how can we map from concrete interface implementation to more abstract representations and viceversa?"* Second, *"how can a Wizard of Oz environment be adapted to a multi-device context?"*

REFERENCES

1. Bailey, B. P., and Konstan, J. A. Are informal tools better?: comparing DEMAIS, pencil and paper, and authorware for early multimedia design. In *Proceedings of the SIGCHI Conference on Human Factors in Computing Systems*, CHI '03, ACM (New York, NY, USA, 2003), 313–320.

2. da Silva, B. S., and Barbosa, S. D. J. Designing Human-Computer Interaction With MoLIC Diagrams — A Practical Guide. Monografias em ciências da computação, Pontifícia Universidade Católica do Rio de Janeiro (PUC-Rio), December 2007.

3. Dahlbäck, N., Jönsson, A., and Ahrenberg, L. Wizard of Oz studies: why and how. In *Proceedings of the 1st international conference on Intelligent user interfaces*, IUI '93, ACM (New York, NY, USA, 1993), 193–200.

4. Davis, R. C., Saponas, T. S., Shilman, M., and Landay, J. A. SketchWizard: Wizard of Oz prototyping of pen-based user interfaces. In *Proceedings of the 20th annual ACM symposium on User interface software and technology*, UIST '07, ACM (New York, NY, USA, 2007), 119–128.

5. de Sá, M., and Carriço, L. Low-fi prototyping for mobile devices. In *CHI '06 extended abstracts on Human factors in computing systems*, CHI EA '06, ACM (New York, NY, USA, 2006), 694–699.

6. Dow, S., MacIntyre, B., Lee, J., Oezbek, C., Bolter, J. D., and Gandy, M. Wizard of Oz Support throughout an Iterative Design Process. *IEEE Pervasive Computing 4*, 4 (Oct. 2005), 18–26.

7. Green, T. R. G., and Petre, M. Usability analysis of visual programming environments: A 'cognitive dimensions' framework. *J. Vis. Lang. Comput. 7*, 2 (1996), 131–174.

8. Hosseini-Khayat, A., Seyed, T., Burns, C., and Maurer, F. Low-fidelity prototyping of gesture-based applications. In *Proceedings of the 3rd ACM SIGCHI symposium on Engineering interactive computing systems*, EICS '11, ACM (New York, NY, USA, 2011), 289–294.

9. Hundhausen, C. D., Balkar, A., Nuur, M., and Trent, S. WOZ pro: a pen-based low fidelity prototyping

environment to support wizard of oz studies. In *CHI '07 Extended Abstracts on Human Factors in Computing Systems*, CHI EA '07, ACM (New York, NY, USA, 2007), 2453–2458.

10. Lawson, J.-Y. L., Al-Akkad, A.-A., Vanderdonckt, J., and Macq, B. An open source workbench for prototyping multimodal interactions based on off-the-shelf heterogeneous components. In *Proceedings of the 1st ACM SIGCHI symposium on Engineering interactive computing systems*, EICS '09, ACM (New York, NY, USA, 2009), 245–254.

11. Lawson, J.-Y. L., Coterot, M., Carincotte, C., and Macq, B. Component-based high fidelity interactive prototyping of post-WIMP interactions. In *International Conference on Multimodal Interfaces and the Workshop on Machine Learning for Multimodal Interaction*, ICMI-MLMI '10, ACM (New York, NY, USA, 2010), 47:1–47:4.

12. Lin, J., and Landay, J. A. Damask: A tool for early-stage design and prototyping of multi-device user interfaces. In *In Proceedings of The 8th International Conference on Distributed Multimedia Systems (2002 International Workshop on Visual Computing*, ACM Press (2002), 573–580.

13. Lin, J., and Landay, J. A. Employing patterns and layers for early-stage design and prototyping of cross-device user interfaces. In *Proceedings of the twenty-sixth annual SIGCHI conference on Human factors in computing systems*, CHI '08, ACM (New York, NY, USA, 2008), 1313–1322.

14. Linnell, N., Bareiss, R., and Pantic, K. A wizard of Oz tool for Android. In *Proceedings of the 14th international conference on Human-computer interaction with mobile devices and services companion*, MobileHCI '12, ACM (New York, NY, USA, 2012), 65–70.

15. Maués, R. A., and Barbosa, S. D. J. Cross-communicability: Evaluating the meta-communication of cross-platform applications. In *Proceedings of INTERACT 2013*, INTERACT '13 (2012).

16. McGee-Lennon, M. R., Ramsay, A., McGookin, D., and Gray, P. User evaluation of OIDE: a rapid prototyping platform for multimodal interaction. In *Proceedings of the 1st ACM SIGCHI symposium on Engineering interactive computing systems*, EICS '09, ACM (New York, NY, USA, 2009), 237–242.

17. Myers, B., Park, S. Y., Nakano, Y., Mueller, G., and Ko, A. How designers design and program interactive behaviors. In *Proceedings of the 2008 IEEE Symposium on Visual Languages and Human-Centric Computing*, VLHCC '08, IEEE Computer Society (Washington, DC, USA, 2008), 177–184.

18. Prates, R. O., de Souza, C. S., and Barbosa, S. D. J. Methods and tools: a method for evaluating the communicability of user interfaces. *Interactions 7*, 1 (2000), 31–38.

19. Sangiorgi, U., and Vanderdonckt, J. GAMBIT: Addressing multi-platform collaborative sketching with HTML5. In *Proceedings of the 4th ACM SIGCHI symposium on Engineering interactive computing systems*, EICS '12, ACM (New York, NY, USA, 2012), 257–262.

20. Sangiorgi, U. B., Beuvens, F., and Vanderdonckt, J. User interface design by collaborative sketching. In *Proceedings of the Designing Interactive Systems Conference*, DIS '12, ACM (New York, NY, USA, 2012), 378–387.

21. Segura, V. C. V. B., and Barbosa, S. D. J. UISK: Supporting Model-Driven and Sketch-Driven Paperless Prototyping. In *Proceedings of the 13th International Conference on Human-Computer Interaction. Part I: New Trends*, Springer-Verlag (Berlin, Heidelberg, 2009), 697–705.

22. Segura, V. C. V. B., and Barbosa, S. D. J. Comparing Widget-based and Sketch-based User Interface Prototyping Tools. In *Proceedings of the 3rd Regional Congress in Interaction Design* (2011), 260–267.

23. Segura, V. C. V. B., and Barbosa, S. D. J. Shape-based versus sketch-based UI prototyping: a comparative study. In *Proceedings of the 10th Brazilian Symposium on on Human Factors in Computing Systems and the 5th Latin American Conference on Human-Computer Interaction*, IHC+CLIHC '11, Brazilian Computer Society (Porto Alegre, Brazil, Brazil, 2011), 162–166.

24. Segura, V. C. V. B., and Barbosa, S. D. J. A Combination of Stroke Manipulation and Recognition Strategies to Support User Interface Construction and Interactive Behavior Definition through Sketching. In *Visual Languages and Human-Centric Computing (VL/HCC), 2012 IEEE Symposium on*, IEEE (2012), 45–48.

25. Segura, V. C. V. B., Barbosa, S. D. J., and Simões, F. P. UISKEI: a sketch-based prototyping tool for defining and evaluating user interface behavior. In *Proceedings of the International Working Conference on Advanced Visual Interfaces*, AVI '12, ACM (New York, NY, USA, 2012), 18–25.

26. Souza, C. S. *The Semiotic Engineering Of Human-computer Interaction*. Acting with Technology Series. Mit Press, 2005.

27. Vellis, G., Kotsalis, D., Akoumianakis, D., and Vanderdonckt, J. Model-based engineering of multi-platform, synchronous and collaborative uis-extending usixml for polymorphic user interface specification. In *Informatics (PCI), 2012 16th Panhellenic Conference on*, IEEE (2012), 339–344.

Audiovisual Perception in a Virtual World: An Application of Human-Computer Interaction Evaluation to the Development of Immersive Environments

Carlos C. L. Silva

Departamento de Informática, Universidade do Minho & HASLab / INESC TEC

Campus de Gualtar, 4710-057 – Braga

carlos.cl.silva@gmail.com

ABSTRACT

Understanding the mechanisms underlying audiovisual perception is crucial for the development of interactive audiovisual immersive environments. Some human perceptual mechanisms pose challenging problems that can now be better explored with the latest technology in computer-generated environments. Our main goal is to develop an interactive audiovisual immersive system that provides to its users a highly immersive and perceptually coherent interactive environment. In order to do this, we will perform user studies to get a better knowledge of the rules guiding audiovisual perception. This will allow improvements in the simulation of realistic virtual environments through the use of predictive human cognition models as guides for the development of an audiovisual interactive immersive system. This system will encompass the integration of two Virtual Reality systems: a Cave Automatic Virtual Environment-like (CAVE-like) system and a room acoustic modeling and auralization system. The interactivity between user and the audiovisual virtual world will be enabled by the using of a Motion Capture system as a user position tracker.

Author Keywords

Immersive Systems; User Interfaces; Audiovisual Perception; Predictive Human Cognitive Models.

ACM Classification Keywords

H.1.2 **[User/Machine Systems]**: Human factors, Human information processing, Software Psychology; H.5.1. **[Multimedia Information Systems]**: Artificial, augmented, and virtual realities; H.5.2 **[User Interfaces]**: User-centered design.

INTRODUCTION

Because of its inherent potential to directly interact with the human senses, immersive environments that make use of Virtual Reality (VR) or Augmented Reality (AR) have long being regarded as in line to become the next predominant human-computer interface [1]. However, in order to turn immersive environments into a serious candidate for the next predominant interface paradigm some current

EICS'13, June 24–27, 2013, London, United Kingdom.
ACM 978-1-4503-2138-9/13/06.

technological limitations have to be overcome and, additionally, developmental approaches more focused on human perception and action on immersive environments should be pursued. Accurate predictions about how users perceive and interact with a computerized environment are of foremost importance in the engineering of computer systems that emphasize usefulness and usability, as any attempt of developing an interactive system should put the human, the *user*, in a central position that defines all the subsequent discussion and design [2].

Computer generated immersive environments are normally classified into two different categories: VR environments and AR environments. The distinction between these two is not a procedural or technical one; rather it is more of a performance-based distinction. In the *reality-virtually continuum* of Milgram and Colquhoun [3] the fundamental distinction is between *Real Environments* and *Virtual Environments*, that are located on the continuum opposite ends (see Figure 1). The positioning of any immersive environment along this continuum coincides with its position along a parallel *Extent of World Knowledge continuum*. Hence, this definition highlights the importance of knowledge about both the physical world and the human mechanisms that allow the perception of these physical signals in order to develop satisfactory immersive systems.

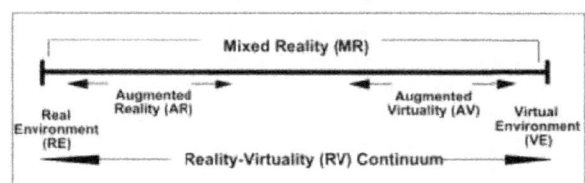

Figure 1. Reality-Virtuality Continuum (from Milgram & Colquhoun, 1999)

When we talk about immersive environments we are addressing any kind of environments that are capable of creating on users' the illusion of being in a place other than where they actually are, or of having a coherent interaction with objects that do not exist in the real world. In other words, we are alluding to all the software and hardware elements, needed to present stimuli to the users' senses, which will elicit this kind of effect in the user – normally referred to as *feeling of presence* [4]. There are some features that an immersive system should have and that are positively correlated with the capability of conveying an adequate feeling of presence: 1) *Unnoticeable hardware*; 2) *Real-time update* of the immersive environment to the user's position; 3) *Multimodal stimulation*; and 4) *User environment interactivity*.

Subjacent to all of these features should be the most important principle in the engineering of immersive environments: The environment should convey an accurately replication of the geometric and temporal characteristic of the real world. This does not mean that computerized environments have to model the exact physical characteristics of a visual or an auditory real world's scenario – in fact this is, and is expectable it will remain being, technologically impracticable. What this principle really means is that the perception that a user has in a VR or AR environment, should be quantitatively indistinguishable of a correspondent scene perception in the real world.

Applying HCI techniques to the development and evaluation of immersive environments becomes an issue of the foremost importance, primarily when we think about the current lack of knowledge on some human perceptual mechanisms that are central to a proper interaction with the natural tridimensional world. The use of HCI research techniques, mostly focused in psychophysical experimentation, can both give us some insight about the human perceptual mechanisms that should be crucial in the engineering of a highly immersive VR or AR environment and, at the same time, allow us to quantitatively evaluate the human performance of an environment user, making possible comparisons with performance in real world situations.

This comparative evaluation had widespread use in the development of Predictive Cognitive Models that have boosted HCI influence in the design of computerized solutions (e.g. Fitt's law [5], Model Human Processor [6], EPIC [7]) and the same should happen in the development of immersive environments. Psychophysical experimentation can be used as a tool in HCI studies, allowing us to construct models of human perception and human performance capable of guiding the development process of a highly immersive and interactive VR or AR system.

OUR GOALS

The project here presented has the generic goal of developing Human Predictive Cognitive Models to guide and evaluate the development of an interactive audiovisual immersive system. Our technological output will be the accurate implementation of aural-visual interaction in a multimodal and interactive immersive system. This development will be guided by psychophysical experimentation and usability tasks that will clarify how we perceive some audiovisual phenomena, such as audiovisual

synchrony, audiovisual depth perception, and audiovisual recalibration phenomena.

The experimental data collected will be integrated in predictive cognitive models for the processes involved in the perception of audiovisual synchrony under different conditions of stimulation. These models will be the quantitative basis for the computational solutions to be integrated in our immersive system.

IMMERSIVE SYSTEM DESCRIPTION

In order to carry out the work, the facilities of the Vision and Perception Laboratory at the University of Minho are being used. In this section we describe the main features of the relevant system to be used.

Visualization System

The visualization system that we are using is composed by a cluster of 3 PCs with NVDIA® Quadro FX 4500 graphics boards, and works with custom projection software running on top of OpenGL and using VR/Juggler as a "virtual platform". Each of the PCs forming the cluster is connected to one image channel using 3chip DLP projectors Christie Mirage S+4K with a resolution of 1400x1050 pixels and a refresh rate of 60Hz up to 101Hz per channel (see Figure 2). The projectors are capable of stereoscopic projection, and the surface of projection can range from a PowerWall of 2.80 m high per 6.30 m wide to a three face (one frontal and two lateral) CAVE-like configuration with each face conveying a projection area of 2.80 m x 2. 10 m.

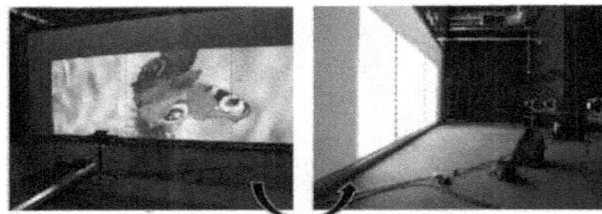

Figure 2. The visualization system in a PowerWall configuration. The red marks delimit the area of projection of each projector. Blending functions are used in order to give the sense of an uninterrupted projection surface.

Room Acoustics Modeling and Auralization Software

The auralization system uses the *Image Source Method* in order to generate sounds corresponding to particular spaces (*Room Impulse Response* – RIR), taking into account the sound source and the listener positions (see Figure 3). Furthermore and depending on the source and listener position the program generates the correct temporal and frequency distribution for the sound presented at each ear (*Head Related Transfer Function*) applying it to a particular RIR. The final binaural sound with the simulated depth cues for a defined room is obtained by convolving the computed RIR with an anechoic binaural sound (a sound recorded in an anechoic chamber – a room design to absorb all the sound reflections and thus allowing the recording of only the direct sound of an auditory event).

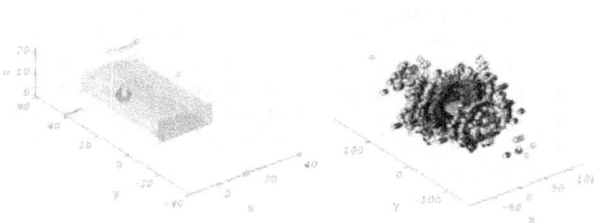

Figure 3.Graphical depiction of the external sound sources generated to simulate the wall reflected sound in a four orders of reflection simulation. Images from a simulation performed in the auralization software currently being developed.

Motion Capture System

The motion capture (MoCap) system that we will use is a Vicon™ MX F20 MoCap system composed by 6 near-infrared cameras with a frame rate of up to 500 Hz, capable of tracking the three-dimensional position of retro-reflective markers with a temporal resolution of 240 HZ and an accuracy of 2 millimeters (see Figure 4). In order to use the Vicon™ MoCap system as a tracker for our interactive immersive environment, we will have to convert the data from the MoCap system into data capable of been read by the virtual platform. This will involve an equalization of the coordinate-axis orientation of both MoCap and visualization system as an equalization of the time stamps and frame rate of both systems. At the moment solutions for coordination between these two systems are being studied.

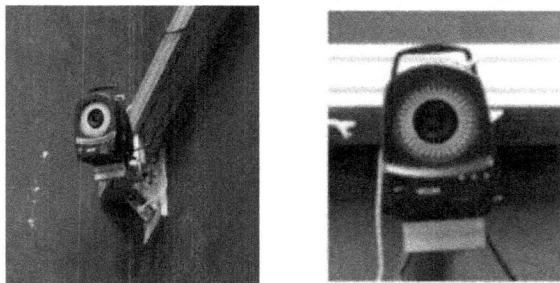

Figure 4. Details on one of the six cameras that integrate the MoCap system at the LVP (UM)

PSYCHOPHYSICAL EXPERIMENTATION AND THE ITERATIVE APPROACH

The interactive audiovisual immersive system in development intends to be a perceptually validated integration between the three above described systems. We will have to develop a connection between the MoCap system and the visualization system in order to convey adequate visualization and auditory stimulation to the user's position. However there are several psychophysical problems that we need to account for.

Audiovisual Synchrony Perception

The perception of audiovisual synchrony is central to the sense of a coherent audiovisual immersive environment and can be quite important in guiding user's action in the world. However this is still a quite intriguing phenomenon. Contradictory data exists on the aural-visual temporal relation that provides the best audiovisual synchrony perception and on its relation with depth perception [8, 9]. We intend to use Simultaneity Judgment Tasks in VR environments in order to develop a Predictive Cognitive Model for human synchrony perception. This model will guide the temporal relation between the visual and the auditory streams of audiovisual events in the final immersive system.

Visual and Auditory Depth Perception

Here we are looking for the visual (pictoric and dynamic) cues and for the features of the acoustic signal (number of reverberation orders, air attenuation, sound pressure level decrement with distance) that are more important to give rise to an accurate judgment of distance in the audiovisual virtual world. In order to accomplish this we are preparing psychophysical experiments with auditory and visual distance judgments tasks, made through both comparisons between real world stimulation and computer generated stimuli, and through absolute estimation tasks. The rational underlying the distance judgment tasks made through real-virtual comparisons is that if we are accurately modeling the world and stimulating the user, there will be no difference on the distance judgment between a real and a virtual, computer generated, stimulus.

Audiovisual Recalibration Processes

The delay between user's movement and audiovisual systems adjustment will have to be the minimum possible, mostly because systems latencies and its visible consequences are fundamental virtual environment deficiencies that can hamper user perception and performance [10]. In this scope, we will also explore the phenomenon of recalibration (i.e. the ability to handle, up to a measurable extend, temporal and spatial inconsistencies in the audiovisual world). Knowing the user recalibration capacity will give us an estimation of what could be the tolerable latencies between the user position and the audiovisual stream update. This is important for systems that have a limited computational capability or a certain network bandwidth.

The Iterative Approach

All the implemented solutions will be guided by Predictive Cognitive Models on the above referred Perceptual phenomena and evaluated by psychophysical experimentation. The idea is to use the results of the real-virtual comparison experiences as a measure of good design and successful human computer interface implementation. This evaluation will be carried out first in each system individually and finally on the integrated interactive audiovisual immersive system. Along with the psychophysical validation others usability tests, like qualitative evaluation of comfort level and feeling of presence, will also be carried out.

The individual systems' evaluation will always be carried out, following some upgrading or development. In this way, we can say that the evaluation is part of the iterative nature of this work's development (Figure 5).

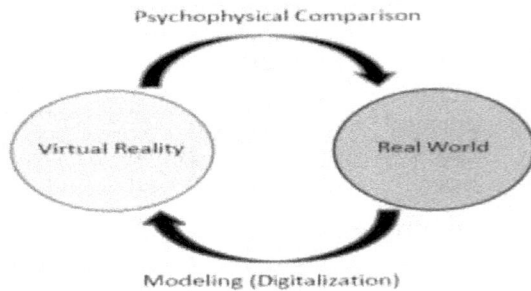

Figure 5. A representation of our iterative approach applied to the development of immersive environments.

After any improvement effort on the immersive system we should experiment and check the perceptual closeness between simulation and the real-world. If not satisfactory, a new cycle of psychophysical experimentation (with the goal of finding the error or lack in the modeling) should begin and then new simulation-reality comparisons should be carried out.

Once a perceptually satisfactory implementation of the interactive immersive system is accomplished, we intend to develop a final audiovisual and interactive system demonstration. This demonstration should consist in a simple task involving audiovisual perception and user's action, preferably capable of being accurately measured in different user's parameters as position, time reaction, and correct interactions. This could be accomplish by using, for instance, a catching task simulation, such as a baseball catch game or a service return in a tennis game, or any other interactive situation that involves accurate perception of the virtual object in order to effectively perform a task.

CONCLUSION

This paper is intended to present a theoretically framed doctoral project description. Our key argument is that a better knowledge about both the physical world and the perceptual mechanisms underlying its perception can improve – and should guide – the development and implementation of interactive immersive systems. HCI has showed us several examples were the study of human cognition ended up in precious contributions for the development of computerized systems and the same should happen with the study of human perception and the improvement of immersive environments.

In the following years of this doctoral project we intend to put together visualization and auralization systems, and demonstrate their interactive capability using a MoCap system. We believe that in the end, enabling users to do a perceptually consistent interactive task using these three systems will provide a quite immersive experience.

ACKNOWLEDGMENTS
The author acknowledges funding by ERDF - European Regional Development Fund through the COMPETE Programme (operational programme for competitiveness) and by National Funds through the FCT - Fundação para a Ciência e a Tecnologia (Portuguese Foundation for Science and Technology) within project FCOMP-01-0124-FEDER-015095.

REFERENCES
1. Cruz-Neira, C., Sandin, D. J., & DeFanti, T. A. "Surround-screen projection-based virtual reality: the design and implementation of the CAVE". *Computer Graphics, SIGGRAPH Annual Conference Proceedings*, 1993. 135-142.

2. Dix, A. "Human-computer interaction: a stable discipline, a nascent science, and the growth of the long tail". *Interacting with Computers*, 22 (2010), 13-27.

3. Milgram, P, & Colquhoum, H. "A taxonomy of real and virtual world display integration". *Mixed Reality – Merging Real and Virtual Worlds*, 1999. Chapter 1. New York: Springer-Verlag.

4. Regenbrecht, H. T., Schubert, T. W., Friedman, F. "Measuring the sense of presence and its relations to the fear of heights in virtual environments". *International Journal of Human-Computer Interaction*, 10(3),1998, 233-249.

5. Fitts, P. M., & Peterson, J. R. "Information capacity of discrete motor responses." Journal of Experimental Psychology, 1964. 67, 103-112.

6. Card, S. K., Moran, T. P., & Newell, A. "*The psychology of human-computer interaction.*" Lawrence Erlbaum Associates, Hillsdale, New Jersey. 1983.

7. Kieras, D., & Meyer, D. "An overview of the EPIC architecture for cognition and performance with application to human-computer interaction." *Human-Computer Interaction*, 1997. Vol. 12, 391-438.

8. Sugita, Y., & Suzuki, Y. "Implicit estimation of sound-arrival time." *Nature*, 2003. *421*, 911.

9. Lewald, J., Guski, R. "Auditory-visual temporal integration as a function of distance: no compensation for sound-transmission time in human perception." Neuroscience Letters, 2004. 357, 119-122.

10. Mania, K., Adelstein, B. D., Ellis, S. R., Hill, M. I. "Perceptual sensitivity to head tracking latency in virtual environments with varying degrees of scene complexity". *Proceedings of the 1st Symposium on Applied Perception in Graphics and Visualization*, 39-47, New York, USA, 2004.

Autonomous Adaptation of User Interfaces to Support Mobility in Ambient Intelligence Systems

Gervasio Varela

Integrated Group for Engineering Research, University of A Coruña

C/ Mendizábal S/N, 15403, Ferrol, A Coruña, Spain

gervasio.varela@udc.es

ABSTRACT

The work presented in this paper is focused on building Ambient Intelligence (AmI) applications capable of moving from one environment to another, while their user interface keeps adapting itself, autonomously, to the variable environment conditions and the available interaction resources.

AmI applications are expected to interact with users naturally and transparently, therefore, most of their interaction relies on embedded devices that obtain information from the user and environment. This work implements a framework for AmI systems that elevates those embedded devices to the class of interaction resources. It does so by providing a new level of abstraction that decouples applications, conceptually and physically, from the different specific interaction resources available and their underlying heterogeneous technologies.

In order to drive the adaptation process to environment changes, the system makes use of a set of models that describe the user, environment conditions and devices, and algorithms for context-aware selection of the interaction devices.

Author Keywords

User Interfaces; Ambient Intelligence; Distributed User Interfaces; Context Adaptation.

ACM Classification Keywords

D2.2 [**Software Engineering**]: Design Tools and Techniques – *User interfaces;* H5. [**Information interfaces and presentation**]: User Interfaces – *Interaction styles, Input devices and strategies, user interface management system (UIMS).*

INTRODUCTION

The operation of an Ambient Intelligence (AmI) system is quite different from a classic software system. An AmI

system is expected to behave proactively and transparently [1], interacting with the users and their environment in the most natural way available. To achieve that, AmI systems must rely on their capacity to use any interaction resource available in a smart environment.

These interaction resources are also quite different from traditional interaction devices. AmI applications use mainly sensing/actuation devices and appliances to interact with the user and the environment [1]. Because of that, they are exposed to a complex world populated by a wide range of different technologies and devices that can be used to implement their user interaction subsystems.

As the user moves from one place to another, the smart environment in which the system is operating is changing, and with it, the available devices, the users and even the environment conditions. Predicting this variability at design time is quite difficult, and because of this, the majority of AmI systems are designed for a specific environment with a specific set of users, devices and conditions.

The main objective of this work is to provide AmI developers with a set of abstractions that isolate them from the user interaction capabilities of the system, which, combined with a distributed UI management system capable of connecting those abstractions to end devices, at runtime, facilitates the development of AmI systems adaptable to different devices/environments/users [2, 3].

This work tries to fulfill this objective by designing and implementing a UI management system integrated into an existing AmI application platform [4]. It uses a model-driven approach [5] to build user interfaces by specifying a series of high level declarative models which, at runtime, are transformed into a set of distributed interaction devices. Applications are decoupled from the specific characteristics and technologies of these devices by using a distributed agent communication protocol called General Interaction Protocol (GIP), which is implemented by the devices and abstracts them as interaction resources.

This paper is organized as follows. Section 2 describes related work; Section 3 explains the contributions of this research and Section 4 presents the current state of development and conclusions.

RELATED WORK

The problem of UI adaptation and reusability in AmI applications has been previously identified by different authors. In [2] Blumendorf et al. introduce the problematic associated with user interaction in Ambient Assisted Living (AAL) environments, which are a subset of AmI. The paper presents a framework for UIs development for those environments that use a model-driven approach and context information to drive the adaptation at runtime. In [3] Abascal et al. identify the necessity of adaptation to the users, because their capabilities and disabilities can greatly impact the performance of the UI of an AmI system. They propose the use of three models, User model, Task model and Environment model, in order to support the autonomous adaptation of the application GUI.

The difficulties associated with user and application mobility in AmI systems have also been studied by many authors. Ranganathan et al. [6] and Satoh et al. [7] provide a similar approach to the migration of applications in Ubiquitous Computing (UC) environments. Even if not specifically related to UI migration, they show that one of the main difficulties when moving a highly distributed system is how to deploy it in a new set of computing devices. They state that the deployment must be achieved bearing in mind the requirements of the system components, as well as the characteristics of the computing resources available. In [8] the authors provide a good overview of the specific problematic of supporting mobility in AmI, while [9] provides a more insightful view of the problems associated with the migration of user interfaces in AmI environments. The two main problems identified are: detecting and integrating the different devices available in each environment; and the need to provide users with an adequate UI able to use the available devices.

UI adaptation to users and devices is also a highly studied topic by the Human-Computer Interaction (HCI) community. In 1999 [10] Thevenin and Coutaz introduced the term 'plasticity of user interfaces' as the capacity of a UI to support changes in the system's physical characteristics and in the environment while preserving usability. They also proposed the use of model-driven engineering techniques in order to support UI adaptation. This proposal has been very successful within the HCI community and many different authors have used it as the basis for their own approach to UI adaptation [5, 11]. Also

in the field of UC and AmI, these kinds of model-driven approaches have been applied with proven results [2, 3].

Another topic of great importance for this thesis is the field of distributed multimodal user interfaces. Due to the intrinsic distributed nature of AmI systems, their UI will operate using devices that are physically distributed throughout the smart environment [1]. Furthermore, these devices will use different modalities to interact with the user. Two prominent approaches to distributed multimodal UIs are: the Cameleon-rt [12] reference model for distributed, migratable and adaptive user interfaces; and the W3C conceptual framework to support multimodal UIs [13]. These two frameworks share some similarities in their way of abstracting distributed UI resources, but the W3C approach ignores the adaptation problem.

INNOVATIVE APPROACH AND RELEVANCE OF TOPIC

As shown by exploring the state of the art, some work has been carried out in the topic of UI adaptation and mobility in UC and AmI systems [2, 3]. The approach followed by these projects is mainly focused on graphical user interfaces and their adaptation to the user characteristics and the displays available. In contrast, the novel approach presented by this work proposes the utilization of sensing/actuation devices and appliances as the interaction resources of an AmI system.

The main contribution of this work to its research field consists in providing a new level of abstraction that isolates applications from devices at the user interaction level. In the proposed framework devices are seen as generic user interaction resources, thus developers can achieve a great level of decoupling between their AmI applications and the hardware devices used to interact with the user and the environment. This decoupling makes applications more easily adaptable to new scenarios.

PROPOSED SOLUTION

The proposed solution, called Dandelion [14], is being developed integrated in the HI^3 general purpose AmI development platform [4]. Dandelion aims to facilitate the migration of HI^3 applications by decoupling them from the interaction devices. An overview block diagram of the solution can be seen in Figure 1. It uses a model-driven approach in which a series of models and device selection algorithms are used to build, at runtime, as the user moves

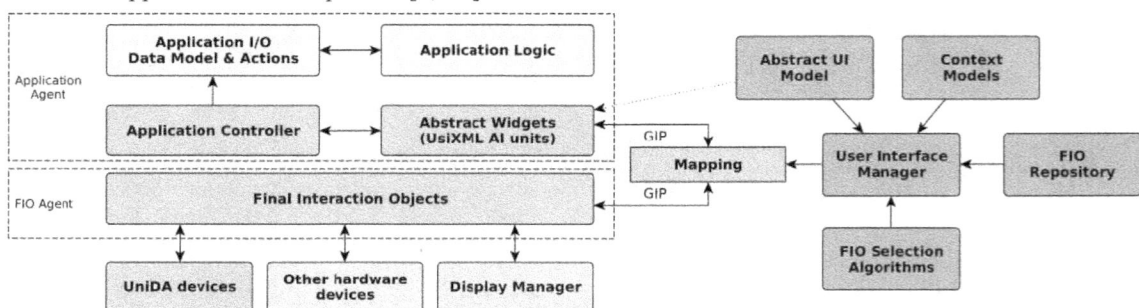

Figure 1. Block diagram of the proposed solution for UI adaptation in AmI

from one place to another, a UI that is appropriate for the user characteristics and preferences, the environment conditions and the devices available in each location.

The HI[3] [4] platform conceptual architecture follows a layer-based design that enables the division of system elements into levels. From bottom to top, the uniform device access layer, UniDA [15], provides homogeneous and distributed access to the physical devices. The sensing and actuation services layer provides virtual representations of sensors and actuators in the physical environment. The service layer is populated by components that provide shared functionalities to other services or applications. Finally, the applications layer is at the highest-level, and hosts the elements implementing applications that provide particular functionalities a user expects from the system.

Inside the HI[3] platform, Dandelion is integrated in the application and device abstraction layers by implementing a distributed user interface system inspired by the principles of the Cameleon-rt [12] reference model.

Dandelion follows a model-driven approach based on the recognized approaches proposed by UsiXML [15] and MASP [2, 11]. It reuses some of the models proposed by UsiXML, but instead of relying on model transformations at design time, it takes the MASP approach, using the models at runtime, along with real-time information of the environment and user, in order to build the user interface. The main difference with MASP is that Dandelion is focused on distributed UIs using not only displays, but every device available in a smart environment, like home automation devices, appliances or sensors. Thus, Dandelion is especially tailored for AmI applications requiring multi-modal interaction using everyday objects, but it can also accommodate GUIs, voice or gesture recognition.

The system is designed to support an arbitrary number of models describing the application domain, its interaction requirements, the user, the environment and the resources available. The information in those models is used to select the interaction elements (mainly automation devices and appliances), available in the environment, that better suit the requirements of the application, the user and the environment. Once selected, those interaction elements are transparently and remotely connected to the application logic, so that it does not need to know anything about the interaction technologies and devices it is using.

The diagram in Figure 1 shows an overview of this process. Along with the application logic, implemented as a multi-agent system in the application layer of HI[3], the developers provide:

1. a description of the UI (AUI), using the UsiXML abstract UI model, that generically describes the user interaction requirements of the application;
2. a set of associations between AUI elements and some data and action objects that will be used as the model to manage data input/output with the user.

Those associations are managed by an application controller using the observer pattern to monitor the data objects. When the application modifies a data object, the controller redirects the change to the UI, and vice versa. The application controller is a physical component of the application agent, so that the Final Interaction Objects (FIO) agents and the application agents interchange messages directly.

As can be seen in Figure 1, the final implementation of the UI is provided by a set of mappings between the AUI elements and the FIOs. This mapping is 1..N, so that the same AUI can be associated with many FIOs. It is stored by the application controller, but it is generated, managed and updated, at runtime, by the User Interface Manager (UIM). It uses the information available in the AUI model, the user model and the environment model, to select among the different interaction resources available in the environment.

FIOs are abstractions of devices and appliances capable of input/output to the user, like switches, lamps, presence sensors, alarm systems, or even higher level interaction resources, like gesture or voice recognition software. They are a key element of Dandelion, because they implement the concrete logic required to interact with a device, and because they provide a generic view of the device as an interaction resource. Their goal is to decouple the rest of the system from the underlying interaction technologies, and this is achieved by hiding the device behavior behind the General Interaction Protocol (GIP) interface

The GIP is another key aspect of this work. It is an event based multi-agent communication protocol which provides a common interface for interaction resources. The set of events defined is inspired by the I/O actions supported by the AUI model of UsiXML. Figure 2 shows an overview of the protocol. Its operation can be summarized with a simple example. An application changes a data object that represents the output state of an alarm. The controller detects the change, and sends an output event to the associated FIO/s. They provide the output to the user depending on the concrete implementation of each FIO, for example powering on a light or playing a sound.

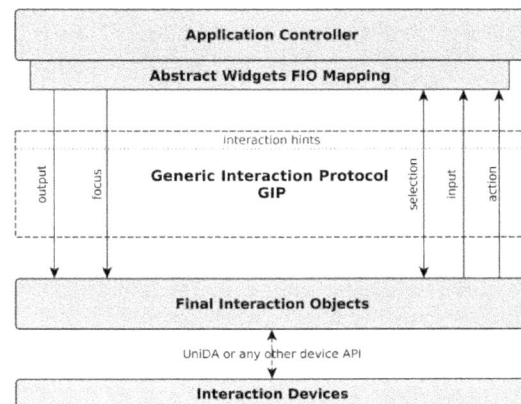

Figure 2. Overview of the GIP for abstracting devices as interaction resources

FIOs are implemented as distributed agents in the sensing/actuation layer of HI³. They implement the GIP interface, but it is not mandatory for a FIO to support all the GIP events, only a subset of them. There can be devices that support only user input, only user output, etc. The supported events are specified in the FIO description, which is used by the AUI during the FIO selection process.

GIP events can have attached a set of variables that are used by developers to provide interaction hits to the FIOs. One example could be an urgent property, or a color property, so that a FIO can adapt (if possible) its response to more specific requirements of an application. Those interaction hints are specified by applications in the association between AUI elements and the I/O data model.

A FIO can encapsulate any kind of interaction resource: a home automation device, a hand-gesture recognition engine or even a GUI. Developers of FIOs are only required to export the interaction capabilities of the resource as GIP events. Thus, for example, a home automatic switch will only provide an action event, while a GUI form for entering data will provide input/output events with a string property for each data field, and maybe an action event for a button.

Even if GUI or other interaction technologies are supported, we are especially interested in supporting user interaction through everyday objects. Therefore, in order to facilitate the development of FIOs that implement the concrete logic required to interact with those kinds of devices. We have developed UniDA [15] as the hardware abstraction layer of HI³, but also as a solution for hardware access within Dandelion. While FIOs provide a common interface for any kind of interaction resource, UniDA provides a common interface to any kind of hardware device. Every kind of device is accessed using the same paradigm and concepts, and each class of devices is reduced to a set of common operations, so it is possible to use entire classes of devices from different manufacturers or technologies using the same exact API.

CONCLUSION

The application of model-driven engineering techniques combined with interaction resource selection algorithms seems a very promising approach to alleviate the problems of developing user interfaces that require the integration and utilization of many different technologies and devices.

The current implementation of Dandelion includes: a device abstraction technology to decouple applications from the hardware technology of their interaction devices; a component migration system to physically move HI³ components from one platform to another and a distributed UI system, allowing applications to operate distributed and decoupled from their interaction resources.

The next step in this work is the development of FIO selection algorithms to adapt the application to changes in the environment by changing the FIOs mapping at runtime.

REFERENCES

1. Dadlani, P, Peregrin Emparanza, J, & Markopoulos, P. Distributed User Interfaces in Ambient Intelligent Environments: A Tale of Three Studies. *Proc. 1st DUI*, University of Castilla-La Mancha (2011), 101-104.

2. Blumendorf, M., & Albayrak, S. Towards a Framework for the Development of Adaptive Multimodal User Interfaces for Ambient Assisted Living Environments. *Proc. 5th UAHCI*, Springer (2009), 150–159.

3. Abascal, J., & Castro, I. F. de. Adaptive interfaces for supportive ambient intelligence environments. *Proc. 11th ICCHP*, Springer (2009), 30–37.

4. Paz-Lopez, A., Varela, G., Becerra, J.A., Vazquez-Rodriguez, S., & Duro, R. J. Towards ubiquity in ambient intelligence: User-guided component mobility in the HI3 architecture. Science of Computer Programming, 11/2012, Elsevier (2012).

5. Collignon, B., Vanderdonckt, J., & Calvary, G. Model-Driven Engineering of Multi-target Plastic User Interfaces. *Proc. 4th ICAS*, IEEE (2008), 7–14.

6. Ranganathan, a., Chetan, S., & Campbell, R. Mobile polymorphic applications in ubiquitous computing environments. *Proc. 1st MOBIQ.*, 2004, 402–411.

7. Satoh, I. Mobile applications in ubiquitous computing environments. IEICE TRANS. COMMUN. VOL.E88-B, NO. 3, 2005, 1026–1033.

8. Aizpurua, A., Cearreta, I., & Gamecho, B. Extending in-home user and context models to provide ubiquitous adaptive support outside the home. User Modeling and Adaptation for Daily Routines, Springer (2013), 25–59.

9. Miñón, R., & Abascal, J. Supportive adaptive user interfaces inside and outside the home. Advances in User Modeling, Springer (2012), 320–334.

10. Thevenin, D., & Coutaz, J. Plasticity of user interfaces: Framework and research agenda. *Proc. INTERACT'99*, IOS Press (1999), 110-117.

11. Blumendorf, M., Lehmann, G., & Albayrak, S. Bridging models and systems at runtime to build adaptive user interfaces. *Proc. 2nd EICS 2010*, ACM (2010), 9-18.

12. Balme, L., Demeure, A., Barralon, N., Coutaz, J. & Calvary, G. Cameleon-rt: A software ar-chitecture reference model for distributed, migratable, and plastic user interfaces. *Proc. EUSAI 2004*, Springer-Verlang (2004), 291-302.

13. W3C Multimodal Interaction Framework. W3C (2011).

14. Varela, G., et al. Decoupled Distributed User Interfaces in the HI3 Ambient Intelligence Platform. *Proc. 6th UCAmI 2012*, Springer (2012), 161-164.

15. Limbourg, Q., Vanderdonckt, J. UsiXML: A User Interface Description Language Supporting Multiple Levels of Independence.Engineering Advanced Web Applications, Rinton Press, Paramus, 2004, pp. 325-338.

16. Varela, G, Paz-Lopez A, Becerra, J. A., Vazquez-Rodriguez, S., & Duro, R. J. UniDA: Uniform Device Access Framework for Human Interaction Environments. Sensors 11 (10), MDPI (2011), 9361–9392

Metric-Based Evaluation of Graphical User Interfaces: Model, Method, and Software Support

Mathieu Zen

Université catholique de Louvain, Louvain School of Management,
Place des Doyens, 1 B-1348 Louvain-la-Neuve (Belgium) - mathieu.zen@uclouvain.be

ABSTRACT

Many factors contribute to ensuring User eXperience (UX) of Graphical User Interfaces, such as, but not limited to: usability, fun, engagement, subjective satisfaction. Aesthetics is a potential element that could also significantly contribute to this user experience. Although aesthetics have been extensively discussed, there is a need to rely on a sound, empirically validated methodology in order to properly evaluate how aesthetics could be measured, namely through metrics. Two main issues need to be addressed: the representativeness and the relevance of aesthetics metrics. In order to address these challenges, this paper introduces a methodology for metric-based evaluation of a graphical user interface of any type. This methodology is based on an underlying model that captures aesthetics aspects and related metrics, a method for computing them based on the underlying model, and software that supports enacting this method on any type of graphical user interface.

Author Keywords

Metrics, visual techniques, aesthetics, ergonomics.

ACM Classification Keywords

D.2.2 [**Software Engineering**]: Design tools and techniques – *User Interfaces*; H.5.2 [***Information Interfaces and Presentation***]: User Interfaces – *Graphical User Interfaces*.

General Terms

Algorithms; Design; Human Factors

INTRODUCTION

In the field of Human-Computer Interaction (HCI), a significant body of knowledge exists that addresses the quality of user of a Graphical User Interface (GUI) in general and its usability in particular [6]. Empirical studies are a major factor that could be used to assess the usability of a GUI. In particular, aesthetics plays an important role that could significantly affect the social acceptance of a GUI by end users [6, 13,16]. Although a complete thorough understanding of the role played by aesthetics in HCI remains to be studied, several references are useful to characterize its facets and to assess whether a GUI could be considered as aesthetic or not [16]. These methods are mostly manual and require a precise and rigorous application in order to guarantee its

appropriate enactment, thus preventing inexperienced designers and developers from applying these methods. One straightforward way to assess the aesthetics a GUI consists in computing metrics addressing visual aspects that are typically considered in aesthetics [3,14,15,17].

This paper discusses the main aspects of a work aimed at automating the GUI evaluation from an aesthetics perspective. A review of key papers that approach concepts related to GUI aesthetics is firstly delivered, including the use of visual techniques and the definition of aesthetics metrics. A methodology for conducting a metric-based evaluation of GUI is provided, based on the assumption that metrics cold be considered as relevant estimators of aesthetics. This methodology consists of three pillars: a model that captures aspects relevant to a metric-based evaluation of a GUI, a structured method in order to compute these metrics based on the aforementioned model, and a software that provides designers and developers with some guidance on how to apply, enact this method on any GUI.

BACKGROUND AND RELATED WORK

Many methods for evaluating a GUI are used today, such as usability guides [4,12] and various software [5,8,11,17] are exploited to automate this process. With respect to metric-based evaluation, GUILayout++ [8] enables the designer to draw a GUI and to evaluate its layout based on BaLOReS [5], a suite of principles and metrics such as unused space, contents of interests, advertising space, website identity elements, and advertisement elements. Results are displayed quantitatively with percentage figures and qualitatively by a "smiley". These metrics, although properly defined in previous work, require substantive validation of their relevance and significance based on user studies [5].

Key references

Two main references were considered as initiators of our method: a set of 30 GUI visual techniques defined on a continuum between two extremes (e.g., regularity vs. irregularity) [18] and a set of 14 characteristics determining GUI aesthetics associated with their significance based on a formula providing a quantitative way of computing each technique:

- A *visual technique* [18] is considered as a commonly accepted visual principle regulating the visual elements of a GUI. It refers to a purely theoretical concept.

- An *aesthetics metric* [9,10] evaluates a visual technique via a mathematical formula for its quantification.

In this regard, we can exemplify the balance property. Considered as a visual technique, balance is a search for horizontal and vertical equilibrium between existing interface objects [18]. Ngo *et al.* [9], guided by their goal to quantify aesthetics, introduce the optical weight in their definition of balance as the perception that one can have of an object weight. In a picture, the human eye perceives objects as more important than others. The metric of balance then results from the difference between the total weight of the various components of each part of the vertical and horizontal axes [9], a mathematical formula (Figure 1).

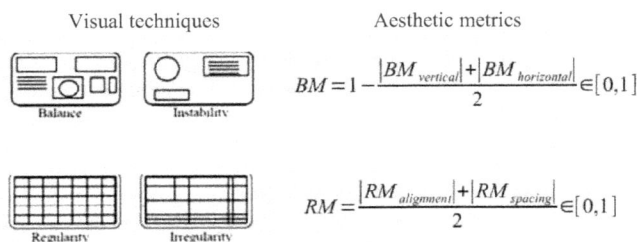

$$BM = 1 - \frac{|BM_{vertical}| + |BM_{horizontal}|}{2} \in [0,1]$$

$$RM = \frac{|RM_{alignment}| + |RM_{spacing}|}{2} \in [0,1]$$

Figure 1. Two metrics associated with a visual technique: balance vs. instability, regularity vs. irregularity).

Many other GUI aesthetics properties could be defined similarly: for each principle (e.g., a visual technique or a general principle), a formalization of its rationale should be obtained that reflects a high value when considered positive by a human and a low value when considered negative. The numerical value of each formula should be correlated to the human estimation of its level.

CONTEXT AND MOTIVATIONS

GUI aesthetics have been extensively studied [1,2,6,7,9,13, 16], with some studies providing empirical evidence that aesthetics influence user experience [7,13]. Table 1 identifies four cases to be investigated where aesthetics could have an influence on user experience. A GUI that is considered both usable and aesthetic will probably be accepted positively, while a GUI that is both unusable and anesthetic will probably be rejected negatively [6]. A GUI that is usable and anesthetic or esthetic and unusable, poses some new challenges for evaluation methods.

Usable UI	Aesthetic UI	User eXperience
Yes	No	Good/Bad (?)
No	No	Bad
No	Yes	Good/Bad (?)
Yes	Yes	Good

Table 1. Cases of aesthetics influence on user experience.

RESEARCH SCOPE, GOALS AND METHODS

In this section, we first describe the scope of the research to be undertaken around the quality standard. Then, we define the research goals and finally propose a methodology to be used. We identify two main issues: the representativeness and the relevance of aesthetics metrics. On the one hand, representativeness explores the extent to which the result of a metric represents end-users opinions. On the other hand, relevance opens a larger question and addresses to what extent an evaluation based on one specific metric is relevant for a GUI in one specific domain, involving one typical task, in one determined environment and/or on one distinctive device. In this regard, an evaluation of GUI balance could be appropriate and appropriate for a well-structured website where information content is the message to convey. On the contrary, it would be non-sense to assess balance of an artist's personal homepage since this visual technique is not on the side of contrast.

Scope of the research

Evaluating a GUI could be achieved by many methods, including standard compliance based on a standard related to quality, such as ISO9126 or ISO 25000 for software quality, or any other framework for quality management.

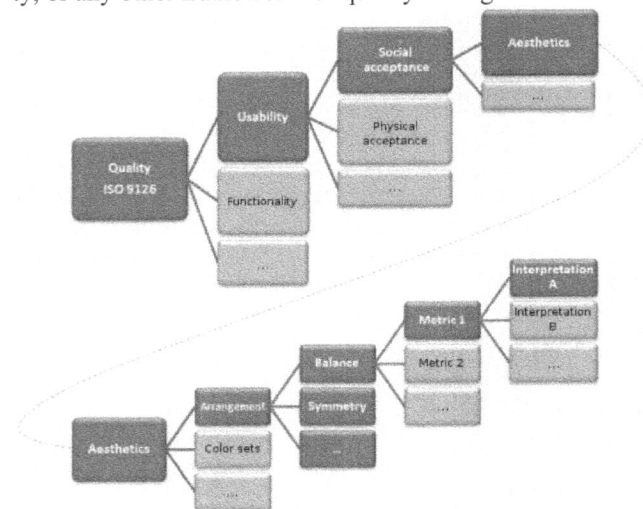

Figure 2. Conceptual map describing scope of research.

The ISO9126 standard for quality management is decomposed into six quality factors: functionality, reliability, usability, efficiency, maintainability and portability. *Usability* itself encompasses various sub-factors such as social acceptance and physical acceptance. One dimension that contributes to social acceptance is aesthetics. Aesthetics cannot be evaluated per se, since it involves multiple criteria that are inter-related: arrangement of objects on a display, used color sets and design of information support. Those criteria could be themselves recursively decomposed in to sub-criteria until a measurable criteria is reached, for instance such as symmetry, balance, density, etc. For each property, one or several metrics may exist.

A *metric* is a quantitative measure linked to a known property. Finally, for each metric, we can find many *interpretations* (e.g. formula). This work is aimed at supporting computation of metrics through their interpretation of formula so as to investigate aesthetics in a computational way. In other words, we seek to point to elements influencing aesthetics through a backward tracking departing from the smallest item (metric formula) in order to establish a general model of aesthetics. The value of a metric must not necessarily be interpreted as good or bad. Its main goal is to describe or compare different interfaces and to generate new solutions.

Research Goals

Metrics used so far are partial and are used to characterize visual quality at a given time. By measuring these metrics, and others to define, we could establish a GUI quality model to estimate and monitor over time evolution of the aesthetics and usability of an interface, whether for a particular information system or for several linked information systems. This work therefore aims at:

- Defining the scope of research around the *quality norm* which is commonly used to characterize good practices in GUI design.
- Motivating, defining and formalizing its *underlying concepts*, such as usability, social acceptance, aesthetics, interpretation, recommendation, and formula.
- Defining a model based on metrics to characterize these concepts in different contexts of use.
- Designing and developing a method to estimate these metrics in various contexts of use.
- Validating the methodology on the basis of experimental studies.
- Developing a tool to proceed to automatic and semi-automatic metrics computations.

The research goal is to demonstrate relevance of using aesthetics metrics to evaluate interface design. Therefore, it is essential to conduct studies on concrete cases throughout the thesis. The following section presents a methodology adopted with this perspective in mind.

Methodology

In this section, we present a methodology to be used to conduct empirical studies under which results may help to answer the main research statement and, more specifically, the question of representativeness.

1. Formulate hypotheses to be empirically verified. Focus on what needs to be validated using statistical tests.
2. Select several concrete GUIs, e.g., webpages, application, based on their differences in terms of goals and, for each one, assess its visible aesthetic orientation in order to establish a corpus of interfaces to be analyzed.
3. Perform a mathematical formalization in order to transform visual techniques, mainly qualitative, into quantitative aesthetics metrics. Some metrics (balance, simplicity...) already have defined mathematical formulas [9], other metrics (e.g., alignment, grouping...) still need to be provided with formula.
4. Compute metrics values for each interface based on these formulas (Figure 3).
5. Conduct a survey among end-users to get reviews about the value of each visual technique for each considered interface.
6. Perform statistical tests to compare quantitative results obtained using defined formulas with user reviews provided by the survey.
7. Analyze the results with further discussions and try to draw relations between metrics results and user perceptions of a UI quality keeping in mind the main research statement.

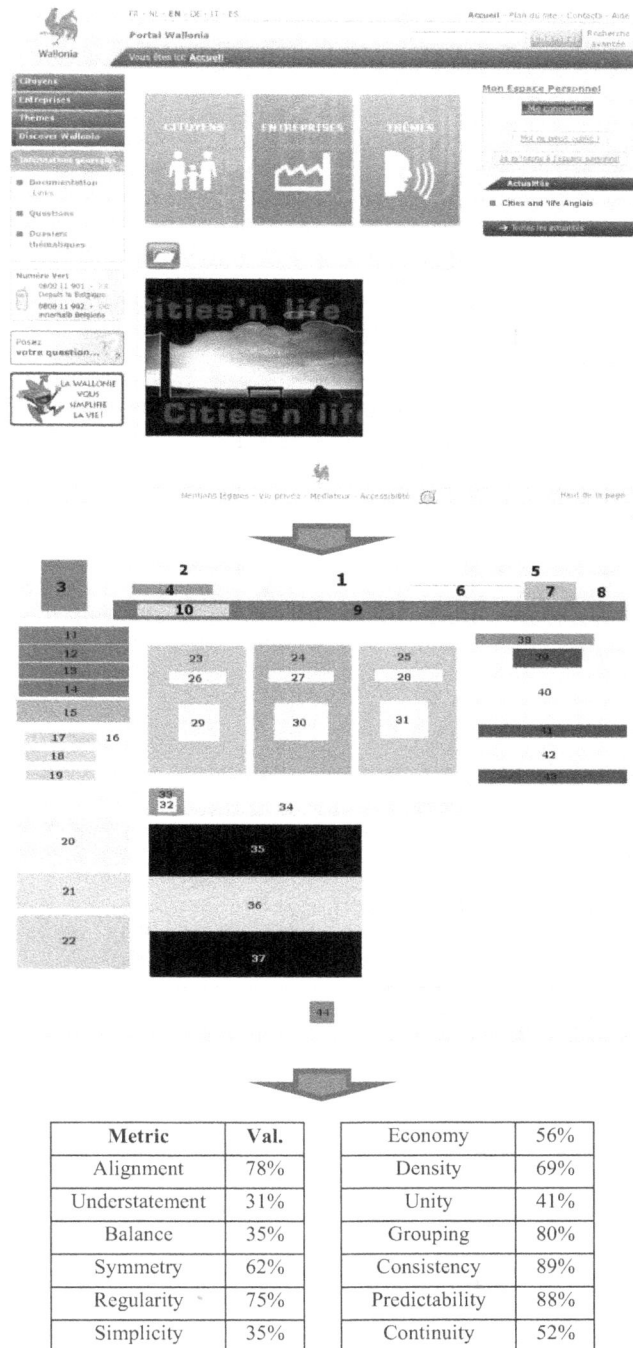

Metric	Val.		Economy	56%
Alignment	78%		Density	69%
Understatement	31%		Unity	41%
Balance	35%		Grouping	80%
Symmetry	62%		Consistency	89%
Regularity	75%		Predictability	88%
Simplicity	35%		Continuity	52%

Figure 3. GUI evaluation method: selecting interface, designing interface grid, computing aesthetics metrics.

RESEARCH SITUATION AND DISSERTATION STATUS

The aforementioned methodology has already been applied to a first pilot experiment. The main finding is: it was not possible to legitimate aesthetics metrics as an exact representation of user reviews. However, we observed that it was possible to obtain a relative similarity; a similarity established on the rankings of metrics rather than on their raw values. Furthermore, we are currently working on the development of a software tool called **QUESTIM** (Quality Estimator Tool using Metrics) in order to support the automatic or semi-automatic computation of metrics. It is a tool for designers requiring an objective evaluation feedback about their work. It is developed as a web service based on Google Web Toolkit, providing an evaluator of GUI quality using aesthetics metrics (Figure 4). The main goal of this tool is to load a website page or screenshot and proceed to automatic metrics computation or semi-automatic computation with objects superimposed by the user on the screenshot.

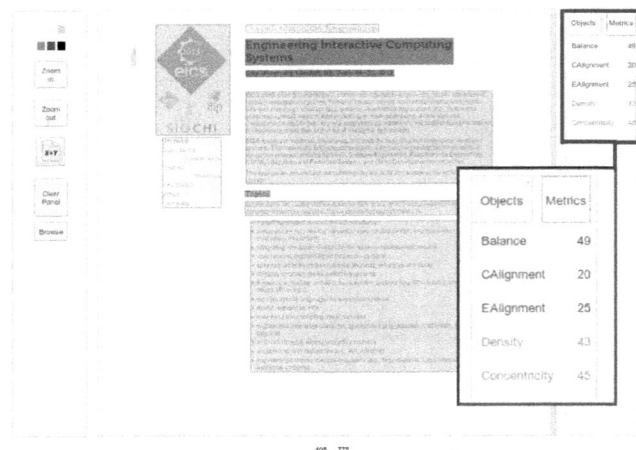

Figure 4. Semi-automatic metrics computation example on EICS2013 web page with QUESTIM.

We already have identified some lines of research to undertake or to further investigate:

- Some metric formulas may be optimized to better reflect human eye perceptions. Indeed, for some metrics, thresholds strongly influencing the outcome were defined empirically. These need to be validated.

- Regarding the automatic evaluation by metrics, we made a small step in providing a tool for drawing objects of an interface and get a quantitative result. It would be interesting to automate most of this evaluation process and propose a system of recognition of shapes and colors. The interest would be, on the one hand, to avoid manual drawing of objects and, on the other hand, the evaluation could be applied to any interface regardless of the language which is used.

- Finally, we developed a model based on five significant aesthetics metrics. The regression coefficient of this model was low (22%). A study on a larger scale (with a larger number of interfaces) could therefore be carried out to define a valid model of aesthetics.

EXPECTED CONTRIBUTIONS

Through this research project, we hope to provide interface designers with a tool using validated assessment items. The lifecycle of GUI usability design could therefore be directly improved. Indeed, designers or developers would be able to get a direct, detailed and objective feedback about their GUI design. In this way, we want to bring a real added value – validated and supported by the scientific world – to their work.

ACKNOWLEDGEMENTS

This work is partially supported by the QualIHM project (Tool-Supported Methodology for the Quality of Human-Computer Interfaces) of the Cwality research programme by Direction Générale DGO6 of Région Wallonne. A special thank goes to our colleagues Ugo Sangiorgi, Vivian Genaro Motti, and Suzanne Kieffer for comments on earlier version of this manuscript.

REFERENCES

[1] Birkhoff, G.D. *Aesthetic Measure*. Harvard University Press, Cambridge, 1933.

[2] Coyette, A., Kieffer, S., Vanderdonckt, J. Multi-Fidelity Prototyping of User Interfaces, *Proc. of INTERACT'2007*. Lecture Notes in Computer Science, Vol. 4662. Springer-Verlag, Berlin, 2007, pp. 149-162.

[3] Florins, M., Montero, F., Vanderdonckt, J., Michotte, B. Splitting Rules for Graceful Degradation of User Interfaces, *Proc. of ACM Conf. on Advanced Visual Interfaces AVI'2006*. ACM Press, New York, 2006, pp. 59-66

[4] Galitz, W.O. *The Essential Guide to User Interface Design*, 3rd ed. John Wiley & Sons, New York, 2007.

[5] González, S., Montero, F. and González, P. BaLOReS: a suite of principles and metrics for graphical user interface evaluation, *Proc. of INTERACCION '12*. ACM Press, New York, 2012, Article 9.

[6] Kurosu, M. and Kashimura, K. Apparent usability vs. Inherent usability, *Proc. CHI '95 Conf. Comp.* ACM Press, New York, 1995, pp. 292-293.

[7] Lavie, T. and Tractinsky, N. Assessing Dimensions of Perceived Visual Aesthetics of Web Sites. *Int. Jour. of Human-Computer Studies*, 60(3), 2004, pp. 269-298.

[8] Montero, F. and López-Jaquero, V. Guilayout++: Supporting Prototype Creation and Quality Evaluation for Abstract User Interface Generation, *Proc. of the 1st Workshop on USer Interface eXtensible Markup Language UsiXML'2010*, Berlin, Thalès, 2010, pp. 39-44.

[9] Ngo, D.C.L., Teo, L.S. and Byrne, J.G. A Mathematical Theory of Interface Aesthetics. *Vis. Math.*, 4, 2000.

[10] Ngo, D.C.L., Teo, L.S. and Byrne, J.G. Modelling interface aesthetics. *Information Sciences*, Vol. 152, 2003, pp. 25–46.

[11] Mahajan, R., and Shneiderman, B. Visual and textual consistency checking tools for graphical user interfaces. IEEE Trans. on Software Engineering, 23(11), 1997, pp. 722-735.

[12] Mullet, K., and Sano, D. *Designing visual interfaces: Communication oriented techniques*. 1994.

[13] Sonderegger, A. and Sauer, J. The influence of design aesthetics in usability testing: Effects on user performance and perceived usability. *App. Erg.*, 41 (3), 2010, pp. 403-410.

[14] Sears, A. AIDE: A step toward metric-based interface development tools, *Proc. of UIST'95*. ACM, pp. 101-110.

[15] Streveler, D.J. and Wasserman, A.I. Quantitative measures of the spatial properties of screen designs, *Proc. of INTERACT'84*. 1994.

[16] Tractinsky, N., Katz, A.S. and Ikar, D. What is beautiful is usable. *Interacting with Computers*, 13, 2000, pp. 127-145.

[17] Tullis, T.S. The formatting of alphanumeric displays: A review and analysis. *Human Factors*, 25(6), 1983, pp.657-682.

[18] Vanderdonckt, J. and Gillo, X. Visual techniques for traditional and multimedia layouts, *Proc. of ACM Conf. on Advanced Visual Interfaces AVI'94*, ACM, 1994, pp. 95-104.

GestIT: A Declarative and Compositional Framework for Multiplatform Gesture Definition

Lucio Davide Spano
Università di Cagliari
Via Ospedale 72,
09124, Cagliari, Italy
davide.spano@unica.it

Antonio Cisternino
Università di Pisa
Largo B. Pontecorvo 3,
56127, Pisa, Italy
cisterni@di.unipi.it

Fabio Paternò
ISTI-CNR
Via G. Moruzzi 1,
56127, Pisa, Italy
fabio.paterno @isti.cnr.it

Gianni Fenu
Università di Cagliari
Via Ospedale 72,
09124, Cagliari, Italy
fenu @unica.it

ABSTRACT
Gestural interfaces allow complex manipulative interactions that are hardly manageable using traditional event handlers. Indeed, such kind of interaction has longer duration in time than that carried out in form-based user interfaces, and often it is important to provide users with intermediate feedback during the gesture performance. Therefore, the gesture specification code is a mixture of the recognition logic and the feedback definition. This makes it difficult 1) to write maintainable code and 2) reuse the gesture definition in different applications. To overcome these kinds of limitations, the research community has considered declarative approaches for the specification of gesture temporal evolution . In this paper, we discuss the creation of gestural interfaces using GestIT, a framework that allows declarative and compositional definition of gestures for different recognition platforms (e.g. multitouch and full-body), through a set of examples and the comparison with existing approaches

Author Keywords
Gestural interaction, Input and Interaction Technologies, Analysis Methods, Software architecture and engineering, User Interface design.

ACM Classification Keywords
H.5.m. Information interfaces and presentation (e.g., HCI): Miscellaneous.

INTRODUCTION
The wide availability of devices with multitouch capabilities (phones, tablets and desktops), together with the spread of sensors that are able to track the whole body for interaction (such as Microsoft Kinect, Creative Interactive Gesture Camera, Leap Motion), has enabled a pervasive introduction of gestural interaction in our everyday life.

From the development point of view, the possibility to exploit such new devices for creating more engaging

interaction has been built on top of existing User Interface (UI frameworks and their reactive programming models. While this is reasonable from a software reuse point of view, applying the event-based management of the UI behaviour is difficult when dealing with gestural interaction, since a gesture is better represented as something varying over time rather than as an event corresponding to an action on a classical WIMP interface (e.g. a button click). Therefore, the application UI usually needs to provide users with intermediate feedback during the gesture performance, and modelling an entire gesture with a single event forces the developers to redefine the gesture recognition logic.

A possible solution for such kind of problem is provided by declarative and compositional approaches for the gesture definition. In this paper, we discuss the advantages and the drawbacks of this type of approach through our experience with the GestIT framework.

CONTRIBUTION
In this paper, we discuss how it is possible to address a set of problems in the engineering and development of gestural interfaces. The first and the second one are related to the gesture modelling in general, while the third is related to the compositional approach for gesture definition. The three problems we address can be summarized as follows:

1. *It is difficult to model a gesture only with a single event raised when its performance is completed.* The need for intermediate feedback forces the developer to redefine the tracking part. From now on, we refer to this issue as the *granularity problem*.

2. In [11], the authors state *"Multitouch gesture recognition code is split across many location in the source"*. This problem is even worse if we consider full-body gesture recognition, which has a higher number of points to track in addition to the other features (e.g. joints orientation, voice etc.). We refer to this issue as the *spaghetti code problem*.

3. A compositional approach for gestures has to deal with the fact that *"Multiple gestures may be based on the same initiating sequence of events"* [11]. This means that a support for the gesture composition has to manage possible ambiguities in the resulting gesture definition. We refer to this issue as the *selection ambiguity problem*.

In this paper, we discuss the advantages of a declarative and compositional approach for gestural interaction, which are able to solve the aforementioned problems. In our examples we use GestIT[1], a supporting framework that allows using the same composition mechanism on different platforms.

The paper is organised as follows: after the discussion of the related work, we compare GestIT with the most complete declarative approach for gesture definition existing in literature [11, 12] and we detail the procedure for creating a gesture-based application through a concrete example. After that, we explain how it is possible to address the problems 1 and 2, leveraging the approach of currently available frameworks, and different solutions for the problem 3. In particular, we discuss the GestIT support for postponing the choice of the actual recognized gesture, offering the possibility to implement the conflicting changes on the UI as long running transactions. Finally, we provide an overview on cross-platform how it is possible to support a cross-platform gesture definition exploiting the discussed approach.

RELATED WORK

Multitouch frameworks
Commercial frameworks for the development of multitouch interfaces (iOS [2], Android [1], etc.) are really similar to each other, and they all manage this kind of interaction at two levels. The first is the availability of common high-level gestures (such as pinch and rotation), which are natively supported by UI controls. The notification is based on a single event at the end of the gesture completion. The second is the possibility to define custom gestures or, as we already explained, to provide intermediate feedback during the gesture performance. This is left to the handling of low-level touch events, which are similar to mouse events.

Full-body frameworks
Different frameworks for the development of full body gestural interfaces exist, and they may be categorized according to the type of devices they support. For depth-camera based devices the most important ones are the Microsoft Kinect SDK [13] and the Primesense NITE framework [16]. Both development kits allow the user's skeleton tracking as a set of joint points, providing the position in 3D and the orientation. The Kinect SDK allows also the tracking of face expressions. NITE instead provides some predefined UI controls that recognize a set of gestures (wave, swipe etc.). The approach for the gesture modelling is the same discussed for the multitouch controls: the controls notify a single event at the completion of the given gesture. SDKs for remote controls provide the access to the low-level data sent by the device, without providing a direct support for the gesture recognition. For instance, WiiLib [19] and WiimoteLib [14] provide the possibility to

interpret correctly the bytes sent by the Nintendo Wiimote controller for developing applications.

DECLARATIVE APPROACHES
We group in the declarative approach category the attempts to provide a formal description of the gesture performance. CoGest [7] exploited context-free grammars in order to describe conversational gestures, while GeForMT [9] exploited the same approach for describing multitouch gestures. Neither of them provides gesture recognition capabilities for the defined grammars. Other approaches such as GDML [5] allow the gesture recognition but provide only a single event when the gesture is completed.

The frameworks Midas [17] and Mudra [8] propose a rule-based definition of multitouch gestures and multimodal input. Both of them are affected by the *spaghetti code* problem, since the definition of the interaction effects on the UI is included in the rules specification. GestIT separates the gesture definition from the UI behavior code. In addition, GestIT provides more flexible handling of the ambiguities, since both approaches solve this problem simply forcing the selection of one gesture through priorities.

GISpL [4] suffers both *granularity* and *spaghetti code* problems, since gestures cannot be decomposed into sub-gestures and the behavior is defined together with the feature tracking. The latter problem affects also the approach in [10]. Shwartz et al. [18] provide a solution for the uncertainty only after the gesture performance. Instead, GestIT manages such uncertainty also during the gesture execution, which is crucial for providing intermediate feedback.

In the following sub-sections, we analyse the two approaches that to the best of our knowledge are the only ones that offer a declarative formalization together with recognition capabilities.

Proton++
Proton++ [11, 12] is a multitouch framework allowing developers to declaratively describe custom gestures, separating the temporal sequencing of the events from the code related to the behaviour of the UI. Multitouch gestures are defined as regular expressions, where literals are identified by a triple composed of 1) the event type (touch down, move and up), 2) the touch identifier (e.g. 1 for the first finger, 2 for the second etc.) and 3) the object hit by the touch (e.g. the background, a particular shape etc.).

It is possible to define a custom gesture exploiting the regular expression operators (concatenation, alternation, Kleene star). The underlining framework is able to identify conflicts between different composed gestures and to return their common longer prefix in order to 1) let the developers remove the ambiguous expression or 2) assign different probability scores to the two gestures. The runtime support receives the raw input from the device, transforms it into a

[1] http://gestit.codeplex.com/

touch event stream that is matched against the defined regular expressions.

When one or more gestures are recognized, the support invokes the callbacks associated to the related expressions, selecting those with higher confidence scores (assigned by the developer in case of conflict between the expression definitions at design time). The improved version of the framework (presented in [12]) included also the possibility for the developer to calculate a set of attributes that may be associated to an expression literal. For instance, it is possible to associate the current trajectory to a touch move event, and let the framework raise the associated events (read recognize the literal) only if its movement direction is the one that the designer specified (e.g. north, north-west, south etc.). Other examples of such attributes are the touch shape, the finger orientation etc. In Proton++ it is possible to define the custom gestures through a graphical notation (called tablature), which has been demonstrated to be more understandable for the developers if compared with normal code.

GestIT

GestIT [20] shares with Proton++ the declarative and compositional approach, and it is able to model gestures for different kind of devices such as multitouch screens or full-body tracking devices. A custom gesture in GestIT is defined through an expression, starting from a set of ground terms that can be composed with a set of operators. The operators are based on those provided by CTT for defining temporal relationships in task modelling [15].

Ground terms represent the single features that are tracked by a given recognition device. For instance, if we consider a multitouch screen, the features that are tracked by the device are the position of the touches, while if we consider a full-body tracking device the features are the skeleton joint positions and orientations. In addition, it is possible to associate a predicate to each ground term in order to constraint its recognition to a given condition, which may be computed considering the current and/or the previous device events (e.g. the trajectory, speed etc.). The composition operators are the following:

- *Iterative* (symbol ∗), which recognizes a given gesture an indefinite number of times
- *Sequence* (symbol ≫), which expresses a sequence relationships among the operands, which are recognized in order, from left to right.
- *Parallel* (symbol ||), which defines the simultaneous recognition of two or more gestures
- *Choice* (symbol []), which allows the recognition of only one among the connected sub-gestures
- *Disabling* (symbol [>), which stops the recognition of another gesture, typically used for stopping the iteration loops.
- *Order Independence* (symbol |=|), which expresses that the connected sub-gestures may be performed in

any order. But when the user starts performing one of the sub-gestures, s/he has to complete it before starting another one.

Comparison

In the next section we demonstrate that the possible gestures modelled using Proton++ are a subset of those that may be defined with GestIT. We prove it showing a general way for mapping Proton++ definition towards the GestIT notation. In addition, we show that there is a class of gestures described by GestIT, which is not possible to define using Proton++. Obviously, since Proton++ describes only multitouch gestures, we define the correspondence between the regular expression literals and the ground terms only for the multitouch platform.

However, it is worth pointing out that the better expressivity of GestIT modelling approach is not due to the multitouch platform domain, but rather to a less expressive set of operators provided by Proton++. Indeed, it is possible to model full-body gestures using the Proton++ approach, providing a set of literals related to a full-body tracking device. Even in this case there is a set of gestures that can be expressed with GestIT but not with Proton++.

Proton++ literals

A Proton++ literal is identified by:

1. An event type (touch down, touch move, touch up)
2. A touch identifier
3. An object hit by the touch
4. A set of custom attributes values (one or more)

In GestIT for multitouch a ground term is identified by an event type (touch start, touch move or end) and by a touch identifier. Therefore the correspondence between the first two elements of the Proton++ literal and the GestIT ground term is straightforward. The third and fourth component of a Proton++ literal can be all modelled constructing a correspondent predicate associated to a GestIT ground term. We recall that a predicate associated to a ground term in GestIT is a boolean condition whether the gesture performance conforms to a set of gesture-specific constraints. According to this definition, the third component can be modelled with a predicate that checks if the current touch position is contained into an object with a given id or belonging to a particular class.

The forth component can be modelled considering, for each Proton++ custom attribute value, the function that computes its value according to the previous and the current position of the touch. Since it has to be defined in Proton++ for being associated to a literal, it is also possible to provide a predicate that compares the current attribute value with the desired one, in order to be used in GestIT. If more than one value is acceptable, the predicate can be defined simply through a boolean OR of the comparison for the different values. Obviously, if both the third and the fourth identification component of the literal need to be modelled, it is sufficient to define a single predicate that is composed by the boolean AND of the corresponding predicates.

Table 1 summarizes how to transform a Proton++ literal into a GestIT ground term.

Proton:	GestIT
$E_{T_{id}}^{O \mid V_1 \dots V_n}$	$E_{T_{id}}[p]$ where: $p = o \wedge (a_1 \vee \dots \vee a_n) \qquad i = 1 \dots n$ $o = true \Leftrightarrow O_{type} = O$ $a_i = true \Leftrightarrow A_i = V_i \qquad i = 1 \dots n$

Table 1: correspondence between the Proton++ literal and the GestIT ground term. E represents an event type, T_{id} a touch identifier. The o predicate models the touched object constraint in Proton++ literals: O_{type} is a property that maintains the current object type, O is a concrete value for the object type (e.g. start, rectangle etc.). The a_i predicates model the custom attribute part of a Proton++ literal: A_i is a property that maintains the value of the attribute, while V_i is the actual attribute value. The p predicate puts all the definitions together and it is associated to the ground term in GestIT.

Proton++ operators

The correspondence between the Proton++ and GestIT operators is straightforward, since for each one defined by the former there is an equivalent in the latter. Table 2 summarizes how to transform the operators from Proton++ to GestIT.

Proton++:	GestIT
Concatenation: $A_P B_P$	Sequence: $A_G \gg B_G$
Alternation: $A_P \mid B_P$	Choice: $A_G [\,] B_G$
Kleene star: A_P^*	Iterative: A_P^*

Table 2: correspondence between the Proton++ operators and the GestIT ones. A_P, B_P and A_G, B_G represent respectively a Proton++ and a GestIT generic expression.

Appling recursively the transformations defined in Table 1 and Table 2 it is possible to build a GestIT gesture definition corresponding to a Proton++ one.

The vice-versa is not possible in general, since there is no way to transform the *Disabling* and the *Parallel* operators from GestIT to Proton++.

The *Disabling* operator is important in order to stop the recognition of iterative gestures, in particular the composed ones. Most of the times, it models how to interrupt the iterative recognition of a gesture. For instance in a grab gesture, the iterative recognition of hand movements is interrupted by opening the hand.

In addition, it may be used also for modelling situations where the user performs an action that interrupts the interaction with the application. For instance, all the Kinect games have a "pause" gesture disabling the interaction. In the application we describe in the next section, the disable operator is used for modelling the fact that the application tracks the user only if she is in front of the screen. Therefore, the gesture "shoulders not parallel to the screen plane" disables the interaction. This is particularly relevant while interacting with devices continuously tracking the user (e.g. Microsoft Kinect), since it is important to provide the user with a way to disable the interaction at any time.

The *Parallel* operator has a clear impact when modelling parallel input for e.g. multi-user applications. For instance, the parallel operator can be useful in a scenario where a user zooms a photo on a multitouch table while another user drags another picture, simply composing two existing gestures. In addition, it is also possible that parallel interaction occurs with a single user. For instance, a user may drag an object through a single-hand grab gesture and point with the other hand for selecting where to drop it.

DECLARATIVE GESTURE MODELLING

In this section, we show how it is possible to create a gestural interface with GestIT, as a sample for the declarative gesture modelling approach. After that, we show how the framework addresses the granularity, spaghetti code and selection ambiguity problems. In order to facilitate the discussion, we refer to two application examples. The first one is a touchless interface for a recipe browser. It allows the cooker to go through the description of the steps for preparing a dish without touching any device. This is particularly useful while cooking, since the user has dirty hands or is manipulating tools. The second one is a simple 3D model viewer, which can be controlled through gestures. The applications have been already discussed respectively in [21] and [20], here we analyse some of the supported interactions that exemplify the recurrent problems in gesture modelling.

Creating a Declarative Gestural Interface

In this section we detail how a developer can use GestIT in order to create a gestural UI. The application is a touchless recipe browser, organised into three presentations: the first one allows the user to select the recipe type (e.g. starter, first dish, main dish etc.), the second is dedicated to the selection of the recipe, while the last one presents the steps for cooking the selected dish with a video and subtitles.

In the latter presentation it is possible to go through the steps back and further or to randomly jump from one point to the other of the procedure. We consider here the C# version for Windows Presentation Foundation (WPF) of the GestIT library.

An interface in WPF is described by two different files. The first one contains the definition of the UI appearance and layout specified using XAML, an XML-based notation that can be used in .NET applications for initializing objects. In this case, it initializes the widgets contained into the application view. The second file involved in the UI definition contains the behaviour, and it is a normal C#

class file. Since the two files are part of the same view class definition, the latter is called the "code-behind" file. Objects defined by the XAML file are accessible in the code-behind file and the methods defined in the code-behind file are accessible in the XAML definition.

In this example, we discuss the implementation of the first presentation, which is shown in Figure 1. The view is composed of a title on the upper part and a fisheye panel in the centre. The bottom part is dedicated to the status messages: the application notifies if it is tracking the user's movements or not.

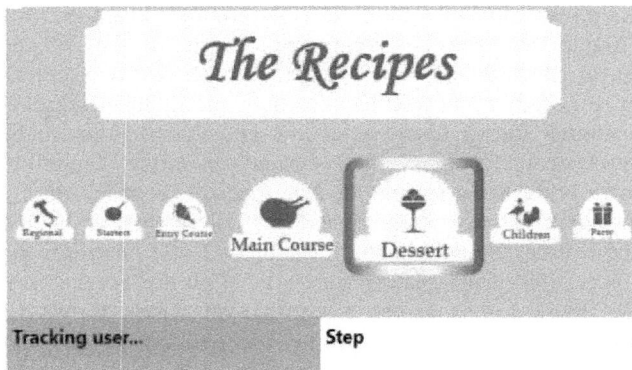

Figure 1: Recipe selection UI

The gestural interaction is defined inside the associated view through a set of custom XAML tags, which are shown in Table 3, and are equivalent to the expression notation we use in this paper. The high level description of the gesture interaction is the following: if the user is not in front of the screen, the application does not track his/her movements. When the user is in front of the screen, s/he can highlight one of the recipe types, which can be selected by a grab gesture (closing the hand).

The interaction is a *sequence* of different gestures, which starts with the user that standing in front of the screen (the screen front gesture, from line 7 to line 13 in Table 3). Such constraint is modelled checking the position of the shoulder points, which have to be almost parallel to the sensor plane on the depth axis. The constraint is computed using a C# method (*screenFront*) that is referenced by the value of the *Accept* attribute and it is defined in the code-behind file associated to a XAML specification.

When this gesture is completed, the user needs to be aware that the application is tracking his/her position, therefore the completion method associated to the gesture changes the message on the label at the bottom of the UI in Figure 1, setting its text to "Tracking user..." with a green background. The definition of this behaviour is again in the code-behind file, and it is linked with the gesture declaration through the *Method* attribute in the *change.completed* tag (from line 9 to 12 in Table 3). The method name in this case is *screenFront_Completed*.

Once this gesture is completed, it is possible to interact with the screen, and the grab gesture implements the selection of the recipe type. First, we listen iteratively to the change of the right hand position (the *Change* tag with *Feature="HandRight"* at line 17 in Table 3). Every time it is completed (read the user moves the hand), the *moveHand_Completed* method is executed. It updates the currently highlighted recipe type (the one with the red border in Figure 1).

After that, the recognition iteration is interrupted in two cases. The first one is when the user closes the right hand (the *Change* at line 24 in Table 3), and the method *rightHandClosed_Completed* handles the completion of the grab gesture, changing the current presentation. The second case is when the user goes away and s/he is not in front of the screen anymore (line 33 in Table 3). This situation is modelled symmetrically with respect to the gesture at line 7, the only difference is the *Accepts* method (*notScreenFront*), which is exactly the logical negation of *ScreenFront*. In both cases, the interruption is modelled using a *disabling*, declared respectively by the inner and the outer *Disabling* tags (line 14 and 16 in Table 3).

In summary, for creating a gestural interface with GestIT is sufficient to:

1. Create the UI view
2. Define the gestures associated to a view (in the same file), composing declaratively existing gestures or creating new ones starting from ground-terms.
3. Provide the methods for calculating the predicates associated to the specified gestures in the code-behind file (if any)
4. Provide the UI behaviour associated to the gesture completion

In the following sections we discuss how such organization solves the problems that are the topic of this paper.

Granularity Problem
The granularity problem derives from the modelling of complex gestures with a single event notification when it completes. Due to the time duration of the interaction gestures, it is usually needed to provide intermediate feedback during the performance, with the consequent need to split the complex gesture in smaller parts.

In order to show the impact of such problem even for simple interactions, here we focus on two specific hand gestures we exploited in the touchless recipe browser: the first one is a simple hand grab, which is used in the first and the second presentation for selecting an object. The second one is a hand-drag gesture we used for controlling the recipe preparation video: the user grabs the knob of the video timeline and then it moves is back and forth before "releasing" it by simply opening the hand.

```
1    <TabItem x:Name="recipeType">
2     <Grid Background="#FF92BCED">
3      <!-- gesture definition -->
4       <g:GestureDefinition x:Name="moveSelection" >
5        <g:Sequence Iterative="True">
6         <!-- turn (front of the screen) -->
7          <g:Change Feature="ShoulderLeft"
8                 Accepts="screenFront">
9           <g:Change.Completed>
10           <g:Handler
11               method="screenFront_Completed"/>
12          </g:Change.Completed>
13         </g:Change>
14         <g:Disabling>
15          <!-- grab gesture  -->
16           <g:Disabling Iterative="True">
17            <g:Change Feature="HandRight"
18                Iterative="True">
19             <g:Change.Completed>
20              <g:Handler
21                method="moveHand_Completed" />
22             </g:Change.Completed>
23            </g:Change>
24            <g:Change Feature="OpenRightHand"
25                  Accepts="rightHandClosed">
26             <g:Change.Completed>
27              <g:Handler
28              method="rightHandClosed_Completed"/>
29             </g:Change.Completed>
30            </g:Change>
31           </g:Disabling>
32          <!-- turn (not in front of the screen) -->
33           <g:Change Feature="ShoulderLeft"
34                   Accepts="notScreenFront">
35            <g:Change.Completed>
36             <g:Handler
37              method="notScreenFront_Completed"/>
38            </g:Change.Completed>
39           </g:Change>
40          </g:Disabling>
41        </g:Sequence>
42       </g:GestureDefinition>
43      <!-- view definition -->
44       <ui:FisheyePage x:Name="heading" />
45       <kt:KinectSensorChooserUI
46         Name="kinectSensorChooser1" />
47      </Grid>
48    </TabItem>
```

Table 3 UI view and gesture definition of the recipe selection presentation

Table 4 shows how it is possible to model such gestures with GestIT. The grab gesture is composed by an iteration of the hand movement ($mH_r{}^*$), which is disabled by a change on the feature that tracks the opened or closed status of the hand (cH_r in the expression). We force the recognition only of a hand closure specifying the *closed* predicate, which accepts only changes from opened to closed. The grab gesture is a prefix for the drag one. Indeed, it is defined by a grab gesture followed in sequence by an iterative movement of the hand, disabled again by a change on the hand status, this time from opened to closed (modelled by the *open* predicate).

Grab	$mH_r^* [> cH_r[closed]$
Drag	$Grab \gg Release$ $Release = mH_r^*[> cH_r[open]$

Table 4: Grab and Drag hand gestures definition using GestIT. The expressions consider only the right-hand, the definition of the same gestures for the left hand is symmetric.

With GestIT it is possible to reuse the definition of the grab gesture for defining the drag one, as it is shown in Table 4. However, the possibility to compose gestures with a set of operators does not guarantee the reusability of the definition. Indeed, even in this simple example, the programmer needs a fine-grained control not only on the gesture itself, but also on it subparts. In the first two screens of the recipe browser application the grab gesture is exploited for an object selection, and the user has to be aware of which object s/he is currently pointing. Therefore, there is the need to provide intermediate feedback during the grab gesture execution. This is supported in the application exploiting the fact that GestIT notifies the completion of the gesture sub-parts. With this mechanism, the application receives a notification when each time mH_r is completed, highlighting the pointed object. The handler associated to the completion of the entire gesture performs the recipe selection and the presentation change. While performing the drag gesture, there is no need to attach a handler to the hand movement in the grab part, but it is sufficient to specify that the position in the video stream is changing after the grab completion, and to update it during the movement of the hand in the release part of the gesture.

It should be clear now how the declarative and compositional pattern offered by GestIT solves the granularity problem: the application developer is not bound to receiving a single notification when the whole gesture is completed. If needed, s/he is able to attach the behaviour also to the gesture sub-parts, handling them at the desired level of granularity.

Spaghetti Code Problem

The previous example may be used also for showing how to address the problem of having the gesture recognition code spread in many places (spaghetti code problem). Indeed, the declarative and compositional approach to the gesture definition allows the developer to separate the temporal sequencing aspect from the UI behaviour while defining a gesture. This allows maintaining the gesture recognition code isolated in a single place.

In the example, the recognition code corresponds to the declaration of the gesture expression. The handlers define the UI behaviour, but they are not part of the recognition code, since they are simply attached to the run-time notification of the gesture completion (or its sub-parts). In this way, it is not only possible to isolate the recognition code into a single application, but it is also possible to provide a library of complex gesture definitions, which may be reused in different scenarios, maintaining the possibility to attach the UI behaviour at the desired level of granularity. In this particular example, it would be possible to model the entire interaction instantiating a single complex gesture. Indeed, the *Grab* and the *Release* gestures differ only for the predicate on the change of the hand status feature. Therefore, it is possible to define with GestIT a complex gesture that is parametric with respect to this predicate.

HandStatus	$HandStatus[p] = mH_r^* [> cH_r[p]$
Grab	$HandStatus[closed]$
Drag	$HandStatus[closed] \gg HandStatus[open]$

Table 5 Grab and Drag gestures defined using a single parametric complex gesture.

Table 5 shows a different definition of the gestures in Table 4, which demonstrates the level of flexibility in the factorization of the gesture recognition code in the proposed framework.

Selection Ambiguity Problem
In this section, we show how the problem of possible ambiguities that may arise when composing gestures is handled in GestIT. We exemplify the problem through a simple 3D viewer application [20]. The interaction with the 3D model is the following: the user can change the camera position performing a "grabbing" the model gesture with a single hand and moving it, while it is possible to rotate the model executing the same gesture with both hands. The complete definition is shown in Table 6. For the sake of simplicity we omit the part related to the left hand in the *Move* definition, but the point we are going to discuss is symmetrically valid also for the left hand.

$$Move [] Rotate$$
$$Move = cH_r[closed] \gg (mH_r^* [> cH_r[open])$$
$$Rotate = (cH_r[closed]||cH_l[closed]) \gg$$
$$((mH_r[d]||mH_l[d])^* [>$$
$$(cH_r[open]||cH_l[closed]))$$

Table 6: Gesture definition for the 3D viewer application

The *Move* and the *Rotate* gestures are composed through a choice operator but, as it is possible to see in the definition, both gestures start with $cH_r[closed]$. Therefore it is not possible to perform the selection immediately after the recognition of the first ground term, but the recognition engine needs at least one "lookahead" term, and the selection has to be postponed to the next event raised from the device. However, the two instances of $cH_r[closed]$ may have different handlers attached to the completion event, which should be executed in the meantime.

In general it is possible that, when composing a set of different gestures through the choice operator, two or more gestures have a common prefix, which does not allow an immediate choice among them. We identified three possible ways for addressing this problem. The different solutions have an impact on the recognition behaviour while traversing the prefix.

The first solution is the one proposed in [11], where the authors define an algorithm for extracting the prefix at design time. After having identified it, it is possible to apply a factorization process to the gesture definition expression, removing the ambiguity. This solution has the advantage that, since there is no ambiguity anymore, the recognition engine is always able perform the selection among the gestures immediately. The main drawback is that it breaks the compositional approach: after the factorization the two gesture definitions are merged and it is difficult for the designer to clearly identify them in the resulting expression. This leads to a lack of reusability of the resulting definition.

The second possible solution is again to calculate the common prefix at design time, without changing the gesture definition. In this case, the recognition support is provided with both the gesture definition and the identified prefix. During the selection phase at runtime, the support buffers the raw device events until only one among the possible gestures can be selected according to the pre-calculated prefix, and then flushes the buffer considering only the selected gesture. This approach has the advantage of maintaining the compositional approach, while selecting the exact match for the gestures in choice: the runtime support suspends the selection until it receives the minimum number of events for identifying the correct gesture to choose. Once the gesture has been selected, the application receives the notification of the buffered events. The latter is the main drawback of this approach: the buffering causes a delay on the recognition that is reflected on the possibility to provide intermediate feedback while performing the common prefix gesture. Another drawback is that the common prefix has to be calculated at design time, which may need an exponential procedure for enumerating all the possible recognizable event sequences, which are needed for extracting the common prefix. For instance, an order independence expression with *n* operands in GestIT recognizes *n!* event sequences, since we should consider that the operands can be performed in any order.

The third solution is based on a best effort approach, and is the one implemented by GestIT. When two or more expressions are connected with a choice operand, the recognition support executes them as if they were in parallel. If the user correctly performed one of the gestures in choice, when the parallel recognition passes the common prefix only one among the operands can further continue in the recognition process. At this point the choice is performed and only one gesture is successfully recognized, and the support stops trying to recognize the others. This approach solves the buffering delay problem of the previous solution, since the effects of the gestures contained into the common prefix is immediately visible for the user. However, in this case the recognition support notified the recognition of the gestures included in the common prefix of all the operands involved in the choice. Consequently, the UI showed the effects associated to all of them, while only the ones related to the selected gesture should be visible. In order to have a correct behaviour, we need a mechanism to *compensate* the changes made by the gestures that were not selected by the recognition support, which means to revert the effects they had on the UI. Such mechanism can be supported through a notification signalling that the recognition of a gesture (to all gestures (ground term or complex) has been interrupted. In this way it is possible for the developer to specify how to compensate the undesired changes. This is the main drawback for this solution: the developer is responsible of handling the compensating actions.

In order to better explain how this solution works, we present a small example of compensation. We consider the gesture model in Table 6, which allows the user to move and to rotate a 3D model. The UI provides intermediate feedback during the gesture execution in the following way: a four-heads arrow while the camera position is changing, and a circular arrow while the user is rotating the model.

We suppose in our example that the user performs the grab gesture with both hands and we describe the behaviour of the recognition support during the recognition of the common prefix (in this case $cH_r[closed]$) and after the gesture selection has been performed. The common prefix handling is depicted in Figure 2: the upper part represents the stream of updates that comes from the device, the black arrow highlights the one that is under elaboration. The central part shows the gesture expression represented as a tree, with the ground terms that can be recognized immediately highlighted in black (we do not show the predicates associated to the ground terms, since for this example we suppose that they are always verified). Some tree nodes are associated to rectangular and circular badges, which represent respectively the completion and the compensation behaviour. Such handlers are external with respect to the gesture description and are defined by the developer. The lower part shows the effects on the UI of the gesture recognition. The left part depicts the UI before the recognition, the middle part shows the intermediate effects, while the right one shows the resulting state after the recognition.

During the recognition of the common prefix, the support behaves as follows: after receiving the update coming from the device, the support executes the two instances of cH_r, highlighted by the black arrows in Figure 2, central part. Since the leftmost one has an associated completion handler (the A rectangular badge), the recognition support executes it. Therefore the UI changes its state and an arrow is shown above the 3D model (Figure 2, lower part). After that, the expression state changes (two ground terms have been

recognized) and we have the situation depicted in Figure 3: the ground terms with a grey background have been completed, therefore the ground terms that may be recognized at this step are mH_r or cH_l. Since the next device update we are considering is cH_l (Figure 3, upper part), the recognition support is now able to perform the selection of the right-hand part of the expression tree, while the left-hand part cannot be further executed.

Therefore, the latter needs compensation, which consists of invoking the handlers associated to all the expressions previously completed (cH_r). In our example this corresponds to the execution of the handler identified with the B circular badge, which hides the four-heads arrow. After that, it is possible to continue with recognition of the gesture: the cH_l ground term in the right-hand part of the expression is completed and also the parallel expression highlighted with a black arrow in Figure 3. Consequently the recognition support executes the completion handler represented with the C rectangular badge, which shows the circular arrow for providing the intermediate feedback during the model rotation, and the gesture recognition continues taking into account only the *Rotate* gesture. The effects of the handlers on the UI for this step are summarized by the lower part of Figure 3: before the recognition of the ground term it was visible on the UI the four-head arrow, which has been hidden by the B compensation handler. The C completion handler instead showed the circular arrow that determines the state of the UI after the ground term recognition.

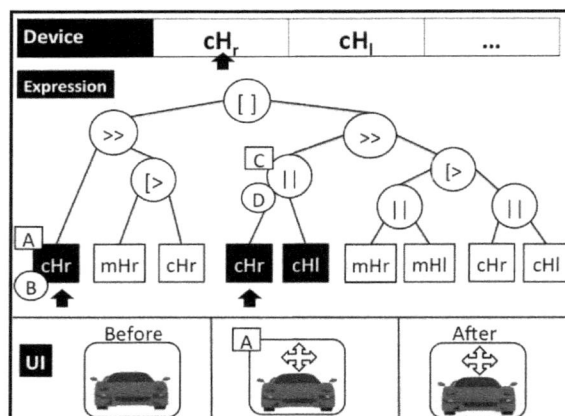

Figure 2: Example of common prefix handling in for the choice operator (part 1).

From a theoretical point of view, the proposed solution considers the set of gestures in choice as instances of long-running transactions [6], but in this case the components involved are not distributed. In case of failure of such kind of transactions, it is not possible in general to restore the initial state, as happens with the effects on the UI of the gestures that are not selected by the choice. Instead, a compensation process is provided, which handles the return to a consistent state. There is a large literature on how to manage long-running transactions, in [3] the authors provide a good survey on the topic.

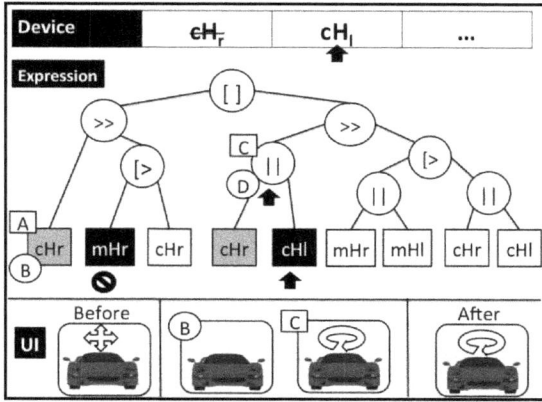

Figure 3: Example of common prefix handling in for the choice operator (part 2).

CROSS PLATFORM GESTURE MODELLING

Since the compositional gesturing model definition is based on a set of building blocks (ground terms), connected through a set of well-defined composition operators, it is possible to create interfaces that share the same gesture definition across different recognition platforms finding a meaningful translation of the source platform ground terms towards the target one. This opens the possibility to reuse the gesture definition not only for different applications that exploit the same recognition device but also, if the interaction provided still makes sense, with different devices that have different recognition capabilities. In order to explain how such reuse is possible, we report here on a first experiment we conducted with the two platforms supported by GestIT: multitouch and full-body.

$$Pan \, [\,] Pinch$$
$$Pan = Start_1 \gg Move_1^* \, [> End_1$$
$$Pinch = (Start_1 |=| Start_2) \gg (Move_1^* \, | \, | Move_2^*) \, [> (End_1 |=| End_2)$$

Table 7: Simple drawing canvas gesture modelling

We started from a simple drawing canvas application for iPhone, which supported the pan gesture for drawing and the pinch gesture for zooming. Such gestures were connected through the choice operator, as defined in Table 7. Notice how it is easy to support the zooming feature while drawing by simply changing the choice operator to the parallel one, without any additional effort for the developer.

The UI behaviour associated to the gesture definition can be summarized as follows:

- To the *Move* block of the pan gesture we associated an event handler that draws a line from the previous touch position to the current one.
- To each one of the *Move* blocks of the pinch gesture, we associated an event handler that computes the difference between the previous and the current distance between the two touches. If it is increased, the canvas zooms in the view, otherwise it zooms out the view accordingly

In order to create a full-body version of the same application, it is not possible to reuse directly the gesture definition, because concepts as pan, pinch, touch etc. do not have any meaning in such platform. However, having a precise definition of the gesture also allows us to define precisely new concepts. In our case, what is missing is a precise definition of what a touch start, a touch move and a touch end are. If we add a precise definition of these concepts, all the gestures that have been constructed starting from such building blocks will be defined consequently. One simple idea is to associate a point that represents a finger position on the iPhone to the position of one hand with the Kinect (therefore, the maximum number of touch points is two). In addition, we have to define a criterion for distinguishing when the touch starts and when it ends. A simple way is to rely on the depth value of the position of a given hand: if it is under a certain threshold, we can consider that the user is "touching" our virtual screen, otherwise we do not consider the current hand position as a touch.

Multitouch Ground Term	Interaction
$Start_1 = r[z_r(t-1) > k \wedge z_r(t) \le k]$ $Start_2 = l[z_l(t-1) > k \wedge z_l(t) \le k]$	
$Move_1 = r[z_r(t-1) \le k \wedge z_r(t) \le k]$ $Move_2 = l[z_l(t-1) \le k \wedge z_l(t) \le k]$	
$End_1 = r[z_r(t-1) \le k \wedge z_r(t) > k]$ $End_2 = l[z_l(t-1) \le k \wedge z_l(t) > k]$	

Table 8: Mapping of the multitouch ground terms to the full-body platform

More precisely, we need to define the multitouch basic gestures according to the 3D position of the left and right hand, indicated respectively as $l = (x_l, y_l, z_l)$ and $r = (x_r, y_r, z_r)$. Moreover, we have to define a plane, which represents the depth barrier for the touch emulation, as $T_p = (x, y, k)$ where k is a constant. The complete definition can be found in Table 8.

It is worth pointing out that, even if we used such definition for a quite "extreme" change of platform, the redefinition of the ground term allows us to support with the Kinect platform all the multitouch gestures that involve no more than two fingers, which are the large majority of those used in such kind of applications. Obviously, from the interaction design point of view it may be a bad idea to port multitouch gestures to the full body gesture platform directly, and the example should be considered only as a proof of concept. However, such kind of approach may be used for those devices that are exploited for recognizing gestures in similar settings. For instance, it can be useful for designing applications that recognize the same full body gestures with a remote or a depth camera-based optical device. In this case, having such kind of homomorphism may reduce the complexity in supporting different devices.

CONCLUSION AND FUTURE WORK

The spread of gesture interfaces both in mobile devices, in game settings and more recently in smart environments is pushing for solving the problem of having a different programming paradigm, with respect to the single-event notification for describing gestures. Declarative and compositional approaches for gesture definition represent a step further towards such a new model, solving the single-event granularity problem and providing a separation of concerns (the temporal sequence definition is separated from the behaviour), which allows a more understandable and maintainable code. In addition, we discussed the selection ambiguity problem, which affects the composition of gestures that have a common prefix through a choice operator. The recognition support has different possibilities for dealing with the uncertainty in the selection while performing this common prefix. We discussed the different solutions using GestIT as a sample framework and we demonstrated that it is more expressive than other libraries in literature.

In the future, we plan to enhance the framework adding the support for more platform and devices (e.g. remotes). In addition we will exploit the declarative approach for identifying gestures that are not used directly for the interaction (*posturing*) but that may be used in order to detect the user's emotional status.

REFERENCES

1. Android Developer, Responding to Touch Events. http://developer.android.com/training/graphics/opengl/touch.html, retrieved 12-10-2012.
2. Apple Inc., Event Handling Guide for iOS. http://developer.apple.com/library/ios/navigation/, retrieved 12-10-2012.
3. Colombo, C., Pace, G. Recovery within Long Running Transaction, ACM Computing Surveys 45 (3), 2013 (accepted paper).
4. Echtler, F., Butz, A. GISpL: Gestures Made Easy. *In Proc. of TEI '12*, pp. 233-240, ACM, (2012).
5. Meyer, A. S., Gesture Recognition. http://wiki.nuigroup.com/Gesture_Recognition, retrieved 12-10-2012
6. Garcia-Molina, H., Gawlick, D., Klein, J., Kleissner, K., Salem, K., Modelling Long-Running Activities as Nested Sagas. IEEE bulletin of the Technical Committee on Data Engineering, 14 (1), 1991.
7. Gibbon, D., Gut, U., Hell, B., Looks, K., Thies, A., and Trippel, T. A computational model of arm gestures in conversation. Proc. Eurospeech 2003, ISCA (2003), 813–816.
8. Hoste, L., Dumas, B., Signer, B. Mudra: a unified multimodal interaction framework. *In Proc. of ICMI '11*, pp. 97-104, ACM, (2011).
9. Kammer, D.,Wojdziak, J., Keck, M., and Taranko, S. Towards a formalization of multi-touch gestures. Proc. ITS 2010, ACM, (2010), 49–58.
10. Khandkar, S. H., Maurer, F. A domain specific language to define gestures for multi-touch applications. *In Proc. of DCM'10 Workshop*, Article No. 2, ACM, (2010).
11. Kin, K., Hartmann B., DeRose. T., and Agrawala, M., Proton: multitouch gestures as regular expressions. In CHI 2012 (Austin, Texas, U.S. May 2012)., 2885-2894
12. Kin, K., Hartmann, B., DeRose, T., Agrawala, M.. Proton++: a customizable declarative multitouch framework. *In Proc of UIST 2012*. ACM, New York, NY, USA, 477-486.
13. Microsoft, Kinect for Windows SDK, http://www.microsoft.com/en-us/kinectforwindows/, retrieved 12-10-2012
14. Brian, P., WiimoteLib, http://www.brianpeek.com/page/wiimotelib, retrieved 12-10-2012.
15. Paternò, F. Model-based design and evaluation of interactive applications. *Applied Computing*, Springer 2000
16. Primesense, NITE, http://www.primesense.com/en/nite, retrieved 12-10-2012
17. Scholliers, C., Hoste, L., Signer, B., De Meuter, W., Midas: a declarative multi-touch interaction framework. *In Proc. of TEI'11*, pp. 49–56, ACM, (2011)
18. Schwarz, J., Hudson, S. E., Makoff, J., Wilson, A. D. A framework for robust and flexible handling of inputs with uncertainty. *In Proc. of UIST 2010*, pp. 47-56, ACM, (2010)
19. Sourceforge, WiiLib, http://sourceforge.net/projects/wiilib/, retrieved 12-10-2012
20. Spano, L.D., Cisternino, A., Paternò F., A Compositional Model for Gesture Definition, *In Proc. of HCSE*, LNCS, 7623, pp. 34-52, Springer, (2012)
21. Spano, L.D., Developing Touchless Interfaces with GestIT, *In Proc. of AMI 2012*, LNCS, 7683, pp. 433-438, Springer (2012).

Designing Disambiguation Techniques for Pointing in the Physical World

William Delamare, Céline Coutrix and Laurence Nigay
CNRS, Joseph Fourier University UJF-Grenoble 1
Grenoble Informatics Laboratory (LIG), UMR 5217, Grenoble, F-38041, France
{William.Delamare, Celine.Coutrix, Laurence.Nigay}@imag.fr

ABSTRACT

Several ways for selecting physical objects exist, including touching and pointing at them. Allowing the user to interact at a distance by pointing at physical objects can be challenging when the environment contains a large number of interactive physical objects, possibly occluded by other everyday items. Previous pointing techniques highlighted the need for disambiguation techniques. Addressing this challenge, this paper contributes a design space that organizes along groups and axes a set of options for designers to relevantly (1) describe, (2) classify, and (3) design disambiguation techniques. First, we have not found techniques in the literature yet that our design space could not describe. Second, all the techniques show a different path along the axes of our design space. Third, it allows defining of several new paths/solutions that have not yet been explored. We illustrate this generative power with the example of such a designed technique, Physical Pointing Roll (P2Roll).

Author Keywords

Physical Interaction; Interactive Physical Objects; Design Space; Selection Techniques.

ACM Classification Keywords

D.2.2. Software Engineering: Design Tools and Techniques - User interfaces. H.5.2. Information interfaces and presentation (e.g., HCI): User Interfaces - Theory and methods, User-centered design.

General Terms

Design; Human Factors.

INTRODUCTION

Ambient Intelligence involves a wide variety of smart objects. For instance, in a domestic context, there is a large range of physical objects that are digitally augmented: TV, light sources, coffee machine, washing machine, etc. These objects are not necessarily within reach of users in everyday situations. Thus, pointing techniques for distal selection of physical objects are important.

However, selecting a physical object by pointing raises several problems that are related to the objects' sizes, their density in the physical environment and the occlusion of the targeted object by other items. For defining an efficient pointing technique, designers can draw their inspiration from studies of the Graphical User Interfaces (GUI) and Virtual Environments (VEs) communities, two communities that extensively studied the pointing task. However, the physical environment defines additional constraints: (1) exocentric techniques [16] that modify the user's point of view or techniques that modify the scene [7][9] are not possible, and (2) in the physical world, the system is not omniscient, whereas in virtual environments, the system creates the virtual world. As a consequence, designers cannot assume that the computer system has all the information about the physical surroundings [13].

Capturing these specificities induced by interaction in the physical environment, we present a design space for the disambiguation of the selection of physical objects by pointing at them. The design space adopts two points of view: the characteristics of the interaction techniques (*Interaction Group*) and the requirements for the disambiguation system to be developed (*Disambiguation System Group*). The identified axes in each group are useful for describing a significant range of existing techniques (descriptive power) as well as for helping designers to create new techniques for selecting physical objects (generative power).

In this paper, we first clarify the steps in a pointing task and highlight the disambiguation stage. After a review of related work, we present our design space. Its descriptive power is shown through concrete examples and its generative power through the design of a new disambiguation technique for the selection of a physical target.

POINTING TASK AND DISAMBIGUATION

When physical augmented objects are more than 1.1m away from the user, a distant interaction by pointing at physical objects is preferred [20, 24]. Nevertheless, pointing tasks in the physical world are difficult for two main reasons: accuracy and occlusion.

Previous studies have reported natural hand tremor and limited human precision as drawbacks for absolute pointing [8]. As a consequence, laser pointer interaction has been proven to be inaccurate, error prone and slow [14]. Jitters appear when trying to maintain a steady position, and drifts of the beam are produced when pressing or releasing a trigger button. Thus, a volume selection (i.e., a cone) can make the selection of physical objects easier by facilitating the aiming action [24] (see Figure 1).

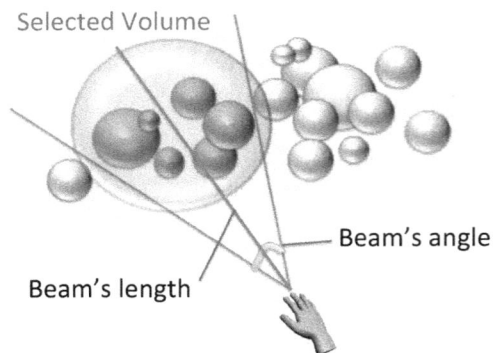

Figure 1: Volume selection: a rough aiming with a pointing gesture. A set of physical objects included in the volume selection (i.e. cone) are selected.

In addition to the accuracy problem, occlusion is another source of difficulty when multiple objects intersect the pointing direction [7].

For the two above cases, volume selection and occlusion, the pointing task requires a disambiguation process.

The finite state machine in Figure 2 models the implementation of a pointing task, including the disambiguation stage. In Figure 2, the initial state corresponds to the state where no physical object is selected. From this initial state, three paths are identified:

- *(t4)* describes a direct pointing, e.g., with an absolute laser pointing system [10, 15, 25, 26]. Direct pointing is possible and efficient for the selection of large physical objects (e.g., a TV) in a non-dense environment.

- *(t5.t6 = t5)* corresponds to an automatic disambiguation mechanism, i.e. performed by the system. The user does not perform any further action in order to reach the final state, that is, the state where a physical object is selected. This is the case for a disambiguation mechanism based on heuristics. Some heuristics rely only on characteristics at the moment of the trigger event (e.g., selecting an object within the selection cone) [17]. Some enhanced approaches define heuristics that are also based on characteristics before the trigger event, e.g., computing scores taking into account the object's size and distance from the selection cone as well as the velocity of the pointing gesture during the entire interaction [22].

- *(t1.t2*.t3)* describes an interactive disambiguation mechanism. Two strategies exist for interactively selecting an object among *n*:

○ *Navigation*: The user cycles through the previously selected set of targets *(t2*)* until reaching and selecting the desired one *(t3)*. For instance, after a pointing gesture in the physical world *(t1)*, the names of the selected objects can be displayed on a handheld device and the user scrolls the list *(t2*)* in order to select the targeted object *(t3)* [24].

○ *Designation*: The user performs another designation *(t3)* in the previously selected set of targets. For instance, the RFIG Lamps system [19] includes such a two-step technique. After a first pointing gesture *(t1)*, the RFIG Lamps system projects tags onto the selected physical objects. Then, the user selects with a laser the targeted object by pointing at its corresponding tag *(t3)*.

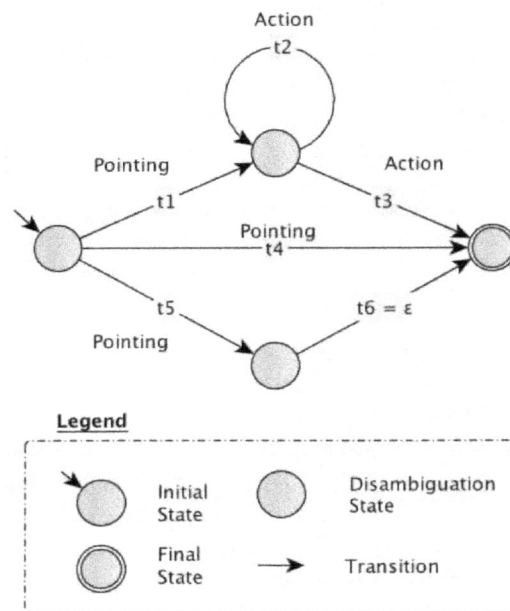

Figure 2: Starting by pointing in the physical world, three paths for the selection of a physical object. (t1t2*t3): pointing gesture followed by an interactive disambiguation process. (t4): single pointing gesture for selecting an object. (t5t6): pointing gesture enhanced by an heuristic method for automatic disambiguation.

Since directly pointing at a physical object *(t4)* reaches its limits when many physical objects can be selected in a dense environment, the selection techniques of a physical object imply a disambiguation stage. An automatic disambiguation stage based on heuristics *(t5.t6)* may lead to the selection of a wrong physical object [7, 17]. Therefore in this paper we focus on techniques that include an initial coarse physical pointing gesture and then an interactive disambiguation stage *(t1.t2*.t3)*. We define a design space for such two-step techniques for selection of a physical object by focusing on the disambiguation stage.

As presented in the following section, a literature review highlights that only five two-step techniques for the selection of a physical object have been developed. Our design space is therefore an analytical tool to empower the designers of interactive techniques in the physical environment, by organizing the design options and by highlighting gaps and under-researched areas.

RELATED WORK

There are two areas of research that are directly relevant to the present paper: (1) the existing two-step selection techniques of a physical object, and (2) the design spaces and taxonomies for the disambiguation stage.

Interactive Disambiguation Techniques for Physical Object Selection

As stated above, only five two-step techniques for the selection of a physical object have been designed. They all include an interactive disambiguation stage after a first pointing gesture. Bold names indicate how we will refer to the corresponding techniques in the remainder of the paper.

GesturePen [23] is a technique using a volume selection metaphor. It is based on an Infrared (IR) beam that is 1.5m long and with a conical angle of 30° (Figure 1). Users can select an IR tag by directing the beam towards a tag. This technique illustrates the problem of volume selection techniques: by easing the pointing task, GesturePen implies unwanted multiple selections. Indeed, GesturePen led to mistakenly selected tags neighboring the targeted object. Nevertheless the limited range of the technique was designed in order to minimize errors due to a too large beam span, but users felt uncomfortable when they had to walk close to the tag. To overcome these difficulties, the authors proposed a disambiguation technique: a dial on the pointing device in order to adjust the beam's length and/or the beam's angle.

Another technique with a similar disambiguation mechanism is **PICOntrol** [21]. With this technique, the user points at a physical object with a visible light projection that activates light sensors attached to physical objects. If several objects are located within the light projection, an envisioned solution is to reduce the projection size.

The Radio Frequency Identity and Geometry Lamps system (**RFIG Lamps**) is a one-handed device that includes a laser, a radio frequency identification (RFID) reader, buttons and a projector [19]. Physical objects are equipped with RFID tags. While the handheld RFID reader scans an area, the system automatically computes the locations of the tags and projects a stabilized interactive graphical presentation of the tags. A user can then more easily disambiguate the selection by pointing with a laser at the projected tags.

While the three above techniques keep the user's actions in the physical world during the disambiguation stage, the two following techniques include a disambiguation stage disconnected from the physical world.

A first solution is to display a list of selected objects on a handheld device [24]. After a coarse pointing gesture in the physical world, if several objects are located within the beam, a **List** of the selected objects' names are displayed on screen and the user selects the targeted object based on its name.

Freeze-Set-Go (**FSG**) proposes an Augmented Reality (AR) technique on a smartphone [11]. The user first places the device so that 2D markers attached to physical targets are visible on the screen through a real-time see-through video. Since several markers can appear on the screen, a touch gesture on the screen is needed for the disambiguation of the selection. In order to ease this disambiguation, FSG provides a custom button that allows users to freeze the video. The real-time see-through video is resumed when the button is pressed again.

With respect to the above five techniques, the authors highlight the need for efficient and usable disambiguation techniques, motivating the need for a design space. We now present the related existing design dimensions.

Design dimensions for Disambiguation Techniques involving 3D Targets in Virtual and Physical worlds

Design dimensions for disambiguation have been studied only for the case of virtual environments. Amongst these studies, the design space [9] for disambiguation mechanisms (selection by progressive refinement) introduces three dimensions:

- The *disambiguation criteria*, characterizing if the disambiguation is *spatial* (e.g., choosing an object based on its location in the scene), *by object attributes* (e.g., choosing red and/or large objects), or *out-of-context* (e.g., choosing objects from a menu).

- The *display* of the selected objects, that can be *in context* (e.g., by freezing the viewpoint as in **FSG** or by relocating targets in order to ease selection) or *out-of-context* (e.g., by using a menu as in **List**). This axis is related to the perceptual continuity criterion as described for Augmented Reality [5].

- The type, characterizing if the disambiguation is:

  o *Discrete*, e.g., if the disambiguation is done through several steps (e.g., *(t1.t2*.t3)* in Figure 2);

  o *Continuous*, e.g., the disambiguation is done through a continuous process implying one continuous action (e.g. *(t5.t6 = t5)* in Figure 2).

A similar axis is found in [7] for describing disambiguation techniques for the case of volumetric displays: the *concurrent/sequential* axis. A *concurrent* (or continuous) disambiguation mechanism means that both pointing and disambiguation tasks are performed at the same time. For instance, with the Depth Ray [7], users control the ray direction and a depth marker along the ray at the same time. Contrastingly, a *sequential* (or discrete) disambiguation mechanism needs a temporal separation between the pointing and the disambiguation tasks. For instance, with the Lock Ray [7], users control the ray direction before locking it so as to then control only the depth marker that appears on the ray.

These design spaces for virtual environments define relevant design dimensions that only partially contribute to our study, i.e. to *disambiguation* techniques for *physical* environments. Nevertheless they lay a foundation for characterizing the design and engineering of the interactive disambiguation stage in the selection of physical targets.

DESIGN SPACE

Our design space is made of 10 axes that are organized according to two groups, *Interaction* and *Disambiguation System*, as shown in Figure 4. The *Interaction Group* characterizes the interaction techniques for the disambiguation stage when selecting physical objects by pointing in the physical world. The *Disambiguation System Group* adopts an engineering point of view by identifying the implications of the *Interaction Group* for the disambiguation system. We first explain the axes of the *Interaction* and *Disambiguation System* groups before concluding on the links between them.

Interaction Group

From an interaction point of view, the designer can operate on two features of the disambiguation mechanism: the display of the targets (i.e. the display space) and the control from the user (i.e. the control space) [2].

Display Space

For the disambiguation phase, the user can (a) focus on the physical targets, or (b) switch her/his focus to a virtual representation (both ends of axis 1 in Figure 4). Between both ends, modifications of the display space can occur in a mixed manner, augmenting the physical target with an additional virtual representation.

Towards the virtual end, augmenting or replacing the physical targets can make the selection easier if selecting the *physical* target is too difficult due to its size, distance or density of objects. For instance, the disambiguation stage of the **RFIG Lamps** system proposes to project a disc onto physical targets for pointing refinement. Indeed the bigger size of the projections as compared to the original tags facilitates the pointing task.

The augmented or virtual representation can be spatially decoupled from the primary physical targets (e.g., the **List** technique, that displays a list of objects' names on a handheld device). However, such a solution divides the users' attention between the physical environment and the virtual representation and creates an additional cost for changing the focus of attention (perceptual discontinuity as described in [5]). To overcome this limitation, the augmented or virtual representation can maintain a spatial link with the physical target (e.g., the **RFIG Lamps** system and an augmented reality technique using the magic lens metaphor such as **FSG**).

For the designer, another way to avoid changes of attention focus between the physical and virtual worlds is to propose a solution towards the physical end of the axis, and allow the user to operate directly in the physical world.

Towards the physical end of the axis, designers will be able in the future to physically modify the display space. For instance, a system such as ZeroN allows actual movements of physical objects in 3D space [12], e.g., to rearrange the targets so that they are easier to point at. Alternatively, Jamming User Interfaces can increase the size of physical objects in order to facilitate the pointing task, while keeping the focus on the bigger primary physical target [6].

Control Space

Designers can help the disambiguation of preselected physical objects by modifying the control, i.e. the actions of the user and the interpretation of these actions by the system. The design approach is to modify the control space assuming that the display space (i.e. physical world) is not modifiable.

To do so, designers can decouple the control from the physical targets by modifying the reference frame (Figure 4, axis 2). Although initially introduced for describing physical pointing gesture [4], the Reference Frame of spatial input can be relevantly applied to disambiguation techniques. The Control Space axis characterizes how the absolute mapping of the pointing step has been transformed for the disambiguation step.

First, if the action of the user is directed to the physical objects, the reference frame is *absolute*. In this case, a disambiguation technique should be based on a Display Space modification (axis 1) in order to ease the pointing task.

Second, if the actions of the user are performed around a user's body part, the reference frame is *relative to the user's body*. The physical objects are abstracted and reorganized according to an origin defined by a body part. For instance the physical objects can be reorganized vertically from the hips to the head. In this example, the user selects a target by moving her/his arm along her/his trunk. The control space hence defines an input space that the user has to mentally map onto the physical world.

Third, if the actions of the user are performed according to the position of a device as a reference point, the reference frame is *relative to the device*. The physical objects are abstracted and reorganized with a neutral position of the device as origin. For instance the physical objects can be reorganized in a clock-manner disposition according to a neutral position of the device. In this example, the user selects a target by rotating the device. Again, the control space defines an input space that the user has to map onto the physical world.

The Control Space axis does not aim to describe in detail all the actions performed by the user: depending on the chosen disambiguation input (e.g., tangible, gesture, gaze, voice command, etc.), previous existing design spaces can further describe specific design characteristics that are not specifically related to disambiguation. Indeed it is an important attribute of our design space that it allows capitalizing on existing design spaces and that it facilitates interconnection between existing approaches.

Disambiguation System Group

We first refine the Extent of World Knowledge [13] of Figure 3. It was introduced by Milgram to characterize how much the system knows about the physical environment. This design dimension defines a continuum from a *world completely un-modeled* to a *world completely modeled*. Between these two extremes is a world partially modeled with *where* and/or *what* data, i.e. localization and identification data. A system knowing only *where* data about an object of interest could precisely place a graphical superimposition onto the physical object. Contrastingly, a system knowing only *what* data could precisely define the augmentation of the physical object, but without correct location, scale or orientation.

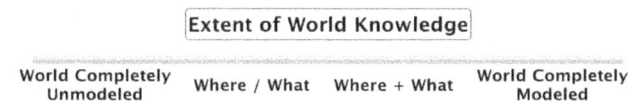

Extent of World Knowledge			
World Completely Unmodeled	Where / What	Where + What	World Completely Modeled

Figure 3: Extent of World Knowledge dimension from [13].

We first define two other types of knowledge, dynamic and static, then refines the *what* and *where* subgroups in our design space.

Knowledge Computation: Static vs. Dynamic

As represented by axes 3 and 8 of Figure 4, we distinguish two kinds of knowledge: the one produced during a setup step and the one produced at runtime. For instance **FSG** needs a registration process of 2D markers. This is an imperative step for further video analysis in order for the system to know what the user is selecting with a tap on the video. Contrastingly, the **RFIG Lamps** system first receives dynamic spatial knowledge for the first pointing step using RFID tags and then the spatial locations of the tags for the disambiguation step using light sensors and encoded projections.

On the one hand, knowledge defined during a setup process will constrain the user to configure and maintain the system, e.g., naming or locating objects and additionally updating the information if the user moves, adds or removes physical objects. On the other hand, knowledge computed at runtime is more flexible but less robust. For example, the **RFIG Lamps** system may know the spatial coordinates of pointed objects by projecting grey codes on light sensors attached to objects. However, these sensors might be visually occluded from the projector's viewpoint, whereas the user can actually see the physical objects (the user's viewpoint being different from the projector's viewpoint).

The *What* and *Where* axes can have different kinds of *knowledge computation*, considering each axis one by one. However, a promising design option is the *dynamic* computation of knowledge, avoiding a setup process from the user. Thus, the *what* and *where* axes are globally qualified to be *static* if at least one of the axes is *statically* computed by the system. Consequently the *what* and *where* corresponding axes (3 and 8 of Figure 4) are qualified to be dynamic if all the information is dynamically computed at runtime.

"What" Subgroup

If the designer chooses to provide a *virtual representation* as a Display Space (axis 1 of Figure 4), then *What* information can enhance the cognitive continuity between the physical object and its representation [5]. The continuity at the cognitive level refers to the user's interpretation of the virtual representation. This interpretation is influenced by the *What* information.

The disambiguation system may know different types of information about the interactive augmented physical objects:

(1) *Identity* of the object (axis 4 of Figure 4) that would allow the disambiguation system to present a label "bedside lamp" instead of "object 1" to the user for example.

(2) *Functionalities* of the object (axis 5 of Figure 4) that would allow the disambiguation system to present another information to the user. For instance, if the user is aiming at two light sources but intends to select the one that can turn blue.

(3) *Appearance information* (axis 6 of Figure 4) such as the aspect of the physical object including its form, its color, its texture. Thus, the disambiguation system could reduce the cognitive discontinuity by representing the target with its actual picture for example.

(4) *State information* about the physical object (axis 7 of Figure 4), including its current power consumption, its on/off state, its dimming level. For instance, if the user is aiming at two light sources – one turned on and another turned off – and intends to select the one that is

turned on: the states of the objects are therefore a key characteristic during this disambiguation step.

Each axis can have several levels of knowledge: for instance *Appearance* includes the object's form, its color (either red-green-blue values or grey levels...), etc. However, in order to avoid too fine-grained descriptions that might be difficult to compare, we only consider two discrete values, namely yes/no, along the four axes [*Identity*, *Functionalities*, *Appearance* and *State*] of Figure 4. This representation allows a clear and simple visualization of *What* knowledge systems have, and is sufficient to compare existing techniques.

"Where" Subgroup
As in Milgram's initial axis, the system may have no spatial information about the physical surroundings (i.e., value none in the *Where Subgroup* of Figure 4). If the system maintains spatial information about the physical surroundings (statically or dynamically) we refine the Extent of World Knowledge axis [13] by defining two new axes:

(1) *Relative vs. Absolute* (axis 9 of Figure 4): In a *relative* situation, the system knows how objects are localized compared with each other (e.g., a target is below another). For example, the system could use a simplified map of the physical world (static knowledge) that only contains left/right relationships between objects. The *relative* situation is well adapted to the *navigation* strategy, when the user has to incrementally navigate through preselected objects, from an object to its neighbor. In an *absolute* situation, the system has absolute spatial coordinates in a common reference frame. For example, the **RFIG Lamps** system determine their spatial coordinates (x,y) in the video. The absolute situation is well adapted to the *designation* strategy, when the user has to directly designate the desired physical target amongst the preselected physical objects.

(2) *Of the world vs. Of a subpart* (axis 10 of Figure 4): In a *World* situation, the system knows spatial information about all the interactive physical objects. For example, a disambiguation technique using an OptiTrack[1] system, composed of IR tracking video cameras, would allow the system to dynamically know where all the interactive objects are (since they are augmented with reflexive markers). In a *Subpart* situation, the system knows only spatial information about a subset of objects. For example, the **RFIG Lamps** system uses dynamically computed spatial coordinates of the preselected objects only.

---

[1] http://www.naturalpoint.com/optitrack/

Links Between the Interaction and Disambiguation System Groups
While describing the 10 axes of our design space, we highlighted the links between the *Interaction Group* and the *Disambiguation System Group*. Indeed, interaction design choices will have an impact on the system to be developed and in particular on the knowledge that the system needs to maintain about the physical objects. But the design space clearly separates the two sets of axes, one set focusing on *interaction* characteristics and one set dedicated to the corresponding *disambiguation system* requirements. Furthermore the *disambiguation system* requirements will in turn have an impact on the technologies to be used for developing the whole system.

Moreover, it is worth noticing that the physical world knowledge may be a constraint for the user. Naming objects, or updating spatial coordinates may be a burden for the users. On the contrary, providing an autonomous system (i.e. value *dynamic* along the axes 3 and 8 of Figure 4 *Knowledge Computation*) might imply a heavy infrastructure and/or might be expensive or simply not feasible for real-world deployment.

Figure 4 illustrates how to use the design space. In order to be able to compare techniques based on the design space, we assume that a proper and complete description of each technique is available. A disambiguation technique for the selection of a physical object defines a path in this multidimensional space. The 10 axes of the design space enable us to precisely define an existing technique by a path in the design space or to design a new one by exploring an unexplored area of the design space. The number of design possibilities defined by the 10 axes is huge (2673 possible paths). In light of our design space, techniques are said to be similar if they have the same characteristics (i.e., the same path) and different if they have at least one difference on one axis. We do not provide any measure yet since we are not able to quantify the importance of the axes. Evaluation of the impact of the axes on usability is future work. The following section describes the existing techniques as paths in the design space (i.e., the descriptive power of our design space), while the next section presents a new technique for which the design is based on the 10 axes (i.e., the generative power of our design space).

DESCRIPTIVE POWER OF THE DESIGN SPACE
Both **PICOntrol** and **GesturePen** propose the same disambiguation mechanism: adjusting the selection volume. Thus, the display space is in the *physical* world, with an *absolute* reference frame since the interaction is the same as the one used for the pointing step, but with a different volume of selection. **GesturePen** proposes to *dynamically* get knowledge of the identity of selected objects using custom tags with an IR transceiver. **PICOntrol** does not have any knowledge about the spatial physical environment. The system uses light sensors attached to

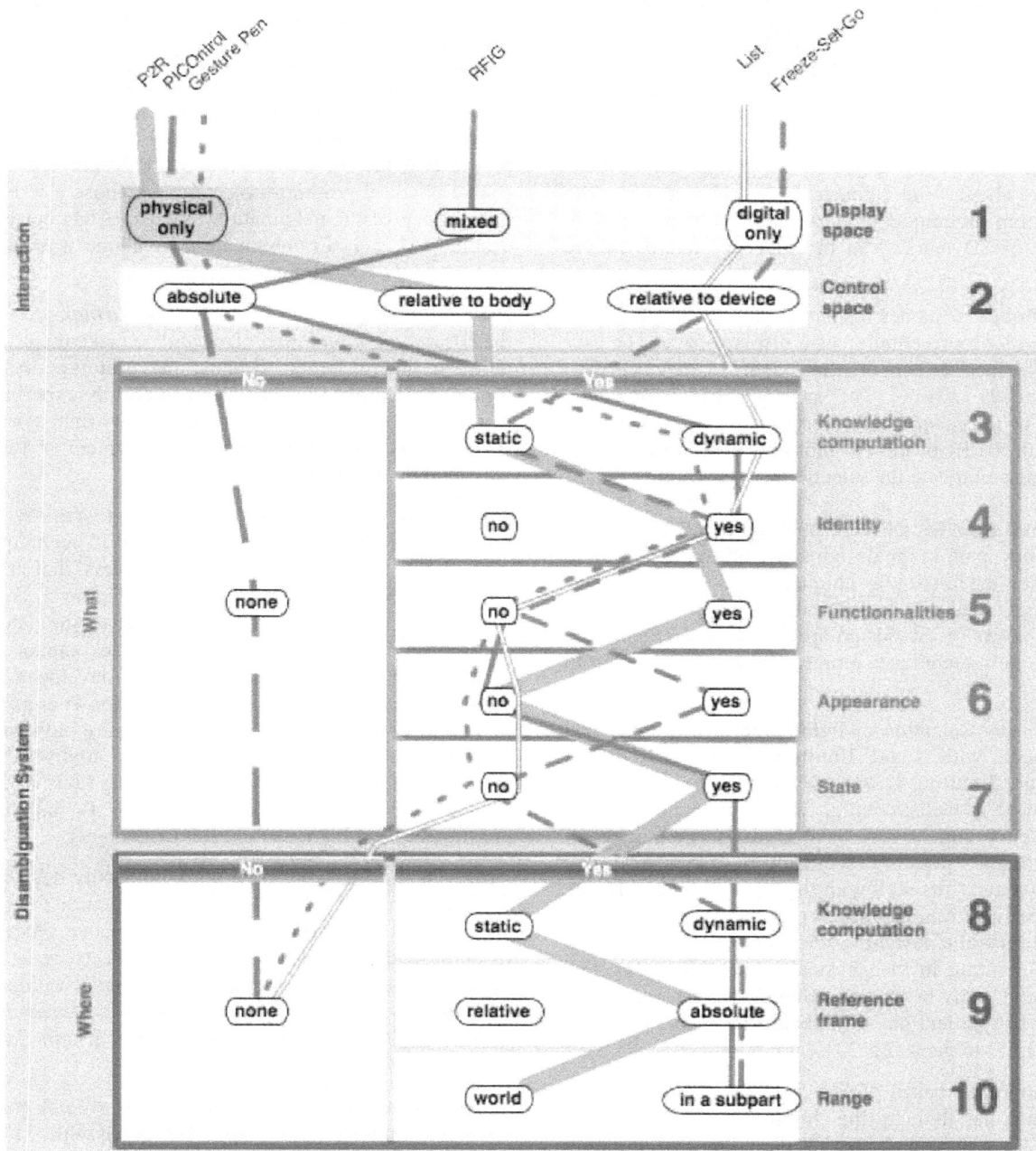

Figure 4: Design Space with 10 axes organized according to two groups: Interaction and Disambiguation System. Classification of existing disambiguation techniques (thin lines). A technique (P2Roll) designed by drawing a new line (under-researched area) in the design space (thick line).

objects in order to directly control the objects, and thus does not need any knowledge about them.

The **RFIG Lamps** system provides a *mixed* display space for the disambiguation step (digital objects projected onto physical ones). The reference frame is *absolute* since the user has to aim these projections with a laser. The system receives *dynamic* knowledge (RFID tags for *what*

information and encoded projection for *where* information) that provides *identity* and *state* information (for the warehouse scenario) and *absolute* tags' locations in the current pointed area – *subpart* of the world.

FSG provides a *virtual* display space for the disambiguation step, i.e. after pressing the button that creates a frozen image of the video, breaking the link with the physical world. The touching gesture for selecting the target is in a reference frame *relative to the device* since the user has to interact with the screen. In order to map the touch input and the content of the image, the system has *static* knowledge of 2D markers, using video-analysis techniques based on the *appearance* of the objects (markers, linked with objects' *identity*). This *What* knowledge about the physical world allows the disambiguation technique to *dynamically* obtain *absolute* coordinates of 2D markers in the video – *subpart* of the world.

The **List** of objects' names displayed on a handheld device defines a *virtual* representation as a display space. The user interacts on the screen of the handheld device, thus *relatively to the device*. The system receives *dynamic* knowledge of the *identity* of objects that are pointed at by the user with the IR beam. No more information is needed in order to disambiguate the selection.

GENERATIVE POWER OF THE DESIGN SPACE

Defining a new path in the design space allows designers to produce a new interaction technique. Based on the 10 axes, many design choices are possible. To illustrate this generative power of the design space, we now explain the design of a new technique, represented by a thick line in Figure 4.

We focus on the selection of light sources in the physical world. Indeed with Light Emitting Diode (LED) and Organic Light Emitting Diode (OLED) technologies, light sources will be in walls, ceiling, floors, furniture or fabric, so that the environment may have a very large number of interactive lights, possibly occluded by other everyday items. This context fits well with the topic addressed by the design space since it brings several problems that designers should address while designing selection techniques of light sources by pointing in the physical world. Moreover, this example could easily be transposed to other contexts since a classic way to augment physical objects for visual feedback is to attach LED to them [21, 23].

A design approach based on the generative power of our design space has led to the following disambiguation technique: a navigation strategy called Physical Pointing Roll (P2Roll). The user first performs a pointing gesture towards the light sources. This defines an initial coarse physical pointing phase. The user then has to precisely select the targeted light source from within the set of selected light sources. To do so, the user navigates through the preselected light sources using a roll gesture of the wrist, as illustrated in Figure 5.

First we made the design choice to keep the focus of the user in the physical world (value *Physical* on axis 1 of Figure 4) so that the user can directly observe LED lights, and more importantly the effect on the ambient lighting.

Concerning the control space, the wrist rolling input covers an unexplored area, with the reference frame having the value *Relative to Body* along the axis 2 of Figure 4. We had to choose an adequate body part as the origin of the reference frame. Since the arm is already used for the rough pointing gesture, we decided to apply the physiologic chain of the arm [1, 3]: Shoulder and elbow are used for the coarse physical pointing task, thus we chose a wrist input. Since the pronation/supination axis (roll) has been proven usable [18], our disambiguation technique is based on a *relative to the wrist* transformation.

Having defined the P2Roll *Interaction Group*, we focus on the *Disambiguation System Group*. We make the distinction between two different systems: the prototype system of Figure 5 that we developed in order to experimentally evaluate the interaction technique and the final system that we will develop for real-world deployment if P2Roll is validated by the in-lab experiments.

Our current lab equipment allowed us to rapidly build a prototype in order to evaluate the P2Roll technique. We used the OptiTrack[2] with six IR cameras that track the instrumented user's hand as shown in Figure 5. Since our LED objects are very close to each other to simulate a very dense physical environment, the OptiTrack cannot be used for tracking LED objects. Thus, the developed system maintains a *static* (axes 3 and 8 of Figure 4) and *absolute* (axis 9 of Figure 4) knowledge of the entire physical *world* (i.e., the LED objects). Since LEDs are controlled by the system itself, the system keeps the *identity* (axis 4 of Figure 4), the *functionalities* (axis 5 of Figure 4), and the *state* on/off (axis 7 of Figure 4) of each LED object.

However, this lab configuration is not easily deployable in the real world: it has a heavy infrastructure for tracking purpose and a significant setup/maintenance process in a dynamic context in which objects can be moved. Thus, if the interaction technique is experimentally validated, we will design another system solution (*Disambiguation System Group*) for the engineering of the designed disambiguation technique.

As part of a collaborative project with a hotel chain, the final setting is a hotel room, designed with LED light sources in walls and furniture. For this particular real-world context, we can assume that the system can have a *static what* and *where* knowledge, the hotel rooms having the same fixed furniture and light sources. However, the key design issue related to the *Disambiguation System Group* is the tracking solution for the pointing and rolling gestures that compose P2Roll. Several design issues based on the axes of our design space are possible, we describe two technological design options: (1) RFID tags hidden in the physical environment for the pointing step that allow the system to *dynamically* receive objects' identities, and then

---

[2] http://www.naturalpoint.com/optitrack/

204

(a)   (b)   (c)   (d)

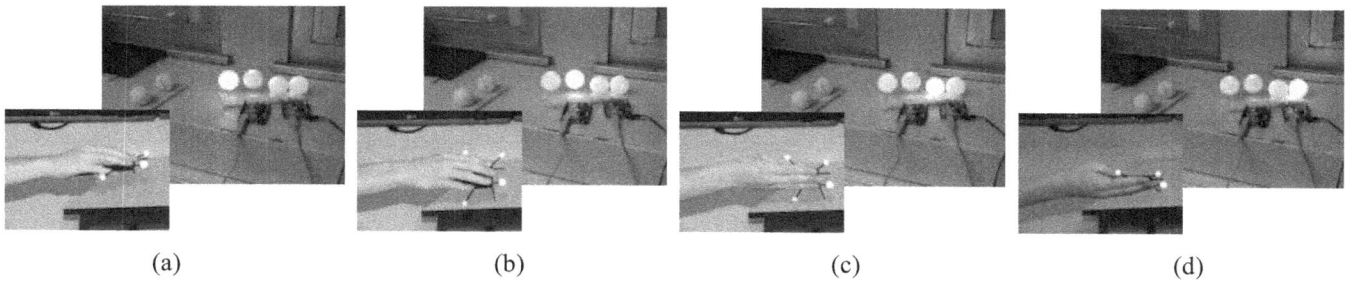

Figure 5: A pointing gesture turns on the lights of the current selected volume at medium brightness (a), and a rolling gesture (b, c, d) changes the current selected object (at maximum brightness) to the next one.

obtain *static* knowledge (e.g., a list of objects ordered from right to left and defined during the setup) for *relative* spatial information amongst the set of preselected objects. (2) Finding a way to communicate with LEDs by switching them on and off at high frequencies not perceived by users but only by the system with a high-frequency video camera. This could lead to *dynamic relative* spatial knowledge of preselected objects (i.e. *subpart* of the world).

CONCLUSION

This paper has introduced and described a design space for pointing in the real world focusing on disambiguation. This novel conception of the design space is intended to support design and research in the field of physical interaction. In contrast to a technology-centered design approach, the design space has introduced a new way of thinking of interaction design for the selection of physical objects in terms of interaction characteristics and their implications for the system.

A first contribution of the paper has been to demonstrate the descriptive power of the design space by precisely classifying existing techniques. This is ongoing work since new techniques are continuously defined. Till now this was successful because the existing techniques show different paths in the taxonomy and we have not found techniques in the literature yet that our design space left out. Moreover the design space capitalizes from existing design spaces of different domains. In particular for characterizing interaction, the design space refines the two main approaches (based on the display and control spaces) that are studied for enhancing pointing tasks in GUI [2] ; and for characterizing the system, it extends existing taxonomies dedicated to Augmented Reality [13]. This contributes to demonstrating the soundness of the underlying concepts of our design space.

A second contribution of the paper has been to demonstrate the generative power of the proposed design space: it allows defining of several new paths/solutions in the taxonomy that have not yet been explored. Although we presented here only one example of such a designed technique, namely the Physical Pointing Roll (P2Roll) technique, this is another form of validation of our design space. The P2Roll technique corresponds to an under-researched area of the design space.

As ongoing work, we are focusing on the design and the evaluation of other techniques in order to measure the benefits of the values along the axes of the design space. In particular we are currently designing techniques for selecting LED light sources, which will be deployed in a hotel room as part of a collaborative project involving a hotel chain. This will allow further testing of the design space.

ACKNOWLEDGMENTS

This work has been supported by the DELight project (French government's FUI -Single Inter-Ministry Fund-program, certified by the cluster Minalogic). The project is dedicated to the study of a new lighting system for Solid State Lighting (SSL) applications and is led by Schneider Electric.

REFERENCES

1. Balakrishnan, R. and MacKenzie, I.S. Performance differences in the fingers, wrist, and forearm in computer input control. In *Proc. CHI 1997*, ACM Press (1997), 303–310.

2. Balakrishnan, R. "Beating" Fitts' law: virtual enhancements for pointing facilitation. *International Journal of Human-Computer Studies 61*, 6 (2004), 857–874.

3. Card, S.K., Mackinlay, J.D., and Robertson, G.G. A morphological analysis of the design space of input devices. *ACM Transactions on Information Systems 9*, 2 (1991), 99–122.

4. Cockburn, A., Quinn, P., Gutwin, C., Ramos, G., and Looser, J. Air pointing: Design and evaluation of spatial target acquisition with and without visual feedback. *International Journal of Human-Computer Studies 69*, 6 (2011), 401–414.

5. Dubois, E., Nigay, L., and Troccaz, J. Assessing continuity and compatibility in augmented reality systems. *Universal Access in the Information Society 1*, 4 (2002), 263–273.

6. Follmer, S., Leithinger, D., Olwal, A., Cheng, N., and Ishii, H. Jamming User Interfaces: Programmable Particle Stiffness and Sensing for Malleable and Shape-

Changing Devices. In *Proc. UIST 2012*, ACM Press (2012), 519–528.

7. Grossman, T. and Balakrishnan, R. The design and evaluation of selection techniques for 3D volumetric displays. In *Proc. UIST 2006*, ACM Press (2006), 3–12.

8. König, W., Gerken, J., Dierdorf, S., and Reiterer, H. Adaptive Pointing–Design and Evaluation of a Precision Enhancing Technique for Absolute Pointing Devices. In Proc. *INTERACT 2009*, 658-671.

9. Kopper, R., Bacim, F., and Bowman, D.A. Rapid and accurate 3D selection by progressive refinement. *In Proc. 3DUI 2011*, IEEE Computer Society (2011), 67–74.

10. De la O Chávez, F., Fernández de Vega, F., Olague, G., and Llano Montero, J. An independent and non-intrusive laser pointer environment control device system. In *Proc. ICPS 2008*, ACM Press (2008), 37–46.

11. Lee, G.A., Yang, U., Kim, Y., et al. Freeze-Set-Go interaction method for handheld mobile augmented reality environments. In *Proc. VRST 2009*, ACM Press (2009), 143–146.

12. Lee, J., Post, R., and Ishii, H. ZeroN: Mid-Air Tangible Interaction Enabled by Computer Controlled Magnetic Levitation. In *Proc. UIST 2011*, ACM Press (2011), 327–336.

13. Milgram, P. and Kishino, F. A taxonomy of mixed reality visual displays. *IEICE Transactions on Information and Systems E series D 77*, 12 (1994), 1321–1321.

14. Myers, B.A., Bhatnagar, R., Nichols, J., et al. Interacting at a distance: measuring the performance of laser pointers and other devices. In *Proc. CHI 2002*, ACM Press (2002), 33–40.

15. Patel, S. and Abowd, G. A 2-way laser-assisted selection scheme for handhelds in a physical environment. In Proc. *UbiComp 2003*, Springer (2003), 200–207.

16. Poupyrev, I. and Ichikawa, T. Manipulating objects in virtual worlds: categorization and empirical evaluation of interaction techniques. *Journal of Visual Languages & Computing 10*, 1 (1999), 19–35.

17. Rahman, A.S.M.M., Hossain, M.A., and Saddik, A.El. Spatial-geometric approach to physical mobile interaction based on accelerometer and IR sensory data fusion. *ACM Transactions on Multimedia Computing, Communications, and Applications 6*, 4 (2010), 1–23.

18. Rahman, M., Gustafson, S., Irani, P., and Subramanian, S. Tilt techniques: Investigating the Dexterity of Wrist-based Input. In *Proc. CHI 2009*, ACM Press (2009), 1943–1952.

19. Raskar, R., Beardsley, P., Van Baar, J., et al. RFIG Lamps: Interacting with a Self-DescribingWorld via Photosensing Wireless Tags and Projectors. *ACM Transactions on Graphics 23*, 3 (2004), 406–415.

20. Rukzio, E., Broll, G., Leichtenstern, K., and Schmidt, A. Mobile interaction with the real world: an evaluation and comparison of physical mobile interaction techniques. *Ambient Intelligence*. Springer Berlin Heidelberg, 2007, 1-18.

21. Schmidt, D., Molyneaux, D., and Cao, X. PICOntrol: using a handheld projector for direct control of physical devices through visible light. In *Proc. UIST 2012*, ACM Press (2012), 379–388.

22. Steed, A. Towards a General Model for Selection in Virtual Environments. In *Proc. 3DUI 2006*, IEEE Symposium on (2006), 103–110.

23. Swindells, C., Inkpen, K.M., Dill, J.C., and Tory, M. That one there! Pointing to establish device identity. In *Proc. UIST 2002*, ACM Press (2002), 151–160.

24. Välkkynen, P., Niemelä, M., and Tuomisto, T. Evaluating touching and pointing with a mobile terminal for physical browsing. In *Proc. NordiCHI 2006*, ACM Press (2006), 28–37.

25. Wilson, A. and Pham, H. Pointing in intelligent environments with the worldcursor. In Proc. *INTERACT* 2003, 495-502.

26. Wilson, A. and Shafer, S. XWand: UI for Intelligent Spaces. In *Proc. CHI 2003*, ACM Press (2003), 545–552.

Formal Description of Multi-Touch Interactions

Arnaud Hamon[1,2], Philippe Palanque[2], José Luís Silva[2], Yannick Deleris[1], Eric Barboni[2]
[1] AIRBUS Operations, 316 Route de Bayonne, 31060, Toulouse, France
[2] ICS-IRIT, University of Toulouse, 118 Route de Narbonne, F-31062, Toulouse, France
(hamon, palanque, silva, barboni)@ irit.fr, yannick.deleris@airbus.com

ABSTRACT

The widespread use of multi-touch devices and the large amount of research that has been carried out around them has made this technology mature in a very short amount of time. This makes it possible to consider multi-touch interactions in the context of safety critical systems. Indeed, beyond this technical aspect, multi-touch interactions present significant benefits such as input-output integration, reduction of physical space, sophisticated multi-modal interaction … However, interactive cockpits belonging to the class of safety critical systems, development processes and methods used in the mass market industry are not suitable as they usually focus on usability and user experience factors upstaging dependability. This paper presents a tool-supported model-based approach suitable for the development of interactive systems featuring multi-touch interactions techniques. We demonstrate the possibility to describe touch interaction techniques in a complete and unambiguous way and that the formal description technique is amenable to verification. The capabilities of the notation is demonstrated over two different interaction techniques (namely Pitch and Tap and Hold) together with a software architecture explaining how these interaction techniques can be embedded in an interactive application.

Author keywords

Tactile interactions, development process, model-based approaches, interactive cockpits

ACM Classification Keywords

D.2.2 [Software] Design Tools and Techniques - Computer-aided software engineering (CASE), H.5.2 [Information Interfaces and Presentation]: User Interfaces - Interaction styles.

INTRODUCTION

The industrial and academic world have been providing prototypes, toolkits and toy systems offering tactile and more recently multi-touch interaction techniques for more than two decades now. However, the actual engineering of multi-touch interactive systems remains a cumbersome task,

as it adds complexity to the design, specification, validation and implementation of interactive systems which is already a difficult task not addressed by current software engineering practice.

As model-based approaches already bring many advantages for the non-interactive part of a software system, it intuitively seems natural that extending these approaches can provide support for a more systematic development of interactive systems featuring multi-touch interactions.

While identifying requirements and user needs for user interfaces in the area of command and control for safety critical systems the designers have to decide either to go for systems with standard and (usually) poor interaction techniques or to embed new (and more sophisticated) interaction techniques. If the users' tasks are complex, requiring, for instance, the execution of multiple commands in a short period of time or the manipulation of large data sets, it is likely that the new interaction techniques will significantly improve the overall performance of the operators. However, in such cases, the development process will at the minimum be more difficult (resources consumption will increase throughout the design, development and evaluation stages) or even be impossible if tools and techniques available for the development do not bring the required level of quality in the final product. In the case of safety critical systems, quality is assessed by the dependability level of the interactive system which must be compliant with the requirements set by the certification authorities.

Beyond the fact that they have reached the adequate maturity level, multi-touch interaction techniques present a set of advantages as identified in [12]:

- The screen content can be completely modified in order to include input management previously devoted to hardware input devices such as keyboard or mouse
- They are by nature multimodal systems taking advantage of these interaction techniques These previous studies (and additional ones such as [14] and [37]) have been proposing and testing the use of multimodal interaction techniques in the field of safety critical systems have **identified and reported several advantages:**
  o Multimodality increases reliability of the interaction as it decreases critical error (between 36% and 50%) during interaction. This advantage alone can justify use of multimodality when interacting with a safety critical system.

o It increases the efficiency of the interaction, in particular in the field of spatial commands (multimodal interaction is 10% more rapid than classical interaction to specify geometric and localization information).

o Users predominantly prefer interacting in a multimodal way, probably because it allows more flexibility in interaction thus taking into account users' variability (especially if equivalence is provided).

o Multimodality allows increasing naturalness and flexibility of interaction so that learning period is shorter

- It is possible to embed a lot of detailed information within a single input such as pressure, orientation of the finger (using the shape of the fingertip) [29];

- They offer a very easy forum for multi-user interaction reducing articulatory coordination effort that is required if input devices are to be shared.

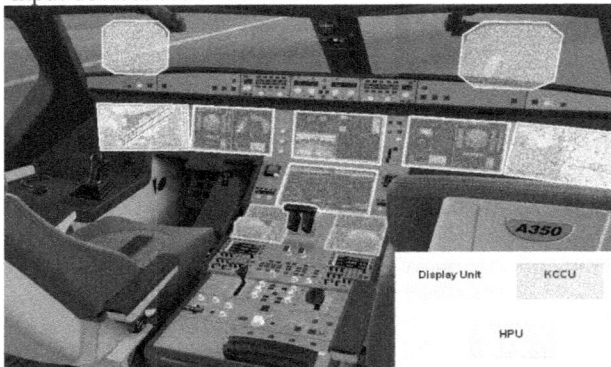

Figure 1 - High level representation of a cockpit

As visible on the Figure 1, the cockpit is made up of 6 large display units, 2 head-up displays and 2 Keyboard Cursor Control Units (an input device integrating a keyboard and a track ball). This paper is part of a study assessing the possible implementation of a map application currently available in the On Board Information System (IOS) with multi-touch interactions. This change of interaction technique (from a standard WIMP interaction as promoted by ARINC 661 specification [4]) to the Multi-Function Display (MFD) which is located in-between the captain and the first officer seats thus allowing collaborative tasks between the two pilots on this shared workspace. However, in order to deploy such interaction techniques in the cockpit of commercial aircraft, it is required to ensure that the dependability level of the cockpit is as reliable as the previous cockpits.

Next section presents and compares previous contributions in the field of multi-touch interactions with a special highlight on expressive power of the notations. The ability of the notation to provide verification techniques and to demonstrate properties on the interaction techniques is also exhibited. The following section presents a quick overview of the ICO formal description technique and highlights how

this description technique is able cover the needs that have been highlighted in related work section. A multi-levels approach is then presented which is able to transform low-level events produced by the multi-touch device into meaningful events such as *Pinch* or *Tap Long* to be received and handled by the interactive application. Section 4 briefly highlights how properties verification can be addressed. Last section identifies a research agenda for future work that still has to be carried before deploying multi-touch interaction in the cockpits of large civil aircrafts.

STATE OF THE ART

In the following paragraphs, we first detail the different conceptual decompositions of multi-touch interactions taking a linguistic point of view on multimodal interactions. Then we compare various notations that have been proposed to describe this interaction paradigm. As the main objective of this paper is to provide a notation for engineering dependable multi-touch interactions, we compare several software architectures that have been proposed for enabling the use of such interaction techniques. This related work analysis is then put into perspective using the more generic point of view of multimodality concepts.

Multi-touch interactions as a language

Linguistic point of view, such as semiotics (description of all phenomena associated with the production and interpretation of signs and symbols) are used in [25] to describe multi-touch gestures. However, this semiotics approach only encompasses some of the multi-touch features not addressing explicitly the production of higher-level events (such as double taps) from low-level events (touch, move, up). This is why, compared to [25], we are following a standard linguistic view based on lexicon, syntax and semantics for addressing multi-touch interactions. The lexicon is composed of the low level users' events while the syntax describes their combination (potentially fusion in the case of multimodal interactions). Regarding semantics (meaning of the interactions) and pragmatics (user mental model), the present work is based on the same definition exposed in [25]. This decomposition allows sorting our various contributions in this paper as follows:

- Lexicon: various event types - elementary vocabulary of the interaction;

- Syntax: combination of interaction models and fusion model;

- Semantic: the dynamic mapping between interaction technique and system command;

- Pragmatics is beyond the scope of the paper.

Notations for multi-touch interaction description

Description

Table 1 – is an extension of the work presented in [35] with additional properties (Analysis…) and references (CPN…).

It summarizes the expressiveness of the UIDL (User Interface Description Language) through ten different properties of the language that are used to characterize this expressiveness. This expressive power is not a goal per se but it clearly defines the type of user interface that can be described using the UIDL and the ones that are beyond their reach. This paper also adds multimodality and formal analysis features as the considered context relies on both usability and reliability aspects of multi-touch. The first three characteristics deal with description of objects and values in the language (this is named "Data Description"), with the description of states ("State Representation") and the description of events ("Event Representation"). For all characteristics, there are four possible values.

- **Yes** means that that characteristic is explicitly handled by the UIDL;
- **No** means that the characteristic is not explicitly handled;
- **Some** means that the property is partly present; and
- **Code** means that the characteristic is made explicit but only at the code level and is thus not a construct of the UIDL.

For instance, data is described in many UIDLs such as ICON [16], which allows modeling data emission and reception from an output port of a device of the model to the input port of another device. Some UIDLs can also represent states of the system, such as ICon [16], which represents the states with nodes in the models. Events are also sometimes explicitly represented as in Wizz'ed [18] where connections between bricks represent event flows.

Time is also an important characteristic for behavioral description of interactive applications.

Time

Qualitative time between two consecutive model elements aims at representing ordering of actions such as precedence, succession, and simultaneity. In OSU [27] a transition between two places represents the fact that the activity represented by the second place will only be active after the first one is achieved. **Quantitative** time between two consecutive model elements represents behavioral temporal evolutions related to a given amount of time (usually expressed in milliseconds). This is necessary for the modeling of the temporal windows in a fusion engine for multimodal interfaces, where events from several input devices are fused only if they are produced within a same time frame. In ICO (in this article), timed transitions express such constraints. Finally, quantitative time over nonconsecutive elements was introduced in [38] for multi-mice double and fusion double click interactions.

Concurrent behavior

Representation of concurrent behavior is necessary when the interactive systems feature multimodal interactions or can be used simultaneously by several users. This can be made explicit in the models like in data flow notations, as in ICon [16] or Whizz'Ed [18] and in all the notations based on Petri nets (last four columns of Table 1. Concurrency representation can also be found in older languages such as Squeak [13], where it is possible to represent parallel execution of processes. This aspect is critical for multi-touch interactions due to the concurrent use of multiple fingers and hands.

		Constraint		Code Based			Flow Based					State Based				Petri Nets			
		ConstraintJS [43]	Squeak [11]	XISL [24]	UsiXml [32]	GeForMT [23]	GWUIMS [39]	Tatsukawa [44]	Marigold [45]	Wizz'ed [16]	ICON [14]	Swinstate [3]	Hierarchical [9]	NiMMiT [13]	Proton++ [26]	Hinckley [20]	MIML [31]	ICO [this article]	CPN [21]
Data Description																			
State Representation																			
Event Representation																			
Time	Qualitative between two consecutive model elements																		
	Quantitative between two consecutive model elements																		
	Quantitative over non consecutive elements																		
Concurrent Behavior																			
Dynamic Instantiation	Widgets																		
	Input devices																		
	Reconfiguration of Interaction technique																		
	Reconfiguration of low level events																		
Multimodality: fusion of several modalities																			
Analysis																			
Dynamic finger clustering																			
Capability to deal with multi-touch interactions	Implicit																		
	Explicit																		

Legend: ■ Yes | ▨ Some | ▦ Code | □ No

Table 1 – UIDL expressiveness and handling of multi-touch interactions

Dynamic instantiation

Dynamic instantiation of interactive objects is a characteristic required for the description of interfaces where objects are not available at the creation of the interface as, for instance, in desktop-like interfaces where new icons are created according to user actions. Supporting explicit representation of dynamic instantiation requires the UIDL to be able to explicitly represent an unbounded number of states, as the newly created objects will by definition represent a new state for the system. Most of the time, this characteristic is handled by means of code and remains outside the UIDLs. Only Petri-nets-based UIDLs can represent explicitly such a characteristic, provided they handle high-level data structures, or objects, as is the case for many dialects [31], [8]; [23]. In the multi-touch context, new fingers are detected during at execution time. Thus, the description language must be able to receive dynamically created objects. In Petri nets this is particularly easy to represent by the creation/destruction of tokens associated to the objects. This way, for instance, for each finger currently touching the multi-touch surface, a corresponding token will be set in a place of the Petri net.

Dynamicity presented is handled at development time i.e. when the system is designed and built. However, dynamicity has also to be addressed at operation time i.e. when the system is currently in use. For instance, to cope with potential hardware failure reconfigurations of the interaction techniques might be required. In [36] we have presented how such dynamic reconfiguration can be modeled and executed. This corresponds to a meta-level representation of interactions which can be dynamically selected at run-time. This is an important aspect to address if multi-touch interactions have to be embedded in safety critical applications. Moreover, in order to ensure the availability of every system commands and maintain a high level of usability, the mapping between interaction techniques and commands (such as presented in a static way in [44]) shall be resolved during run-time.

Multimodality

This row refers to the capability of a language to support the fusion of several distinct modalities such as the combination of pen and multi-touch in [19]. Fusion engines have been a focal point of the research in the area of multimodal interactions and they are of prime importance as far as multi-touch interactions are concerned. A survey about the characteristic of fusion engines can be found in [32] and the requirements expressed there are directly applicable to multi-touch interaction.

Analysis

Analysis of the interaction techniques is a critical aspect in order to reduce time and resources spent on user studies and if reliability is considered an important property of the final system. Typically, analysis requires a formal description of the interactions and can be separated into three groups addressed by different types of analysis techniques:

- **validation**, accomplished by interactive simulation (step by step), invariant, structural and reachability/coverabiliy graph analysis;
- **verification**, accomplished by invariant, structural and reachability/coverabiliy graph analysis;
- **performance analysis,** accomplished by simulation.

The results of the analysis aim at detecting errors in the formal description, to validate the existence of required properties and to study the performance of the proposed interaction techniques.

As stated in Table 1 only few approaches for UIDL provide support analysis. Marigold [49] addresses limited validation and verification analysis based on reachability graph analysis. Verification analysis results are based on the verification of properties such as deadlock-free or liveness and the validation by a step by step interactive simulation of the model. By using time in the models (timed colored Petri nets) CPN Tools [23] provides performance analysis support.

Architectures to support multi-touch

Various software architectures for multi-touch applications have been proposed such as in [24] where a taxonomy describes them. Most interactive software architectures are layer-based [17] in order to enrich low level user events into high level events and then interactions techniques. To resolve the computational delays introduced by these architectures and allowing most immediate feedback which is needed by user during direct manipulation, [17] introduced a low-latency subsystem computing the fingers' trace to be immediately displayed. Most of these architectures address hardware/software integration. We argue that these technical solutions only provide local solutions to the issue of development of multi-touch interaction technique and the key point is to integrate them seamlessly with the description technique. This is the reason why, this paper proposes a more generic architecture model that enables all features listed in Table 1 and is based on the Arch model [7] represented on Figure 2.

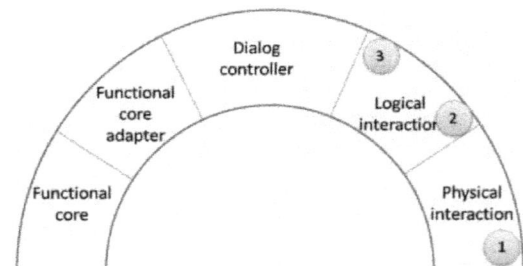

Figure 2 - Arch Model from [7]

Multi-touch as multi-modality: fusion engines

As stated above, multi-touch interaction techniques are by nature multimodal as their event stream meanings "can vary according to the context, task, user and time" [32]. In this paper we will address two of the important features of fusion engines from [32]: the temporal combinations of multiple events and error handling.

MODELLING MULTI-TOUCH INTERACTION TECHNIQUES WITH THE ICO FORMALISM

ICO: Informal definition

ICOs (Interactive Cooperatives Objects) are a formal description technique dedicated to the specification of interactive systems. It uses concepts borrowed from the object-oriented approach (dynamic instantiation, classification, encapsulation, inheritance, client/server relationship) to describe the structural or static aspects of systems, and uses high-level Petri nets [20] to describe their dynamics or behavior. The ICO notation is based on a behavioral description of the interactive system using the Cooperative objects formalism that describes how the object reacts to external stimuli according to its inner state. This behavior, called the Object Control Structure (ObCS) is described by means of Object Petri Net (OPN). An ObCS can have multiple places and transitions that are linked with arcs as with standard Petri nets. As an extension to these standard arcs, ICO allows using test arcs and inhibitor arcs. Each place has an initial marking (represented by one or several tokens in the place) describing the initial state of the system. As the paper mainly focuses on behavioral aspects, we do not describe them further (more can be found in [35].

It is important to note that ICOs have been used for other types of interfaces than multimodal ones. The notation is supported by a CASE tool called PetShop [9]. As it goes beyond the scope of this paper that focuses on the fusion engines aspects, more information about the tool structure and integration in a software development process is available in [40].

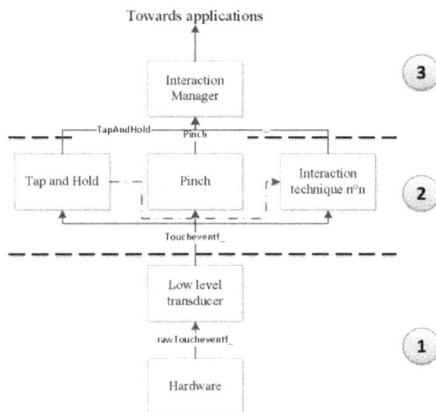

Figure 3 – Software architecture dedicated to the management of multi-touch events

Managing the event chain from hardware to application

From raw data events to object manipulation and system commands

As we demonstrated in the section introducing multi-touch architecture principles, the architecture we propose here (see Figure 3) can be directly mapped onto the ARCH architecture presented in Figure 2. The 3 circles in the ARCH model are thus explicitly represented on that architecture.

The first level corresponds to the low level transducer while the second one is composed by the various interaction technique models. Finally, the fusion engine model ensures consistency between the recognized events and is in charge of triggering these events to the dialog part for system command construction. In the following parts, we will use the following graphical hints to ease the reading of the models' descriptions: **places**, *events*, transitions. As there is a Java binding to ICOs and Petshop the detailed elements are given with respect to that binding. Each element of the architecture is presented in details together with its modeling using the ICO notation introduced above.

Low level transducer

The low level transducer is the one model linked to the hardware touch events. An excerpt of this model is presented Figure 4. It parses the features of the received event into a java finger object. The **FingerPool** place acts as a limiter on the allowed number of distinct fingers input. This transducer packages events, forwards them to models listners (i.e. higher level events handlers) such as TapAndHold, Pinch... as defined in [1]. Indeed, a "*toucheventf_move*" or "*toucheventf_up*" event will only be triggered if the event corresponds to a registered finger.

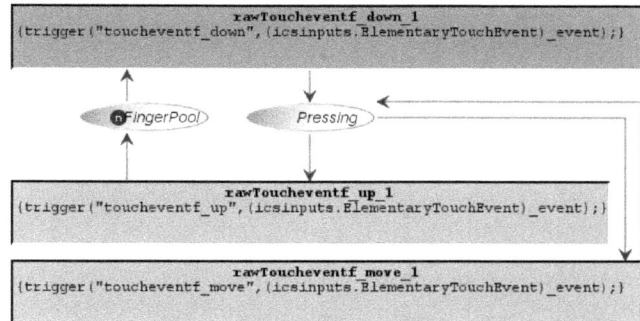

Figure 4 - Low Level event transducer

Interaction technique description

The following paragraph describes the model of the "standard" interaction technique called Pinch and presented in Figure 5. When the interaction transducer is in initial state, all places of the models are free of tokens. The model may receive the low level event "*toucheventf_down*" handled by the synchronized transition toucheventf_down_1. When this event occurs, a token is set in the place **p1**. This token comprises a finger object synthetizing the touch information encompassed by the low level event. Another token (empty this time) is added in the place **nbFingerModel** and enables to toucheventf_up_1 transition, allowing the model to handle "*toucheventf_up*" events. In this configuration, two low level events may be handled:

- "*toucheventf_down*": another "*toucheventf_down*" received event behaves the same way on the PetriNet. Then if two token are stored in the **p1** place, the eagerFusion transition is automatically crossed, grouping both fingers into the same token in place **p2**.

- "*toucheventf_up*": as long at the transducer contains information about at least one finger, the event handler toucheventf_up_1 is fireable. Each time such an event is received, a token containing the corresponding finger information is added to **temp** place, leading to two cases:
  - The "*toucheventf_up*" event corresponds to a finger stored in place **p1**: the transition endInteraction1 is fired, removing the finger's related token in **p1** and temp as well as one token from **nbFingerModel** place.
  - The "*toucheventf_up*" event corresponds to a finger stored in place **p2**: the transition endInteraction2 is fired, subtracting the finger's related token in **p2** and temp; and two tokens from **nbFingerModel** place since to fingers are composing tokens in place **p2**.

While waiting in place **p2**, the transition toucheventf_move_1 is enabled and can handle move events from the low level transducer. When such an event occurs, the transition is fired and updates the corresponding finger's information. Finally the transition triggers a "pinch" event.

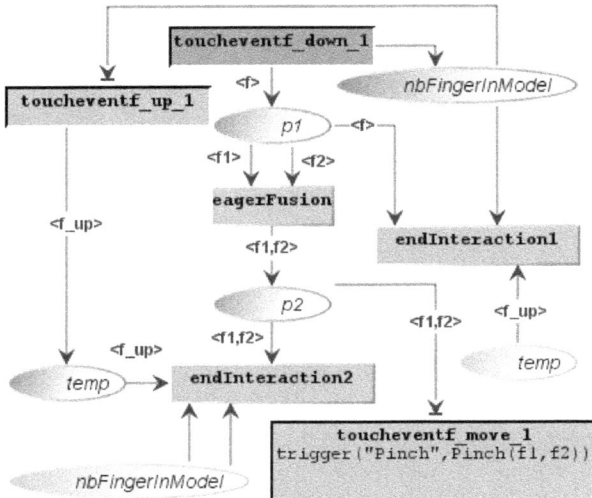

Figure 5 - Pinch Interaction transducer's model

Combining interaction techniques

The ICO notation together with the related architecture (presented in Figure 3) allows the design of complex interaction techniques using the events triggered by models other interaction techniques such as the uniform scale interaction proposed in [29] and combining a "one-touch on the object, together with a two-touch pinch". Due to the space constraint, we will not present the corresponding model in this paper. However, its principle is identical to the other interaction technique models.

Interaction Manager

The interaction manager acts as a supervisor entitled to generate coherent user events from its lower level transducers towards the application. This model may act as a fusion or fission engine depending on the type of rules it implements. Figure 6 details the model of another role of

the interaction manager i.e. conflict management between interaction techniques. Indeed, in early design phases, interaction designers specify standalone interaction techniques which might, in the end, be conflicting. Such conflicts can be identified and corrected later on using regular expression analysis as demonstrated in [28]. We argue that this course of action may alter the usability of the initial standalone interactions in order to cope with local and identified conflicts. The interaction manager aims at resolving these local conflicts preserving usability by implementing simple resolution rules. An example of such conflict may occur when two interaction techniques interfere. For instance Pinch could interfere with a TapAndHold interaction if one of the fingers used for the Pinch does not move enough and thus is treated as a TapAndHold even though involved in a Pinch. Such a scenario is part of the interaction specification process we presented in [21] and applied to the interaction techniques fusion engine. To solve this conflict a possible modification is to give priority to Pinch and thus disabling TapAndHold interaction when a Pinch interaction is being recognized.

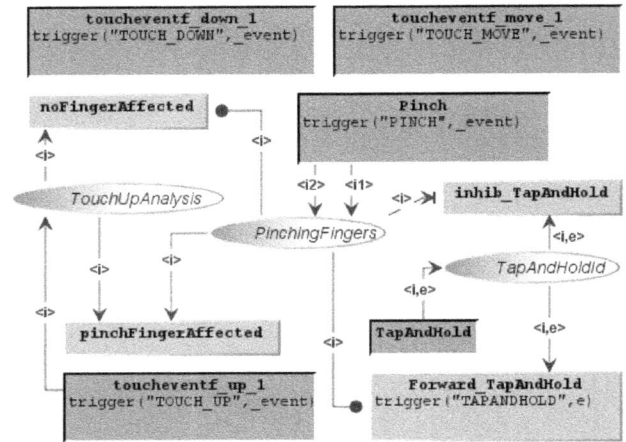

Figure 6 – Interaction Manager

When the interaction manager receives a "*Pinch*" event, the synchronized transition Pinch_1 forwards the event (trigger PINCH) and puts two tokens in the **PinchingFingers** place, each token being compose by an int value corresponding to one of the Pinch finger. In parallel, each time a "*TapAnhHold*" is received, the event is stored in the **TapAndHoldId** place with the corresponding finger id. Then, the transitions inhibTapAndHold and ForwardTapAndHold which are in mutual exclusion test if the finger from the received event is involved in a Pinch interaction and process it according to the rule presented above. When a "*toucheventf_up*" is received, if it impacts on finger involved in a Pinch interaction, the pinchFingerAffected transition subtracts the **PinchingFinger** token with the same id; otherwise the transition noFingerAffected discards the token.

In addition of the conflict resolution rules, the interaction manager acts by default as an event forwarder towards the applications. This allows the applications to be registered only to this one model which keep them independent from the various transducers and their architecture. This forwarding role is instantiated by the trigger actions in the various synchronized transitions.

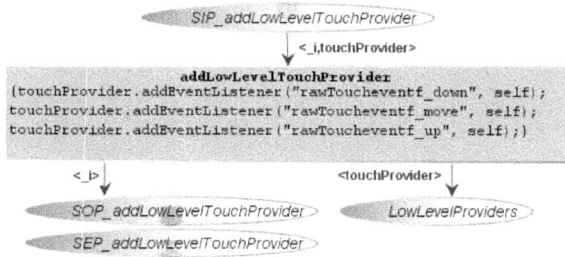

Figure 7 - ICO services for dynamic registration to low level events providers

Handling multi-touch specificities

Dynamic instantiation and management
During multi-touch interactions, fingers are by definition detected dynamically. We argue that the most natural manner to fully specify multi-touch interactions is for UIDL to support dynamic instantiation (creation of inputs devices and GUI components at run time). Indeed, most operating systems handle plug and play devices. Therefore a notation for multi-touch application specification should be able to dynamically detect and manage input devices. Figure 7 presents one ICO service called addLowLevelProvider. This handles a list of LowLevelProviders (stored in place with the same name) and can be added to the ICO transducer presented in Figure 4. It also allows the transducer to listen to "*rawToucheventf_down*" (*move*s and *up*s) fired by the providers it is a listener of. Due to space constraints, the service to remove providers it not presented.

Finger clustering
In purely multi-touch interaction techniques, determining a correct mapping between fingers of the same hand/user is critical as demonstrated in [30]. Therefore we present how our notation is able to formally address this aspect at run-time. The initial Pinch transducer model Figure 5 matches fingers in the order they are pressed. This specific model works for a single user that interacts with one object at the time. In the context of our application domain the presented model will suffer shortcomings when two users will start to interact on a multi-touch surface at the same time. The model shall be able to resolve the correct finger clustering i.e. which fingers are paired. The model we present Figure 8 is one possible specification that can handle dynamic finger re-clustering and resolve possible inconsistencies of the previous model and is divided into four different parts:

- The first part is the same as the Pinch interaction model presented in Figure 5 (augmented only with the transition remaingPinch).
- The second part is in charge of managing clustering. When the model receives a "*toucheventf_move*", the

related pinching fingers trajectories are analyzed to verify their match. If such is the case, the clustering_ok transition is crossed and the pinching fingers are stored back in the **PinchReady** place; otherwise, they are put in the **Re-Clustering** place. From this point, the analysis is recursive as long as the **PinchReady** place is empty or a correct match for the finger trajectories is found which leads to four possibilities after taken a pair of pinching fingers from the **PinchReady** place: a match is found (two possibilities), no finger corresponds and either the **PinchReady** place is empty or not. In this last case, the finger clustering is let as is until a next "*toucheventf_move*" event is received.

- The third part is composed of meta-event listeners capable to monitor the state of particular transitions and places in the model.
- Once the re-clustering has been computed, the fourth part's behavior is designed to re-locate all pinching fingers in their idle state setting the corresponding tokens in place **PinchReady**.

Gesture recognition
Formal description of multi-touch gestures is proposed in PROTON++ is based on regular expressions [28]. To enable such specifications, PROTON++ introduces directions (South, North...) to the touch events used by the gesture recognizer. A gesture is a sequence of finger movement which directions match its description. The ICO formalism addresses such specification even though it is not presented in this paper due to space constraints. The events represented in PROTON++ by means of regular expressions are described in the synchronized transitions in ICO. The touch direction attributed computed in PROTON++ by combining position associated to previous touch events past with the position of the current touch event is represented in ICO adding the same mechanisms in the low-level transducers.

The main advantage of ICO with respect to PROTON++ is that on one hand it makes explicit the various states the interaction techniques can be in and, on the other hand explicitly supports concurrency both in terms of fork and join. Such elements remain implicit in PROTON++ as interaction techniques are handled independently and it is even recommended to remove them at design time as they are not recognized by regular expressions[1]. However, for sake of readability of the models this direction management has not been represented in the models.

Adding Resilience to manipulation errors
Many studies such as [2] have highlighted limitations of touch manipulations and have considered solutions to overcome then ([2, 10]).

---

[1] "Proton++ recognizes a gesture when the entire touch event stream matches a gesture regular expression. Each time a match is found, Proton++ executes the callback associated with the gesture expression and flushes the stream. Thus, with a single stream, Proton++ is limited to recognizing at most one gesture at a time." Paragraph "SPLITTING THE TOUCH EVENT STREAM "Page 6 from[28]

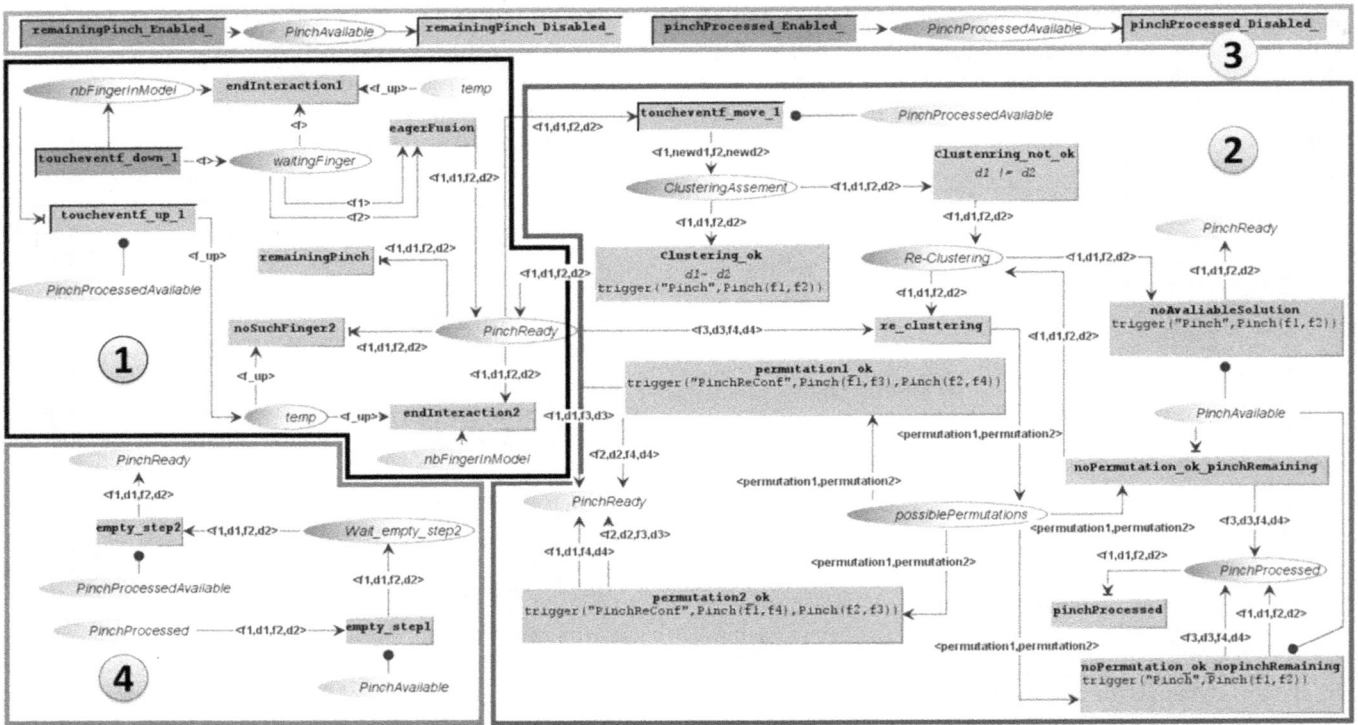

Figure 8 - Pinch interaction model with dynamic re-clustering

However, less work has been published on false touch handling which is the purpose of this paragraph. While interacting and more frequently in case of turbulences, users may inadvertently and briefly touch the screen triggering false touches events.

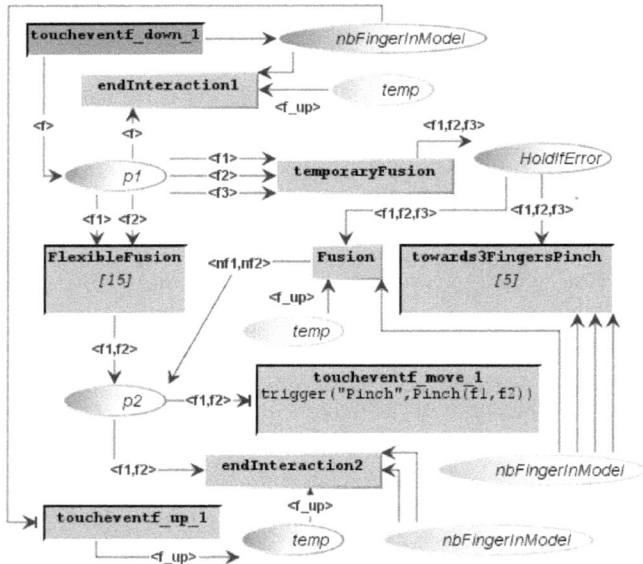

Figure 9 - An error-tolerant model for the Pinch interaction

In order to maintain high usability level and not display blinking feedback, interaction models shall be resilient to such manipulations errors. Figure 9 presents such a behavior applied to the initial detection of a Pinch interaction

technique. If a "*toucheventf_down*" is received less than Xms after the second down, a temporary fusion is processed. This 3 fingers fusion is validated and sent to the 3 fingers pinch model after 5ms unless a "*toucheventf_up*" is received within this time frame.

ANALYSIS

The Petri net formalism enables the use of several analysis capabilities provided by the community. Petshop tool is used to perform the invariant analysis directly on ICO models. CPN Tools together with the work of Silva et al. [43] is used to accomplish the structural analysis and reachability graph analysis to CPN models converted from ICO models. Invariants, standard properties (e.g. liveness) and properties based on patterns (e.g. consistency, precedence) were identified in the presented models but are not presented due to space constraints.

CONCLUSION AND PERSPECTIVES

This paper has presented how multi-touch interaction techniques can be modelled using ICOs which is a Petri net based formal description technique dedicated to the modelling, verification and simulation of interactive systems. The paper has emphasised how some of the constructs of the formal description technique fit with the needs for multi-touch interactions modelling. More precisely we demonstrated how dynamic instantiation of input devices (fingers), dynamic reconfiguration of interactions, fusion of multiple events, clustering (grouping of input devices involved in the same interaction) and explicit handling of true concurrency enable multi-touch interaction specification. Gesture recognition has only been mentioned even though it is easily manipulated thanks to the capability of ICO to handle complex tokens carrying values. The examples given have presented in detail how multi-touch interactions modelled with ICOs can cooperate in order to produce high-level events such as Pinch and TapAndHold meaningful for the interactive application.

This work belong to more ambitious research programme aiming at producing methods, tools and techniques for the engineering of multimodal and multi-touch interfaces in the field of safety critical interactive systems. Indeed, ICOs provide a complete, concise and un-ambiguous description of the fusion engine that makes it possible to assess the performance, the efficiency and the reliability of multimodal interfaces thus providing a way of broadening the application of multi-touch interfaces to the area of safety critical systems.

ACKNOWLEDGEMENTS

This work is partly funded by Airbus under the contract CIFRE PBO D08028747-788/2008

REFERENCES

1. Accot J., Chatty S., Maury S. and Palanque P. Formal Transducers: Models of Devices and Building Bricks for Highly Interactive Systems DSVIS 1997, Springer Verlag, pp. 234-259.
2. Albinsson, P.A. and Zhai, S. High Precision Touch Screen Interaction. Proc. CHI '03, 2003, pp. 105-112.
3. Appert, C. and Beaudouin-Lafon, M. 2006. SwingStates: Adding state machines to the swing toolkit. In Proc. of the 19th Annual ACM Symp. on User Interface Software and Technology (UIST '06). ACM, N-Y, 319–322.
4. ARINC 661-4, Prepared by Airlines Electronic Engineering Committee. Cockpit Display System Interfaces to User Systems. ARINC Specification 661-4; (2010)
5. Barboni E., Jean-François Ladry J-F., Navarre D, Palanque P, & Marco Winckler M. 2010. Beyond modelling: an integrated environment supporting co-execution of tasks and systems models. In Proc. ACM SIGCHI symp. EICS '10. ACM, 165-174.
6. Barboni E., Conversy S., Navarre D. & Palanque P. Model-Based Engineering of Widgets, User Applications and Servers Compliant with ARINC 661 Specification. Proc. 13th conf. on Design Specification and Verification of Interactive Systems (DSVIS 2006), LNCS Science, Springer Verlag. p25-38
7. Bass, L., Pellegrino, R., Reed, S., Seacord, R., Sheppard, R., and Szezur, M. R. The Arch model: Seeheim revisited. Proc. of the User Interface Developpers' workshop. 91.
8. Bastide, R. and Palanque, P. 1990. Petri nets with objects for specification, design and validation of user driven interfaces. Proc. of the 3rd IFIP Conf. on Hum.-Comput. Interact. (Interact'90).
9. Bastide, R., Navarre, D., and Palanque, P. 2002. A model-based tool for interactive prototyping of highly interactive applications. CHI '02., demo., ACM, 516-517
10. Benko H., Wilson A.D. & Baudisch P. 2006. Precise selection techniques for multi-touch screens. In Proc. of CHI '06, ACM, 1263-1272.
11. Blanch, R. and Beaudouin-Lafon, M. 2006. Programming rich interactions using the hierarchical state machine toolkit. In Proc. of the Working C. on Advanced Visual Interfaces: AVI'06, ACM N-Y, 51–58.
12. Buxton B. Multi-touch systems that I have known and loved. http://billbuxton.com/multitouchOverview.html, 2009
13. Cardelli, L. and Pike, R. 1985. Squeak: A language for communicating with mice. SIGGRAPH Comput. Graph. 19, 3, 199–204.
14. Cohen, P. R., Johnston, M., McGee, D., Oviatt, S., Pittman, J., Smith, I., Chen, L., and Clow, J. 1997. QuickSet: multimodal interaction for distributed applications. In Proc. of the Fifth ACM int. Conf. on Multimedia. Multimedia '97. ACM, 31-40.
15. Coninx, K., Cuppnes, E., De Boeck, J., and Raymaekers, C. 2007. Integrating support for usability evaluation into high level interaction descriptions with nimmit. In Interactive Systems: Design, Specification, and Verification. Lecture Notes in Comput. Sc. Springer.
16. Dragicevic, P. and Fekete, J. 2004. Support for input adaptability in the ICON toolkit. 6th Int. Conf. on Multimodal Interfaces (ICMI'04). ACM, N-Y, 212–219.
17. Echtler F. & Klinker G.. 2008. A multitouch software architecture. In Proc. of the 5th Nordic Conf. on Hum.-Comput. Interact: building bridges (NordiCHI '08). ACM, 463-466.
18. Esteban, O., Chatty, S., and Palanque, P. 1995. Whizz'Ed: A visual environment for building highly interactive interfaces. In Proc. of the Interact'95 Conf. 121–126.
19. Frisch M., Heydekorn J., & Dachselt R. 2009. Investigating multi-touch and pen gestures for diagram editing on interactive surfaces. In Proc. of the ACM Int. Conf. on Interactive Tabletops and Surfaces (ITS '09). ACM, 149-156.
20. Genrich, H. J. 1991. Predicate/Transitions Nets. In High-Levels Petri Nets: Theory and Application. K. Jensen and G. Rozenberg, Springer Verlag (1991) pp. 3-43
21. Hamon A., Palanque P., Deleris Y., Navarre D. & Barboni E.. A Tool-supported Development Process for Bringing Touch Interactions into Interactive Cockpits for Controlling Embedded Critical Systems. Int. Conf. on Hum.-Comput. Interact. in Aeronautics (HCI'Aero 2012), ACM DL, p. 25-36, 2012.
22. Hinckley, K., Czerwinski, M., and Sinclair, M. 1998. Interaction and modeling techniques for desktop twohanded input. In Proc. of the 11th Annual ACM Symp. on User Interface Software and Technology (UIST'98). ACM, N-Y, 49–58.

23. Jensen, K., Kristensen, L. M., & Wells, L. (2007). Coloured Petri Nets and CPN Tools for modelling and validation of concurrent systems. Int. Journ. on Software Tools for Technology Transfer, 9(3-4), 213-254.

24. Kammer D., Keck M., Freitag G. & Wacker M. Taxonomy and Overview of Multi-touch Frameworks: Architecture, Scope and Features. In Proc. of Workshop on Engineering Patterns for Multi-Touch Interfaces, Berlin, Germany, June 2010.

25. Kammer D., Wojdziak J., Keck M., Groh R., & Taranko S. 2010. Towards a formalization of multi-touch gestures. In ACM Int. Conf. on Interactive Tabletops and Surfaces (ITS '10)

26. Katsurada, K., Nakamura, Y., Yamada, H., and Nitta, T. 2003. XISL: A language for describing multimodal interaction scenarios. In Proc. of the 5th Int. Conf. on Multimodal Interfaces (ICMI'03). ACM, N-Y, 281–284.

27. Keh, H. C. and Lewis, T. G. 1991. Direct-Manipulation user interface modeling with high-level Petri nets. In Proc. of the 19th Annual Conf. on Comput. Sc. (CSC'91). ACM, 487–495.

28. Kin K., Hartmann B., DeRose T., and Agrawala M.. 2012. Proton++: a customizable declarative multitouch framework. In Proc. Of ACM Symp. on User Interface Software and Technology (UIST '12). ACM, 477-486.

29. Kin K., Miller T., Bollensdorff B., DeRose T., Hartmann B.& Agrawala M. Eden: a professional multitouch tool for constructing virtual organic environments. Proc. of (ACM CHI '11). ACM, New-York, 1343-1352.

30. Kin-Chung Au O. & Tai C-L. 2010. Multitouch finger registration and its applications. Proc. of (OZCHI '10). ACM DL, 41-48.

31. Lakos C. 1991. Language for object-oriented Petri nets. #91-1. Dep. of Comput. S., Univ. of Tasmania.

32. Lalanne D., Nigay L., Palanque P., Robinson P., Vanderdonckt J., & Ladry J-F. 2009. Fusion engines for multimodal input: a survey. In Proc. of the 2009 Int. Conf. on Multimodal Interfaces (ICMI-MLMI '09). ACM, New-York, 153-160.

33. Latoschik, M. E. 2002. Designing transition networks for multimodal VR-interactions using a markup language. In Proc. of the 4th IEEE Int. Conf. on Multimodal Interfaces. 411–416.

34. Limbourg, Q., Vanderdonck, J., Michotter, M., Bouillon, L., and Lopez-Jaquero, V. 2005. USIXML: A language supporting multi-path development of user interfaces. In Proc. of EHCI-DSVIS'04 Conf. Lecture Notes in Comput. Sc., vol. 3425. Springer, 200–220.

35. Navarre D., Palanque P., Ladry J-F., & Barboni E. ICOs: A model-based user interface description technique dedicated to interactive systems addressing usability, reliability and scalability. ACM Trans. Comput.-Hum. Interact. 16, 4, Article 18 (Nov. 2009), 56 pages.

36. Navarre, D., Palanque, P., Basnyat, S. Usability Service Continuation through Reconfiguration of Input and Output Devices in Safety Critical Interactive Systems.

Int Conf. on Comp. Safety, Reliability and Security (SAFECOMP 2008), LNCS 5219, pp. 373–386.

37. Oviatt, S. Ten myths of Multimodal Interaction Comm. of the ACM; 42: 11: 74-81, 1999.

38. Palanque P., Barboni E., Martinie De Almeida, Navarre D., Winckler M. A Tool Supported Model-based Approach for Engineering Usability Evaluation of Interaction Techniques. ACM (EICS 2011), Pisa, Italy.

39. Palanque P., Bastide R. & Sengès V. Validating interactive system design through the verification of formal task and system models. In Proc. of the IFIP TC2/WG2.7 Working Conf. on Engineering for Hum.-Comput. Interact., Chapman & Hall, Ltd., UK, 189-212.

40. Palanque P., Ladry J-F, Navarre D. & Barboni E. High-Fidelity Prototyping of Interactive Systems can be Formal too 13th Int. Conf. on Hum.-Comput. Interact. (HCI International 2009) Springer Verlag, LNCS 5610

41. Roch, S. and P. H. Starke (1999, April). INA Integrated Net Analyser (V. 2.2). Humboldt-Universitat zu Berlin

42. Sibert, J. L.,Hurley,W. D., and Bleser, T.W. 1986. An object-oriented user interface management system. In Proc. of Conf. on Comput. Graph. and Interactive Techniques (SIGGRAPH'86). ACM, 259–268.

43. Silva J. L., Campos J.C., & Harrison M. D., Formal Analysis of Ubiquitous Computing Environments through the APEX Framework," in EICS '12: Proc. of the 4th ACM SIGCHI symp. 2012, pp. 131-140.

44. Songyang Lao, Xiangan Heng, Guohua Zhang, Yunxiang Ling, and Peng Wang. 2009. A gestural interaction design model for multi-touch displays. Proc. of the BCS HCI Conf. (BCS-HCI '09), 440-446.

45. Starke P. H.: Analyse von Petri-Netz-Modellen. Stuttgart : B. G. Teubner, 1990 (Leitfäden und Monographien der Informatik).

46. Oney S., Myers B. and Brandt J. 2012. ConstraintJS: programming interactive behaviors for the web by integrating constraints and states. ACM symp. on User interface software and technology (UIST '12). ACM, New-York, 229-238.

47. Szekely, P. and Myers, B. 1988. A user interface toolkit based on graphical objects and constraints. In Proc. of the Conf. on Object-Oriented Prog. Systems, Languages and Applications (OOPSLA'88). ACM, 36–45.

48. Tatsukawa, K. 1991. Graphical toolkit approach to user interaction description. In Proc. of the SIGCHI Conf. on Hum. Fact. in Comput. Syst. (CHI'91), S. P. Robertson, G. M. Olson, and J. S. Olson, Eds. ACM, N-Y, 323–328.

49. Vorobyov, K. & Krishnan, P. (2010). Comparing model checking and static program analysis: A case study in error detection approaches. 5th Int. Workshop on Systems Software Verification (SSV '10).

50. Willans, J. S. and Harrison, M. D. 2001. Prototyping pre-implementation designs of virtual environment behavior. In Proc. of the 8th IFIP Int. Conf. on Engineering for Hum.-Comput. Interact., Lecture Notes In Comput. Sc., vol. 2254. Springer, 91–10.

What If Everyone Could Do It?
A Framework for Easier Spoken Dialog System Design

Pierrick Milhorat
Institut Mines-Télécom
Télécom ParisTech
CNRS LTCI
Paris, France
milhorat@telecom-paristech.fr

Stephan Schlögl
Institut Mines-Télécom
Télécom ParisTech
CNRS LTCI
Paris, France
schlogl@telecom-paristech.fr

Jérôm Boudy
Institut Mines-Télécom
Télécom SudParis
Paris, France
jerome.boudy@telecom-sudparis.eu

Gérard Chollet
Institut Mines-Télécom
Télécom ParisTech
CNRS LTCI
Paris, France
chollet@telecom-paristech.fr

ABSTRACT

While Graphical User Interfaces (GUI) still represent the most common way of operating modern computing technology, Spoken Dialog Systems (SDS) have the potential to offer a more natural and intuitive mode of interaction. Even though some may say that existing speech recognition is neither reliable nor practical, the success of recent product releases such as Apple's *Siri* or Nuance's *Dragon Drive* suggests that language-based interaction is increasingly gaining acceptance. Yet, unlike applications for building GUIs, tools and frameworks that support the design, construction and maintenance of dialog systems are rare. A particular challenge of SDS design is the often complex integration of technologies. Systems usually consist of several components (e.g. speech recognition, language understanding, output generation, etc.), all of which require expertise to deploy them in a given application domain. This paper presents work in progress that aims at supporting this integration process. We propose a framework of components and describe how it may be used to prototype and gradually implement a spoken dialog system without requiring extensive domain expertise.

Author Keywords
SDS Design; Language Technology Components; WOZ.

ACM Classification Keywords
H.5.2 User Interfaces: Natural language; H.5.2 User Interfaces: Prototyping; D.5.2 User Interfaces: Voice I/O

General Terms
Human Factors; Design.

INTRODUCTION

Spoken Dialog Systems (SDS) are booming, with products such as Apple's *Siri*[1], Google's *Voice Search*[2] or Nuance's *Dragon Solutions*[3] demonstrating how current (and future) technologies may change the way we interact with our devices. Even though a lot of these potential applications might also be achievable using traditional Graphical User Interfaces (GUI), a reasonably 'intelligent' computer system that (sufficiently) understands spoken input would simply convey a better user experience [23]. Yet, the design of this type of systems is complex and so we see a pressing demand for tools and techniques that better support this task. SDSs usually consist of several language technology components, ranging from speech recognition and generation to dialog management and artificial intelligence. Building functioning solutions may therefore require sufficient expertise in several different domains. While some tool-support for stand-alone components exists (e.g. [14, 27, 30, 8, 9, 26, 4]) only few attempts have been undertaken to generate a more holistic framework for SDS design (e.g. [15, 16, 7, 3]).

This paper discusses an SDS prototyping framework that has been implemented by our research group. The goal of our approach is to exclude 'hand-crafting' work as much as possible and use a combination of machine learning algorithms and Wizard of Oz (WOZ) experimentation [13] to build SDS solutions from scratch. Integrating existing open-source technology components with WOZ we aim for the creation of a flexible and easy to use prototyping environment, that can be used not only by speech engineers, but also by designers/researchers outside the signal processing community. The paper starts with an overview of the proposed framework architecture which is followed by a description of its different components. After that we discuss our current employment of the framework and conclude the paper with planned future directions.

---

[1] http://www.apple.com/ios/siri/
[2] http://www.google.com/mobile/voice-search/
[3] http://www.nuance.com/dragon/

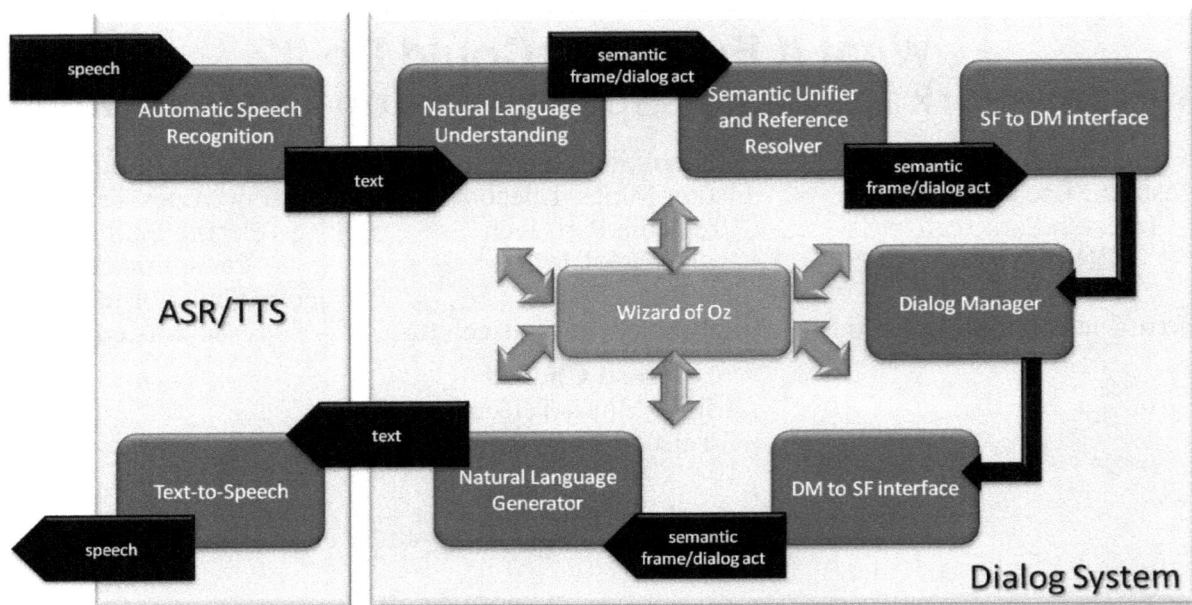

Figure 1. A framework architecture for Spoken Dialog System design

FRAMEWORK COMPONENTS

The overall architecture of our prototyping framework closely resembles the state of the art processing chain of a modern SDS (cf. Figure 1). On the input side we find the Automatic Speech Recognition (ASR) module, a Natural Language Understanding (NLU) component, as well as a novel component which we call the Semantic Unifier and Reference Resolver (SURR). The output side consists of a Natural Language Generation (NLG) component and a Text-to-Speech synthesis (TTS) module. The core of the system is represented by a Dialog Manager (DM) which is connected to the input and output chain via two formatting interfaces. These interfaces offer additional flexibility with respect to possible future framework extensions (e.g. a potential integration of multi-modality).

At runtime the ASR module decodes speech input, producing natural language text utterances and passes them on to the NLU component. The NLU component then extracts from these utterances so-called Semantic Frames (SF), which consist of a goal and *0 to n* instantiated slots. Next, the SURR component filters these SFs, replaces relative values like dates, times or locations by absolute ones and resolves references. Then an interface component translates the SURR output into a format that can be processed by the DM. The DM, which represents the core of the overall system, is responsible for keeping track of the dialog progress, taking into account the given context, and consequently triggers the request for additional input; i.e. it is aware of the current tasks and therefore demands the relevant variables to be defined. It takes the output of the SURR and, based on the currently loaded task model, selects appropriate actions (i.e. it initiates utterances to be produced by the NLG component or commands to be sent to a back-end application). Again, a dedicated formatting interface is used to translate the DM output

into a format that can be interpreted by the NLG component. Such consequently produces the requested text utterance. Finally, the TTS module takes the NLG output and converts it into synthesized speech.

In order to offer this work flow we have integrated a set of open-source language technology components, augmented by various 'home-made' software modules, into a flexible SDS prototyping framework. The following sections will describe the different components of this framework and their roles in some more detail, and highlight which extensions and adaptations were necessary in order to create a cohesive interaction pipeline.

Automatic Speech Recognition Module

SDSs are different from other dialog systems in that speech represents their single interaction modality. Thus, an SDS's first processing stage has to generate hypotheses about the orthographic content that is encoded in a user's spoken input. Despite decades of research and commercial deployment this processing is still regarded as highly error-prone. Current best practice is to search for the best matching sequence of stochastic models using the digitized input signal. Mel-Frequency Cepstrum Coefficients (MFCC) (and their deltas) are widely used descriptors for such speech signal analyses (e.g. [6, 2, 1]). The distribution of the coefficients' vectors for the contextualized phonemes or triphones (i.e. the smallest units of the processed sound signal) are usually encoded as Hidden Markov Models (HMM) [11], which were trained from already transcribed speech segments. These models constitute the first ingredient for building a working ASR module – the so called Acoustic Model (AM). Next, in order to construct words out of a sequence of phonemes, a Pronouncing Dictionary (PD) is required, which consists of the decomposition of a language's words into phonemic units. Finally, the last ingredient that is necessary to build the ASR module is a so-called Language Model (LM) which provides probabilities for given word sequences to appear in a sentence. Those probabilities are based on existing linguistic structures and encoded as n-grams. The combination of the three knowledge sources (i.e. AM, PD and LM) is then used by the recognition engine to produce one or several hypothesis of recognized text for a given (segmented) speech signal [1].

Given these requirements one may argue that building ASR systems for distinct application scenarios is time consuming and very much dependent on both the availability of required knowledge sources (i.e. AM, PD and LM), and the quality and amount of data that was used to construct them. Yet, existing Large Vocabulary Continuous Speech Recognition systems (LVCSR) often already cover a great amount of general purpose vocabulary (as long as their training has been performed on such data). Hence, extending such a general system (and its knowledge sources) to fit the vocabulary space of a specific application scenario may be quicker and more effective than building an entirely new recognizer from scratch. What is needed, however, are appropriate interfaces that allow for the adaptation of the general models so that they better facilitate the recognition of expected utterances related to a specific application scenario. Milhorat et al. [17] proposed a filtering method to favor such a recognition of 'correct' utterances while discarding mis-recognized or out-of-context ones. Results could then further be augmented with features like the dialog state, the dialog history and, a user's personalized settings, and eventually be used to dynamically update/replace an LVCSR's general engine configuration with a more specific, application dependent one.

In order to offer a solution that allows for such a dynamic adaptation of knowledge sources our prototyping framework integrates the Julius ASR engine, an LVCSR engine developed by the Kawahara Lab at Kyoto University [14]. The current setup supports the recognition of spoken input in English, French, Spanish and Dutch. In addition we have acquired the necessary databases to build recognizers for German and Italian. Using this setting we plan to create adapted language models for a number of application scenarios, including the speech-based operation of a calendar program, the use of communication services such as email and text messages, and the interaction with several health and well-being applications (e.g. a well-being diary).

Natural Language Understanding Component
Although all uni-modal dialog systems work with only one input modality (i.e. either direct text input or text recognized by an ASR component) the meaning representation they employ can differ greatly between solutions [9, 18]. The outptut that has to be produced by an integrated NLU component therefore depends on the purpose of the overall system as well as its DM formalism. Specific implementations can take on various forms and notations. For our prototyping framework we have chosen a frame-based semantic representation of language understanding. Semantic Frames (SF) are often used because of their versatility. An SF (cf. Figure 2) consists of a

goal (i.e. the user's intent) and is further defined by a number of relevant parameters, represented by slot-value pairs. Given a textual input, the task of and SF-based NLU component is to select a matching SF (i.e. a goal and its parameters) from a predefined set of possibilities. It does this by applying a number of rules which are usually learned from an annotated corpus.

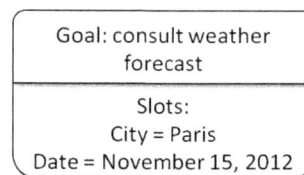

Figure 2. The example of a Semantic Frame (SF)

The NLU component we have integrated employs an algorithm developed by Jurcicek et al. [12]. It is based on sequential transformation rules which are applied to find a match between an input utterance and an SF. Rules consist of triggers and transformation operations. A trigger contains one or more conditions such as an n-gram or a skipping bigram in the user utterance, a goal value, or a slot-type in the (temporary) paired SF. The transformation is applied if all the conditions of a rule's trigger match the input utterance-SF pair. An utterance to be processed is initialized with the default dialog act i.e. no slot and the most common goal as determined by the annotated training corpus. The training algorithm then looks for one rule that maximizes the value of the optimization function (i.e. it follows a transformation-based learning principle). In our case the optimization measure is the distance between each temporary SF and the 'true' SF in the corpus. This is computed as the sum of required addition, deletion and substitution operations (i.e. Levenshtein distance). Once this best rule is found, it is applied to the current state of the corpus and the algorithm is re-initiated for the resulting new training database. The process is stopped when the best rule's increase of the optimization function is below a given threshold.

Semantic Unifier and Reference Resolver
The Semantic Unifier and Reference Resolver (SURR) is not a standard SDS component but rather one of the features that was needed to fill the gap between the NLU component integrated with our prototyping framework and its DM component. In particular, it transforms the NLU output, which is out of context, so that it can be processed by the following DM. For example, if we want to add a valid event entry to a calendar application the system usually requires an event name (i.e. a title), a starting as well as an ending point in time (i.e. a date and a time) and maybe an optional note. A user, however, might interact with the system as follows:

- User: "Add the birthday of my daughter, on Saturday the 15th of November from 2 pm"

- System: *[asks the user for the ending-point-in-time slot's value]* "When will it be finished?"

- User: "I think I'll be there for 6 hours"

In this situation, even if the system would create an SF with a duration slot of 6 hours instead of an ending time, the DM would not be able to process the data as it requires a precise ending. What we see here is an SF space difference between the semantic interpreter (NLU) and the decision-making component (DM). To solve this mismatch we would need to augment the entire dialog task model, which consequently might also require significant changes to be made to the back-end application. Instead, however, our framework uses a dynamic mapping component (i.e. the SURR) that allows for a duration slot to be converted into an ending-point-in-time slot. We call this process the semantic unification. Furthermore we use what we call a reference resolution process to convert the 'tomorrow' that is used in the above example into 'today's date incremented by one day'. Both operations, semantic unification and reference resolution, are contained in the same tree structures which are searched by the SURR algorithm. These trees are handcrafted from situations that happen in experiments with real users, and then further expanded according to a designer's/researcher's ideas. For instance, after having implemented the 'tomorrow' branch one may think of adding the 'yesterday' one.

The current version of the SURR module is based on data collected through a set of initial experiments. It employs a tree-climbing algorithm that is applied to a structure of additive and converting branches. Every link between nodes represents a predicate. Figure 3 shows an example of a tree and Figure 4 its associated implementation. The initial function looks for *1 to n* slot-value pair(s) for which a transforming predicate exists and subsequently applies the defined operation. The resulting (transformed) SF is then processed again and such is repeated until no further predicate match is found. The algorithm succeeds if the final SF contains only those pairs that are declared as roots. All parameters of an SF which cannot be replaced by a root slot (i.e. where the algorithm fails) are subsequently discarded.

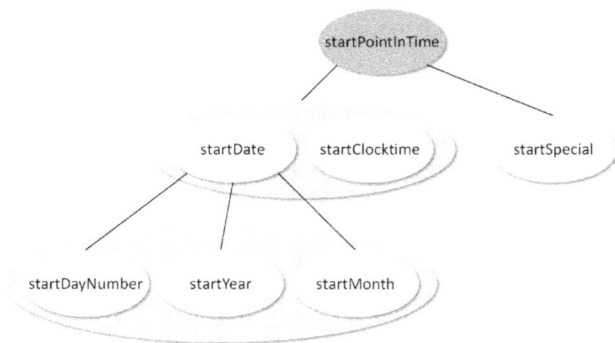

Figure 3. The tree structure of the Semantic Unifier and Reference Resolver (SURR)

Dialog Manager

To date several probabilistic DM components are available (e.g. [10, 28]). Yet, most of them require a significant amount of data to produce viable results, and their scalability is often limited to a few slots, user dialog acts and system actions. An alternative can be found in fully deterministic DM components whose functional breadth is pre-defined. Such,

```
/**root definitions*/
root([slot(startPointInTime,_)]).

/**start point in time(current date + current clocktime) -> start special(now)*/
rewrite([slot(startPointInTime, C)], [slot(startSpecial, [now])]) :-
        append(A, B, C), append(D, E, A), append(F, G, E),
        slot(currentMonth, D), slot(currentDayNumber, F),
        slot(currentYear, G), slot(currentClocktime, B).

/**start point in time -> start date + start clocktime*/
rewrite([slot(startPointInTime, P)], [slot(startDate, D), slot(startClocktime, C)]) :-
        append(D, C, P).

/**start date -> start day number + start month + start year*/
rewrite([slot(startDate, D)], [slot(startMonth, M), slot(startDayNumber, Dn), slot(startYear, Y)]) :-
        append(X, Y, D), append(M, Dn, X).
```

Figure 4. An example implementation of the Semantic Unifier and Reference Resolver (SURR)

however, requires greater knowledge of the supported dialog space and is therefore only suitable for well defined interaction domains. Since the goal of our framework is to support the development of dialog systems for specific application scenarios we decided to integrate Disco [21, 22], a representative of the later approach. It requires a task model compliant with the ANSI CEA-2018[4] standard, which essentially demands a recursive decomposition of tasks into atomic actions. Disco integrates a so-called inference engine which, if provided with one or more task models, is able to manage a mixed-initiative dialog. It processes a hierarchy of tasks (applying plan recognition), guiding the user towards the completion of macro tasks (consisting of several subtasks). Planning is performed automatically, supported by static task models and a dynamic focus stack. Task models contain the task structure, the temporal constraints for the dialog and the data flow within the models. They are implemented in XML and usually require expertise to be built. In order to help with their creation we investigated two notation languages. These languages aim at the automatic extraction of suitable task models based on the description of the given back-end application, where the back-end applications is represented by a form-filling service with attached commands. The first such language is a set of first-order logic formulas. It enables the designer/researcher to specify incompatibilities between slots, as well as optional and mandatory slot attributes. While such certainly helps the design process its application is somewhat limited. Additional manual edits are still required in order to support all the essential information a task model might need to encode. Hence a second, more advanced language is currently under development, which supports conditional relationships between slots, reusable subapplication descriptions, and computed values. Here, an application's command is described as a form containing an ID, a set of slots, sub-forms (i.e. links to other forms) and an action triggered by the completion of the form. Sub-form attributes are boolean optional, ignore and default, which respectively set the linked form to non mandatory, ignored (in the case the applicable condition is not fulfilled), or default (in the case of ambiguity). This process may allow for a richer formalism and should enable the designer/researcher to focus more thoroughly on the actual application.

---

[4]http://www.ce.org/Standards/Standard-Listings/R7-Home-Network-Committee/CEA-2018-(ANSI).aspx

Formatting Interfaces (SF to DM and DM to SF)

In addition to the earlier highlighted semantic ambiguities which exist between NLU and DM (we tackle them with the described SURR component), we often also find certain formatting incompatibilities between those two components (as well as between the DM and the following NLG component). Such is usually caused by the use of different input/output interface standards or diverging forms of knowledge representation. Generally the task of a DM component is to trigger output-dialog-acts and accompanying actions based on input provided by the NLU. The anticipated input as well as the produced output are, however, context dependent so that the current dialog state is often required for better disambiguation. To tackle this problem we have introduced two formatting interfaces; one of which translates an SF (delivered by the SURR) into a context-specific input-dialog-act (i.e. factoring in the current dialog state), and a second one that takes the output-dialog-act delivered by the DM and translates it back into an SF (i.e. the format that can be processed by our NLG component). While these interfaces do not modify the actual input/output content they can be regarded as necessary formatting components, implemented as an overlay to the actual DM. As such, they also offer more flexibility with respect to the modularization of our framework (Note: A future replacement of single components might require additional input/ output formatting).

Natural Language Generation Component

While NLG is generally an important aspect of an SDS it is currently not our main area of interest. Our framework therefore only implements a very basic generation engine. It uses the output of the DM (i.e. the output that has been converted by the output formatting interface described above) to select a human-readable response sentence form a set of possible templates. Each template uses a goal ID that is matched with the dialog act produced by the DM. The SDS designer has to provide at least as many templates (cf. Fig. 5) as dialog acts exist. In case there are more possible templates for a given dialog act, the NLG component randomly selects one and forwards it to the TTS.

```
goal:text /slot1/ text /slot2/ text.
time:Today is the /dayNuber/th of /month/.
```

Figure 5. Natural Language Generator templates

Text-to-Speech Synthesis Module

Finally, in order to generate speech from the text fragments produced by the NLG component, our framework integrates the OpenMary TTS [19, 25]; a state-of-the-art, open source, synthesis platform which supports several languages. We currently use the platform to produce speech output in German, Italian, French and English.

Wizard of Oz Component

One last important aspect of our proposed framework architecture is the integration of a Wizard of Oz (WOZ) component. WOZ constitutes a prototyping method that uses a human operator, the so-called wizard, to simulate a system (or part of it) in order to collect relevant interaction data [5]. To support this task we have integrated the WebWOZ prototyping platform [24]; a tool that permits the wizard to replace one or several components of an SDS. Such should offer an easy and efficient solution for various sorts of data gathering. For example, the training corpus for our NLU component consists of possible inputs and its matching outputs. Replacing this component by a human wizard who transforms spoken input into relevant dialogue acts (i.e. SFs), may alleviate the fastidious work of manually searching and annotating corpus data that matches a given application domain.

CURRENT FRAMEWORK EMPLOYMENT

The framework described above is currently used to build a multi-lingual SDS for an application scenario situated in the ambient assisted living domain. Experiments are conducted in which the WOZ component acts as a substitution for the ASR as well as the NLU component. Doing this we are able to collect various types of interaction data (mainly training data that is used for building and improving the NLU component and user experience data that helps to obtain initial end-user feedback). While our initial sessions are in French, experiments in German and Italian are planned for the next couple of month. Once sufficient data for a language is collected, one only needs to re-configure the ASR and re-train the NLU to integrate it with the system. Such demonstrates the flexibility we are aiming for with our framework composition. Another aspect of this flexibility is reflected by the amount of control the human operator (i.e. the wizard) can take over. Set-ups in which *1-n* parts of the framework are simulated/augmented/controlled should allow for accurate refinements of faulty or weak components as well as support user studies at any stage of the development process; an aspect which, we believe, may enable also non-experts to use our framework as a means for designing and building novel SDS solutions.

CONCLUSION AND FUTURE WORK

We presented a flexible SDS prototyping framework that aims to support the easy and quick construction of voice user interfaces for different application scenarios. The implementation of this framework is achieved through the integration of a set of interchangeable open-source language technology components. While the different components are not by default ready to be used with any application domain, their configuration and adaptation to fit a specific purpose requires only little knowledge and expertise.

Future work will focus on the adaptability and flexibility of the presented framework, particularly exploring its employment by non-expert users. Furthermore we will investigate possible ways of improving single framework components. For example, we aim for increasing the robustness of the ASR by using the feedback produced by post-processing components (i.e. NLU, SURR, DM). Another planned improvement is the use of parametric HMMs [29, 20]. Those can be controlled by a set of external shared parameters and therefore would match more closely the acoustic phenomenons of spoken language. Finally, we are also investigating the use of several speech recognition hypothesis.

ACKNOWLEDGEMENTS

The research presented in this paper is jointly supported by vAssist, a project funded by the European Ambient Assisted Living Joint Programme and the National Funding Agencies from Austria, France and Italy (AAL-2010-3-106), and ARHOME, a French national research project.

REFERENCES

1. Anusuya, M. A., and Katti, S. K. Front end analysis of speech recognition: a review. *International Journal of Speech Technology 14*, 2 (2011), 99–145.

2. Baker, J. M., Deng, L., Glass, J., Khudanpur, S., Lee, C.-h., Morgan, N., and O'Shaughnessy, D. Research Developments and Directions in Speech Recognition and Understanding, Part 1. *IEEE Signal Processing Magazine 26*, 3 (2009), 75–80.

3. Bohus, D., Raux, A., Harris, T. K., Eskenazi, M., and Rudnicky, A. I. Olympus: an open-source framework for conversational spoken language interface research. In *Proc. of ACL-HLT* (2007).

4. Churcher, G. E., Atwell, E. S., and Souter, C. Dialogue management systems: a survey and overview. *Research Report Series - University of Leeds School of Computer Studies* (February 1997).

5. Dahlbäck, N., Jönsson, A., and Ahrenberg, L. Wizard of oz studies - why and how. In *Proc. of ACM IUI* (1993), 193–200.

6. Davis, S. B., and Mermelstein, P. Comparison of parametric representations for monosyllabic word recognition in continuously spoken sentences. *IEEE Transactions on Acoustics Speech and Signal Processing 28*, 4 (1980), 357–366.

7. Galibert, O., Illouz, G., and Rosset, S. Ritel: an open-domain, human-computer dialog system. In *Proc. of INTERSPEECH* (2005), 909–912.

8. He, Y., and Young, S. Semantic processing using the Hidden Vector State model. *Computer Speech & Language 19*, 1 (2005), 85–106.

9. He, Y., and Young, S. Spoken language understanding using the hidden vector state model. *Speech Communication 48*, 3-4 (2006), 262–275.

10. Henderson, J., and Lemon, O. Mixture model POMDPs for efficient handling of uncertainty in dialogue management. In *Proc. of ACL-HLT* (2008), 73–76.

11. Juang, B.-H., and Rabiner, L. R. Hidden Markov models for speech recognition. *Technometrics 33*, 3 (1991), 251–272.

12. Jurčíček, F., Mairesse, F., Gašić, M., Keizer, S., Thomson, B., Yu, K., and Young, S. Transformation-based Learning for semantic parsing. *Evaluation* (2009), 2719–2722.

13. Kelley, J. F. An empirical methodology for writing User-Friendly Natural Language computer applications. In *Proc. of ACM CHI* (1983), 193–196.

14. Lee, C., Jung, S., and Lee, G. G. Robust dialog management with n-best hypotheses using dialog examples and agenda. In *Proc. of ACL-HLT* (2008), 630–637.

15. Leuski, A., Pair, J., and Traum, D. How to talk to a hologram. In *Proc. of IUI* (2006), 360–362.

16. Leuski, A., Patel, R., Traum, D., and Kennedy, B. Building effective question answering characters. *Proc. of SIGDIAL* (2009), 18–27.

17. Milhorat, P., Istrate, D., Boudy, J., and Chollet, G. Hands-free speech-sound interactions at home. In *Proc. of EUSIPCO* (2012), 1678–1682.

18. Mori, R. D., Béchet, F., Hakkani-Tur, D., McTear, M., Riccardi, G., and Tur, G. Spoken language understanding: A survey. In *Proc. of IEEE ASRU* (2007).

19. Pammi, S., Charfuelan, M., and Schröder, M. Multilingual voice creation toolkit for the MARY TTS platform. In *Proc. of LREC* (2010).

20. Radenen, M., and Artieres, T. Contextual hidden markov models. In *Proc. of ICASSP* (2012), 2113–2116.

21. Rich, C. Building task-based user interfaces with ANSI/CEA-2018. *Computer 42*, 8 (2009), 20–27.

22. Rich, C., and Sidner, C. L. Using collaborative discourse theory to partially automate dialogue tree authoring. In *Proc. of IVA* (2012), 327–340.

23. Schalkwyk, J., Beeferman, D., Beaufays, F., Byrne, B., Chelba, C., Cohen, M., Garret, M., and Strope, B. Google search by voice : A case study. *Visions of Speech: Exploring New Voice Apps in Mobile Environments, Call Centers and Clinics 2* (2010), 1–35.

24. Schlögl, S., Doherty, G., Karamanis, N., and Luz, S. WebWOZ: a wizard of oz prototyping framework. In *Proc. of ACM EICS* (2010), 109–114.

25. Schröder, M., and Trouvain, J. The German text-to-speech synthesis system MARY: A tool for research, development and teaching. *International Journal of Speech Technology* (2003).

26. Seneviratne, V., and Young, S. The hidden vector state language model. In *Proc. of INTERSPEECH* (2005), 1–4.

27. Stolcke, A. SRILM-An extensible language modeling toolkit. In *Proc. of ICSLP* (2002).

28. Williams, J. D., and Young, S. Partially observable Markov decision processes for spoken dialog systems. *Computer Speech & Language 21*, 2 (2007), 393–422.

29. Wilson, A. D., and Bobick, A. F. Parametric hidden markov models for gesture recognition. *IEEE Transactions on Pattern Analysis and Machine Intelligence 21*, 9 (1999), 884–900.

30. Young, S., Evermann, G., Gales, M. J. F., Hain, T., Kershaw, D., Liu, X., Moore, G., Odell, J., Ollason, D., Povey, D., Valtchev, V., and Woodland, P. C. The HTK Book (for HTK Version 3.4), 2006.

RefactorPad: Editing Source Code on Touchscreens

Felix Raab
University of Regensburg
Chair for Media Informatics
felix.raab@ur.de

Christian Wolff
University of Regensburg
Chair for Media Informatics
christian.wolff@ur.de

Florian Echtler
University of Regensburg
Chair for Media Informatics
florian.echtler@ur.de

ABSTRACT

Despite widespread use of touch-enabled devices, the field of software development has only slowly adopted new interaction methods for available tools. In this paper, we present our research on *RefactorPad*, a code editor for editing and restructuring source code on touchscreens. Since entering and modifying code with on-screen keyboards is time-consuming, we have developed a set of gestures that take program syntax into account and support common maintenance tasks on devices such as tablets. This work presents three main contributions: 1) a test setup that enables researchers and participants to collaboratively walk through code examples in real-time; 2) the results of a user study on editing source code with both finger and pen gestures; 3) a list of operations and some design guidelines for creators of code editors or software development environments who wish to optimize their tools for touchscreens.

Author Keywords

Editor; source code; IDE; gestures; pen; touchscreen; tablet; surface; refactoring.

ACM Classification Keywords

D.2.3 [Software Engineering]: Coding Tools and Techniques - Program Editors; D.2.6 [Software Engineering]: Programming Environments - Interactive environments.

INTRODUCTION

As devices with touchscreens have become mainstream, an increasing number of application domains have taken advantage of interaction via multi-touch and gestures. One of the applications areas that has remained comparatively cautious with respect to widespread use of new interaction paradigms is the field of software engineering: most of the existing development tools like integrated development environments (IDEs) heavily rely on keyboard and mouse interaction in the traditional GUI style and have yet to be optimized for touch-enabled devices. In comparison with other domains, development tools stand out due to *feature-rich user interfaces* or, for

developers reluctant to use graphical editors, reliance on *efficient text input*. Both usage patterns call for input techniques that do not hinder productivity when those tools need to be compatible with touchscreens in the future. Some tablets, for instance, provide high-quality text rendering that might work well for code reading and maintenance tasks. Entering and editing source code, however, is challenging without hardware keyboards.

So far, research in this field has concentrated on creating new development environments that radically differ from traditional desktop environments, in some cases by integrating visual programming concepts [7]. Despite the benefits of improving overall interaction, this approach might suffer from low acceptance among developers who are used to development environments as well as programming styles in which they have become proficient over the years. In addition, porting existing tools to multi-touch interaction is challenging: on the one hand, features cannot be simply carried over and applied to touchscreens. Codebases and user interface concepts would need a considerable amount of rework to be viable on such devices. On the other hand, pure text-based environments and editors require efficient keyboard input. While some advances in touch-typing research can improve certain aspects, almost all currently available devices still provide standard on-screen keyboards. Entering and editing large amounts of text for programming tasks can quickly get difficult and time-consuming without hardware keyboards.

Rather than fundamentally change development tools by introducing workbenches with new user interface concepts, we attempt to enhance standard text-based editors with gestural interaction. New code has to be entered via the on-screen keyboard as usual. However, code selection, editing and refactoring is supported through gestures which take programming language syntax into account. Such gestures take the place of hotkeys in traditional interfaces and therefore make common code editing tasks easier to perform on touchscreens. Since code is generally read more than it is written [8], maintenance-oriented development tools might be well-suited for portable, touch-enabled devices. Furthermore, maintenance activities such as refactoring have been shown to play a significant role in the development process. For instance, up to 70% of the structural changes of the Eclipse IDE source code can be attributed to refactoring [17]. It has been reported that

Microsoft uses about 20% of their development efforts for code rewriting [12].

Prior to implementing a working prototype of *RefactorPad*, we have conducted a user study to determine which gestures programmers find convenient for common maintenance tasks in a code editor. In addition, we were interested in pen or finger input preferences and in what the respective performance characteristics were. For this purpose, we have created an interactive and collaborative test setup that allowed us to walk through code examples with participants in real-time. The results of the study can be used as guidelines for implementers of touch-enabled code editors. Moreover, our test setup might be useful for other research projects that examine interaction in software development tools.

We outline related work in section 2, describe how we identified relevant editor operations in section 3 and show the test setup and experiment in section 4. In section 5, we present our results and conclude with design recommendations derived from our experiments.

RELATED WORK

In this section, we highlight some of the more recent research projects that are related to our work as they both present software development tools and integrate *natural interaction* [15] methods into their systems.

Although the project *Code Bubbles* [1] has not been built for touchscreens, it has introduced novel user interface concepts for understanding and maintaining code. The system abandons the file-oriented nature of existing tools and instead shows connected source code fragments as bubbles on a canvas. Editable fragments are grouped into simultaneously visible working sets that have shown to significantly reduce the time spent navigating and the time needed to complete code understanding tasks. A similar project, *Code Canvas* [3], leverages spatial memory to reduce disorientation. Using connected documents, semantic zoom and information overlays, it serves as an interactive map for developers. Since both projects share some ideas, a collaboration finally lead to the commercial tool *Debugger Canvas* [4]. A map-like zoomable surface supports debugging by displaying call paths and execution traces in a set of connected bubbles. Developers can then step back and forth through the code and visually explore relationships. The tool is currently used as a separate mode within the main IDE window. Since the previously mentioned projects use a zoomable canvas and do not rely exclusively on traditional user interface elements, they might work well on touchscreens when support for multi-touch interaction and gestures is added.

CodePad [10] provides interactive spaces for various programming-related tasks on secondary multi-touch-enabled devices. The devices are connected to the main IDE and are meant to support development scenarios such as refactoring, visualization or navigation. While it was mainly introduced as a vision, a prototype demonstrates some of their interaction concepts. *Code Space* [2] takes the application of natural interaction even further by enabling teams to use in-air-gestures and cross-device communication at developer meetings. *Touching Factor* [5] and *TouchDevelop* [13] present solutions for writing code on small mobile screens. However, in order to enable efficient input of code, both projects limit developers either to a certain programming language or to a specific syntax, enhanced by predefined code blocks.

IDENTIFICATION OF EDITOR OPERATIONS

Since the test system is built upon a standard code editor component that is not coupled to idiosyncrasies of certain programming languages, we first compiled a list of common editor operations that participants later had to perform during the study. Even though we did not use a strictly systematic approach of identifying these operations, we are confident that our choices reasonably represent general usage since we 1) examined some of the major editors, 2) took the personal experience of the authors and colleagues into account and 3) evaluated qualitative feedback during and after the study which did not reveal any important commands that were missing. For 1) we mainly examined the "Edit" menus of *Eclipse*, *Visual Studio*, *Xcode* and the popular text editor *Sublime Text*. Table 1 shows a list of operations used in the study.

Basic Operation	Refactoring Task
Move Caret	Extract Method (Without Locals)
Select Identifier	
Select Multiple Identifiers	Extract Method (With Parameter)
Select Line	Inline Method
Select Multiple Lines	
Select Block	Inline Temp
Move Lines	Replace Temp With Query
Duplicate Line	
Delete Line	Introduce Explaining Variable (Extract Local)
Toggle Comment	
Copy/Paste	Rename (Multiple Variables)
Undo/Redo	
Goto Method Declaration	

Table 1. List of basic operations and refactoring tasks that we selected for participants to perform in the study.

The second part of the list includes common refactoring commands. In addition to the approach we used for identifying basic edit operations, we took recent research of refactoring practice [6, 9, 14] into account. As a result, this list contains some of the refactoring tasks that are regarded as frequent and important based on interviews with developers and collected usage data. The list could be extended by various other commands, however, we did not want to further increase the number of tasks.

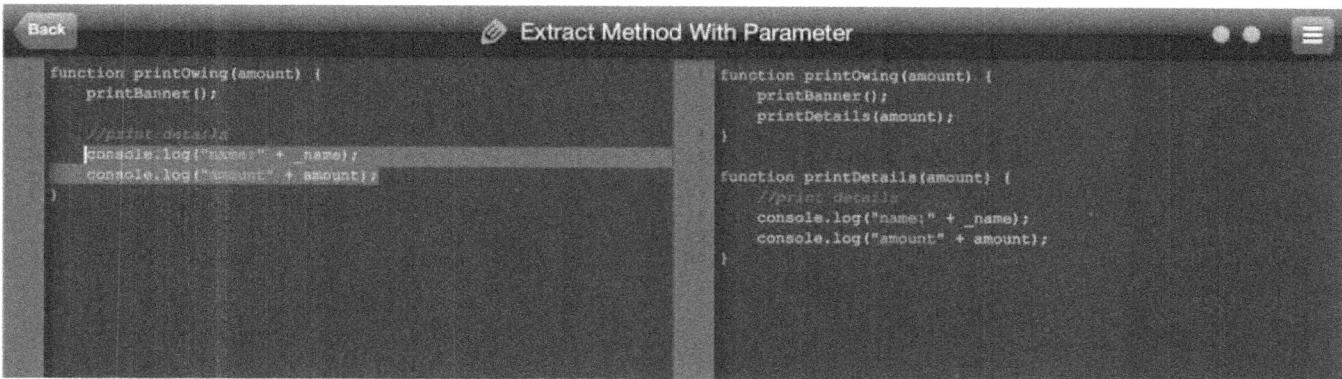

Figure 1. Editor view on the participant's tablet. The caption displays the current task, the left pane shows the initial code with highlights for emphasis and the right pane the desired result. An enhanced view with task instructions, controls to toggle the on-screen keyboard and touch/pen events in an overlay is shown on the experimenter's laptop.

TEST SETUP AND USER STUDY

Our test system consisted of two main parts: an editor running on an iPad 3 tablet showing JavaScript source code and a second, connected editor running on the laptop of the experimenter (Figure 1). We selected JavaScript, a weakly typed language, to reduce participants' mental load regarding issues such as variable declarations, return types etc. By means of a socket connection between the two systems, all touch events on the tablet and key press events of pen buttons were visualized as overlay on the experimenter's editor. In addition, the experimenter could act as a "wizard" and control different aspects on the tablet editor in real-time: modifications of the source code, selections of parts of the source code, cursor position, scrolling to certain lines, and showing or hiding the on-screen keyboard were all directly reflected on the tablet editor. A split view on both systems showed the initial state of the source code on the left side and the desired state on the right side. In order to ensure that all participants received the same instructions, additional notes were displayed on the experimenter's system for each task. This somewhat resembled a "Wizard-of-Oz" experiment except that the participants were fully aware of interacting with a remotely controlled system.

Using this setup, the experimenter could track all tablet interaction on the laptop. At the same time, we could better introduce each code example by highlighting certain code lines, thereby avoiding inconvenient pointing on the small screen in front of the participant. For later analysis, all interaction events were logged to a database on the tablet. The pen used in this study was a *Adonit Jot Touch* with two hardware buttons and a transparent touch-disk attached to the pen tip. Since not all characteristics of interaction can be reconstructed from logged touch events, we captured the area around the tablet on video so that the participant's hands and pen usage could be seen.

Participants

All participants filled in a questionnaire before the actual test. They were asked to specify their experience in certain programming languages, IDEs and their usage of devices with touchscreens. We recruited 16 participants (14 male, 2 female), aged between 21 and 32 years (Mean: 24), all right-handed. While all but one of the participants indicated (on a 5-Point Likert scale) that they use devices with touchscreens "always" or "frequently", 9 stated that they "never" use a pen for input. 12 participants had between 2 and 5 years of programming experience, 2 more than 10 years. 11 participants were "quite experienced" in the programming language Java, 4 selected "very experienced". As for JavaScript, 7 participants indicated "quite experienced" and 4 "very experienced". 10 participants were "quite experienced" in using the Eclipse IDE, 2 "very experienced". In addition, participants named programming languages and IDEs in which they were at least "somewhat experienced": PHP (8), C++ (7), C (5), C# (5), Visual Studio (5), NetBeans (4) and Objective-C (3).

Procedure

The procedure itself was mainly based on a "guessibility study" by Wobbrock et al. [16]. They achieved good results by showing users the effect of surface gestures and then letting them perform their cause. Since the test system did not respond to user input and accepted all input, the users' behavior was not affected by technical aspects such as gesture recognition. In our study, participants were first introduced to the test setup and could then try a demo task. Each of the 20 different tasks had to be done once with the pen and once using only normal touch interaction without the pen. Consequently, each participant completed 40 tasks in fully randomized order. The total number of tasks performed was: 16 participants x 20 tasks x 2 input types = 640 tasks. Participants took 75 minutes on average (including filling in the questionnaires).

A single task consisted of the following stages: First, the experimenter introduced the code example using the previously mentioned features of the test setup and made sure that the participant understood both the initial state of the source code and the desired state (instruction phase). The participant should then try to find a suitable gesture while thinking aloud (preparation phase). As soon as the participant was ready to articulate the gesture again (articulation phase), pressing the title button started the recording of this phase, and another press stopped recording and displayed two post-task questions. Similar to the study in [16], the first question asked if the participant thought the performed gesture was a "good match for its intended purpose" ("goodness" on 7-Point Likert scale). As for the second question, we used the SMEQ (Subjective Mental Effort Question) version developed in [11] where users should indicate perceived effort by moving a slider on a scale ranging from "not at all hard to do" to "tremendously hard to do". This scale has been shown to be reliable and easy for participants to use in its interactive form. After all tasks had been performed, the test persons filled out a final questionnaire indicating which input method they preferred (pen, fingers or both) and which commands they frequently use in their development environments.

RESULTS

Agreement

In order to classify performed gestures and determine agreement scores, we examined all video captures and visualized touch events. Agreement was calculated using the same formula as in [16], using the number of participants, of gesture classes and of participants in each class. Figure 2 shows an example of all combined touch events for the task "Select Multiple Lines". This figure clearly shows two prevalent gesture classes: one group selected lines by swiping over the lines numbers in the gutter on the left side of the editor, the other group swiped across the code block from top left to bottom right. For this example, the final gesture was the gutter swiping gesture since it was used by the highest number of participants and did not conflict with other interactions.

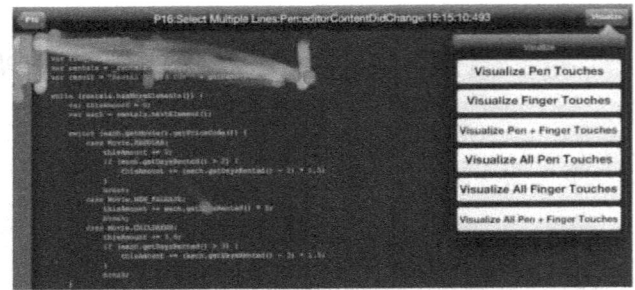

Figure 2. Visualization tool on the experimenter's system showing two patterns for the task "Select Multiple Lines".

Overall, agreement scores were lower (Mean: 0.20) than in [16] which might be due to the more complex application domain in our study. Users generally agreed most on selection gesture for identifiers, lines and blocks, "Move Caret" and "Move Lines".

Goodness – SMEQ – Agreement – Articulation Time

The relationships between the two post-task values for "goodness" and SMEQ, the calculated agreement score and the measured articulation time are illustrated in the two bubble charts in Figure 3. The diagrams show that the most agreed upon gestures were those that users perceived as good matches and least effortful. Further, those gestures were also articulated fastest. This is contrary to some of the results in [16] where articulation time did not affect goodness ratings and gestures that took longer to perform were perceived as easier. We also got different results for the number of touch events: gestures with more touch events were perceived as more effortful in our study (but did not have lower goodness ratings). Again, we suppose that these differences are due to different target groups and application domains. We could also confirm previous results: Better gestures are apparent to participants more quickly (less preparation time) and popularity (high agreement) can identify better gestures.

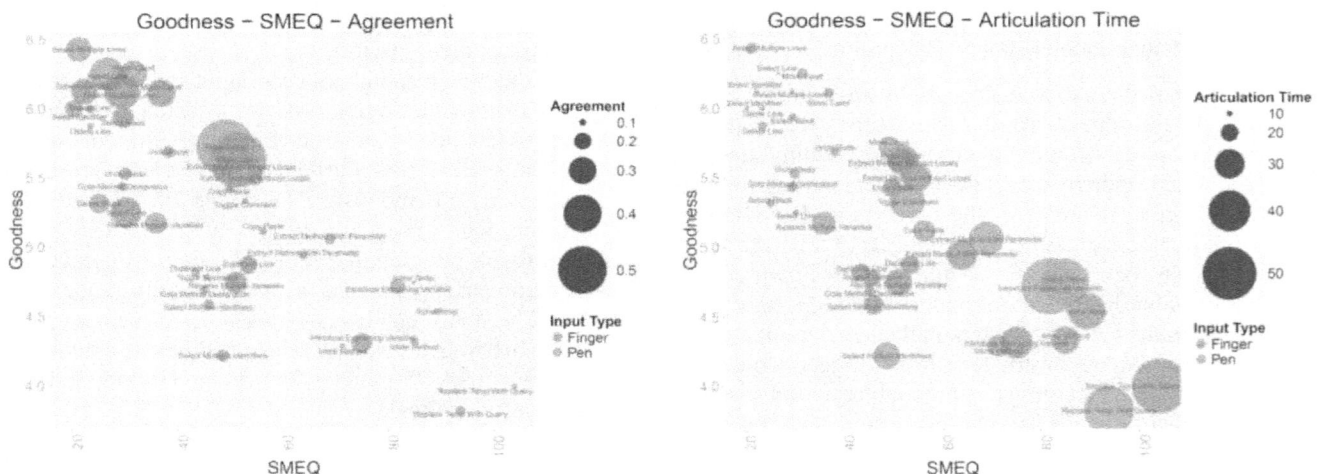

Figure 3. Left: Bubble chart showing aggregated values for gesture goodness (vertical), SMEQ (horizontal) and agreement (size). Right: Bubble chart showing aggregated values for goodness (vertical), SMEQ (horizontal) and articulation time (size).

We could not detect significant differences between pen and finger interaction in any of the mentioned values.

Input Preference and Frequently Used IDE Features

In the post-study questionnaire, 44% of the participants chose the pen as their preferred input method, 25% chose interaction with fingers and 31% preferred mixed pen and finger interaction. Since in the pre-study questionnaire, 56% said that they never use a pen for touch input, this somewhat suggests that support for pen interaction might be a worthwhile addition to touch-enabled code editors. IDE features that participants frequently use at their own judgement, are (*number of mentions in brackets*): Rename (6), Auto-complete (5), Navigation to method or class (5), Auto-format (4), Save (3), Extract method (2), Create new method (2).

Qualitative Observations

During the study, we observed that the users' mental models are strongly influenced by interaction concepts of mobile operating systems. Most of the participants could easily be identified as "Android users" or "iOS users". Additionally, users frequently asked for context menus since they either could not think of a suitable gesture or found a menu more convenient in certain cases. At the same time, however, they expressed their dislike for menus that contain too many items. Some participants were concerned that selection and gesture recognition might not be precise enough in a working system, leading to a lot of re-selection and adjustments in the editor. Most users seemed to prefer one-handed gestures and used

multi-touch interaction only conservatively (only few gestures were performed with more than two fingers). According to participants' comments, the pen was generally perceived as more accurate than interaction with the fingers. Users often decided to perform the same gesture for both the pen and finger version of the task. The two hardware buttons of the pen were sometimes used as left and right mouse buttons.

As far as specific refactoring operations are concerned, users generally seemed to find it easier to extract than to inline code. Some inline operations resulted in sequences of unnecessary steps to complete the task. For users without prior knowledge of inline refactoring, it was not apparent that this transformation could be automated and hence only needed a gestural trigger to be initiated.

Design Recommendations

Based on results from the user study, we propose a set of gestures (Figure 4) for the operations used in this study. This could serve as starting point for implementers of touch-enabled code editors. The set also shows some user interface elements that should be considered as interactive zones: For instance, the majority of users chose the gutter with line numbers as selection target for multiple lines and code blocks by swiping over the corresponding area. Without involving users, we probably would not have predicted this area to be a popular line selection target. Although we tried to remove context menus from the set, integrating more commands would certainly need some form of touch-optimized menu or sidebar that could be displayed on demand. As another subtle, yet important,

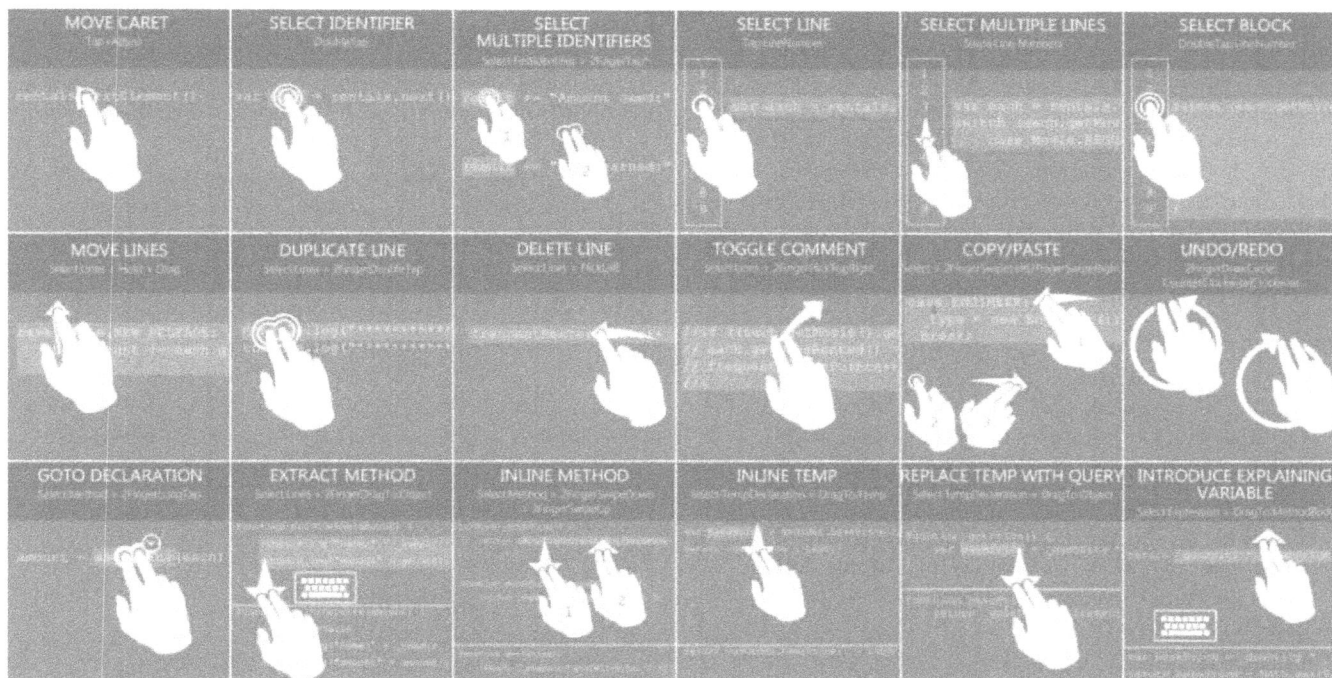

Figure 4: Gesture set for basic selection, editing and refactoring operations for text-based editors on touchscreens.
(*SelectFirstIdentifier* > *2FingerTap* * means: Select the first identifier, then (>) perform multiple (*) taps using 2 fingers.)

usability aspect the study revealed the need for additional "buffer zones" at the top and bottom of the editor area: Almost all participants touched buttons in the navigation bar by accident when they tried to perform their gestures in the editor area.

DISCUSSION

Our current work can be extended in several directions. First, we propose gestures only for a basic subset of commands. Integration of more functionality requires additional selection triggers since not all commands can easily be mapped to gestures. Second, the code examples in our tasks included only "intra-file" source code. It remains open how certain commands would best work with multiple files. Third, some of the common refactoring tasks need additional configuration or user input with the keyboard. Our current command set, however, focuses on the interaction used to trigger the command. Fourth, the lab setting might have prevented users from using two-handed interaction since the tablet could not be picked up by participants to freely interact with the test system. Finally, our work does not address the problem of entering large amounts of new code and still relies on existing on-screen keyboards.

CONCLUSION

With the continuing adoption of touchscreens and mobile devices, it seems logical that development tools need to be optimized for multi-touch and gestural interaction in the future. In addition, approaches such as visual programming have led to interesting concepts but have not gained much acceptance among professional programmers. This might partly be due to the fact that developers wish to keep working with programming languages and tools they have become experienced in over the years. Therefore, rather than radically changing development tools, we suggest to enhance existing text-based code editors with gestural interaction for basic selection and edit operations. This work presents a test setup that involves users to find suitable ways of interacting with source code on touchscreens and proposes design recommendations for implementers of touch-enabled development environments.

REFERENCES

1. Bragdon, A., Zeleznik, R., Reiss, S. P., Karumuri, S., Cheung, W., Kaplan, J., Coleman, C., Adeputra, F., LaViola, J. J. Code bubbles: a working set-based interface for code understanding and maintenance. In *Proc CHI '10*, 2503-2512.

2. Bragdon, A., DeLine, R., Hinckley, K., Morris, M. R., CodeSpace: Touch + Air Gesture Hybrid Interactions for Supporting Developer Meetings. In *Proc ITS'11*, 212-221.

3. DeLine, R., Rowan, K. Code Canvas: Zooming towards Better Development Environments. In *Proc ICSE'10*, 207-210.

4. DeLine, R., Bragdon, A., Rowan, K., Jacobsen, J., Reiss, S. P. Debugger canvas: industrial experience with the code bubbles paradigm. In *Proc ICSE'12*, 1064-1073.

5. Hesenius, M., Medina, C. D. O., Herzberg, D. Touching Factor: Software Development on Tablets. In *Lecture Notes in Computer Science 7306 (2012)*, 148-161.

6. Kim, M., Zimmermann, T., Nagappan, N. A Field Study of Refactoring Benefits and Practice. In *Proc. FSE'12*.

7. Knaus, C. Interaction design for software engineering: boost into programming future. In *Interactions* 15, 4 (July 2008), 71-74. http://doi.acm.org/10.1145/1374489.1374508

8. Ko, A., Aung, H. H., Myers, B. Eliciting Design Requirements for Maintenance-Oriented IDEs: A Detailed Study of Corrective and Perfective Maintenance Tasks. In *Proc. ICSE '05*, 126-135.

9. Negara, S., Chen, N., Vakilian, M., Johnson, R. E., Dig, D. Using Continuous Change Analysis to Understand the Practice of Refactoring. *Technical Report*, http://hdl.handle.net/2142/30759.

10. Parnin, C., Görg, C., Rugaber, S. CodePad: Interactive Spaces for Maintaining Concentration in Programming Environments. In *Proc. SOFTVIS'10*, 15-24.

11. Sauro, J., Dumas, J. S. Comparison of Three One-Question, Post-Task Usability Questionnaires. In *Proc. CHI'09*, 1599-1608

12. Shatnawi, R., Li, W. An Empirical Assessment of Refactoring Impact on Software Quality Using a Hierarchical Quality Model. *International Journal of Software Engineering and Its Applications* 5, 4 (2011), 127-149.

13. Tillmann, N., Moskal, M., de Halleux, J. TouchDevelop: programming cloud-connected mobile devices via touchscreen. In *Proc. ONWARD'11*, 49-60.

14. Vakilian, M., Chen, N., Negara, S., Rajkumar, B. A., Bailey, B. P., Johnson, R. E. Use, disuse, and misuse of automated refactorings. In *Proc. ICSE'12*, 233-243.

15. Wigdor, D., Wixon, D. *Brave NUI World: Designing Natural User Interfaces for Touch and Gesture*, Morgan Kaufmann, Burlington, MA, USA, 2011.

16. Wobbrock, J. O., Morris, M. R., Wilson, A. D. User-defined gestures for surface computing. In *Proc. CHI'09*, 1083-1092.

17. Xing, Z., Stroulia, E. Refactoring Practice: How it is and How it Should be Supported – An Eclipse Case Study. In *Proc. ICSM'06*, 458-468.

Interactive Prototyping of Tabletop and Surface Applications

Tulio de Souza Alcantara
University of Calgary
Calgary, Canada
tuliosouza@gmail.com

Jennifer Ferreira
University of Calgary
Calgary, Canada
jen.ferreira@ucalgary.ca

Frank Maurer
University of Calgary
Calgary, Canada
frank.maurer@ucalgary.ca

ABSTRACT

Physically large touch-based devices, such as tabletops, afford numerous innovative interaction possibilities; however, for application development on these devices to be successful, users must be presented with interactions they find natural and easy to learn. User-centered design advocates the use of prototyping to help designers create software that is a better fit with user needs and yet, due to time pressures or inappropriate tool support, prototyping may be considered too costly to do. To address these concerns, we designed ProtoActive, a tool for designing and evaluating multi-touch applications on large surfaces via sketch-based prototypes. Our tool allows designers to define custom gestures and evaluate them without requiring any programming knowledge. The paper presents the results of pilot studies as well as in-the-wild usage of the tool.

Author Keywords

Prototyping tool; gesture definition; NUI

ACM Classification Keywords

H.5.2 [Information Interfaces and Presentation]: User Interfaces - Interaction styles, prototyping

INTRODUCTION

Designing *Windows, Icons, Menus and Pointers* (WIMP) based applications is a well-known challenge. This challenge becomes even greater when designing for touch and gesture based applications [3, 5, 6, 8, 9, 28] due to different size, orientation and ways to interact with these gesture based applications. The increasing availability of multi-touch tabletop and surface computing opens up new possibilities for interacting with software systems. Interactions with multi-touch surfaces through gesture and touch-based interactions can either improve or hamper the user experience [1, 2, 3]. When creating gestures for interacting with *Interactive Tabletop and Surface* (ITS) applications, interaction designers have to determine if users consider them natural, understandable and easy to use [6]. These gestures might drastically hamper the user experience if *Human Computer Interaction* (HCI) principles are not taken

into consideration [2]. Designers should be able to follow HCI principles not only for the designing how ITS applications look but also for designing how these applications can be interacted with. Previous research on gesture-based interaction has shown problems with the design of the interactions, the meaning of touch and gestures and how context influences them [3, 5, 6, 8, 9, 28].

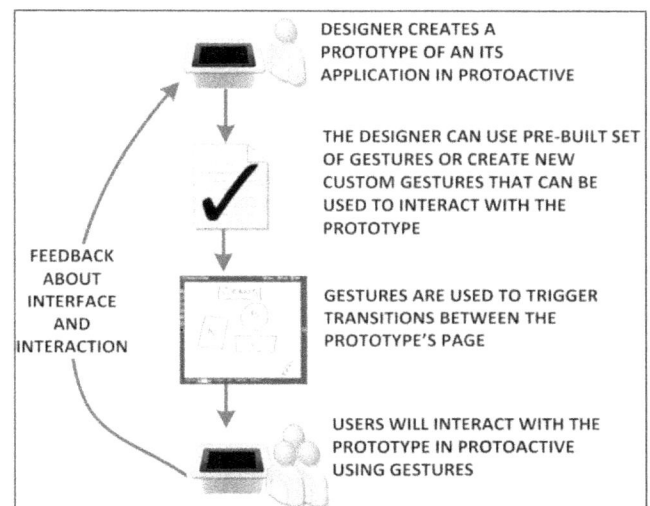

Figure 1 ProtoActive evaluation cycle

There are two main challenges with gesture design:

- the cost (effort, time and technical expertise) required to create gestures [10, 12, 13];
- the design of gestures that are suitable for specific tasks, context and users [5, 9].

The current state of design of multi-touch applications lacks processes and tools to support the design of the interaction of these applications [3, 5, 14]. Studies show a lack of proper tools and methods (such as user-centered design) to improve the design of multi-touch applications [3, 5, 28]. Having users involved early in the process through the use of prototypes has been widely researched and the advantages of sketching and prototyping to improve the design of applications has proved successful [4, 14, 17, 18, 19, 20, 21, 22, 23, 24, 25, 32]. Paper prototypes allow designers to evaluate the output of a system, while the input (how the user interacts with a system) is assumed to be obvious; they allow designers to evaluate what users want to do. With non-trivial interactions, paper prototypes are not sufficient [17, 22].

Tool support for ITS application design has to make it easy to design gestures, respecting the time and cost constraints of prototyping, and make it easy to evaluate the usability of those gestures. The aim of our research is to provide designers with a tool that will help them deliver highly usable ITS applications. In order to do so, we developed a sketch-based tool for evaluating ITS interfaces and interactions in the context of the tasks in the application. This paper presents two contributions: first, ProtoActive, which is composed of

- a storyboarding sketching tool, designed to draft prototypes for ITS applications, based on *Active Story Touch* (AST) [35];
- an integrated gesture learning tool – *Intelligent Gesture Toolkit* (IGT) that uses a specialized anti-unification method[41] to create gesture definitions based on samples of gestures;
- a tool that emulates ITS applications and allows designers to gather feedback on their usability.

Second, this paper presents studies that evaluate the benefits and limitations of ProtoActive. Figure 1 shows the design cycle supported by our tool: a designer creates a prototype of an ITS application and defines how a user will interact with it. The designer can then evaluate the design with the interactions built into it, gathering early user feedback about the application. The whole cycle shown in Figure 1 can be performed without any programming effort or any of the associated costs of programming (e.g.: setting up a work station or managing source code).

To gather requirements for ProtoActive (as a sketch-based prototyping tool), the authors used existing research about computer-based prototyping tools, problems found in existing tool support for prototyping and a qualitative study that consisted of semi-structured interviews with five *User Experience* (UX) designers from different companies.

BACKGROUND
This background section will explain the application domain of the tool proposed here. This will be followed by defining our prototyping tool based on the current taxonomy of prototyping. Finally, the authors provide a definition of gestures and tangibles that will be used in this paper.

Application domain and technical aspects
ProtoActive is a prototyping tool designed to help designers create and evaluate ITS applications and their interactions. In this paper these interactions will be referred to as *gestures* and are described in further detail in the following section. ProtoActive is currently supported by Microsoft Surface 1, Microsoft Surface 2 (PixelSense) and tabletops, tablets or desktop computers with touch enabled monitors, running Microsoft Windows 7 or Microsoft Windows 8. ProtoActive's gesture learning and recognition mechanisms use a modified version of Gesture Toolkit and its *Gesture Definition Language* (GDL) [10].

Gestures
The gestures defined with IGT, differently from stroke based gesture recognizers such as $N [11] and RATA [13], contain information about order, direction and time, which allows IGT to recognize both types of gestures (static and dynamic). In this paper, gestures are considered as single or multi-touch 2D touches; hand postures; detection of fiduciary markers; and concurrent interactions that occur on the surface of an ITS device. Gestures do not include interactions above or in front of a display that do not touch the surface.

Tangibles
The detection of fiduciary markers allows the definition of a subset of interactions: tangible interactions. By allowing designers to define gestures that incorporate fiduciary markers, ProtoActive allows designers to prototype the detection of physical tangibles. By attaching a fiduciary tag to a physical object, a designer can use it as a tangible in ProtoActive and have users evaluate the physical tangibles. Figure 7 illustrates tangibles that can be detected on ProtoActive by their fiduciary markers. Any physical object with a flat surface where a fiduciary tag can be attached can be used as a tangible in ProtoActive.

Prototypes
Buxton [24 p.139] makes a distinction between sketches and prototypes as having different purposes due to the difference between the time spent on them; even though both are tools that can be used in early stages of the design, sketches are earlier drafts whereas prototypes are created later in the design process when ideas are starting to converge. Having more sophisticated and interactive sketches allows designers to take advantage of having users involved and providing feedback about the interactions in ITS applications. Rudd *et al.* [27] suggests advantages and disadvantages of low and high-fidelity prototypes. The design of ProtoActive aims to leverage the advantages of low-fidelity prototypes and it proposes to address the disadvantages: this research aims at providing a prototyping tool that incorporates interactivity at the level of high-fidelity prototypes allowing usability tests based on interaction but having the low effort cost of low-fidelity prototypes allowing the evaluation of multiple design and interaction concepts.

Prototypes created in ProtoActive are sketch based with a low *level of visual refinement* following Buxton's [24] principle that prototypes with a low level of detail and refinement encourage users to provide more feedback. In later stages of design, ProtoActive can also be used in collaboration with image editors and tools to create prototypes with a higher level of visual refinement. Different *breadths of functionalities* [20] can be covered with ProtoActive as it allows designers to easily create several pages in the prototype that can cover a wide range of functionality. Different *depths of functionality* [20] can also be achieved with ProtoActive; in the same fashion that a whole application can be prototyped using ProtoActive, a single task or behavior can be designed in depth and evaluated using ProtoActive. ProtoActive allows a *rich interactivity* [20] evaluation as it allows designers to create their own interaction techniques through custom gestures and use them to interact with the prototype, simulating the behavior of the application through page transitions triggered by gestures. In ProtoActive, there is no mechanism to communicate with any form of *data model* [20]; this was done to keep designers from spending too much time with details such as populating data sources.

Lim *et al.* [21] focused on the support for design exploration in the prototype. This study reveals two key dimensions: *prototypes as filters* (leading the creation of meaningful knowledge about the final design as envisioned in the design process) and *prototypes as manifestations of design ideas.* ProtoActive allows designers to create interaction-based prototypes, where the design and visual details can be evaluated along with the gestures used to interact with the application.

RELATED WORK

Research on design of ITS applications
Hesselmann and Boll propose *Surface Computing for Interactive Visual Applications* (SCIVA), a user-centered and iterative design approach addressing some challenges in designing ITS applications [3]. Their design process gives a general overview of the most important aspects in design of ITS applications. The solution in this paper provides a tool suite that allows designers to follow three steps of the SCIVA design process: defining manipulation functions, conducting user studies to create gestures and evaluating the system with the user to detect flaws from previous steps.

Studying ways to interact with tabletops, Hinrichs and Carpendale found that the choice and use of multi-touch gestures are influenced by the action and social context in which these gestures are performed, meaning that previous gestures and the context of the application influence the formation of subsequent gestures [5]. Also supporting the contextualization of interaction is Krippendorff [23] highlighting that design is not only about making things but also about making sense of things. Both studies suggest that to evaluate interactions it is necessary to contextualize them in the scenario that they will be used.

Trying to understand users' preferences for surface gestures, Morris *et al.* [28] compare two gesture sets for interactive surfaces: one created by end-user elicitation and one authored by three HCI researchers. Their results showed that their participants had similar gesture preference patterns and these preferences were towards physically and conceptually simple gestures. The most popular gestures were designed by larger sets of people, even though the participants did not know who or how many authors created the gesture. Their findings suggest that participatory design methodologies involving user input should be applied to gesture design, such as the user-centered gesture elicitation methodology.

Studying the inconveniences that can be generated by touch based interactions, Gerken *et al.* [29] focus on how users compensate for conflicts between non-interactivity and interactivity created by unintended touch interaction when using a multi-touch enabled tabletop. They conclude that touch-enabled devices can lead to "*touch-phobia*", reducing pointing and leading to less efficient and fluent communication. Their suggested solution is to make touch smarter and more context-aware, which supports the need for better design principles in the creation of touch and gesture-based interactions.

Norman and Nielsen [2] highlight the new concerns that should be addressed by designers when creating touch-based interfaces and ways of interacting with them. The authors propose a balance between creative means of interacting while preserving basic HCI principles, but guidelines for processes that can help designers follow a user centered design approach in the development of ITS applications are limited [3]. Hence, there needs to be a way to evaluate the usability of gesture-based applications in early stages of the design, to preserve HCI principles and have users involved in early stages of the design. There is a need for a tool that supports designers following a user-centered approach.

In order to help the prototyping of tangible tabletop games, Marco *et al.* propose *ToyVision* [15]. *ToyVision* is a toolkit that helps the prototyping of tangible tabletop games. It utilizes a practical implementation of the tangible user interface description language (TUIDL) [16] to model the playing pieces in an XML specification. This toolkit offers a valuable aid in designing tangible based applications as it proposes a classification of the tangibles (tokes) that can be used in the prototypes, which expands the interaction options for tangible based prototypes. To the contrary of ProtoActive, this toolkit requires programming effort.

Research on prototyping
Derboven et al. show the importance of creating prototypes for ITS applications [22]. Their study introduces two prototype methods for multi-touch surfaces. By comparison, their approach consists of physical materials such as paper, cardboard and markers, while our approach proposes an ITS tool, allowing users to create and evaluate the prototypes on the device the applications are designed for.

Sefelin *et al.* [18] compare paper prototyping with prototyping using software tools. Their study suggests three scenarios where paper prototyping would be a preferable medium: when the available prototyping tools do not support the components and ideas which a designer wants to implement; when a designer does not want to exclude members of the design team who do not have sufficient software skills; and when evaluations can lead to a big amount of drawings, which then can be discussed inside the design team. ProtoActive allows designers to create free-hand sketches on a drawing canvas that allows designers to better explore their creativity. In order to simulate the paper-based experience, ProtoActive has an interface that allows designers to create prototypes without requiring much time to learn to use the application, reducing required expertise.

Drawbacks of current prototyping tools

A drawback among the current prototyping tools is the lack of customization of interactions. ProtoActive provides a set of pre-built gestures that can be expanded by allowing designers to provide samples of a gesture to create new gesture definitions that can be used to interact with the prototypes. This feature was implemented to overcome drawbacks from the following tools: *CrossWeaver* [30], *Balsamiq Mockups* [36] and *Fore UI* [39].

Prototyping tools that allow custom interactions also come with the cost of requiring a programming step for customization. This was seen as a drawback as it adds to the cost of prototyping. ProtoActive does not require any programming effort: creating prototype pages, linking them through gestures, creating custom gestures and evaluating them can be accomplished in ProtoActive through its GUI. The need for this feature was gathered from limitations of the following tools: *Raptor* [31], *Sketchify* [32] and *Microsoft Sketch Flow* [38]. By allowing designers to sketch in a similar fashion as sketching on paper, ProtoActive allows designers to create interfaces that are not constrained by a pre-built set of controls. Among the tools studied, another limitation was the lack of a feature that allows designers to free-hand sketch pages. Having pre-built UI widgets might increase the productivity and the speed of creating prototypes, but this comes at the cost of constrained creativity, especially of concern for the design of ITS applications that is a field that is still evolving (and so are the UI widgets used in these applications). ProtoActive is a sketch-based prototyping tool that proposes to mimic the visual refinement of paper prototypes. This was done according to Buxton's principles about sketching and low-fidelity prototypes looking quick and dirty which encourages users to provide more feedback [24]. Having a sketch-based prototyping tool was gathered from drawbacks from *UISKEI* [33], *SILK* [32], *DEMAIS* [34], *Balsamiq Mockups* [36], *Axure Rp* [37], *Microsoft Sketch Flow* [38] and *Fore UI* [39].There is however a way to also help designers in further steps of the design, by allowing them to import high-fidelity images of prototypes into ProtoActive and link these pages using ProtoActive's features.

PROTOACTIVE

ProtoActive is based on *Active Story Touch* (AST) a tool developed by Hosseini-Khayat *et al.* that targets the creation of low-fidelity prototypes for touch-based applications [35]. AST had to be modified in order to cover the needs of an ITS application and to allow designers to define their own gestures. Designers in ProtoActive elicit user feedback through sketch-based prototypes that take into consideration the size constraints of the target ITS device the application will be used on. These prototypes allow the evaluation of how users will interact with the application by having a pre-

built set of gestures that can be expanded through a gesture recorder tool (IGT) that allows the creation of custom gestures without requiring the designer to write any programming code. These gestures can be used by the user to interact with the prototypes.

Design guidelines based on interviews

A qualitative study was conducted in order to gather requirements for ProtoActive. We conducted semi-structured interviews with UX designers from industry. The semi-structured interviews lasted around 40 minutes each and covered usability issues of sketching on a multi-touch device. The interviews aimed to collect experiences with other prototyping tools from the designers and gather their opinions about desirable features for a sketch-based prototyping tool for touch-based applications. During the interviews, participants could use paper, tablets or tabletop devices that were available at the interview location, to demonstrate behavior and functionalities. Based on the interviews, ProtoActive was designed to be a sketch based prototyping tool. Prototyping tools with pre-built drag and drop *User Interface* (UI) widgets would bias designers to use these widgets thus constraining creativity. From one of the participants: *"I've been working with 3D applications* (for ITS) *for a while and the concept of these components* (pre-built widgets), *they don't quite apply"*. In ProtoActive, sketches are performed on touch-based screens, meaning that in a similar fashion to paper, the sketches are visualized on the same display where they are made.

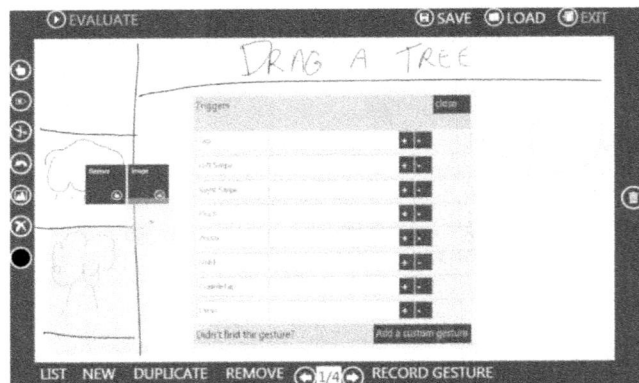

Figure 2 ProtoActive gesture menu

ProtoActive functionality

Prototypes in ProtoActive can be interacted with via gestures and this can be done through the use of *gesture areas*. *Gesture areas* are movable and resizable areas defined on the page of a prototype that can be bound to one or multiple pairs of gesture and page.

ProtoActive comes with a pre-built set of gestures (Figure 2): *Tap* (a single tap with the finger on the surface), *Double tap* (subsequent taps with the finger on the surface), *Pinch* (gesture using two fingers moving towards each other), *Swipe left* and *Swipe right (*single finger moving in the swipe direction), *Lasso* (single finger gesture of an arbitrary shape establishing a closed loop), *Zoom* (gesture using two fingers moving in opposite directions). If a designer wants to use a gesture that is not listed, he can create custom gestures using IGT [41]. IGT (Figure 3) has a canvas where the designer can perform the gesture he wants ProtoActive to learn (involving multi-finger,hand postures and fiduciary markers). The designer can provide as many samples as he wants, as different samples allow the anti-unification algorithm [41] to identify the different nuances that the gesture definition should cover. For each sample provided (and for the anti-unified definition created) ProtoActive shows the primitives (properties) of the gesture provided as a sample.

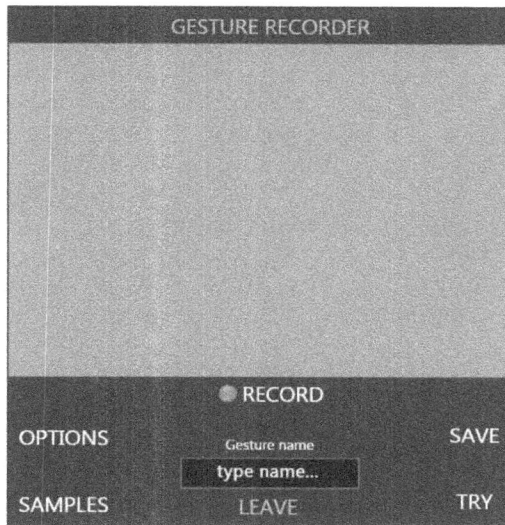

Figure 3 Gesture recorder (IGT) screenshot

For example: length, orientation, number of fingers, basic shapes (circle, line), detection of fiduciary tags, detection of a hand and how these primitives relate to each other. This is the only mechanism that designers have to see how a provided sample was recognized by ProtoActive. Alcantara *et al.* described how IGT integrates with ProtoActive (previously named as ASG) and how it creates gesture definitions without requiring any programming expertise by using samples of the gesture performed by the designer [41]. The main purpose of a prototyping tool is to elicit user feedback about design ideas, so in order to allow designers to evaluate their prototypes, ProtoActive has an *evaluation mode* where the only way to move through pages is through the defined *gesture areas*. If a gesture from the gesture-page binding is recognized on the *gesture area*, the prototype will show the corresponding page of the binding. Figure 4 illustrates how a designer can use a sequence of pages to simulate the behavior of the application. When evaluating the prototype in Figure 4, the first screen (quadrant 1) is a login screen that has a *gesture area* that is activated when a certain tag is placed over the gesture area. Quadrant 2 shows a scan image screen with images A, B and C. Image B has a *gesture area* that is bound to two gestures: place *open right hand* gesture that navigates to quadrant 3, where it shows

image B selected and with a menu; and a *"X"* gesture, that navigates to quadrant 4, meaning that image B was deleted. Both *open right hand* detection and *"X"* gesture can be created using IGT, thus making these two gestures available in ProtoActive. It is important to mention that making use of the features of ProtoActive: pages creation, gestures creation, gesture binding to specific areas of the prototype and gesture recognition can be done without writing one single line of code. The machine learning process to create gestures was described in Alcantara *et al.* [41].

EVALUATION

In order to evaluate ProtoActive, the evaluation was conducted in three stages: first, a pilot study was conducted to evaluate ProtoActive in designing ITS applications having developers with experience in developing multi-touch applications for tabletops. The second study incorporates the results of the first pilot study and was conducted with designers experienced in designing tangible applications and focused on getting qualitative feedback about using ProtoActive to design tangible applications for tabletops. Finally, the third stage was an evaluation of ProtoActive *in the wild* [40], where ProtoActive was used by designers for a period of at least two weeks in their projects.

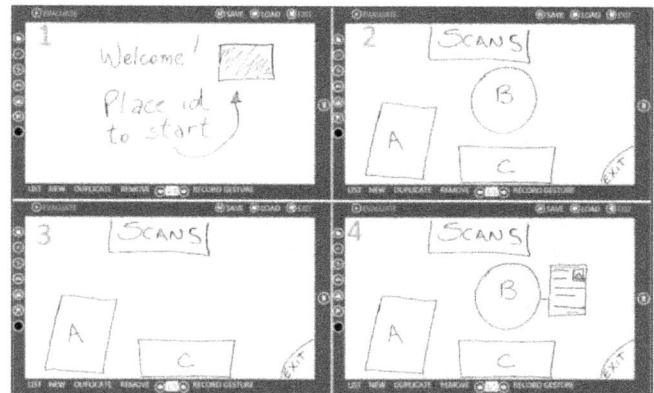

Figure 4 Navigating between the pages in ProtoActive

Pilot study of gesture based prototypes

A pilot user study of ProtoActive was conducted with seven participants. Each one of the participants had a minimum of six months of experience developing ITS applications for academic projects. Participants were presented with a demo of the features of ProtoActive that lasted on average ten minutes. The demo explained how to draw, navigate between pages in ProtoActive and how to create a gesture. In order to avoid biasing participants, the pre-built set of gestures was not offered to the participants. Participants were asked to create a prototype for an ITS medical application to select MRI scans. The scenario given to participants covered three main functionalities in a similar fashion as shown in Figure 4: a log in screen; a selecting a scan image; and bringing up a menu over an image to delete it. The participants were asked to create the prototypes using ProtoActive on a Microsoft Surface and view their designs by clicking *"evaluate prototype"* when done. According to the *Think Aloud Protocol* [42], participants were encouraged to verbalize their impressions and comment throughout their experience with ProtoActive. By the end of the evaluation, participants were asked to complete a survey that asked their impression of using ProtoActive.

Time spent on tasks

The average time to build the prototype for the login page was four minutes and forty six seconds with a *standard deviation* of one minute and thirty seven seconds (SD=1:37); the *select image* took an average of five minutes and twenty seconds (SD=2:59) and finally the last page of the prototype that should show a menu and delete a scan image took an average of five minutes and fifteen seconds (SD=1:52). The longest time was spent when the participant was not satisfied with gesture recognition.

Defining and evaluating gestures

Defining a gesture in IGT had usability issues regarding the information that is shown to participants. While providing a sample gesture to IGT, the only feedback that participants used for checking whether the provided sample was properly analyzed was the canvas that contained the strokes from the gesture. One of the participants that tried to look at the GDL of the gesture, said that it did not mean a lot to him and that *"it seemed fine"*. Another participant mentioned that *"(GDL) it doesn't look clear enough to read it"*. The participants were asked to create any gesture they thought to be appropriate for the task. Figure 5 and Figure 6 show the gestures created for each task and the occurrence of the gesture for that task. For the last task, the combination of opening a menu and deleting an image produced a different combination of gesture for each participant: *square and tap; tap and swipe right; z shaped gesture; swipe up and swipe left; swipe up-left and tap; swipe right and tap.*

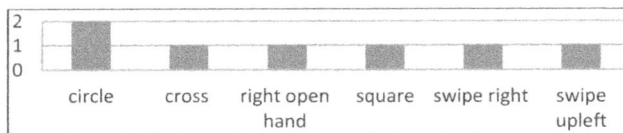

Figure 5 Gestures used for login

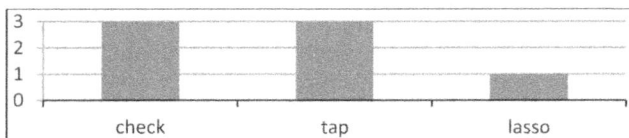

Figure 6 Gestures used for selecting an image

Discussion of pilot study results

The study shows the potential of different interaction approaches that can be used for the same task and emphasizes the need for a tool like ProtoActive that allows designers to explore different interaction approaches but evaluating these interactions in user studies using prototypes. For the first (logging in) and the last task (opening a menu and deleting), the different ways that an interaction can be designed for the same task illustrate how ProtoActive could help designers explore and evaluate different ways for a user to interact with an ITS application. The survey showed that, overall, the participants were satisfied with both IGT and ProtoActive, with IGT eliciting a few remarks when it appeared that a gesture was not recognized: feedback about the samples recognized for a gesture definition and problems with sketching in ProtoActive.

Improving gesture definition

Due to inconsistent hardware performance in touch recognition, it is necessary to provide designers with feedback about how a sample of a gesture was recognized. The problem of showing designers how a sample was recognized is not a trivial aspect, as having detailed information about the recognized sample might require expertise from designers to understand it; and without any information designers cannot identify potential recognition problems. In order to solve this problem, the chosen approach was to show a thumbnail of the print of the sample (the stroke generated while providing the sample) next to the definition of the sample in GDL. A designer isn't required to read the GDL of each sample but if he wants to see the gesture definition, he can look for detailed information of the steps recognized in the provided sample that might affect the gesture recognition.

Improving prototyping on a touch-based device

Another problem noticed during this evaluation was caused by a design decision about the sketching features of ProtoActive: to take advantages of a multi-touch device, selecting strokes, erasing and defining *gesture areas* needed a combination of two hands to happen; while one finger stays pressing the correspondent button, the other would perform the action on ProtoActive drawing canvas (*e.g.*: one hand holds the selection button while the other performs a lasso on canvas to select strokes). This feature was not well accepted by participants, due to hardware limitation, in some occasions an event would be miss-triggered, detecting that a finger was moved up from the device; depending on the distance between the button and the place on the canvas that the action was performed, it felt uncomfortable for participants; and in some other occasions, participants would move up the finger holding the button by mistake. The solution was to change this functionality to a regular button on the screen that doesn't need to be held.

Pilot study of prototyping TUI applications

This pilot study investigated the value of prototyping in the design of tangible applications. The study was conducted with five UX designers that had experience in the design of tangible applications; four designers from academia and one from industry. In order to validate prototypes in the tangible application context, designers were asked to create a prototype in ProtoActive and include the use of some clay, printed tags and plastic toys with tags attached to them (which were provided for the study). The aim of this study was to have participants think aloud about prototyping for tangible applications, to collect information about the value of prototyping for tangible applications and how a tool could better improve this process. Participants were given a scenario where they needed to design functionalities of a *Geographical Information System* (GIS) application. Participants were asked to prototype a login screen and a map that would change layers when specific tags were placed on the surface tabletop. According to the *Think Aloud Protocol* [42], participants were encouraged to verbalize their impressions and comment while creating the prototypes in ProtoActive. After creating the prototypes, a semi-structured interview was conducted. The interview covered the importance of prototyping for tangible applications, regarding the application and the physical tangibles; the participant's impressions about ProtoActive and how they think ProtoActive could have aided them in their previous tangible-based projects. The participants had never previously used prototypes for the design of the tangible applications. Participants' design ideas had always been communicated through paper sketches and tangibles were used with a trial and error approach.

Time spent on creating prototypes
The participants were impressed with the amount of design ideas that could be covered in a prototype that took less than thirty minutes to be created with ProtoActive. When asked about how useful ProtoActive would be to quickly evaluate design ideas for tangible applications, one of the participants commented: *"coding the interface and the interactions would take forever (...) but if I would use sketches on a paper, I am not sure that I could represent it* (tangibles interactions) *just as nicely"*. Using ProtoActive, as mentioned by the participants, consumed less time than some bad design decisions had cost them in previous projects and could even help to discuss design ideas between teammates: *"*(to discuss ideas between teammates) *it is so much easier if you can see what you're talking about"*.

Designing and evaluating tangibles
Figure 7 shows tangibles that were provided to participants and could be used in the evaluation; Figure 7 compares a tree created by a participant with a fiduciary tag and a plastic toy that could be used to activate the vegetation layer on the study. The participants' comments on these two options allowed the researcher to understand how crucial to this stage of design the shape of the tangible is. This was mentioned by one of the participants: *"sometimes the concept is still too abstract that the shape of the tangible doesn't matter (...) but there are other cases when it might be important to differentiate, some shapes automatically represent what you want to show, for example, this is a tree and represents vegetation"*. The interviews showed that participants found that creating clay prototypes of the tangibles is a valuable asset, especially for tangibles that imply movement and require ergonomics studies. For situations where a tangible does not need any special shape, the clay did not seem necessary, and the participants chose to use tags simply attached to colored plastic toys.

Participants also commented that a valuable asset of this approach is to also bring clay and printed tags for the evaluation of the prototypes with users, allowing them to make suggestions and even have them create their own clay prototypes during the prototype evaluation. As mentioned by one of the participants: *"you need to prototype it* (the tangible) *as well as it might affect the interaction"*.

Evaluations in the wild
Finally, an evaluation of ProtoActive's efficacy for designing applications *in the wild* [40] was conducted by asking two UX designers in industry and academia to use ProtoActive in their design process. The aim of this evaluation was to have designers use ProtoActive in their own environment and to assist with the design of applications they care about. The evaluation was structured in two phases. First, we provided the tool installation and a brief explanation of the tool, in video format, explaining the features of the tool. When the participant had spent at least two weeks becoming familiar with ProtoActive, the author contacted the participants individually, sending a survey. The responses on the survey was used as a guide for a semi-structured interview aiming to collect data about the gestures created using ProtoActive, the application being designed by the participant and the sketches created.

Figure 7 Clay custom tangibles and the plastic toy tangible

Using ProtoActive to design for a vertical multi-touch device to be used in oil platforms
A UX designer used ProtoActive to evaluate design ideas of a gesture-based commercial application to be used in a proprietary dual-capacitive touch display that supports two simultaneous touch points. The display was created to resist extreme temperature conditions. The participant is a UX designer who has eight years of industry experience and no experience in programming gestures for touch-devices. The participant uses low-fidelity prototypes regularly in his job, has used different prototyping tools including pen and paper and considers prototyping a critical part in the design of ITS applications. The designed application is a main system navigation to be used in oil platforms that will likely be used by users wearing protective gloves. In this scenario, besides evaluating interface and gestures, ProtoActive was used to study how designers in an environment with extreme temperature conditions interact with a touch-based device: using gloves or stylus pens. Also, since the designer was working directly with the proprietary custom device during design of the applications in ProtoActive, he was able to test

the device capabilities and identify a problem when working with two simultaneous touch points. The overall comment from the UX designer was: *"Overall it's a very promising tool. We had no other tools at all for looking at gestures, so it fills a necessary void. We are unfortunately in an early development stage of our device and with ProtoActive discovered some issues with our touch screen drivers with dual touch and gestures".*

Regarding the drawbacks and problems found using ProtoActive, the UX designer found that it is not clear how many samples would be enough for a good gesture definition. He suggested that for the anti-unified gesture definition, an image was shown illustrating a heat map of an overlap between all the gestures, where overlapping strokes would have higher temperature visualization.

```
validate as step 1
        Touch state: TouchUp
        Touch shape: Circle
        Touch direction: Right
        Touch path length: x
validate as step 2
        Touch state: TouchUp
        Touch shape: Circle
        Touch direction: Right
        Touch path length: 1.5x ..2x
validate
        Touch limit: 2
        Relative position between 1 and 2: Left
```

Figure 8 Circle gesture defined by participant

Regarding reading GDL the UX designer said that he grew more comfortable and could understand better the language after the time he spent using it. The participant's only suggestion to how this could be improved would be to provide a list with all the possible primitives that can be identified in GDL, but overall, the participant was satisfied with reading GDL and said that it was a good way to determine if a sample was properly recognized. Regarding usability issues with ProtoActive, the participant's only suggestion was to have a way to fix the position of some *gesture areas*, avoiding unintended drags on the page.

Using ProtoActive to design a tabletop game
The participant in this evaluation is a PhD candidate who used ProtoActive to prototype a new version of the high automation interface for tabletop of the pandemic game described by Wallace *et al.* [43]. The participant had no previous experience in designing ITS applications or programmatically creating gestures, but with experience in using pen and paper to prototype interfaces. In order to design the prototypes, the participant used a tablet that supports up to two touch points.

The final application will be used in a tabletop device, but according to the participant, a tablet was used for prototyping due to:

- availability of the device, as the tabletop that could be used to prototype is shared among other teammates for different projects;
- portability, as sometimes the design had to be shown or evaluated in different locations, having a tabletop would impair the evaluation process.

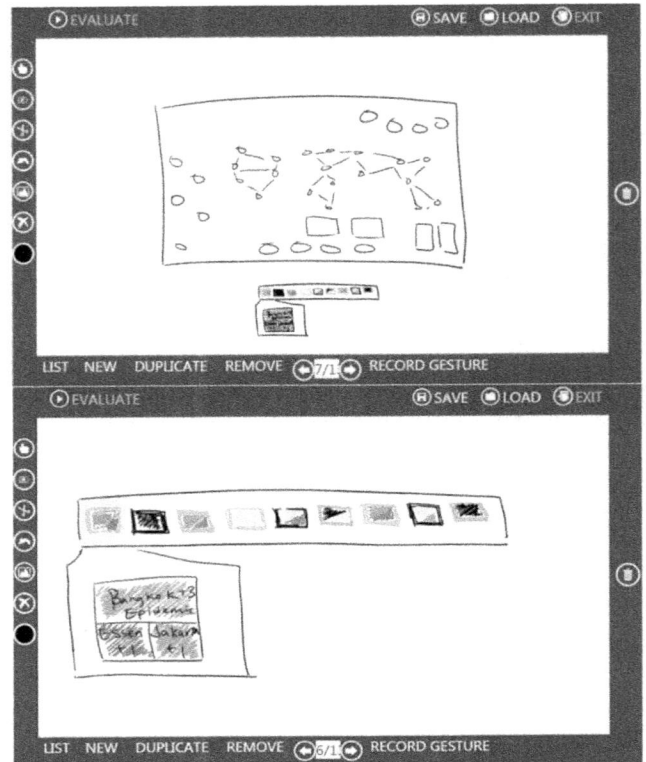

Figure 9 Using ProtoActive to provide more detail about items

According to the participant, ProtoActive was used in the following scenarios:

- using ProtoActive as a tool to brainstorm and sketch different ideas. Later, if needed, interactivity can be added to the sketches on ProtoActive and they can be evaluated;
- creating a prototype of small tasks and guide users to play with the prototype to elicit discussion about the interface and the interactions in it;
- using the prototypes to transmit ideas about design and interaction options. In this scenario the designer was the one interacting with the prototypes and was mostly used during meetings to communicate the design ideas to supervisors and teammates.

In total, the participant estimated to have used ProtoActive for fifteen hours spread along three weeks, generating twenty different prototypes, and having four users that evaluated the prototypes. Regarding the gesture definition feature, the participant commented: *"I think the defining custom gesture functionality was pretty good. It is unclear what order to carry out actions for first time users. However, once learnt,*

I think it is pretty good". The participant mentioned that for most of the interactions used in the prototypes the gestures pre-built in the tool sufficed and only three custom gestures were created: *two fingers hold* and *two fingers swipe*.

Figure 9 illustrates how the participant used ProtoActive to better illustrate specific points of a prototype. The top of Figure 9 shows how a menu will appear contextualized within the game screen; the bottom of Figure 9 shows the menu in more detail, showing how a designer can obtain feedback about different depth of functionalities. Also, as can be seen in Figure 9, a prototyping tool based in pre-built UI widgets would change the level of abstraction as most of the interface items in the prototypes are undefined shapes.

DISCUSSION AND LIMITATIONS
Allowing designers to create custom gestures allows the evaluation of different interaction ideas contained in the costs and time constraints of low-fidelity prototyping. This was shown by the evaluations in the pilot studies that contained gestures that do not exist in the prototyping tools investigated in related work. Providing designers with ways to evaluate these gestures in the final application context (through using the custom created gestures in interactive prototypes) allows these innovative interactions to be developed following a user-centered approach as recommended by Norman and Nielsen [2]. The different evaluations showed that ProtoActive fills the need for creating prototypes for ITS applications, but it arguably has limited support for gathering data during evaluation. Designers often rely on their own equipment to record the video and audio of evaluation sessions of the prototypes. ProtoActive support for evaluation relies on the same as paper prototyping.

ProtoActive uses Gesture Toolkit [7] for gesture recognition and definition. This means that some of the limitations in Gesture Toolkit are inherited. While the GDL supports multi-step gestures, it is currently limited to gestures with sequential steps and that need to fit in the toolkit gesture primitives. The feature to allow the gesture recognizer to break the gesture into parts facilitates the sequential process but it requires some experience from the designer to decide if dividing a gesture into steps or not will generate the best gesture definition for its needs.

CONCLUSION AND FUTURE WORK
This research offers two main contributions. The first is ProtoActive, a sketch-based prototyping tool for ITS applications. ProtoActive allows designers to evaluate not only the output of sketch-based prototypes (namely what happens when a user wants to accomplish a task) but also the input on the prototypes and how a user wants to interact and accomplish a task. In order to allow the evaluation of this input, the prototypes in ProtoActive can be interacted with via a pre-built set of gestures or through customized gestures. ProtoActive supports designers following user-centered design of ITS applications. The second contribution in this paper is an evaluation of ProtoActive consisting of two pilot studies and two evaluations in the wild. The first pilot study gathered the different gestures that participants created to perform similar tasks. The variety of gestures created for the same task suggests that designers benefit from a tool like ProtoActive to evaluate different and innovative interactions. The second pilot study evaluated ProtoActive features for prototyping TUI applications, using fiduciary markers. One of the participants stated that by using such a tool, hours of development could be saved by evaluating the tag-based gesture in a prototype that took thirty minutes to be created. This shows that potential problems and design issues could be addressed before the implementation phase. Feedback from the second pilot study shows that by being so easy to use, such a tool could also be used to explain a design idea and act as a communication artifact between team members (which was in fact used by the evaluation in the wild for the tabletop game). Our participants recognized the value of using ProtoActive to experiment and evaluate design ideas in an early stage of application development. Future work should address the usability issues found during the evaluations of ProtoActive. Our method of defining and recognizing gestures could be improved to be adaptable to other gesture recognizers. Also, a mechanism for resolving conflicting gestures during gesture recognition should be created. In the current version of ProtoActive a *gesture area* can support multiple gestures, but does not detect potential conflicts between gesture definitions. The future conflict resolution mechanism should also then have a way of warning designers about conflicting gestures.

REFERENCES
1. Norman, D.,A. (2007). The Design of Future Things. Ed. Basic Books.
2. Norman, D., Nielsen, J. (2010). Gestural interfaces: a step backward in usability. Interactions, vol 17, issue 5.
3. Hesselmann, T., & Boll, S. (2011). SCIVA: designing applications for surface computers.EICS 2011, 191-196.
4. Moggridge, B. (2007). Designing Interactions. MIT, Ch 10 – People and Prototypes. Press, Cambridge, MA.
5. Hinrichs, U., Carpendale, S. (2011). Gestures in the Wild : Studying Multi-Touch Gesture Sequences on Interactive Tabletop Exhibits. CHI'11, 3023-3032.
6. Wobbrock, J. O., Morris, M. R., & Wilson, A. D. (2009). User-defined gestures for surface computing. *CHI '09*. Pages 1083-1092.
7. Khandkar, S. H., & Maurer, F. (2010). A Domain Specific Language to Define Gestures for Multi-Touch Applications, DSM '10, Article 2 , 6 pages.
8. Lao, S., Heng, X., Zhang, G., Ling, Y., Wang, P. (2009). A gestural interaction design model for multi-touch displays. BCS-HCI '09, 440-446.
9. Allan Christian Long, Jr., James A. Landay, and Lawrence A. Rowe. (1999). Implications for a gesture design tool. CHI '99. 40-47.

10. Lyons,K., Brashear,H., Westeyn,T., Kim,J.S., Starner, T. (2007). GART: the gesture and activity recognition toolkit. HCI'07. 718-727.

11. Anthony, L.,Wobbrock. J.O. (2012). $N-protractor: a fast and accurate multistroke recognizer. GI'12.117-120.

12. Kin, K., Hartmann B., DeRose T., Agrawala M.. Proton: Multitouch Gestures as Regular Expressions. CHI'12, ACM 978-1-4503-1015-4/12/05.

13. Plimmer, B., Blagojevic,R., Hsiao-Heng Chang,S., Schmieder,P., Zhen, J.S. (2012). RATA: codeless generation of gesture recognizers. BCS-HCI '12, 137-146.

14. Wiethoff, A., Schneider, H., Rohs, M., & Butz, A. Greenberg, S. (2012). Sketch-a-TUI: low cost prototyping of tangible interactions using cardboard and conductive ink. Embodied Interaction, 1, 309-312.

15. Marco,J., Cerezo,E., Baldassarri,S. (2012). ToyVision: a toolkit for prototyping tabletop tangible games. EICS '12. 71-80.

16. Shaer,O., Jacob, R.J.K. (2009). A specification paradigm for the design and implementation of tangible user interfaces. CHI'09. 16, 4, Article 20, 39 pages.

17. Rudd, J., Stern, K., Isensee, S. (1996). Low vs. high-fidelity prototyping debate, interactions, v.3 , p.76-85.

18. Sefelin, R., Tscheligi, M., Giller, V. (2003). Paper prototyping - what is it good for?: a comparison of paper and computer-based low-fidelity prototyping, CHI '03.

19. Virzi, R.A., Sokolov, J.L., Karis, D. (1996). Usability problem identification using both low- and high-fidelity prototypes, CHI'96, p.236-243.

20. McCurdy, M., Connors, C., Pyrzak, G., Kanefsky, B., Vera, A. (2006). Breaking the fidelity barrier: an examination of our current characterization of prototypes and an example of a mixed-fidelity success. CHI '06. 1233-1242.

21. Youn-Kyung Lim, Stolterman, E., Tenenberg, J.. (2008). The anatomy of prototypes: Prototypes as filters, prototypes as manifestations of design ideas. CHI'08. 15, 2, Article 7 , 27 pages.

22. Derboven, J., Roeck, D. D., & Verstraete, M. (2010). Low-Fidelity Prototyping for Multi-Touch Surfaces. . Presented in the workshop Engineering Patterns for Multi-Touch Interfaces held in EICS'10.

23. Klaus Krippendorff. (2006). The Semantic Turn: A New Foundation for Design. Taylor & Francis, Boca Raton, FL.

24. Bill Buxton. (2007). Sketching User Experiences: Getting the Design Right and the Right Design.Morgan Kaufmann Publishers Inc., San Francisco, CA, USA.

25. Constantine, L. L. (2004). Beyond user-centered design and user experience: Designing for user performance. Cutter IT Journal, 17, 2.

26. Robertson, S., Robertson, J. (2006). Mastering the Requirements Process (2nd Edition). Chapter 12. Addison-Wesley Professional.

27. Rudd, J., Stern, K., and Isensee, S. (1996) Low vs. high fidelity prototyping debate. Interactions, 3, 1, 76-85.

28. Morris, M., R., Wobbrock,J., O., Wilson., A.,D. (2010). Understanding users' preferences for surface gestures. GI '10. 261-268.

29. Gerken,J., Jetter,H.C., Schmidt,T., Reiterer, H. (2010) Can "touch" get annoying?. ITS '10. 257-258.

30. Sinha, A.K., Landay,J.A. (2003). Capturing user tests in a multimodal, multidevice informal prototyping tool. ICMI '03. 117-124.

31. J. David Smith and T. C. Nicholas Graham. (2010). Raptor: sketching games with a tabletop computer. Futureplay '10. 191-198.

32. Obrenovic, Z., Martens, JB.(2011). Sketching interactive systems with sketchify. ACM Trans. CHI'11. 18, 1, Article 4, 38 pages.

33. Segura V.C.V.B., Barbosa,S.D.J., Simões, F.P. (2012). UISKEI: a sketch-based prototyping tool for defining and evaluating user interface behavior. AVI '12. 18-25.

34. Bailey, B.P., Konstan, J.A., Carlis, J.V. (2001). DEMAIS: designing multimedia applications with interactive storyboards. MULTIMEDIA '01. 241-250.

35. Hosseini-Khayat, A., Seyed, T., Burns, C., Maurer, F. (2011). Low-Fidelity Prototyping of Gesture-based Applications. EICS'11. 289-294.

36. Balsamiq Mockups – Available at www.balsamiq.com. Accessed July 2012

37. Axure RP: Interactive wireframe software and mockup tool. Available at http://www.axure.com/. Accessed October 2012.

38. Microsoft Sketchflow. Available at http://www.microsoft.com/expression/products/sketchflow_overview.aspx. Accessed March 2012.

39. ForeUI: Easy to use UI prototyping tool. Available at http://www.foreui.com/. Accessed October 2012.

40. Johnson,R., Rogers, Y., van der Linden, J., Bianchi-Berthouze, N. (2012). Being in the thick of in-the-wild studies: the challenges and insights of researcher participation. In Proceedings of CHI '12. 1135-1144.

41. Alcantara, T., Denzinger, J. , Ferreira, J. , Maurer, F. (2012). Learning gestures for interacting with low-fidelity prototypes. RAISE'12,.32-36.

42. Lethbridge, T. C., & Sim, S. E. (2005). Studying software engineers: Data collection techniques for software field studies. Empirical Software Engineering, 10(3), 311–341.

43. Wallace, J.R., Pape, J., Yu-Ling Betty Chang, McClelland,P.J., Graham,T.C.N., Scott, S.D. and Hancock, M. (2012). Exploring automation in digital tabletop board game. CSCW '12.231-234.

Toward Rapid and Iterative Development of Tangible, Collaborative, Distributed User Interfaces

Chris Branton, Brygg Ullmer, Andre Wiggins, Landon Rogge,
Narendra Setty, Stephan David Beck, Alex Reeser
Louisiana State University
Baton Rouge, LA, USA 70803
{branton, ullmer, awiggi5, lrogge1, nnary3, sdbeck, areese2}@lsu.edu

ABSTRACT

Distributed, tangible, collaborative applications involve potentially complex interactions of users, computing platforms, and physical artifacts. Realizing the necessary connections for these interactions can create hardware and software dependencies early in development, resulting in a system that is difficult to adapt to design changes. The Ensemble architecture is designed to encourage exploratory development of these systems by limiting the impact of changing components. Ensemble is a product of the exploratory design process it supports, evolving through use in two distinct application domains. The experience gained from these implementations has shaped Ensemble's structure and design priorities, resulting in a component-based architecture that includes: (i) an application framework and graphical user interface support; (ii) a service framework, including service publication and discovery; (iii) local and remote event handling; (iv) distributed user and resource coordination; and (v) a structured configuration language shared by all Ensemble components.

Author Keywords

Multi-platform user interfaces; Multi-device user interfaces; Distributed user interfaces; Software architecture; Tangible interfaces

ACM Classification Keywords

H.5.2. Information Interfaces and Presentation: User interface management systems

General Terms

Human Factors; Design; Experimentation.

INTRODUCTION

The value of iterating user interface designs is well established. During these iterations, it can be difficult to make structural changes to systems that feature novel user interaction techniques and technologies. Advanced user interfaces are increasingly distributed and heterogeneous. Tangible, multi-modal, and distributed interfaces can comprise a broad array of devices, network environments, programming languages, operating systems, runtime frameworks, and both automated and human agents. Complex systems quickly become hard to modify as hardware and software dependencies make changes increasingly difficult to execute. Too often, the resulting systems are brittle and difficult to adapt, constraining designers' ability to adjust early design decisions.

The Ensemble architecture is designed to shorten iteration times for exploratory development of distributed and multi-modal interfaces, limiting the impact of changes to specific components, technologies, or aspects of a system while still providing considerable UI design flexibility. Ensemble can be used as the basis for complete applications, or serve as a prototyping tool to explore different software or hardware design patterns.

A number of frameworks and applications have been developed to create collaborative, distributed, multimodal, or tangible systems, but few of these focus on iterative exploratory development [24, 25, 33, 29]. Unlike other architectures or frameworks in this area, Ensemble is geared toward initial rapid development of experimental systems that are loosely-coupled, fault tolerant and relatively resilient to component substitution, without the overhead of autonomic features.

To this end, Ensemble defines a simple component model with compact APIs; a messaging and event system intended to integrate easily with existing UI toolkits (e.g. Java Swing) and remote peers; a service framework based on an established grid computing model; and an extensible configuration language for specifying properties and relationships of ensemble members.

The Ensemble architecture is comparatively lightweight, cross-platform, and capable of modeling a number of interaction styles and design patterns. The current implementation directly supports integration of Java Swing graphical user interfaces with external devices and applications, inter-host communication via Open Sound Control (OSC) [36], and member service publication and discovery.

Ensemble and its predecessors have been used in the exploration of core tangibles [32], multiple display systems, interactive digital posters, computer-human musical performance [5], and interactive high performance computing. The architecture has been used to compose entire applications, and increasingly as a glue architecture to combine existing components and systems. Ensemble applications have been deployed at international conferences, science education centers, public events, and in college classrooms.

RELATED WORK

Multi-device and distributed interfaces [22, 12] are an important topic of research in several areas, including ubiquitious computing [35], computer supported cooperative work [10], tangible and embodied interaction [26], and the number of architectures, frameworks, and systems being developed is growing rapidly. Complete coverage of this work will not be attempted here. We have instead selected a small number of relevant examples to illustrate the potential role of Ensemble in this landscape.

Relatively few systems target prototyping and early development of tangible distributed interfaces, and most of these are focused on a particular platform, type of interface, or specific technology. For example, Toyvision [24] supports prototyping of tangible games, but is specifically targeted for multi-touch tabletops. The Proximity Toolkit [25] focuses on distance and orientation in multi-device interaction. Microsoft's .NET Gadgeteer [33] supports structured prototyping of tangible devices using the .Net Micro Framework and the Visual Studio IDE. We are unaware of another prototyping architecture designed to integrate tangible applications across a spectrum of devices, host platforms, and interaction types.

The OpenInterface platform [29] was created for prototyping multimodal systems. The OpenInterface focus on device abstraction through common API's and transformations is well aligned with Ensemble's design strategy. OpenInterface is not primarily designed for distributed interfaces, and is focused on interaction device integration. Squidy [19] is a platform with similar goals. Like OpenInterface, Squidy uses the type of dataflow approach that motivated early iterations of Ensemble, and includes a full-featured graphical development environment. And like Ensemble, Squidy defines a common programming interface and makes use of OSC for communication between remote instances of the toolkit [37].

DynaMo [1] is a framework for engineering pervasive multimodal systems, and features an autonomic manager for dynamic device integration. Like Ensemble, DynaMo is service-oriented, dynamic, and specifies component properties with structured text (i.e. XML). DynaMo is not primarily intended for protoyping, and requires substantial software infrastructure.

HephaisTK [13] is also used for multimodal system development, designed primarily to serve as a testbed for multimodal fusion algorithms [14]. HephaisTK uses SMUIML to specify and integrate multiple levels of program behavior, but does not support distributed applications directly.

ReticularSpaces [3] supports development of distributed interfaces in multi-display environments. ReticularSpaces provides direct support for the activity-based computing (ABC) concept [2], which organizes tasks, users, and resources around the construct of collaborative activities.

Shared Substance [16] is a system for creating multi-surface interfaces in ubiquitous computing environments. Shared Substance and Ensemble share a focus on flexibility and separation of interaction and data, and several of the design goals of the instrument interaction model [4] upon which Shared Substance is based. Commands (instructions), instruments (devices), and targets are explicitly represented in Ensemble. Shared Substance is a language level framework requiring its own runtime environment and programming framework, while Ensemble is primarily an application level system.

PuReWidgets [8] is a programming toolkit for development of interactive applications for public displays. This usage scenario is similar to several of Ensemble's early implementations, and its focus on local and remote browser-based interfaces reflects a growing direction in Ensemble development.

Ensemble's focus on breadth and flexibility engenders a preference for lightweight and adaptable infrastructure, and a compact set of features in comparison to the more mature or specialized systems mentioned here. For example, while Ensemble is intended to be used with various types of input and output devices, the architecture is not specifically engineered for multimodal interaction like DynaMo [1] or HephaisTK [13], and does not provide direct support for multimodal features like autonomic management or data fusion. Instead, Ensemble defines architectural constructs to facilitate integration of such capabilities. And while Ensemble is service-oriented like DynaMo and ReticularSpaces [3], the design focus is on providing service publication, discovery, and supporting capabilities rather than specific service definitions or infrastructure. For instance, Ensemble services are not necessarily stateful like those of ABC, but state modeling and tracking APIs are available through the grid framework classes. A comparison of key features of Ensemble with some related examples is given in Table 1.

	Distributed	Multimodal	Service oriented	Prototyping focus
Ensemble	✓	○	✓	✓
DynaMo	✓	✓	✓	
HephaisTK		✓		✓
OpenInterface		✓		✓
ReticularSpaces	✓		✓	
PuReWidgets	✓		✓	
Shared Spaces	✓	○		○
Squidy		✓	✓	
ToyVision	✓	○		✓

Table 1: Comparison of design focus for related frameworks and systems. (✓ = supports; ○ = partially supports.)

Recent Ensemble design has been influenced by its use with Grendl, an application for coordinating performances of laptop orchestras [5]. A number of languages and environments have been developed either specifically for laptop orchestras, or to support the collaborative performance paradigm of laptop orchestras, including ChucK [34] and NRCI [7]. These languages and systems focus primarily on interactions of the instruments themselves, and do not consider the context of the performance as a whole.

MOTIVATION AND BACKGROUND

An important motivator of this work is what Edwards et al. refer to as "the infrastructure problem in HCI" [15]. This is the idea that every layer of a system has some impact on the interaction aspect. This can be especially vexing in the area of tangible systems research, where relatively minor changes in interaction hardware can cause significant changes to system structure, often degrading system design [9].

The features of Ensemble are perhaps best understood in the context of its origins. Ensemble evolved through the intersection of two initially independent research threads. The first was an exploration of the concept of core tangibles in distributed environments [31, 32]. These projects often made use of purpose-built hardware, firmware, and software [28], and feedback was gathered by installing working systems in public spaces and at special events. Later iterations have focused on utilizing consumer electronics (e.g. tablet computers) in the construction of core tangibles.

The developing architecture was subsequently adapted to address a different set of challenges faced by computer music ensembles, whose performances incorporated a continuously changing array of musicians, machines, computer instruments, and interaction devices. The current architecture works to address requirements common to the two domains.

Ensemble is currently being used to test the hypothesis that a number of user interaction types can be modeled as a collaborative computer-human performance, in pre-scripted, improvisational, or hybrid forms. Ensemble views a distributed system as a performing group, a workflow as a script or playlist, and the user interface as a set of linked performance spaces.

Prototyping multi-modal and distributed interfaces

The genesis of Ensemble was a series of projects exploring interaction strategies and technologies for informal science education, deployed as kiosks in public venues. The research focus of these applications was to advance understanding and development of core tangibles in a period of rapidly changing technology [32]. Figure 1 shows four variations.

Design refinements and lessons learned from each installation motivated changes to the physical platforms, interaction hardware, firmware, or software, and most often all at once. Planning, implementing, and tracking the changes consumed an increasing fraction of project time and effort. Changes to interaction device hardware or firmware often dictated wholesale redesign and reimplementation of otherwise functional application software.

The initial version of Ensemble, called ContentServer, was meant to help address these issues and return focus to designing effective user interfaces, enabling faster turnaround for each iteration, and more thorough evaluation of each deployment. ContentServer included thin wrappers for several Java Swing and Python-based graphical user interface (GUI) components, and support for runtime configuration of multiple displays. This allowed developers to hot-swap new design variations during program execution by editing text files. ContentServer included the common messaging system and instruction format that form the core of Ensemble, and allowed developers to quickly create adaptors for new interaction devices, whether local or remote. Applications deployed to this generation of kiosks were similar to those created using PureWidgets [8], with a Java Swing client substituted for PureWidgets' thin client implementation.

Grendl: Grid computing for music ensembles

Laptop ensembles use computers – often combined with specialized interface hardware – to create instruments for live musical performances (Figure 2). These performances often require musicians to launch, configure, and synchronize multiple custom software applications on a number of networked computers. This process may be repeated for each piece, all while an audience watches and waits. Grendl was developed to help distribute and execute music software, and manage application environments for a university laptop orchestra [5].

(a)   (b)

(c)   (d)

Figure 1: Generations of tangible kiosk designs contributed to the Ensemble architecture. (a) First generation kiosks made heavy use of custom electronics for tangible interaction technologies. (b,c) Second generation kiosks distributed the user interface between large displays and mobile computing platforms (i.e. smartphones and tablets). (d) Current generation combines large displays, mobile platforms, custom electronics, multitouch tabletops, and tangible interaction devices to create distributed interactive systems.

Immediately before (or during) a performance, Grendl reads the program (i.e. play list) and issues instructions that transfer all of the necessary components for each composition to every member of the ensemble. The conductor uses Grendl during the concert to issue instructions for members to launch and configure each piece at the proper time, and to stop execution and restore the environment when each piece is completed.

Figure 2: Laptop ensembles combine music, computation, and novel interaction techniques. In this piece, the orchestra creates a single instrument, with each player contributing a part. OSC messages connect the players, and projectors allow audience members to track each player's contribution.

Grendl views a laptop ensemble as a distributed computing platform. The first incarnation relied heavily on the SAGA grid computing framework [17] to deliver distributed functionality. Subsequent versions replaced SAGA with a variant of the Ensemble system adapted to retain many of the features of the grid service model. Ensemble members are modeled as grid nodes, with each composition seen as a job, and individual instructions as tasks.

Requirements and Objectives

The realization that ContentServer could be readily adapted to implement the performance-inspired grid model of Grendl shaped the overall design of Ensemble, and shifted focus for the architecture. Using ContentServer and Grendl as a foundation, subsequent design decisions were influenced primarily by the overarching goal of maintaining flexibility across technologies and interaction models during early development. This push for adaptability led to a decision to integrate the treatment of players, devices, content, and processes.

Ensemble is designed primarily to minimize required infrastucture and prerequisites, allowing developers to create working systems quickly. The objective motivating this approach is to facilitate exploration of design choices. In the same way

that HephaisTK [13] is designed to facilitate testing of fusion algorithms and OpenInterface [29] enables experimentation with interaction device choices, Ensemble seeks to facilitate testing of different combinations of interaction technology, application structure and interaction design.

Ensemble is targeted to work in the application-layer to the degree possible, avoiding the need for elevated privileges. Security is an important aspect of network applications, and we wished to preserve the ability to integrate existing access control schemes. The need to work with diverse collections of software and devices required us to abstract both data and flow of control (i.e., program structure) as much as possible, and create a system that is portable across operating systems and programming languages. To complement the desired architectural flexibility, we wanted to be able to add and remove users, devices, or content dynamically, ideally using a single mechanism.

ARCHITECTURE

From its beginnings as a small group of convenience classes, Ensemble has evolved into an architecture that includes a GUI component model, messaging and event model, service model, and configuration language. The grid computing framework and interactive performance model inspired by the Grendl experience have contributed a number of infrastructure classes and organizing constructs, broadening the types and complexity of applications that can be realized. One important strength of Ensemble is that only a few of these classes are required to create an application. This feature contributes to the ability of developers using Ensemble to create working systems quickly.

Ensemble applications are made up of collections of Players, Devices, and GUI components, collectively referred to as Interactors for the programming interface they share. The only responsibility of an Interactor is to process Instructions, as illustrated in Figure 3. Virtually all Ensemble components support the Interactor interface, allowing information to pass freely between the different types of interaction participants.

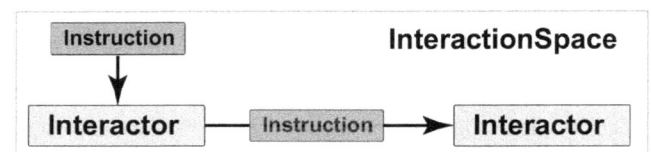

Figure 3: The heart of Ensemble applications consists of Players, Devices, and GUI components (collectively known as Interactors) processing Instructions. Interactors can send Instructions to each other directly, or through the Ensemble routing infrastructure.

The Interactor interface generalizes a given component to a node in a directed graph, allowing developers to model a large number of abstract constructs. Interactors were originally envisioned to implement a data flow structure similar to the components of OpenInterface [21] and Squidy [19]. This property was a core objective of the ContentServer architecture.

Interactors normally communicate within the context of an InteractionSpace. An InteractionSpace defines a collection of Interactors that can be referenced by name, and provides the infrastructure to deliver requests to named targets. InteractionSpace allows both absolute and context-aware addressing of members. For example, a control named 'touch5' on the 'poster_cartouche' device belonging to the 'surface' View is addressed as 'surface/poster_cartouche/touch5'. If a message is addressed only to 'touch5', the InteractionSpace attempts to find an Interactor with that name among active or currently selected components.

Interprocess Communication

For distributed systems, an OSCSender converts Instructions to OSC messages, and a RemoteInteractor component reverses the process at the receiving end. This is illustrated in Figure 4. OSC messages include an address part and one or more typed arguments [36]. Ensemble messages normally include a single text argument that is converted to an Instruction by the RemoteInteractor. The OSC message address is mapped to an Interactor name. The Instruction is passed to the local event routing framework for delivery to the named Interactor. Subclasses of the default message class could be used to process TUIO (Reactable) [18], LusidOSC (Trackmate) [20], and other OSC-based message formats.

In addition to OSC delivery of Instructions, Ensemble includes facilities for service advertisement and discovery. Grendl was the first Ensemble implementation to make use of dynamic service discovery. With the decision to replace SAGA, we selected the Apple Bonjour implementation of Zero Configuration Networking [38] as an interim technology for this purpose. Bonjour allows participants to publish services for joining and configuring ensembles, as well as services to establish direct connections for specific roles or pieces.

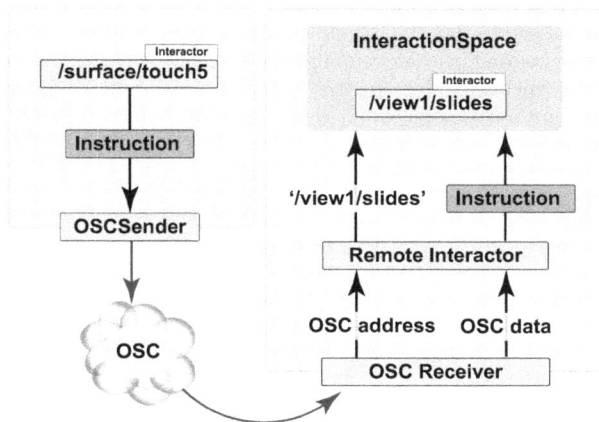

Figure 4: Instruction processing for distributed applications. Instructions are converted to OSC messages, transmitted, and converted back to Instructions. The address of the message identifies the message target.

As an example, the kiosk installation shown in Figure 5 combines a computer controlling a 42-inch LCD display, a Samsung SUR40 multitouch table, and custom built touch sensors with RGB LED strips installed on the SUR40 bezel. Users can select and interact with content on the SUR40 by touching the sensor elements on the bezel, placing cartouches on the display surface, or using mobile applications on smartphones or tablets. Placing a cartouche on the tabletop creates a GUI panel with widgets corresponding to cutouts in the cartouche. The application on the vertical display was created entirely from Ensemble components. The SUR40 applications and bezel elements were integrated by wrapping Javascript and C++ applications with Ensemble-derived APIs.

Figure 5: Kiosk combining vertical display with Samsung SUR40 and custom electronic controls. SUR40 recognizes tangible elements (cartouches) on its surface and displays corresponding content, relaying appropriate instructions to other components via OSC. Capacitive sensors and LED arrays on the SUR40 bezel mirror the software controls delimited by cutouts in the cartouches.

For this example, the SUR40 application is modeled as a remote View named 'surface'. Each of the cartouche interfaces and bezel sections are configured as Devices, including a list of controls or widgets associated with each Device. The vertical display contains 'view1', the Ensemble application's primary View. Messages from the 'surface' devices trigger GUI events in 'view1', and vice-versa. For instance, placing the 'poster_cartouche' element on the tabletop and touching the space defined as 'touch5' causes 'view1' to display a specific image.

Configurations and YAML

The information carried by Instructions is managed by the Configuration class. Configurations are used to specify screen layouts and events, devices, middleware, network configuration, players and the services they offer, and instructions. The Configuration class in turn functions as a wrapper for Ensemble's data serialization language. Ensemble uses

YAML [6] for this purpose. The relationship of Instructions, Configurations, and YAML is shown in Figure 6.

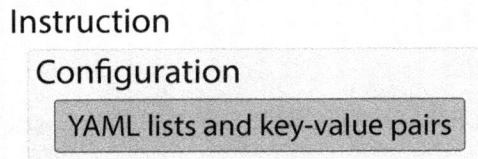

Instruction

Configuration

YAML lists and key-value pairs

Figure 6: The principal data member of Instruction is a Configuration object. Configurations function primarily as wrappers for YAML key-value pairs.

A snippet of a YAML InteractionSpace configuration is shown in Figure 7. The example creates a two member ensemble consisting of a single player (an event clock) and a single view containing a slide show and a button. The slide show will display the images specified in its 'contents' field. The configuration also lists a type for each InteractionSpace member. Types that are not native to Ensemble are created using Java reflection.

The InteractionSpace provides simple service publication and discovery capabilities, so that the 'slideShow' component can subscribe to the 'Simulation.EventClock' service (e.g., to advance slides at predetermined intervals), as long as both components are contained in the same InteractionSpace.

We developed an original configuration language using YAML instead of adopting a mature user interface description language (UIDL) such as UIML [23] to better align with our goals for exploratory development. YAML's design goals include being human-readable, simple, versatile, and available for a number of programming languages. YAML is a proper subset of JSON [11], which greatly simplifies the integration of Ensemble applications with RESTful web services [27]. YAML implementations are available for a large number of programming languages including C/C++, Java, PERL, Python, JavaScript and Ruby. Configurations figure prominently in Ensemble system development, and it is important for developers to be comfortable modifying the files using a text editor.

Also, the Ensemble GUI development classes are intended to normally function as adaptors to existing technology, rather than as a fully developed UI toolkit. For example, the Java version of an Ensemble View inherits from Swing's JFrame class. This made flexibility a more pressing requirement than completeness in specifying GUI-related Configurations. The choice of a minimal configuration language over a UIDL also simplified the integration of GUI, Player, and Device configurations.

While YAML has been the language of choice for our applications to this point, the architecture views the configuration language as an implementation choice, which is one of the main reasons it is encapsulated in the Configuration class. It is likely that implementers in some domains would select a different (e.g. XML-based) language.

```
                          # '#' begins a YAML comment
Alias 'frame' is          frameType: &frame `ensemble.ui.Frame'
defined with '&'          ##########
                          players:            Only player is a
Indentation                 name: mainClock   simulation clock
defines                     type: clockType
hierarchy                   ########
                            playerServiceName: 'Simulation.EventClock'
'views' specifies         views:              Service name for
GUI classes                 name: view1         subscribing to
                            type: View          clock events.
                            primary: True
Primary view is the         bounds: {x: 0, y: 0,  width: 1920, height: 1080}
main GUI window             backgroundcolor: &bgcolor {r: 10, g: 10, b: 16}
                            contents :  'contents' of views are
'-' delimits YAML           -             primarily Swing Components
list elements                 name: zoomButton
                              type: *frame
'command' specifies         backgroundcolor: *bgcolor
events and response.        command: {event: 'click', command: 'zoom',
In this case, click            amount: 1.1, target: 'view1/slides'}
zooms image by 10%          contentType: 'image'
                            contents: './data/ui/buttonZoom.jpg'
                            -
'*' dereferences            name: slides
'frame' alias             type: *frame
defined above             bounds: {x: 0,  y: 100, width: 1920,
                              height: 1080}
'slideShow' contents      contentType: 'slideShow'
lists series of images    contents: { './data/posters/p1-1920-norm.jpg',
                            './data/posters/p2-1920-norm.jpg'}
```

Figure 7: YAML Ensemble configuration. This snippet defines a simple slideshow application with a single player (an event clock) and a single view (window) that displays slides. Command elements define responses to specific Instructions.

Events and Instruction Processing

The listing in Figure 7 specifies an event handler for the zoom button, identified by the key 'command'. In this case, clicking the button zooms the image by ten percent. When the button is created, the 'command' YAML string is used to bind an Instruction object to the 'click' event handler. Instructions are used as parameters for event-initiated communication throughout the Ensemble system. The semantics of the instruction contents are program-specific, with the exception of three parameters that are used for instruction routing.

In the Figure 7 command example, the target name is fully qualified. When the zoom button initializes, it will query the View for an Interactor reference to its target. If a reference is returned, the button will send Instructions directly to the slide show element. Otherwise, the button will pass the event (including the target name) to its default handler for processing.

The default model for instruction processing is asynchronous with no guaranteed delivery, reflecting a purposeful decision to place more responsibility for successful communication on the issuer of instructions. Conversely, once an instruction is accepted for processing, it is the responsibility of the target to complete the task, including any state tracking that may be necessary. There is, however, no universal requirement to acknowledge that a message has been received or processed.

Interactive Performance Grid

Inspired by the Grendl experience, Ensemble adopted the analogy of an interactive performance grid as an organizing structure. The interaction is modeled as a collaborative performance of the ensemble members, with each device, software component, and human participant contributing a part. Computational grids are designed to be service-oriented and dynamic in structure [17], organized to meet the requirements of the current problem. To support this model, Ensemble adopted the SAGA practice of organizing work by jobs, tasks, and resources.

A job is a goal-driven unit of work, with a role comparable to the ABC [2] concept of an activity. Like ABC, Ensemble explicitly models tasks, materials (resources), and users (performers). The job can function as the central driver of an interaction, but because of Ensemble's emphasis on flexibility, there is no requirement for an interaction session to include a job at all. Jobs are accomplished by Interactors (i.e. Players, Devices, Views) performing tasks. Ensemble defines roles for performers that are stable for a given task, and can evolve as the job progresses.

The integration of the grid service model partially transformed the Interactor interface from a data flow connector to a service interface. Individual Interactors were already addressable, and Instructions were designed to carry structured data, so the transition was made with minimal changes to the interface. Depending on application requirements, Interactors may be used in both roles more or less simultaneously.

Ensemble can be used to build applications from scratch, or as a glue architecture to combine pre-existing components or systems. The architecture has been used to create model-view-controller (MVC) applications, small grids, workflow applications, and simple content delivery systems.

EVOLUTION AND IMPLEMENTATIONS

Like the projects it is built to support, the Ensemble architecture has evolved through a number of iterations, with key implementations providing new insights and direction, and helping to validate the architecture's contributions. Subsets of Ensemble functionality have been developed in a number of languages, with the most extensive GUI implementations using Java Swing. The Swing implementation utilizes JFrame as the base class for View, and ScreenElement extends JPanel. These are examples of the Ensemble preference for wrapping existing technology where possible. Localizing changes in wrapper classes like View is intended to favor flexibility and portability over other design considerations.

The first ContentServer implementations focused on single user interactions with predefined content and simple UI widgets, similar to the types of interactions described for PuReWidgets [8]. Smartphone or tablet client interfaces were used to load and manipulate text, images, and visualizations. In the most common configuration, OSC messages were relayed between mobile devices and one or more workstations driving two to four vertical displays.

These applications tested the Interactor concept using a slightly modified MVC pattern, created by defining a Controller subclass of Interactor and requiring all View and Device event listeners to be of this class. While this approach was effective for creating an MVC system, the pattern proved limiting for our purposes, and was replaced with the InteractionSpace concept.

Initial iOS user interfaces for Ensemble were created with TouchOSC [30], an iOS app for interacting with OSC-enabled software and devices. TouchOSC messages map readily to the Ensemble message addressing scheme, and these early GUI's were instrumental in developing the name-based messaging capabilities of the InteractionSpace.

To deal with the growing number of content types across multiple platforms, a provider (or bridge) pattern was used with abstract class factories to separate Ensemble classes from specific widget or device implementations. As with MVC, the architecture was capable of implementing the patterns with few changes, but the result was determined to be too cumbersome for exploratory prototyping and the change was rolled back in favor of a small and extensible set of content types. The most commonly used types include captioned images, slideshows, QR code generators, image arrays, and web content. The class factory concept was retained for integration of higher level GUI components and task handlers.

The Grendl implementations demonstrate the suitability of Ensemble for service-oriented and multi-user applications. In the current version, a Java client running on each laptop publishes a Bonjour service that enables players to transmit and receive Instructions via OSC and the RemoteInteractor interface. One application instance, identified as the Conductor, publishes an additional service that identifies it as the instruction source for the current composition. The Conductor role may be changed as many times as needed during a performance. The workflow for a performance is specified in the *program*, a YAML file that includes an instruction list for each composition to be played. The Conductor issues instructions and optionally monitors completion of each task.

The Grendl client application is composed primarily of relatively complex Swing components connected via Ensemble. While adopted initially as an expedient way to reuse the components of the original (i.e. non-Ensemble) Grendl GUI, the implementation first demonstrated Ensemble's potential as a connecting architecture for higher level components, a role in which it is increasingly being used.

The most recent Ensemble implementation, described previously and shown in Figure 5, combines a vertical display with a Samsung SUR40 and custom electronic controls. Events generated by software on the SUR40 cause Instructions to be sent to the Ensemble application on the vertical display computer, and to software adaptors for the Arduino microcontroller responsible for the LED strips and capacitive touch sensors on the SUR40 bezel.

This installation further validates Ensemble's potential as a glue architecture for system composition. The software applications and electronics were designed and developed largely in isolation, and integrated immediately before deployment.

Integration and testing of the combined functionality was completed within a few hours.

The product of Ensemble's evolution can be seen in Figure 8, which provides an overview of the current architecture. The classes shown (and their descendants) demonstrate an array of capabilities, while only the three core classes are required to begin building an Ensemble application.

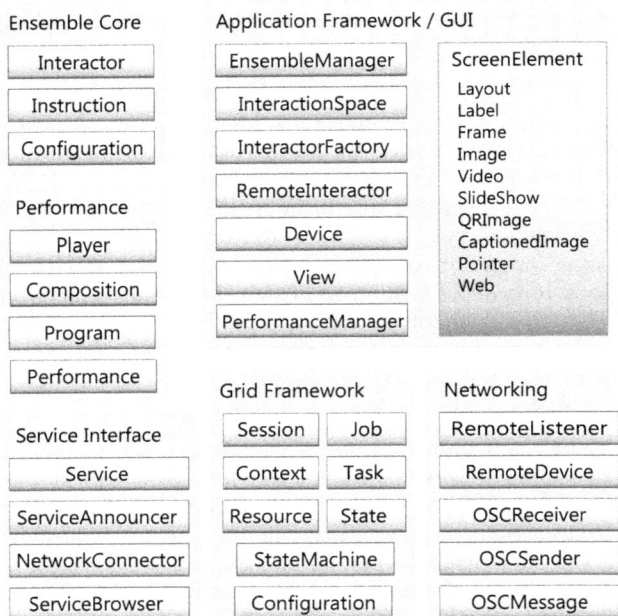

Figure 8: Overview of Ensemble classes.

Assessment and future directions

Ensemble began as a limited scope effort to reduce the amount of time and effort needed to create and modify reliable tangible applications, allowing designers more freedom to explore and refine application concepts and interaction models. The introduction of the grid computing model added significant capabilities for distributed collaboration, resulting in a flexible architecture that is neither application runtime, network infrastructure, nor development toolkit, but combines elements of all of these.

While applications can be implemented entirely using Ensemble classes and components, its most natural role is as a glue architecture, creating a common method for composing and linking lower level components and environments. For instance, the current Grendl UI is composed of several Java Swing components occupying a single Ensemble View. Instructions are integrated at various points with the Swing event handling system, providing a thread safe interface between the local and distributed UI, and mediating the interaction of each top level Swing component with the others. In the latest kiosk incarnation, the use of Ensemble in the software adaptors for the touch sensors and LED strips on the bezel of the SUR40 is limited to sending and receiving OSC messages, while the vertical display utilizes virtually all of the features of the architecture.

With the rise of web and cloud services, mobile computing, and the increased capabilities available with advanced Javascript toolkits and HTML 5, we will be defining additional service interfaces and thin client components for Ensemble, with primarily content-centric applications likely evolving to an architecture similar to that described for PuReWidgets [8]. As an example, the latest kiosk installation utilized a transparent HTML canvas overlay to mediate interaction between the SUR40 and other components.

Given the nature of exploratory development, it remains important to be able to create direct connections between components. While direct OSC connections over UDP have worked well in a controlled research environment, a more flexible connection mechanism will be required. A lightweb web service bus is being developed to replace the Bonjour services currently used for service publication and discovery.

The next priority for Ensemble will be the creation of development tools and supporting infrastructure. This will likely require individual aspects of the architecture to be further formalized. Ideally, Ensemble can be developed for use as an evaluation tool to compare variations of (sub)systems, combinations of modalities, or competing interaction models.

DISCUSSION

Architectures can be shaped as much by their designers' goals and priorities as they are by the problems they are intended to address. It is tempting to believe that the somewhat accidental nature of Ensemble's origins and evolution may have mitigated some of this effect. The exploratory character of Ensemble's development, and the development of the applications for which it was used, provided ample opportunities to test opinions and beliefs concerning the design of distributed, tangible, collaborative systems.

One lesson learned early and repeatedly is that there is no substitute for executing code when trying to understand a complex software system. Virtually every recent design choice for Ensemble has been influenced by the goal of creating working systems quickly. This focus has led us to defer investigation of some specific features in favor of capabilities for experimentation. Compared to many other systems in this domain, Ensemble strives more for flexibility and comprehensibility than advanced features. Ensemble does not currently possess an information resource management framework like ReticularSpaces' principle of Activity-Centric Resource Aggregation [3], or autonomic multimodal mediation facilities like DynaMo [1]. Instead, Ensemble provides capabilities to allow systems such as these to interact.

In this context, we found comprehensibility and ease of use to be important requirements for an exploratory architecture. Enabling Ensemble systems to be created using only a few base classes helps new users to see see initial results quickly, and expand their understanding of the architecture as needed. Maintaining this commitment required forgoing some desired features, and removing others that existed in earlier iterations.

Interaction models and design patterns can be important tools for managing system complexity and creating reliable and usable applications and environments. The ability to explore different options and variations quickly may help avoid premature choices. Ensemble is not meant to provide or enforce a particular interaction model or design pattern on applications; rather it is designed to enable a number of models, or even combinations of models, to be used. The goal has been to create a modular and reconfigurable space that accommodates a number of design patterns and objectives. For example, the flexible control and dynamic addition of components may encourage creation of applications that are innovative and playful. Another system might make heavier use of the embedded grid classes to create an application focused on reliability and security, or with a more formal structure. Perhaps most important, these patterns can be combined in a number of ways within a single system, depending on the goals of the designers. The system is intended to impact existing applications and technology as little as practical. It is also quite possible that realizing smart spaces and other distributed systems in practice will require integration of two or more disparate infrastructures. The design of Ensemble makes it a candidate for such integration.

The performance grid interaction model is one of the most recent additions to Ensemble, and its impact and potential are the focus of ongoing research. While the model shares many of the attributes of ABC [2], the effects of casting ensemble members primarily as performers, rather than participants in an activity, are not completely understood. The model has a greater impact on the architecture's nomenclature than its organization at present, but this will undoubtedly change as Ensemble matures.

Very few architectures, no matter how elegantly designed, survive deployment unscathed. Late ad hoc changes (i.e., hacks) may be required, especially during early iterations. A welcome benefit of Ensemble has been a tendency to isolate these changes to a few specific locations in the code, simplifying the process of redesign and refactoring for the next iteration. This specific feature has likely been responsible for much of the system's rapid iteration capability. At the same time, localization of functionality changes could indicate a potential bottleneck as the system scales, a possibility that is currently being evaluated.

CONCLUSION

Ensemble began as a focused project to reduce the time and effort required to add an additional digital display to an existing application, substitute a smartphone for a microcontroller, or configure a network connection while an audience looked on. The architecture developed from these origins has shown encouraging potential for exploratory development. The integration of the grid computing framework with the performance ensemble interaction model, combined with an overarching goal of flexibility and distribution of capability, have resulted in an architecture that is lightweight, portable, and capable of implementing a number of interaction models. The component integration aspect of the architecture has been stable, and the single programming interface used for performers, content, and devices has allowed developers to test and adopt interaction patterns in domains other than those for which they were created.

There are still a number of questions to be answered. For example, the grid ensemble combination has mapped naturally to the small set of domains we have addressed to this point, but we are still establishing its suitability for other application domains. Also, the flexibility of text-addressable components comes at a cost to performance. Developing a model of this cost as system size and distribution increases will be important if the architecture is to be used as part of an evaluation of fusion toolkits or interaction frameworks.

Finally, the greatest potential of Ensemble may be as a service-oriented integration architecture for disparate systems and infrastructures, but we have only begun evaluating this conjecture. We are also testing Ensemble's suitability for entangling groups of room-sized and larger interaction spaces.

ACKNOWLEDGMENTS
This work was partially funded by the Arts, Visualization, Advanced Technologies and Research Initiative (AVATAR), the NIST Center for Digital Innovation, and the Louisiana State University Center for Computation and Technology. Additional support was provided by the National Science Foundation program for Creative-IT (IIS-0856065), and Major Research Instrumentation grants (MRI-1126739, MRI-0521559). The authors wish to thank the Laptop Orchestra of Louisiana for their support, and Shantenu Jha and Sharath Madinenni for their assistance with SAGA integration.

REFERENCES
1. Avouac, P., Lalanda, P., and Nigay, L. Autonomic management of multimodal interaction: Dynamo in action. In *Proc. of EICS 2012*, ACM (2012), 35–44.

2. Bardram, E. Activity-based computing: support for mobility and collaboration in ubiquitous computing. *Personal and Ubiquitous Computing 9*, 5 (2005), 312–322.

3. Bardram, J., Gueddana, S., Houben, S., and Nielsen, S. ReticularSpaces: Activity-based computing support for physically distributed and collaborative smart spaces. In *Proc. of CHI 2012*, ACM (2012), 2845–2854.

4. Beaudouin-Lafon, M. Designing interaction, not interfaces. In *Proceedings of the working conference on Advanced visual interfaces*, ACM (2004), 15–22.

5. Beck, S., Branton, C., and Maddineni, S. Tangible performance management of grid-based laptop orchestras. In *New Interfaces for Musical Expression (NIME)*, vol. 11 (2011), 13.

6. Ben-Kiki, O., Evans, C., and Ingerson, B. *YAML Ain't Markup Language (YAML^{TM})*. Tech. Rep, 2005.

7. Burns, C., and Surges, G. NRCI: Software tools for laptop ensemble. In *Proc. of ICMC 2008* (2008).

8. Cardoso, J., and José, R. Purewidgets: a programming toolkit for interactive public display applications. In *Proc. of EICS 2012*, ACM (2012), 51–60.

9. Carter, S., Mankoff, J., Klemmer, S., and Matthews, T. Exiting the cleanroom: On ecological validity and

ubiquitous computing. *Human–Computer Interaction 23*, 1 (2008), 47–99.

10. Christian, D., and Rotenstreich, S. An evaluation framework for distributed collaboration tools. In *Information Technology: New Generations (ITNG), 2010 Seventh International Conference on*, IEEE (2010), 512–517.

11. Crockford, D. The application/json media type for javascript object notation (JSON). Tech. rep., RFC 4627, July, 2006.

12. Demeure, A., et al. The 4c reference model for distributed user interfaces. In *Fourth International Conference on Autonomic and Autonomous Systems*, IEEE (2008), 61–69.

13. Dumas, B., Lalanne, D., and Ingold, R. HephaisTK: a toolkit for rapid prototyping of multimodal interfaces. In *Proceedings of the 2009 international conference on Multimodal interfaces*, ACM (2009), 231–232.

14. Dumas, B., Signer, B., and Lalanne, D. Fusion in multimodal interactive systems: an HMM-based algorithm for user-induced adaptation. In *Proc. of EICS 2012*, ACM (2012), 15–24.

15. Edwards, W., Newman, M., and Poole, E. The infrastructure problem in HCI. In *Proc. of CHI 2010*, ACM (2010), 423–432.

16. Gjerlufsen, T., Klokmose, C., et al. Shared Substance: developing flexible multi-surface applications. In *Proc. of CHI'11*, ACM (2011), 3383–3392.

17. Goodale, T., Jha, S., Kaiser, H., Kielmann, T., Kleijer, P., Merzky, A., Shalf, J., and Smith, C. A simple api for grid applications (saga). In *Grid Forum Document GFD*, vol. 90 (2007).

18. Kaltenbrunner, M., Bovermann, T., Bencina, R., and Costanza, E. TUIO: A protocol for table-top tangible user interfaces. In *Proc. of the The 6th Int'l Workshop on Gesture in Human-Computer Interaction and Simulation*, Citeseer (2005).

19. König, W. A., Rädle, R., and Reiterer, H. Squidy: a zoomable design environment for natural user interfaces. In *CHI'09 extended abstracts on Human factors in computing systems*, ACM (2009), 4561–4566.

20. Kumpf, A. *Trackmate: Large-scale accessibility of tangible user interfaces*. PhD thesis, Massachusetts Institute of Technology, 2009.

21. Lawson, J., Al-Akkad, A., Vanderdonckt, J., and Macq, B. An open source workbench for prototyping multimodal interactions based on off-the-shelf heterogeneous components. In *Proc. of EICS 2009*, ACM (2009), 245–254.

22. Luyten, K., and Coninx, K. Distributed user interface elements to support smart interaction spaces. In *Multimedia, Seventh IEEE International Symposium on*, IEEE (2005), 8–pp.

23. Luyten, K., Meskens, J., Vermeulen, J., and Coninx, K. Meta-gui-builders: generating domain-specific interface builders for multi-device user interface creation. In *CHI'08 extended abstracts on Human factors in computing systems*, ACM (2008), 3189–3194.

24. Marco, J., Cerezo, E., and Baldassarri, S. Toyvision: a toolkit for prototyping tabletop tangible games. In *Proc. of EICS 2012*, ACM (2012), 71–80.

25. Marquardt, N., Diaz-Marino, R., Boring, S., and Greenberg, S. The proximity toolkit: prototyping proxemic interactions in ubiquitous computing ecologies. In *Proc. of UIST 2011*, ACM (2011), 315–326.

26. Merrill, D., Kalanithi, J., and Maes, P. Siftables: towards sensor network user interfaces. In *Proc. of TEI 2007*, ACM (2007), 75–78.

27. Richardson, L., and Ruby, S. *RESTful web services*. O'Reilly Media, 2007.

28. Sankaran, R., Ullmer, B., Ramanujam, J., Kallakuri, K., Jandhyala, S., Toole, C., and Laan, C. Decoupling interaction hardware design using libraries of reusable electronics. In *Proc. of TEI 2009*, ACM (2009), 331–337.

29. Serrano, M., Nigay, L., Lawson, J.-Y. L., Ramsay, A., Murray-Smith, R., and Denef, S. The OpenInterface framework: a tool for multimodal interaction. In *CHI'08 extended abstracts on Human factors in computing systems*, ACM (2008), 3501–3506.

30. TouchOSC. http://hexler.net/software/touchosc.

31. Ullmer, B. Entangling space, form, light, time, computational steam, and cultural artifacts. *interactions 19*, 4 (2012), 32–39.

32. Ullmer, B., Dell, C., Gil, C., Toole Jr, C., et al. Casier: structures for composing tangibles and complementary interactors for use across diverse systems. In *Proc. of TEI 2011*, ACM (2011), 229–236.

33. Villar, N., Scott, J., and Hodges, S. Prototyping with Microsoft .Net Gadgeteer. In *Proc. of TEI 2011*, ACM (2011), 377–380.

34. Wang, G., Cook, P., et al. ChucK: A concurrent, on-the-fly audio programming language. In *Proceedings of International Computer Music Conference*, Citeseer (2003), 219–226.

35. Weiser, M. The computer for the 21st century. *Scientific American 265*, 3 (1991), 94–104.

36. Wright, M., Freed, A., and Momeni, A. Opensound control: State of the art 2003. In *Proc. of NIME 2003*, National University of Singapore (2003), 160.

37. Zeitler, A. Survey and review of input libraries, frameworks, and toolkits for interactive surfaces and recommendations for the Squidy interaction library, 2009.

38. Zeroconf. http://www.zeroconf.org/, 2012.

A Framework for the Development of Distributed Interactive Applications

Luca Frosini
HIIS Laboratory – ISTI-CNR
Via G. Moruzzi, 1
56124 Pisa (Italy)
luca.frosini@isti.cnr.it
+39 050 621 2602

Marco Manca
HIIS Laboratory – ISTI-CNR
Via G. Moruzzi, 1
56124 Pisa (Italy)
marco.manca@isti.cnr.it
+39 050 621 3117

Fabio Paternò
HIIS Laboratory – ISTI-CNR
Via G. Moruzzi, 1
56124 Pisa (Italy)
fabio.paterno@isti.cnr.it
+39 050 621 3066

ABSTRACT

In this paper we present a framework and the associated software architecture to manage user interfaces that can be distributed and/or migrated in multi-device and multi-user environments. It supports distribution across dynamic sets of devices, and does not require the use of a fixed server. We also report on its current implementation, and an example application.

Author Keywords

Multi-device User Interfaces, Multi-user User Interfaces, Distributed and Migratory User Interfaces.

ACM Classification Keywords

H.5 Information Interfaces and Presentation; H.5.2 User Interfaces, H.5.3 Group and Organization Interfaces.

INTRODUCTION

In the last decade mobile devices have increased in number, and people spend more and more time using them. This has made it possible to create many environments where people spend long time interacting with various devices in sequential or in parallel [4].

In order to better exploit such technological offer often people would like to dynamically move components of their interactive applications across different devices with various interaction resources. Thus, there is a need for novel frameworks that facilitate the development of interactive applications that can be dynamically distributed across various devices.

This is an area in which some research contributions have already been proposed. Some contributions have been dedicated to investigating design spaces indicating various important relevant dimensions for this type of applications [3][6]. Such dimensions can be addressed in different ways. For example, some authors [1] proposed a solution for migrating existing Web applications, while herein we put

forward a new solution for supporting distribution and migration in the development of new applications. A toolkit for peer-to-peer distribution of user interfaces was presented in [5], but it requires the use of specific libraries, while our framework can be exploited in different implementation environments. DeepShot [2] is a framework for migrating tasks across devices using mobile phone cameras, but it does not support user interface distribution across multiple devices at the same time.

In particular, our work aims to provide designers and developers with a framework that allows them to obtain applications in which the interactive components can be dynamically distributed across various devices. It allows developers to obtain applications that can have multiple instances at the same time for different groups of devices and users.

In the paper we first introduce our approach, then we describe the distribution manager and the commands that it is able to handle. We report on the underlying architecture, and the protocol used for the communication among the components. The last part is dedicated to describing the current implementation, an example application, conclusions and future work.

OUR APPROACH

We propose an environment called *Distribution Manager* composed of a client-side library for the development of Distributed User Interfaces (DUI), and run-time support for the management of the dynamic distribution. One advantage of our approach is that it does not require the use of a fixed server, as in [1], but it allows dynamic sets of devices to organize themselves in order to support the distribution. In addition, the versions of the distributed interactive applications for the various devices should not be pre-developed at design time, but can be created dynamically at run-time according to the indications defined by the developers.

The ultimate goal of the work is to provide developers with a framework to easily develop applications supporting distribution without having to implement the necessary protocol of communication and the run-time support to manage the distribution.

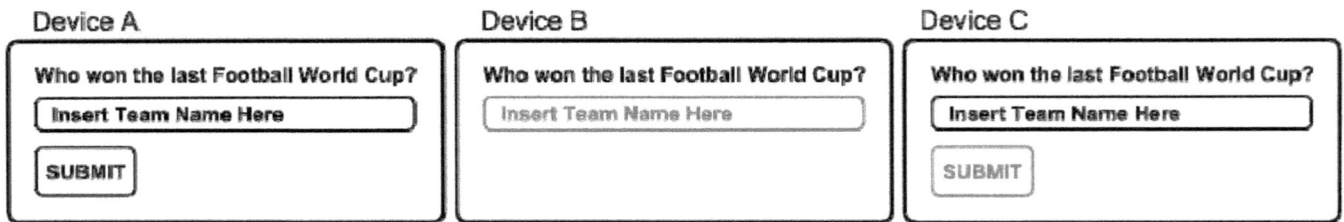

Figure 1. Example of Components Distribution.

With our framework the application can be distributed through dynamic sets of devices. The first device accessing the distribution service provides the initial distribution configuration. If later on new devices access the distribution service for the same application instance then they inherit such distribution, and can modify it if they have the appropriate access rights.

In general, it is possible to create different distribution groups composed of different devices for the same application.

THE DISTRIBUTION MANAGER

The framework is logically divided into two main components: one running on the devices where the application interactive parts are presented (we will refer to this as *client side*) and the other in a device which behaves as distribution manager (*engine side*). Using our framework the engine part does not necessarily reside on a fixed server, but when the application starts the user can configure the application to access a distribution engine running on their own mobile device or in another device. For example, in a situation where external network availability is not guaranteed, the devices can create a LAN and set one of the devices as *master*, which will act as the distribution *engine*.

The *client side* part is a library which provides application developers with facilities to:

- subscribe a device to the UI distribution service;
- request a UI distribution change to the *engine side;*
- receive notification from the *engine* of UI distribution changes for the device.

The *engine side* part provides capabilities to:

- subscribe devices to distribution changes;
- filter (depending on configurations and credentials provided by the client) and process requests for UI distribution changes;
- notify UI distribution changes to involved devices.

The requests for distribution changes can be specified by one command called **ASSIGN**. It has been designed in such a way to be easy to understand, compact, and with the possibility of obtaining flexible results. The command takes three parameters as follows:

$$\textbf{ASSIGN}(\textit{what}, \textit{inputEnabled}, \textit{target});$$

Where:

- *what* : identifies an interface part, typically the ID of the element or the container of elements that has to be distributed.
- *inputEnabled* : is a Boolean value. If this parameter is set to *False,* any UI events assigned to the element identified by *what* are not enabled.
- *target* : specifies to which device(s) the interface part identified by *what* should be distributed.

The *target* devices can be identified by lists of:

- Device Types (e.g. Mobile, Desktop), so that all the devices of the type indicated that have been subscribed to the service will receive the updates;
- Device IDs (e.g. Device 1, Device 54);
- Device Roles (e.g. Guide, Tourist, Widescreen), in this case groups of devices can be identified for the role that they play within the application.

Figure 1 shows an example in which a UI composed of one *container* and 3 internal elements: a *Label*, a *TextInput*, a *Button*. Three devices are subscribed to the distribution service (**A**, **B**, **C**). Suppose that we want to show the *container* on all devices and the other elements in the following way:

- Device **A** shows all the elements contained in *container* and all element are *enabled* to receive input events;
- Device **B** shows only *Label* and *TextInput* (but does not show the *Button*). *TextInput* receives the feedback of the entered input from other devices but the user cannot insert any value through it.
- Device **C** shows all the elements, the *Button* is visible, but is deactivated.

Such assignments are then transmitted to the relevant devices through distribution update commands defined in our protocol, each of them can contain multiple assign commands. The distribution commands requested for this configuration are the following:

250

- **ASSIGN**("*Container*", True, [A, B, C])

- **ASSIGN**("*Label*", True, [A,B,C])

- **ASSIGN**("*TextInput*", True, [A,C])
  ASSIGN("*TextInput*", False, B)

- **ASSIGN**("*Button*", True, A)
  ASSIGN("*Button*", False, C)

In general, a distribution command on an application element clears the previously defined assignments. Thus, for example if we want to move one object from one device to another then it is sufficient to assign it to the second device. This implicitly removes the element from the initial device. If the element needs to be redundant over multiple devices then it is sufficient to indicate such devices in the target field.

ARCHITECTURE

Figure 2 shows the proposed architecture divided into its two main components: *engine side* and *client side*. Furthermore, there is a component that represents the application that uses the *client side* library; the application logic is responsible for associating UI events with distribution change commands.

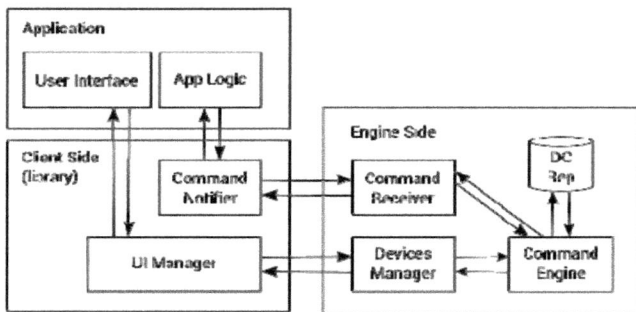

Figure 2. Overview of the Distribution Manager architecture.

Engine Side

The *engine side* part of the architecture is logically composed of three main components: **Command Receiver**, **Command Engine**, **Devices Manager**.

The **Command Receiver** is the one responsible for:

- receiving new device subscriptions to the UI distribution service;

- receiving requests of distribution changes commands;

- filtering and controlling if the received request can be made by the device sent it.

The **Command Engine** is the component responsible of taking in charge the requests of UI distribution changes (from Command Receiver), and process them to calculate the new distribution status.

The processing consists in: expanding the list(s) identified by the *target* (when the ASSIGN command *target* is a list

of *Device Types* and/or *Device Roles*) to obtain the actual devices involved; checking if the ASSIGNMENT command (for *what*) is compatible with the ASSIGNMENT of the ancestor elements in the interactive application structure.

Once the new state of the distribution has been processed, it is passed to the **Devices Manager,** which is the component responsible for communicating to each subscribed device the new distribution status.

There is also a **Distribution Configuration Repository (DC Rep)**, which is used by the Command Engine to retrieve application specific information. For example, it can provide the description of the actual distribution state, allowed roles for the application, and the needed credential to get such a role. The DC Rep is also the component responsible to maintain the status of distribution at any time (we will refer to this as *Actual Status*).

Client Side

The *client side* part is logically composed of two components: the **Command Notifier** and the **UI Manager.**

The **Command Notifier** is the component responsible to send:

- device subscription commands;

- distribution update commands;

The **UI Manager** is the component responsible for:

- receiving UI update commands;

- receiving the *Actual Status* of UI distribution when a device is subscribed. The *Actual Status* is the distribution description in a certain moment;

- perform actions to make UI update commands effective (i.e. show or hide the UI element, enable or disable event associated to elements, enable or disable input elements).

COMMUNICATION PROTOCOL

The content of the distribution communication protocol is encoded in XML. Each request from client to the engine contains an *Application ID* defined at development time. The engine uses this ID to retrieve the configuration for the specific application on DC Rep.

Some application can be session based. This means that for the same application more than one session can be created, which may be even active at the same time. For this reason each request created by the client contains a *Session ID* as well. In this way it is possible to identify the group of devices running the same application instance.

A session is newly created by the first device that subscribes with a certain *Session ID*. To create a new session a device should have the right to do it. If the new session is accepted the engine requests the initial distribution status to the client.

Sequence Diagram

Figure 3 shows a sequence diagram that represents the communication flow between clients and engine.

The diagram describes a case where Device D creates a new session, and the engine requests it to send the initial distribution state. Then, device A registers successfully to distribution and another one (C) is refused, because it did not provide acceptable credential.

After the subscription Device A receives from the *engine* the *Actual Status* of distribution and it shows the UI accordingly. Then, device A requests a distribution change. In the example the request has effect on all devices subscribed in that moment (A, D).

After this event, device B requires to be subscribed, and once the request is accepted, it asks for a new distribution change. In this case we can notice that this request has effect only on devices A and B.

We can notice that after a new request of subscription to the distribution service the *Actual Status* of distribution is sent to the subscribed device. This allows a device to subscribe itself at any time and not only at the beginning of the session.

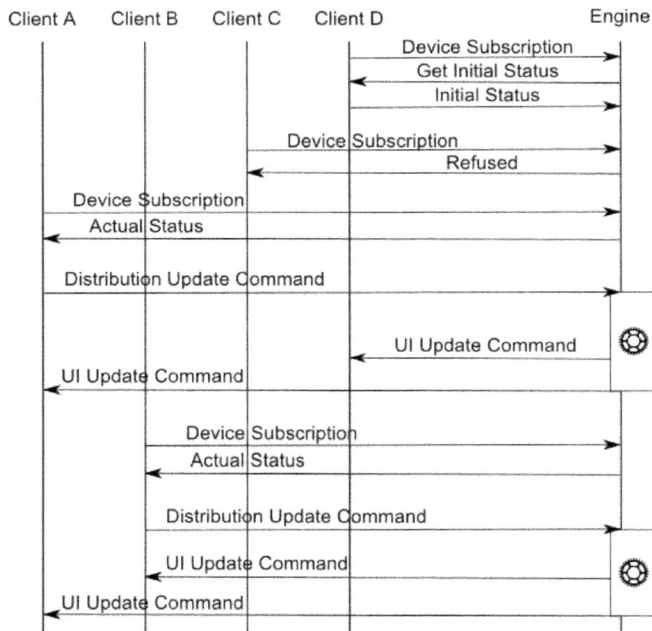

Figure 3. Sequence Diagram describing an example of interactions among multiple devices.

MESSAGE TYPE

Device Subscription

The following XML snippet shows an example *Device Subscription* Request.

```
<DeviceSubscription
    applicationID="4071d6cb-f11e-4f37-9f1d "
    sessionID="fec8e5bd-12f1-4c8b-9bee">
    <Device id="JDQ39015d2a5018500202"
        name="Nexus 7" type="MOBILE">
        <Connectors>
            <Connector type="HTTP"
                uri="http://146.48.107.155:5454/" />
        </Connectors>
    </Device>
</DeviceSubscription>
```

When a device requests a subscription it communicates its own ID, a name and the device type it belongs to. Furthermore it also sends the connector type that will be used by the engine to contact the client for notification of distribution changes. The choice of the connector is made by the developer and depends on the device capabilities and the current configuration.

One example is when the application recognizes that it is running on the same device of the engine, in this case an API connector is preferred because the direct API call consumes less resources (e.g. battery, memory and CPU, bandwidth) than the HTTP connector.

In the XML example the device requesting the subscription is a Mobile device that can be contacted by the engine using HTTP at the URL provided.

On device subscription, the *engine* elaborates the new *Actual Status* of distribution for the device. The *Actual Status* is communicated as a list of *UIUpdateCommands* described below.

Distribution Update Command

When a user accesses an application developed using our framework some user-generated events can trigger requests for distribution changes in one or more devices subscribed.

Such requests are communicated to the *engine* using the **Command Notifier** through distribution update commands that can include various assignments. An example of the information sent for such requests is presented in the following XML snippet

```
<DistributionUpdateCommand
    applicationID="4071d6cb-f11e-4f37-9f1d "
    sessionID="fec8e5bd-12f1-4c8b-9bee">
    <Assign>
        <What>
            <id>Image54</id>
        </What>
        <InputEnabled>True</InputEnabled>
        <Targets>
            <Target>
                <ID>
                    JDQ39015d2a5018500202
                </ID>
```

```
                    </Target>
                </Targets>
            </Assign>
            <Assign>
                <What>
                    <id>Image54</id>
                </What>
                <InputEnabled>False</InputEnabled>
                <Targets>
                    <Target>
                        <ID>
                            5018500202KH5J99
                        </ID>
                    </Target>
                </Targets>
            </Assign>
        </DistributionUpdateCommand>
```

The example XML shows a case where the element with ID (Image54) is distributed in different ways on two devices: in the first one the element is enabled to receive the events associated by the developer (i.e. tap or long press), in the second one the events are not enabled.

UI Update Command

When the engine receives a new distribution request, if accepted this has potential side effects on one or more devices, which are notified through update commands.

The following XML snippet shows an example of *UI Update Command*

```
<UIUpdateCommand>
    <elementID> Image54</objectID>
    <visible>True</visible>
    <inputEnabled>False</inputEnabled >
</UIUpdateCommand>
```

The snippet is received by the device identified with *5018500202KH5J99* in the previous example. The *UI Update Command* informs the device to show (visible is True) the element identified by the *Image54* ID and to disable the events associated to it.

IMPLEMENTATION

We have developed a prototype as proof-of-concept supporting the proposed approach.

Our prototype is implemented in Java and has been developed to run on Android and Desktop platforms. On both implementations the *engine* responds to requests thought a Servlet.

We have tested the library with different Android devices, which have different computational capabilities, screen resolution and size ranging from small mobile phones to large tablets, and desktop systems with screens with various sizes.

Another capability in our implementations is the API connection. The API connection is used when the *engine* and the *client* are running on the same device because it avoids access to the network and thus saves resource consumption.

In addition to the advantage that the framework does not require a fixed server, another important contribution is that the development of a client supporting the distribution requires limited effort.

Fig. 4 shows an example of code that can be used to register the device to distribution.

```
public void subscribeDevice() {
    CommandNotifier notifier = CommandNotifier.getInstance();

    ClientConnector clientConnector = new ClientConnector(master);
    EngineConnector engineConnector = new EngineConnector(master);

    Device thisDevice = new Device(Utility.getDeviceName(),
            Utility.getDeviceID(), clientConnector);

    notifier.setDevice(thisDevice);
    notifier.setEngineConnector(engineConnector);
    notifier.subscribeDevice();
}
```

Figure 4. Example of code to subscribe a device to distribution.

For each event that generates a distribution change just a few lines of code are needed to notify it to the engine as shown in Fig. 5

```
public void notifyDistributionUpdateCommand(What what,
                    boolean inputEnabled, Target target) {
    CommandNotifier notifier = CommandNotifier.getInstance();

    Assign assign = new Assign(what, inputEnabled, target);

    notifier.notify(command);
}
```

Figure 5. Example of code to notify a distribution update to the engine.

EXAMPLE APPLICATION

We have applied our framework prototype for a mobile guide. The resulting application runs on mobile devices and can be used to enrich the visit experience of tourists inside a museum.

The scenario considered aims to exploit opportunistically large screens that can be encountered during the user visit and are identified through QR codes.

The application selects the large screen acquiring the QR code and allows users to select images, video or textual information to show on the large screen to enrich the visit experience by sharing them with other visitors. Figure 6 shows the user interfaces in the two devices before (top) and after (bottom) the distribution.

Figure 6. Example of distribution involving a mobile device (smartphone) and a large screen.

In the mobile application the tap event is associated to a *DistributionUpdateCommand*. In this case, the *command* contains two ASSIGN commands: one to the sending device with *InputEnabled* to *True* and the other to the large screen (identified by its ID which is known thanks to the QR code) with *InputEnabled* to *False*. This situation corresponds to that described as an example in the Distribution Update Command paragraph.

A long press event on a resource instead results in an assignment only to the mobile device, removing it from large screen if present.

It is important to highlight that this application is not just a solution to share multimedia content but it also changes dynamically the interaction capabilities of the various parts of the application distributed across multiple devices.

CONCLUSION & FUTURE WORK

We have presented a framework for dynamic distribution of interactive components, composed of a library and a run-time support. We have also reported on the current implementation and its use for a specific application.

The main contribution of our framework is that it eases the development of applications that support UI distribution, and does not require a fixed server to support runtime distribution.

Future work will be dedicated to investigating further improvements to our solution able to make it even more flexible, optimize the battery consumption on mobile devices, and address security issues by introducing customizable security policies in the architecture presented.

We also plan to carry out a study with application developers in order to gather further empirical feedback regarding the easiness of distributed UI development and suggestions for improvements.

ACKNOWLEDGMENTS
This work is part of a project co-funded by Regione Toscana, ISTI-CNR, IIT-CNR and Softec s.p.a which aims to create a framework to develop applications able to support distributed user interfaces in mobile environments. More info at http://giove.isti.cnr.it/IUDSM/index_en.html.

We also thank Zeno Amerini (Softec s.p.a.) for useful discussions.

REFERENCES
1. Bellucci, F., Ghiani, G., Paternò, F., Santoro, C. Engineering JavaScript state persistence of web applications migrating across multiple devices, In *Proc.* ACM SIGCHI 2011, ACM Press (2011), 105-110.

2. Chang, T.H., and Li, Y. Deep Shot: A Framework for Migrating Tasks Across Devices Using Mobile Phone Cameras. In *Proc.* CHI 2011, ACM Press (2011), 2163-2172.

3. Demeure, A., Sottet, J.-S., Calvary, G., Coutaz, J., Ganneau, V., and Vanderdonckt, J. The 4C Reference Model for Distributed User Interfaces, in *Proceedings of ICAS '08*, IEEE, 2008, 61-69.

4. Google. The new multi-screen world: Understanding cross-platform consumer behavior. Technical report, August 2012.
http://www.google.com/think/research-studies/the-new-multi-screen-world-study.html

5. Melchior, J., Grolaux, D., Vanderdonckt, J., Van Roy, P. A toolkit for peer-to-peer distributed user interfaces: concepts, implementation, and applications, In *Proc.* ACM SIGCHI 2009, ACM Press (2009), 69-78.

6. Paternò, F., Santoro, C. A logical framework for multi-device user interfaces. In *Proc.* ACM EICS 2012, ACM Press (2012), 45-50.

CrowdStudy: General Toolkit for Crowdsourced Evaluation of Web Interfaces

Michael Nebeling, Maximilian Speicher and Moira C. Norrie
Institute of Information Systems, ETH Zurich
CH-8092 Zurich, Switzerland
{nebeling,norrie}@inf.ethz.ch, maximilianspeicher@gmx.de

ABSTRACT

While traditional usability testing methods can be both time consuming and expensive, tools for automated usability evaluation tend to oversimplify the problem by limiting themselves to supporting only certain evaluation criteria, settings, tasks and scenarios. We present CrowdStudy, a general web toolkit that combines support for automated usability testing with crowdsourcing to facilitate large-scale online user testing. CrowdStudy is based on existing crowdsourcing techniques for recruiting workers and guiding them through complex tasks, but implements mechanisms specifically designed for usability studies, allowing testers to control user sampling and conduct evaluations for particular contexts of use. Our toolkit provides support for context-aware data collection and analysis based on an extensible set of metrics, as well as tools for managing, reviewing and analysing any collected data. The paper demonstrates several useful features of CrowdStudy for two different scenarios, and discusses the benefits and tradeoffs of using crowdsourced evaluation.

Author Keywords

Web usability; user testing; crowdsourced evaluation

ACM Classification Keywords

H.5.2 Information Interfaces and Presentation: User Interfaces—*Evaluation/methodology*

INTRODUCTION

Usability evaluation is an important part of the user interface design process. Particular attention has been devoted to web usability, where specific design methods [19] and evaluation metrics [10] have been crafted over the years. While the most commonly used evaluation method is user testing [9], it is heavily constrained by available time, money and human resources. At the same time, an evolving set of tools for automated usability testing have emerged over the years [11]. However, there are still several limitations of current usability evaluation tools that we aim to address in this work.

First, given today's proliferation of web-enabled devices, the usability of a web site is largely determined by its ability to adapt to the specific device in use. Existing guidelines such as WCAG, the Web Content Accessibility Guidelines[1] by W3C, consist of a set of recommendations on making content accessible with the focus on meeting special needs of users. The W3C web site lists different evaluation and issue reporting tools, but none of them consider the rapidly evolving range of use contexts. In particular, there is a need for tools that also support mobile settings and make use of the rich input sensing techniques available on modern touch devices.

Second, while there are advanced frameworks for user activity tracking [1], available implementations such as Web-Quilt [7] and Web Usability Probe [3] are often restricted to event logging and usually support this on either the server or client side. Therefore, information is generally collected at a very low level semantically which means that post processing and special log analysis tools are required to visualise and make sense of the collected data.

Third, essential tasks such as subject recruitment including qualification tests and many key aspects of remote usability testing including task distribution within or between subjects are generally out of scope of existing tools. Rather than allowing tools to be configured for different settings, often special solutions need to be developed for testing under the required conditions.

Recently, crowdsourcing services such as Amazon Mechanical Turk[2] have received a lot of attention as a platform for conducting online user tests [12]. Research has started to investigate the benefits and tradeoffs of crowdsourced user testing by comparing lab and remote studies [4, 16]. Our goal is to tightly integrate support for crowdsourcing into usability testing tools in order to support a wide range of evaluation methods and scenarios.

In this paper, we present CrowdStudy, a general framework and comprehensive web site testing toolkit that integrates with crowdsourcing services such as Mechanical Turk to advertise and facilitate online evaluations. CrowdStudy evolved out of several research projects that required user testing for a wide range of use contexts in a short amount of time [22, 23]. While it was first specifically developed to conduct these studies [21], we have now built several mechanisms

---

[1] http://www.w3.org/TR/WCAG20
[2] http://mturk.com

into CrowdStudy that allow it to be configured for different tasks and additional metrics required for particular evaluation scenarios. As examples of important scenarios that pose interesting challenges, we report on two evaluations conducted with CrowdStudy, where it was used for usability testing in large-display environments and on mobile touch devices.

The next section discusses related work. This is followed with two scenarios that are difficult to address with existing tool support. We then present the CrowdStudy framework, its architecture and implementation, together with example studies illustrating its use. Finally, the paper analyses the contributions made with CrowdStudy, compares traditional usability testing and crowdsourced evaluation, and discusses the benefits and trade-offs of each technique.

BACKGROUND

CrowdStudy builds on existing frameworks for automatic usability evaluation [1, 3, 7]. Common to most approaches is logging of user interface events with the goal of extracting usability-related information [5]. While a comprehensive overview is given in [11], here we limit our review to a selection of tools and highlight differences to CrowdStudy.

An early tool is WebQuilt [7] which supports logging and user activity tracking based on server-side components using a proxy-based solution to intercept the interaction with a web site. WebQuilt records the communication between client and server in terms of navigation and access paths within and between web pages. This information can then be visualised in a graph showing web pages as nodes and actions as edges. Given this information, it is possible to detect certain user interaction patterns as well as issues with the document structure and navigation. Compared to client-based solutions, one of the greatest disadvantages of WebQuilt is that recording and handling of JavaScript-based actions is not supported. This is especially problematic given the increased popularity of libraries such as jQuery[3] and that many modern web sites make extensive use of AJAX for dynamic content.

The general framework developed in [1] also builds on a proxy server so that no manual modification of the web site under investigation is necessary. In contrast to WebQuilt, the approach focuses on JavaScript-based, client-side interaction tracking techniques. This is motivated by the fact that such client-based techniques tend to provide richer information in terms of the interaction within a web page. The data that can be collected with that framework includes mouse movements and clicks, element focus and selection, form input and the required time for different form fields. It can then be mapped to the respective page elements and may be used to visualise the interaction paths of users within a web page.

More recently, Web Usability Probe (WUP) [3] was proposed. WUP extends the principles described above in that it not only supports data logging and visualisation, but also automatic analysis. The approach is based on "optimal" logs defined by the evaluator for the test scenario. These logs then provide a reference for comparisons with the logs produced by participants. Similar to other solutions, WUP enables evaluations across web sites while capturing most of the standard mouse and keyboard events. In addition, also custom client-side events can be registered for tracking, giving more flexibility to evaluators. However, visualisation of the recorded data is limited to timelines, which is only useful for time-related performance measurements.

The aforementioned solutions provided good starting points for our framework. However, they lack support for context-awareness which is a core component of CrowdStudy. Specifically, we show how to make use of state-of-the-art sensing techniques [6] to obtain more information on the use context, which is particularly important in mobile settings. In addition, our solution integrates support for crowdsourcing, which has only recently been considered for usability testing [16].

Crowdsourcing refers to the idea of outsourcing a task to a larger group of people in the form of an open call [8]. As already mentioned, much attention has been devoted to paid micro-task crowdsourcing markets such as Amazon Mechanical Turk (MTurk). First studies have assessed it as a general platform for conducting online user studies [12], some of which replicated previous lab studies and obtained similar results [4, 13].

While other methods for usability evaluation might produce more reliable results, MTurk is commonly regarded a useful tool and arguably has advantages over traditional lab experiments, such as easy and quick access to a large user pool, relatively low cost, and faster iteration between initial and follow-up experiments to refine the evaluation procedure [18]. To address the shortcomings of MTurk as a platform for experiments, many different toolkits have been developed on top of it, ranging from TurKit [15] for programming iterative and parallel crowdsourcing task designs, over Turkomatic [14] for using crowds to do the "programming" of tasks, to AutoMan [2] for fully automatic crowd programming.

CrowdStudy is similar to these works in that it also aims to leverage existing crowdsourcing services such as MTurk to facilitate large-scale web site user testing under time and monetary constraints. However, in contrast to these toolkits, CrowdStudy was specifically designed to provide flexible support for crowdsourced evaluation of existing web sites independent of other services, using MTurk as an additional, but optional, channel for conducting online experiments.

The closest to CrowdStudy in terms of the overall design is TurkServer [17]. TurkServer aims to be a general platform for synchronous and longitudinal online experiments, addressing common challenges such as the technical setup of online experiments, user and data tracking across experiment sessions, and filtering of incomplete and invalid data. It does this by providing suitable abstractions and infrastructure, which is similar to CrowdStudy. However, CrowdStudy implements tasks and metrics that are specific to web usability evaluation, and also addresses the proliferation of new devices and how they may impact user experience. As a result, CrowdStudy can be configured to target and recruit more users with devices that are poorly supported by the current web design.

---

[3]http://jquery.com

This helps developers to target usability problems on specific devices and ultimately provide more flexible web interfaces that can adapt to a greater variety of use contexts.

SCENARIOS

To better illustrate the problems and motivate the techniques developed for CrowdStudy, we present two scenarios that pose different requirements and help to explain the roles of the different components defined in our framework.

Scenario 1: Designing Web Pages for Large Screens

A team of HCI researchers have developed a new prototype of a system that provides end-users with tools for customising a web page specifically for larger viewing sizes. For evaluating the tool support and studying many possible layouts in a short amount of time, they decide to conduct a remote user study and hope to recruit a large number of participants. At first, participants are randomly given one out of three possible tasks—one asking them to adapt the web page, another to compare layouts based on aesthetic considerations and a third for reading using a specific layout and answering questions on the text. Participants are encouraged to work on additional tasks, but task distribution depends on the tasks that a participant has already worked on as well as the number of layouts contributed by other participants. Each task starts by showing instructions and finishes with a post-task questionnaire collecting subjective feedback. The researchers need to be able to closely monitor and inspect the results during and after the study.

Scenario 2: Touch Interaction on Mobile Devices

The same team of researchers have also developed a second prototype specifically for mobile browsers using new techniques for touch interaction tracking and adapting web pages based on user performance measures. Again, they need to evaluate their new system with a large number of participants in a short amount of time, but now for a wide range of different mobile devices. For the study, participants will be given 50 small tasks (e.g. clicking a link) that need to be randomised and counterbalanced. To guide users through the study, respective parts of the web page are highlighted and the window scrolled to the required position. After the study, participants are asked to fill in a questionnaire providing feedback in terms of ratings and comments. The researchers want to review and visually inspect the collected data for convenient and fast analysis. Moreover, a follow-up lab study using a similar set of tasks is planned to validate their findings in a more controlled setting.

Requirements

The above scenarios not only differ in terms of the use context (large screen vs. mobile touch), but also regarding the types of tasks (rather complex tasks such as designing & comparing web pages vs. rather simple, mechanical tasks such as clicking links), task distribution (randomised & controlled vs. randomised & counterbalanced) and assignment (within-subjects vs. between-subjects). Based on these scenarios and our experience with conducting usability studies, we have derived the following set of requirements for CrowdStudy:

(R1) **Context-awareness** The system must be able to detect the client context as well as being compatible with all major browsers, both on desktop PCs and mobile touch devices.

(R2) **Easy integration** The system must be easy to integrate into a web site under investigation. Moreover, smaller changes to the web interface (e.g. for annotating page components part of a task) should be supported.

(R3) **Subject recruitment** The system must support easy recruitment of a potentially large number of participants over a short period of time.

(R4) **Simple and complex tasks** The system must enable both simple and complex tasks, e.g. by splitting tasks and automating irrelevant sub-tasks to keep the cognitive load and participant distraction at a minimum.

(R5) **Controlled testing** The system must support different modes of task distribution and assignment, e.g. randomisation and counterbalancing, within or between subjects.

(R6) **Qualification checks** The system must ensure that only participants fulfilling certain requirements (e.g. usage of a specific browser or device) can take part in the study.

(R7) **Pre/post-conditions** The system must support optional pre and post-conditions for the overall study and individual tasks. For example, conditions could be questionnaires asking for demographics and feedback.

(R8) **Different metrics** The system must provide automatic logging of all kinds of available data, including demographics, user feedback and task-related data (such as task completion time, task success rates etc.). These must be made available in aggregated forms through metrics for convenient statistical processing.

(R9) **On-the-fly data inspection** Based on the metrics just described, the system must provide means for easy and convenient inspection of the gathered data during and after the study, both in terms of individual data sets from single participants, and in configurable aggregated ways.

(R10) **Different types of evaluation** The system must enable easy preparation of different study methods, i.e. asynchronous remote studies as well as controlled lab studies.

CROWDSTUDY

In this section, we give a first overview of our framework from a higher level of abstraction. Figure 1 illustrates the main components of CrowdStudy. The design of these components was informed from previous work [1] and different scenarios including those mentioned previously, but the overall framework design was generalised and also extended to provide support for context-awareness and crowdsourcing. On the one hand, the tasks and metrics components allow for the configuration of usability evaluation scenarios and the information to be collected by the framework. Based on this configuration, it is then possible to automatically control subject recruitment, task distribution and other aspects of a running study. On the other hand, the administrative tools and components for viewing, analysing and visualising user data are typically used during and after a study in order to monitor tests and evaluate the results. Below we discuss the different aspects of web usability testing addressed by specific components of our framework.

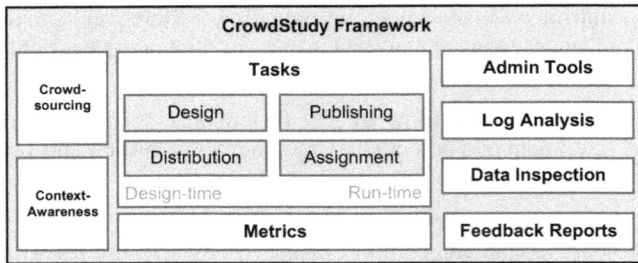

Figure 1: Framework Components

Task Design, Distribution and Assignment (R4–R5)

The **Task Design** component allows test developers to define different task designs where each task may involve one or several web site components as well as navigation between pages. Additionally, tasks can be designed for different use contexts and input modalities. Using client-side scripting, some aspects of a task may also be automated to allow users to focus on others. For example, we provide tools that can automatically scroll to a component of interest and annotate and highlight certain parts that require interaction or the attention of users. The **Task Publishing** component refers to the part of the framework that coordinates the invitation of web site visitors to participate in studies. This can also mean to generate task descriptions and publish them on crowdsourcing services such as Mechanical Turk. Finally, the task management components also provide design and run-time support for **Task Distribution** and **Task Assignment**. This means that evaluators can use randomisation or controlled assignment of tasks at design-time and the framework enables automatic counter-balancing at run-time based on the test coverage so far.

Abstract Model for Different Studies (R6–R7,R10)

While our framework also enables "traditional" lab studies, it was specifically designed to support asynchronous remote usability evaluation and parallel user tests. This requires special components for task distribution among participants and assignment within or between subjects according to the study design. The task management components of our framework provide flexible support for evaluators to design test scenarios. To support this in a uniform way, we first generalised the basic process of user studies into a simple model that defines the most common steps. We show the abstraction underlying our framework in Figure 2.

Following this model, each step of a study can be introduced by a set of instructions, consists of the user performing one or several tasks and usually ends with a post-task questionnaire before continuing to the next step. Additionally, users may be asked to fill in questionnaires before and after the study to provide information on their background and overall feedback. Since different studies have different requirements, we provide support for varying the basic steps involved. For example, qualification tests are not

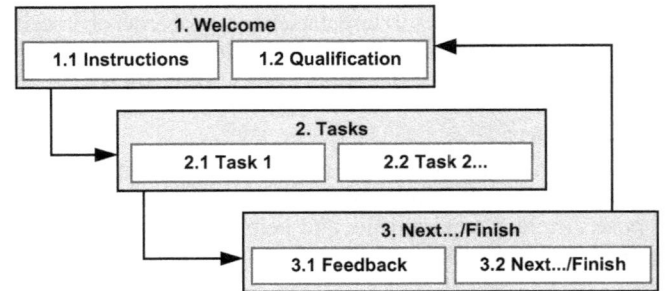

Figure 2: Abstraction of Study Process

required, but depending on the kind of study, they can be implemented either programmatically using technical checks or by means of collecting information explicitly from users. The central entity in this study process is a task defined as $T = < precon, (action)+, postcon >$ where the first and last components refer to the pre and post-conditions, while the actual task is defined in terms of a series of actions the user is asked to perform. Actions may be specifically scripted or can be defined by marking web site elements with pre-defined task classes, e.g., for clicking links, navigating the page or reading text and answering questions. As part of the conditions, tasks can also be configured to require other tasks to be completed first or select the appropriate next task depending on the previous result. This is helpful in the case that they depend on each other and may even be required to enforce a certain workflow in the scope of the investigation.

Extensible Set of Metrics (R8)

In addition to this flexible design of studies, our framework supports an extensible set of metrics through the **Metrics** component that can generally be divided into the following classes.

- **Device-related metrics** like the device model and type, display size, resolution and orientation, supported input modalities, browser agent and version, OS, etc.

- **User-related metrics** such as self-reported experience levels in general or specifically with the web site under investigation as well as a user's gender, age, background, skills and preferences

- **Time-based metrics** including time-on-task and intermediate or accumulated times for subsets of tasks or larger parts of a study

- **Counter-based metrics** useful for measuring error and success rates as well as controlled task assignment and distribution, e.g. within and between subjects

- **User activity metrics** including server-side requests and client-side interactions

- **Ratings and comments** for subjective feedback typically collected through questionnaires

Device-related and *user-related* metrics generally describe the use contexts of participants. The device-related ones may be collected automatically by extracting the relevant information from browser information or using device input sensing techniques based on event listeners. The user-related ones mostly need to be provided by participants and can also be used to define a demographic profile of participants. These may include aspects such as a user's handedness and potential motor impairments to address special needs in addition to a user's cultural background and location. As stated previously, such components have not been an integral part of existing evaluation tools even though they may be used to enrich the information that can be collected based on user activity tracking alone [1, 3, 7].

Time-based and *counter-based* metrics are general indicators as they may be used to measure the time a certain task or aspect of a study required—or to set a time limit for completing a certain task or sets of interrelated tasks—and to then build and compare the error and success rates between participants. Timers and counters may therefore help control the testing environment which is important in remote usability testing. Our framework provides a set of timer and counter components that generate time information and update counters per user session, which can be used to control the time-on-task and task flow. They are usually hidden from users and the control typically remains with the evaluator running the study. The quantitative information collected by these components is typically indicative of user performance and normally used in combination with other metrics as part of a statistical analysis and to help the interpretation of results.

The *user activity* metrics are among the most distinct features of our usability evaluation framework. The framework can be configured to capture client-side events similar to [1, 3]. However, our activity tracking mechanisms operate at a semantically higher level. By this we mean that, rather than simply recording each client-side event together with its type and data in a timeline, we capture interactions that may consist of multiple events and log them on a per-component basis. This allows us to organise the tracking data associated with the components involved in the interaction and also enables our framework to reduce the amount of tracking data. For example, we may aggregate and combine multiple consecutive events, such as scrolling in the same direction, or aggregate individual touch events to higher-level gestures (such as tap-and-pan). In addition, our tools can track, not only click or touch events that successfully activated a link or other kinds of active content, but also those that occurred nearby within a specified range around the target as instances of a potentially intended action that did not get triggered. To support this, we have tools that instrument the page with additional tracking areas surrounding the respective elements. At the same time, our framework automatically registers any changes of the viewport due to scrolling or zooming of the page, changes of the orientation or auto-focus and user-zoom actions. While the latter are primarily supported by mobile browsers and typically performed in response to rotating the device or performing gestures on a touch surface, all of them provide valuable information concerning the use context.

Finally, *user ratings* and *comments* can be collected using single and multiple-choice as well as open questions. However, since the focus of our framework was on other aspects, we only provide basic means for authoring questionnaires, such as JavaScript methods for validating input for required fields. Alternatively, evaluators may combine CrowdStudy with advanced questionnaire tools, e.g. SurveyMonkey[4].

Admin and Data Analysis Tools *(R9)*
As the last set of components, our framework provides **Admin Tools** for creating, managing, testing and deploying new user studies. The analysis tools range from a **Log Analysis** component that allows evaluators to access the data for each test and filter it by certain criteria, e.g. class of device or user experience level, to **Feedback Reports** that summarise questionnaire data provided by participants. In addition, CrowdStudy provides a component for **Data Inspection** of the evaluation data which may be aggregated per task over all participants or per participant for all completed tasks. It is possible to develop different visualisations of the data such as a heat map for touch interaction data aggregated from smartphone or tablet users, as shown in [23].

ARCHITECTURE
Figure 3 shows the typical client/server infrastructure around an existing web application and how the architecture underlying our framework extends it with additional components (marked in grey). Some components of our framework such as the ones for user activity tracking are implemented on the client side, while the context engine and other parts of our framework remain on the server side. The figure also illustrates the integration with existing crowdsourcing platforms such as Mechanical Turk that provide interfaces for programmatic access to their services. Below we describe how each of the components implement parts of our framework and relate to each other.

CrowdStudy Client
First note that clients can either be *users*, i.e. "normal" web site visitors, or *workers* specifically recruited using crowdsourcing services. The components responsible for **User Activity Tracking** are provided by our **CrowdStudy Client** running on the user's device. Depending on the specific metrics and tasks configured for a web site test, CrowdStudy may collect data related to some or all of the metrics described earlier. The data is therefore buffered and cached locally before it is sent to the server side at suitable intervals. Also part of the client-side components is the **Test Pilot** which implements parts of the task management logic for instructing users and guiding them through the tests, e.g. by highlighting and navigating to certain page elements.

CrowdStudy Server
The server-side extensions are grouped into a **CrowdStudy Configuration** and the **CrowdStudy Server**—the heart of CrowdStudy's architecture. The configuration is used for setting up the client-side tool and connecting it to the server.

---

[4]http://www.surveymonkey.com

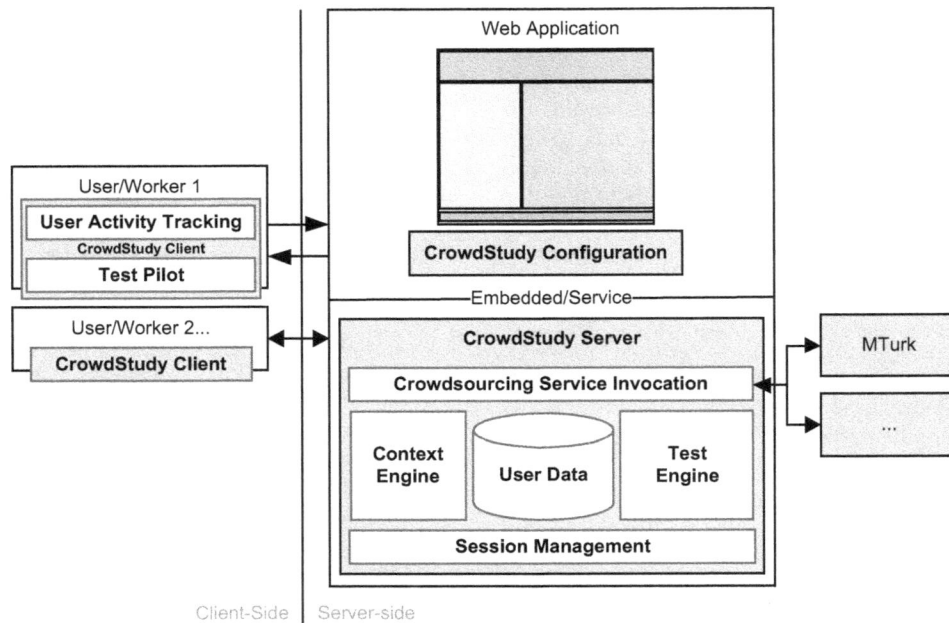

Figure 3: Architecture

The server implements the **Context Engine** that is responsible for associating any data gathered from clients with the corresponding client context. This means that device and user-related metrics from our framework are managed mainly by this component. The server also contains the **Test Engine** which implements the task manager logic responsible for assigning and distributing tasks to participants. All information collected by these components is managed as part of the **User Data** in a database. The **Session Management** component is necessary for identifying and keeping track of users as required for logging. If external, paid crowd workers are to be recruited, the **Crowdsourcing Service Invocation** component enables crowdsourced evaluation via selected platforms.

Integration with Mechanical Turk

Using the MTurk SDK[5] for Amazon Mechanical Turk for example, CrowdStudy can generate and publish so-called *Human Intelligence Tasks* (HIT) on behalf of the evaluator. To generate a HIT, our **MTurk** component accepts several configuration parameters. First, the external URL where Crowd-Study is hosted needs to be specified. Second, a requester needs to decide how long workers can work on a task and how high their reward should be. Each HIT generated by our framework maps all three phases of the study process to MTurk concepts. For the first phase, the qualification ensures that a candidate user is eligible to participate in the study. This can either be done by asking users to answer certain questions, completing sample tasks or based on an assessment using MTurk's own qualification tests setting conditions for HIT completion rate or required a certain demographic profile. In addition, CrowdStudy's context information can be used, e.g. to determine whether the device characteristics match the study requirements. In the second phase,

the actual user testing takes place by redirecting workers to a CrowdStudy instance asking them to go through a one or multiple tasks as specified by the evaluator. Finally, the third phase typically includes a feedback questionnaire to gather data about the user's background and experience as well as self-reported measures. CrowdStudy then redirects back to MTurk to allow participants to check the data collected during the study and submit it for review to the evaluator.

Figure 4 illustrates the interaction for a generated HIT from the worker perspective. The management of the HIT is done through Amazon's web site which provides the worker with interfaces for accepting, returning and submitting HITs. To the evaluator, Amazon provides management tools to accept or reject the HITs submitted by the workers (not shown here). The *User Study* and *Questionnaire* parts of the study are hosted on the CrowdStudy Server which collects all measures along the defined metrics including user feedback. The two back-ends are synchronised by consistently using MTurk's assignment identifiers which uniquely describe a (HIT, worker) pair. Currently, evaluators need to manually accept or reject HITs after analysing the data users have submitted to the CrowdStudy Server. Automatic validation could be implemented based on MTurk's API to aid scalability.

Deployment

While most existing frameworks are proxy-based, our solution can either be directly embedded into web sites by the providers or be made available to users in the form of a browser plug-in. The first embedded deployment only requires linking the CrowdStudy Client to the web site using a single line of code similar to including JavaScript libraries such as jQuery. The latter service deployment is similar to Mozilla's Test Pilot[6] which is a plug-in for collecting struc-

---

[5]http://aws.amazon.com/mturk

[6]http://testpilot.mozillalabs.com/

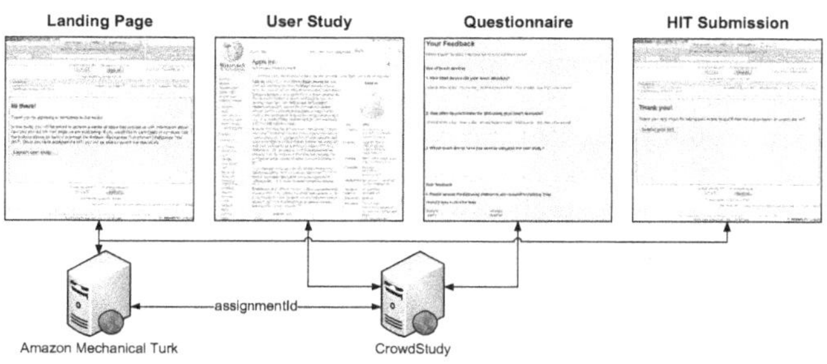

Figure 4: Integration with Amazon Mechanical Turk

tured user feedback through Firefox. Using the CrowdStudy plug-in, other developers could create and exchange test scenarios for an existing web site independent of the provider.

The embedded deployment mode can be useful for focus tests of new parts of a web site before they are rolled out to the entire user community. The service deployment mode is required for platforms such as WordPress and Facebook, where third-party application developers may want to test how their solutions integrate with the kernel application and platform, but have no control over the hosting site.

IMPLEMENTATION AND USE

CrowdStudy is a lightweight framework and does not impact web site performance. To achieve this, it uses asynchronous synchronisation with the server and implements client-side buffering mechanisms not to interfere with the collection of timing data during active tasks. The CrowdStudy Client is implemented using jQuery in combination with jQMulti-Touch [20] for handling touch events and device orientation on mobile devices. The CrowdStudy Server is implemented in PHP, using MySQL as the database backend.

CrowdStudy can be added to an existing web site simply by embedding the CrowdStudy Client as external JavaScript and providing a configuration. CrowdStudy works best on web sites implemented in HTML/CSS, where all elements involved in tasks are accessible via the DOM. Notable exceptions are Flash, Silverlight and custom HTML5 canvas implementations, where interaction tracking is limited to the container element that renders the inner-content. The highly dynamic nature of modern web sites is generally not a problem for CrowdStudy's interaction tracking, but may require additional techniques for conditional data inspection and visualisation. Next to recording user interactions, CrowdStudy can also collect qualitative data in the form of questionnaires.

All data collected by the CrowdStudy Client is associated with OS and browser information, screen dimensions and display orientation. In addition, CrowdStudy uses MobileESP[7] for detecting mobile device classes and further distinguishes portrait and landscape mode using a combination of JavaScript and CSS3 media queries. For the integration with MTurk, CrowdStudy generates HITs using an *external question* to point to the CrowdStudy URL that MTurk embeds by using an HTML iframe of configurable size.

---

[7]http://mobileesp.com

Figure 5: CrowdStudy Example

CrowdStudy offers several pre-defined tasks and metrics. Web page elements part of a task only need to be annotated with special CSS marker classes. New types of tasks can be implemented using jQuery callbacks. Likewise, additional metrics can be registered by implementing the relevant tracking functions in the form of callback handlers on the client and/or server side as required.

Figure 5 illustrates the steps required for setting up a CrowdStudy instance for a simple example page. Similar to the second scenario, crowdsourced evaluation is used in a mobile context. The **welcome.html** page implements a simple browser and device check using JavaScript and welcomes participants or shows a corresponding error message. The **test.html** page defines several tasks by associating links and text paragraphs in the page with pre-defined CrowdStudy task classes. By linking jQuery and **crowdstudy.js**, the CrowdStudy Client will automatically analyse the DOM and compile a set of tasks accordingly. The **questionnaire.html** page collects user feedback once all tasks are completed.

Interested readers are referred to the the project web site[8] for more technical information and the CrowdStudy source code.

EXAMPLE STUDIES

This section presents two experiments that we conducted using CrowdStudy based on the scenarios described earlier. We focus on these examples because they demonstrate different

---

[8]http://dev.globis.ethz.ch/crowdstudy

aspects of CrowdStudy due to different study requirements. The first experiment illustrates how CrowdStudy can be configured for task distribution and assignment according to the requirements and different phases of a study and dependencies between tasks. The second study shows examples of how CrowdStudy was extended with new metrics specifically designed for multi-touch interaction and additional visualisation techniques for touch input tracking data. The tasks used in the experiments are shown in Figure 6 and the metrics in Figure 7. Note that the two studies are not a contribution of this paper, but the fact that CrowdStudy supported them is meant to demonstrate its usefulness and that it can be configured for different scenarios. Rather, this section contributes an analysis and comparison of the two experiments in terms of the tasks and metrics implemented using CrowdStudy. Interested readers are referred to [22, 23] for details on these studies.

Study 1: Designing Web Pages for Large Screens

The first study concerned the quality of new web page layouts created by end-users as well as the set of new tools proposed for adapting web sites to particular viewing conditions. The experiment consisted of three tasks illustrated in Figure 6 (left) and was divided into two phases.

The *design* task asked participants to use the design tools to adapt the layout of a news article so that it best supported their viewing situation. The *compare* task asked participants to rate a number of layouts for the news web page by comparing two layouts in each step and choosing the better one for reading the article. The *evaluate* task asked participants to read the news article using one of the layouts and then answer five questions on the text by clicking on the text paragraph that contained the answer, rather than typing it.

For each task, CrowdStudy showed instructions and measured the time for completion. In the *design* task, CrowdStudy was also used for logging how users made use of the design tools as well as when the window was resized. In the *compare* task, participants were not allowed to vote on their own layout, and CrowdStudy only counted one rating per pair for each participant even though it was possible that the same pair was compared multiple times. In the *evaluate* task, the times for reading and answering were measured separately. The *design* and *evaluate* tasks finished with a post-task questionnaire, where CrowdStudy was used for data collection.

CrowdStudy also controlled task distribution and assignment within and between subjects. The experiment initially started with the original design of the news article used as the basis for designing and reading. This was switched in the second phase of the experiment, then using the currently best-matching user-generated layout for the tasks. CrowdStudy randomised between the three tasks, but the *design* and *evaluate* tasks were allowed only once within subjects. The *compare* task was only enabled for client contexts that matched at least three different layouts to reduce the chance that participants would see their own layout in comparisons.

We recruited a total of 93 participants using CrowdStudy. Users had to pass a CrowdStudy qualification page checking whether their browser settings met the technical requirements of the experiment as only Firefox and no mobile devices were supported. Overall, CrowdStudy monitored the design of 28 custom layouts, collected 143 ratings and 42 answers providing reading feedback for several layouts. It also helped us to coordinate switching to the second phase once we had received sufficient user-generated layouts and ratings [22].

Study 2: Touch Interaction on Mobile Devices

The goal of our second study was to conduct a comparative evaluation of the original Wikipedia web site and a new version generated for touchphones and tablets. The study involved both crowdsourced usability evaluation and a smaller follow-up lab study to test the validity of results. Since participants were allowed to use their own touch devices in the remote evaluation, CrowdStudy was tested in terms of compatibility with a wide range of mobile devices and different browsers. Using CrowdStudy, we implemented device and browser checks as part of the qualification test to make sure that users had a touch-enabled device and adequate browser support before they were allowed to participate.

The experiment consisted of four different types of tasks illustrated in Figure 6 (right). In *click link* tasks, participants were asked to tap on a specific link that was underlined and highlighted as well as marked by an arrow pointing at the link. For *find link* tasks, the article was scrolled to the top and participants then had to find a link within the main article text marked by our framework. The time required to locate and click the correct link was measured, as well as the number of times the scrolling direction changed. In *read text* tasks, participants were asked to read a highlighted part of the article text. In this case, the instructions box additionally provided a "Done" button for users to indicate that they finished reading, after which we logged the required time. In *describe image* tasks, users answered a multiple-choice question for which it was necessary to view details of an image. The image was scrolled into the viewport and marked. CrowdStudy counted correct responses and recorded the time required to answer.

In contrast to the first study, all tasks were carried out within the same page. A total of 33 tasks of different types were defined, randomised and counterbalanced between subjects using CrowdStudy. In order that users only had to focus on the actual interaction that was required to complete a task, CrowdStudy automatically scrolled to the respective part of the web page except for the *find link* task that started from the top. For each task, CrowdStudy showed instructions at the bottom of the page and guided users through the experiment.

The first part of the study using crowdsourcing involved 84 participants in total; 39 tested the original version, 45 the adapted one. Here, we used CrowdStudy for closely monitoring the experiment and specifically recruiting smartphone and tablet users to focus testing on mobile settings: 64 participants used a smartphone (we detected a number of different models such as iPhone, HTC Desire, Motorola Defy, Samsung Galaxy S and Nokia N9), the other 20 used a tablet device including iPad, Lenovo ThinkPad, Motorola Xoom and Archos 70. 50 completed the study with questionnaire feedback providing their gender, age and ratings concerning device usage in general and specifically for web browsing. In

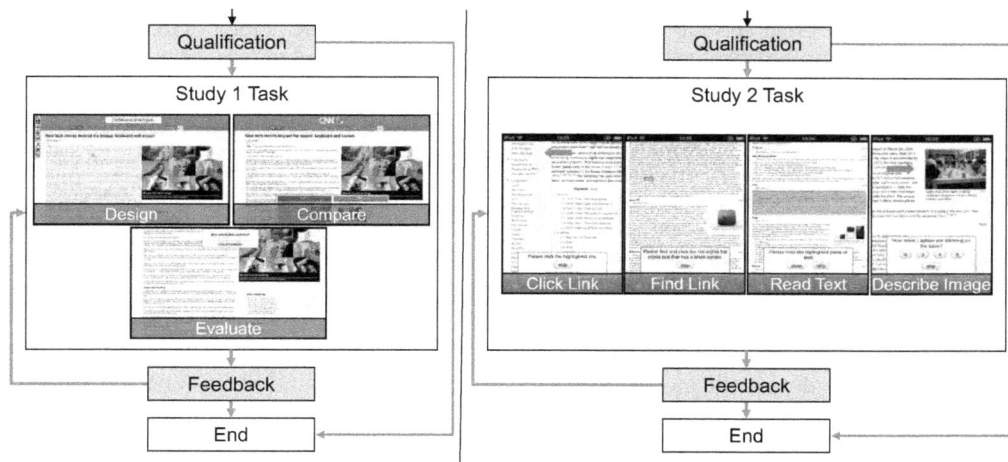

Figure 6: Tasks used in Study 1 (left) and Study 2 (right)

Metrics	Study 1: Designing Web Pages for Large Screens	Study 2: Touch Interaction on Mobile Devices
Device-related	Detected browser and screen resolution; recorded window width and height; collected other system information including language, OS version, and location in terms of the IP address.	Detected mobile operating system, browser and screen resolution as well as device type (using MobileESP); **Per task**: logged the zoom level and device orientation.
User-related	Demographics (gender, age, etc.); also asked for level of expertise in design, development and user experience.	Demographics similar to Study 1; frequency of touch device use in general and for web browsing specifically.
Time and counter-based	**All tasks**: measured completion times for *design, compare* and *evaluate* tasks (with separate times for reading and answering); **Compare task**: number of votes per layout and participant; **Evaluate task**: number of questions answered or skipped.	**All tasks**: measured task completion times; counted skipped tasks.
User activity and interaction-based	**Design task**: recorded all customisations in terms of design actions and how web page elements were changed (position, size, spacing, font size, visibility etc.); **Evaluate task**: logged scrolling actions; **All tasks**: logged when and how the window was resized while working on a task.	**Click link task**: measured missed-links and zoom-factor ratios to see how often participants misclicked links and zoomed into certain areas of the page; **Find link task**: additionally logged scroll actions including how often the scroll direction changed; **Read text and describe image tasks**: monitored zoom level.
Ratings and comments	**All tasks**: collected ratings on whether task was easy to understand and easy to perform; question on further comments; **Design task**: also ratings on usefulness of each tool; **Evaluate task**: additional questions on reading efficiency using the layout; **Design and evaluate tasks**: different ratings of layout.	Post-study questionnaire asking participants to rate statements concerning the ease and efficiency of tasks; question on further comments.

Figure 7: Metrics used in the two example studies

the follow-up lab study with 13 participants, a simpler version of CrowdStudy and an iPod touch were used. Based on the collected data obtained in both phases, we developed simple, touch-related usability metrics and visualisation techniques that, not only allowed visual inspection of the collected data by aggregating the results obtained from different users, but also identifying critical components that required adaptation for the particular use context. This is detailed in [23].

DISCUSSION AND CONCLUSION

This paper presented CrowdStudy, a flexible framework for designing and conducting web site evaluations in the lab or remotely, then using crowdsourcing techniques and services such as Mechanical Turk for large-scale user testing. To demonstrate the novelty and flexibility of our framework at the technical level, the studies spanned many different use contexts including different kinds of mobile touch devices.

CrowdStudy is not yet another framework on top of Mechanical Turk (MTurk). Rather, CrowdStudy is a general framework designed for conducting web usability tests that can also be used in combination with crowdsourcing services such as

MTurk. While MTurk already provides support for qualification tests, the level of support and implementations vary between different crowdsourcing platforms. CrowdStudy's tests can be similar to MTurk's, but are configured independently of crowdsourcing services and are also available if Crowd-Study only recruits web site users rather than crowd workers. Also note that CrowdStudy tests can go beyond the worker history and their performance, making it possible for usability testers to specifically recruit users and conduct tests for undersupported use contexts. In particular, the two studies show that it is possible to realise dependencies between tasks and control whether and how tasks are assigned to users depending on their background and qualification as well as the device in use and progress of the experiment.

A central question is how crowdsourced evaluation compares with usability evaluation using experts or lab subjects. While this is generally discussed in [18, 16], our experience with using CrowdStudy suggests that the benefits outweigh the trade-offs. For example, the second study conducted with Crowd-Study showed that our mobile test version came very close to the original in terms of reading experience and efficiency, with similar results in both the online and lab setting. The lab study confirmed the findings of the crowdsourcing experiment, but did not provide any new insights. However, the more controlled setting produced higher validity of results. For example, the reading times showed generally less variance in the lab study. On the other hand, crowdsourced evaluation provided additional insight into how participants used the test page on many different smartphones and tablets under diverse and realistic conditions. This allowed us to detect use patterns and differences, not only between different types of devices, but also between portrait and landscape, which would be difficult in a lab setting.

While CrowdStudy does not provide specific mechanisms for quality control in the form one might expect from crowdsourcing frameworks, it provides tools for reviewing and analysing collected data. In particular, via the admin tools, it is possible to block users and exclude selected contributions by marking them as incomplete or invalid. A possible extension to CrowdStudy is a tool for replaying the user interactions as a basis for qualitative analysis. It could also be interesting to combine CrowdStudy with more advanced crowdsourcing frameworks such as Turkomatic [14] or AutoMan [2]. We plan to extend the framework in mainly two ways. First, we are currently exploring the extension of our framework with additional tracking techniques such as 3D skeletal tracking using Kinect. This will provide additional support for studies with a focus on collaboration that were out of scope at this stage. Second, we aim to support both co-located and remote user studies in multi-device environments by developing new concepts and techniques for interaction tracking across devices. This includes scenarios where the user interface is dynamically distributed and migrated between devices, which requires additional mechanisms.

Acknowledgements

We thank Michael Grossniklaus for his help with the Mechanical Turk integration. This work was supported by the Swiss NSF under research grant 200020_134983.

REFERENCES

1. Atterer, R., Wnuk, M., and Schmidt, A. Knowing the User's Every Move – User Activity Tracking for Website Usability Evaluation and Implicit Interaction. In *Proc. WWW* (2006).

2. Barowy, D. W., Curtsinger, C., Berger, E. D., and McGregor, A. AutoMan: A Platform for Integrating Human-Based and Digital Computation. In *Proc. OOPSLA* (2012).

3. Carta, T., Paternò, F., and de Santana, V. F. Web Usability Probe: A Tool for Supporting Remote Usability Evaluation of Web Sites. In *Proc. INTERACT* (2011).

4. Heer, J., and Bostock, M. Crowdsourcing Graphical Perception: Using Mechanical Turk to Assess Visualization Design. In *Proc. CHI* (2010).

5. Hilbert, D. M., and Redmiles, D. F. Extracting Usability Information from User Interface Events. *CSUR 32*, 4 (2000).

6. Hinckley, K., Pierce, J. S., Sinclair, M., and Horvitz, E. Sensing techniques for mobile interaction. In *Proc. UIST* (2000).

7. Hong, J. I., Heer, J., Waterson, S., and Landay, J. A. WebQuilt: A Proxy-based Approach to Remote Web Usability Testing. *TOIS 19*, 3 (2001).

8. Howe, J. The Rise of Crowdsourcing. *Wired 14*, 6 (2006).

9. Insfran, E., and Fernandez, A. A Systematic Review of Usability Evaluation in Web Development. In *Proc. WISE Workshops* (2008).

10. Ivory, M., and Megraw, R. Evolution of Web Site Design Patterns. *TOIS 23*, 4 (2005).

11. Ivory, M. Y., and Hearst, M. A. The State of the Art in Automating Usability Evaluation of User Interfaces. *CSUR 33*, 4 (2001).

12. Kittur, A., Chi, E. H., and Suh, B. Crowdsourcing User Studies With Mechanical Turk. In *Proc. CHI* (2008).

13. Komarov, S., Reinecke, K., and Gajos, K. Z. Crowdsourcing Performance Evaluations of User Interfaces. In *Proc. CHI* (2013).

14. Kulkarni, A. P., Can, M., and Hartmann, B. Collaboratively Crowdsourcing Workflows with Turkomatic. In *Proc. CSCW* (2012).

15. Little, G., Chilton, L. B., Goldman, M., and Miller, R. C. TurKit: human computation algorithms on mechanical turk. In *Proc. UIST* (2010).

16. Liu, D., Lease, M., Kuipers, R., and Bias, R. G. Crowdsourcing for Usability Testing. *CoRR abs/1203.1468* (2012).

17. Mao, A., Chen, Y., Gajos, K., Parkes, D., Procaccia, A., and Zhang, H. TurkServer: Enabling Synchronous and Longitudinal Online Experiments. In *Proc. HCOMP* (2012).

18. Mason, W., and Suri, S. Conducting behavioral research on Amazon's Mechanical Turk. *Behav Res 44*, 1 (2011).

19. Matera, M., Rizzo, F., and Carughi, G. Web Usability: Principles and Evaluation Methods. *Web Engineering* (2006).

20. Nebeling, M., and Norrie, M. C. jQMultiTouch: Lightweight Toolkit and Development Framework for Multi-touch/Multi-device Web Interfaces. In *Proc. EICS* (2012).

21. Nebeling, M., Speicher, M., Grossniklaus, M., and Norrie, M. C. Crowdsourced Web Site Evaluation with CrowdStudy. In *Proc. ICWE Demos* (2012).

22. Nebeling, M., Speicher, M., and Norrie, M. C. CrowdAdapt: Crowdsourced Web Page Adaptation for Individual Viewing Conditions and Preferences. In *Proc. EICS* (2013).

23. Nebeling, M., Speicher, M., and Norrie, M. C. W3Touch: Metrics-based Web Adaptation for Touch. In *Proc. CHI* (2013).

Complex activities in an Operations Center: A Case Study and Model for Engineering Interaction

Judith M. Brown
Carleton University
Ottawa, Canada
mmjbrown@connect.carleton.ca

Steven Greenspan
CA Labs, CA Technologies
200 Princeton S. Corp Center
Steven.Greenspan@ca.com

Robert Biddle
Carleton University
Ottawa, Canada
Robert_Biddle@Carleton.Ca

ABSTRACT

Data operations and command centers are crucial for managing today's Internet-based economy. Despite advances in automation, the challenges placed on operations professionals continue to increase as they work individually or in teams to repair or proactively avoid service disruptions. Although there have been a few studies of collaborative work in military supervisory control centers, due to the sensitive nature of work in operating centers, there have been few studies on the activities that take place in commercial data centers. In this case study of a large, complex data operations and control center, activity theory is used to guide and interpret observations of individual and collaborative work. This resulted in a model of data operations activities, and the identification of tensions that arise within and between these activities. This model is of value to interaction engineers in the first phase of a user-centered engineering methodology. Using this model, we provide some recommendations for reducing some of the tensions we found, and discuss significant opportunities and challenges in this new domain for the HCI community.

Author Keywords

Modeling; activity theory; attention; data operations centers.

ACM Classification Keywords

H.5.m. [Information interfaces and presentation]: Miscellaneous.

INTRODUCTION

Individual and collaborative work in data operations and command centers is increasingly complex and crucial for managing today's Internet-enabled economy. The work in operations centers is therefore expected to undergo rapid transformation to meet rising demands. Emerging technologies in automation, network monitoring, and analytics, together with user-oriented trends in handheld mobile computing, wall-sized and tabletop shared displays, and visualization, show great promise in meeting this demand if the application of these technologies are

carefully integrated into current workplace practices.

This paper describes a case study of current software usage in a large control center. The goal is to understand successes, problems, and challenges as a basis for future engineering-based interaction design work. Rather than evaluate each software application and user interface individually we are concerned with how all the parts fit together into goal-oriented activities and how these activities support or inhibit one another. From this vantage point we can gain insights to guide future design, as well as identify gaps in software usefulness and usability.

In today's operations and command centers, human operators are needed to monitor networks and facilitate corrective actions, despite increasing automation [20]. The automated responses to network and platform anomalies are not perfect. To maintain IT services, operators must contend with the problems created or amplified by automation [7], as well as with the root causes of IT service disruptions. Supporting IT services is thus a complex job requiring sophisticated pattern matching, situation awareness, decision-making, as well as endurance, dedication, and sustained multitasking skills [7][20].

Figure 1: Example of a command and control center [27].
Image provided by the Highways Agency,
under the Open Government License,
http://www.nationalarchives.gov.uk/doc/open-government-licence/

The operations and command center environment can be visually complex with many competing cues and activities (see Figure 1), and can induce cognitive overload and stress [18]. Operators must manage multiple distractions, rapidly switch between problem solving and monitoring activities, keep track of where other team members are focused, and maintain social cohesion within their team, their customers and their management [18].

Despite its central importance in modern economies and in today's human-computer interactions, little is known about how operators collaborate and how teams of operators interact with automated control software. Within this context, as researchers, we are particularly interested in attention allocation and distributed decision-making through team coordination; topics which were mentioned as two of ten top human supervisory control issues in network-centric operations [5].

The research described below is part of a three-pronged approach to improving attention allocation and collaboration in operations and command centers. In this approach we are designing tools that make it easier to (a) visualize the interactions between services and network resources, (b) identify problems and understand the business context, and (c) introduce tools and processes that enable the operations managers and staff to work together more effectively. To ensure usability and usefulness, these tools and processes must be based on a firm understanding of the activities and workflow in today's operations and command centers, i.e., it must be based on careful observations of the way work is accomplished and the way tools are used in context.

This paper describes the findings of an initial field study. Our goal was to conduct an analysis at the level of Calvary et al.'s task and context analysis [4] and to produce domain-dependent models that could later serve as starting points for other work, such as producing Abstract UI models [16].

In the next section the methodology is explained along with the theoretical frameworks that guided our observation and analytic processes. We then consider the results, identifying the different activities we observed, and the tensions within and between activities that disrupted the workflow. Following this, recommendations for reducing the identified tensions are discussed. We conclude by considering how the nature of work in operating and command centers might change as network and system automation evolves.

METHODOLOGY

Our study aimed to understand and solve problems arising out of human activity under stressful conditions. In our work we use a combination of methodological and theoretical approaches to guide field observations, interviews, data collection and interpretation. We first describe our theoretical foundations and then details of the design of our study.

Divided attention

In studies of operating centers, issues of attention figure prominently, e.g. [18]. Because divided attention is a key characteristic of work with the operations center we drew on the research on attention mechanisms [13][14][29] and in particular multi-tasking [23]. Current research suggests that an individual's supervisory attentional system controls endogenous orientation to external stimuli [21], and is responsible for managing working memory and effortful mental activities [2][25]. However, multitasking can occur with little or no supervisory involvement in practiced tasks, and in novel tasks that do not require the same cognitive, perceptual or motor resources at the same time [23]. For example, and relevant to operations and command centers, recent research suggests that although text chat is perceived by many to be less disruptive than voice communication while working on concurrent pattern-matching (non-communication) tasks, text chat has been shown to significantly decrease concurrent pattern matching performance [28]. Multitasking ability can also be affected by individual and personality differences. For example, extroverts are better at multitasking when communication tasks are involved [15].

Activity theory

To understand operating center activities holistically we drew on activity theory which was developed from Vygotsky's cultural historical psychology. Activities exist to meet human needs. Activity theory provides a framework that allows for the identification of the distinct activities occurring in a complex environment. It also helps to identify the essential elements of activities as they have been structured by individuals or groups over time. Within this framework, *activities*[1] are seen as systems of inter-related parts that adapt and change in response to any one of its elements changing. The concepts of individual and group activity are well integrated; in this research both are important because many of the activities of the center are accomplished by groups of people working together.

An activity theory framework directs us to focus on certain *elements*, such as the people, their tools, the makeup of groups or teams, implicit or tacit rules in the workplace, and the way their work is divided between members of a team. It also draws attention to the *motive* (or motives) for the activity, (which addresses the reason for its existence) and the *object* or focus of the activity [11].

For example, in the center we observed the primary activity was Incident Resolution. The motive for the activity was to ensure customers and end users are not impacted by any IT problems. The object of the activity was the tickets that

---

[1] "Task", used in the previous section, is a term not commonly used in activity theory. Tasks are roughly equivalent to scripted sequences of goal-oriented actions, which are directed towards advancing activities.

operators create and continuously update in their work, as well as an abstract understanding of the specific incident, which allows operators to assemble the right team to solve the problem.

Activity theory directs attention to disturbances, which are common occurrences in any activity. *Disturbances* are disruptions to the free flow of an activity. For example, disturbances may be observed in the operators' work of Monitoring Alerts that relate to matters of attention, such as missed alerts, or people experiencing stress because of poorly configured tools that make alerts visible in unhelpful ways.

Disturbances are indicators of *tensions* in an activity. A "bad fit" between elements, is evidenced by repeated disturbances of various types. The frequency of these disturbances can be reduced or eliminated by identifying the underlying tensions or conflicts, and changing one or more elements in the activity to eliminate these conflicts. Conflicts arise for multiple reasons, including conflicting motives, conflicts between "human nature" and the social or technological environment. All activities have underlying tensions.

The *location* of tensions in an activity are the points at which an activity is in need of development and change. The location is specified by identifying the two elements where there is a bad fit. Modifying the elements in an activity can alter the tensions between elements, thus reducing or eliminating the underlying tensions and *evolving the activity*. In the case of the bad fit between the operators and the tools they use to monitor alerts, it is possible to evolve an activity by changing the tools to monitor alerts or training individuals.

Activity theory also draws attention to disturbances and tensions *between* activities. This results because of a bad fit between activities. For example, there may be a tension between the Incident Resolution activity and the Monitoring Alerts activity due to a workplace rule for operators that make monitoring alerts a much lower priority than Incident Resolution. The observed disturbance may be that impacting alerts are sometimes missed.

In this study, the main goal was to accurately identify the principal activities in the daily work environment and to locate the underlying tensions that create disturbances in the workflow.

Design of the Field Study

We designed a field study to develop understandings of the complex environment within operator centers. Our approach is most similar to influential workplace studies conducted by Engeström [11] and Turner and Turner [26] whose field studies, which were informed by an activity theoretical framework, were used to generate understandings of workplaces [8][11]. Our study is also like the field studies conducted by the Mitre Corporation on Military Command Centers [3], which was guided by the concept of 'activity levels' and 'situation awareness', although those studies served a completely different purpose.

The co-authors visited an operations and command center that was responsible for a data center in June 2012 (we also visited 3 other centers where we did not collect data). The operating center was large and during the field study approximately 30 to 40 people worked during the day shift handling incidents that arose in their clients' data processing and transaction services. One team of operators monitored batch processes that were scheduled daily, while other teams monitored platforms and networks that supported a broad array of business services. Operators were notified about problems (i.e., incidents) through calls from affected business customers, by noticing system log anomalies, alarms or alerts generated by performance monitoring tools, or through emails and text chats from other operators or business partners.

Participants varied in their roles and years of experience. Most had a decade or more of experience in control centers. Operators had different skills, some were also team leads and some were managers.

We conducted 16 observations ranging from short 15-minute observations at handover times to more typical observations lasting 2 or 3 hours, totaling to about 32 hours. We took extensive notes detailing the direct and technology-mediated interactions of the operators, especially noting the arrangements of their tools across various displays. In this way we captured the concrete nature of this work. Ten semi-structured interviews, inspired by Nardi and Kaptelinin's checklist [9] and lasting about 1 hour each, provided a broader perspective on the center's activities because they contained information on how operators reflect on their work and their past, current and future work context. The observation notes and the interview data were entered into a qualitative analysis tool called NVivo. This allowed us to code our data, query it, and write memos capturing our thoughts.

To analyze observations and report our results, we followed a four-step process described by Turner and Turner [26]:

1. Describe the activities
2. Find disturbances in and between activities
3. Locate and identify underlying tensions that are the causes of the disturbances
4. Resolve the tensions by suggesting changes to an activity (i.e. Generate recommendations)

Details of these steps and the results of taking the steps are described in the Results section. The results of steps 1-3 is a model of value to interaction engineers developing software tools for operators and who are in the first phase of a user-centered engineering methodology. Step 4, recommendations to improve work efficiency, is considered in the Discussion section. (Alternate fourth steps that could follow from the model generation steps could be for example, a task analysis or the application of a clearly delineated method for designing peripheral displays [17], which would be equally valid.

RESULTS

Step 1: Activities

The center we observed is a well-run, complex organization with a strong commitment to business service continuity and customer satisfaction. It is a large, well-designed facility staffed by dedicated operators who daily do a remarkable job of juggling multiple activities to maintain operations and maximize service quality. Figure 2 depicts the activities within the center, which were determined as a result of an activity systems analysis. This analysis involved identifying all the elements of each activity although we only name the activities here [11]. The activity Incident Resolution was the exception and key elements are shown in Figure 3.

Activities and Tensions

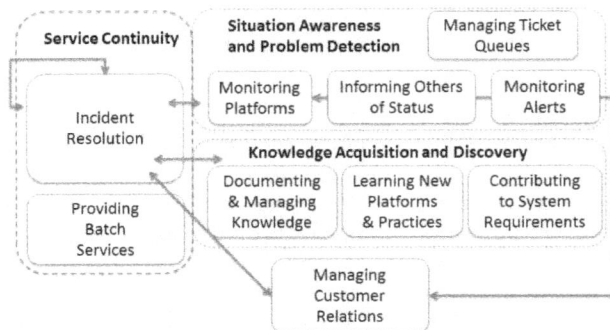

Figure 2: Model of observed operating center activities and tensions between them. Blocks represent activities. Key service continuity activities are highlighted with a dashed line. Tensions between activities are indicated with arrows.

The essential activities we observed were 1) Incident Resolution (depicted in detail in Figure 3) and 2) Providing Batch Services. These two activities directly provided service continuity to customers. Other activities supported the aforementioned essential services.

A corollary goal to service continuity is maintaining situation awareness [10]. Operators need to stay aware of activities around them, detect problems, and track problem solving work. This need motivated several activities: (a) monitoring alerts, (b) monitoring platforms and job queues, (c) informing others of problem resolution status typically through phone calls, text chats or face-to-face conversations, and (d) managing ticket queues.

Another class of activities was motivated by knowledge acquisition and discovery. These included: (a) Documenting and Managing Knowledge and (b) Learning New Platforms and Practices and (c) Contributing to System Requirements. Operators were incident-resolution enablers and system monitors and, from this perspective, they attempted to capture and expand collective knowledge.

They used this knowledge to transform the monitored systems, and to aid others in doing so.

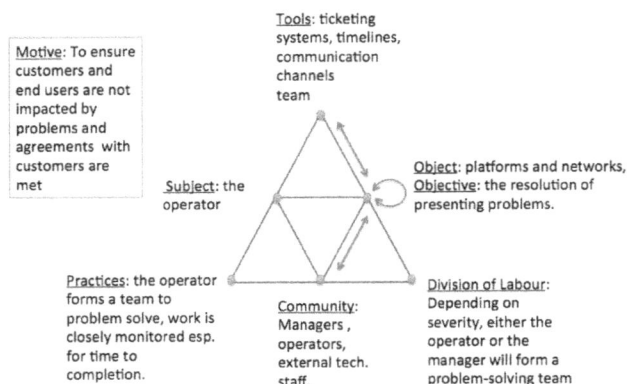

Figure 3: The Incident Resolution activity. Critical elements are identified. Arrows indicate tensions between elements.

A final activity we identified was Managing Customer Relations. This took many forms ranging from prioritizing incidents to carefully crafting the information conveyed to customers. The good relationships the operators developed with customers built goodwill, which was essential to incident resolution.

Step 2: Disturbances

As we watched individual operators for several hours and focused on issues of attention, we noticed workflow disturbances or disruptions or interruptions to the free-flow of an activity that had to do with attention. In all of our data we captured 208 disturbances, but when we considered only the disturbances recorded in our observational notes, we found we had ninety-six. Because observational data is a better record of what actually occurs in day-to-day operations, we focused on analyzing these disturbances.

The following is a disturbance noted while observing a Batch operator Providing Batch Services:

> "While [the Batch operator] is working on the request, they are also checking the job queues on the different batch systems about every 30-60 seconds. They are primarily looking at job status and CPU states, and are determining if any jobs are halted or significantly slowed. The [operator says s/he] knows what jobs are run routinely and can recognize problems."

This is a disturbance because the Batch operator's work Providing Batch Services is interrupted every 30-60 seconds to check logs which means she can't attend fully to the batch jobs she is running. To analyze our data we began by creating a corpus of ninety-six disturbance descriptions similar to the one just described, although the descriptions were in many cases much longer.

Step 3: Tensions

To analyze the ninety-six disturbances we asked, "What is the nature of the disturbance?" i.e., the underlying tension? From the ninety-six disturbances we identified twenty-six 'tensions'. *Tensions* are a misfit between two elements within an activity or a misfit between two activities. Multiple disturbances frequently point to a single tension.

The vast majority of the observed disturbances were connected with individual and joint attention. To show how we found the nature of the disturbance, i.e., the underlying tension, we return to the example of the Batch Operator:

> Frequent checking of the batch systems was drawing this operator's attention away from the request s/he was working on. Although alerting tools were available to the operator, this operator, and others, preferred to view the activity logs. One commented that s/he knew which jobs should be running and when they should be running. For this person it was cognitively easier to observe the logs than to trust (and also interpret) the alerts.

We coded this as a tension between the Monitoring Platform activity and the activity of Providing Batch Services since the disturbance showed that information does not flow particularly well between these two activities.

We reflected on each of the 96 disturbances and created notes about the location of the underlying tension. This lengthy process "kept us grounded in our data", and kept us aware of the real day-to-day work practices and difficulties we actually observed.

Step 3a: Tensions within Activities
Within the activity Incident Resolution we observed nine tensions. One of the tensions is provided below, along with the multiple disturbances that indicated its existence.

Incident Resolution often required teamwork and individuals often found themselves working on multiple incident resolution teams. Each team conferred with one another through telephone conference bridges, text chats, and collaboration software.

> *Tension*: The goal of resolving multiple incidents simultaneously and Managing multiple bridge calls. The goal of resolving incidents was not well supported by the teleconference system that was in use.

> *Disturbances*: There were many disturbances supporting this assertion. Sometimes operators were unsure which call they were on. There were also mistakes made when reporting back on the wrong conference call. We also observed the accidental creation of more than one conference call for the same incident. Often people did not know who was the on the call and had to ask, or had to go looking through various other means (by asking a colleague or by looking up someone's role). It was also not always clear who was working on what and why they were doing it.

Despite these disturbances, bridge calls were typically efficient and led to incident resolutions within demanding time limits. However, because severe financial penalties are incurred when contracts are broken and deadlines for service agreements are not met, the disturbances listed above were potentially not minor events.

Next we continue by listing the tensions we observed in the various activities beginning with other tensions in the Incident Resolution activity.

Incident Resolution tensions (depicted in Figure 3):

1. The goal of resolving incidents simultaneously and Managing multiple bridge calls.
2. The goal of resolving an incident and Inadequate tools for communication.
3. The goal of resolving incidents and Getting the right person's attention.
4. The goal of resolving incidents simultaneously and Too many incidents to respond to.
5. The goal of resolving incidents simultaneously and Too many platforms with their own specialized tools.
6. Developing an understanding of incidents and The tools available for communication.

One operator was addressing tension #4 and #5 when she said: "… I monitor different platforms so if something's going on this platform and I'm working on an issue here, I have to make sure my coworkers' got, you know, got the other steps [i.e., her colleague needs to know how to resolve the issue on that other platform]."

Informing Others of Status tensions:

7. The goal of informing others of a problem's status and Managing multiple bridge calls.

8. The goal of informing others of a problem's status and The communication infrastructure.

Managing Ticket Queues tensions:

9. Different sources of ticket and Maintaining a consistent ticketing structure.
10. Maintaining tickets for intermittent problems and Alerting tools.

Monitoring Alerts tensions:

11. The intermittent problems of alerting system tools and Writing a ticket.
12. Understanding alerts and Knowledge of batch schedules.
13. Understanding alerts and Knowledge of client norms for maintenance.
14. Managing frequent multiple alerts that do not require a response, but can't be cleared.
15. Monitoring multiple devices for alerts simultaneously.
16. The display space for alerts and The number of alerts.

Documenting and Managing Knowledge tension:

17. Documenting knowledge of how problems are resolved and The nature of text chats that are used to retrieve past information.
18. Documenting knowledge of how problems are resolved and Scanning an incident.

Step 3b: Tensions Between Activities

A tension between activities often occurs when information needs to be moved between activities.

Other tensions between activities occur because individuals must switch from one activity to another. The multiple demands made on operators frequently required them to switch rapidly between activities. This creates the need for triage and makes demands on memory. There were multiple issues here. We saw that operators could sometimes be overloaded with information, but also that they sometimes did not have enough information. We also saw operators distracted by multiple sources and operators focusing too much on a single activity.

For example, each operator had three to four monitors on their desktops. Each monitor was used for a different purpose. One might be used for alerts, another for email and text chats, and a third for ticket management and resolution. This enabled operators to switch from one activity to another by redirecting their attention. However, they often needed to be watching multiple monitors simultaneously. As an example, managers would routinely monitor alerts while working to close a ticket, moving their attention back and forth between multiple monitors. This created problems such as this one we recorded in our notes:

The operator has many windows iconized in [the middle screen], and is concerned about alerts from iconized windows. The icons open to different displays, which is confusing, although the operators have adapted by developing routines such as rules about how they will use their displays.

In total, we found eight tensions between activities. Hence in addition to the 18 within activity tensions we found the following between activity tensions:

19. Monitoring and Incident Resolution.

Operators could sometimes be overloaded with information, but also they sometimes did not have enough information. Operators could be distracted by multiple sources or operators could experience attention tunneling. Operators focused on an incident sometimes did not know where other team members were focused.

20. Incident Resolution and Documenting & Managing Knowledge.

This tension addresses the problem of distilling the knowledge from an incident to make it useful in the future and also the problem of reporting issues to

evolve practices in the center. The copious amounts of information and the manner in which they're recorded do not make it easy to create repositories that can be mined.

21. Incident Resolution and Incident Resolution.

This is the problem of cascading problems and detecting that there are cascading problems. Not uncommonly, incidents were related to each other, but it was hard to discern this especially when operators were working on separate but related incidents. This tension is also about the management of multiple bridge calls. We saw it was sometimes hard to keep track of the details of an individual call, but even harder to keep track of it all when there were multiple calls.

For example one operator describes how the center learned about the same incident from different sources. "some of the links that went through, for example for the [Company X] issue, … So we kind of knew that it was [Company X], but we didn't know what was going on. Then we got a call from [Company Y who was] … seeing it too."

22. Incident Resolution and Monitoring and Learning New Platforms and Practices.

Because incident resolution and monitoring always took priority, there was no time to learn on the job. Because knowledge was important to performing Incident Resolution and Monitoring activities there was a tension here.

23. Incident Resolution and Managing Customer Relations

It was not uncommon for operators to launch separate "parallel" bridge calls for non-customer relevant chats to discuss an incident and create palatable stories for customers about the incident. This would require them to then track two bridge calls for the incident.

24. Incident Resolution and Maintaining Software and Hardware (an external activity to the command center).

On occasion we saw there was a culture clash between operators and engineers. For example, one time we saw an engineer dump far too much information in a ticket, making it impossible for an operator to make any kind of sense of it and resulting in cognitive overload, which was indicated by the operator's comments. It also made the ticket harder to work with. There were also other small indicators of a culture clash within the global command center itself, between engineers capable of resolving incidents and other operators on the floor.

One operator who was an Incident Manager told us "Generally, you're dealing with a lot of smart people on a call, 'cause they're mostly engineers and architects and things like that. And generally the things that force you off from ceasing impact are: them wanting to dig into the problem even deeper."

25. Incident Resolution and Managing Ticket Queues

The Incident Resolution activity is centered on tickets. We saw some operators managing ticket queues in idle moments. One problem we saw was ticket duplication, but we heard about others.

26. Monitoring and Customers Maintaining their IT Networks and Servers (an external activity to the global command center)

While monitoring alerts, operators had to have some knowledge of the state of customers' IT networks and servers, because alerts and platform states had to be interpreted with this knowledge in mind. The channels for finding out about activities external to the global command center that could for instance generate alerts that were false-alarms or cause erratic behavior on platforms, appeared haphazard at times.

DISCUSSION OF TENSION RESOLUTION

An analysis of the aforementioned tensions suggested the following areas for improvement. This list below does not address all of the tensions identified above, but does focus on areas where engineered solutions could improve collaboration and attention allocation.

1. *Integration of voice conference and text chat tools with task management tools is essential for better coordination of activities.*

As noted above, most operators were engaged in concurrent text sessions. The display used for text chats was typically covered with open text chats, and one text chat session frequently obscured other text chats. To ensure that new text communications were noticed, operators needed to repeatedly scan the monitor displaying the chats (which was typically not the monitor used for their main activity). This recommendation speaks to several of the tensions noted above. The first is tension #7 the within-activity tension arising between the goal of Informing others of problem status and Managing multiple bridge calls. The second is tension #8 the within-activity tensions arising from the communication tools (i.e., text chat and conference calls) that support actions that inform others of a problem's status that eventually leads to incident resolution.

Text chat interfaces could be used to create conferences and notify participants about who is on a call. It could also help operators multi-task by allowing them to switch from one call to another simply by selecting an option on the text chat window. Interestingly, operators were very aware of, and had access to, popular online collaboration tools, but considered these tools awkward for their use. Also, we do not know of any existing commercial product that meets all of the requirements, but recent integrations between

Microsoft® Microsoft Lync Server and Cisco® VOIP technology, and research by Boiney [3] are pointed in the right direction.

Better integration between voice, text and text management tools could also reduce tension that arises within the Documenting & Managing Knowledge activity when text chat is used to retrieve past information, and between Incident Resolution and Documenting & Managing Knowledge, because the Documenting & Managing Knowledge activity is a secondary activity and must often be done long after the incident was resolved.

Text chats were used to retrieve past information in order to document how problems were resolved. This resulted in substantial numbers of text chat sessions being left open for no other reason than for end-of-day report writing (adding to the stress of monitoring conversations and the muddle of tools "iconified" on the desktop). As a repository for history, text chat tools are typically not optimized as repositories for recent conversations. Although text chats may contain significant amounts of information, these can be difficult to find when they are embedded in large amounts of irrelevant conversation.

2. *Sharing visualizations and drawings needs to be easier.*

Visualization and collaboration technology has evolved quickly over the past 10 years, but usability is still an issue, as is the ability to share common data that is visualized differently for different users. This created a tension within the Incident Resolution activity, because the tools for visual communication interfered with the goal of resolving incidents (tension #2).

Several operators noted that it was not easy to share visualizations with others in the room, or in other locations. We saw occasions where it would have been useful to share a drawing, but this was not done because the drawing was on paper and there was no easy mechanism for scanning or sharing visuals. We also noted cases in which a software tool provided relevant information in a tabular or graphic form, but the communication tools (text chats and conference calls especially) did not provide easy ways to share screenshots or other visuals. Popular commercial collaboration tools provided these capabilities, but were considered cumbersome by the operators we talked with.

3. *Face-to-face communication should not be hindered through room or desk design.*

The communication infrastructure and physical arrangement of desks, in some centers, do not facilitate face-to-face interactions. This can create a within-activity tension as operators attempt to use the available tools to communicate and share insights (tension #6).

We were initially told that all operators work at their desktop, that they have everything they need on their

271

screens, and that primary activities (e.g., Incident Resolution) do not require face-to-face interaction.

In contrast we observed the following: 1) People listen-in on other conversations and provide running commentaries to co-workers. 2) People sense the activity in the room, in part, through the amount of murmuring. 3) Face-to-face, backchannel communications are common, sometimes to get the status of an incident a co-worker is handling, sometimes to problem-solve, and sometimes for team building. 4) When phones and text chats are not answered, people are sometimes approached directly to get their attention.

Most face-to-face interactions were with neighbors, but some involved one co-worker walking over to the desk of another co-worker.

There are good reasons for wanting to reduce face-to-face interactions: (a) many co-workers are remote and need to be kept in the loop as the incident resolution progresses, and (b) when physical motion is required, it takes time and reduces opportunities for multitasking. Future research should expand on when and why face-to-face communication is sometimes required to facilitate incident resolution.

4. Tools need to be better adapted to multi-monitor desktops

Monitoring to maintain situation awareness is a major activity that is required for identifying and understanding incidents and other anomalies. This activity coexists with the primary activity, incident resolution and batch processing services and the activities are in constant tension with one another (tension #19). This requires many open applications each with one or more user interface windows that typically overlap and obscure one another. In today's environment, to reduce the between-activities tension between monitoring and resolving incidents, operators often have three or four monitors on their desktop. While this reduces the overlap between application windows, it creates other problems.

Operators often needed to watch multiple displays, routinely shifting attention back and forth among different log and alert widows and their tools for managing incident resolution.

Unfortunately, most applications assume a single monitor will be used for its graphical user interface. When multiple monitors are used, the primary window for the application may be on one monitor, but the associated error and system messages may be displayed on a different monitor. This can cause confusion and mistakes when the second monitor is not in the user's line of vision. In addition, the ergonomics of multiple monitors are not completely understood. Some multi-monitor configurations, for example, may lead to neck strain because the top of the top screen is above eye-level.

Nonetheless, operators prefer multiple screens. Multiple screens may reduce cognitive load because users do not have to switch between applications on a single screen as often and therefore can more easily compare the content of two application windows. This hypothesis is confirmed in a number of studies suggesting that multiple screens provide better support for multitasking, peripheral awareness and recognition memory [6][22][24]. However, research described in Czerwinski et al. [6] and Owens et al. [19] suggest that as screen size or the number of monitors increases,

- Cursor-based access to icons, windows become more time-consuming,
- Notifications and dialog boxes appear in the wrong window, and
- The number of open windows increases, leading to more complex multitasking and more time determining the purpose of these open documents.

Thus, too many windows are iconized without proper alert indicators in the icon, icons and pop-up windows appear on screens that the operator is not observing, and alarms are missed because the operator was attending to one monitor but not others.

Notably, we are not aware of any study, other than the present research, that documents the use of three or more monitors in an environment that requires rapid decision-making and frequent monitoring of platform status and alarms (cf., Andrews et al. [1], where the goal was to analyze a large set of new articles). There is a need for application software that is designed for multi-monitor, multi-device user experiences [12], and multi-monitor management software that more effectively manages icons, dialog windows and notifications.

CONCLUSION

Throughout their history, data operations and command centers have complemented IT automation with human intelligence. As advances in IT automation continue to lessen the need for human supervision in many areas, the need for oversight (situation awareness, decision monitoring and intervention) is expected to increase (see Figure 3).

In this paper, we have described our methodology and findings, following the four steps outlined by Turner and Turner:

1. Describe the activities
2. Find disturbances in and between activities
3. Locate and identify underlying tensions that are the causes of the disturbances
4. Resolve the tensions by suggesting changes to an activity (i.e. Generate recommendations).

Ten types of activities were found to represent most of the work we observed (see Figure 2). The operators were very skilled in accomplishing these activities. However, twenty-seven tensions were observed within and between the activities. These tensions reflect issues in the structural aspects of the workflow. Based on this analysis, several areas were identified for improvement

- Tools that integrate asynchronous text and synchronous voice communication, with workflow,
- Collaborative visualization tools,
- Tools that help users manage complex, multi-monitor workspaces

Each of these areas requires consideration because they address aspects of work where attention, collaboration, and cognitive overload are an issue, and because they are likely to become more problematic as the operations environment becomes more complex. For example, monitors with a dozen or more text chat sessions place a strain on human memory and attention. The same is true with conference calls. Not knowing who is on a conference bridge, or not knowing which of several bridges is associated with a particular incident, strains attention and comprehension.

The tensions identified in this study also suggest the importance of studying proposed engineering solutions *in situ,* because many of the identified tensions would be difficult to recreate in laboratory studies or in simple field observations of a single application. However, careful case studies of current activities with the current technical and process solutions can provide HCI specialists or usability engineers with deep insights into user experiences, goals, and activities.

In many case studies the usability of a new tool is studied in the context of its use. In contrast the present work was undertaken to develop a rich description of attention allocation and collaboration across may different software tools in order to gain an unbiased view of the work and needs of the operations professionals.

As this work progresses it will form the basis of a ontological model of operations and command centers and can be used in model-based user interface design, as described by [4].

In conclusion, IT automation will change the nature of work in operations and command centers. As the boundary shifts between decision making by human operators and automated, self-healing IT, the tasks delegated to human operators will evolve. We have seen this already in IT departments as they shift from in-house services that entail machine-level management to cloud services that only require monitoring and confirmation of service-level agreements. Thus we can expect human operators to take on more strategic roles in maintaining IT, discovering anomalies and resolving incidents. They will be helped by resilient, automatic processes that discover patterns, predict failures or disturbances, and suggest repair options for nontrivial incidents. We hypothesize that the basic

activities identified in this case study, and some of the intrinsic tensions between those activities will remain. They can be reduced and managed through careful modeling of behaviors and rigorous engineering of the solutions.

LIMITATIONS OF OUR STUDY

The results discussed above should be considered within limits of generality attending any singular case study. In particular, field studies of more operations centers are needed to derive fundamental patterns and strong recommendations. As such, the recommendations in the present work must be considered tentative. In addition, the time we spent at the operations center was brief, and we were not able to observe the work under intense strain (e.g., during the busy seasons). Therefore we were particularly cautious in interpreting disturbances as reflecting the true stresses in the work. Much more time in the center would be needed to unearth more disturbances and to derive a more complete picture of their patterns. Further, although we have developed a solid model of activities in the center we have observed, we do not claim to have exposed all tensions nor have we addressed how to resolve all the tensions we have exposed.

Despite the limitations of this research, the significant contribution of this work is providing an initial contextual model of value to interaction engineers, and opening up a domain that presents opportunities and challenges for the HCI and human factors communities.

ACKNOWLEDGMENTS

We thank all of the operators and managers in the data and operations center, for allowing us to observe and interview them, and for their gracious hospitality.

REFERENCES

1. Andrews, C., Endert, A., and North, C. Space to think: Large high-resolution displays for sensemaking. In *Proc.CHI 2010*, ACM Press (2010), 55-64.

2. Baddeley, A.D. *Working memory.* Clarendon Press, Oxford, 1986.

3. Boiney, L. G. Taming multiple chat room collaboration: Real-time visual cues to social networks and emerging threads. Mitre Corporation, http://www.iscramlive.org/dmdocuments/ISCRAM200 8/papers/ISCRAM2008_Boiney_etal.pdf. (2008).

4. Calvary, G., Coutaz, J., Thevenin, D., Limbourg, Q., Bouillon, L., Vanderdonckt, J.: A Unifying Reference Framework for Multi-Target User Interfaces. Interacting with Computers 15,3 (2003) 289–308.

5. Cummings, M. L., Bruni, S., and Mitchell, P. J. Human supervisory control challenges in network-centric operations. *Reviews of Human Factors and Ergonomics*, 6, 1 (2010), 34-78.

6. Czerwinski, M., Robertson, G., Meyers, B., Smith, G., Robbins, D and Tan, D. Large display research overview. *CHI 2006*, ACM Press (2006), 69-74.

7. Dan, C. S., Cullen, R. H., Rogers, W. A., and Fisk, A. D. Exploring strategy use in a multiple-task environment: Effects of automation reliability and task properties. In *Proc. of the Human Factors and Ergonomics Society Annual Meeting*, SAGE Publications. (2012, Sept), 2123-2127.

8. Daniels, H. *Vygotsky and Research*, Routledge, UK , 2008.

9. Duignan, M., Noble, J., and Biddle, R. Activity theory for design: From checklist to interview. In *Designing for Human Work*: IFIP (Series); 221. IFIP (2006), 1-25.

10. Endsley, M.R. Design and evaluation for situation awareness enhancement. In *Proc. of the Human Factors Society Annual Meeting*, Human Factors and Ergonomics Society (1998), 97-101.

11. Engeström, Y. Activity theory as a framework for analyzing and redesigning work. *Ergonomics*, 43(7), Taylor & Francis (2000), 960-974.

12. Greenspan, S. Collaborating Through Shared Displays and Interacting Devices. *CA Technology Exchange*: Post-PC Era, 5, (2012) 61-64

13. Kahneman, D. *Thinking, fast and slow*. Doubleday Canada, 2011.

14. Kahneman, D., and Treisman. A. Changing views of attention and automaticity. In R. Parasuraman and D. A. Davies (Eds.), *Varieties of attention*. Academic Press, New York (1984) 26- 61.

15. Lieberman, M. D., and Rosenthal, R. Why introverts can't always tell who likes them: multitasking and nonverbal decoding. *Journal of Personality and Social Psychology*, 80(2), (2001), 294.

16. Limbourg, Q. and Vanderdonckt, J. Addressing the mapping problem in user interface design with UsiXML. In *Proc.of Task models and diagrams* (TAMODIA '04). ACM (2004), 155-163

17. Matthews, T., Rattenbury, T. and Carter, S. Defining, designing, and evaluating peripheral displays: An analysis using activity theory. *Human-Computer Interaction* 22, 1-2 (2007), 221-261.

18. Mitchell, P. J., M.L. Cummings, T.B. Sheridan. Human supervisory control issues in network centric warfare. Report HAL2004-1 *MIT, Humans and Automation Laboratory*, Cambridge, MA. (2004).

19. Owens, J.W., Teves, J. Nguyen, B., Smith, A., and Phelps, M.C. (2012) Examination of dual vs. single monitor use during common office tasks, *Proc. of the Human Factors and Ergonomic Society*, Boston, MA (2012), 1506-1510.

20. Parasuraman, R., and Wickens, C. D. Humans: Still vital after all these years of automation. Human Factors: *The Journal of the Human Factors and Ergonomics Society*, 50,3, (2008) 511-520.

21. Posner, M. I., and Rothbart, M. K. Research on attention networks as a model for the integration of psych. science. *Annual Rev. Psychol.*, 58, (2007), 1-23.

22. Robertson, G., Czerwinski, M., Baudisch, P., Meyers, B., Robbins, D., Smith, G., and Tan, D. (2005) The large-display user experience. *Computer Graphics and Applications*, 25, 4, IEEE (2005) 44–51.

23. Salvucci, D. D., and Taatgen, N. A. Threaded cognition: An integrated theory of concurrent multitasking. *Psychological Review*, 115, (2008), 101–130.

24. St. John, M., Harris, W.C., Osga, G. Designing for multi-tasking environments: Multiple monitors vs. multiple windows. *Human Factors and Ergonomics Society Annual Meeting* (1997), 1313-1317.

25. Stanovich, Keith E., and Richard F. West. "Individual differences in reasoning: Implications for the rationality debate?" Behavioral and brain sciences 23, 5 (2000), 645-665.

26. Turner, P., and Turner, S. A web of contradictions. *Interacting with Computers*, 14, 1, (2001) 1-14.

27. UK Highways Agency. Traffic Officer operator at a Regional Control Centre, August 2009. Source: http://www.flickr.com/photos/highwaysagency/600856 6262.

28. Wang, Z., David, P., Srivastava, J., Powers, S., Brady, C., D'Angelo, J., and Moreland, J. Behavioral performance and visual attention in communication multitasking: A comparison between instant messaging and online voice chat. *Computers in Human Behavior*. (2012), 968-975.

29. Wickens, C. D. Multiple resources and performance prediction. *Theoretical Issues in Ergonomics Science*, 3, (2002) 159–177.

Insights into Layout Patterns of Mobile User Interfaces by an Automatic Analysis of Android Apps

Alireza Sahami Shirazi, Niels Henze,
Albrecht Schmidt
University of Stuttgart, Stuttgart, Germany
firstname.lastname@vis.uni-stuttgart.de

Robin Goldberg,
Benjamin Schmidt, Hansjörg Schmauder
University of Stuttgart, Stuttgart, Germany
firstname.lastname@studi.informatik.uni-stuttgart.de

ABSTRACT

Mobile phones recently evolved into smartphones that provide a wide range of services. One aspect that differentiates smartphones from their predecessor is the app model. Users can easily install third party applications from central mobile application stores. In this paper we present a process to gain insights into mobile user interfaces on a large scale. Using the developed process we automatically disassemble and analyze the 400 most popular free Android applications. The results suggest that the complexity of the user interface differs between application categories. Further, we analyze interface layouts to determine the most frequent interface elements and identify combinations of interface widgets. The most common combination that consists of three nested elements covers 5.43% of all interface elements. It is more frequent than progress bars and checkboxes. The ten most frequent patterns together cover 21.13% of all interface elements. They are all more frequent than common widget including radio buttons and spinner. We argue that the combinations identified not only provide insights about current mobile interfaces, but also enable the development of new optimized widgets.

Author Keywords

mobile applications; user interface; design, pattern; widget; android; reverse engineering; apps

ACM Classification Keywords

H5.2 [Information interfaces and presentation]: User Interfaces. - Graphical user interfaces.

INTRODUCTION

Over the last decade, mobile phones became the most ubiquitous devices. Worldwide mobile phone subscriptions grew to almost 6 billion in 2011 [25]. Recently, mobile phones evolved from simple phones to sophisticated smartphones with various sensors, powerful processors, and run third-party applications. In particular, with the emergence of the iPhone, Android, and recently Windows Phone, smartphones became open for third-party developers. The market share of smartphones is dramatically increasing. According to Nielsen half of the mobile subscribers in the US own a smartphone [21].

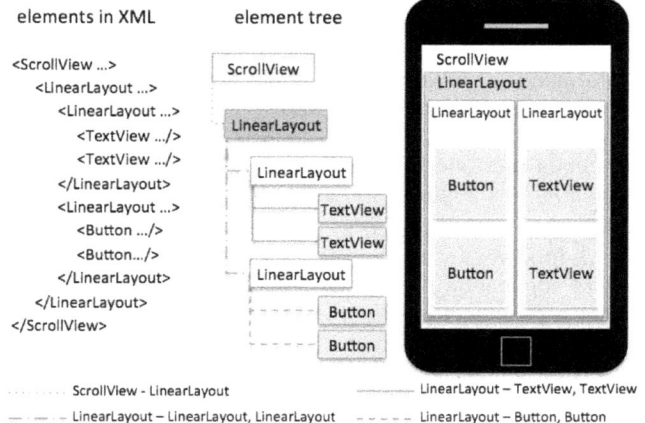

Figure 1. Four common UI element combinations extracted from 400 popular apps downloaded from Google Play. Combinations are describe as follows: *<parent element>-<child element1>,<child element2>*

Smartphone users are no longer limited to the applications provided by the phone's manufacturer. One of the main aspects that differentiate smartphones from their precursor is the app model. Users can easily install third-party applications from application stores. Development environments and centralized application stores are available for all major smartphone platforms. They enable developers to easily build and distribute mobile applications. Together, over a million applications are available for current smartphones in the most prominent stores, i.e., Google Play and Apple's App Store. The most popular apps have been installed several million times. In September 2012, Google reported "... *We've now crossed 25 billion downloads from Google Play* ..." [3].

Today, popular smartphone applications are among the most widely used applications in general. A number of disciplines try to learn about the nature of mobile applications from their own perspective. The general approach is to collect a large number of mobile applications and develop automatic means to analyze them. Software engineering researchers, for example, developed techniques that automatically find privacy leaks in Android applications [10]. They show that widely used applications leak private data. Obviously, it is crucial that applications are not only trustworthy but also usable by a diverse population. It is therefore important to investigate the nature of existing mobile applications from a user interface design perspective. Previous work developed techniques for model driven engineering [23], investigated formal methods for prototyping and simulating mobile and ubiquitous systems [29] and presented interactive tools for reverse engineering UI code [28]. While previous work formalizes and generates UIs through model-driven design it is necessary to learn about currently used patterns to close the gap between formal approaches and commercial systems.

In this paper, we investigate a large number of popular Android applications. We automatically download and analyze 400 popular Android applications from Google Play, Google's official application store for Android devices. We decode the application to reconstruct their source. We retrieve and assess the layouts, user interface elements, and the features used. We determine common interface elements and identify patterns how they are combined and used. The contribution of this paper is threefold: (1) we describe the disassembling of Android application packages (APK) and how information can be retrieved from the decoded files, (2) we report the most common features and components used by popular mobile applications, and (3) we determine the most common user interface elements and identify common combinations (see Figure 1 for an example).

The paper is constructed as follows: first we discuss related work followed by an explanation of how to disassemble Android application packages. Then, we describe the data set used for our investigation. We report features and components extracted from the data set. Later, we discuss the analysis of user interface elements and the patterns retrieved. We address the limitations we come across. Finally, we conclude our findings and describe potential future work.

RELATED WORK

Mobile applications are currently distributed through market places, such as Apple's App Store and Google Play. Users access these marketplaces to download applications. Researchers continually investigate, collect data, and monitor users' application usage behavior to gain insights into how users interact with their mobile phones. For example, Cui and Roto investigated how people surf the mobile web [8]. They state that the duration of web sessions is short in general, but browser usage is longer if users are connected to WiFi. Böhmer et al. conduct a large-scale study and log detailed application usage information from mobile Android devices [7]. They report basic and contextual descriptive statics. Moeller et al. analyze the update behavior and security implications in the Google Play market [20]. They describe that users do not install an update even seven days after it is released. The usage of smartphone-based services is examined by observing 14 teenage users in [22]. It is reported that usage is highly mobile, location dependent, and serves multiple social purposes. Verkasalo [31] also shows that users use certain types of mobile services in certain contexts. He finds that users mostly use browsers and multimedia services when they are on the move, but play more games while they are at home. Balagtas et al. assess different user interface designs and input techniques for touch-screen phones [6].

Another strand of work explored users' behavior while using and interacting with mobile applications. Henze et al., for example, assess the touch performance on mobile applications [13]. They derive a compensation function that shifts the users' touches to reduce the number of errors. Further, they investigate the typing behavior using a virtual keyboard on mobile phones [14] and conclude that visualizing the touched positions using a simple dot decreases the error rate of the Android keyboard. Leiva et al. [17] investigate mobile application interruptions caused by intentional switching back and forth between applications and unintended interruptions caused by incoming phone calls. They report that these interruptions rarely happen. But when they do, they may introduce a significant overhead.

Furthermore, various projects have investigated dynamic analysis of mobile applications. Szydlowski et al. discuss challenges for dynamic analysis of iOS applications [30]. The challenges are mainly driven from graphical user interfaces. Lim and Bentley use *AppEco*, an artificial life model of mobile application ecosystems, to simulate the Apple's iOS app ecosystem [18]. Researchers have presented methodologies for automatically analyzing applications to find possible security problems and user interface bugs. Gilbert et al. propose a security validation system that analyzes applications and generates reports of potential security and privacy violation [11]. Permissions requested by Android applications are used to detect potentially malicious applications [9]. Di Cerbo et al. present an approach to detect malware Android applications. The approach relies on the comparison of the Android security permissions of each application with a set of reference models for applications that manage sensitive data. *Andromaly* is another framework for detecting malware on Android mobile devices [27]. It collects various features and events from the phone and classifies them using machine learning anomaly detectors. Mahmood et al. describe an analysis technique for automated security testing of Android apps [19]. The technique generates a large number of test cases for fuzzing an app and testing its security. Hu and Neamtiu introduce an approach to verify graphical user interface (GUI) bugs in Android applications [16]. It automatically generates test cases and feeds the application random events to generate trace files and analyze them. *AndroidRipper* is an automated technique that test Android apps via their GUI [5]. An app's GUI is explored with the aim of exercising it in a structured manner. Zhang et al. also present technique to find invalid thread access errors in multithread GUI applications [32].

In contrast to previous work and instead of accessing certain users' interaction or application usage, we analyze Android applications' source code to obtain insight into common components, features, and user interface elements used. To achieve this goal, we downloaded 400 of the most popular Android application packages (APKs) from the marketplace and analyzed them to extract valuable information.

DISASSEMBLING ANDROID APPLICATIONS

At the conception of this paper, the Android ecosystem is the most popular smartphone platform. Like other mobile platforms, the Android system is centered on the concept of apps that usually focus on a set of specific services. Android phones come with a number of pre-installed apps, including the phone app used to make and receive phone calls and the web browser app for surfing the web. Android users can install additional apps from Android marketplaces such as Google Play, Google's application store for the Android platform. Android apps are developed using the Android Software Development Kit (SDK). It provides a frame for developing apps and ensures that a certain structure and metadata is provided by the developer. An app is then packaged into an Android application package (APK) file. APKs are file archives used to install applications on the Android system.

Structure of Android applications

Android applications are typically written in the programming language Java using the Android SDK. The Android SDK compiles the source code along with all data and resource files, into an APK file, which is an archive file with an .apk suffix. All of the code and resources in a single APK file is considered as one application.

The essential building blocks of an Android app are the application components. While there are different types of applications components, users only interact with so called activities, directly. The Android developer guidelines [1] recommend that each activity represents a single screen with a user interface. An application often consists of multiple activities but typically, one activity of an app is specified as the "main" activity, which is presented to the user when the application is launched. Having more main activities in an app allows users to enter the app from different starting points (e.g., launch the Skype app from the home screen or from the address book). An activity can start other activities to perform different actions. Only one activity can be in the foreground and thus, users can only interact with one activity at a time.

An activity's user interface is structured by a hierarchy of views. Each view controls a rectangular space within the activity's window and can respond to user input. For example, a view can be a button that initiates an action when the user touches it. The most common way to define a layout (according to the developer guidelines) is to use XML layout files. These XML layout files offer a human-readable structure for the UI's layout, similar to HTML. However, it is also possible to define a layout programmatically.

Android developers can use resources to separate graphical objects and texts from the source code. Most importantly, resources include the XML layout files that describe the user interface, images, and texts. All resources are organized in files and folders that are located in the 'res' folder of the application project. An app can contain resources for different languages, screen resolutions, and screen sizes. The resources enable to provide a single APK that supports a range of devices and is localized to different regions. Resources are referenced in the source code and the layout files.

An app's important metadata is specified in the 'manifest' file. This file specifies all activities and, in particular, defines an app's main activities. Having no main activity means that the app is started without any user interfaces (e.g, a service runs in the background). Furthermore, it declares which security permissions the app requests (e.g., Internet access, activation of the vibrator, or retrieval of location information).

Decoding Android application packages

To analyze Android apps from third parties, we extract the content from APKs and convert the included files to a human-readable form. To decode an APK, we use the *apktool* [2], an

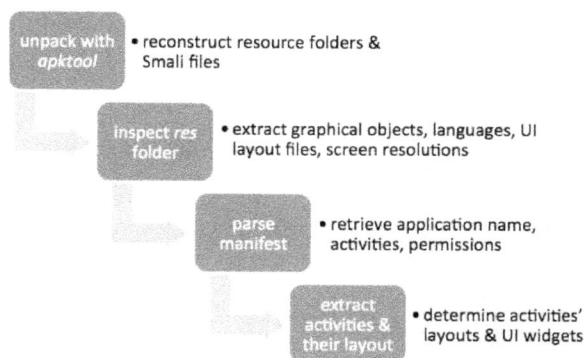

Figure 2. Steps to decode Android application packages

open-source tool for reverse engineering binary APK files. This tool decodes APK files almost to the original Android application project. The *apktool* reconstructs the complete resource folders including all layout files, pictures, animations, and string files. Furthermore, it provides the source code of the app in the intermediate '*Smali*' format [4]. Smali is an assembler language that is equivalent to the byte code for Android's Java Virtual Machine. The files resulted from unpacking an APK are used for analysis of its source code and to obtain insights into features and components used. Figure 2 shows the steps required to unpack an AKP file.

Inspecting decoded application packages

After decoding an APK file, we then analyze the app's files and folders. Next, we analyze the metadata specified in the app's manifest. Finally, we determine the interface layouts included. In the following we describe the information that we retrieve in each step.

Analysis of files & folders structures

To determine information about resources, we first parse the APK's *res* folder to inspect the names of the files and folders. An Android application can have multiple sets of resources, for example, to support multiple languages. Each resource set is customized for a different device configuration. The Android OS automatically chooses the resources that best match the device. To create alternative resources, specific suffixes are used in the files' and folders' name. Suffixes can be languages indicated by region codes (e.g., DE for German, FR for French), screen sizes (e.g., small, normal, large, xlarge), and screen orientation (e.g., port for portrait mode, land for landscape mode). Analysis of the *res* folder reveals the following information:

Graphical Objects: Static images are located in the *res/drawable/* folder and animations are located in the *res/anim/* folder. We can determine the number of images and animations as well as their formats.

Languages: The *res/value–<suffix>/* folders contain the texts used by the application. We use the names of the folders to determine the number of languages supported in an app.

User Interface layouts: The XML files that describe the layout of the user interface are located in *res/layout–<suffix>/*.

By parsing this folder, we can estimate how many user interfaces the application has.

Screen resolutions: We examine the suffixes of the *res* folder to identify devices an app specifically addresses (with a specific screen size or a screen pixel density). If no specific suffix is used, it can be assumed that the application's layouts support all screen sizes. However, it is also possible to optionally specify screen sizes an app supports in the *manifest* file.

Analysis of the Metadata

We determine an app's metadata by analyzing its *manifest* file. The manifest includes the application name and describes the components of the application. We extract the permission(s) an app requires. In addition, the manifest also contains the app's minimum and the maximum application programming interface (API) level. This API level is equivalent to a specific version of the Android platform. All activities of the app are also declared in the manifest. We determine the number of activities as well as the main activities that can be identified through the *android.intent.action.MAIN* attribute.

User Interface Layouts and Elements

To determine which activities use which layouts, we combine activities declared in the manifest file with the activity's corresponding Smali file. For each activity, we parse the Smali file to find the call of the *SetContentView()* method. This method includes an ID for the layout file that is used to render the user interface on the screen. With this ID, it is possible to determine the respective XML layout file. Thus, it is possible to parse the layout files and extract UI elements used in the layouts. The elements in the layout are either Android standard elements such as a <TextView>— a widget for displaying texts—or custom elements implemented by developers.

DATA SET

To analyze typical Android applications we downloaded APKs from the Google Play market. We implemented a script that downloads APKs using the android-market-api[1]. The script connects to the market's server using an existing Google account that is linked to an Android device. The script can download all free apps that are not protected. Using the API, we downloaded and stored the APKs of the top 400 highest ranked apps from the Google Play market on August 20th, 2012.

We configured the query to the Google Play server to receive free applications ordered by descending popularity. We also store additional information provided by the market while downloading the APKs such as the application name, its category, users' average rating, and its popularity rank. The used Android Market API requires an Android device ID in order to download apps from the store. We used a HTC Wildfire's device ID to download apps and did not explicitly specify any locale information. However, the device's locale used was German. Also the SIM card installed on the device and the IP address of the server were both from Germany. Among the

---

[1]The android-market-api is an open-source API for the Android Market. It is not affiliated with Google: **http://code.google.com/p/android-market-api/** accessed 17.12.2012

Category	N	Rating	Activities	Layouts	Images
Tools	58	4.37	14.00	29.64	34.47
Communication	37	4.29	36.65	88.16	65.22
Entertainment	34	4.17	21.41	49.68	23.56
Efficiency	34	4.38	25.32	65.38	60.29
Social Networks	34	4.11	44.44	118.88	74.71
Music & Audio	31	4.19	24.97	66.35	59.77
Photography	21	4.34	24.57	60.76	61.81
Shopping	19	4.03	36.89	106.53	56.89
Books & References	16	4.25	18.94	54.81	50.50
Travel & Locales	15	4.21	40.73	131.47	73.73
Lifestyle	14	4.30	37.57	89.43	41.43
Health & Fitness	13	4.28	50.77	93.92	55.38
Media & Videos	12	4.34	22.92	53.08	37.75
Personalization	11	4.44	15.45	55.82	29.55
News & Magazines	11	4.10	24.73	66.09	40.09
Finances	10	4.26	61.10	118.40	44.20
Office	8	4.12	25.25	99.38	69.38
Weather	8	4.24	18.13	36.25	166.50
Sports	7	3.98	40.00	136.29	46.86
Software & Demos	4	4.28	1.25	1.75	0.00
Learning	3	3.72	39.33	88.00	78.67

Table 1. The distribution of the apps downloaded and analyzed within the different application categories. The last three columns show the average number of activities, layouts, and images in the respective category.

400 apps downloaded, some were clearly associated with locales outside Germany, e.g., "Domino's Pizza USA" or "FOX News". Therefore, we assume that our approach did not distort the popularity order due to our language or locale configuration.

We downloaded APKS from 21 different categories. Categories with the highest numbers of apps are "Tools" (14.5 %) and "Communication" (9.2 %). Table 1 shows the number of applications in each category. We intentionally did not download games. The average rating of the applications was 4.25 (Median = 4.36, SD = 0.45). 80 % of the applications had a rating of four or higher. It is obvious that popular apps are likely to be highly rated. However, there were few applications with low ratings, i.e., the app "More for me" from the "Shopping" category with a 1.88 rating and a rank of 131. The three categories with the best average rating were "Personalization", "Efficiency", and "Tools" (ratings from 4.37 to 4.44). Lowest average ratings were found in the categories "Shopping", "Sports", and "Learning" (3.72 to 4.03).

STATISTICS OF POPULAR ANDROID APPLICATIONS

After downloading the APKs, we decoded them using the aforementioned process. This resulted in 778,071 files organized in 47,706 folders.

Languages

We assessed the applications' resources that can be used to internationalize them to determine which languages an app explicitly supports. For all inspected apps, English is the default language. Including regional variation (e.g., "en_us" and "en_gb") we found a total of 235 other languages. On average, an app supports 12.74 languages (SD=16.42). 47 apps support only the default English and 56 support an additional language. More than half of the apps (216) support five or more languages. Figure 3 shows the 12 most frequently supported languages (without the default English). The most common languages besides English are Chinese (63.8 %),

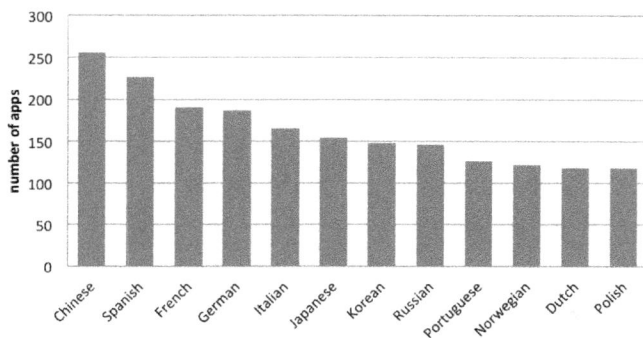

Figure 3. The 12 most frequently supported languages (besides English).

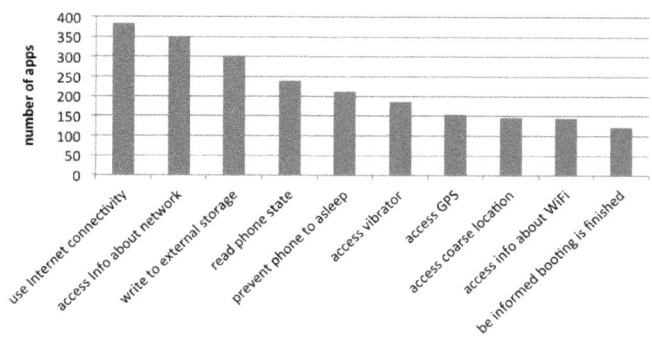

Figure 4. The most frequent Android standard permissions.

Spanish (56.6 %), and French (47.6 %). In total, 30 different languages are supported by more than 50 apps (12.5 %).

Supported screen

Parsing the resource files' suffixes reveals which applications support devices with different pixel densities and screen sizes. For the pixel density (dpi) there are four suffixes: ldpi (low dpi), mdpi (medium), hdpi (high dpi), and xhdpi (extra high dpi). The analysis shows that only 173 apps explicitly support all four variants and 26 apps do not specifically address any density type. 93% of the applications support hdpi, 75% mdpi, 70% lpdi, and 50% xdpi. Four suffixes are used for the screen size: small (low-density QVGA screen), normal (medium-density HVGA screen), large (a medium-density VGA screen), xlarge (medium-density HVGA screen). Nine apps support all four screen sizes explicitly and 215 apps do not specify any screen size. The screen size "large" is the most common size supported by 170 apps.

It should be mentioned that a screen size or screen density suffix does not imply that the resources are only for screens of that size or density. If resources with suffixes that match the current device configuration are not provided, the system may use whichever resources match best. This can be a reason that most apps do not explicitly provide specific resources.

App's launchers (main activities)

As previously mentioned, apps can have more than one main activity. Parsing the manifest files shows that 10 apps have no main activity, 300 apps have one main activity, and 90 apps that have more than one main activity. The *Kayak* app has the highest number of main activities (64).

Analysis of the permissions

We investigated the metadata provided by each application by analyzing their manifest files. In total, we extracted 355 different permissions (M=11.2 permissions per app, SD=7.83). In particular, we looked at Android standard permissions the applications require. From the 355 permissions, 121 are Android standard permission (M=9.6 permissions per app, SD=6.6). Figure 4 shows the ten most common Android standard permissions. The three most frequently used permissions are Internet access (8.7% of all extracted permissions), the permission to determine if network access is available (7.9%), and the permission to store data on the mobile phone's external storage (6.8%).

Tactile Feedback. Most Android devices are equipped with a vibration motor that is used to provide tactile feedback. A permission is required to activate the vibration motor. The results show that 47.25% of the applications use vibration motor to provide tactile feedback.

Location Information. We were also interested in the use of contextual information such as the user's location. In total, 190 applications can access the device's location. 154 apps use the fine location information provided by the GPS sensor and 147 accessed coarse location details (e.g., determined via the phone network's Cell-ID or visible WiFi networks). 111 applications can access both, the fine location and the coarse location of the device.

Connectivity. 96.25% of the applications use the Internet access permission. Further analysis reveals that 10.25% of the applications use the Bluetooth connectivity, 8.25% have the permission to send SMS, and 2.5% use near field communication (NFC). It should be mention that not all mobile phones support the NFC technology.

Number of User Interfaces

To examine whether the user interface of applications from various categories differ, we conducted a statistical analysis of the most frequent categories in our data set. Because of the small sample size for some categories we focus on the ten most frequent categories (N>=15). We use the number of activities, the number of layouts, and the number of images as indicators for the complexity of the user interface. Table 1 provides an overview of the number of activities, layouts, and images for each category. To determine if categories are different we did an analysis of variance (ANOVA). As we were doubtful that the variances are equivalent, a Games-Howell post hoc test is used for the pairwise comparison.

Activities

After extracting the number of activities for each app, we assessed if the average number of activities differ between the ten most frequent categories. Levene's test indicates that the assumption of homogeneity is violated $F_{(9,289)}=3.89$, $p<.001$. An ANOVA test reveals a significant difference between the categories, $F_{(9,289)}=5.14$, $p<.001$. Games-Howell post hoc test shows six pairwise significant differences between the categories. Applications in the category Tool (M=14.00, SD=17.34) have fewer activities than applications in the categories Social Networks (M=44.44, SD=27.64,

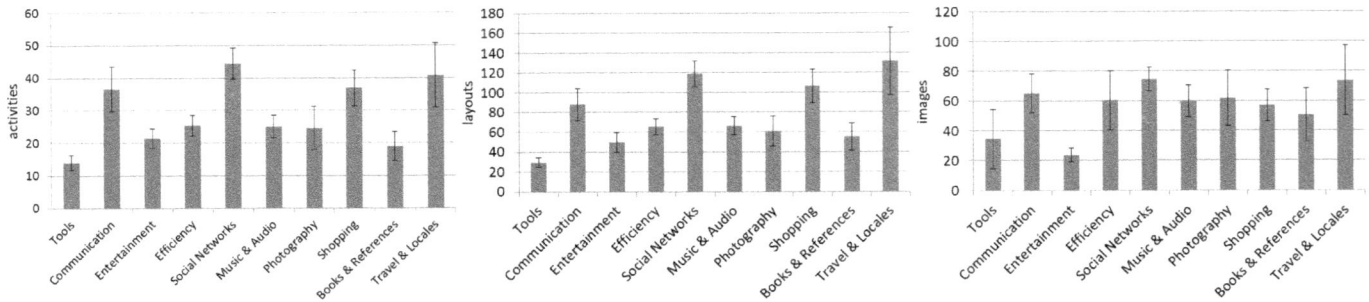

Figure 5. The average number of activities (left), layouts (center), and images (right) for the ten categories with the most frequent applications in our data set. Error bars show standard error.

p<.001) and Shopping (M=36.89, SD=24.07, p<.05). Entertainment apps (M=21.41, SD=17.34) have significantly less activities than Social Networks applications (p<.01). Furthermore, applications in the Social Networks category have significantly more activities than Music & Audio apps (M=24.97, SD=19.41, p<.05) and Books & References apps (M=18.94, SD=17.83, p<.01).

Layouts

We further investigated if the average number of layouts per application statistically differ between the categories. Again, Levene's test indicates that the assumption of homogeneity is violated F(9,289)=4.44, p<.001. An ANOVA reveals a significant difference between the categories, F(9,289)=6.87, p<.001. Games-Howell post hoc test reveals eight pairwise significant differences between the categories. Applications in the category Tool (M=29.64, SD=35.52) have less layouts than applications in the categories Communication (M=88.16, SD=98.72, p<0.05), Efficiency (M=65.38, SD=45.99, p<.01), Social Networks (M=118.88, SD=76.21, p<.001), Music & Audio (M=66.35, SD=51.13, p<.05), and Shopping (M=106.53, SD=74.39, p<.01). Applications in the Entertainment category (M=49.68, SD=57.74) have fewer layouts compared to applications in the category Social Networks (p<.01). Efficiency applications have fewer layouts than Social Network applications (p<.05).

Images

Further, we compared the average number of images per application. Levene's test shows that the assumption of homogeneity is not violated F(9,289)=0.64, p=.77. An ANOVA test revealed no significant difference between the categories, F(9,289)=1.03, p=.413. We therefore, refrained from conducting a post hoc analysis.

Correlations

Looking at the charts shows in Figure 5 suggests that there might be a correlation between the number of activities, layouts, and images of an application. Therefore, we further investigate the correlation between the number of activities, the number of layouts, and the number of images. The Pearson correlation reveals that there are significant pairwise correlations between all three parameters. There is a strong correlation between the number of activities and the number of layouts (r=0.79, p<.0001). Furthermore, there is a correlation between the number of activities and the number of images (r=0.29, p<.0001) and between the number of layouts and

the number of images (r=0.39, p<.0001). While it is not surprising that an application with a larger number of activities has a larger number of layouts, the strong correlation suggest a common pattern.

Discussion

Of the Android applications we analyzed, we found that 88.25% support more languages in addition to English. Furthermore, we determined that a diverse range of languages is supported and the majority supports five or more languages. The results suggest that popular Android applications are diverse in terms of supported languages. It can be assumed that the chance to become popular is much higher if an application supports languages in addition to English.

We analyzed the applications' number of activities, layout files, and images. It is shown that applications from different categories use significantly different number of activities and layout files. We show that tools and as well as applications from the categories Entertainment, Efficiency, Music & Audio, Photography, and Books & References have fewer views and interface layouts than applications from the categories: Communication, Social Networks, Shopping, and Travel. The strong linear correlation between the number of activities and the number of layout files suggests a linear factor. Further, it is not common that an app provides more than one entry point. Only 20% of the apps have more than one main activity. With 96.25%, the overwhelming majority of the applications analyzed require Internet access and almost half of the applications (47.50%) access location information. While there are different reasons why an application requires Internet access (e.g., to display advertisements), the very high number of applications that require it still suggest that the majority of the applications rely on dynamic content. In particular, if ads are considered dynamic content. Notably, almost half of the applications (47.25%) can provide tactile feedback through the phones' vibration motor. Furthermore, the apps explicitly support various devices based on screen pixel densities rather than screen sizes.

Applications from the categories differ in terms of interface complexity. Tools, for example, have distinctly fewer views and layouts compared to social networks. Tools, as the name of the category suggests, address specific use cases. A typical example is the application "Spirit Level Plus" that enables use of the device as a spirit level. However, the few numbers of activities and layouts of other categories (i.e., Entertainment, Efficiency, Music & Audio, Photography, and Books &

Layout	Apps	Percent	Total
LinearLayout	390	66.95	51780
RelativeLayout	365	24.20	18716
FrameLayout	307	7.82	6048
ScrollView	332	2.35	3733
ListView	325	1.77	2814
TableLayout	167	0.92	710
AbsoluteLayout	35	0.12	89

Table 2. The seven standard layout containers. The columns show the name of the layout container, the number of applications that use the layout, the percent of the total number of layout containers, and the total number of times they are used.

Widget	Apps	Percent	Total
TextView	383	35.50	56467
ImageView	380	15.59	24794
Button	355	9.37	14912
View	271	4.35	6917
EditText	318	2.91	4628
ImageButton	294	2.71	4308
ProgressBar	300	1.67	2662
CheckBox	285	1.54	2443
RadioButton	176	0.76	1213
Spinner	178	0.48	759

Table 3. The ten most frequently used widgets used by the applications. The columns show the name of the widget, the number of applications that use the widget, the percent of the total number of widgets, and the total number of times they are used.

References) suggest that they also address specific use cases.

USER INTERFACE ELEMENTS & PATTERNS

We are further interested in common UI elements and potential design patterns used in the applications. The user interfaces of Android applications are typically defined in XML layout files. These files help to define the interface elements and their structures. In the following, we briefly describe Android user interfaces. We determine which interface elements are most frequently used in Android applications. By analyzing the hierarchy of interface elements, we identify common interface elements combinations.

Android User Interface Layouts

The user interface of an Android application consists of a set of activities. Each activity represents a single screen with an interface. Each of these interfaces is a composition of widgets such text boxes, checkboxes, and buttons. These widgets are embedded in layout containers that define the visual structure of the interface. By nesting layout containers in other layout containers, the developer creates a tree of UI elements. While it is also possible to define the user interface directly in the source code, the Android developer guidelines recommend declaring the trees of UI elements in XML layout files.

The Android API provides a number of different layout containers that structure the arrangement of the embedded elements. In addition, developers can define their own widgets and layout containers. The five most common layout containers are briefly described in the following. The *Linear-Layout* arranges its elements in a single column or a single row. The *RelativeLayout* allows for relative positioning of its elements in relation to each other or the parent. The *Frame-Layout* blocks out an area on the screen to display a single item. The *TableLayout* is similar to the *LinearLayout* but can

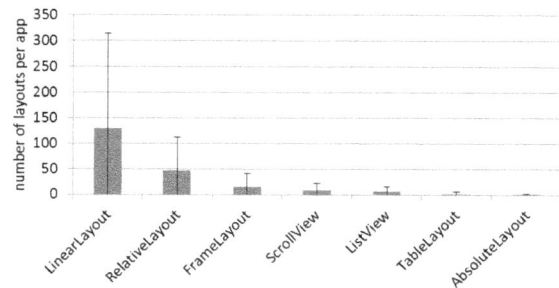

Figure 6. The average number of layouts per application for the seven standard Android layout container. Error bars show standard deviation

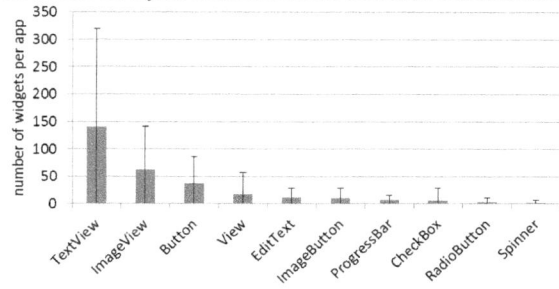

Figure 7. The average number of widgets per application for the most frequent widgets in our data set. Error bars show standard deviation

arrange its elements in rows and columns. The *AbsolutLay-out* enables specification of the exact locations of it elements and, hence, it is less flexible and harder to maintain.

While the layout containers provide the structure of the interface, the user only interacts with the embedded widgets. Android provides typical widgets that are also used in Desktop applications and the Web. Typical examples are the TextView (a text label), ImageView (an image), the Button, EditText (to enter text), and the ProgressBar (visual indicator of progress). One can also implement and use customized elements.

User Interface Elements

In total, we retrieved 29,086 XML layout files from the 400 Android applications. We analyzed the XML layout files to determine the most frequent layout containers and widgets. In total, the layout files contain 77,343 Android standard layout containers and 159,072 widgets. Thus, there are about twice as many widgets than layout containers.

Table 2 shows all standard layout containers in our data set. The LinearLayout accounts for 66.95% of all layout containers and is used by 390 applications. The RelativeLayout accounts for 24.20% of all layout containers and is used by 365 applications. The FrameLayout and the ScrollView are used by the majority of the applications (307 and 332 applications) but account for only 7.82% and 2.35% of all layout containers. The TableLayout is used by 167 applications and the AbsoluteLayout is used by 35 applications. Both account for less than one percent of the total number of standard layout containers. Figure 6 shows the average frequency of a layout is used by an application.

We also extracted the Android standard widgets used in the applications. From the 159,072 widgets retrieved, *TextView* is by far the most common element (35.5%) followed by *Im-*

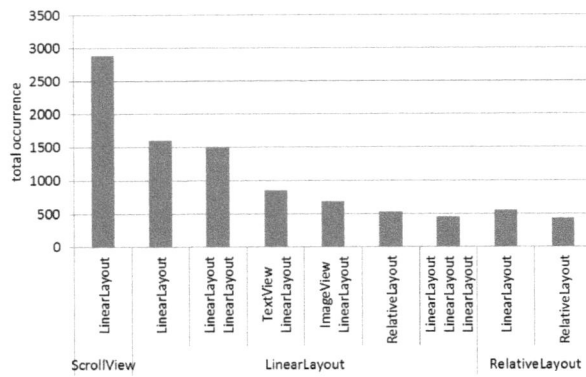
Figure 8. The most common layout patterns.

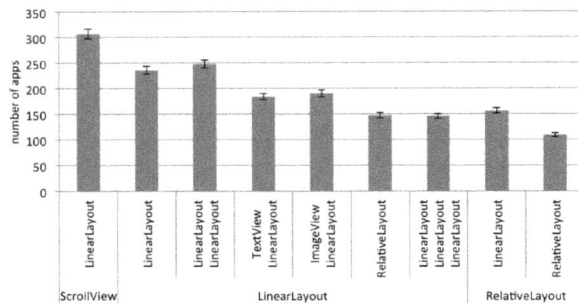
Figure 9. The use of common layout patterns by the apps.

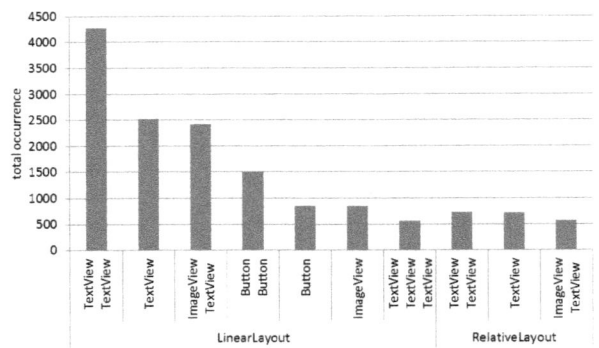
Figure 10. The most common widget patterns.

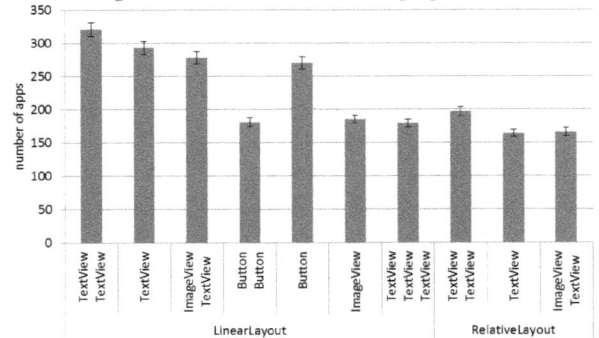
Figure 11. The use of most common widget patterns used by the apps.

ageView (15.6%), and *Button* (9.4%). Table 3 shows the ten most frequent widgets. Together, these frequently used widgets account for 74.87% of the total number of the extracted widgets and are used by more than half of the 400 applications. Figure 7 further depicts how often on average a widget is used by an application.

In addition to the standard Android elements, we found 4,022 custom layout and widget elements used in layout files. These layout containers and widgets are often custom buttons or layouts, but also complete gallery views or a date-time picker.

User Interface Patterns

After extracting all widgets and layouts, we further analyzed the layout files. We determined how elements are combined together and used to obtain potential user interface design patterns. We inspected the combination of widget elements as well as combination of elements and their layout types.

To achieve this, we assessed layouts and their embedded elements. The elements in a layout file are hierarchically structured. Therefore, we parsed the hierarchy of the layout files to retrieve parents and their child elements. This means that for an element, we had its parent element as well as its siblings (if any exist). This allowed us to extract available combinations of elements. Then, we counted how often the combinations are used in order to find the common patterns.

In total we identified 22,870 unique combinations of elements. 75.8% of these combinations are used only once. The patterns can be classified in two different types. One type of pattern consists of a layout container that contains another layout elements as well as widgets. The most common pat-

tern is a ScrollView that contains a LinearLayout. This combination can present more content in a linear fashion then the screen can show at once. Figure 8 shows the nine most frequent layout patterns. We also checked how many apps used these patterns. The most frequent pattern is used in 307 applications. Interestingly, the second most frequent pattern, which is a linear layout nested in a linear layout, is used in fewer applications than the third pattern, i.e., two linear layouts nested in a linear layout (236 vs. 248 applications). The use of the frequent patterns is shown in Figure 9. The applications in the Learning category use the patterns on average, more often than other categories.

The second type of pattern consists of layout elements that only contaion widget elements. Figure 10 presents the ten most frequent combinations. Having two TextViews in a LinearLayout is the most frequent pattern used in the applications. The second frequent pattern is a LinearLayout that has one TextView, and the third one is an ImageView together with a TextView in a LinearLayout. We also observed the use of ButtonViews in different patterns. The use of patterns by the applications reveals similar trend for the top three patterns. However, the pattern which consists of two buttons nested in a linear layout (forth most frequent pattern) is used less than the pattern which has single button nested in a linear layout (fifth frequent pattern). Figure 11 shows the use of patterns in the applications. The applications in the Social Network category use this type of pattern on average more often than other categories.

Implications

We analyzed the interface layouts of the 400 most popular Android applications. We determined which interface wid-

282

gets and layout containers are most frequently used. We found that the two widgets TextView and ImageView that are just used to show labels and images account for over 50% of all widgets. While it is rather obvious that widgets that display information are more common than interactive widgets, the proportion is still surprising. We found, for example, 47 times more TextViews than RadioButtons. Some interactive standard widgets, such as the ToggleButton and the SeekBar, can even be considered as esoteric. The Toggle-Button accounts for only 0.37% and the Seekbar accounts for 0.25%. The most frequent interactive widgets (Button and EditText) suggest that the layouts of the analyzed applications are mainly used by entering text and pressing buttons.

We further identify frequent patterns of interface elements. The patterns retrieved are commonly used across all apps. We found that the most frequent patterns are more common than a number of standard widgets. Altogether, 21.13% of all widgets and layout containers in our data set are part of at least one of the 10 most frequent patterns. Since 77.28% of all ScrollViews contain a LinearLayout, replacing this combination by a layout container that combines the two would be the fifth most frequent layout container. The second most frequent layout pattern combines a LinearLayout with another LinearLayout. Interestingly, one of the layout containers in this combination is useless[2].

The most common widget pattern in our data set consists of a LinearLayout that includes two TextViews and covers 5.43% of all interface elements. This pattern alone is almost as frequent as check boxes, radio buttons, toggle buttons, and seek bars together. Development of a new widget that substitutes this pattern would rank it as the sixth most frequent widget. Thus, identification of frequent patterns in general will enable development of new optimized widgets.

LIMITATIONS

We rely on the ranking of the Google Play market to select popular applications. The parameters that influence the ranking and the algorithm itself are unknown. However, the same ranking is used if users browse Google Play. Therefore, the 400 selected applications might not be the 400 most widely used applications, but we assume that there is a very strong overlap. In addition, to the best of the authors' knowledge, 400 is the highest number of mobile interfaces that have been systematically analyzed. While selecting and downloading applications, we had to use a specific device ID and a specific locale. Developers can restrict applications to certain devices, locales, and configurations. In addition, we only downloaded free applications. We assume, however, that popular applications are widely available across devices and locales.

We only analyze UIs created through XML layout files. User interfaces and further enhancements can be developed programmatically beyond the XML files and can thus also be dynamically be created. However, the Android developer guidelines recommend using XML layout files to define the user

interface. Accordingly, all of the analyzed apps use this approach. We therefore assume that this approach is so common that the analysis enabled general conclusions.

CONCLUSION & FUTURE WORK

In this paper we show how to disassemble Android APK files to retrieve information about mobile interfaces. We downloaded and analyzed 400 apps from Google Play, Google's application store for Android devices. We disassembled the application packages to reconstruct the content. We found that 88.25 % of the apps support more than one language and 93% of the app explicitly support screens with high pixel density. We showed that tools as well as apps from different categories vary in the number of views and interface layouts. This can be used as indicators for the complexity of apps' use interfaces.

By analyzing the apps' interface layouts, we determined the interface widgets and layout containers used most often. We further identified frequent combinations of interface elements. Aggregatively, the ten most frequent combinations cover 21.13% of all interface elements. They are all more frequent than some common widgets, including radio buttons and Spinner. If the four most common widget combinations would be considered as separate widgets, they would all be among the ten most frequent widgets. The most common combination that consists of three nested elements covers 5.43% of all interface elements. It is more frequent than progress bars and checkboxes. This means, a new widget that substitutes this combination could replace all occurrences of the combinations. In this case, this new widget would be the sixth most frequent widget. The identification of frequent UI elements combinations provide the possibilities of optimizing widgets and introducing new widgets.

Determining how frequently different interface elements are used can motivate further research. We only investigated the parent and siblings of an element to find possible parents. However, it would be interesting to take into account other information such as the child elements to retrieve other type of patterns. Researchers might consider focusing on common interface elements. Furthermore, the patterns identified motivate the development of new widgets that ease the interface development and improve the usability. We conducted a static analysis of the user interface. Executing the downloaded application in an emulator would enable to also observe the applications' dynamic behavior. A user's input can be simulated to combine the static analysis with an analysis of the visual appearance. The static analysis combined with an analysis of UI interaction paths [33], observations of actual user behavior collected on a large scale [7, 12, 24, 26], and consideration of biomechanics [15] could ultimately result in a holistic understanding of mobile interaction. In general, the presented approach suggests a new method to understand user interface designs that may help to implement new development tools for designing more successful and more usable applications.

Acknowledgment: This work was funded by the German Research Foundation within the SimTech Cluster of Excellence (EXC 310/1).

---

[2]If a developer adds a LinearLayout as the only child of another LinearLayout the Android SDK suggest that "This LinearLayout layout or its LinearLayout parent is useless"

REFERENCES

1. *Android Developer Guideline*, accessed 17.12.2012.
   `http://developer.android.com/guide/practices/`
   `ui_guidelines/index.html`.

2. *apktool Software*, accessed 17.12.2012.
   `http://code.google.com/p/android-apktool/`.

3. *Google Blog*, accessed 17.12.2012.
   `http://officialandroid.blogspot.de/2012/09/`
   `google-play-hits-25-billion-downloads.html`.

4. *smali - An assembler/disassembler for Android's dex format*, accessed 17.12.2012.
   `http://code.google.com/p/smali/`.

5. Amalfitano, D., Fasolino, A., Tramontana, P., De Carmine, S., and Memon, A. Using gui ripping for automated testing of android applications. In *Proc. ASE* (2012).

6. Balagtas-Fernandez, F., Forrai, J., and Hussmann, H. Evaluation of user interface design and input methods for applications on mobile touch screen devices. In *Proc. Interact* (2009).

7. Böhmer, M., Hecht, B., Schöning, J., Krüger, A., and Bauer, G. Falling asleep with angry birds, facebook and kindle: a large scale study on mobile application usage. In *Proc. MobileHCI* (2011).

8. Cui, Y., and Roto, V. How people use the web on mobile devices. In *Proc. WWW* (2008).

9. Enck, W., Ongtang, M., and McDaniel, P. On lightweight mobile phone application certification. In *Proc. CCS* (2009).

10. Gibler, C., Crussell, J., Erickson, J., and Chen, H. Androidleaks: Automatically detecting potential privacy leaks in android applications on a large scale. *Trust and Trustworthy Computing* (2012).

11. Gilbert, P., Chun, B., Cox, L., and Jung, J. Vision: automated security validation of mobile apps at app markets. In *Proc. MCS* (2011).

12. Henze, N., Pielot, M., Poppinga, B., Schinke, T., and Boll, S. My app is an experiment: Experience from user studies in mobile app stores. *IJMHCI* (2011).

13. Henze, N., Rukzio, E., and Boll, S. 100,000,000 taps: analysis and improvement of touch performance in the large. In *Proc. MobileHCI* (2011).

14. Henze, N., Rukzio, E., and Boll, S. Observational and experimental investigation of typing behaviour using virtual keyboards on mobile devices. In *Proc. CHI* (2012).

15. Hrabia, C.-E., Wolf, K., and Wilhelm, M. Whole hand modeling using 8 wearable sensors: biomechanics for hand pose prediction. In *Proc. AH* (2013).

16. Hu, C., and Neamtiu, I. A gui bug finding framework for android applications. In *Proc. SAC* (2011).

17. Leiva, L., Böhmer, M., Gehring, S., et al. Back to the app: The costs of mobile application interruptions. In *Proc. MobileHCI* (2012).

18. Lim, S. L., and Bentley, P. J. How to be a successful app developer: lessons from the simulation of an app ecosystem. In *Proc. GECCO* (2012).

19. Mahmood, R., Esfahani, N., Kacem, T., Mirzaei, N., Malek, S., and Stavrou, A. A whitebox approach for automated security testing of android applications on the cloud. In *Proc. AST* (2012).

20. Möller, A., Diewald, S., Roalter, L., Michahelles, F., and Kranz, M. Update behavior in app markets and security implications: A case study in google play. In *Proc. MobileHCI* (2012).

21. Nielsen. *Smartphones Account for Half of all Mobile Phones, Dominate New Phone Purchases in the US*, accessed 17.12.2012. `http://blog.nielsen.com/`
    `nielsenwire/online_mobile/smartphones-account-`
    `for-half-of-all-mobile-phones-dominate-new-`
    `phone-purchases-in-the-us/`.

22. Rahmati, A., and Zhong, L. Studying smartphone usage: Lessons from a four-month field study. *IEEE Transactions on Mobile Computing* (2012).

23. Raneburger, D., Popp, R., and Vanderdonckt, J. An automated layout approach for model-driven wimp-ui generation. In *Proc. EICS* (2012).

24. Sahami Shirazi, A., Rohs, M., Schleicher, R., Kratz, S., Müller, A., and Schmidt, A. Real-time nonverbal opinion sharing through mobile phones during sports events. In *Proc. CHI* (2011).

25. Saylor, M. *The Mobile Wave: How Mobile Intelligence Will Change Everything*. Vanguard, 2012.

26. Schleicher, R., Sahami Shirazi, A., Rohs, M., Kratz, S., and Schmidt, A. Worldcupinion experiences with an android app for real-time opinion sharing during soccer world cup games. *IJMHCI* (2011).

27. Shabtai, A., Kanonov, U., Elovici, Y., Glezer, C., and Weiss, Y. andromaly: a behavioral malware detection framework for android devices. *Journal of Intelligent Information Systems* (2012).

28. Silva, C. E. Reverse engineering of gwt applications. In *Proc. EICS* (2012).

29. Silva, J. L., Campos, J., and Harrison, M. Formal analysis of ubiquitous computing environments through the apex framework. In *Proc. EICS* (2012).

30. Szydlowski, M., Egele, M., Kruegel, C., and Vigna, G. Challenges for dynamic analysis of ios applications. *Open Problems in Network Security* (2012).

31. Verkasalo, H. Contextual patterns in mobile service usage. *Personal and Ubiquitous Computing 13*, 5 (2009).

32. Zhang, S., Lü, H., and Ernst, M. D. Finding errors in multithreaded gui applications. In *Proc. ISSTA* (2012).

33. Zheng, C., Zhu, S., Dai, S., Gu, G., Gong, X., Han, X., and Zou, W. Smartdroid: an automatic system for revealing ui-based trigger conditions in android applications. In *Proc. SPSM* (2012).

Engineering Works: What is (and is not) "Engineering" for Interactive Computer Systems?

Ann Blandford

University College London

Dept. of Computer Science, Gower Street, London WC1E 6BT

A.Blandford@ucl.ac.uk

ABSTRACT

What does it mean to "engineer" an interactive computer system? Is it about the team doing the work (that they are engineers), about the process being followed, about the application domain, or what? Is engineering about managing complexity, safety or reliability? For physical artifacts, it may be possible to achieve consensus on how well engineered a product is, but this is more difficult for digital artifacts. In this talk, I will offer some perspectives, both positive and negative, on the nature of engineering for interactive computer systems and, at least implicitly, the nature and future of the EICS conference series.

Author Keywords

Engineering; HCI; safety; reliability; professionalism.

ACM Classification Keywords

H.5.2 [Information Interfaces and Presentation]: User Interfaces - Interaction styles.

General Terms

Human Factors; Design; Reliability; Verification.

INTRODUCTION

The aim of this short paper is to facilitate discussion on the role and value of engineering in relation to interactive computer systems. It arises, in part, from an activity at the most recent IFIP WG2.7 / 13.4 (User Interface Engineering) working meeting: to develop a short video to communicate the value of engineering for user interfaces. It also arises from discussions I have had with various people on the nature and scope of the EICS conference. Both activities have generated more heat than light. It is, intentionally, not a well engineered argument for a particular position, but a series of vignettes putting forward different cases, for and against particular views of engineering in relation to interactive computer systems (ICS). My intention, which may or may not be realized, is that the community should establish a better shared understanding of the nature, value and role of engineering in the ICS context.

IF IT'S DONE BY ENGINEERS THEN IT IS ENGINEERING

I am a Chartered Engineer. I started my career as a Graduate Trainee Engineer, at about the time the Finniston report [7] was published. That report emphasized the importance of engineering to the future of the economy, and also argued strongly for the status of professional engineers. Within the UK, that is a battle which has now been lost: "anyone in the UK may describe themselves as an engineer. Seeking to regulate or legislate on the use of a now common term is recognized by the Engineering Council as totally impractical." [6] So, at least in the UK, anyone can call themselves an engineer, and – by extension – claim that what they are doing is engineering. A subset can make a stronger claim: that we are accredited as professional engineers. But is what any of us do "engineering"? Let us consider definitions of engineering.

ENGINEERING: DEFINITIONS

A dictionary definition of engineering is: "The application of scientific and mathematical principles to practical ends" [14]. The emphasis in the Engineering HCI Community of ACM is on "the application of scientific knowledge and rigorous design methodology to reliably predict and, thus, help improve the consistency, usability, economy and safety of solutions to practical problems" [1]. Both of these definitions focus on principles and rigor for addressing practical problems. Clearly, these principles should apply in the design of complex, safety-critical systems [10]. It is much less clear what it means to engineer the user experience, in terms of fun or affect (a theme in this year's call for papers). The science of fun is poorly developed, the mathematics of fun even more so. User experience is not so well understood that it can be reliably predicted or delivered consistently without extensive iterative testing, which is standard ICS development practice, and not particular to an engineering approach.

THE IMPORTANCE OF ITERATION IN ICS

Most HCI text books assert that iteration is essential in the design of ICS. Rogers et al [12] focus on four main phases of developing interactive systems: establish requirements; design alternatives; prototype; and evaluate. Iteratively. Best practice in the development of ICS includes requirements gathering and user testing, neither of which is particularly amenable to the application of scientific or mathematical principles, although both can be done rigorously and are essential to the delivery of systems that are safe and usable.

EICS'13, June 24–27, 2013, London, United Kingdom.

ACM 978-1-4503-2138-9/13/06.

Tools such as CogTool [13] bring an engineering rigor and prediction to important aspects of user interaction with interactive devices, based on task performance. Similarly, model-based approaches to system development [9] support the task-based development of ICS. However, none of these "engineering" approaches take account of the softer, but equally important, aspects of the use of ICS, including the full user experience, how the ICS fits within its broader context of use, and how people conceptualise the activity the ICS is designed to support [2]. Without taking such aspects of use into account, the engineering of ICS runs the risk of delivering solutions to the wrong practical problems.

A CASE STUDY: CHI+MED

The CHI+MED programme [5] provides an interesting object of study in terms of engineering ICS. CHI+MED is studying the design and use of interactive medical devices: safety-critical devices such as infusion pumps that are themselves moderately complex, and are used in highly complex settings. There are many aspects of these devices that can be subjected to an engineering approach, including modeling their safety properties [4] and formal verification [8]. Such approaches are necessary, but not sufficient. There are many aspects of the use of such devices in practice [11] that need to be understood and designed for. Without systematic study of the use of devices in context, and rigorous description of the "problem", which defines requirements for the next generation of systems, and without careful testing of device prototypes, it is easy to deliver solutions that are verified by not validated [3]. There is a risk that by separating off "engineering" approaches to ICS, the engineering becomes distanced from the practical problems that it is intended to address.

CONCLUSION

There is an argument, based on the above, that engineering is the servant of design – that the user needs are identified outside the engineering process, that the engineer's job is just to make the design as conceived by others *work* (ensuring that the system performs as intended – traditionally referred to as 'verification'). This seems at odds with the broader view of software development lifecycles that development is iterative [3], and is concerned with considerations of usability, utility and experience (all of which are arguably elements of 'validation'), which should also be concerns for engineering.

The title of this paper, "Engineering works", is a play on words. One reading is a claim: that engineering makes things better; that it provides assurance that the proposed solution to a problem (an ICS) is well engineered: that it will not crash or permit the system to get into unsafe states, and will manage complexity well. The second reading is as a noun, "works", qualified with an adjective, "engineering"; engineering work is needed when things have gone wrong, or need maintenance. In the context of EICS, I suggest that both meanings pertain: that engineering can make complex systems work well, but that the engineering approach needs active maintenance to remain relevant to other aspects of ICS design and to avoid becoming narrow and irrelevant.

ACKNOWLEDGMENTS
This paper has benefitted from discussions with many people, but the viewpoints put forward are my own. CHI+MED is funded by EPSRC EP/059063/01.

REFERENCES

1. ACM (n.d.) chi2013.acm.org/communities/engineering/ accessed 17/4/13.

2. Blandford, A., Green, T. R., Furniss, D., & Makri, S. (2008). Evaluating system utility and conceptual fit using CASSM. *Int. J. Human-Computer Studies*, 66(6), 393-409.

3. Boehm, B. W. (1988). A spiral model of software development and enhancement. *Computer*, 21(5), 61-72.

4. Bowen, J. & Reeves, S. (in press) Modelling Safety Properties of Interactive Medical Systems. *Proc. EICS 2013*. To appear.

5. CHI+MED (n.d.). www.chi-med.ac.uk.

6. Engineering Council (n.d.). *Status of Engineers*. www.engc.org.uk/statusofengineers.aspx ac. 17/4/13.

7. Finniston, H. M. (1980). *Engineering our future: report*. HM Stationery Off.

8. Masci, P., Ayoub, A., Curzon, P., Harrison, M., Lee, I., Sokolsky, O. & Thimbleby, H. (in press) Verification of Interactive Software for Medical Devices: PCA Infusion Pumps and FDA Regulation as an Example. *Proc. EICS 2013*. To appear.

9. Meixner, G., Paternò, F., & Vanderdonckt, J. (2011). Past, Present, and Future of Model-Based User Interface Development. i-com, 10(3), 2-11.

10. Navarre, D., Palanque, P., Ladry, J. F., & Barboni, E. (2009). ICOs: A model-based user interface description technique dedicated to interactive systems addressing usability, reliability and scalability. *ACM Trans. CHI*, 16(4), 18.

11. Rajkomar, A., & Blandford, A. (2012). Understanding infusion administration in the ICU through Distributed Cognition. *J. biomedical informatics*, 45(3), 580-590.

12. Rogers, Y., Sharp, H., & Preece, J. (2011). *Interaction design: beyond human-computer interaction*. Wiley.

13. Teo, L. H., John, B., & Blackmon, M. (2012). CogTool-Explorer: a model of goal-directed user exploration that considers information layout. *Proc CHI*. 2479-2488.

14. The Free Dictionary (n.d.) www.thefreedictionary.com/engineering accessed 17/4/13.

Improving Software Effort Estimation with Human-Centric Models: a comparison of UCP and iUCP accuracy

Rui Alves
Madeira Interactive Technologies
Institute
Caminho da Penteada,
9020-105 Funchal, Madeira, Portugal
rui.alves@m-iti.org

Pedro Valente
University of Madeira
Campus da Penteada,
9020-105 Funchal, Madeira, Portugal
pvalente@uma.pt

Nuno Jardim Nunes
University of Madeira
Campus da Penteada,
9020-105 Funchal, Madeira, Portugal
njn@uma.pt

ABSTRACT

Bringing human-centric models into the software development lifecycle provides unique opportunities to enhance development practice. Modeling the interactive aspects of a software system ensures a better understanding of user requirements leading to improved user interface and general usage and acceptance of the system. It also provides a unique opportunity to enhance conventional software development practices, such as effort estimation, which is known to have major deviations. In this paper we illustrate this mutual benefit presenting a statistical analysis of the effort estimation for seven real world software development projects. We contrast a conventional use-case points (UCP) method with iUCP an HCI enhanced method Here we propose an enhancement of the iUCP original effort estimation formula. This results in an improved mean deviation of iUCP over UCP supporting the claim that reflecting HCI concerns into internal SE artifacts generates more accurate estimations of software development effort. Our results provide additional evidence of the benefits of using human-centric models to enhance the software development practice, in particular for long lasting challenges like generating accurate project estimates early in the development lifecycle.

Author Keywords

Software engineering; user-centered design; effort/cost estimation; use case points; interactive use case points.

ACM Classification Keywords

D.2.9

INTRODUCTION

In recent years the software engineering (SE) and human-computer interaction (HCI) communities have tried to bridge methods and techniques that are successful for both software development and interaction design. The cross-fertilization of these disciplines is hard. Methods and techniques are developed independently and are underused largely because of a lack of common understanding between the two communities. Despite the fact that practitioners often must work together in multidisciplinary teams, examples of the lack of communication are still evident. Many mature and successful HCI techniques are unknown and unrecognized by software developers – for instance user roles and personas, human-activity modeling and contextual inquiry/design [20]. Although these techniques tackle a major problem of SE (requirements and user-involvement) they are understood by too few software practitioners and are still far from large-scale adoption.

Creating product cost estimates, early in the development lifecycle, is a challenge for the software industry. In this paper we focus on software effort estimation, one of the software development practices, which is known to have major deviations often resulting in important wastes of time and money [4, 10, 17, 19]. They require that developers agree on the concepts driving the estimations and rely on substantial data from past projects as well as constant feedback and fine-tuning. On top of failing to comply with developers' and managers' expectations, these inaccuracies can ultimately lead to company collapse. Therefore, the ability to estimate development effort early in the project lifecycle is critical to the SW industry [17]. However, with few exceptions [3], existing estimation methods fail to produce reliable results. Several authors reported on how estimation techniques perform when compared to real project data. Kemerer has identified huge estimation errors, in the range of 500-600% [17] while Collopy analyzed 12 studies in which the average estimation error ranged from 13% to 413% [4]. Specifically for UCP the literature provides contradictory data. Carroll reported a widely positive study on 200 projects, conducted in one company, with less than 9% deviation in 95% of the projects [3]. On the opposite side, Crosby, in a study conducted with students, found large variations with a maximum of 500% difference between two estimates, for the same set of requirements [8]. Consequently, early estimates are a relevant challenge and an opportunity to bridge the gap between HCI and SE early in the lifecycle [20].

In this paper we explore how bringing an HCI insight to the effort estimation SE technique can improve the accuracy of the assessment. We build on previous work [22] proposing changes to the popular Use Case Points (UCP), estimation method by Karner [16]. These changes take advantage of the cross-fertilization of disciplines leveraging the enhanced information that can be extracted from HCI techniques - like actors, roles and essential use-cases - to improve the software estimation model. Our research with data from seven real-world projects also provides additional evidence by comparing the original UCP method with the HCI enhanced Interactive UCP (iUCP), by Nunes et al. [22].

The next section provides a brief review of the software effort estimation state of the art, as well as an assessment of the estimation accuracy reported in the literature. The following section defines the main concepts of software estimation followed by a description of the UCP and iUCP methods used in the scope of our study. We then present our research question and hypothesis, as well as the data gathering process and methodology described in our experiment design. The results section includes the raw data collected and the statistical analysis. In the discussion section we present the factors impacting our results building on this to present an improvement proposal, which was latter tested by reassessing the results with the new formula. Finally we present our conclusions and the envisioned future work.

Background and State of the art

There are many different software estimation methods from those that rely on analogies, expert estimations and artificial intelligence techniques [17]. The UCP methods discussed in this paper are classified as parametric models and follow the long-lasting tradition of other popular methods like Function Point Analysis (FPA), proposed by Albrecht [1], and the Constructive Cost Model (COCOMO), pioneered by Boehm [2]. FPA assigns points to each function in an application, further adjusting it for environmental and technical factors like complexity, developer skills and risk. COCOMO, which is still evolving today under the sponsorship of the Center for Systems and Software Engineering at USC [4], uses statistical returns to calculate project cost and duration within a given probability. The underlying assumption of parametric models is that statistically significant historical data exists to drive the factoring of the models. However, companies struggle to find a consistent definition of functions and environmental factors across multiple projects and development platforms.

With the advent of object-oriented software engineering, use-cases emerged as the dominant technique for structuring requirements [10]. This technique, established by Jacobson, was further integrated in the Unified Modeling Language (UML) and the commercial Rational Unified Process (RUP) thus becoming the *de facto* standard for requirements modeling in SE. Later, Karner, also from Rational, created a software estimation technique that assigns points to use-cases in much the same way that FPA assign points to functions. This technique was named UCP and was integrated in the unified process, receiving tool support from popular UML tool vendors. The UCP model became popular due to its relative simplicity and

applicability at early stages of development. UCP was practical for early estimation of software size and effort at the end of the analysis phase (requirements specification in the cone of uncertainty [2]).

In the last years several proposals to enhance UCP were published, namely the Simplified UCP by Ochodek [23] and iUCP by Nunes [22]. The simplified UCP suggests a set of simplifications to UCP, in particular: i) estimation with and without unadjusted actor weights (UAW) with similar prediction accuracy; ii) estimation of use case complexity based on steps instead of transactions; and iii) a reduction of the number of adjustment factors from 21 to 6 (two environmental factors and four technical complexity factors) maintaining accuracy [23]. Conversely iUCP provides an enhancement of UCP incorporating HCI concerns and claims to contribute to more consistent effort estimation. iUCP is based on revised actor and use-case assessment criteria emerging from enhanced human-centric models of requirements such as the ones proposed by the Wisdom method [21]. The rationale is that for interactive system development, early estimates based on models of requirements, can only be accurate if they reflect the HCI concerns related to users and their interaction with the system [20].

Foundations

In this section we present the core concepts used by UCP and iUCP, namely actors, roles, use cases, user intentions and system responsibilities. Since both UCP and iUCP rely on these constructs to provide the basic parametric estimation, their clear definition is important to accurately apply the methods. In fact, a major source of inaccuracy introduced by these methods comes from the different interpretation of what is a use-case or an actor. This is one of the improvements of iUCP, which bases the estimation on the HCI definitions of actor and use-case, thus providing a more consistent baseline and consequently more accurate estimations. An actor specifies a role played by a user or any other system that interacts with the subject [24]. A role constitutes a relationship between a user and a system and is defined by a set of characteristic needs, interests, expectations, behaviors and responsibilities [28]. There are many definitions of use-case and this is reportedly a problem with this widespread concept. A traditional use case is "a specific way of using the system by using some part of the functionality and constitutes a complete course of interaction that takes place between an actor and the system" [10]. On the other hand, essential use cases are "single, discrete, complete, meaningful, and well-defined task of interest to an external user in some specific role or roles in relationship to a system, comprising the user intentions and system responsibilities in the course of accomplishing that task, described in abstract, technology-free, implementation independent terms using the language of the application domain and of external users in role" [8]. As prescribed in [21] a use case can be detailed with an activity diagram, which is composed by two major sections:

user's intentions and system responsibilities. User intentions are meaningful and complete sets of actions required to achieve a goal [21] (completion of the use case). System responsibilities are system components (objects) that make the "coordination, sequencing, transactions and control of other objects" [21].

The UCP and iUCP Estimation Methods

Both UCP and iUCP rely on five major components to estimate effort: unadjusted actor weight (UAW), unadjusted use case weight (UUCW), technical complexity factor (TCF), environmental complexity factor (ECF), and productivity factor (PF). iUCP differs from UCP on the complexity assessment and weighting of UAW and UUCW. The UAW is the point size of the software that accounts for the number and complexity of actors.

In the original UCP there are three actor weights [16]:

- simple (weight 1) for actors representing another system with a defined API.

- average (weight 2) for actors that interact with another system through a protocol, or a human interaction with a line terminal.

- complex (weight 3) for actors that interact through a graphical user interface.

In the revised iUCP there are six actor weights [22], which reflect the HCI understanding of the complexity of the interaction:

- simple system actors (weight 1) communicate through an API.

- average system actors (weight 2) communicate through a protocol or data store.

- simple human actors (weight 3) are supported by one user role.

- complex system actors (also a weight of 3) communicate through a complex protocol or data store.

- average human actors (weight 4) are supported by two or three user roles or one focal role.

- complex human actors (weight 5) are supported by more than three user roles or more than one focal role.

The UUCW is the point size of the software that accounts for the number and complexity of use cases and relies on the number of transactions. In UCP the transactions are the total number of activities or steps (user intentions and system responsibilities) in the use case [5]. Instead, iUCP considers transactions as the system responsibilities only. Both UCP and iUCP weight the UUCW levels equally [22]:

- simple use cases (weight 5): three or less transactions.

- average use cases (weight10): four to seven transactions.

- complex use cases (weight15): eight or more transactions.

Thus, both UCP and iUCP rely on this generic formula to calculate the estimated effort (EE), in hours:

$$EE = UCP * PF$$

Where PF is the Productivity Factor (the number of hours an organization needs to implement one use case point) and the UCP is the number of points. The UCP formula is then:

$$UCP = UUCP * TCF * ECF$$

The UUCP is the Unadjusted Use Case Points, calculated by this formula:

$$UUCP = UAW + UUCW$$

The Unadjusted Actor Weight (UAW) formula is:

$$UAW = \sum_{i=1}^{k} (n_i * W_i)$$

Where i is a category of actor and k is the maximum number of categories an estimation method admits. n_i is the number of items of category i and W_i is its weight.

The Unadjusted Use Case Weight (UUCW) formula is:

$$UUCW = \sum_{i=1}^{3} (n_i * W_i)$$

Where i is a category of use case, n_i is the number of items of category i and W_i is the weight of category i.

The TCF is the factor that is used to adjust the size based on technical considerations and the ECF is used to adjust the size based on environmental considerations. The overall effort estimation formula is:

$$EE = (UAW + UUCW) * TCF * ECF * PF$$

Which fully expanded as follows:

$$EE = \left(\sum_{i=1}^{k} (n_i * W_i) + \sum_{i=1}^{3} (n_i * W_i) \right) * \left(C_1 + C_2 * \sum_{i=1}^{l} (TF_i * W_i) \right) * \left(C_3 + C_4 * \sum_{i=1}^{m} (EF_i * W_i) \right) * PF$$

The modifications proposed by iUCP preserve the original UCP model integrity but introduce a deeper understanding of the HCI concerns captured in human-centric models of the software system under construction. The goal of iUCP is to help software developers and interaction designers to apply heuristics that are suitable for interactive applications and work consistently across and within projects [22]. In the next section we present the research question that drove our current study.

RESEARCH QUESTION

Combining SE and HCI provides new opportunities for collaboration between interaction designers and software developers. This helps developers to see the advantage of using HCI techniques early on. Conversely, interaction designers can better understand their models' impact and recognize user interface (UI) elements' impact at the architecture level. This builds common ground for activities such as prioritizing development and planning releases.

Our research question builds on previous work where we provided evidence that iUCP produces size estimations more consistent in their assessment of use-case complexity and overall UCP unadjusted complexity. This claim was verified with reported less variance between estimations produced by iUCP when compared with UCP [22].

Here we want to test if iUCP actually produces better estimates than the conventional UCP method, grounded in the possibility that the HCI perspective introduced by iUCP will produce more accurate estimations than the original method. Hence, we have formulated the following hypothesis, H_1: iUCP estimation accuracy is better than UCP. Its corresponding null hypothesis, H_0, is that iUCP accuracy is not better than UCP. In this setting, our independent variable is the estimation method, which has two levels (UCP and iUCP) while our dependent variable is the estimation accuracy, i.e., the estimation deviation from real effort reported in each project analyzed.

DATA GATHERING

We realized that most of the publications in this area are studies carried out in a single organization, either academic or from industry. In order to improve our contribution and reduce bias we tried to include projects from different sources in this study. Consequently, we contacted several organizations but, mainly due to confidentiality issues, data gathering proved to be a major difficulty.

Project selected for our study were required to include detailed use case models, which complied with the essential use case modeling directives (allowing the identification of the users and roles, user intentions and system responsibilities). In addition projects were required to have detailed *post-mortem* actual effort reports. The use-case models were required to calculate the estimates while the reported effort was used to assess the estimation deviation, by comparing the calculated estimation with the actual effort. These constraints impacted our study by reducing the sample size due to a number of rejected projects that failed to comply with the study requirements. Access to the real effort reports proved to be difficult, not only because of the underlying costs but also because several companies were not willing to disclose their confidential project data.

The study procedure included four major activities:

1. Collect project documentation.

2. Produce iUCP and UCP estimates for each project.

3. Compute the deviation from reported effort.

4. Examine the significance of the results.

In the end our study included seven projects from three organizations: Logica [18], GMV [12] and GDAI [12]. Logica is a leading multinational business and technology service company employing 41,000 people in 41 countries. The company delivers business-consulting, systems development and integration, and outsourcing across several industries. GMV is a multinational software house mainly devoted to aerospace, defense and security markets, which employs more than 1000 people worldwide. GDAI is an internal software development unit of the University of Madeira (UMa) involving a team of one coordinator and five software engineers. GDAI develops and manages the University information systems, which support all the academic activities and integrates with third parties standard business applications.

GDAI contributed with five projects (including one project previously analyzed in [27]) and both Logica and GMV provided one valid project each. Table 1 summarizes the seven projects analyzed in terms of their duration and general description. Three projects had duration of three months and the others 10, 13 and 30 months.

ID	Description	Duration (months)
P1	Facilities access control	3
P2	Billing system integration with the financial management	13
P3	Student's accreditations request and approval	3
P4	Disciplines accreditation	3
P5	Automation of the Academic Office's requests	3
P6	An infrastructure occurrences management tool	30
P7	A web based accounting system	10

Table 1.Analyzed projects.

Despite the fact that our sample was small, we decided to proceed with the experiment to understand the problems impacting estimation and pave the way for future work. Next, we describe the methodology used in this study.

METHODOLOGY

In this section we discuss how the study was conducted and identify the main problems, as well as the rational behind the decisions made in order to overcome them.

Experiment Design

In this study we measure the iUCP method performance against UCP by comparing the estimation results alongside the real effort reported for each project analyzed. A within-subjects design was selected, where there are no ordering effects. In order to make this comparison possible we had to comply with some trade-offs. For instance, the complexity of the uses cases assessment was based exclusively on the number of transactions, because most of the projects did not produce the robustness (architecture) model, making it impossible to consider the number of entities in each use case, as required by the iUCP method. Moreover, in order to factor out the impact of the TCF and ECF we decided to level these factors, setting them to one in both iUCP and UCP. The rational for this decision is related to the fact that we lacked data to accurately assess all the 21 factors involved in calculating the TCF and ECF factors. In addition, to avoid additional bias, the PF used was leveled to 30 hours, as experimentally suggested by Karner from the of 20-30 hours range [16]. These modifications resulted in the following effort estimation formula:

$$EE = (UAW + UUCW) * 1 * 1 * 30$$

In summary our analysis singles out the three factors that do not change the unadjusted actor and use case estimations. This way we are able to compare the methods in what they really differ and not the implication of the technical, environmental and productivity factors. The deviation, i.e., the accuracy of each method in each project, will be calculated using the magnitude of relative error (MRE):

$$MRE = (Real\ effort - Estimated\ Effort) / Real\ Effort$$

In the next section we present our study results with both the raw data and the statistical analysis conducted.

RESULTS

In order to compute the unadjusted actor and use-case weights we collected information about the models of all the projects involved in this study. That data was then used to perform the categorization of actors and use cases leading to the statistical analysis performed to test H_1.

Raw Data

We categorized actors (Table 2) and use cases (Table 3) according to each method (iUCP and UCP), as previously described. Then we calculated the UAW, UUCW and the UUCP for each project (Table 4).

Table 2 presents the actors' raw data categorization, according to both iUCP and UCP methods. In iUCP the majority of actors (55%) are categorized as simple human actor, whereas in UCP the vast majority of actors (85%) are categorized as complex, yet leading to the same weight (3). iUCP adds an extra weight to the UAW value by categorizing six more actors (30%) as average human actors, with a weight of 4.

	iUCP						UCP		
	a	b	c	d	e	f	g	h	i
W	1	2	3	3	4	5	1	2	3
P1		1			1			1	1
P2			2	2	1			2	3
P3			2		1				3
P4			3		1				4
P5					2				2
P6			2						2
P7			2						2

a) Simple System Actor,   b) Average System Actor,
c) Simple Human Actor,   d) Complex System Actor,
e) Average Human Actor, f) Complex Human Actor,
g) Simple Actor, h) Average Actor, i) Complex Actor
w) Weight

Table 2. Actors categorization.

Table 3 presents the use cases' raw data categorization, according to both iUCP and UCP methods. The collected data shows that iUCP tends to categorize the vast majority of use cases as simple (84%), whereas UCP tends to distribute more evenly this categorization (47% as simple, 23% as average and 30% as complex use cases). As a result UCP adds an extra weight to the UUCW, when compared to iUCP.

	iUCP			UCP		
	j	k	l	J	k	l
w	5	10	15	5	10	15
P1	1					1
P2	5	2		1	1	5
P3	4					4
P4	1	4				5
P5	1	2				3
P6	34	2		24	11	1
P7	8			5	3	

j) Simple Use Case,   k) Average Use Case,
l) Complex Use Case, w) Weight

Table 3. Use Cases categorization.

Table 4 presents the calculated points for actors (UAW), use cases (UUCW) and the resulting UUCP. The figures confirm that in iUCP the UAW exceeds UCP in 14%. Regarding UUCW, iUCP accounted for 37% less than UCP. The resulting UUCP is always smaller for iUCP. The total number of points of iUCP is 32% less than UCP.

291

	UAW		UUCW		UUCP	
	iUCP	UCP	iUCP	UCP	iUCP	UCP
P1	6	5	5	15	11	20
P2	16	13	45	90	61	103
P3	10	9	20	60	30	69
P4	13	12	45	75	58	87
P5	8	6	25	45	33	51
P6	6	6	190	245	196	251
P7	6	6	40	55	46	61

Table 4.UAW, UUCW and UUCP calculation.

The estimation deviations to the reported real effort are presented in Table 5. The projects real effort duration for the complete development of the requirements spans a wide range. For instance P6 is 29 times larger than P5. The estimated hours are the UUCP presented in the previous table, multiplied by the PF (30 hours). The absolute deviation column presents the deviations obtained for both iUCP and UCP.

	Real Effort (Hours)	Estimated		Deviation	
		iUCP	UCP	iUCP	UCP
P1	598.5	330	600	44.9%	0.3%
P2	2357.4	1830	3090	22.4%	31.1%
P3	2282.0	900	2070	60.6%	9.3%
P4	1134.0	1740	2610	53.4%	130.1%
P5	434.0	990	1530	128.1%	252.5%
P6	12889.5	5880	7530	54.4%	41.6%
P7	3170.0	1380	1830	56.5%	42.3%

Table 5. iUCP and UCP real effort, estimated effort and absolute deviations (MRE).

The deviations obtained range from 0.3% to 252.5%, including three results with deviations above 100% (UCP in P4, and both iUCP and UCP in P5). The mean of deviations was 60.0% for iUCP and 72.5% for UCP. In the following section we detail our statistical analysis.

Statistical Analysis
We used SPSS 20 [11] to analyze the deviation data normality with the Skewness and Kurtosis and Kolmogorov–Smirnov tests ($p<0.05$). We concluded that our data is not normal. The deviations mean favored iUCP over UCP (60% versus 72.5%). Regarding data dispersion, iUCP standard deviation (32.6%) was also more consistent than UCP (89.9%), as depicted in Figure 1.

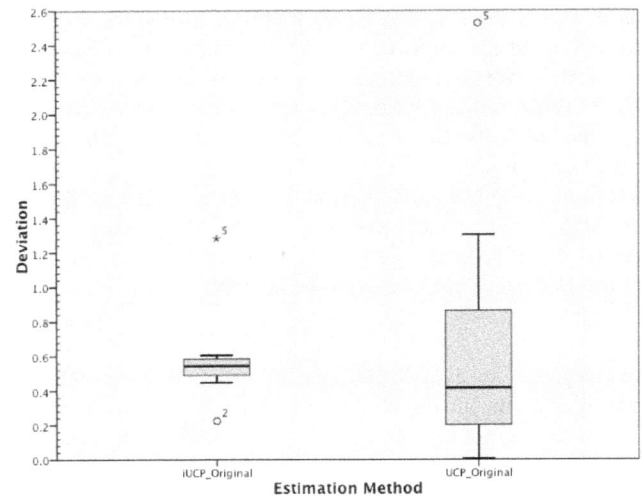

Figure 1:Box plot.

The non-parametric Wilcoxon T was applied to evaluate UCP and iUCP deviation differences. No significant results were obtained as both ranks had a T of 14. According to the two-tailed significance test table [6] the $T_{critical}$ is 2 (14 > 2), resulting in an asymptotic significance of p=1 (p>0.05), meaning that the result is not significant and we cannot reject the null hypothesis, i.e. that iUCP accuracy is not better than UCP.

Using the G*Power application [11] we computed the effect size by performing a *post hoc* analysis, identifying a small effect size (dz = 0.171). The effect size is the magnitude of the effect investigated [6], in our case the effect of the estimation method (iUCP over UCP) in the accuracy achieved (deviation to real effort reported). We further investigated, by using an *a priori* power analysis, based on the aforementioned values, which would lead to the required sample size in order to achieve statistical significance ($\alpha=0.05$) with a power of 0.8 (the probability of detecting an effect if a real effect exists [6]). This resulted in a sample size of 223 projects. Despite the fact that we could not obtained statistical evidence to sustain our hypothesis, the measured effect size is also small. This led us to further investigate these results, a process that we present in next section.

DISCUSSION
The major outcome of our statistical analysis is that we cannot reject the null hypothesis. In fact, the only result that point towards H_1 is the average deviation, in which iUCP result is better than UCP (60.0% versus72.5%).

Based on our findings and the previous experience applying UCP and iUCP, we concluded that the results were almost unacceptable for both methods thus suggesting that other factors should have impacted the estimations. This is in line with the idea that the original UCP, largely applied in software engineering industry, should provide better results. In fact Carroll supported this claim in a study involving more than 200 projects, in which an average deviation of

9% was obtained in about 95% of the sample [3]. Moreover, the cone of uncertainty reports that by the end of the requirements specification phase, where UCP and iUCP are applicable, the deviation should be less than 50% [2].

As a consequence of these results, and the close analysis and discussion of our projects, we considered two different approaches to draw more conclusions from our study. Firstly, we calculated what would be the sample size needed in order to reach statistical significance. Considering that we cannot control either the effect size or the power, but admitting an increased sample with a hopefully large effect size of 0.5, the minimum required sample size would be 28 projects (maintaining a power of 0.8 and $\alpha=0.05$,). This possibility is far more encouraging than the 223 sample size stated in the previous section. Secondly, we inspected which factors impacted the results and how we could generate an improved proposal for effort estimation. These factors are discussed in the next section based on the available information of the software development process for each project.

Factors Impacting Results

During our study we found that deviations were influenced both by the estimation method applicability and by the real effort reporting. We also found that the estimation could be influenced by factors impacting the productivity factor, such as the requirements volatility, the software framework and the project type.

Moreover, the lack of standardization in the use case modeling techniques also impacts the estimation, because the number of transactions (system responsibilities in iUCP) and steps (the total number of activities in a use case, in UCP) has a direct impact on the final UUCP and varies significantly across organizations. For instance, iUCP estimation of average complexity use cases differed from 40% in one organization to 4.5% in another.

Furthermore, TCF and ECF are prone to bias influenced by the estimator experience [19]. Our study did not explore the estimation of these factors and hence this bias is not present in our results. However, the real effort conveyed is impacted by over-reporting, which could happen due to organizational issues, such as the financing sources, and the method used by the team to report the time spent on the project. All these issues are interdependent and complex and should be further explored. The PF significantly impacts the final effort estimation since it is multiplied by the resulting UCP (use case points). For instance, if the UUCP is 100, by applying a PF of 30, the estimation results in 3000 hours, whereas applying a PF of 15, the final estimation will change to 1500 hours. As a result of our analysis we concluded that there were three major factors impacting the estimation: 1) requirements volatility, 2) software framework, and 3) project type. This analysis led to a new proposal, that we present in the next section.

An Improvement Proposal

Requirements volatility (RV) (1) refers to the changing of requirements before the project is concluded. RV is a factor that affects negatively the productivity of a software development team. On average the RV impacts the development costs of a project by nearly 50% [9]. The original UCP method [16] addresses this with the ECF, namely in the sixth factor (T6 – Stable requirements) resulting however, in a minor impact in the final estimation. We argue that this factor is undervalued. Thus, we propose PF to normalized where a factor of 0.5 should be added to the PF of the projects affected by this situation (Table 6).

The software framework (SF) (2) refers to the development tools supporting the software development process, and in particular important issues like separation of concerns leading to n-tier software architectures [25]. Taking the 3-tier architecture, we consider that if changes are made to any of the three components (database, internal logic or user-interface) during the project development, a 25% extra value should be added to the PF (i.e., 25% if changes are made in the database, 25% if changes are made in the user-interface, plus 25% if the internal logic is changed). Moreover, if a new SF is created to develop the project, a value of 50% should be considered (Table 7).

The project type (PT) (3) describes the project nature whether it is new (adds functionality) or is it maintenance (changes existing functionality). Regarding maintenance, Cote and St-Pierre reported a 20% effort reduction when dealing with modified components, 66% when dealing with suppressed components, 94% when dealing with untouched components and 0% for new components [9]. Since maintenance projects involve dealing with a mixture of the aforementioned situations, we settled for an initial value of -25% for this project type (Table 8).

Requirements Volatility	Description	RV
Volatile	Requirements changed	0.50
Stable	Requirements remained stable	0

Table 6. Requirements Volatility Proposed Weights.

Software Framework	Description	SF
Established Development Framework	The project is developed using an already established software framework	0
Improvement of the existing software framework	1 MVC component changed	0.25
	2 MVC components changed	0.50
	3 MVC components changed	0.75
New Software Framework	Development of a new software architecture	0.50

Table 7. Development Framework Proposed Weights.

Project Type	Description	PT
Perfective maintenance	Enhancement of existing system modules	-0.25
New Requirements	New system modules	0

Table 8. Project Type Proposed Weights.

The application of the mentioned factors results in the following estimation formula, where TCF and ECF are replaced by (RV+SF+PT+1):

$$Effort = (UAW + UUCW) * (RV + SF + PT +1) * PF$$

The experiment was repeated using the new formula, which is presented in the following section.

Reassessing the Results with the New Proposal

We recalculated the estimations, considering the factors that impacted each project (Table 9).

Project	RV	SF	PT	Final PF
P1	0%	0%	0%	30.0
P2	50%	0%	-25%	37.5
P3	0%	50%[1]	0%	45.0
P4	0%	25%	0%	37.5
P5	0%	0%	-25%	22.5
P6	50%	50%[2]	0%	60.0
P7	50%	50%[2]	0%	60.0

Table 9.Corrected PF.

Considering the new PF we calculated the new effort estimation (Table 10) and the related deviations (Table 11).

In Table 10, we summarize the two estimates against the real reported effort. In the new proposal there is a clear increase in the estimated effort.

	Real Effort	Original		Proposal	
		iUCP	UCP	iUCP	UCP
P1	598.5	330.0	600.0	330.0	600.0
P2	2357.4	1830.0	3090.0	2287.5	3862.5
P3	2282.0	900.0	2070.0	2250.0	3105.0
P4	1134.0	1740.0	2610.0	2175.0	3262.5
P5	434.0	990.0	1530.0	742.5	1147.5
P6	12889.5	5880.0	7530.0	11760.0	15060.0
P7	3170.0	1380.0	1830.0	2760.0	3660.0

Table 10. Estimated effort in hours, with the original and the new formula (per project).

---

[1] Software framework changes in two levels (MV)

[2] New software framework

In Table 11 we compare how the new proposal affected each method's performance. In iUCP the estimation accuracy, was better in five out of seven projects, whereas in UCP the results were worst in four out of seven.

	iUCP			UCP		
	Original	Proposal		Original	Proposal	
P1	44.9%	44.9%	=	0.3%	0.3%	=
P2	22.4%	3.0%	+	31.1%	63.9%	-
P3	60.6%	1.4%	+	9.3%	36.1%	-
P4	53.4%	91.8%	-	130.2%	187.7%	-
P5	128.1%	71.1%	+	252.5%	164.4%	+
P6	54.4%	8.8%	+	41.6%	16.8%	+
P7	56.5%	44.9%	+	0.3%	15.5%	-

=) No changes, +) Better, -) Worst

Table 11.Absolute deviations (MRE) with the original and the new formula (per project).

Analyzing the new data normality trough Skewness and Kurtosis, as well as the Kolmogorov–Smirnov test, we conclude that our data is now normal ($p>0.05$).

The mean results favored again iUCP over UCP (33.4% versus 69.2%) - the original means were 60% and 72.5%, respectively. Regarding data dispersion, iUCP standard deviation (36.4%) was also more consistent than UCP (76.0%), as depicted in Figure 2. Again the original standard deviation values were 32.6% and 89.9%, respectively. A closer analysis of the box-plot in Figure 2 shows that the "iUCP_Proposal" and "UCP_Proposal" charts (for iUCP and UCP respectively, for the new proposal) present better results when compared to the original ones ("iUCP_Original" and "UCP_ Original"). Since there are no outliers, the maximum deviations are lower in both cases, and especially in "iUCP_Proposal" the first and second quartile are much closer to zero.

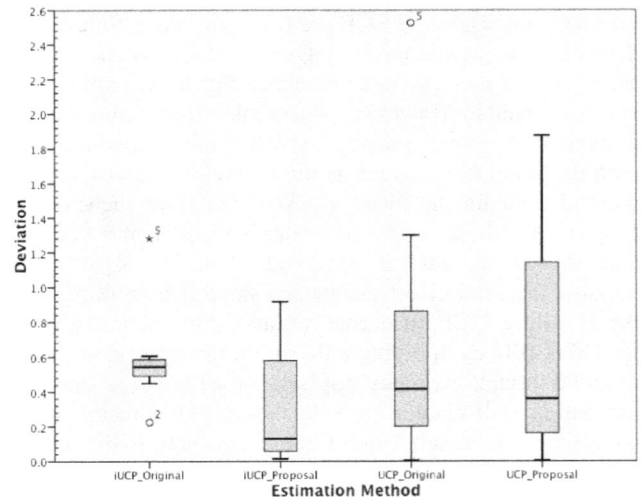

Figure 2: Box plot, comparison between the old and the new formula.

We further used a parametric t-test to evaluate UCP and iUCP deviation differences. According to the two-tailed significance test table [6] t(6)=2.447>-1.560, with a significance value of p=0.17 (p>0.05), is not statistically significant.

Finally using the G*Power application [11], we computed the new effect size (dz = 0.589) which is now bigger than the previously identified (dz = 0.171), configuring a large effect size. In our case this large effect of the estimation method points towards an improved accuracy achieved by iUCP over UCP. The power achieved by this new proposal is now 0.397 (which is still half of the conventional 0.8 target).

We further investigated, conducting an *a-priori* analysis, with an effect size of 0.589, and concluded that in order to achieve a significance of 0.05 (with a power of 0.8), the new required sample size would be 20 projects. This is yet a significant improvement when compared to the 28 projects calculated in the beginning of this section, which provide a more practical research target.

However and despite the improvements our new proposal still does not provide enough statistical evidence to support the original research hypothesis. In the next section we present our conclusions.

CONCLUSION

In this paper we presented a statistical analysis of the cost estimation results for seven real world projects using a conventional SE estimation method (UCP) and a modified HCI method (iUCP). Our research was motived by the need to provide evidence that human-centric models can be used to enhance the software development practice, and that creating project cost estimates early in the development lifecycle is still a challenge for the software industry. Here we tried to improve the state of the art, with further empirical evidence that benefits can emerge from the cross-fertilization of the SE and HCI fields.

The main conclusion of our experiment is that we cannot statistically support the hypothesis that iUCP produces more accurate estimates than the original UCP method. This motivated a *post-experiment* analysis resulting in a new estimation proposal, which improves the estimation results for the iUCP method. The obtained mean deviation (34.3% for iUCP, and 69.6% for UCP) seems to provide indications that support that the interactive perspective introduced by iUCP can be more adequate for modern software development requirements. The assumption that reflecting HCI concerns into internal SE artifacts used to generate more accurate estimation models stands, and could generate value for both the SE and HCI communities.

Another relevant conclusion is that iUCP tends to estimate less effort than UCP, as denoted in the data presented both in Table 5 and Table 11. This fact is explained by the more refined assessment of actors and use cases proposed by iUCP.

Our decision to conduct a multi-organization study revealed several new issues to be tackled in the future. For instance, we found that deviations were influenced by the estimation method applicability, the lack of standardization in the use cases modeling technique, and by the real effort reporting, which is influenced both by organizational and procedural factors. On top of these factors, we also found the requirements volatility, the software development framework and the project type to play a major role on the software development team productivity, and consequently on effort estimation. This is the reason why we propose a revised formula for effort estimation.

The initial calculations using the original methods and our sample size of only seven projects resulted in a low effect size and statistical power. Therefore a sample size of 223 projects was required to achieve statistical significance. This implies a tremendous effort for future research in particular considering the difficulties obtaining data on real-world development projects. The improvements proposed here reduce the sample size to 20 projects which is an achievable target even for intensive research effort like the one required to calculate effort estimation from use-case models. This opens-up interesting perspectives for expanding this research in the future.

Future Developments

We plan to expand this experiment to a minimum of 20 projects, in order to apply both the original and the new proposal. Our goal would be to further enhance our revisions, producing a new version of iUCP that better reflects the needs of modern software development effort estimation for interactive systems.

Moreover, we plan to assess the implications of modeling interactive systems requirements using conventional and essential use cases and its implications on effort development and estimation. Furthermore, we plan to verify if there is a correlation between the project size and effort estimation deviation, in order to infer the range of project size to which the estimation methods are applicable.

ACKNOWLEDGMENTS

We thank GDAI, Logica and GMV for contributing with real projects to be analyzed. As well, author 1 gratefully acknowledges the grant from +Conhecimento (MADFDR-01-190- FEDER-000004).

REFERENCES

1. Albrecht, A. A New Way of Looking at Tools. IBM, 1979.

2. Boehm, B.W. *Software Engineering Economics*. Prentice Hall, 1981.

3. Carroll, E.R. Estimating software based on use case points. Companion to the 20th annual ACM SIGPLAN conference on Object-oriented programming, systems, languages, and applications, (2005), 257–265.

4. Center for Systems and Software Engineering, University of Southern California. http://csse.usc.edu/.

5. Clem, Roy. Project Estimation with Use Case Points - CodeProject. http://www.codeproject.com/Articles/9913/Project-Estimation-with-Use-Case-Points.

6. Coolican, H. Research Methods and Statistics in Psychology. Hodder Education, 2009.

7. Collopy, F. Difficulty and complexity as factors in software effort estimation. International Journal of Forecasting 23, 3 (2007), 469–471.

8. Constantine, L.L. and Lockwood, L.A.D. Structure and style in use cases for user interface design. In Object modeling and user interface design. Addison-Wesley Longman Publishing Co., Inc., 2001, 245–279.

9. Cote, V. and St.-Pierre, D. A model for estimating perfective software maintenance projects. (1990), 328–334.

10. Crosby, L.L., Schwalb, J., Coe, D.J., et al. CrossTalk: The Journal of Defense Software Engineering. Volume 21, Number 3. DTIC Document, 2008.

11. G*Power. http://www.psycho.uni-duesseldorf.de/aap/projects/gpower/.

12. Gabinete de Desenvolvimento de AplicaçõesInformáticas. https://gdai.uma.pt/.

13. GMV. http://www.gmv.com/en.

14. IBM SPSS Statistics. http://www-01.ibm.com/software/analytics/spss/products/statistics/.

15. Jacobson, I. Object Oriented Software Engineering: A Use Case Driven Approach. Addison-Wesley Professional, 1992.

16. Karner, G. Resource estimation for objectory projects. Objective Systems SF AB 17, (1993).

17. Kemerer, C.F. An empirical validation of software cost estimation models. Commun. ACM 30, 5 (1987), 416–429.

18. Logica Iberia. http://www.logica.pt/.

19. Morgenshtern, O., Raz, T., and Dvir, D. Factors affecting duration and effort estimation errors in software development projects. Information and Software Technology 49, 8 (2007), 827–837.

20. Nunes, N.J. iUCP - estimating interaction design projects with enhanced use case points. Proceedings of the 8th international conference on Task Models and Diagrams for User Interface Design, Springer-Verlag (2010), 131–145.

21. Nunes, N. Object Modeling for User-Centered Development and User Interface Design: The Wisdom Approach. Phd Thesis, Universidade da Madeira, (2001).

22. Nunes, N.J., Constantine, L., and Kazman, R. iUCP: Estimating Interactive-Software Project Size with Enhanced Use-Case Points. Software, IEEE 28, 4 (2011), 64–73.

23. Ochodek, M., Nawrocki, J., and Kwarciak, K. Simplifying effort estimation based on Use Case Points. Information and Software Technology 53, 3 (2011), 200–213.

24. O.M.G. Unified Modeling Language, Superstructure. 2007.

25. Reenskaug, T. Models - Views – Controllers, Xerox PARC, (1979).

26. Seffah, A. and Metzker, E. The obstacles and myths of usability and software engineering. Communications of ACM 47, 12 (2004), 71–76.

27. Valente, P. and Sampaio, P. Analysis of Interactive Information Systems Using Goals. Innovative Information Systems Modelling Techniques, InTech, (2012), Available from: http://www.intechopen.com/books/innovative-information-systems-modelling-techniques/analysis-of-interactive-information-systems-using-goals

28. Wirfs-Brock, R. The art of designing meaningful conversations. Smalltalk Report, (1994).

Validating an Episodic UX Model on Online Shopping Decision Making: A Survey Study with B2C e-Commerce

Abdullah A.M. Al Sokkar
University of Leicester
LE1 7RH Leicester, U.K.
aama4@leicester.ac.uk

Effie Lai-Chong Law
University of Leicester
LE1 7RH Leicester, UK
elaw@mcs.le.ac.uk

ABSTRACT

Existing online shopping decision-making models (OSDMs) do not address adequately the role of experiential qualities in customer satisfaction. The awareness of this scoping issue has become stronger due to the recent User Experience (UX) research. We have developed an OSDM called 'Episodic UX Model on Decision-Making' (EUX-DM) by integrating the established technology acceptance model, emerging UX models, and expectation-confirmation theory. EUX-DM covers three phases: before interaction, after interaction, and confirmation. To validate the model, we designed and conducted a web-based survey, which comprises eight main constructs. Five (i.e. usefulness, ease-of-use, aesthetic quality, trust and experiential quality) were measured in all three phases, two (i.e. usage attitude, intention to purchase, overall satisfaction) were measured in the 'during' phase, and one (i.e. overall satisfaction) was measured only in the 'confirmation' phase. Results from analysing 278 responses suggest the validity of our model. Implications for augmenting EUX-DM are discussed.

Author Keywords

E-Commerce; Trust; Expectation; Confirmation; User experience; Decision-making; Satisfaction;

ACM Classification Keywords

H.5.m. Information interfaces and presentation (e.g., HCI): Miscellaneous.

INTRODUCTION

E-Commerce has sustained its growth globally since its inception in the early 1980s, albeit at different rates in different countries (e.g. [14, 33]). A key question "Which *factors* contribute to deciding on intended, actual and repeated purchases in a particular online shopping environment?" has been investigated by researchers primarily from two related fields: Human-Computer Interaction (HCI) (e.g. [28, 35]) and Management Information Systems (MIS) (e.g. [21, 26]) for more than twenty years. Consequently, a range of structural and measurement models on the relationships among such

factors have been developed. Presenting in-depth reviews of these online shopping decision making (OSDM) models is beyond the scope of this paper. Nonetheless, we have identified an emerging trend of this research inquiry that several concepts - *expectation, trust, aesthetic quality* - have received increasing attention in the related studies during the last decade. The observed change can be attributed to the recent shift of emphasis from usability to user experience (UX) in HCI at the turn of the millennium, stimulating research interest in experiential qualities in its neighboring fields. Reciprocally, the field of MIS has somehow influenced UX modeling, especially the role of expectation (e.g. branding) in shaping user experience *before, during* and *after* an interaction event (e.g. [36]).

Earlier OSDMs were built on the traditional frameworks such as technology acceptance model (TAM) and its variant [7, 38] and information systems success model (ISSM) [9]; some of the recent ones were grounded in the expectation-confirmation theory (ECT) [4, 26] and some focused on the affect-emotion aspect [10]. But there is a lack of an OSDM model integrating these related concepts. Besides, the experiential aspect of interaction design needs to be addressed more adequately by referencing the most recent work in the field of UX (e.g. [16], [24]). Hence, we aim to develop an integrated OSDM to study the relationships among the constructs with the right level of abstraction while attempting to strike the delicate balance between authenticity and completeness on the one hand and manageability and understandability on the other hand.

Our model is known as *Episodic UX Model on Decision Making* (EUX-DM). The term 'episodic' implies that there is a clear beginning and end of an interaction event. Essentially, it addresses three main phases of the online shopping decision-making process: *pre-interaction* where expectation is hypothesized to play a significant role in estimating the qualities of the online shopping environment concerned; *during-interaction* where the expected qualities are revised against the perceived qualities; *after interaction* where the overall user experience is further shaped by the confirmation between the expected and perceived qualities.

Overall, the main contribution of our current study is modeling the multifaceted relationships between users' expected and perceived qualities of e-commerce websites and decision-making. We synthesize the related approaches into an integrated framework, break it down into constructs, and then group them under the phases of our process model. This operationalisation enables us to validate the assumption how user experience is related to expectations, which can be structured as a special type of requirements [3, 44] for engineering the practical interaction design.

In the following sections, we first present the related work on UX, TAM and ECT. Then we present our own model: EUX-DM. Next we will describe the design of our web-based survey. Finally, we present our results and discuss our main findings and implications.

RELATED WORK
User Experience (UX)
A number of research efforts have been undertaken to define UX (e.g. [19, 23]), especially how it can be demarcated from usability (e.g. [18], [40]). Two major stances on the relationship between usability and UX are: first, usability is subsumed by UX; second, UX is an elaborated form of *satisfaction* – one of the three usability metrics. Nevertheless, recognizing the uniqueness of UX does not imply abandoning the traditional usability approaches, which should actually serve as the base for incorporating some new requirements of UX. In accord with the common understanding of UX as *subjective, dynamic* and *context-dependent* [23], UX measurement should essentially be *self-reported, trajectory-based* and *adaptive* [41]. Traditional techniques such as questionnaire, interview, and think-aloud remain important for capturing self-reported data.

Furthermore, a major challenge in UX is to operationalise non-instrumental qualities, experiential qualities (for a detailed review see [1]) and system appraisal, thereby rendering UX more manageable in product/service creation processes to enhance user satisfaction and loyalty [27]. In our model EUX-DM, we study how the salient non-

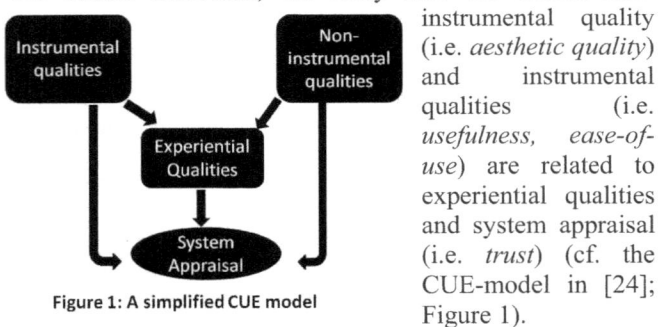

Figure 1: A simplified CUE model

instrumental quality (i.e. *aesthetic quality*) and instrumental qualities (i.e. *usefulness, ease-of-use*) are related to experiential qualities and system appraisal (i.e. *trust*) (cf. the CUE-model in [24]; Figure 1).

Non-instrumental quality: Aesthetic quality (AQ) has empirically been found to be a factor for user enjoyment, perceived ease-of-use and perceived usefulness. Several research studies have investigated the fuzzy relations between beauty and usability (e.g. [10, 16]). For instance, [2] show that users' preference for products with different perceived usability levels and aesthetic qualities can be biased by the expected effect that their judgement may have on themselves. This finding is somewhat corroborated by Hassenzahl's [17] conjecture about hedonic identification (i.e. the social value of beauty). Aesthetics have a strong

halo effect for user preference, depending on the perceived seriousness of the usage context (e.g. games vs. formal classroom learning) [8]. Whether and how such halo effect works in e-commerce contexts, which can be informal as well as formal, is not clear. Further, Lavie and Tractinsky's [22] have developed a measurement tool for perceived aesthetics; their work has stimulated others to evaluate aesthetic qualities quantitatively (see [1]).

Instrumental qualities (IQ): TAM has extensively been used in the field of MIS and HCI since the initial version was published in 1989 [42]. Its variants, namely TAM2, UTAUT and TAM3 [43], with increasing complexity as a result of including more constructs (e.g. personal attributes, social influence) have been developed. There is a large volume of literature on the applications of these models; conducting an in-depth review on them is beyond the scope of this paper. But it is crucial to point out that not all the constructs of the extended TAMs are relevant to a particular usage context such as online shopping. To address our research questions pertaining to aesthetic quality and trust, we consider that the original TAM constructs are sufficient. Otherwise, an overly complex model would loosen the focus of our research study.

Experiential qualities (EQ) are known as emotional reactions in the CUE model [24]. They are manifest as subjective feelings, motor expressions and physiological responses. Basically, EQ cover a broad range of affective and emotional reactions such as enjoyable, pleasant, fascinating, fun, surprise, to name just a few. A review on the recent UX research studies [1] shows that EQs have mostly been evaluated with qualitative approaches; measuring EQs objectively remains challenging [41].

System Appraisal: Trust (T) has stimulated many discussions in the UX community in the last decade with reference to a range of use contexts, from technical agents for the internet security to human peers in social networking sites (e.g. [5, 12, 13, 15, 35]. In e-commerce, the objects of trust are essentially the information provided by the web retailer (i.e. information quality) and the system with which the information is delivered (i.e. system quality). This is the tenet of ISSM [9], which shares certain attributes with TAM. Specifically, we have mapped information quality to perceived usefulness and system quality to perceived ease-of-use. Furthermore, among others, the reputation and size of an online store are determinants of customer trust in it [20]. Pavlou [32] revealed a direct effect of trust and a stronger moderating effect of usefulness and ease of use (i.e. TAM) on intention to purchase. Apart from system trust, it is important to consider the personal dimension of trust (e.g. dispositional trust) [15]. Another dimension of trust is dynamicity, implying that it is not a static quality but evolves over longer-term interaction [39].

Expectation Confirmation Theory (ECT)
Building a strong trustful relationship between e-commerce companies and their customers is the key point to ensure

customer loyalty [31]. Other critical success factors in e-commerce include enabling customers to have *realistic expectations* about the quality of interaction with the system and about the quality of product/service purchased, and providing them positive user experience to confirm their expectations [31, 34, 37]. In marketing research, expectation has been studied as a factor influencing customers' post-purchase satisfaction and behaviour [26] as well as their trust and loyalty towards e-commerce companies ([4, 6, 29]). Specifically, the Expectation-Confirmation Theory (ECT) has been applied in these studies to assess customers' expectations in four different phases: (i) initial expectation towards the product/services prior to purchase; (ii) product/services acceptance, where customers perceive the products/service quality and performance in this stage; (iii) expectation assessment: customers compare their original concept-based expectations with their interaction-based perceptions and assess the extent to which their expectations is confirmed; (iv) customers satisfaction, which is partially shaped by the (dis)confirmation of expectations. Further, the ECT can serve as a relevant theoretical backdrop for the work of temporal UX [40] where the role of expectation in shaping the experience of subsequent phases of interaction is explicitly acknowledged.

EPISODIC UX MODEL ON DECISION MAKING (EUX-DM)
With our goal of investigating the relationships between the expected and perceived qualities of interacting with an online shopping environment, we have developed an OSDM. The model is built upon the existing literature on consumer decision-making that highlights the relevance of trust [21, 26, 28, 31], TAM [7], and ISSM [9]. In brief, perceived trust may facilitate a consumer's intention to complete an online purchase. As our research focuses on individual usage episode with a specific start and an end, our structural model is called 'Episodic UX Model on Decision Making' (cf. momentary or cumulative UX) [40]. The proposed model comprises three phases (Figure 2):

- *Before Interaction (expected online shopping experience)*: Customers' expectations towards aesthetic quality and pre-purchase knowledge of an online shopping website (e.g. previous experience, familiarity, brand image, advertisements, friends, review reports and/or recommendations) can influence their expectations of the experiential quality (e.g. pleasant) and their expected instrumental qualities such as information quality (e.g., usefulness) and system quality (e.g., ease of use) of the website, which in turn shape their expectation toward trust. Such expectations can also influence actual interactions with the website and eventually the overall online shopping experience.

- *During Interaction (online shopping experience assessment):* Perceived instrumental qualities and perceived aesthetic quality of an online shopping website affect directly customer experience, including perceived trust and perceived experiential qualities. Furthermore, actual interactions with the website enable customers to assess

their expectations and influence their intention to purchase as an outcome of decision-making influenced by usage attitude (UA). UA can be defined as customers' general tendency to appreciate the value of the website and to use it. UA is influenced by perceived experiential qualities. Some research work has already highlighted the direct influence of customers' trust on their intention to purchase and UA (e.g. [21, 28, 31]). Besides, it has been found that trust is directly related to customers' UA. The unified model for e-commerce relational exchange [31] suggests that customers' overall satisfaction is positively related to their intention to purchase.

- *Confirmation;* Based on the experience and knowledge gained through the interactions, customers can review and compare their expected instrumental qualities, aesthetic quality, experiential qualities and trust of the website against the corresponding perceived ones. In fact, a significant factor contributing to user satisfaction is the outcome of the expectation-confirmation assessment. There are two main approaches to measuring confirmation: *indirect* (i.e. subtracting the assessment of expectation from the assessment of perceived values) or *direct* (i.e. assessing the extent to which an expectation is (dis)confirmed) [39]. In our study, we have adopted both approaches to substantiate the validity of our empirical findings.

METHODS
Based on the above discussions pertaining to our EUX-MD model, we have derived a set of 13 hypotheses (Figure 2). They were verified with a web-based survey, which was implemented with an open-source software application *Limesurvey*. A link to this study survey was distributed via the authors' personal contacts and several mailing lists (e.g. CHI-Announcement, British Computer Society HCI) of which the recipients are primarily HCI researchers.

Instrument
While most of the items of the survey were adapted from the related literature (Table 1), the items for the experiential qualities were developed based on our earlier pilot usability study with the B2C retailer website 'IKEA.com'. The pilot study was conducted with 24 participants (50% male, age-range: 18 to 45) who had previous experience with online shopping. Each participant was required to perform five different tasks with the website (e.g., "You have recently moved to a one-room apartment, you want to look for a suitable sofa-bed."). There was a short interview before each task and another one right after it in order to elicit user expectation and experience, respectively. Specifically, we extracted from the responses certain positive experiential qualities that the participants had or would like to have with the retailer website. Several instrumental qualities (IQs) (e.g. helpful, simple, understandable), non-instrumental qualities (NIQs) (i.e. beautiful), and experiential qualities (EQs) (i.e. fascinating, pleasant, curious) were identified. The IQs and NIQs were consistent with the literature and thus integrated into the items of the respective constructs. The EQs constituted the items of this construct in this survey (for all items, see **Appendix I**).

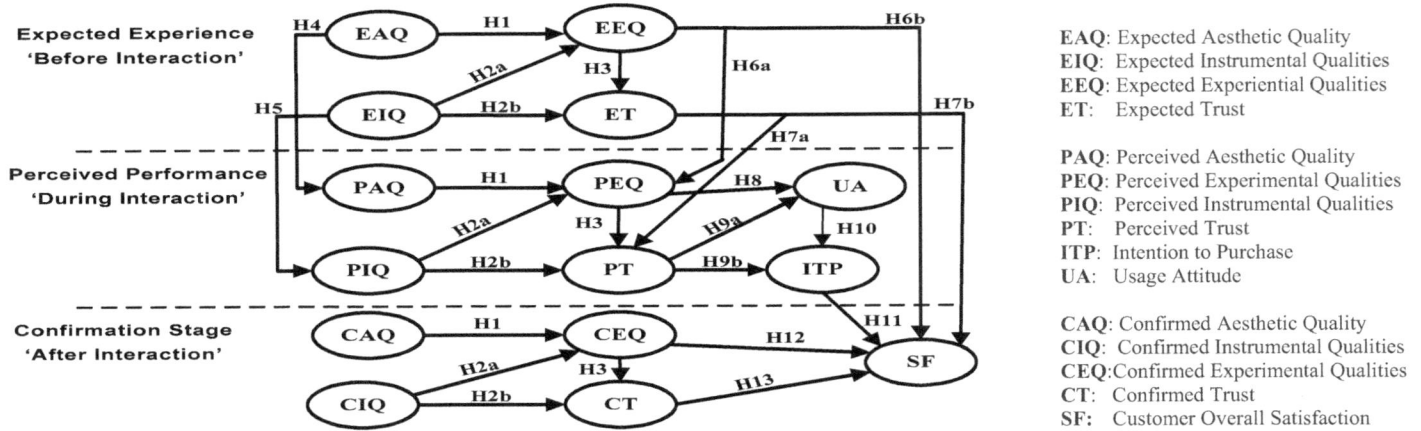

Note: The prefix of each abbreviated construct represents the corresponding interaction phase where: **E** = Expected, **P** = Perceived, and **C** = Confirmed

EAQ: Expected Aesthetic Quality
EIQ: Expected Instrumental Qualities
EEQ: Expected Experiential Qualities
ET: Expected Trust

PAQ: Perceived Aesthetic Quality
PEQ: Perceived Experimental Qualities
PIQ: Perceived Instrumental Qualities
PT: Perceived Trust
ITP: Intention to Purchase
UA: Usage Attitude

CAQ: Confirmed Aesthetic Quality
CIQ: Confirmed Instrumental Qualities
CEQ:Confirmed Experimental Qualities
CT: Confirmed Trust
SF: Customer Overall Satisfaction

UX-related Hypotheses

H1. In each phase of EUX-DM, *Aesthetic Quality (AQ)* positively affects *Experiential Qualities (EQ)*;
- In 'before-interaction' phase: *Expected AQ* positively affects *Expected EQ*.
- In 'during-interaction' phase: *Perceived AQ* positively affects *Perceived EQ*.
- In 'confirmation' phase: *Confirmed AQ* positively affects *Confirmed EQ*.

H2a. In each phase of EUX-DM, *Instrumental Qualities (IQ)* positively affects *Experiential Qualities (EQ)*:
- In 'before-interaction' phase: *Expected IQ* positively affects *Expected EQ*.
- In 'during-interaction' phase: *Perceived IQ* positively affects *Perceived EQ*.
- In 'confirmation' phase: *Confirmed IQ* positively affects *Confirmed EQ*.

H2b. In each phase of EUX-DM, *Instrumental Qualities (IQ)* positively affects customer *Trust (T)*:
- In 'before-interaction' phase: *Expected IQ* positively affects *Expected T*.
- In 'during-interaction' phase: *Perceived IQ* positively affects *Perceived T*.
- In 'confirmation' phase: *Confirmed IQ* positively affects *Confirmed T*.

H3. In each phase of EUX-DM, *Experiential Qualities (EQ)* positively affects customer *Trust (T)*:
- In 'before-interaction' phase: *Expected EQ* positively affects *Expected T*.
- In 'during-interaction' phase: *Perceived EQ* positively affects *Perceived T*.
- In 'confirmation' phase: *Confirmed EQ* positively affects *Confirmed T*.

Expectation Confirmation Theory Related Hypotheses

H4. *Expected Aesthetic Quality* of the 'before-interaction' phase positively affects *Perceived Aesthetic Quality* in the 'during-interaction' phase.
H5. *Expected Instrumental Qualities* in the 'before-interaction' phase positively affect *Perceived Instrumental Qualities* in the 'during-interaction' phase.
H6a. *Expected Experiential Qualities* in the 'before-interaction' phase positively affect *Perceived Experiential Qualities* in the 'during-interaction' phase.
H6b. *Expected Experiential Qualities* in the 'before-interaction' phase positively affect the customer *overall Satisfaction*.
H7a. *Expected* customer *Trust* in the 'before-interaction' phase positively affects *Perceived* customer *Trust* in the 'during-interaction phase'.
H7b. *Expected* customer *Trust* in the 'before-interaction' phase positively affects the customer *overall Satisfaction*.
H12. *Confirmed Experiential Qualities* in the 'confirmation' phase positively affect the customer *overall Satisfaction*.
H13. *Confirmed* customer *Trust* in the 'confirmation' phase positively affects the customer *overall Satisfaction*.

Decision Making and TAM Related Hypotheses

H8. *Perceived Experiential Qualities* in the 'during-interaction' phase positively affect customer *Usage Attitude*.
H9a. *Perceived* customer *Trust* in the 'during-interaction' phase positively affects the customer *Usage Attitude*.
H9b. *Perceived* customer *Trust* in the 'during-interaction' phase positively affects the customer *Intention to Purchase*.
H10. Customer *Usage Attitude UA* in the 'during-interaction' phase positively affects the customer *Intention to Purchase*.
H11. Customer *Intention to Purchase* in the 'during-interaction' phase positively affects the customer *Overall Satisfaction*.

Figure 2: Episodic UX Model on Decision-Making and Related Hypotheses

Component	Construct	Remarks
Instrumental qualities (IQ)	Usefulness [26,31]	Mapping TAM [42] to the information quality of ISSM [9]
	Ease of use [26,31]	Mapping TAM [42] to the system quality of ISSM [9]
Non-instrumental quality (NIQ)	Aesthetics Quality (AQ) [28]	AQ is a salient NIQ; the other NIQ such as identification [24] are not included in this study to keep the scope of the model manageable
Experiential qualities (EQ)	Empirical data of our usability study on IKEA.com	Several EQs, which the participants considered important for their online shopping experience, were identified from the data
System appraisal	Trust (T) [21, 31, 39]	Items have been adapted from several studies, which were in turn based on TAM, ISSM, ECT and other frameworks.
	Usage Attitude (UA) [31]	
	Intention to purchase (ITP) [21, 31, 39]	
	Satisfaction (SF) [26, 31]	

Table 1. Sources of items used in the survey

Participants

We received altogether 278 valid responses after the survey had been run for about one month. The profiles of the participants are shown in Table 2. All participations were voluntary. On average it took 26 minutes (SD = 11.28) to complete the whole survey.

Gender	Female: 43.4%; Male 56.6%		
Age	(Less than 24): 21%	(25-34): 60.6%	
	(35-44): 9%	(45-54): 6.4%	
	(50 and more): 3 %		
Highest educational level attained	(High school):1.9%	(College):4.1%	
	(Bachelor):30.7%	(Master):48.3%	
	(Doctorate):15%		
Country of origin	(U.K.):62.5%	(USA):10.8%	(Jordan):9%
	(South Korea):4.1%	(Others):13.6%	

Table 2. Sample demographics

Procedure

Participants were asked to respond to all four sections of the survey:

Section 1- Background: Basic demographic data, online purchase experience, familiarity with the 'IKEA.COM' website, and disposition to trust people;

Section 2- Pre-purchase: Online customers tend to refer to previous shopping experiences, others' feedback and review reports on the product or the retailer website of interest when they are considering a purchase [21, 26]. We prepared a short and somewhat neutrally phased description of the IKEA website.

IKEA is a privately held, international home products company that designs and sells ready-to-assemble furniture such as beds and desks, appliances and home accessories. The company is the world's largest furniture retailer. The IKEA website contains about 12,000 products and is the closest representation of the entire IKEA range. There were over 470 million visitors to the IKEA websites in the year from Sep.2007- Sep. 2008. The company is keen to show leadership in adopting more environmentally friendly manufacturing processes. (Wikipedia.org)

Participants were asked to read it before responding to the items on their expectations about the constructs (Table 7, Appendix I). Each item was evaluated with a 7-point Likert scale with the leftmost and rightmost anchors being "not likely at all" and "highly likely", respectively.

Section 3 - During Interaction: In this third section, participants were asked to visit the 'IKEA.com' website to carry out a task of looking for a specific product and to report the task completion time when finishing it (mean = 6.1 minutes; SD =6.7). Based on their experience of interacting with the website, participants were asked to respond to the same set of items used in Section 2 as well as some extra items related to the constructs *Intention to Purchase* and *Usage Attitude UA*. The 7-point Likert scale used here had different descriptors with the leftmost and rightmost anchors being "very poor" and "very good". Besides, participants were asked whether they were familiar with that specific product and whether its price had affected their decision making.

Section 4 - Confirmation: In this last section, participants were asked to respond to the same set of items used in Section 2. But the 7-point Likert scale descriptors were different with leftmost and rightmost anchors being "much lower than I thought", "much higher than I thought" and the middle point being "the same as I expected". This measurement could reflect the participants' ability to assess their overall satisfaction with the website by comparing their expectations with perceived qualities [25, 34]. Also, the participants were asked to answer a set of items related to the construct *Customer Overall Satisfaction*.

Construct Reliability and Validity

While most of the items of the survey were validated in the earlier research studies, we further tested their reliability and validity. In Appendix 1, Tables 7 to 10 we list all the items, which are grouped under their respective constructs. The Cronbach alpha reliability coefficients of all the items exceeded the minimum value of 0.70, indicating high internal consistency [20]. Furthermore, convergent validity for each construct was tested. Results of factor analysis showed that the item loading for each construct was greater than 0.5 and the eigenvalue exceeded the acceptable minimum score of 1.00.

RESULTS AND DISCUSSION

In this section we report and discuss only major findings of our survey, leaving out some details due to the space limit.

Multiple Regression Analysis of Constructs

Multiple regressions were performed to assess how much variance and unique variance in each construct in the confirmation phase could be explained by the same construct measured in the before-interaction and during-interaction phases. As mentioned earlier, there are two approaches to measuring confirmation: *direct* and *indirect*. The direct measurement of confirmation showed that *Aesthetic Quality, Instrumental Quality(IQ), Experiential Quality, and Trust* in the confirmation phase could be explained 38.3%, 32.3%, 40.2%, and 19.4%, respectively by their corresponding measures taken in both the before-interaction and during-interaction phases (Table 3). For instance, *IQ* in the before-interaction and during-interaction phases could explain 32.0% of *IQ* in the confirmation-phase, and the differences in the values of the construct among the three phases were statistically significant (F=50.43, *p*<.001).

Construct measured in the confirmation phase (direct measures of confirmation)	Construct measured in *before-* and *during-* interaction phases (indirect measures of confirmation)		
	F	*R²*	*p*
Aesthetic quality (AQ)	65.439	0.383	< 0.001
Instrumental quality (IQ)	50.43	0.323	<0.001
Experiential quality (EQ)	72.183	0.406	<0.001
Trust (T)	25.34	0.194	<0.001

Table 3. Multiple regressions of the constructs measured in the three phases and confirmed by direct/indirect measures

Transformation of Confirmation Measures

McKinney and associates [26] discussed the two main methods for measuring the confirmation construct: First, computing confirmation by subtracting expectation from perceived performance; second, measuring confirmation directly as an independent construct of the perceived gap. They argued that direct measurement of confirmation would be a better, established approach in the expectation-confirmation paradigm and thus developed a 11-point Likert scale to measure confirmation, where 0 = 'much lower than I thought', 5= 'the same as I expected' and 10= 'much higher than I thought'. However, we found both approaches problematic. For instance, if the participant's expectation for a specific item was rated as 2 out of 7 (0 = 'not likely at all') and then rated the same item after interacting with the website to be 3 out of 7 (0 = 'very poor'), the subtraction result would be +1, though the participant tended to regard the website negatively. Furthermore, the scale for direct measurement of confirmation is confusing with respect to overall satisfaction. The middle point (6 = 'the same as I expected') could be rated by participants when they perceived what they had expected, no matter whether their ratings for both expectation and perceived performance were in the negative or positive side of the scale. To address this issue, we developed a simple means called *indexing approach* to transform the data (Table 4).

Results with the indexing approach showed that *Aesthetic Quality, Instrumental Quality, Experiential Quality, and Trust* in the confirmation phase could be explained 84%, 92.8%, 86.7%, and 91.9%, respectively by their corresponding measures taken in both the before-interaction and during-interaction phases (Table 5).

(E)	(P)	(P)-(E)	(C)	(E)	(P)	(P)-(E)	(C)
1	7	+6	7	5	7	+2	7
	6	+5	7		6	+1	6
	5	+4	6		5	0	5
	4	+3	5		4	-1	3
	3	+2	4		3	-2	2
	2	+1	3		2	-3	1
	1	0	1		1	-4	1
2	7	+5	7	6	7	+1	7
	6	+4	7		6	0	6
	5	+3	6		5	-1	4
	4	+2	5		4	-2	3
	3	+1	4		3	-3	2
	2	0	2		2	-4	1
	1	-1	1		1	-5	1
3	7	+4	7	7	7	0	7
	6	+3	7		6	-1	5
	5	+2	6		5	-2	4
	4	+1	5		4	-3	3
	3	0	3		3	-4	2
	2	-1	2		2	-5	1
	1	-2	1		1	-6	1
4	7	+3	7				
	6	+2	6				
	5	+1	5				
	4	0	4				
	3	-1	3				
	2	-2	2				
	1	-3	1				

Table 4: The indexing approach to transforming confirmation data (E = expectation rating, P = performance rating; C= computed result of confirmation).

Construct measured in confirmation- phase 'Indexing approach'	Construct measured in *Before* and *During-* Interaction phases		
	F	*R²*	*P*
Aesthetic quality	552.913	0.840	< 0.001
Instrumental quality	1364.53	0.928	<0.001
Experiential quality	688.287	0.867	<0.001
Trust	1203.54	0.919	<0.001

Table 5. Multiple regressions of the constructs measured in the three phases and confirmed by the index table

In comparing the results computed based on the direct measurement with those on the indexing approach, the latter proved to be more valid and powerful (details are not shown due to the space limit). Hence, subsequent analyses were performed using the data transformed by the indexing approach. Results suggest that the ECT can be considered as a relevant theoretical backdrop for the work of temporal UX, because individual constructs measured in the during-interaction phase had a strong unique contribution to the corresponding constructs measured in the confirmation phase. For instance, as shown in Table 6, the perceived *Instrumental Quality* measured in the during-interaction phase had a strong unique contribution to the confirmed *Instrumental Quality* in the confirmation phase (beta=1.147, $R^2 = 0.927$, $p < 0.001$). However, the constructs measured in the expectation (before-interaction) phase had less and negative significant unique contribution to the corresponding constructs in the confirmation-phase.

Constructed measured in Confirmation phase	Construct measured in before-interaction phase			Construct measured in during-interaction phase		
	beta	R^2	p	beta	R^2	p
Aesthetic quality	-0.283	0.290	<.001	0.980	0.820	<.001
Instrumental quality	-0.401	0.130	<.001	1.147	0.927	<.001
Experiential quality	-0.437	0.150	<.001	0.680	0.864	<.001
Trust	-0.447	0.040	<.001	1.108	0.900	<.001

Table 6. The unique contribution of the constructs measured in the two phases to the confirmation values estimated by the indexing approach (Table 4)

In summary, results of the above multiple regressions suggest that the EUX-DM model is largely verified and that the confirmation measurement proposed in [26] needs to be revised or replaced; the indexing approach is a viable alternative.

Structural Paths and Hypothesis Testing

All the hypotheses derived from the EUX-DM were tested using SmartPLS 2.0 (beta) [30]. Figure 3 presents the results of structural equation modeling for EUX-DM after removing the two non-significant paths between *Expected Experiential Qualities* and *Customer Overall Satisfaction* (H6b), and between *Expected Trust* and *Customer Overall Satisfaction* (H7b). The non-significant paths (H6b and H7b) suggest that a customer's expectation has no direct effect on shaping their overall satisfaction with the online shopping website. All the other hypothesized paths were supported and the correlations were significant at $p<0.05$.

For the three phases of EUX-DM, the results indicate a high direct contribution of *Instrumental Quality (IQ)* and *Aesthetic Quality (AQ)* to predict *Experiential Quality (EQ)*. For instance, in the before-interaction phase; R^2 for *Expected Experiential Quality (EEQ)* was 0.87, implying that the *Expected Instrumental Quality* (EIQ) and *Expected Aesthetic Quality (EAQ)* could predict 87% of the total variance of *EEQ*, where the direct path between *EIQ* and *EEQ* was significant ($\beta= 0.31$, $t = 4.49$, $p<0.01$), and the direct path between *EAQ* and *EEQ* was significant ($\beta= 0.71$, $t = 11.52$, $p<0.001$). Also, *IQ* and *EQ* on the three phases of EUX-DM were significant predictors of *Trust (T)*. These results suggested that trust could be shaped by the user experience that was essentially based on perceived usefulness, perceived ease of use as well as the experiential qualities of the retailer website. Furthermore, decision-making and TAM related hypotheses were also supported. The two hypothesized paths between *Perceived Trust (PT)* and *Intention to Purchase (ITP)* ($\beta= 0.76$, $t =12.42$, $p<0.001$), and between *PT* and *Usage Attitude (UA)* ($\beta=0.28$, $t =2.47$, $p<0.01$) were significant. The path leading from *Perceived Experimental Qualities (PEQ)* as one of the central component of UX to UA ($\beta= 0.69$, $t = 7.84$, $p<0.001$) was also significant. It could explain the positive, direct effect of *EQ* on the usage of the website as a consequence of the user experience that led to a positive direct effect on *ITP*.

The results of the structural model also showed that a customer's expectations of all the constructs in the before-interaction phase had an impact on their perceptions of all the constructs in the during-interaction phase. For instance the direct path between *Expected Aesthetic Quality (EAQ)* and *Perceived Aesthetic Quality (PAQ)* was significant ($\beta= 0.41$, $t = 4.01$, $p<0.001$). Furthermore, not all of the ECT related hypotheses were supported: H6a and H7b were non-significant paths, indicating that neither *Expected Experiential Quality (EEQ)* nor *Expected Trust (ET)* could significantly predict *SF*. These findings can be attributed to the participants' unfamiliarity with the website; 54.7% of the participants of this study were not familiar with the IKEA website. *ET* was not built on any pre-knowledge. Furthermore, the recency effect [18] – the most recent experience has the strongest impact on the overall judgment of the system - may explain the insignificant contribution of *EEQ* to *SF*, given the time gap as *EEQ* was measured in the earliest phase of the process. However, results confirmed that *Confirmed Experimental Qualities (CEQ)* and *Confirmed Trust (CT)* were significant predictors of *SF*. Figure 3 presents the explanatory powers of the constructs. For instance, the model indicates that *ITP*, *CEQ*, and *CT* can account for 80.7% of the total variance of *SF*.

The EUX-DM can be used as a basis for further research on UX, and online shopping decision making (OSDM) models. The results of this study provided perhaps a better comprehensive understanding of the role of the realistic expectation in user performance at a more abstract level.

In particular, investigating the three phases of user interaction enabled us to know more about the direct positive effect of the experiential qualities and the indirect positive effect of aesthetic qualities on customer trust and usage attitude.

For the TAM-related hypothesis, 55.4% of the variance in *Usage Attitude* was explained by *Perceived Trust* and *Perceived Experimental Qualities*. *Perceived Trust* together with *Usage Attitude* in turn accounted for 72.3% of the variance in customer *Intention to Purchase*, implying that there is a strong need for the B2C retailer website designers to identify effective strategies and approaches to enhancing trust as well as the quality of pleasantness, fascination and curiosity. Some of the ECT-related hypotheses were supported, indicating the direct positive influence of both *Confirmed Trust* and *Confirmed Experimental Qualities* on shaping the *Customer Overall Satisfaction*.

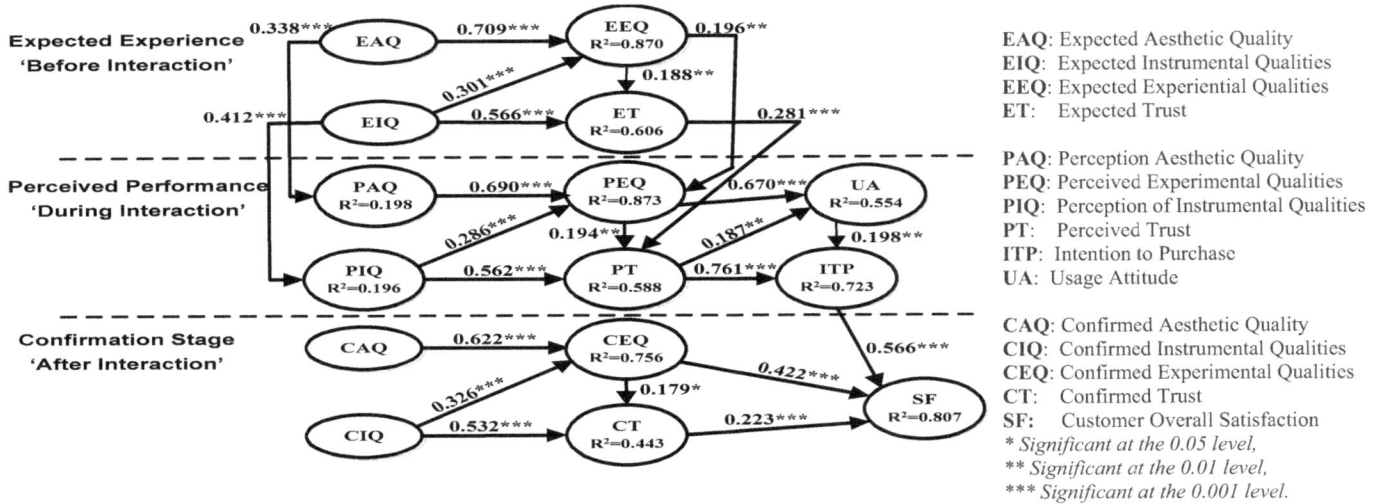

Figure 3: Result for the structural model for Episodic UX Model on Customer Decision-Making

EAQ: Expected Aesthetic Quality
EIQ: Expected Instrumental Qualities
EEQ: Expected Experiential Qualities
ET: Expected Trust

PAQ: Perception Aesthetic Quality
PEQ: Perceived Experimental Qualities
PIQ: Perception of Instrumental Qualities
PT: Perceived Trust
ITP: Intention to Purchase
UA: Usage Attitude

CAQ: Confirmed Aesthetic Quality
CIQ: Confirmed Instrumental Qualities
CEQ: Confirmed Experimental Qualities
CT: Confirmed Trust
SF: Customer Overall Satisfaction
* Significant at the 0.05 level,
** Significant at the 0.01 level,
*** Significant at the 0.001 level.

CONCLUSION

The proposed EUX-DM model was empirically validated, lending further support to the assumption about the important role of expectation in shaping user experience before real interactions take place (H4, H5, H6a and H7a). It substantiates the notion of temporal UX that experiential qualities evolve over time. But the insignificant correlations between the constructs measured in the before-interaction and confirmation phase suggest the 'decaying' influence of initial perceptions (cf. the recency effect). The dynamicity of trust is also attested. Particularly intriguing is the direct and indirect effects of expected as well as perceived aesthetic quality on trust. This resonates with the ongoing debate about the fuzzy relationship between beauty and usability in the field of UX. The verified hypotheses H4 for all the three phases (Figure 2) suggest that the halo effect of the perceived aesthetic quality [8] is applicable in the context of e-commerce.

The empirical results demonstrated that expectation for the critical qualities (*Expected Aesthetic Quality, Expected Instrumental Qualities, Expected Experiential Qualities, and Expected Trust*) effected as a strong determinant of the perception of the corresponding qualities in the during-interaction phase (H4, H5, H6a and H7a). Therefore, we recommend that requirement engineers consider customers' expectations as critical requirements informing the design of a B2C retailer website.

There are several limitations of the study. The web-based survey did not enable us to observe how the participants behaved, for instance, the way the given search task was performed could vary much with individuals. The quantitative data allow us to describe the relationships between the constructs but do not allow us to analyse the underlying causes. The scope of the study, though more comprehensive than the earlier ones, needs to be extended in the future work. In particular, the three phases of EUX-DM model should be augmented to include phase 4: *post-purchase,* where an extended period of interacting with the item bought may lead to the revision of user experience and evaluation of the purchase decision. Longitudinal empirical

studies to investigate this augmented aspect of the model are called for.

APPENDIX 1
Measurement scale for Expectations phase (before interaction) All items (Table 7) were measured with a 7-point Likert scale, where 1= not likely at all, and 7 = highly likely. A general question was asked after the participants read the short report; Based on the short description provided about the website, do you expect the website to:

Constructs	Item	Loading
Usefulness [26,31]	be informative to your purchase decision	0.950
	be valuable to make your purchase decision	0.961
	in general, useful in purchase decision	0.949
Eigenvalue = 2.728, AVE = 0.91, Cronbach α= 0.950,		
Ease of use [26,31]	have as a simple layout for its content	0.866
	be easy to use	0.940
	be well organised	0.931
	have a clear design	0.890
	in general, be user-friendly	0.901
Eigenvalue = 4.104, AVE= 0.81, Cronbach α=0.945,		
Trust [21, 31, 39]	the website to be trustworthy	0.914
	the website vendor to give the impression that keeps promises and commitments.	0.937
	the website vendor would have my best interest in mind	0.887
Eigenvalue= 2.500, AVE= 0.84, Cronbach α= 0.901		
Experiential Qualities	fascinating	0.881
	pleasant	0.849
	Curious	0.852
Eigenvalue = 4.533, AVE= 0.71, Cronbach α = 0.931		
Aesthetics Quality [28]	aesthetically appealing	0.900
	visually appealing especially the screen layout	0.923
	in general, attractive	0.927
Eigenvalue = 1.759, AVE= 0.83 , Cronbach α =0.863,		

Table 7. Measurement Constructs for before interaction phase

Measurement scale for perceived performance phase (during interaction) All items (Table 8) were measured on with a 7-point Likert scale, where 1= very poor and 7 =very good. A general question was presented to the participants: "*Based on your experience of using the website, do you find the website*":

Usefulness [26,31]	informative to your purchase decision	0.960
	valuable to make your purchase decision	0.959
	in general, useful in purchase decision	0.958
Eigenvalue= 2.760, AVE= 0.92 , Cronbach α = 0.956		
Ease of use [26,31]	have as a simple layout for its content	0.920
	be easy to use	0.922
	be well organised	0.905
	have a clear design	0.915
	in general, be user-friendly	0.933
Eigenvalue =4.121, AVE= 0.82, Cronbach α =0.945		
Trust [21, 31, 39]	the website to be trustworthy	0.893
	the website vendor to give the impression that keeps promises and commitments.	0.953
	the website vendor would have my best interest in mind	0.892
Eigenvalue = 4.223, AVE= 0.84, Cronbach α = 0.953		
Experiential Qualities	fascinating	0.883
	pleasant	0.890
	curious	0.852
Eigenvalue= 4.917, AVE= 0.71, Cronbach α=0.924,		
Aesthetics Quality [28]	aesthetically appealing	0.934
	visually appealing especially the screen layout	0.967
	in general, attractive	0.959
Eigenvalue = 2.728, AVE= 0.91 , Cronbach α=0.949,		
Usage Attitude [29]	I like to use the website of IKEA	0.910
	I like the layout of the website of IKEA	0.934
	the IKEA's website is valuable to you	0.845
Eigenvalue = 2.712, AVE= 0.82, Cronbach α=0.902		
Intention to purchase [21, 31, 39]	I would like to purchase the product on the IKEA's website	0.949
	I would recommend the IKEA's website to friends	0.921
	I am likely to make another purchase from the IKEA's website if I need the products that I will buy	0.943
Eigenvalue = 2.637, AVE = 0.88, Cronbach α=0.931		

Table 8. Measurement Constructs for during interaction phase

Measurement scale for confirmation phase (after interaction) All items (Table 9) were measured with a 7-point Likert scale, where 1= much lower than I thought and 4 =the same as I expected and 7= much higher than I thought. A general question was presented to the participants to validate their experience after they finished the interaction with the given website: "*My experience with using the IKEA's website was better than I had expected regarding the following items*":

Usefulness [26,31]	Informative to your purchase decision	0.917
	valuable to make your purchase decision	0.948
	in general, useful in purchase decision	0.954
Eigenvalue = 2.648, AVE= 0.88, Cronbach α = 0.933,		
Ease of use [26,31]	have as a simple layout for its content	0.880
	be easy to use	0.890
	be well organised	0.933
	have a clear design	0.934
	in general, be user-friendly	0.912
Eigenvalue = 4.140, AVE = 0.82, Cronbach α = 0.948		
Trust [21, 31, 39]	the website to be trustworthy	0.916
	the website vendor to give the impression that keeps promises and commitments.	0.948
	the website vendor would have my best interest in mind	0.874
Eigenvalue = 2.501, AVE= 0.83, Cronbach α = 0.900		
Experiential Qualities	fascinating	0.866
	pleasant	0.870
	curious	0.842
Eigenvalue = 5.116, AVE= 0.73, Cronbach α = 0.938		
Aesthetics Quality [28]	aesthetically appealing	0.974
	visually appealing especially the screen layout	0.947
	in general, attractive	0.969
Eigenvalue = 2.785, AVE= 0.85 , Cronbach α = 0.925		

Table 9. Measurement Constructs for Conformation phase

Measurement scale for satisfaction: All items related to the satisfaction construct (Table 10) were measured with a 7-point Likert scale, where 1= complete disagreement and 7 =complete agreement.

Customers Satisfaction [26, 31]	I would be very pleased with making purchase with the IKEA's website	0.916
	I am likely to make another purchase from this website If I need the products that I will buy	0.927
	I am likely to recommend this website to others	0.953
	Overall, I am satisfied with the IKEA's website	0.902
Eigenvalue = 3.779, AVE= 0.84, Cronbach α = 0.939,		

Table 10. Measurement items for Customer's Satisfaction

REFERENCES

1. Bargas-Avila, J. A. and Hornbæk, K. Old wine in new bottles or novel challenges: a critical analysis of empirical studies of user experience. In *Proc. CHI 2011*, (2011), 2689-2698.

2. Ben-Bassat, T., Meyer, J., and Tractinksy, N. Economic and subjective measures of the perceived value of aesthetics and usability. *TOCHI, 13*, 2 (2006), 210-234.

3. Bergman, M., King, JL., and Lyytinen, K. Large-scale requirements analysis revisited: the need for understanding the political ecology of requirements engineering. *Requirements Engineering* 7, 3 (2002), 152–171.

4. Bhattacherjee, A. Understanding Information systems Continuance: An Expectation-Confirmation Model. *Management Information Systems Research Centre 25*, 3 (2001), 351-370.

5. Corritore, C.L., Kracher, B. and Wiedenbeck, S. Trust and technology. *Special issue of International Journal of Human-Computer Studies, 58*, 3 (2003).

6. Dabolkar, P. A., Shepard, C. D., Thorpe, D. I.: A Comprehensive Framework for Service Quality: An Investigation of Critical conceptual and Measurement Issues Through a Longitudinal study. *Journal of Retailing 76*, 2 (2000), 139-173.

7. Davis, F. D. Perceived usefulness, perceived ease of use, and user acceptance of information technology, *MIS Quarterly 13*, 3 (1989), 319–340.

8. De Angeli, A., Sutcliffe, A., and Hartmann, J. Interaction, usability and aesthetics: What influences users' preferences? In *Proc. DIS 2006*, Penns. USA. (2006).

9. DeLone, W.H., and McLean, E.R. Measuring E-Commerce Success: Applying the DeLone & McLean Information Systems Success Model, *International Journal of Electronic Commerce* 9,1 (2004) 31-47

10. Diefenbach, S., and Hassenzahl, M. The "Beauty Dilemma": beauty is valued but discounted in product choice. *Proc. CHI 2009*, (2009), 1419-1426.

11. Egger, F. N. Affective Design of E-Commerce User Interfaces: How to Maximise Perceived Trustworthiness. *The*

International Conference on Affective Human Factors Design Asean Academic Press, London, (2001).

12. Folstad, A. and Rolfsen, R.K. Measuring the effect of User Experience design changes in e-Commerce web sites: A case on customer guidance. *the Second COST294-MAUSE Workshop User Experience Towards a Unified View, 10,* 15(2006)

13. French, T., Liu, K., and Springett, M. A Card-Sorting Probe of E-Banking Trust Perceptions. In *People and Computers XXI – HCI.* (2007).

14. Gartner inc. Magic quadrant for e-Commerce 2011. http://www.gartner.com/id=1839418

15. Gräbner-Krauter, S., and Kaluscha EA. Empirical research in on-line trust: A review and critical assessment. *International Journal of Human-Computer Studies, 58* (2003), 783-812.

16. Hassenzahl, M. and Monk, A. The inference of perceived usability from beauty. *Human Computer Interaction, 25,* 3 (2010), 235-260.

17. Hassenzahl, M. The interplay of beauty, goodness, and usability in interactive products. *Human-Computer Interaction, 19* (2004), 319-349.

18. Hassenzahl, M. The Thing and I: Understanding the Relationship between User and Product. Funology (2005) 31-42.

19. ISO DIS 9241-210:2010. Ergonomics of Human System Interaction – Part 210: Human-centred design for interactive systems. *International Standardisation organisation (ISO).*

20. Jarvenpaa, SL., and Tractinsky N. Consumer trust in an Internet store: A cross-cultural validation. *Journal of computer mediated communication, 5,* 2 (1999).

21. Kim, DJ., Ferrin DL., and Rao, HR. A trust-based consumer decision-making model in electronic commerce: the role of trust, perceived risk and their antecedents. *Elsevier Decision Support Systems 44* (2008), 544-564.

22. Lavie, T., and Tractinsky, N. Assessing dimensions of perceived visual aesthetics of web sites. *International Journal of Human-Computer Studies, 60* (2004), 269-298.

23. Law, E., Roto, V., Hassenzahl, M., and Vermeeren, A. P. O. S.: Understanding, Scoping and Defining User eXperience: A Survey Approach. In *Proc. CHI 2009.*

24. Thüring, M., and Mahlke, S. Usability, aesthetics and emotions in human–technology interaction. *International Journal of Psychology, 42,*4 (2007), 253–264.

25. Maltby, J., Day L.: Early Success in Statistics. *Person Education Limited* (2002).

26. McKinney, V., Yoon, K., and Zahedi, F. The Measurement of Web-Customers Satisfaction: An Expectation and Disconfirmation Approach. *Information System Research 13,* 3 (2002), 296-315.

27. Nielsen, J. E-Commerce Usability. Oct 2012 http://www.useit.com/alertbox/ecommerce.html

28. O'Brien, H. L. The influence of hedonic and utilitarian motivations on user engagement: The case of online shopping experiences. *Interacting with Computers, 22* (2010), 344-352.

29. Oliver, R. L.: A Cognitive Model for the Antecedents and Consequences of Satisfaction. *Journal of Marketing research 17,* 1980, 460-469.

30. Ringle, C.M., Wende, S., and Will, A: SmartPLS (Version 2.0 (beta) (2006). Hamburg, Germany.

31. Palvia, P.: The role of trust in e-Commerce relational exchange: A unified model. *Information & Management 46* (2009), 213-220.

32. Pavlou, P.A. Consumer Acceptance of Electronic Commerce Integrating Trust and Risk with the Technology Acceptance Model. *International Journal of Electronic Commerce, 73* (2003), 69–103.

33. PriceWaterCoopers. Customers take control, Dec 2012. http://download.pwc.com/ie/pubs/2011_customers_take_control.pdf

34. Reichheld, FF., Schefter, P,: E-loyalty: your secret weapon on the web. *Harvard Business Review 78,* (2000), 105–113.

35. Riegelsberge, J. and Vasalou, A. Trust 2.1: advancing the trust debate. *CHI Extended Abstracts, ACM* Press (2007), 2137-2140

36. Roto, V. User Experience from Product Creation Perspective. *Towards a UX Manifesto workshop* (2007)

37. Turban, E., King, D., Vieheland, D., Lee, J.: Electronic Commerce. *Pearson Prentice Hall.* Fourth Edition (2006), 1-75.

38. Venkatesh, V., Bala, H. Technology Acceptance Model 3 and a Research Agenda on Interventions, *Decision Sciences 39,* 2 (2008), 273–315.

39. Zhang, X., and Zhang, Q. Online trust forming mechanism: approaches and an integrated model. In *Proc. of the 7th International Conference on Electronic Commerce* (2005) 201-209.

40. Roto, V., Law, E., Vermeeren, A. and Hoonhout, J. (2011). UX White Paper. http://www.allaboutux.org/uxwhitepaper

41. Law, E. L-C., and Schaik van, P. Modelling user experience - An agenda for research and practice. *Interacting with Computers 22,* 5(2010), 313-322

42. Davis, F. D. Perceived usefulness, perceived ease of use, and user acceptance of information technology, *MIS Quarterly 13,* 3 (1989), 319–340

43. Venkatesh, V.; Bala, H.), Technology Acceptance Model 3 and a Research Agenda on Interventions, *Decision Sciences 39,*2 (2008), 273–315

44. Quartel, D., Engelsman, W. and Jonkers, H., A Goal-Oriented Requirements Modelling Language for Enterprise Architecture. *Proceedings of the 13th IEEE International Enterprise Distributed Object Computing Conference, EDOC* (2009).

Assessing the Support Provided by a Toolkit for Rapid Prototyping of Multimodal Systems

Fredy Cuenca, Davy Vanacken, Karin Coninx, Kris Luyten

Hasselt University - tUL - iMinds

Expertise Centre for Digital Media, Diepenbeek, Belgium

{fredy.cuencalucero,davy.vanacken,karin.coninx,kris.luyten}@uhasselt.be

ABSTRACT

Choosing an appropriate toolkit for creating a multimodal interface is a cumbersome task. Several specialized toolkits include fusion and fission engines that allow developers to combine and decompose modalities to capture multimodal input and provide multimodal output. Unfortunately, the extent to which these toolkits can facilitate the creation of a multimodal interface is hard or impossible to estimate, due to the absence of a scale where the toolkit's capabilities can be measured on. In this paper, we propose a measurement scale, which allows the assessment of specialized toolkits without need for time-consuming testing or source code analysis. This scale is used to measure and compare the capabilities of three toolkits: CoGenIVE, HephaisTK and ICon.

Author Keywords

Multimodal systems; User interface toolkits; Visual languages; Domain specific languages;

ACM Classification Keywords

H.5.m. Information Interfaces and Presentation (e.g. HCI): Miscellaneous

INTRODUCTION

For a traditional WIMP system, the detection of a single user event is enough to identify the user's intent. For instance, a click on a button *Accept* or *Cancel* of a GUI is enough to realize whether a user wants to process or close a form respectively. For the case of a multimodal system, its users are allowed to dissociate a command so that it can be conveyed through multiple modalities. For example, the users can simultaneously utilize speech and pointing to issue commands, such that the action to be executed on an object is indicated by the speech input whereas the object itself is pointed out. Thus, the identification of the user's intent is not that simple since it requires the evaluation of multiple events in order to decode what the user is requesting. A multimodal system is a computer system capable of collecting the information provided by a user through multiple input modes, integrating these inputs in order to interpret the user's intent, and responding to him/her via multiple outputs. Some input modes that can be used to enter information into a multimodal system are speech, touch, hand gestures, handwriting or sketching. Output modes can include images, audio, synthesized voice, video or haptics.

The development of a multimodal system is time-consuming, and therefore expensive. It involves the creation and iterative adaptation of prototypes. Therefore, the development phase of a multimodal system can be shortened by facilitating the creation and modification of prototypes, which is precisely the purpose of the toolkits under study. In the remainder of this work, these toolkits will be referred to as toolkits for rapid prototyping of multimodal systems.

Some existing toolkits for rapid prototyping of multimodal systems are ICon [5], Squidy [13], CoGenIVE [4], HephaisTK [6] and PetShop [9]. They are rather different one from another, since they provide different features, target different domains, use different programming paradigms and/or expect different skills from their users. Some aspects of these toolkits have already been assessed. De Boeck et al. [3] evaluated the abstraction, difuseness, role-expressiveness, viscosity and premature commitment of the visual languages of two toolkits. Later, Dumas et al. [7] used the architecture traits, reusability easiness and other characteristics as criteria for assessing a set of toolkits. Even though the results of these evaluations deepen our understanding of rapid prototyping toolkits, their practical application is not always obvious.

From a pragmatic viewpoint, the evaluation of a toolkit for rapid prototyping of multimodal systems leads us to the concrete question 'To what extent is the use of this toolkit going to facilitate the implementation of a multimodal prototype?'. Unfortunately, the absence of a scale for measuring the functionalities incorporated in a specialized toolkit prevents us from accurate answers. Such measurement scales will be proposed in this work and use to evaluate the support provided by CoGenIVE, HephaisTK, and ICon for the implementation of prototypes.

ARCHITECTURE OF A MULTIMODAL SYSTEM

The parts that comprise a multimodal system, and their interrelations are shown in Figure 1.

In this architecture, user inputs are recognized by a group of specialized software components called recognizers. Each recognizer is continuously sensing and decoding the infor-

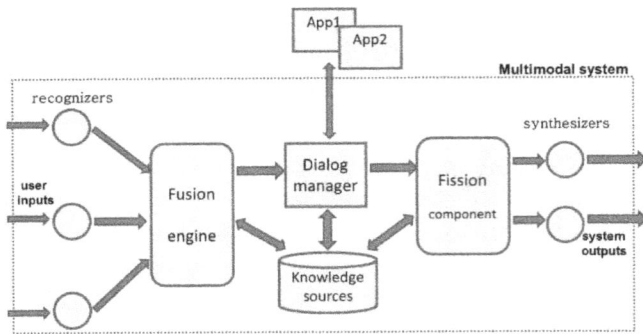

Figure 1. Architecture of a multimodal system

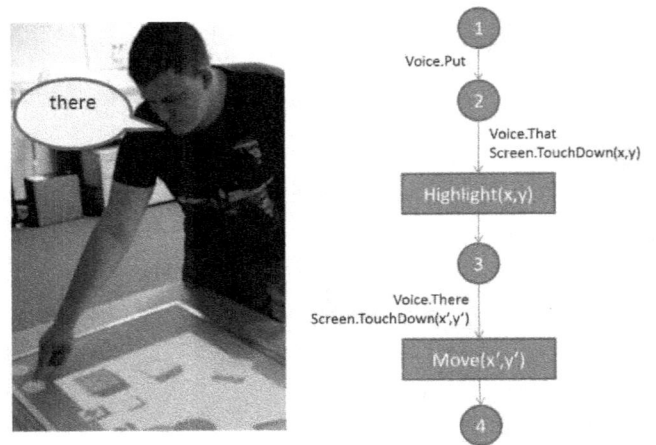

Figure 2. Left. End user interacting with a multimodal system. Right. Visual model used for specifying human-machine interaction.

mation provided by the user via the modality it is intended to sense. Some examples of these components are gesture, handwriting and voice recognizers.

Whenever a recognizer has interpreted a stream of user inputs, it informs the fusion engine, which is in charge of merging the information provided by all the recognizers in order to interpret the user's request.

Once the dialog manager is notified of the user's request, it must decide how to handle it. Since the same input may result in different responses, depending on the context, the dialog manager must track the status of the human-machine dialog so that user requests can be addressed correctly.

After the dialog manager has decided on the response to be sent, it delegates this task to the fission component. This must then choose the synthesizers (computer programs that control rendering devices) that are best suited for the situation. The generation and coordination of multimedia output is the responsability of the fission component.

Finally, the response to a user command may depend on the user profile (e.g. gender, age, preferences, etc.), on the domain of the problem, or on the history of the human-machine dialog. All the relevant information needed by the system is available in data storages called knowledge sources.

When using a toolkit for rapid prototyping of multimodal systems, its users do not have to implement all the aforementioned functionalities from scratch. Rather, they can use its visual language to invoke some functions that are pre-programmed in its framework, as shown below.

TOOLKIT FOR RAPID PROTOTYPING OF MULTIMODAL SYSTEMS

A toolkit for rapid prototyping of multimodal systems includes a framework and a graphical editor. It aims to enhance an external application, herein called client application, with multimodal capabilities. On the one hand, the client application is developed by means of a textual programming language and with no support from the toolkit. It must implement the particular functionalities of the intended prototype. On the other hand, the graphical editor allows the depiction of visual models that will be interpreted and executed by the framework. These visual models specify the tasks the prototype must perform during its interaction with the end user. Some of these tasks are present in a wide variety of multimodal systems (e.g. speech recognition or tracking of sys-

tem state) and are already pre-programmed in the framework. Other tasks are application-specific and have to be carried out by the subroutines of the client application.

Consider a multimodal prototype that supports the *put-that-there* interaction technique [1]. This prototype displays a series of objects on a touch-sensitive screen, and its user can move any of these objects by using speech and pointing (Figure 2). The user must utter the sentence 'put that there' to move an object from its original position to a new one. In order for the system to correctly interpret the meanings of the utterances 'that' and 'there', the user must point out an object and any arbitrary position while pronouncing these words respectively.

The layout of the GUI and the algorithms for highlighting and moving an object must be implemented in a client application. This application does not need to detect voice commands or pointing events. Nor does it have to verify the temporal co-occurrence of the speech input 'that' (or 'there') and the touch on the screen. These functionalities can be delegated to the framework through a visual model like the one shown on the right side of Figure 2. It specifies that the occurrence of the speech input 'put' followed by the co-occurrence of the speech input 'that' and a touch on the screen will cause the execution of the subroutine *Highlight*. Afterwards, the co-ocurrence of the speech input 'there' and a touch on the screen will trigger the execution of the subroutine *Move*, which will have to change the position of the currently selected (highlighted) object. *Highlight* and *Move* have to be programmed in the client application.

MEASURING THE SUPPORT OF A TOOLKIT TO THE IMPLEMENTATION OF MULTIMODAL PROTOTYPES

Through a visual model, users can delegate some tasks to the framework of a toolkit, as illustrated in the previous section. We now want to identify and classify these tasks in accordance to the software components (recognizers, fusion engine, etc.) that are in charge of their execution.

The study of several toolkits shows that they all incorporate software for detecting the inputs coming from a myriad of hardware devices. Since this is the responsability of the recognizers, it can be claimed that the use of a toolkit can release its users from implementing the recognizers of a multimodal prototype. Another point in common is that none of the studied toolkits supports the implementation of synthesizers or knowledge sources. Thus, their users have to include software for synthesis of modalities in their client applications, and to create and fill the data storages containing the information needed by the prototype. However, the support offered for the implementation of the fusion engine, dialog manager and fission component varies with each toolkit.

Scale for measuring toolkit's support

We propose to map the support provided by a toolkit to the set of components whose implementation can be facilitated through its use. For instance, the support of a toolkit T will be $\{recognizers, fusion\ engine\}$ if the functionality in charge of both components can be delegated to the framework of T through the use of its visual language. Then, the set of all the possible combinations of components is the scale of measurement we are proposing. For the sake of formality, let C be the set of components shown in Figure 1, the scale on which the support of a toolkit will be measured on is the power set 2^C. Even though the nature of this scale is qualitative, it will still lead to more precise assessments of a toolkit's capabilities, which is of interest for its potential users.

The use of the proposed measurement scale requires finding out whether some functionalities of the fusion engine, dialog manager or fission component are incorporated in a toolkit, and available to be invoked by its users through the depiction of visual models. Indications to create such awareness are given below.

The detection of a user's request, which is a task of the **fusion engine***, can be delegated to the framework of a toolkit if its visual language allows the specification of composite events.* A composite event is a set of events and the temporal constraints among them. It occurs whenever its constituent events are detected in a predefined order. By including composite events in the specification of a human-machine dialog, the user exploits the framework's capacity to evaluate streams of events, seeking for those meaningful patterns that are of interest for the client application to handle.

Managing context-dependent human-machine dialogs entails identifying the current state of the prototype throughout its interaction with the end user. *The management of context-dependent human-machine dialogs, which is the responsability of the* **dialog manager***, can be supported by the framework of a toolkit if its visual language allows representing the states the prototype may ever be in.* Without using a toolkit, tracking the state of a multimodal prototype would imply the maintenance of global variables across different event handlers. Furthermore, choosing the subroutines that will handle a user's request would imply the implementation of complex convoluted logic, i.e. sets of nested if-else statements, involving the aforementioned global variables. By using an appropiate toolkit, users can release their client applications from this spaghetti code, entailing the creation of easy-to-maintain client applications.

The generation and coordination of multiple outputs, which

is a task of the **fission component***, can be delegated to the framework of a toolkit if its visual language offers constructs for concurrency and synchronization.* Concurrency is required to convey the returning message through multiple outputs, and synchronization is required to keep these outputs coordinated at every moment. For instance, a multimodal system displaying an animated character capable of talking must concurrently activate a display manager and a speech synthesizer. Additionally, in order to display the lips of the animated character such that they can always be in accordance with its speech [12], both outputs have to be constantly synchronized.

Scale for measuring toolkit's fusion, dialog management and fission capabilities

The preceding subsection proposed measuring the support provided by a toolkit in terms of the components of a multimodal system. In addition, it gave us indications to realize whether the fusion of inputs, the human-machine dialog management or the fission of a returning message can be handled by the framework of a toolkit. This subsection proposes additional metrics to increase the precision of toolkit assessment. For a toolkit supporting the implementation of a fusion engine, we can identify the type of fusion it can support. According to the **CASE classification space** [10], a system can fuse data that is conveyed sequentially or simultaneously. The fusion of sequential (simultaneous) data allows identifying multimodal commands issued through consecutive (parallel) user actions. The CASE space can also be used to obtain a more precise gauge of the toolkit's fission capabilities. Indeed, the fission ability of a toolkit can be measured in terms of whether the toolkit can render a returning message through consecutive and/or parallel outputs.

For a toolkit capable of handling context-dependent human-machine dialogs, it is pertinent to detail whether these dialogs can involve complementary, assigned, redundant or equivalent modalities. Formally speaking, we can use the **CARE properties** [2] for providing more precise assessments of the toolkit's dialog management capabilities.

Unlike the previous subsection, we cannot give generic indications about how to infer the CASE and CARE properties of a toolkit from its visual language. The reason is that the language constructs required to exploit these properties vary from toolkit to toolkit. The identification of the type of fusion, dialog management and fission provided by a toolkit has to be done on an ad hoc basis.

ASSESSING COGENIVE, HEPHAISTK AND ICON

The diagrams depicted with the graphical editor of a toolkit for rapid prototyping of multimodal systems are variations of some well-known model. For the studied toolkits, these models are state diagrams and block diagrams.

State diagrams

State diagrams are graphs that can be utilized to model the interaction between a system and its end user. In this case, the nodes represent the states the system may ever be in, and the arcs represent its state transitions. Every arc of a state diagram can hold two annotations. One annotation is intended to indicate the event that makes the system changes its state, and the other to specify the subroutine(s) the system must execute during this transition. The models created with the editors of CoGenIVE and HephaisTK are variants of state diagrams.

CoGenIVE

The model shown on the left side of Figure 3 was depicted with the graphical editor of CoGenIVE [11, 4]. It specifies the behavior of a prototype implementing the *put-that-there* interaction technique described above.

This model shows that the prototype can be in four states, which are depicted as circles and labeled *Start, Put, Put-That* and *Put-That-There*. Once up and running, the prototype is in the state *Start*. Thereupon, the user commands will make it change its state. For instance, when the prototype is in the state *Put*, it will ignore every command except for the selection of the object to be moved, which is characterized by the co-occurrence of the speech input 'that' and a mouse click, i.e. by the occurrence of the composite event *Voice.That & Mouse.ButtonPressed*. As a response to this user command, the prototype will invoke some subroutines (represented as the rectangles labelled *CollisionWithPointer* and *SelectObject*) that will lead to the identification of the selected object. After performing these actions, the system will change its state to a new one labelled *Put-That*.

The possibility to include composite events in a CoGenIVE model permit us to delegate the **fusion of inputs** to the CoGenIVE's framework. In CoGenIVE, a composite event is a label annotated in an arrow of a visual model. It specifies those events whose co-occurrence must be detected by CoGenIVE's framework. This detection indicates that the end user has requested a service to the prototype.

CoGenIVE's editor allows us to place circles to represent each potential state of the prototype. Thus, the **management of context-dependent human-machine dialogs** is more easily implemented when using CoGenIVE. Its users must only program those subroutines implementing the particular functionalities of the intended prototype. Then, the CoGenIVE's framework will decide which of these subroutines must be executed and when this is the case.

As to the **fission component**, its functionality cannot be delegated to CoGenIVE's framework. This is due to the impossibility of specifying concurrency with the CoGenIVE's visual language, i.e. CoGenIVE's framework can only execute one subroutine per time. This limitation stems from the fact that state diagrams only experience one transition at a time and thus, only one subroutine can be executed in a given moment. Of course, one subroutine can be programmed so that it can handle concurrent computation but this would put all the burden on the programmer instead of on the framework.

At a more detailed level, we observe that CoGenIVE can fuse information coming from modalities used in parallel as seen in Figure 3. A sequence of events can also be interpreted as a multimodal command [4]. Finally, CoGenIVE's framework can handle human-machine dialogs exhibiting the four CARE properties. In view of space limitation, we cannot elaborate upon this point, but interested readers can refer to [11].

HephaisTK

The concise model of the right side of Figure 3, depicted with the editor of HephaisTK [6], specifies the behavior of a prototype implementing the *put-that-there* interaction technique. The prototype will initially be at state *Start* awaiting for the sequence of events whose detection will cause the movement of an object. This movement is executed by the subroutine *put_that_there_action* whereas the stream of events that will cause the execution of this subprogram is represented as a set of nested rectangles.

HephaisTK's notation allow four different types of rectangles to declare composite events [6]. Each type of rectangle indicates the temporal constraints among the events annotated within it. Thus, a wide variety of composite events can be defined by nesting these four types of containers. For instance, the yellow rectangles shown in the aforementioned figure mean simultaneous complementarity whereas the white one means sequential complementarity. Therefore, the model specifies that the sequential detection of the voice command 'put' followed by the co-occurrence of the voice command 'that' and a mouse click, and by the co-occurrence of the voice command 'there' and a mouse click will cause the execution of the subroutine *put_that_there_action* (implemented at the client side).

As mentioned above, the HephaisTK's editor allows representing composite events by nesting different types of rectangles. Thus, some functionalities of the **fusion engine** can be delegated to the HephaisTK's framework in benefit of its users. More specifically, users release their client applications from examining streams of events. Rather, it is the responsability of HephaisTK's framework to seek for those meaningful patterns of events specified as composite events.

Implementing the **management of context-dependent human-machine dialogs** can be facilitated when using HephaisTK. The states and subroutines to be called by HephaisTK's framework can be specified by means of a visual model. Each state is depicted as a circle, and the subroutines are annotated next to a zigzagged arrow. Models like the one shown in Figure 3, contain enough information so that HephaisTK's framework can always choose the subroutine that will correctly handle a multimodal command.

As regards the **fission component**, it has to be implemented at the client side with no support from HephaisTK. As mentioned in the previous subsection, this is due to the limitation of state diagrams to model concurrency.

At a more detailed level, HephaisTK can fuse information conveyed through sequential or simultaneous user actions. Finally, the appropiate use of the HephaisTK's visual language leads to the creation of prototypes supporting the four CARE properties[6].

Block diagrams

A block diagram is a set of blocks connected by directed arcs. It represents the transformations suffered by the data that flows within a system. Whereas the arcs can be seen as the channels through which the data flows, the blocks can be thought of as entities performing operations on the data that flows through them. The data enters into a multimodal prototype whenever its user issues some recognizable command. ICon models resemble block diagrams.

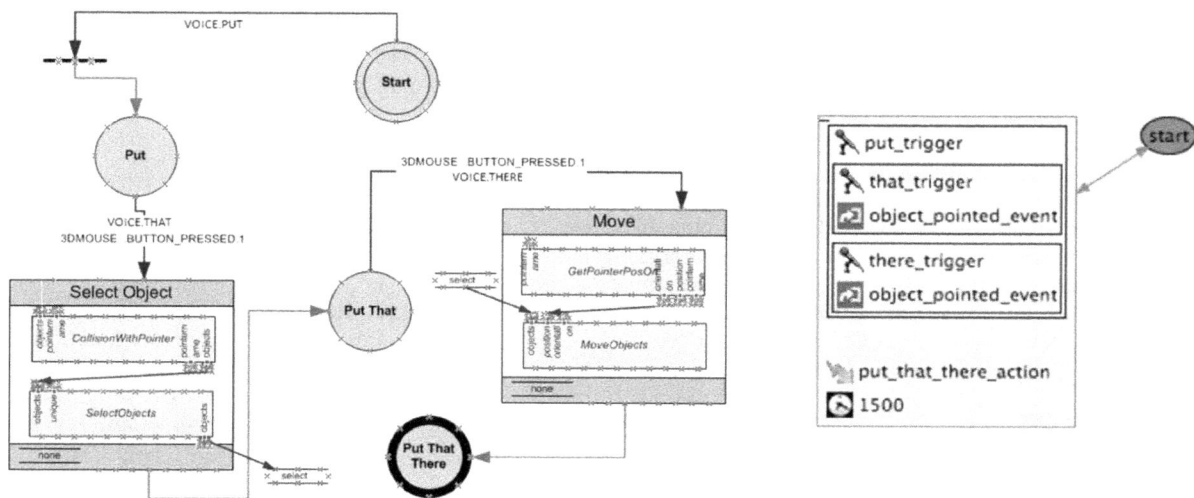

Figure 3. Specification of the put-that-there interaction technique in CoGenIVE (left) and HephaisTK (right) [8].

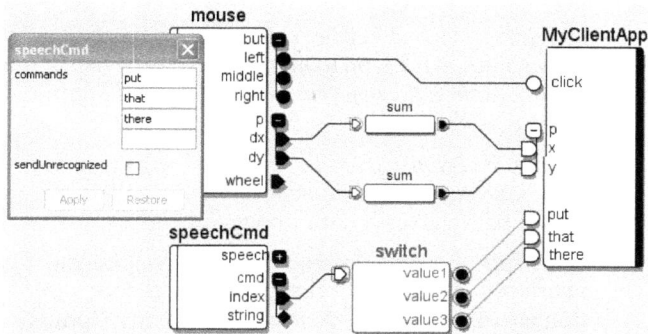

Figure 4. Specification of the put-that-there interaction technique in ICon.

ICon

Figure 4 shows how a client application called *MyClientApp* can be enhanced with speech recognition by means of a ICon's model. Instead of listening to system events, the client application expects to be notified, by the framework of ICon [5], about the user activities: clicking the mouse or uttering a voice command. The nodes labelled as *speechCmd* and *mouse* represent the recognizers that sense the voice and pointing commands issued by the end user. The data provided by these recognizers is then transformed by the nodes *switch* and *sum* before being sent to the client application. Nodes *sum* transform delta values (dx, dy) into cursor locations (x, y). The node *switch* activates one flag to identify the utterance -*put*, *that* or *there*- issued by the end user. ICon does not verify whether the speech and pointing inputs satisfy the temporal constraints expected during the put-that-there interaction technique. Rather, the client application must be programmed to check whether the sequence of events that will lead to the movement of an object has been detected or not. In short, ICon does not support the implementation of fusion of inputs [5].

As seen in Figure 4, ICon models do not contain symbols to represent the state of the prototype or to specify composite events. Moreover, the semantics of its visual language establishes that the data entering a block must be processed and inmediately reinjected to the net, thus preventing the users to model synchronization.

ICon successfully accomplishes its goal of providing its users an easy way to extend their applications so that they can support a wide set of heterogeneous devices. Its work consists of informing the client application about the events ocurring in the environment. Later, the client application will be responsible for interpreting the user's request from these events, tracking the state of the dialog, and responding the user. In other words, all the functionalities of the **fusion engine**, **dialog manager** and **fission component** have to be implemented without support from ICon.

DISCUSSION

This work is the first stage of a research intending to advance the state of the art of toolkits for rapid prototyping of multimodal systems. Such attainment would not be possible without a deep understanding of toolkits, which entails their precise assessment and objective comparison. The absence of metrics for measuring a toolkit's functionality, and our need for precise evaluations are the reasons that made us define the measurement scales presented in this paper.

We proposed to measure the support provided by a toolkit in terms of the components whose implementation it can facilitate. In order to foster the use of this scale, we described a heuristic method that helps us to uncover the capabilities of a toolkit from its visual modeling language. It consists of evaluating the visual language of a given toolkit, seeking for a series of features whose presence reveals the functionality incorporated in its framework. For instance, the presence of composite events in a visual model discloses the toolkit's capability to fuse multimodal inputs.

The support provided by three toolkits was measured on the aforementioned scale by using the proposed heuristics.

311

The results obtained (Table 1) show that the use of Co-GenIVE and HephaisTK leads to a higher reduction of the programming code at the client side. More precisely, Co-GenIVE, HephaisTK and ICon all allow their users to invoke the recognition capabilities incorporated in their frameworks, thus releasing them from implementing the recognizers of the intended multimodal prototype. But CoGenIVE and HephaisTK can also detect the multimodal commands issued by an end user (through a series of consecutive or parallel actions). Moreover, both also allow the specification of context-dependent human-machine dialogs (where the messages can be conveyed through complementary, assigned, redundant and equivalent modalities).

	ICon	CoGenIVE	HephaisTK
Recognizers	✓	✓	✓
Fusion Engine	✗	✓	✓
Dialog Manager	✗	✓	✓
Fission component	✗	✗	✗
Synthesizers	✗	✗	✗
Knowledge Source	✗	✗	✗

Table 1. Checkmarks are used to indicate the components whose implementation is supported by a toolkit.

Although the results summarized in Table 1 give us an overall idea of what can be expected from a toolkit during the implementation of multimodal prototypes, they are still coarse-grained and call for extending our measurement scale with additional criteria.

Finally, it seems to be a correlation between the gains provided by a toolkit and the formalism on which its visual language is based on, i.e. CoGenIVE and HephaisTK may exhibit similar functionalities because their visual models are based on state diagrams. Indeed, in an ongoing study we are looking into the existence of classes of toolkits. Such finding will facilitate the understanding, and permit an organized study of toolkits; both can hopefully lead to the design of simpler visual languages and/or more efficient toolkits.

CONCLUSIONS

The novelty of this work is the proposal of a scale for measuring the support provided by a toolkit for the implementation of multimodal prototypes. Such scale is not only a useful reference for the evaluation, but also for the comparison of toolkits. Since the use of this scale requires infering the functionalities that are pre-programmed in the framework of a toolkit, heuristic rules were provided to accomplish this task. We have discussed the results obtained from the evaluations of three toolkits with the proposed scale.

ACKNOWLEDGMENTS

We want to thank the BOF financing of Hasselt University for supporting this research, and our colleague, Jan Van den Bergh, for his valuable feedback.

REFERENCES

1. Bolt, R. Put-that-there: Voice and gesture at the graphics interface. In *SIGGRAPH' 80 Proc. of the 7th annual conference on computer graphics and interactive techniques*, ACM (1980).

2. Coutaz, J., Nigay, L., Salber, D., Blandford, A., May, J., and R., Y. Four easy pieces for assessing the usability of multimodal interaction: The care properties. In *Proc. of INTERACT'95* (1995).

3. De Boeck, J., Raymaekers, C., and Coninx, K. Comparing nimmit and data-driven notations for describing multimodal interaction. In *TAMODIA' 06 Proc. of the fifth International Conference on Task Models and Diagrams for User Interaction Design*, Springer Verlag (2007).

4. De Boeck, J., Vanacken, D., Raymaekers, C., and Coninx, K. High level modeling of multimodal interaction techniques using NiMMiT. *Journal of Virtual Reality and Broadcasting 4*, 2 (2007).

5. Dragicevic, P., and Fekete, J. Support for input adaptability in the icon toolkit. In *ICMI'04 Proc. of the 6th International Conference on Multimodal Interfaces*, ACM (2004).

6. Dumas, B. *Frameworks, Description Languages and Fusion Engines for Multimodal Interactive Systems*. PhD thesis, University of Fribourg, 2010.

7. Dumas, B., Lalanne, D., and Oviatt, S. Multimodal interfaces: A survey of principles, models and frameworks. In *Human Machine Interaction*, Springer Verlag (2009).

8. Dumas, B., Signer, B., and Lalanne, D. A graphical uidl editor for multimodal interaction design based on smuiml. In *Proc. of the Workshop on Software Support for User Interface Description Language*, WISE publication (2011).

9. Navarre, D., Palanque, P., Ladry, J., and Barboni, E. ICOs: A Model-Based User Interface Description Technique dedicated to Interactive Systems Addressing Usability, Reliability and Scalability. *ACM Transactions on Computer-Human Interaction 16*, 4 (2009).

10. Nigay, L., and Coutaz, J. A design space for multimodal systems: Concurrent processing and data fusion. In *Proc. of INTERACT'93*, ACM (1993).

11. Vanacken, D. *Touch-based interaction and collaboration in walk-up-and-use and multi-user environments*. PhD thesis, Universiteit Hasselt, 2012.

12. Wahlster, W., Reithinger, N., and Blocher, A. Smartkom: Multimodal communication with a life-like character. In *Proc. of the 7th European Conference on Speech Communication and Technology*, DKFI (2001).

13. Werner, K., Raedle, R., and Harald, R. Interactive Design of Multimodal User Interfaces - Reducing technical and visual complexity. *Journal on Multimodal User Interfaces 3*, 3 (2010).

Echo: The Editor's Wisdom with the Elegance of a Magazine

Joshua Hailpern & Bernardo Huberman
HP Labs
1501 Page Mill Rd, Palo Alto, CA 94304
{joshua.hailpern,bernardo.huberman}@hp.com

ABSTRACT

The explosive growth of user generated content, along with the continuous increase in the amount of traditional sources of content, has made it extremely hard for users to digest the relevant pieces of information that they need to pay attention to in order to make sense of their needs. Thus, solutions are needed to help both professionals (e.g lawyers, analysts, economists) and ordinary users navigate this flood of information. We present a novel interaction model and system called Echo which uses machine learning techniques to traverse a corpus of documents and distill crucial opinions from the collective intelligence of the crowd. Based on this analysis, Echo creates an intuitive and elegant interface, as though constructed by an editor, that allows users to quickly find salient documents and opinions, all powered by the wisdom of the crowd. The Echo UI directs the user's attention to critical opinions using a natural magazine style metaphor, with visual call outs and other typographic changes. Therefore, this paper present two key contributions (an algorithm and interaction model) that allow a user to "read as normal," while focusing her attention on the important opinions within documents, and showing how these opinions relate to those of the crowd.

Author Keywords

opinions; alignment; documents; collective intelligence; typography; call out; reading; economics of attention

ACM Classification Keywords

H.5.m. Information Interfaces and Presentation (e.g. HCI): Miscellaneous

INTRODUCTION

In the information age, few documents live in a vacuum, especially documents that express opinions or evaluations. Knowledge workers (e.g., political analysts, financial investors, economists, CEOs), legal professionals (e.g., clerks, lawyers, judges) and other consumers of topical information have to navigate hundreds, or perhaps thousands of opinion documents and meet the challenge of sorting out the relevant information that actually requires attention. The addition of

user-generated content to this mix has added tremendous diversity to this ecology of documents, which, while empowering at some level, also leads to a poverty of attention [38, 45]. This implies that potentially relevant content is missed when foraging for information among large corpuses of interlinked documents.

Solutions must therefore be created to help the recipients of this information "allocate their attention effectively among the overabundance of information sources that might consume it" [38]. This problem is known as the economics of attention, and directly relates directly to how users access key information in an ever-growing digital information space [22, 23, 1]. This problem has two main challenges: how to browse and find the most salient documents in a large corpus, and how to quickly find critical opinions within each document and situate them within the "big picture." Three critical limitations of the broad class of existing solutions pertaining to document and opinion browsing are that they do not situate each document's opinions in a broader context, they do not present key opinions in a natural manner, and they do not provide a corpus browsing UI that focuses on finding the most representative or out-of-line documents with respect to crucial opinions. Furthermore, many of the existing software solutions add to the information overload by presenting the user with more information (e.g. multiple documents side by side) in increasingly smaller areas of screen real-estate.

In response, we created a novel interaction model, algorithm and system called **Echo** that enables a user to easily traverse a corpus of documents and naturally read individual documents while maintaining a broader context. Echo utilizes a rich series of Machine Learning techniques that we refer to as the **Echo System**. The Echo System examines a large corpus of documents, extracts the content and gathers the collective opinions and intelligence of the crowd on key topics. In addition, we developed two key User Interfaces for Echo: the **Echo Locator**, which shows the user how each *document* fits in with the document database; and the **Echo Reader**, which allows the user to see how each *opinion in a document* fits into the opinions of the crowd. The Echo Locator allows users to peruse a corpus and find documents that have opinions (on a specific topic or overall) which are representative or out-of-line as compared to the crowd. The Echo Reader UI calls the user's attention to critical opinions using a natural magazine style metaphor, with visual call outs and other typographic changes. This technique allows a user to "read as normal," while focusing her attention on important opinions that have a very small or very large difference in opinion as compared to the crowd. Echo has been tested on multiple data sets to ensure the breath of its flexibility, including political news, financial reports, and movie reviews.

The foremost contribution of this work is an algorithm and interaction technique (demonstrated in a functional system) that allows the user to focus on the most important opinions in any article, quickly analyze and synthesize a document corpus, and see how each article and opinion fits into the broader context in a natural way. To the authors' knowledge, Echo is the first UI system to present opinions by alignment or divergence from the sentiment distribution on that specific topic/word. We first discuss how Echo builds on the existing literature and is situated within the broader context of solutions. We then present Echo's features and implementation, followed by very positive results from a preliminary pilot study we conducted, and conclude with a discussion of future ongoing work.

RELATED WORK

While much work in the machine learning community has focused on creating algorithms for document summaries[4, 29, 40], Echo is not a summarization tool. Rather, this paper focuses on user interaction design, and systems to support the navigation of opinions within a corpus. In this section, we discuss literature that explores *how* people read, and some existing UI solutions to help people navigate a large document or opinion space.

Economics of Attention

While the original relationship between attention and information was described in 1971 [38], numerous research since then has continued to explore, expand and quantify his observations across many disciplines, including the digital domain [22]. Based on these findings, some research has been done to explore how to adapt information presentation based on these economics of attention. We therefore wish to build on their findings and further increase the speed and access of users to large document corpuses and the key opinions within them.

Reading & Document Corpuses

The rich set of real-world activities that surround document corpuses can be organize into four groups of interactions: reading, annotating, collaborating, and authoring[11]. While issues of annotation, collaboration, and authoring are important problems, this work focuses specifically on the economics of attention [38] as it pertains to exploring the overwhelming collection of documents in a corpus and situating each document/opinion within a broader context.

We therefore must consider not just *what* information should be brought to the user's attention, but *how* to do so in the most natural manner. When users move within and between documents, they begin with a critical "planning phase" [32]. While planning, users quickly scan through a document to get an overall sense of structure and important facts, in order to connect key "bits" of information. When the medium of paper is used to present information, the physical layout of content on a page leads to incidental memory (e.g. remembering a key fact as being on a specific page, and specific column)[32]. These contextual cues [9] actively support

this planning phase, which can help users serendipitously encounter information through browsing[30]. In print media, editors actively take advantage of typographic changes and other visual callouts to call readers' attention to what they deem as key content. We can leverage visual callouts can help users navigate by bringing key opinions to their attention while working within a reader's natural planning phase.

In online media, this information recall is paralleled with textual relationship to navigation UI and pictures [16, 32]. However, reading online documents brings up new limitations. While paper readers commonly compare and contrast content by physically arranging documents or flipping back and forth, presenting documents side-by-side on a computer is problematic in that the reduced screen real-estate makes it more difficult to traverse content [32]. Further, reading documents in parallel (rather than jumping between them) may lead to issues of practice inference in working memory [24]. We can therefore see that there is a need to create a method for allowing a user to read a single digital document without losing context. Furthermore this solution should follow a known style metaphor (e.g. magazine callouts) because using a metaphor on top of new technology is a powerful way of conceptualizing interaction, especially for novice users [16].

Reading Documents in Context

Providing context for a document in a broader space is a challenging technological problem. For example Souneil Park [34, 35] has attempted to explore bias in news events by showing pairs of documents on contrasting ends of a political spectrum side-by-side. While this technique helps with directly comparing two *known* contrasting opinions (via two documents), it makes no affordances for bringing forward critical information, since all information is at the same visual level). Nor does it help place the key opinions within a larger context or present the full "large" corpus of opinions, as the technique just shows the user *one* contrasting opinion. Further, by showing contrasting documents side-by-side, the literature suggests that this UI decision makes it more difficult to traverse content[32].

Other tools such as AKTiveMedia [13], Fishnet [7], and others [37, 39, 8]) use vibrant color highlighting within a document to draw users' attention to keywords based on queries issued. While this does draw a user's attention to key information, it is visually jarring and can be distracting, adding to issues to attention rather than resolving them. However, given the generally highly promising results of these systems, we seek to build upon their work by combining their successful use of highlighting with the metaphor of magazines.

Abstracting documents to a corpus level reveals a class of tools that help users organize a document space. Popcorn [14] and many other tools [20] employ a wide range of visualizations to help users traverse a collection based on hierarchical semantic relationships (e.g. tree maps, network graphs). However, many of these visualization styles can be confusing [20, 12]. For example, Tag Clouds are actively used in many systems (e.g. [26, 46, 18, 28, 27]) and are intended to provide a high level view of a document space. However, evidence suggests that while they may be aesthetically pleasing, from

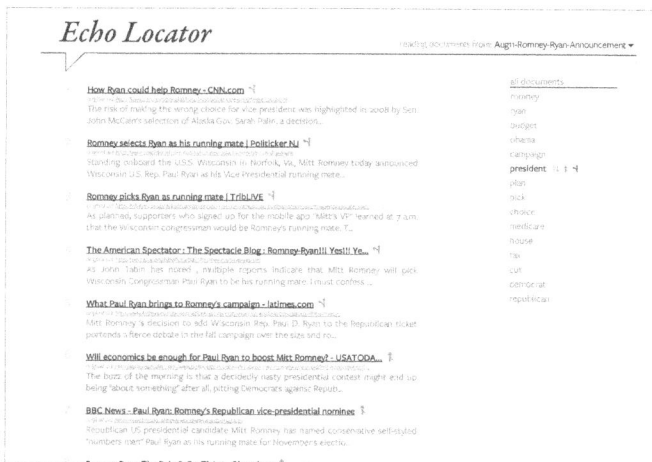

Figure 1: Screenshot of User Interacting with Echo Locator
Screenshot shows documents that have opinions on the subject "President" sorted by how Out-Of-Line their opinions on the president are. Corpus can be switched by clicking the corpus name in the top right corner of the UI.

a content consumption perspective they are unusable, misrepresentative, and inferior to simple sorted lists [21, 26, 36, 19]. An alternative Tag Cloud visual summarizations are systems that utilize textual summaries/synopsis[29, 25] or key quote lists (e.g. Yelp or Amazon.com) to provide smoother, more natural means of conveying key critical information and assisting users in finding salient information. While text summaries are useful for generally understanding a corpus at a high level, they do not help users trace those summaries back to specific documents/opinions; nor do they allow users to traverse a document space itself. Further, none of these approaches allow interaction based on opinion alignment or divergence from those of the crowd[1] It is in the space of these unfulfilled needs that we situate our work on Echo.

IMPLICATIONS FOR DESIGN
From on the above literature in reading, memory and HCI, we can distill a set of four design guidelines:

G1 Contextual Cues: Leverage contextual cues such that users can recall information easier [9, 30]

G2 Planning Phase: Help readers quickly find important facts with little cognitive effort [32] from a range of opinions from the perspective most applicable to a given user's needs

G3 Callouts: Leverage visual callouts [16, 32] to help users find key information in the document text

G4 Alignment: allow users to find opinions and documents based on relation to crowd's opinion (unlike existing solutions which focus on summary only)[33]

SCOPE & MOTIVATION

[1]Rather, opinion sentiment itself are treated as the end deliverable (e.g. stating that the "beds" were rated positively in hotel reviews).

Echo is not a document or corpus summarization tool, nor is the underlying algorithm performing summarization. Rather, Echo is the first algorithm and a UI for opinion alignment. Echo places individual opinions in document context and crowd context, allowing users to quickly find those opinions. Unlike existing approaches that display documents side-by-side, or focus on summarizing a document or corpus at a birds-eye level (visually and algorithmically), Echo takes an orthogonal approach. We allow a user to read any document in their corpus as they normally would, with crucial opinions in *each* document brought to attention akin to a magazine's metaphor. Given the broad set of potential applications of Echo, the system can consume and render any type of document (e.g. blogs, online news, forums, reports, court documents) or format (e.g. HTML, PDF, DOC).

In this paper, we will refer to these visual distortions that are used to highlight key opinions as **Callouts**. Traditionally, an editor would make a series of subjective decisions on what to call out, and how to bring each word or phrase to the reader's attention. This is an expensive process, time consuming, and the decisions are entirely subjective. Echo automates this process by gathering the collective intelligence of the crowd (via a corpus of documents), distilling what "the crowd" is talking about, and noting what opinions the crowd have about the main topics. Echo then visually distorts the text of a document, bringing to the user's attention the key opinions in *each* document. In this paper, we will refer to key opinions that are representative of the crowd as **Representative** opinions, and well as opinions that go against the grain as **Out-Of-Line** opinions. A weighting algorithm determines the degree to which each opinion is visually brought to the forefront or left in the periphery, based on how important each topic is, and how much an opinion is in-line or out-of-line with the crowd.

ECHO
Echo is comprised of three key components: the **Echo Reader**, the UI that a user sees when they read a given document in a corpus; the **Echo Locator**, which is the UI that allows a user to browse the corpus of documents (and open them in the Echo Reader) based on both topic and opinion representativeness; and the **Echo System**, which is the backend algorithm and system that performs the data mining analysis of the document corpus. The UI is HTML based, and is rendered in a web browser. In the following section, we detail the Echo Reader and the Echo Locator UI interactions as perceived by the user. The section following the UI discussion covers the specifics of *how* the underlying Echo System makes its calculations and models. Echo has been tested on political and financial reports, as well as the more mundane domain of movie reviews.

DESIGN & INTERACTION
We designed the first-load form of a document in Echo to require no explicit user interaction while still providing a majority of the benefits of the Echo System's analysis. Yet with simple and non-intrusive mouse-hovers, documents in Echo can become an interactive and exploratory experience.

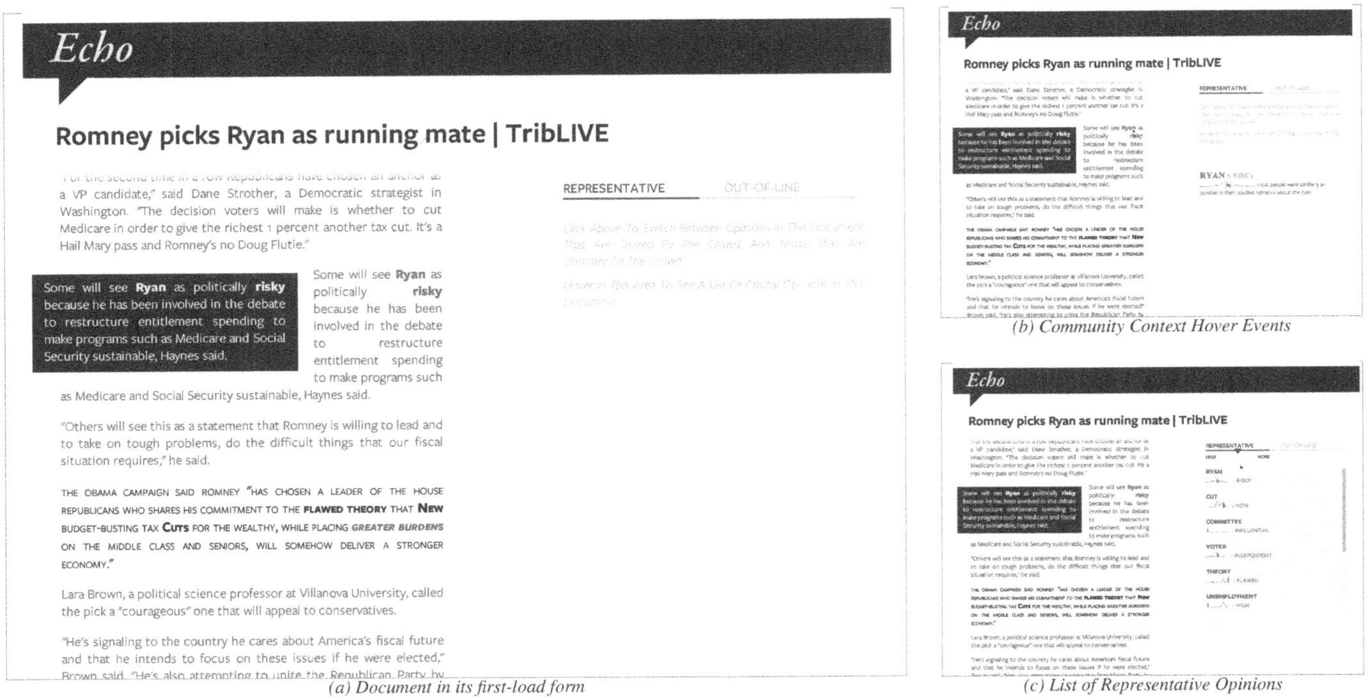

Romney picks Ryan as running mate | TribLIVE

For the second time in a row Republicans have chosen an anchor as a VP candidate," said Dane Strother, a Democratic strategist in Washington. "The decision voters will make is whether to cut Medicare in order to give the richest 1 percent another tax cut. It's a Hail Mary pass and Romney's no Doug Flutie."

Some will see **Ryan** as politically **risky** because he has been involved in the debate to restructure entitlement spending to make programs such as Medicare and Social Security sustainable, Haynes said.

Some will see **Ryan** as politically **risky** because he has been involved in the debate to restructure entitlement spending to make programs such as Medicare and Social Security sustainable, Haynes said.

"Others will see this as a statement that Romney is willing to lead and to take on tough problems, do the difficult things that our fiscal situation requires," he said.

THE OBAMA CAMPAIGN SAID ROMNEY "HAS CHOSEN A LEADER OF THE HOUSE REPUBLICANS WHO SHARES HIS COMMITMENT TO THE **FLAWED THEORY** THAT **NEW** BUDGET-BUSTING TAX **CUTS** FOR THE WEALTHY, WHILE PLACING *GREATER BURDENS* ON THE MIDDLE CLASS AND SENIORS, WILL SOMEHOW DELIVER A STRONGER ECONOMY."

Lara Brown, a political science professor at Villanova University, called the pick a "courageous" one that will appeal to conservatives.

"He's signaling to the country he cares about America's fiscal future and that he intends to focus on these issues if he were elected," Brown said. "He's also attempting to unite the Republican Party by

(a) Document in its first-load form

(b) Community Context Hover Events

(c) List of Representative Opinions

Figure 2: Three Screenshots of a User Interacting with a Document in the Echo Reader
From corpus of political articles about the August 11th 2012 Romney nomination of Paul Ryan.
These are high resolution screenshots, and can be zoomed in when viewed digitally.

We illustrate the functionality and features of the Echo Reader and Echo Locator through a scenario that follows Fran, a political analyst. To illustrate the breadth of the features in the Echo Reader and Echo Locator, the following scenario is overly extensive to cover multiple approaches and uses of Echo. In practice, users can apply any subset of the following techniques, at any time, in any order or any type of data source.

Fran is a political analyst for the WeSaySo TV News Network. Fran is working on a story about Republican presidential candidate Mitt Romney's selection of Paul Ryan as his running mate in the 2012 US election. To get a handle on what the news media is saying about this announcement, she loads a document corpus of political news articles related to the announcement into Echo. Fran first needs to get a general sense of, "what are people saying?"

Corpus Browsing with Echo Locator
Fran begins by loading her document corpus into Echo, and opening up the Echo Locator user interface (Figure 1). Fran really wants to see those documents that have the most representative opinions so she can get a high level view of the document space. The Echo Locator interface will allow Fran to browse her entire corpus of over 300 documents quickly and easily by mitigating information overload.

On page-load, Fran can see all documents in the corpus sorted alphabetically. For each document, its title, original URL (source of the content), and a a preview of the body copy is shown. Along the right side of the user interface are the

words "all documents," followed by a list of all the subjects of discussion sorted by how important the subject is within the corpus. This list is scrollable upon hover. Should she wish to filter the document space, Fran can click any subject (or "all documents") to show only documents that have opinions on the clicked subject. The currently selected filter (or "all documents") is in dark gray. Whichever subject (or "all documents") that is selected, three sort controls appear to its right. By clicking on any of these icons, the current list of documents is filtered alphabetically (default) $\updownarrow$, by how Representative they are on the given subject ($\uparrow$) or how Out-Of-Line they are on the current subject ($\searrow$). The opinion based sorts are in defending order, so that the most Representative/Out-Of-Line document is at the top[2].

Because Fran wishes to gather the best "high level" view on this corpus, she leaves the filter as "all documents," and re-orders the list based on how Representative they are by clicking the $\uparrow$ icon (G4). Skimming the list, Fran can then opens a documents at the top of the list that catch her eye.

Page-load and Crucial Opinion Call-Outs
Upon page-load in Echo Reader, the document appears like any standard web-based article that has been laid out well by an Editor (Figure 2A). Some of the document's most Representative opinions are called out for Fran's attention (G3).

---

[2] The Echo Locator places a small icon to the right of each title to indicate for the given filter, if the document is Representative ($\uparrow$) or Out-Of-Line ($\searrow$) on the specific subject.

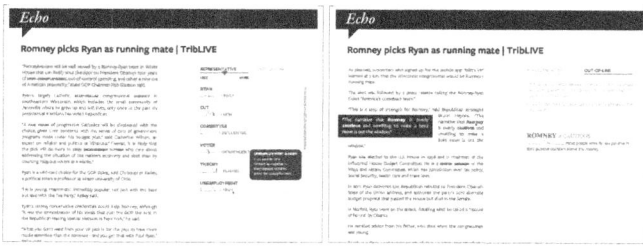

(a) Interactions with Opinion List   (b) Out-Of-Line Opinions

Figure 3: Additional User Interactions with Echo Reader
High resolution screenshots can be zoomed in when viewed digitally.

The degree of visual callout is proportional to how important the subject is, and how Representative the opinion is.

Thus, from the moment a page loads, Fran does not need to interact with the document and can still reap a large portion of Echo's benefits by scanning and reading the text as she normally would (G2). Immediately, Fran quickly scrolls through the document and quickly finds the most representative opinion in the document, which is brought to her attention in a black box (G3). Less noteworthy opinions are brought to her attention in a smaller degree visually, through the use of small caps, bold, italic, or even darker shades of gray based on the hierarchy of visual and typographic changes by Bringhurst[10]. The less the body copy is called out, the less Representative the opinion is. This allows Fran to quickly check the pulse of the community within the context of the document she is reading, for any particular opinion she encounters. By borrowing well known style metaphors from magazine layouts, the Echo Reader directly facilitates Fran's planning phase (G2), incidental and contextual memory (G1).

Community Context Hover Events

After scanning the document, Fran is intrigued by the comment that, "Some will see [Paul] Ryan as politically risky..." which was called out in a black box. To find out exactly why this is opinion is so Representative, Fran moves her cursor on top of the phrase in the text. Upon hovering, a sparkline[42] and english sentence explanation situating this opinion in the broader context appears on the right side of the page (Figure 2B). The sparkline allows Fran to see the distribution of opinion sentiments on the subject of Ryan across all documents in the corpus (G4): the negative part of the distribution appear in red, the positive in blue, and neutral in gray:

RYAN *is* RISKY

most people were similarly as
positive in their positive opinions about the *ryan*

The portion of the distribution which contains this particular opinion on Ryan (which is just slightly more positive than neutral) is filled in with dark blue. This allows Fran to visually place opinions within a given document in the broader context of the corpus/crowd.

Opinion Sliders

Upon load, the Echo Reader calls a subset of all Representative opinions to the reader's attention. Because Fran wishes to get the broadest overview of the crowd's opinions (G4),

she wants to see more of the Representative opinions in this document. She moves her cursor over the right hand side of the screen, and a slider under the word Representative fades in (Figure 2C). Fran can use this slider to adjust (more or less) the amount of Representative opinion callouts in the text. Increasing this slider causes new callouts to emerge which, though still Representative, are on somewhat less important subjects, or situated slightly further away from the mean community opinion on the topic.

Opinion Overview List

After spot-exploring a handful of opinion callouts in the document, Fran wants to see an overview of *this* document's Representative opinions. She once again moves her cursor over the right hand side of the screen. During a slightly longer hover event (as compared to the shorter hover event that produced the opinion sliders), a scrollable list of Representative opinions then appears (Figure 2C). The list consists of a series of subjects, with the modifying opinions appearing below the subject (G2). If Fran now manipulates the slider under the word Representative, not only would more/less opinions callouts appear in the text, but more/less opinions would populate this list. When the document has more than one opinion on a subject, they both appear bellow the subject word:

CUT
_/ᴠᴌ ᵢₛ DEEP
_/ᴠᴌ ᵢₛ NEW

Each opinion appears in italic, and has a opinion distribution sparkline next to it. Fran can now find noteworthy opinions she may have missed. Because each opinion in the list corresponds to a specific word/sentence in the text, when Fran hovers over an opinion in the list, the Echo Reader auto scrolls to where that opinion occurred in the text, highlights the sentence with the opinion (in yellow like a highlighter) and provides an brief english sentence explanation situating this opinion in the broader context[3] (Figure 3a). Highlighting or pointing to text from a list has been empirically shown to be a powerful interaction to improve document browsing[16]. Thus with this overview and interaction, Fran can quickly survey the Representative opinions in this document, quickly gauge their sentiment, see the document context, and place the opinions within the spectrum of the crowd's.

Out-Of-Line Opinions

Now that Fran has a good grasp on this document's Representative opinions, she wants to see where this document differs from the crowd (G4). Next to the word Representative on the right hand side of the Echo Reader, is a grayed-out word Out-Of-Line. By clicking on Out-Of-Line, the Echo Reader switches from bringing Representative opinions to the reader's attention, to calling out Out-Of-Line opinions. Fran now can visually see the contrasting opinions in the document (Figure 3b) through visual callouts. Just as with the Representative opinions, she can use community context hover events in the body copy (Figure 3b), explore with a summary list, and move the Out-Of-Line slider to adjust the amount of callout. By keeping Representative and Out-Of-Line opinions

---

[3]This is the same text that appear in the community context hover events, but without the sparkline.

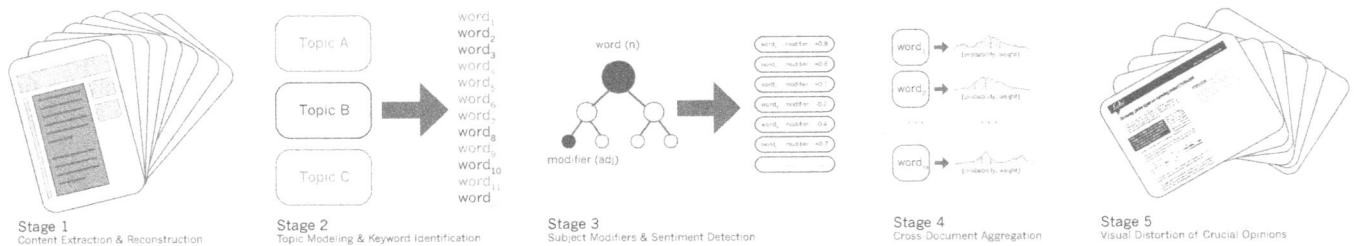

Figure 4: Echo Five-Stage Algorithm Overview

separate through two modes, the Echo Reader avoids confusion as to what type of opinion callout (or what element in the list) is currently being shown.

Continued Exploration

When Fran finishes reading her document, she wishes to continue exploring the corpus by returning to the Echo Locator (Figure 1). After reading the first document, Fran has decided she needs more information about how people talk about the office of the president. She quickly filters her list of documents by clicking on the word "president," and gets an alphabetically sorted list of documents that have opinions of the topic "president." To signify the filter is active, "all documents" becomes light gray, and "president" darkens. Fran can now re-sort her list, find documents that are highly Out-Of-Line or Representative of the crowd's opinion on the president, and begin reading those documents in the Echo Reader.

IMPLEMENTATION

The Echo interface is built in HTML, CSS and JavaScript. Document corpora undergo a Java-based five-stage algorithm, the (Echo System), in order to generate the Echo UI (Figure 3): 1) Content Extraction & Reconstruction; 2) Topic Modeling & Keyword Identification; 3) Subject Modifiers & Sentiment Detection; 4) Cross-Document Aggregation; and, 5) Visual Distortion of Crucial Opinions. Figure 4 presents a overview of the five-stage process.

It should be noted that the Echo System assumes that a corpus of documents (PDFs or links to webpages) on the same subject have been collected.[4]

Stage 1. Content Extraction & Reconstruction
Finding The Text in Each Document, and Building Indexable Content

First, we must crawl and clean every document in a corpus to identify the body copy[5]. Body copy is needed to perform the ML analysis and generate the re-rendered document in Echo.

PDF body copy extraction[3] is relatively easy, as most PDF documents do not contain copious amounts of non-body copy

---

[4]Grouping and clustering articles by subject matters is an active area of research for those in the IR and ML communities, and is outside the scope of this work. The Echo System implementation does have a crawler for recent Google News stories and a PDF uploader so as to facilitate the core contributions of Echo itself.

[5]*Body copy* is a term from the layout and design community used to describe the main text of a document, as compared to logos, images, title, advertisements, comments etc.

material. Unlike PDFs, web content is not as "clean." The raw HTML for any given webpage has navigation elements, ads, comments, or other non body copy content. Further complicating body copy extraction is that every webpage uses different CSS markup for its content. While templates, hand-coded or auto-generated, are often used to identify body copy [6], the number of templates needed would grow quite large. Consider the diversity of the set of all sources from a Google News query. In response, we utilized the CETR algorithm [43] which extracts body-copy from webpages using HTML tag ratios and multidimensional clustering. Thus, we can extract body-copy from any source, whether it has seen a given layout before or not.

Once the body copy of a given document is extracted, we reconstruct each document fully marking-up the content, with each sentence and word[6] within a distinct HTML <span>. Thus, any element of text can be easily found using JavaScript lookups, so that their visual weight can be modified.

Stage 2. Topic Modeling & Keyword Identification
Finding What the Corpus is Talking About

Next we attempt to identify *what* the articles within a given corpus are talking about. We limit our word selection to Nouns, as they are generally considered the "subject" of a sentence, by applying POS tagging[2] as a filter[7]. With filtered documents, we apply Latent Dirichlet Allocation (LDA) topic modeling[31] to extract topics and associated keywords across all documents.

LDA topic modeling considers each document as being the outcome of a mix of topics which each generate some portion of the document's content. In order explain our use of LDA, consider T to be the set of all topics ($t_0 \ldots t_k$), D to be the set of all documents in our corpus ($d_0 \ldots d_l$), and W to be the set of all unique words ($w_0 \ldots w_m$) across all documents. Every document (d_i) consists of a subset of words from W. Every topic (t_j) consists of a subset of words from W, each with a probability $P(w_q|t_j)$ that if a word is randomly chosen from t_j, it is that particular word (w_q). In this way, t_j is a probability distribution over W:

$$\sum_{q=0}^{m} P(w_q|t_j) = 1 \qquad (1)$$

---

[6]Sentence and Word detection is done through use parser from [41].
[7]While an alternative to filtering by Noun could be Named Entity Recognition[17], entity disambiguation is an open challenge, and we opted to utilize a more conservative approach.

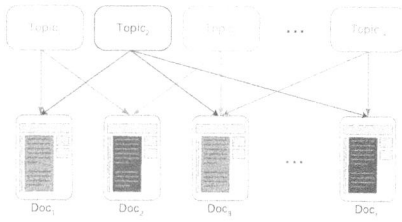

Figure 5: Latent Dirichlet Allocation (LDA)

and a document (d_i) consists of a probability distribution over all topics T:

$$\sum_{j=0}^{k} P(t_j|d_i) = 1 \qquad (2)$$

In layman's terms, every word in a document is contributed by one of the topics.

Our goal is to rank order all words in W based on how "important" they are across all topics and documents. LDA gives us the rank ($P(w_q|t_j)$) of each word (w_q) given a particular topic (t_j). However, these word probabilities cannot be compared across topics as they are conditional. We therefore marginalize out the topics for each word:

$$P(w_q) = \sum_{j=0}^{k} P(w_q|t_j)P(t_j) \qquad (3)$$

This calculates for each word a rank that is topic independent, and therefore valid across our document corpus. This ranking provides the most important subjects of discussion in the corpus.

Stage 3. Subject Modifiers & Sentiment Detection
Finding the Opinions on Key Subjects

Next we attempt to identify the opinions on each of the important subjects of discussion. We apply a statistical parser[15] to each sentence in each document, generating a full parse tree, a dependence parse tree, and the part of speech for each word. These sentence parse trees are akin to sentence diagraming done in grade school. From these parse trees we can programmatically uncover which modifiers (e.g. adjectives) were applied to any sentence subject.

For each modifier uncovered, we calculate a sentiment score by looking up its value in Senti-WordNet[5]. Senti-WordNet is a hand-compiled list covering a large selection of common word modifiers. Each word is evaluated on two 0.0-1.0 scales, Positive and Negative. We maintain both positive and negative values because if combined on a single scale, on average, most results would trend towards neutral. Modifier lookup does not have word sense disambiguation (context). However, it does allow us to explicitly associate a modifier with a subject in a sentence. Thus we are able to calculate the opinion on a subject within a sentence, rather than the holistic sentiment of the entire sentence.

During the sentiment analysis stage, we also identify negations in the parse tree, so we can invert the opinion of the modified subject. For example, in the phrase *"the stock is*

not a good buy," the subject "stock" is modified by "good." However there is a negation - "not" - requiring us to swap the opinion's positive and negative scores.

Thus, for each of the important subjects in Stage 2 (w_q), we uncover the set of opinions $O(w_q)=[o_1(w_q)\ldots o_n(w_q)]$ within each sentence where the subject occurs.

Stage 4. Cross-Document Aggregation
Finding the Opinion Trends Across the Corpus

Next, we aggregate all opinions on each subject over all documents. First we find all instances of each subject by computing the base form of each word[41] and americanizing all spelling. Thus, for a given corpus, we have a weighted list of subjects (from stage 2) and for each subject a distribution of opinions (from stage 3).

From these per-subject distributions ($O(w_q)$), we can calculate a mean positive $\mu_{pos}(w_q)$ and negative sentiment $\mu_{neg}(w_q)$, as well as the standard deviation $\sigma_{pos}(w_q)$ and $\sigma_{neg}(w_q)$. We refer to this mean as the crowd's opinion on a given subject. For each subject-opinion instance in each document $o_v(w_q)$, we calculate that instance's distance:

$$F_{pos}(o_v(w_q)) = \frac{|o_{pos,v}(w_q) - \mu_{pos}(w_q)|}{\sigma_{pos}(w_q)}$$

$$F_{neg}(o_v(w_q)) = \frac{|o_{neg,v}(w_q) - \mu_{neg}(w_q)|}{\sigma_{neg}(w_q)} \qquad (4)$$

$$F(o_v(w_q)) = <F_{pos}(o_v(w_q)), F_{neg}(o_v(w_q)) >$$

We therefore consider a specific subject-opinion to be "representative" of the crowd if the opinion's distance is less than or equal to one (within one SD). If the opinion distance is greater than one, we consider the subject-opinion to be "out of line" from the crowd.

Stage 5: Visual Distortion of Crucial Opinions
Showing the User Crucial Opinions

Finally, for each document, we must determine what subject-opinions should be called out, and how much to visually bring them to the user's attention. From Stages 1-4, every subject-opinion $o_v(w_q)$ has an importance value $P(w_q)$ and an opinion distance $F(o_v(w_q))$. To find the most crucial "representative" and "out of line" subject-opinions, we use the following ranking equations:

$$F_L(o_v(w_q)) = MAX(F_{pos}(o_v(w_q)), F_{neg}(o_v(w_q)))$$
$$R_{out}(o_v(w_q)) \propto P(w_q) * F_L(o_v(w_q))$$
$$R_{rep}(o_v(w_q)) \propto \frac{P(w_q)}{F_L(o_v(w_q))} \qquad (5)$$

Based on the rankings in Equation 5, within each document, we place each subject-opinion instance in a ranked-tier (separately for both representative and out of line subject-opinions): 1) Normalize the ranking values of all subject-opinions in the document; 2) Sort the normalized ranking values in defending order; 3) Based on cumulative sum, distribute the subject-opinion instances into 10 tiers, such that each tier must have at least as many words as the tier index (at least one word in tier one, two words in tier two, etc).

While the user specifies *which* tier of subject-opinions is called out via the UI sliders, the rendering of said call out is determined by the relative importance of typeface/weights combinations [10]. Robert Bringhurst outlines the hierarchy of visual and typographic changes that can be made to text to call salient information to the user's attention at various degrees. For tiers 2-10, we adhere closely to [10], visually distorting the subject and modifiers in the crucial opinions. Tier 1 (being the most crucial "representative" or "out of line" opinion) is additionally called out by the entire sentence containing the subject and modifier, being replicated in a black box with white type. This extreme, though sparse, callout parallels the large callouts commonly found in magazine articles. Any element of text in the body copy that needs to be visually distorted or undistorted, can be easily found using the tags created in Stage 1, during the document recreation.

This same ranking algorithm (5) is used for the Echo Locator UI generation. To sort documents by how representative or out-of-line they are, we simply sum all rankings on a given subject within a document to get a document level rank. For cross subject rankings, we sum across all subject-opinions in a document. By using sum, rather than mean, we give more weight to documents that have many representative or out-of-line opinions, rather than just one strongly opinion.

INITIAL USER REACTIONS

In order to explore the benefits of and the reaction to Echo, we conducted a preliminary pilot study to evaluate the reaction to and value of this approach. We gauged the user reaction, and examined the initial interaction with the Echo UI related to aspects of information overload, and discovery so as to support the main contribution of this work, our system and algorithm.

To ecologically ground our pilot study, we recruited 12 knowledge workers (eight female and three male, ages 33 to 56) from a large US corporation (3 from the legal department, 4 administrative assistants and 5 from marketing and outreach). All of our participants reported using large collections of documents daily or a few-times a week, with self reported average corpus size of 1,262 documents. None of the participants had prior knowledge of, or experience with, Echo.

To provide further grounding, our study task followed O'Hara [32] and Winograd[44] who suggest that text summarization requires a deep understanding of text, relates to the skills required to comprehend a document space, and has a "strong connection with many of the kinds of reading tasks... knowledge workers [carry] out" [32]. Further, to demonstrate the breadth of the Echo, we demonstrated its use with 3 data sets from 3 different domains during this experiment.

Dependent and Independent Measures

This experiment followed a within subject design that manipulated one independent variable, the UI for reading documents, which consisted of two levels 1) The Echo Reader UI (referred to as the *Echo Condition*) and 2) A plain text UI with the same general layout and typeface as the Echo

Reader without any call-outs or interactive components (referred to as the *Traditional Condition*)[8]. The primary dependent variable measure was the time taken to read a small collection of (5) documents with each UI. Given the small size of our dataset, we utilized a Two-Sample Wilcoxon Rank-Sum (Mann-Whitney) test, a more conservative metric than the Student's T-Test as it makes no assumptions about the data distribution. In addition, we also recorded the user's screen and administered questionnaires to understand users' interactions, satisfaction and preferences.

Set-up & Methods

Participants were first presented with the Echo Locator UI and the Google News UI as two methods for finding a document in a corpus. They were then asked to complete a brief questionnaire focused on how they navigate document collections, and how each of the just demonstrated UIs could benefit their own work. The document collection was a corpus of financial analyst articles about the August 8th HP announcement that the company was writing down the value of its enterprise-services business by $8 billion, and changing people in upper management. While gaining feedback on Echo Locator was valuable, the primary purpose of this phase was to situate the task of reading documents in a large corpus.

Next, participants were shown the Echo Reader UI using the same dataset. Following the opportunity to explore the UI or ask questions, participants were asked to read two sets of five documents,[9] each on a different topic. One document set was a collection of movie reviews about the 2009 film *Star Trek*, and the other was a collection of political news articles about the pick of Paul Ryan as Mitt Romney's running mate in the 2012 US election.

For each participant, one set of five documents was in the *Echo Condition* and the other was in the *Traditional Condition*. The assignment of topic and presentation order was counterbalanced across participants to mitigate ordering and topic effects. Thus, there were four possible combinations of topic and order, and each group had three participants.

Based on the readings of the two sets of documents, participants were then asked to write a 2-3 sentence summary of the opinions within each set. After completing the summaries, participants were asked to complete a questionnaire about their experience with both interfaces. The experiment was run using a full-screen Chrome Browser on a 24" monitor. On average, the study took 45 minutes per participant.

Quantitative Results

For each participant, the total time to read each set of five documents was calculated in order to control for potential differences between each individual document. Document reading with the Echo Reader had a mean time of 466.08 seconds (σ=226.87) while reading with the Traditional UI had a mean time of 289.75 seconds (σ=116.92). Statistical

---

[8]The articles in both conditions used the same layout, typography, and sizing. Thus, users were comparing interactivity and highlights not UI design.

[9]Each set of 5 documents were drawn from a collection of over 100 documents fed into Echo.

	Mean	(SD)
In Terms of Ease of Use, Which was Better? †	1.25	(0.62)
In Terms of Usefulness, Which was Better? †	1.08	(0.29)
Which Would Give the Most Benefit for Your Own Work? †	1.17	(0.58)
Which Was Best for Making Sense of a Document Collection? †	1.25	(0.62)
How Helpful were Callouts in Finding Key Information? ‡	4.42	(1.16)
How Well Did the Callouts Pick Important Information? ‡	4.17	(1.11)

Table 1: Reader UI Comparisons
Rated From: † 1 = Echo, 3 = neutral, 5 = Traditional UI
Rated From: ‡ 1 = "Not at All," 5 = "Extremely"

significant differences were found (Wilcoxon Rank-Sum) between the two UIs ($p=0.02$), though there appeared to be no order effects ($p=0.27$) nor topic effects ($p=0.21$).[10] Participants were asked to rate their satisfaction with the two UIs and the value of callouts (Table 1). In addition, when examining the videos, 10 of the users employed the Community Context Hover Events, 10 of the users employed the Opinion Overview List, and 9 users clicked to view the Out-Of-Line opinions. When using the Echo Reader, two of our participants' entire method of document reading was traversing the opinions using the Opinion Overview List, and letting the document auto-scroll. While it did appear that many users performed an initial scroll through of the document in Echo Reader looking for key callouts, we are hesitant to include a quantitative count, since we are unable to categorically state that this was the users' intent.

Qualitative Results & Discussion

Participants were overwhelmingly positive in their quantitative and qualitative feedback regarding Echo:

Wow, that was really really great... You know when you're in school, and you buy a used book thats been highlighted. You have to hope that its an A student [that highlighted it], not a D student.... its almost like you are cheating. - P2

When participants were asked why they thought they took longer with the Echo Reader, responses tended to focus on not missing information, ease of finding information, and taking advantage of Echo's intelligence;

[I]t was easier to note the essential information and I spent more time lingering on it and thinking about it than when I was trying to wade through lots of homogeneous material - P11

I wanted to make sure that I got the key point of the callouts and it led me to want to see the opinions associated with the callouts. - P5

While our data showed that reading with Echo took longer, half of the participants did not notice this difference and were surprised that Echo took longer. P4 stated that she thought the Echo Reader was *"faster and [gave a] more accurate summary of keywords than skimming."* This suggests that the reading experience with Echo was not only more powerful, but users did not feel that it was tedious or were wasting their time on the unnecessary information in the documents. This would need to be confirmed in a longer-term study.

---

[10]Lack of significance does not mean lack of statistical difference.

In addition, we asked participants to come up with applications of the Echo Reader and Echo Locator interaction models. Most participants suggested applications in the legal domain (litigation, and IP), medical, finance, education, and news aggregators. When asked if there were any benefits to the traditional UI, participants generally focused on being "forced to read the whole thing," and drawing their own conclusions on document text without bias from the crowd.

It is important to note that while the individual algorithmic components in Echo make use of straightforward approaches from the ML and NLP domains, participants explicitly stated that the callouts were helpful and appeared to pick out key information well. We strongly believe that this is due to the power of aggregating opinions based on the wisdom of the crowd, combining both subject importance in a topic model with sentiment detection and delta from the mean.

LIMITATIONS & FUTURE WORK

While the Echo System employed standard Machine Learning techniques, there are more powerful topic and sentiment tools that exist on the "bleeding edge." As we continue to develop Echo, we'll seek to improve the Echo System algorithm with more advanced techniques for sentiment analysis (taking sentence context into account), keyword extraction (with n-gram phrases and Named Entity Recognition) and topic modeling (combining supervised and unsupervised techniques). However, participants did report that the callouts were highly accurate, even with our current approaches.

Another direction of future work would be the inclusion of document traversal in the Echo Reader, such that users could select a called out keyword, and request to see a list of documents that further support, or go against that opinion. In addition, based on feedback from users in our Pilot Study, we wish to include in keyword search in Echo Locator, allowing users to filter based on topics as well as keywords. These additional features would expand both the usability of Echo, and the ability of users to traverse their datasets.

Given the small size of this pilot study, our initial investigation is not intended as a validation of Echo. rather to gauge initial Echo's potential utility. We would like to perform a long-term ecological valid study of Echo, integrating it within a corporate or legal environment allowing us to better understand how impact on job performance.

CONCLUSION

In the information age, it is often hard to sort out the relevant information that one needs to pay attention to. With so many sources of documents at our digital fingertips, we enjoy enormous diversity of sources but at the cost of suffering from a poverty of attention. In this paper, we provide a novel automated system and interface to help users navigate and find relevant content when foraging for information. This system, Echo, leverages the "wisdom of the crowd," to create elegant magazine-style interfaces to documents. Through natural layout and typographic techniques, key information that can be displayed in any platform is brought to the attention of users. This is an important consideration, given that the problem with attention is often exacerbated by the small visual real estate of small devices such as smart phones. Further, positive results from a pilot study offer support for the benefits offered by Echo's design. Thus, the foremost contribution of this work is a interaction model and algorithmic approach that allows users to place each document and opinion within the larger echo of voices.

REFERENCES

1. Adar, E., and Huberman, B. A. The economics of surfing. *Quarterly Journal of Electronic Commerce* (2000).

2. Aphache.org. Apache OpenNLP.

3. Aphache.org. Apache PDFBox.

4. Archak, N., Ghose, A., and Ipeirotis, P. G. Show me the money!: deriving the pricing power of product features by mining consumer reviews. In *KDD '07*, ACM Request Permissions (Aug. 2007).

5. Baccianella, S., Esuli, A., and Sebastiani, F. Sentiwordnet 3.0: An enhanced lexical resource for sentiment analysis and opinion mining. In *Proceedings of the 7th Conference on Language Resources and Evaluation* (2010).

6. Bar-Yossef, Z., and Rajagopalan, S. Template detection via data mining and its applications. In *the eleventh international conference*, ACM Press (New York, New York, USA, 2002), 580.

7. Baudisch, P., Lee, B., and Hanna, L. Fishnet, a fisheye web browser with search term popouts: a comparative evaluation with overview and linear view. In *AVI '04: Proceedings of the working conference on Advanced visual interfaces*, ACM (May 2004).

8. Billsus, D., Hilbert, D. M., and Maynes-Aminzade, D. Improving proactive information systems. In *the 10th international conference*, ACM Press (New York, New York, USA, 2005), 159–166.

9. Bjork, R. A., and Richardson-Klavehn, A. *On the puzzling relationship between environmental context and human memory*. Lawrence Erlbaum Associates, Inc, 1989.

10. Bringhurst, R. *The Elements of Typographic Style*, 3rd ed. Hartley and Marks Publishers, Oct. 2004.

11. Brush, A. J. B., Bargeron, D., Gupta, A., and Cadiz, J. J. Robust Annotation Positioning in Digital Documents . In *the SIGCHI conference*, ACM Press (New York, New York, USA, 2001), 285–292.

12. Carenini, G., Ng, R. T., and Pauls, A. Interactive Multimedia Summaries of Evaluative Text . In *the 11th International Conference*, ACM Press (New York, New York, USA, 2006), 124.

13. Chakravarthy, M., and Ciravegna, P. Cross-media document annotation and enrichment.

14. Davies, S., Allen, S., Raphaelson, J., Meng, E., Engleman, J., King, R., and Lewis, C. Popcorn: the personal knowledge base. In *the 6th ACM conference*, ACM Press (New York, New York, USA, 2006), 150–159.

15. De Marneffe, M. C., and MacCartney, B. Generating typed dependency parses from phrase structure parses. In *Proceedings of LREC '06* (2006).

16. Dillon, A., Richardson, J., and McKnight, C. Navigation in hypertext: a critical review of the concept. *Navigation* (1990).

17. Finkel, J. R., Grenager, T., and Manning, C. Incorporating non-local information into information extraction systems by gibbs sampling. *ACL'05* (2005).

18. Ganesan, K. A., Sundaresan, N., and Deo, H. Mining tag clouds and emoticons behind community feedback. In *WWW '08*, ACM (Apr. 2008).

19. Halvey, M. J., and Keane, M. T. An Assessment of Tag Presentation Techniques . In *the 16th international conference*, ACM Press (New York, New York, USA, 2007), 1313.

20. Hearst, M. A. User interfaces and visualization. *Modern information retrieval* (1999).

21. Hearst, M. A., and Rosner, D. Tag clouds: Data analysis tool or social signaller? … *on System Sciences* (2008).

22. Huberman, B. A., Pirolli, P., Pitkow, J., and Lukose, R. Strong Regularities in World Wide Web Surfing. *Science 280*, 5360 (Apr. 1998), 95–97.

23. Huberman, B. A., and Wu, F. The economics of attention: Maximizing user value in information-rich environments. *Advances in Complex Systems* (2008).

24. Keppel, G., and Underwood, B. J. Proactive inhibition in short-term retention of single items. *Journal of Verbal Learning and Verbal Behavior* (1962).

25. Kriplean, T., Morgan, J., Freelon, D., Borning, A., and Bennett, L. Supporting reflective public thought with considerit. In *CSCW '12*, ACM Request Permissions (Feb. 2012).

26. Kuo, B. Y.-L., Hentrich, T., Good, B. M., and Wilkinson, M. D. Tag clouds for summarizing web search results. In *the 16th international conference*, ACM (May 2007).

27. Lee, S. E., Chun, T., and Han, S. S. Using Qtag to Extract Dominant Public Opinion in Very Large-Scale Conversation. In *2009 International Conference on Computational Science and Engineering*, IEEE (2009), 753–758.

28. Lee, S. E., Son, D. K., and Han, S. S. Qtag: tagging as a means of rating, opinion-expressing, sharing and visualizing. In *SIGDOC '07*, ACM Request Permissions (Oct. 2007).

29. Liu, B., Hu, M., and Cheng, J. Opinion observer: analyzing and comparing opinions on the Web. In *the 14th international conference*, ACM Press (New York, New York, USA, 2005), 342.

30. Marshall, C. Saving and using encountered information: implications for electronic periodicals. In *CHI'05* (2005).

31. McCallum, A. K. Mallet: A machine learning for language toolkit.

32. O'Hara, K., and Sellen, A. A Comparison of Reading Paper and On-Line Documents. In *the SIGCHI conference*, ACM Press (New York, New York, USA, 1997), 335–342.

33. Otterbacher, J., Radev, D., and Kareem, O. News to go: hierarchical text summarization for mobile devices. In *SIGIR '06* (2006).

34. Park, S., Kang, S., Chung, S., and Song, J. NewsCube: delivering multiple aspects of news to mitigate media bias. In *CHI '09: Proceedings of the 27th international conference on Human factors in computing systems*, ACM Request Permissions (Apr. 2009).

35. Park, S., Ko, M., Kim, J., Liu, Y., and Song, J. The Politics of Comments: Predicting Political Orientation of News Stories with Commenters' Sentiment Patterns. In *the ACM 2011 conference*, ACM Press (New York, New York, USA, 2011), 113.

36. Rivadeneira, A. W., Gruen, D. M., Muller, M. J., and Millen, D. R. Getting our head in the clouds: toward evaluation studies of tagclouds. In *CHI '07: Proceedings of the SIGCHI conference on Human factors in computing systems*, ACM Request Permissions (Apr. 2007).

37. Sereno, B., Shum, S. B., and Motta, E. ClaimSpotter: an environment to support sensemaking with knowledge triples. In *the 10th international conference*, ACM Request Permissions (Jan. 2005).

38. Simon, H. A. Designing organizations for an information-rich world. *Computers, Communication, and the Public Interest*, The Johns Hopkins Press (1969).

39. Suh, B., Woodruff, A., Rosenholtz, R., and Glass, A. Popout prism: adding perceptual principles to overview+detail document interfaces. In *CHI '02: Proceedings of the SIGCHI conference on Human factors in computing systems: Changing our world, changing ourselves*, ACM Request Permissions (Apr. 2002).

40. Sun, J.-T., Wang, X., Shen, D., Zeng, H.-J., and Chen, Z. CWS: a comparative web search system. In *WWW '06*, ACM (May 2006).

41. The Stanford Natural Language Processing Group. Stanford CoreNLP.

42. Tufte, E. R. *Beautiful evidence*, 1st edition ed. Graphics Pr, 2006.

43. Weninger, T., Hsu, W. H., and Han, J. CETR: content extraction via tag ratios. *WWW 2010* (2010).

44. Winograd, P. Strategic Difficulties in Summarizing Texts. *Reading Research Quarterly 19* (1984), 404–425.

45. Wu, F., and Huberman, B. A. Novelty and Collective Attention. *PNAS 104*, 45 (Nov. 2007), 17599–17601.

46. Yatani, K., Novati, M., Trusty, A., and Truong, K. N. Review Spotlight: A User Interface for Summarizing User-generated Reviews Using Adjective-Noun Word Pairs . In *the 2011 annual conference*, ACM Press (New York, New York, USA, 2011), 1541.

Hardware-in-the-Loop-Based Evaluation Platform for Automotive Instrument Cluster Development (EPIC)

Sebastian Osswald
TUM CREATE
1 Create Way,
Singapore 138602
sebastian.osswald@tum-create.edu.sg

Pratik Sheth
TUM CREATE
1 Create Way,
Singapore 138602
pratik.sheth@tum-create.edu.sg

Manfred Tscheligi
CD Laboratory,
University of Salzburg
Sigmund-Haffner-Gasse 18,
5020 Salzburg, Austria
manfred.tscheligi@sbg.ac.at

ABSTRACT

This paper offers a contribution for platform-based evaluation techniques by proposing a hardware-in-the-loop-based approach for automotive instrument cluster (IC) development. An automotive IC interface requires for special attention as it provides the driver with safety-relevant information like speed or state of charge that is critical for the driving situation. As state of the art in-vehicle Human-Machine-Interfaces (HMI) are mostly embedded systems that make time-consuming research and development processes necessary, we propose a development platform that allows for a more rapid interface implementation and analysis. The evaluation platform for ICs (EPIC) is targeted at supporting engineers and researchers during the development phase of novel interface solutions that are reliable regarding their hardware connectivity and signal communication. It consists of a model-based vehicle simulation combined with automotive hardware to enable a real-time vehicle structure through a controller area network (CAN). Interchangeable, Android-based interfaces illustrate the flexibility of the approach and show the operability of the evaluation platform. To illustrate the applicability of the approach, the platform was embedded in an engineering process for an electric vehicle to address the challenge of user interface development.

Author Keywords

Automotive user interfaces; prototyping; hardware-in-the-loop; evaluation platform; interactive system development.

ACM Classification Keywords

D.2.11.b [Software Engineering]: Domain-specific architectures; H.5.2 [Information Interfaces and Presentation]: User Interfaces - Prototyping.

General Terms

Human Factors; Design.

INTRODUCTION

When talking about user interfaces development for a vehicle, the safety of the driver and the passengers is one of the most important issues. Driver distraction through continuous warnings from assistant systems and the inattention that arises when a driver perform secondary tasks with information systems challenge the development of appropriate devices. It motivates on the other hand, engineers and researchers to increase the effort in developing less distractive interface solutions and find ways to support the drivers with the appropriate information in the right situation. The development of such interfaces thus requires powerful software tools and suitable platforms that allows developers to continuously accompany the development process.

Among the various available interfaces in cars, an instrument cluster (IC) is present in every vehicle and dedicated to present critical vehicle-related information to the driver. The interface has to fulfill high quality standards and reliability demands but also needs to meet aesthetic requirements. The quality of displayed information ranges from basic data such as the vehicle speed, rounds per minute (RPM), fuel consumption or warning telltales to more detailed information about trip calculations, fuel efficiency and other similar details. As the IC is always in the view of the driver and essential for the driving task, the interface design of the HMI and the data representation is a subject of considerable importance to address safety.

In the industry driven development process of ICs, development cycles often exceed a period of 18 months [19]. These cycles involve multiple iterations of requirements and changes, most often carried out by suppliers [2] as the majority of devices are not developed by the vehicle original equipment manufacturer (OEM) itself. The iterations are time consuming and resource-intensive [10] as different tools and varying simulation-based environments are used during the development phases of an interface. The drawback of these prototyping tools and simulations for the development cycle are that they are decoupled from actual vehicle data interfaces and only represent design elements. As a result, implementation issues like data communication rates and system behavior peculiarities are difficult to consider and evaluate in the same cycles. Due to cost efficiency and the time consuming implementation process for the mostly embedded systems, issues that arise from system peculiarities are commonly not addressed after a system has reached a certain degree of maturity. In research the same issues appear when novel systems are evaluated and system-specific drawbacks are not taken into account. Most often these drawbacks are not considered as research approaches mainly focus on a rapid conceptual verification. It would be nevertheless advantageous to reflect these issues to enhance the validity of evaluation results especially for certain research areas that deal with attention management and cognitive processing.

In an effort to further ease the work for engineers and researchers in the IC development, research has begun to support tools that help to consider the vehicle system behavior. Early work [8] has utilized a computer-simulated instrumentation based on a back-projected image onto a screen in front of the driver. The described UMTRI Driver Interface Research Simulator applied LabVIEW[1] for the construction of the graphical interface to rapidly generate and test new display designs.

It is our aim to describe a new evaluation platform, which is intended to build on the success of the above work and at the same time address some of their limitations. The platform described in this paper is in its core a tool for rapid automotive IC user interface development and evaluation. It aims at the engineering phase and is designed for early prototyping without the need of an overall vehicle structure. It can be utilized during the whole development process and it can replace a variety of simulation and prototyping tools as the conceptual structure can be transferred directly to the final reassembling stage of a vehicle. The tight integration into the development cycle further eases the communication between engineers and designers as the platform provides a reliable framework to access the necessary data that allows the designers to iterate interfaces much quicker while the engineering support can be significantly reduced.

RELATED WORK
In this section we give a brief overview of the context and the framework conditions of the development platform. We present the main components deployed and identify weaknesses of earlier processes we observed in the past.

Instrument cluster development
The motivation for evaluating ICs certainly can be manifold. Regarding the rapid development in the automotive domain, a range of new technologies make their way in the vehicle that are unfamiliar to the drivers. The drivers will encounter completely new concepts that e.g. inform about the charging time or charging procedure of their vehicle. As drivers will experience these and other aspects of the changing vehicle properties most often through the available user interfaces in the vehicle, appropriate concepts and proper evaluation processes are required.

The IC which is mainly responsible for displaying information that is immanently driving-related. To support the IC

design cycles, rapid prototyping tools and platforms are required. In the beginning of automotive user interface evaluation, tools like HyperCard or SuperCard were the most popular choices for prototyping interactive control-panel interfaces [7]. Other approaches utilize system design software like LabView to rapidly create facsimiles of existing ICs [8], make use of reprogrammable interfaces [4] and use digital displays to simulate a system behavior based on triggered events [18]. Platforms like Ford's OpenXC platform[2] and OnStar's ATOMS platform[3] are advanced programmable interfaces to vehicles and allow to extend a vehicle with pluggable modules and custom applications. These OEM-driven approaches primarily target aftermarket solutions and do not concern the engineering process, restrict the access for developers and only work for certain vehicle brands. Focusing on the interface, HMI tools like Vaps[4] or Altia[5] give the possibility to design GUIs and further take care about the embedded system requirements. These tools are useful to a certain extent but have drawbacks due to the difficulties in servicing embedded systems, which are implemented into another machine, the low reusability rate of developed products and the inflexibility towards technology advancement.

We address the advantages and disadvantages of the listed tools by defining the main characteristics of choosing an appropriate platform as (1) the ease of use of the piece of software, (2) the reusability of produced content, (3) the level of data accuracy and the (4) transferability of the built interface into a vehicle structure. Our proposed platform addresses these four challenges to generate a valuable platform for engineers and researchers. As the communication between engineers and designers is known as difficult, this platform is further targeted to support the cooperation among the different groups who are involved in the process. To support the platforms flexibility we believe that utilizing a mobile operating system (OS) as basis will be beneficial in terms of cost efficiency as the platform can be used throughout different vehicle models. Further, the platform will benefit from the development effort of third-party developers who are extending the capabilities of the OS. Based on the extensively documented resources and available libraries we decided for the Android OS. The lightweight set of XML resources in Android as well as the non-restricted access to resources is beneficial for UI development, like the Android feature of automatically adapting the UI to look best for varying devices.

Instrument cluster objects and structure
Sensors and software-controlled electronics are nowadays the core of any vehicle's subsystem that enables a flawless communication between different hardware components and also between the driver and the vehicle. To communicate the vehicle status, the IC is one of the most important interfaces as it is in sight of the driver and does not require for further interaction.

---

[1]http://www.ni.com/labview/

[2]http://openxcplatform.com/
[3]https://www.onstar.com/
[4]http://www.presagis.com/
[5]http://www.altia.com/

The IC traditionally shows analog gauge rings to display the speed of the vehicle and the rounds per minute of the engine. Additionally, an analog odometer, a fuel gauge, a motor temperature gauge, warning telltales, indicators and a beam status light are most often included. In nowadays vehicles it can be observed that mechanical ICs are going to be replaced by hybrid solutions with mechanical elements as well as digital parts. The input for these interfaces can be separated into four broad segments: analog inputs (e.g. the ignition voltage), discrete inputs (switches), digital pulses (sensor output) and serial data (module data such as fuel used, malfunction warnings).

Reconfigurable, more sophisticated digital display can be altered in manifold ways e.g. to customize the interface for using the same hardware for different car models. Digital ICs have further the advantage to handle purely digital input, which can be directly provided through the vehicle network. Additionally, hardware components such as different micro controllers, stepper motors and communication modules are getting obsolete. Among experts, an important issue is the question if sensor-based input which is relevant for the IC is gathered centrally through e.g. a *Car PC* or if the respective module receives the data directly because the information is just required by the IC. A decentralized structure very much rely on purpose built hardware that integrates the necessary receiver in e.g. a custom wire board. These systems are lightweight and stable to be implemented in a car, but lacks in flexibility due to their hardware limitations when it comes to more sophisticated functions like location-based support or persuasive systems. In this paper, we favor a central solution as we want to reduce the amount of required components and give way for advanced solutions.

More than 50 electronic control units (ECU) developed by different suppliers are integrated in a vehicle nowadays that measure and provide data for the vehicle subsystem to support e.g. the functionality of the IC [10]. Coordinating such a multi-peered development process makes detailed specifications in advance of the development work necessary which stretches the time necessary for the requirement engineering process. As the development of the IC relies on the data provided by the ECUs, changes in the requirements raise the need of iterative development throughout the whole engineering and development process [2]. Figure 1 documents a basic development process for an IC. The iterative cycles between the OEM and the suppliers document the time which is necessary to coordinate the work throughout the process stages. The challenge here would be to find a reliable basis to support the requirement engineering process for the IC development and further provides access for contractors to react to requirement changes. While the IC functions are going to be developed on module level, a flexible platform can also support the system and integration level. To achieve this, evaluation must be done as early as possible in the development process.

Hardware in the loop

A Hardware-In-the-Loop (HIL) system is a development paradigm that is widely accepted in the industry to ease and expedite the development process of various ECUs [9], [3],

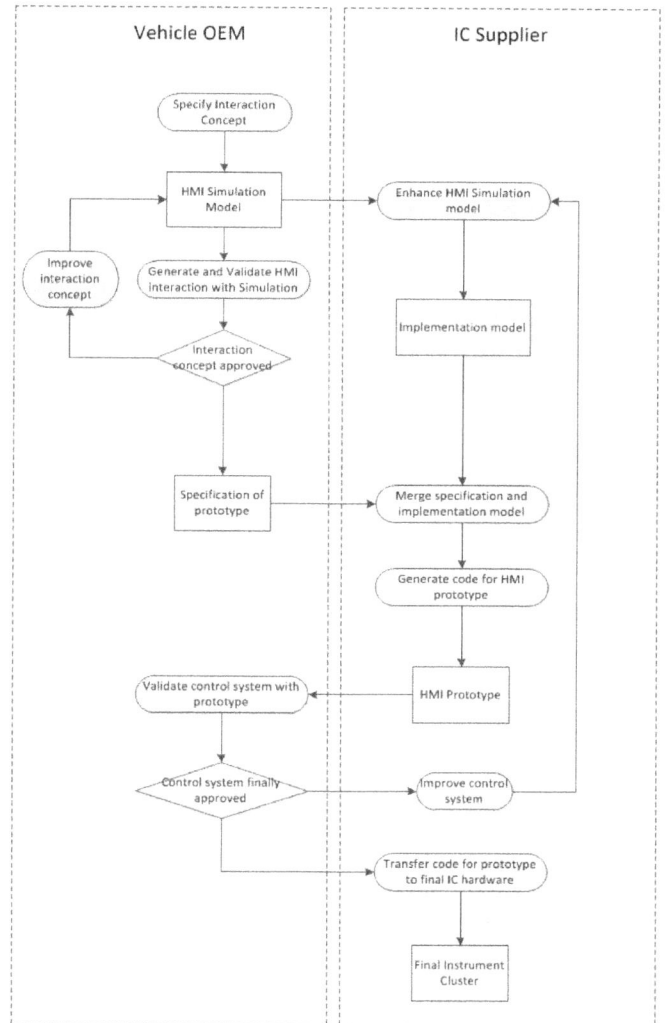

Figure 1. Example of an instrument cluster development process between OEM and suppliers

[16]. The HIL technique allows to exercise real control systems against simulations of a vehicle-under-control and replaces many aspects of traditional vehicle testing [15]. Especially in an early stage of software development, it reduces the dependence on prototype vehicles, which reduces on the other hand resources required to support and build a prototype. The integration of the targeted software/hardware can be done much later in development process and does not require major modifications before volume production [14]. Figure 2 shows an example HIL system structure. This structure documents how behavior of various dynamic systems and ECUs of a vehicle are simulated to test a particular Device Under Test (DUT) (e.g. an IC), which can be done throughout all development stages. A HIL system is generally scalable and it can be used in all stages of development, starting from a model based simulation on a computer to verify the functional control aspects of the DUT. As an example, the initial testing for an engine controller for a vehicle might involve testing its control algorithm on a model-based offline simulation. This

gradually progresses to more advanced simulations containing different vehicle hardware in mature stages of their development as described in [11]. In this work, the authors applied a HIL set-up supported by a model-based approach that simulates vehicle network in real-time to give way for a machine vision system to perform function tests.

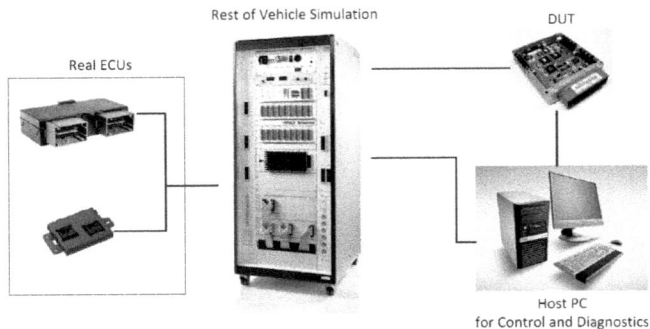

Figure 2. Example of a generic HIL system

Integrating electrical or communication interface hardware into the simulation allows for different levels of integration testing. For an engine controller this might mean testing a prototype version of the electronics and/or software with planned electrical and communication interfaces to simulated signals representing other ECUs, sensors and actuators in a vehicle. As the vehicle development progresses, some of the simulated ECUs may be replaced by real prototypes or units to investigate issues related to their integration with the engine controller. The HIL stage of the vehicle development is then followed up by a vehicle prototype to test the integration-related issues of all the systems of the vehicle.

HIL systems, while commonly used to test the device hardware and software, are not so commonly used to evaluate the user interfaces of HMI systems like an IC. However, the proposed platform is a way to extend the use of HIL systems.

DEFINING THE EVALUATION PLATFORM FOR INSTRUMENT CLUSTERS (EPIC)

The proposed platform consists of a *back end* and a *front end*. The back end is composed of a HIL system that generates the vehicle data. An automotive communication protocol is used to transmit the signals and data from the HIL set-up to the *front-end*. The front end of the platform consists of a gateway device to interface a freely programmable Android-based IC interface (see Figure 3).

We selected the Controller Area Network (CAN) as the communication protocol to interface the back end with the front end of the platform. CAN is a time-multiplexed, multi-master, messaged-based serial communication protocol developed by Bosch in 1983 [5]. CAN has become the most widely used serial communication protocol in the automotive industry. While newer, more robust options like MOST and Ethernet are gaining popularity, they are targeted to specific applications like multimedia for MOST and high-bandwidth

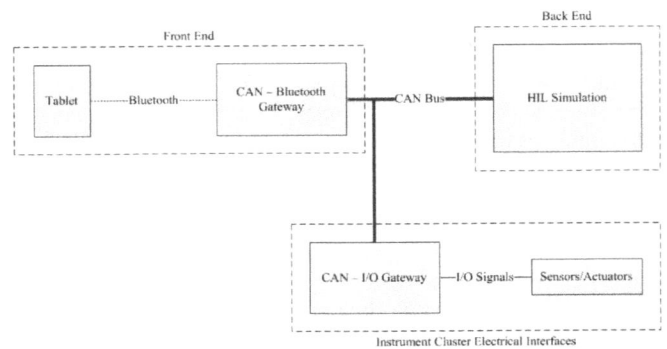

Figure 3. The structure of the hardware-in-the-loop-based evaluation platform for automotive instrument clusters

drive-by-X systems for Ethernet. For ECUs with more moderate bandwidth needs, including IC, CAN is thus the communication protocol of choice for the near future due to the wide variety of development tools available and the comparatively low overall system costs [12].

The most prominent challenge we were faced with was the definition of the interface hardware. A variety of aftermarket solution as well as OEM produced IC are available and offer manifold possibilities to build the targeted evaluation platform. The decision of using an Android-based solution to generate the interface was justified by the stability and reusability of the programming language characteristics. An advantage of Android is the high flexibility and reliability of its emerging development platform targeted at mobile devices, which also receives a lot of support in the development community. In addition, Android is well supported by Google and detailed documentations can be accessed online. Android compatible hardware ranges nowadays from clock-sized devices (e.g. Sony Smart clock) up to 11 inch tablets (e.g. Galaxy Tab 2) which allows us to use differently scaled devices as interface references in the evaluation platform.

Another challenge we were faced with, was the required connectivity bridge between the CAN bus and the IC. A popular approach for prototyping interfaces in a vehicle is the usage of the standardized on-board diagnostics (OBD2) interface, which provides access to parts of CAN message transfer. As the focus of our platform is the support of the vehicle engineering and evaluation process, this solution was not feasible as the OBD2 interface is not available in the targeted development stages that the platform should be supportive with. We thus decided for a Bluetooth CAN interface gateway module. This approach supports the mobility of the platform as we in respect to other mobile CAN interfaces like CAN-to-USB remain flexible in positioning the output interface It was further beneficial as Android devices are mostly powered via the USB interface, which is why it was not necessary to reduce the current intake to use the data connection.

With respect to the wireless gateway, security issues that even persist for prototyping vehicles were taken into account. Several aspects of security were considered during the development process through applying message filters, a secured pairing process, a customized handshake procedure between the devices, preset MAC IDs and a secured Bluetooth socket connection. The motivation for choosing a Bluetooth connection was grounded in the advantages of the wireless connection in terms of flexibility and range. Compared to Wifi, Bluetooth radio is more reliable and less failure-prone as it hops faster and use shorter packets, which makes the transmission very robust against typical interference phenomena [17]. Compared with other systems operating in the same frequency band, the Bluetooth radio typically hops faster and uses shorter packets, which makes a Bluetooth transmission very robust against typical interference phenomena.

Back end: generating the CAN message framework

The platform is designed in a way that the back end is scalable, starting from a model-based HIL simulation during the starting phases of the project through to the prototype vehicle, while maintaining the same interfaces to the front end. This makes it possible to rapidly evaluate newly developed solutions and design requirements for the IC as the project proceeds.

Figure 4 shows in detail a standard CAN frame we used for communicating between the different ECUs in the vehicle. A frame is transferred bit field by bit field, starting with its start of frame field. Within a field the most significant bit is transmitted first [12]. The definitions for all the CAN messages as required by the different applications on the CAN serial bus are contained in a worksheet or database, often called the CAN matrix. This CAN matrix is developed and maintained by a network architect and undergoes significant changes and additions as the development cycle of the vehicle proceeds. An important aspect during the development cycle of the vehicle is to keep the development of the various ECUs in sync with the overall development process. This is quite pronounced in the maintenance of the CAN matrix as well. However, the parameters of the network itself like the baud rate and the message format hardly change after their initial definition. Thus, the CAN network is a valuable choice as communication medium of the platform and its development can furthermore be adjusted according to the development of the network for the vehicle.

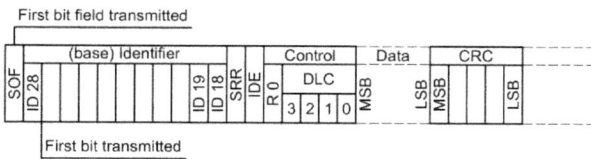

Figure 4. CAN standard frame format of bit transmission.

An important part of the back end in our platform is a CAN simulation tool called CANoe developed by Vector Informatik GmbH [6]. The tool is one of the most widely used CAN development tools in the automotive industry. It is used to simulate all the ECUs on the CAN bus that exchange data with the IC. The CAN matrix for CANoe is contained in a unique CAN database file with the extension .dbc editable

[6]http://www.vector.com/

by the CANdb++ tool which is part of the tool suite in CANoe. To automatically generate the CAN database file from the CAN matrix, an additional tool is provided to make it easy to generate and update the database when the CAN matrix is reconfigured. We have developed this tool to also automate the generation of the basic CAPL scripts that transmit the data over CAN. This otherwise time-consuming process is thus faster to perform.

Regarding the transmitted data, the user of the platform can dynamically change the data through panels in CANoe. These panels are generated automatically by CANoe from the .dbc files. We therefore created a CANoe configuration for the CAN simulation. Figure 5 shows the three file sources that are required for the overall process of the CAN simulation. The configuration for the simulation only needs to be updated if there are changes to the number of ECUs connected to the CAN bus. Thus the entire back end of the simulation is generated automatically from the CAN matrix spreadsheet, and this results in an easy to scale overall system. The system can be kept updated to the changes in the CAN message definitions without fear of errors due to synchronization between the various files.

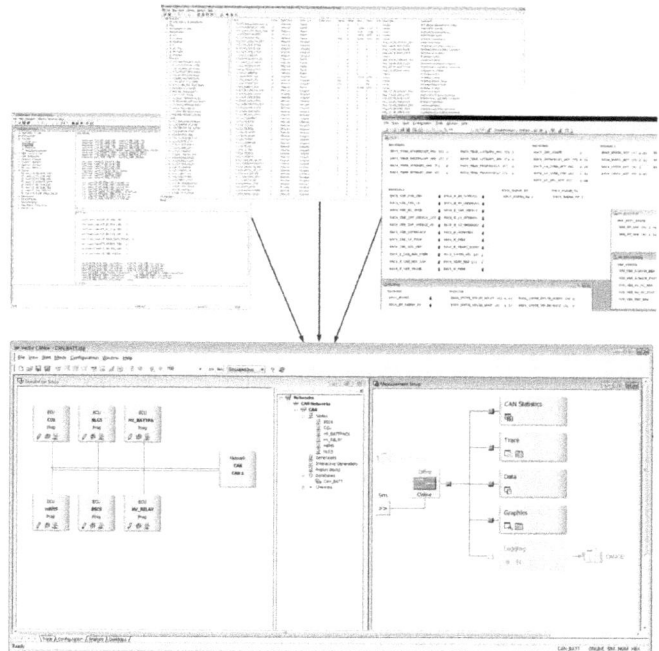

Figure 5. The CAN simulation developed from the CAPL, DBC and Panel-based input files.

Front end I: Bluetooth CAN bridge preparation

We interfaced the front end of the platform with the communication channel over a wireless network. This enabled us to have a more portable evaluation front end which can be mounted on rapidly changing mechanical designs rather easily, without facing issues of harness redesign. We selected a CAN to Bluetooth gateway called *CANblue II* from Ixxat[7] as the interface between the CAN communication channel and

[7]http://www.ixxat.com/

the front end. CANblue II is an easily configurable device which can be used for a wide range of applications. It is Bluetooth 2.1 compliant which enables a reasonable range without consuming too much power, which might become a factor when using the platform with an electric vehicle, where total power consumption might be an issue.

Filtering the appropriate CAN messages is further supported by the Bluetooth gateway hardware itself. Based on the previous CAN network preparations we were able to define the appropriate filters and save these setting on the gateway micro controller. We set a unique paring code for the devices to restrict external connection. As this is a weak protection in terms of security, a MAC address filter was additionally enabled to allow connections from the IC only. After successfully adding a Bluetooth media address of a SPP server to the CANblue II, the device tries to establish a connection to the serial port protocol server of a Bluetooth device with the added media access control address. The module itself creates an RFCOMM BluetoothSocket which enables the module to start a secure outgoing connection with a remote device using a service discovery protocol lockup of the universal unique identifier (UUID). This procedure is designed to be used with listenUsingRfcommWithServiceRecord(String, UUID) for peer-peer Bluetooth applications.

Front end II: Android CAN interpretation

The CAN messages for the IC interface components are the basis for different user interface objects and functions that make use of plain CAN message values or of calculated values that are generated in the application itself. For this, the overall concept mudt consist of a proper message channel, an interpreter for the CAN messages on the receiver site, the main application for handling the data input and the interface for visual output. It needs to address further the challenge of an increased information flow provided by the ECUs [1]. The software architecture should handle the in-vehicle information through integrative and adaptive functions that control the information flow.

To establish the connection between the Android application and the Bluetooth module, the Bluetooth specific configurations needed to be taken into account. In detail, this comprises establishing the appropriate communication channel, which requires for a custom hand shake procedure. Included in this procedure is the the initializing of the CAN controller and the choice of a standard baud rate (in our case 100kbaud). Proceeding in establishing the communication channel, the application determines the data protocol, as the module itself provides either an ASCII-based protocol or a binary format to permit a better data rate for transmitting the Bluetooth CAN messages. When the up to 8 byte long CAN messages are received at the application side, they are processed by a proper translation structure that takes care about the various requirements that determine the further processing to the respective interface. As an example this can be the translation of vehicle speed CAN values that are subsequently send to the interface object to display the information in a speedometer gauge. On the other hand more sophisticated processing is done to provide values that are determined by combining

CAN-based message sources as for the energy meter. The energy meter displays the energy consumption of the vehicle based on the consumption of the different energy consumers (e.g. motors) in the car. Accordingly, a set of values needs to be considered and processed in a way that accurate output for the visual interface is possible.

The interface objects are fragmented to provide an easy to customize interface structure. We designed accordingly several standard objects, which can easily be adapted due to the results of a previous requirement engineering process. The graphical resources as an example, were implemented in a way that the interface elements can be set on top of the functional structure to allow for interchangeable skins. It thus allows for quickly redesigning already known interface designs for evaluation purposes or to quickly generate interface designs for different cars that need to maintain the same basic structure of interface elements.

The functional structure on the other hand determines aspects such as the ration of data translation according to the data source. For the basic gauge design, we implemented a zero position identifier based on the pivot center and an angle calculation algorithm to allow for different needle-like designs. These elements are especially useful for the often referenced gauge designs, which are still popular in the interface design of semi-analog interfaces. In detail, we further paid special attention on determining the needle speed/indicator speed. This was done as the direct reflection of data values needs to be smoothed from case to case (e.g. for the energy meter, as the values are changing frequently and thus would not allow for a correct visual interpretation).

To ensure the application's stability and support developers in the same way throughout the user interface implementation, we further generated a reliable exception handling management. This includes on the one hand a reliable application structure that incorporates drawback mechanisms for encountered problems such as connection losses, message errors and application misbehavior. We provided on the other hand exception messages for a broad variety of commands which can be caught and used in the debugging process.

A further decision we made concerning the software design, was targeted at the arrangement of the interface objects. The speedometer was defined as the minimum requirement of the interface object that needs to be displayed continuously while driving due to safety reasons and legal specifications in almost every country in the world. According to that we designed a basic framing structure that defines layers of interchangeable interface objects that either surrounds a static top layer or is displayed side by side to a static element. The same interchange approach was taken for the telltales, as they can be displayed in the most cases in the same defined area in the interface.

Apart from the interfaces objects that are reliant on vehicle data, we also acknowledged the wide range of possibilities an Internet connection offers for vehicular applications as demonstrated e.g. in [20] for navigational purposes. We implemented and established an additional Wifi connection to

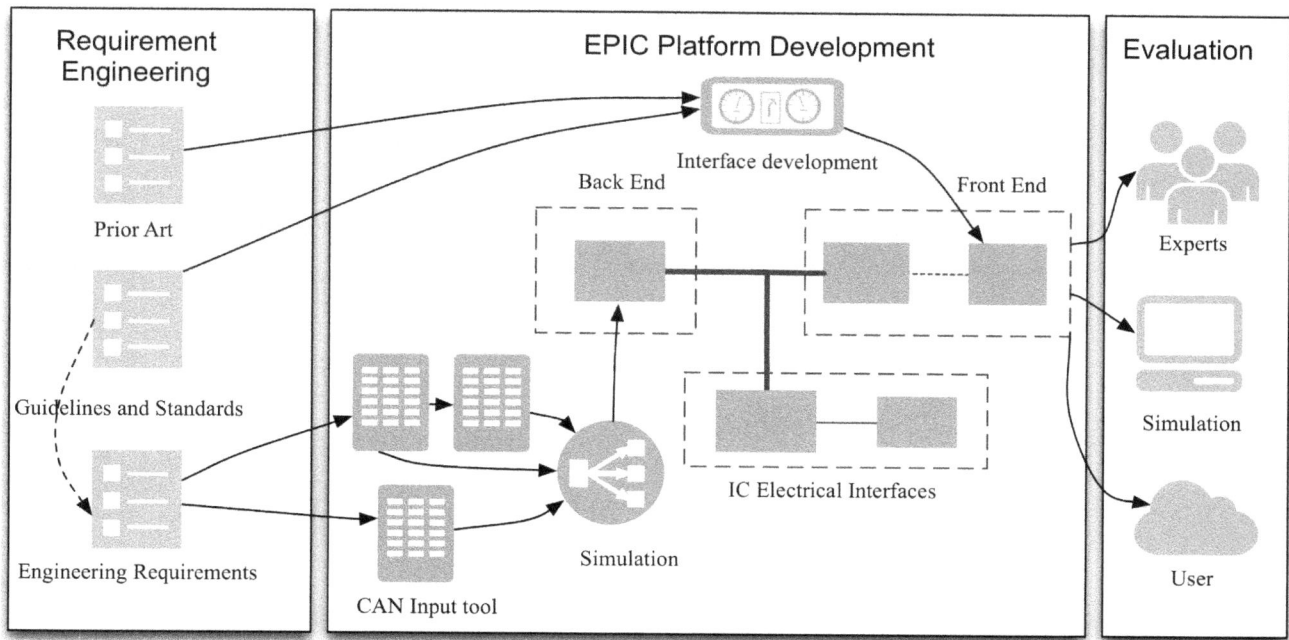

Figure 6. The workflow for the evaluation platform for instrument clusters (EPIC)

a CarPC to benefit from an Internet connection. The CarPC was part of the general vehicle infrastructure and routes the required Internet connection to provide the IC with access to a variety of online services. As this connection is less reliable than the Bluetooth connection, only online information which does not affect the driving task was gathered. This criteria is only fulfilled by non-real time data and by information which just needs to be received once. As an example this could be useful for persuasive systems that are targeted to persuade the driver to a more ecological driving behavior. For that purpose it might be necessary to provide the persuasive system with information about the driving performance of other drivers to generate a competitive situation.

The overall workflow of the platform targeted engineering process is shown in Figure 6. The above described development steps of the EPIC platform are embedded between the requirement engineering and the evaluation phase, whereby a iterative development cycle needs to be considered.

USER INTERFACE GENERATION
In order to test our platform, we decided to generate two sets of interfaces as reference examples. They were built with the purpose to analyze the platform regarding the (1) ease of use of the piece of software, (2) the reusability of produced content, (3) the level of data accuracy or the (4) transferability of the built interface into a working environment. The major input to this step is the set of selected user interface components as a result of the user interface requirement engineering. The output is a comprehensive user interface which is consistent with the currently available knowledge [6] about individual user needs and context requirements in a vehicle that might influence the interaction. In total we present here two interfaces that were designed for electric vehicles and

implemented for the evaluation platform. One IC interface was designed to display the necessary, driving-related information in a conservative way that correlates with what is already known from former IC designs. The second interface was designed to enhance the drivers' experience about driving an electric vehicle and elevate the characteristics of the vehicle itself through focusing on the vehicles' range and state of charge.

The I/O values that we used for the user interface are defined by the available CAN messages. Nevertheless, they can be reduced and filtered depending on the values required for the overall concept. According to the context of use which was in our case an electric vehicle, the advantage of the overall parametrization of the system is strongly bond to the interface concept. Further ideas require additional data which can be supported by accessing the Internet. This might be of use in scenarios like car sharing, electric vehicles with special purposes (like e-taxis that need information for pickup points, waiting customers or route optimization). In our case, we defined the message parameters for an electric vehicle shown in Table 1. These messages and signals were support by the earlier mentioned CAN matrix and the filter mechanisms on the receiver side, and it represents the core variables necessary for most of the required IC interface functions.

EPIC-based IC Development
The IC interfaces were implemented in Android according to the platform requirements. Due to the broad variety of available Android API classes, no additions to the available libraries needed to be made for our concepts. The well-documented Android API allows for easy modifications and additions to the interface descriptors. Simple interface adjustments like color, size, fonts, positioning and exchange of

Level	Transmitter	Analog Signal/bitmap Name
Msg	CCU	Warning and Indicator Tell tales
Sig	IC	Vehicle Master Warning
Sig	IC	Vehicle Master Warning
Sig	IC	Seat Belt Warning
Sig	IC	Low LV Warning
Sig	IC	Battery Temperature Warning
Sig	IC	Low Beam Active Tell Tale
Sig	IC	Park Brake Tell Rale
Sig	IC	Indicator Tell Tales
Sig	IC	Door Ajar Tell Tales
Sig	IC	Boot Open Tell-Tale
Sig	IC	Bonnet Open Tell Tale
Msg	CCU	Battery Information
Sig	IC	HV Battery State of Charge
Sig	IC	Battery State of Health
Sig	IC	Battery Current
Msg	CCU	EMOTOR Information
Sig	IC	EMOTOR Axle Speed
Sig	IC	EMOTOR Torque Actual
Sig	IC	EMOTOR DC Current
Msg	CCU	Vehicle Status
Sig	IC	Vehicle Mode
Sig	IC	HV Status
Sig	IC	Motor Status
Sig	IC	Aircon Status
Sig	IC	HV Battery Error

Table 1. The parametrization of CAN messages for the platforms instrument cluster

graphical elements can be done instantly. Due to a comprehensive documentation of the underlying functional control of the CAN communication, adjustments and additions can be done as fast as the interface alterations. To ease the understanding of how to connect to the underlying services that interpret the CAN messages, the evaluation platform already provides basic code for interfaces elements like the speed gauge, odometer or range indicator that rely on CAN-based input. This includes the code for data interpretation as well as the code for translating the data into visual cues (e.g. a charging bar).

As the platform requires a certain level of programming skills, the ease of use of the piece of software heavily depends on the available knowledge about Android. Nevertheless, when a system's complexity rises the difficulty level remain on a moderate level as the solid communication structure can be used in various ways and adapted to changing requirements. For simple to medium complex interfaces with basic Internet data inbound, the setup of an interface structure can be described as easy to handle. This is mainly justified through the available examples and the well-documented structure that allow for a high reusability of designed interface objects from one interface concept to another.

To elevate similarities to state of the art interface, the first interface was designed with the aim of generating a conservative gauge-based design that incorporates user interface elements for an electric vehicle. The design shown in Figure 7

displays the speed on the right and the energy meter on the left side in a prominent way. The Arabic numerals as well as the charging bars on both sides are used to display the respective values. The center of the interface is separated in three stacked elements. The first from the top shows telltales that sit on top of a message box, which is displaying text-based information about upcoming warnings. The central element is used to present navigation information, while the lower element presents the odometer and tripmeter. The left charging bar displays the state of charge, while the charging bar above displays the battery temperature. The lower right charging bar is intended to display the energy meter. The energy meter displays the amount of used energy which correlates with the experience drivers have with the common RPM gauge object.

Figure 7. Interface concept for an electric vehicle instrument cluster

The second design was intended to enhance the drivers' experience of electric vehicles by elevating the characteristics of the vehicle itself compared to other user interface characteristics that have been prominent in past design concepts. The concept was created in an iterative design session with industrial designers and engineers. The requirements for this process were based on prior art [18] and an extensive evaluation of interface designs from electric and hybrid vehicles. One of the concepts that was implemented in our platform is presented in Figure 8. The concept shows a charging bar each on the left and the right side, whereas the left one shows the state of charge and the right the available range of the vehicle. We focused on the direction of the charging bar flows, as both elements grow from the bottom to the top. This was done to be consistent in going from negative (low battery charge - low range (e = empty)) to a positive state (fully charged battery - high range (f = full)). The difference between both elements is that the range is determined not only by the state of charge, it further incorporates the driving behavior and energy consumption over time. The center element shows the actual driving speed of the vehicle in a prominent way, to enhance the awareness of the driving situation. The overall design is kept in light colors to reduce distraction.

INTEGRATION AND IC ANALYSIS

Besides the design and implementation task for the two interfaces we described in the previous section, a further goal was to demonstrate the flexibility of the platform. For this purpose, we integrate the platform in an engineering process, which is aimed at building an electric vehicle. This process incorporates all stages of engineering the vehicle from scratch, designing the interior and the exterior and also facing the challenges of defining an appropriate infrastructure.

Figure 8. Interface concept variation for an electric vehicle instrument cluster

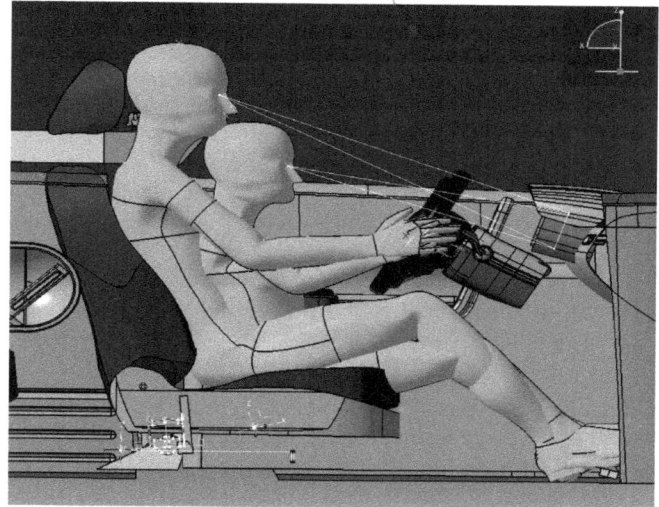

Figure 9. RAMSIS ergonomic analysis of the viewing angles based on a case study vehicle structure

Integrating an IC into such an overall engineering process requires a proper communication structure and the physical placement in an overall vehicle package. In our case this was done in a computer-aided design approach (CAD) using CATIA[8]. We measured the dimensions of the development platform and placed the Android-based interface in the 3D model of a vehicle. For the preliminary analysis of the prototype IC interface we then followed a two-step approach.

First we made use of the 3D-CAD ergonomic tool RAMSIS[9] which can be run in CATIA to assess the direct and indirect views of a driver. This was done in order to determine requirements for the interface design (e.g. text size, visibility). Due to the lightweight Android-tablet solution, we were able to maintain these values throughout the development process. This is an advantage as compared to former approaches because state of the art IC solutions most often needed to be physically rearranged due to their large volume which led to a change in the measured values. To determine the viewing angles we placed two CAD manikins in a 3D vehicle model as a reference for our analysis (see Figure 9). In doing so, one manikin represents the tallest average male driver and the other one represents the smallest average female driver. In the second step, we placed the platform in a seating box. This basic prototype setup of a vehicle was built to give engineers and researchers a physical impression about the dimensions of a targeted vehicle (see Figure 10).

The results of the RAMSIS evaluation led to a resizing of the column size as they were to small. This was justified trough the assessed viewing angle distance between the eyes of the manikin and the interface. Based on ISO 15008:2009 [13] the column size for small letters was calculated. Following the ISO15008 recommendation for the optimal viewing angle dimension of 20 arc minutes and, the in our case, measured distance value of 813.64 mm for the tallest manikin, the angular values expressed in radiant (α_R) is thus 0.0058, which calculates in a text hight of 4.73 mm. The seating box evaluation further led to a rearrangement of the gauges as they were initially placed too low and were partially covered by the instrument panel. The space usage of different interface elements (e.g. the odometer) within the display was additionally optimized regarding their overall distribution.

The analysis exhibits the properties and binding conditions for integrating an IC concept into an overall engineering pro-

cess. In this case, we documented how rapidly engineers are able to integrate the platform into a computer-aided design approach to derive interface design criteria based on an ergonomic analysis. Additionally, the seat box approach allowed for evaluating the hardware integration characteristics that might also affect the visibility, which gives a proper subjective impression about the final product. Both procedures form a proper foundation for further detailed evaluations that addresses the users' perspective. As an example, the platform can be easily combined with simulation tools like DYNA4[10] to obtain realistic driving data. The platform can also be connected to driving simulator software like OpenDS[11], to carry out user studies for evaluating interfaces with methods like eye tracking to determine gaze time and workload.

Figure 10. Seat box setup with portable instrument cluster for ergonomic evaluation

---

[8]http://www.3ds.com/products/catia/
[9]http://www.appliedgroup.com/ramsis/

[10]http://www.tesis-dynaware.com/
[11]http://www.opends.eu/

CONCLUSION

In this paper, we have presented a development platform to support engineers and researchers in developing and evaluating automotive IC interfaces. The main feature of this platform is that it is based on an adaptable vehicle simulation, a flexible communication structure and a freely programmable Android-based interface. This platform is targeted to support novel and complex interface solutions (including multimodal solutions as the platform is extendable). The main advantage of this platform is that its development process addresses the ease of use of the software, the reusability of already available content, the level of data accuracy and the transferability of built interfaces into a working environment.

Regarding the overall development cycle of instruments clusters, the platform further targets all stages of development and reduces the need for different prototyping tools or simulation environments. Future work might address other, non-driver-related interfaces in the car that can benefit from vehicle data. As there is a trend towards front seat passenger interfaces recognizable in research, it seems to be valuable to extend the platform based on front-seat passenger interface requirements. Due to the proper communication structure, the platform is also suitable to be deployed in a driving simulator environment for user studies. The HIL simulation can rapidly be interfaced with a simulator environment where it can receive values like speed from the driving simulator setup.

The functionality and setup of the platform is aimed at supporting the development and evaluation of driver-vehicle interaction aspects in order to increase driving safety and enhance the driver's experience. Within the research project this work is based on, the platform and its components are being implemented in a demonstrator vehicle, namely EVA.

ACKNOWLEDGMENTS
This work was financially supported by the Singapore National Research Foundation under its Campus for Research Excellence And Technological Enterprise (CREATE).

REFERENCES
1. Amditis, A., Kubmann, H., Polychronopoulos, A., Engstrom, J., and Andreone, L. System architecture for integrated adaptive hmi solutions. In *Intelligent Vehicles Symposium, 2006 IEEE*, IEEE (2006), 388–393.

2. Bock, C. Model-driven hmi development: Can meta-case tools do the job? In *Proc. of HICSS 2007*, IEEE (2007), 287b–287b.

3. Dhaliwal, A., Nagaraj, S., and Ali, S. Hardware-in-the-loop simulation for hybrid electric vehicles–an overview, lessons learnt and solutions implemented. *SAE Technical Paper Series* (2009).

4. Ecker, R., Holzer, P., Broy, V., and Butz, A. Ecochallenge: a race for efficiency. In *Proc. of MobileHCI*, ACM (New York, NY, USA, 2011), 91–94.

5. Führer, T., Müller, B., Dieterle, W., Hartwich, F., Hugel, R., and Walther, M. Time triggered communication on can (time triggered can-ttcan). In *Proc. of CAN Conference* (2000).

6. Green, P. In-vehicle UI standards. In *Adjunct Proc. of AutoUI*, ACM (2012).

7. Green, P., Boreczky, J., and Kim, S. Applications of rapid prototyping to control and display design. *SAE paper 900470* (1990).

8. Green, P., and Olson, A. Practical aspects of prototyping instrument clusters. *SAE transactions 105* (1996), 657–670.

9. Hanselmann, H. *Hardware-in-the Loop Simulation as a Standard Approach for Development, Customization, and Production Test of ECU's*. Society of Automotive Engineers, 1993.

10. Heumesser, N., and Houdek, F. Experiences in managing an automotive requirements engineering process. In *Proc. of Requirements Engineering Conference*, IEEE (Washington, DC, USA, 2004), 322–327.

11. Huang, Y., Mouzakitis, A., McMurran, R., Dhadyalla, G., and Jones, R. Design validation testing of vehicle instrument cluster using machine vision and hardware-in-the-loop. In *Proc. of ICVES*, IEEE (2008), 265–270.

12. International Organization for Standardization (ISO). *ISO 11898-4:2004 Road vehicles – Controller area network (CAN) – Part 4: Time-triggered communication*, 2004.

13. International Organization for Standardization (ISO). *ISO 15008:2009 Road vehicles - Ergonomic aspects of transport information and control systems - Specifications and test procedures for in-vehicle visual presentation*, 2009.

14. Kendall, I., and Jones, R. An investigation into the use of hardware-in-the-loop simulation testing for automotive electronic control systems. *Control Engineering Practice 7*, 11 (1999), 1343–1356.

15. Köhl, S., and Jegminat, D. How to do hardware-in-the-loop simulation right. *SAE Technical Paper* (2005), 01–1657.

16. Lu, B., Wu, X., Figueroa, H., and Monti, A. A low-cost real-time hardware-in-the-loop testing approach of power electronics controls. *Industrial Electronics, IEEE Transactions on 54*, 2 (2007), 919–931.

17. Nusser, R., and Pelz, R. Bluetooth-based wireless connectivity in an automotive environment. In *Proc. of Vehicular Technology*, vol. 4, IEEE (2000), 1935–1942.

18. Strömberg, H., Ericsson, J., Andersson, P., Karlsson, M., Almgren, S., and Nåbo, A. Driver interfaces for electric vehicles. In *Proc. of Automotive User Interfaces and Interactive Vehicular Applications* (2011), 177–184.

19. Winters, F., Mielenz, C., and Hellestrand, G. Design process changes enabling rapid development. *Proc. of Convergence* (2004), 613–624.

20. Ziegler, J., Hussein, T., Münter, D., Hofmann, J., and Linder, T. Generating route instructions with varying levels of detail. In *Proc. of AutoUI*, ACM (2011).

Creativity on a Shoestring – Concept Generating in Agile Development

Neil Maiden
Centre for Creativity in
Professional Practice
City University London
Northampton Square
London, EC1V0HB, UK
N.A.M.Maiden@city.ac.uk

Bianca Hollis
Telegraph Media Group
111 Buckingham Palace Road
London SW1W ODT, UK
Bianca.Hollis@gmail.com

ABSTRACT
This tutorial presents creativity techniques that can be applied with limited resources including time in agile development projects.

Author Keywords
Agile; creativity techniques; tutorial

ACM Classification Keywords
D.2.1 [Requirements/Specifications]: Elicitation methods

CREATIVITY ON A SHOESTRING
Developing interactive systems has seen a substantial growth in the use of agile development methods such as scrum, lean and extreme programming over the last decade intended to meet requirements through the continuous delivery of software of value to customers [3]. One claim for agile is that it can produce innovative software in uncertain situations [4]. However, the concrete evidence that agile methods lead to novel requirements as the precursors of innovative products is lacking, and commentators are increasingly questioning whether agile techniques can deliver innovation, for example [7].

Requirements in agile methods are normally expressed as user stories. Each user story is expected to describe one requirement, often a user requirement, on a A5 card made visible to the project team on a wall or similar shared space. These physical cards enable the agile team to manage requirements without the administrative tasks usually associated with requirements documents: each card enables communication of the requirement to developers and is used to track progress to deliver it. Often a system called Kanban, meaning visible card, is employed to display and track requirements as they move from in-progress to done [5].

However, Cao and Ramesh's [2] empirical investigations of agile projects revealed many requirements-related problems including the omission of non-functional requirements, poor requirements validation practices and a failure to develop scalable prototypes that deliver large numbers of requirements to customers. Developing software that satisfied requirements was not possible without high-quality interactions with stakeholders. On the positive side, agile requirements practices did enable customers to steer the project in unanticipated directions, especially when their requirements evolved owing to changes in the environment or their own understanding of the software solution. Such flexibility suggests a development process in which creative thinking can flourish, yet there remains little evidence of creative outcomes from agile development methods.

One obvious weakness is that current agile development methods tend not to exploit working software for creative thinking about new requirements and opportunities. Indeed the short durations of sprints can discourage the incubation and reflection needed for creative thinking. Often the principle of simplicity, eliminating waste and reducing complexity is taken too far. Beck [1] advises agile developers to think of the simplest solution. For many features the simplest solution may be the best. But unless a concerted effort is made to see the potential beyond the simplest solution, customers will continue to settle for just enough. This problem is reinforced by agile adoption of data-driven techniques such competitor analysis and personas that focus on current practices, and techniques such as model storming that give little consideration to alternatives to core functions.

Whilst more linear requirements processes have increased their adoption of creativity techniques, for example [6], a key challenge that we explore in this tutorial is how to integrate creative thinking effectively into shorter, more iterative and resource-light agile development methods. The aim of this tutorial is to provide guidance on how to select user stories with the greatest creative potential, then provide practice and reflection on creativity techniques selected for agile development projects. These techniques include Hall of Fame, Constraint Removal, Back to the Future, Creativity Triggers, and Story Writing.

REFERENCES

1. Beck, K. 2005, Extreme Programming Explained: Embrace Change: Embracing Change. 2 edition, Addison Wesley.

2. Cao L. & Ramesh B., 2008, 'Agile Requirements Engineering Practices: An Empirical Study, IEEE Software, 25(1), 60-67.

3. Fowler, M. Highsmith, J 2001, The Agile Manifesto, Software Development, August 2001, retrieved 11/01/11 from: http://www.agilemanifesto.org/

4. Highsmith, J. 2004, Agile Project Management: Creating Innovative Products. Addison-Wesley Professional.

5. Kennaley, M. 2010, SDLC 3.0: Beyond a Tacit Understanding of Agile. Fourth Medium Press.

6. Maiden N.A.M., Ncube C. & Robertson S., 2007, 'Can Requirements Be Creative? Experiences with an Enhanced Air Space Management System', Proceedings 28th International Conference on Software Engineering, ACM Press, 632-641.

7. Oza N. & Ambrahamsson P., 2011, Building blocks of agile innovation, http://www.agileinnovationbook.com/welcome.

3rd Workshop on Distributed User Interfaces: Models, Methods and Tools

**María D. Lozano, Jose A. Gallud,
Ricardo Tesoriero,
Víctor M. R. Penichet**
Univ. of Castilla-La Mancha
Computing Systems Department
02071, Albacete, Spain
[maria.lozano, jose.gallud,
ricardo.tesoriero,
victor.penichet]@uclm.es

Jean Vanderdonckt
Université catholique de Louvain
Louvain School of Management
Place des Doyens, 1
B-1348, Louvain-la-Neuve,
Belgium
jean.vanderdonckt@uclouvain.be

Habib Fardoun
Faculty of Computing and
Information Technology
King AbdulAzziz
University
Saudi Arabia
hfardoun@kau.edu.sa

ABSTRACT

This document describes the most relevant issues regarding development approaches for computer systems based on distributed user interfaces (DUIs). DUIs have brought about drastic changes affecting the way interactive systems are conceived and this fact affects the way these novel systems are designed and developed. New features need to be taken into account from the very beginning of the development process and new models, methods, and tools need to be considered for the correct development of interactive systems based on Distributed User Interfaces. The goal of this workshop is to promote the discussion about the development of DUIs, answering a set of key questions: How current UI models can be used or extended to cover the new features of DUIs?. What new features should be considered and how should they be included within the development process?. What new methods and tools do we need to develop DUIs in a correct way following the quality standards for interactive systems?.

Author Keywords

Distributed User Interfaces; Interactive Systems; Model-Based UI Development; User Interface Models and Tools.

ACM Classification Keywords

H.5.2 User Interfaces (D.2.2, H.1.2, I.3.6); Theory and methods; User Interfaces Management Systems (UIMS); Input devices and strategies.

INTRODUCTION

Distributed User Interfaces (DUIs) have recently become a new field of research and development in Human-Computer Interaction (HCI). The DUIs have brought about drastic changes affecting the way interactive systems are conceived. DUIs have gone beyond the fact that user interfaces are controlled by a single end user on the same computing platform in the same environment.

The term "Distributed User Interface" or "DUI" can be found in literature since just a few years ago [6, 7, 8], although the term has not been formally defined yet. According to [1] and synthesizing across different informal definitions in earlier works, they get the following definition: "A distributed user interface is a user interface whose components are distributed across one or more of the dimensions input, output, platform, space, and time" [1].

All this concerns affect the way these novel systems are designed and developed. New features need to be taken into account from the very beginning of the development process and new models, methods, and tools need to be considered for the correct development of interactive systems based on Distributed User Interfaces.

The goal of this workshop is to promote the discussion about the emerging topic of DUIs, answering a set of key questions: How current UI models can be used or extended to cover the new features of DUIs?. What new features should be considered and how should they be included within the development process?. What new methods and methodologies do we need to develop DUIs in a correct way following the quality standards for interactive systems?.

MODEL-BASED DUI DEVELOPMENT CHALLENGES

Looking back retrospectively to the evolution of concerns in Human-Computer Interaction (HCI) from a Software Engineering (SE) point of view, we can observe that different models have appeared over time in order to address the shortcomings observed in the previous generation of models.

Today, we have reached a point where the prevalent models used to characterize a User Interface (UI) are task, domain, abstract UI, concrete UI, and final UI, if we consider for example the Cameleon Reference Framework (CRF) [5]. Other approaches include also a user model to characterize users' features.

The $\mu 7$ concept summarizes the essential aspects to consider regarding DUIs [3]. These aspects are the multi-device, multi-platform, multi-user, multi-language / culture, multi-

335

organization, multi-context and multi-modality implementation.

Multi-device and Multi-platform usage
A single user employs different devices at the same time, whether they are running the same operating system or not. Besides, multi-device usage subsumes a multi-platform usage (since there are different machines) but the reciprocal does not hold: a user could use several computers (hence, multi-platform) that are similar (hence, no multi-device). In a DUI scenario, the user takes advantage of these resources to improve the user experience [2].

Multi-user and organization support
One or many users may want to distribute parts or the whole UI among several monitors, devices, platforms, or displays. For instance, in a control room setup, users may want to direct portions of a UI to other displays of others users depending on the context of use.

Multi-language / culture support
The distribution of the UI among different users leads to the cultural adaptation of the UI. The distribution of the elements according to the cultural and the language aspects of the user is an important issue to take into account. For instance, the layout of the controllers for Chinese users differs from the English users.

Multi-context of use
The distribution of the UI depends on different aspects regarding the context the UI is being executed. These aspects may be related to the proximity of the environmental resources (i.e. the distance to displays), or may be related to the user profile (i.e. capabilities, role in the session, etc.) among many others.

Multi-modality implementation
The distribution of the UI is not limited to GUIs since vocal user interfaces may be directional. For instance, games developed for the Kinect platform are controlled using vocal and gesture –based UIs.

Indeed, the emergence of new interactive resources affects the development and evaluation of distributed user interfaces (DUIs) and introduces new aspects that should be taken into account regarding software engineering methods, models and tools.

Apart from these dimensions and concerns regarding DUIs, it is also important to consider quality factors within the development process. The software product quality model presented in the ISO/IEC 25010 categorizes software quality attributes into eight characteristics (*functional suitability, reliability, performance, efficiency, operability, security, compatibility, maintainability and transferability*). These attributes should be also considered when developing DUIs

CONCLUSIONS
The aim of this workshop is to conclude with a common development framework where we try to find out the answer on how the µ7 concepts affect the way in which software systems based on DUI should be developed. How µ7 concepts do influence every phase of the software life cycle starting from requirements to the final implementation.

ACKNOWLEDGEMENTS
We thank ITEA2 Call 3 UsiXML Project and SERENOA FP7 Project; CICYT-TIN 2011-27767-C02-01 Spanish National Project; and the PPII10-0300-4174 and PII2C09-0185-1030 JCCM Projects, for partially supporting this research.

REFERENCES
1. Niklas Elmqvist. Distributed User Interfaces: State of the Art. 1st workshop on Distributed User Interfaces. CHI 2011. Vancouver, Canada. 2011.

2. Gallud, J. A., Tesoriero, R., Penichet, V. M. R., Distributed User Interfaces: Designing Interfaces for the Distributed Ecosystem. Springer HCI Series, Berlin, 201. 2011.

3. Vanderdonckt, J. Distributed User Interfaces: How to Distribute User Interface Elements across Users, Platforms, and Environments. Proc. of XI Interacción 2010. 20-32.

4. Aquino, N., Vanderdonckt, J., Condori-Fernández, N., Dieste, Ó., Pastor, Ó. Usability Evaluation of Multi-Device/Platform User Interfaces Generated by Model-Driven Engineering, Proc. of 4th Int. Symposium on Empirical Software Engineering and Measurement ESEM'2010 (Bolzano, 16-17 September 2010), ACM Press, New York, 2010, Article #30.

5. Calvary, G., J. Coutaz, D. Thevenin, Q.Limbourg, L. Bouillon, and J. Vanderdonckt, A Unifying Reference Framework for Multi-Target User Interfaces, Interacting with Computers 15, 3 (June 2003), pp. 289-308.

6. Luyten, K. and Coninx, K. 2005. Distributed User Interface Elements to support Smart Interaction Spaces. Proc. of the 7th IEEE Int. Symposium on Multimedia, IEEE Comp. Society, Washington, DC, pp. 277-286.

7. Balme, L., Demeure, A., Barralon, N., Coutaz, J., Calvary, G.: CAMELEON-RT: A software architecture reference model for distributed, migratable, and plastic user interfaces. In: Proceedings of the Symposium on Ambient Intelligence, Lecture Notes in Computer Science, vol.3295, pp. 291–302. Springer (2004).

8. Sottet, J.S., Calvary, G., Coutaz, J., Ganneau, V., Vanderdonckt, J.: The 4C reference model for distributed user interfaces. In: Proceedings of the International Conference on Autonomic and Autonomous Systems, pp. 61–69 (2008).

Formal Methods for Interactive System (FMIS 2013)

Judy Bowen
Department of Computer Science
The University of Waikato
Hamilton
New Zealand
jbowen@cs.waikato.ac.nz

Steve Reeves
Department of Computer Science
The University of Waikato
Hamilton
New Zealand
stever@cs.waikato.ac.nz

ABSTRACT
The workshop focuses on use of formal methods in the development and analysis of Interactive Systems. The workshop is particularly concerned with issues relating to Human Computer Interaction and to the analysis of interaction in a variety of computing environments (safety-critical, ubiquitous etc.). In the latter case the complexities of dynamic context, including location and large numbers of interacting entities, pose particular challenges to formal modelling.

Author Keywords
Software engineering; formal methods; interactive systems

ACM Classif cation Keywords
D.2.4 Software/Program Verif cation: Formal methods

INTRODUCTION TO THE WORKSHOP
Reducing the risk of human error in the use of interactive systems is increasingly recognised as a key objective in contexts where safety, security, f nancial or similar considerations are important. These risks are of particular concern where users are presented with complex or novel interactive experiences in already challenging environments. Formal methods are required to analyse these interactive situations. In such complex systems analysis and justif cation that risk is reduced may depend on both qualitative and quantitative models of the system.

The aim of this workshop is to bring together researchers from a range of disciplines within computer science (including HCI) and other behavioural disciplines, from both academia and industry, who are interested in both formal methods and interactive system design. An aim of the workshop is to grow and sustain a network of researchers interested in the development and application of formal methods and related verif cation and analysis tools to HCI and usability aspects of complex systems.

The focus of the workshop is, though not restricted to, general design and verif cation methodologies, which take account of models or accounts of human behaviour, as well as application areas such as pervasive and ubiquitous systems, augmented reality, scalability and resilience, mobile devices, embedded systems, safety-critical systems, high-reliability systems, shared control systems, digital libraries, eGovernment.

Previous Workshops were held in 2006, 2007, 2009 and 2011. These were located in Macau SAR China in October 2006 (organised by the United Nations University UNU-IIST), in Lancaster in September 2007 (in conjunction with HCI 2007), in Eindhoven in November 2009 (in conjunction with FM2009) and in Limerick in June 2011 (in conjunction with FM2011).

All these events were documented in (for the f rst two) ENTCS proceedings (volume 183 and 208) and (for the last two) in Electronic Communication s of the European Association of Software Science and Technology (EASST, volumes 22 and 45). Two special issues of a selection of the workshop contributions have been published: one in "Innovations in Systems and Software Engineering" (ISSE) and the other in "Formal Aspects of Computing". A third special issue (based on FMIS 2009 and 2011) is about to appear in "Innovations in Systems and Software Engineering".

THE ORGANISERS
This issue of the workshop is organised by:

- Professor Steve Reeves
  University of Waikato
  Department of Computer Science
  Hamilton 3240 New Zealand
  Tel: + 64 (0) 7 838 4398
  Fax: +64 (0) 7 858 5095
  Email: stever@cs.waikato.ac.nz
  Homepage: http://cs.waikato.ac.nz/~stever

Steve Reeves's main research areas are formal methods for program development and for integrating with user-centred design (UCD). He has published over 80 journal and ref ereed conference papers and a textbook with Addison-Wesley on logic in computer science. He has previously conducted research in automated theorem-proving (via semantic tableaux) and program construction in intuitionistic theories. He has experience as programme committee member and co-Chair on many conferences and workshops over the years, and has co-edited conference proceedings and special journal issues. He has held a series of NZ government-funded grants (from FRST, the Foundation for

Research, Science and Technology) over the last 14 years, all in the area of formal methods, ref nement and UCD. He is a member of the ASWEC (Australasian SE Conference) Steering Committee and a Fellow of both the British and New Zealand Computer Societies. He is a member of the Editorial Board of the journal Innovations in Systems and Software Engineering, Springer..

- Dr. Judy Bowen
  University of Waikato
  Department of Computer Science
  Hamilton 3240 New Zealand
  Tel: + 64 (0) 7 838 4547
  Fax: +64 (0) 7 858 5095
  Email: jbowen@cs.waikato.ac.nz
  Homepage: http://cs.waikato.ac.nz/~jbowen

Judy Bowen's main research area is the use of formal methods with user-centred design approaches for interactive systems. She has published a number of journal and refereed conference papers and has been on several programme committees. She has been involved in creating and running workshops on both logic and programming and has given invited talks on her research on a number of occasions. She was a holder of a BuildIT post-doctoral fellowship award and was previously selected for the BuildIT emerging researchers mentor programme. She is a member of IFIP Working Group 2.7/13.4 devoted to User Interface Engineering.

THE PROGRAMME COMMITTEE FOR THE WORKSHOP

Judy Bowen, University of Waikato, New Zealand
Paul Cairns, University of York, UK
Jos Creissac Campos, University of Minho, Portugal
Antonio Cerone, UNI-IIST, Macau SAR China
Paul Curzon, Queen Mary, University of London, UK
Anke Dittmar, University of Rostock, Germany
Michael Harrison, Newcastle University, UK
Chris Johnson, University of Glasgow, UK
Paolo Masci , Queen Mary, University of London, UK
Mieke Massink, CNR-ISTI, Italy
Gerrit Meixner, Heilbronn University, Germany
Philippe Palanque Universit Paul Sabatier, Toulouse, France
Steve Reeves, University of Waikato, New Zealand
Rimvydas Rukšėnas, Queen Mary, University of London, UK

FORM OF PROCEEDINGS

There will be informal proceedings of the workshop handed out during the workshop, followed by post-proceedings in EASST (if accepted) and/or a journal special issue of selected, extended and high-quality contributions. Depending on the kind of contributions we receive candidate journals are "Formal Aspects of Computing", "Innovations in Systems and Software Engineering" or another relevant journal following the tradition of previous years.

Context-Aware Service Front-Ends

Francisco Javier Caminero Gil
Telefonica I+D -Distrito C,
Edificio Oeste 1, Planta 5
Ronda de la Comunicación, s/n
28050 Madrid (Spain) - fjcg@tid.es

Fabio Paternò
CNR-ISTI, HIIS Laboratory
Via Moruzzi 1 56124 Pisa, Italy
fabio.paterno@isti.cnr.it

Vivian Genaro Motti
Université catholique de Louvain
Place des Doyens 1, 1348
Louvain-la-Neuve Belgium
vivian.genaromotti@uclouvain.be

ABSTRACT
Context-aware adaptation of user interfaces have been investigated since the early 80's to provide mechanisms for stakeholders to propose, implement and execute adaptation, enabling users to efficiently interact with adaptive and adaptable applications. Today, adapting UIs according to the context of use becomes inevitable. Not only because users interact with applications from many distinct environments (platforms, devices and users' profile vary significantly), but also because such applications must provide a high usability level regardless of the contexts of use, efficiently adapting themselves according to the context. In this sense, Serenoa project proposes its 2nd workshop, to join experts in the domain of context-aware adaptation to exchange experiences, discuss current trends, promote approaches, and raise awareness for this field.

Author Keywords
Context-Awareness; Service Front End; User Interface Adaptation; Adaptivity; Adaptability.

ACM Classification Keywords
D2.2 [**Software Engineering**]: Design Tools and Techniques – *Modules and interfaces; user interfaces.* D2.m [**Software Engineering**]: Miscellaneous – *Rapid Prototyping; reusable software.* H.5.1 [**Information interfaces and presentation**]: Multimedia Information Systems. H5.2 [**Information interfaces and presentation**]: User Interfaces – *User-centered design.*

INTRODUCTION
In a context in which users with different profiles interact by using different devices, modalities, platforms, systems, from distinct environments (concerning light, noise and stability level), it is neither scalable nor feasible for stakeholders to implement dedicated versions of interactive systems which provide high usability levels. Aiming to address this issue, the contextual information must be gathered and take into account in to adapt user interfaces (UIs), i.e. the content, navigation and presentation of interactive systems must be modified according to the context of use in which the user is located aiming to provide high usability levels. To support context-aware adaptation, several techniques, methods and strategies have been proposed in the last 30 years. Languages, frameworks, toolkits, architectural approaches and algorithms have been

continuously proposed, created and published since the early 80's. However, now, more than ever before, users interact from contexts that significantly vary, and considering such variations to appropriately adapt applications becomes a great challenge. In this context, Serenoa project proposes its second workshop. Named CASFE'2013, Context-Aware Services Front End, this workshop is dedicated to join experts in this field to discuss, comment, review, publish and analyze the latest achievements, current issues, and future trends for adaptation.

WORKSHOP
Several works attempted to address the challenge of context-aware adaptation including valuable inputs from various disciplines, such as: ubiquitous computing, pervasive applications, ambient intelligence, artificial intelligence, engineering interactive computing systems, mobile human-computer interaction. These contributions are often expressed in a format that prevents them to be compared with others, mainly because they are heterogeneous and their format is inconsistent. This workshop is aimed at addressing context-aware adaptation of user interfaces via an interaction model according to three dimensions (adapted from [1]): a *descriptive* power that consists in characterizing a sufficiently large spectrum of adaptation techniques according to a unified format, an *evaluative* power that consists in comparing different adaptation techniques based on the same format, and a *generative* virtue that is intended to identify holes in the resulting design space to foster further research and development of new interaction techniques. "A good interaction model must strike a balance between generality (for descriptive power), concreteness (for evaluative power) and openness (for generative power)" [1]. This means that there is a need for creating a design space for context-aware adaptation of any kind of user interface that should exhibit enough expressiveness (for guarantying enough descriptive power), decidability (for ensuring the ability to assess any adaptation technique), and flexibility (for accommodating new adaption techniques that were previously unforeseen). There is also a need for discussing and reviewing the state of the art in the domain of UI adaptation under the viewpoint of context-awareness since most surveys are either obsolete [2] or do not address context-awareness [3]. This state of the art will be namely focusing on models, methods,

EICS'13, June 24–27, 2013, London, United Kingdom.
ACM 978-1-4503-2138-9/13/06.

and tools that support context-aware adaptation of UIs, in particular in order to address existing challenges [4].

Aims and Goals. This workshop is targeted at industrial and academic participants, with interest in the adaptation field, belonging to different domains of expertize, as: computer scientists, engineers, architects and psychologists.

Format. The workshop will last half day dedicated to discuss and review the state of the art in the area of context-aware adaptation: criteria, requirements, design spaces, rules, techniques, tools and languages for context-aware adaptation of user interfaces. Selected papers will be presented, and discussed, resulting into an updated and accurate version of the workshop material. A projector will be used.

Participants. Participants are welcome from any background or discipline that is concerned by context-aware adaptation ranging from psychology, social sciences to computer science. The expected amount of participants will be around 15, but could be extended depending on the interest of the topic.

ORGANIZERS

Francisco Javier Caminero Gil is the project coordinator of the FP7-ICT5-Serenoa (Multidimensional context-aware adaptation of Service Front-ends) project funded by the European Commission.

Fabio Paternò is research director of the Laboratory on Human Interfaces in Information Systems at ISTI, CNR in Pisa, Italy. He has been Co-Chair of the ACM CHI 2000, INTERACT 2003 and 2005, and chair of MobileHCI'2002, EICS'2011 and AmI'2012.

Vivian Genaro Motti is a PhD candidate at Université catholique de Louvain where she is a member of the Louvain Interaction Laboratory (LILab). She works as a research assistant for FP7-ICT5-Serenoa project and has publications on ICWE, EICS, AVI, Interact, and WWW.

POTENTIAL OUTCOMES

We intend to discuss at the workshop the following topics:

• What are the major challenges (e.g., conceptual, methodological, technical, organizational) for developing context-aware adaptation of user interfaces?

• For which kinds of systems or applications are context-aware user interfaces particularly useful?

• When and how could we measure the effectiveness, the efficiency of context-aware adaptation?

• How could we measure the quality of the user interface resulting from a context-aware adaptation process?

• In which ways will context-aware adaptation affect user interfaces in the future and how will they evolve?

• What kinds of context-aware adaptation do you see as particularly promising?

CALL FOR PAPERS

We will accept participants based on the paper quality and the diversity of their backgrounds, aiming at an interdisciplinary group. The authors of accepted papers will be asked to provide a refined version of their paper one month before the workshop based on a preliminary version of workshop material: a design space, an adaptation specification language, some example of adaptation rules. These position papers will be circulated in advance for participants to get an understanding of the mutual views and to provide a starting point for the discussion. The papers should be submitted via EasyChair.

CONCLUSION

Although there is a great motivation for the topic of interest of this workshop, there are still many open issues and a lot of room from improvement. That is why we propose a second release of Serenoa workshop. To bring together experts in this domain, promote discussions, exchange of experiences and raise awareness for this relevant topic.

ACKNOWLEDGMENTS

This workshop is supported by Serenoa, funded by the European Commission's Seventh Framework Programme under grant agreement n° 258030 (FP7-ICT-2009-5).

REFERENCES

1. Beaudouin-Lafon, M. Designing interaction, not interfaces. In: Proc. of ACM Working Conf. on Advanced Visual Inter-faces AVI'2004 (Gallipoli, May 25-28, 2004). ACM Press, New York (2004), pp. 15-22.

2. Dieterich, H., Malinowski, U., Kuhme, T., and Schneider-Hufschmidt, M. State of the art in adaptive user interfaces. In: Schneider-Hufschmidt, M., Kuhme, T., Malinowski, U. (Eds.), Adaptive User Interfaces Principles and Practice. Elsevier Science Publishers B.V., Amsterdam (1993), pp. 13–48.

3. López-Jaquero, V., Vanderdonckt, J., Montero, F., and González, P. Towards an Extended Model of User Interface Adaptation: the ISATINE framework. In: Proc. Of EIS'2007 (Salamanca, 22-24 March 2007), J. Gulliksen, M.B. Harning, Ph. Palanque (Eds.). LNCS, Vol. 4940. Springer-Verlag, Berlin (2008), pp. 374-392.

4. Vanderdonckt, J. Model-Driven Engineering of User Interfaces: Promises, Successes, and Failures. In: Proc. of 5th Annual Romanian Conference on Human-Computer Interaction ROCHI'2008 (Iasi, September 18-19, 2008). S. Buraga, I. Juvina (Eds.). Matrix ROM, Bucharest (2008), pp. 1–10.

Author Index

www.ingramcontent.com/pod-product-compliance
Lightning Source LLC
Chambersburg PA
CBHW08090822O326
41598CB00034B/5516